Staff Development and Clinical Intervention in Brain Injury Rehabilitation

Edited by

Charles J. Durgin, MS
Director of Education and Clinical Training
Community Integrated Programs
NovaCare Comprehensive Rehabilitation Services
King of Prussia, Pennsylvania

Nancy D. Schmidt, MS
Program Administrator for Head Injury Services
New England Rehabilitation Hospital
Woburn, Massachusetts

L. Jeanne Fryer, PhD
Corporate Director of Development and Regulatory Affairs
NovaCare Comprehensive Rehabilitation Services
King of Prussia, Pennsylvania

with Foreword by
Neil Brooks, PhD

AN ASPEN PUBLICATION®

Aspen Publishers, Inc.
Gaithersburg, Maryland
1993

Library of Congress Cataloging-in-Publication Data

Staff development and clinical intervention in brain injury
rehabilitation / edited by Charles J. Durgin, Nancy D. Schmidt, L.
Jeanne Fryer.
p.   cm.
Includes bibliographical references and index.
ISBN 0-8342-0359-6
1. Brain damage—Patients—Rehabilitation.   2. Brain damage-
-Patients—Rehabilitation—Study and teaching.   3. Neurologists-
-Training of.   4. Neurological nurses—Training of.
5. Rehabilitation counselors—Training of.   I. Durgin, Charles J.
II. Schmidt, Nancy D.   III. Fryer, L. Jeanne.
[DNLM: 1. Brain Injuries—rehabilitation—handbooks.   2. Staff
Development—methods—handbooks.   WL 39 S779 1993]
RC387.5,S73   1993
617.4'81044—dc 20
DNLM/DLC
for Library of Congress
92-48478
CIP

The authors have made every effort to ensure the accuracy of the information herein. However,
appropriate information sources should be consulted, especially for new or unfamiliar
procedures. It is the responsibility of every practitioner to evaluate the appropriateness of a
particular opinion in the context of actual clinical situations and with due consideration to new
developments. Authors, editors, and the publisher cannot be held responsible for any
typographical or other errors found in this book.

Editorial Resources: Barbara Priest

Library of Congress Catalog Card Number: 92-48478
ISBN: 0-8342-0359-6

Printed in the United States of America

1 2 3 4 5

Table of Contents

Contributors

Charles V. Arokiasamy, RhD, CRC, NCC
Assistant Professor
Department of Rehabilitation Counseling
Louisiana State University Medical Center
New Orleans, Louisiana

Carol Ann Balch, MN, RN
Director of Program Services,
    Western Division
Management Services Division of National
    Medical Enterprises
Santa Monica, California

John D. Banja, PhD
Associate Professor
Department of Rehabilitation Medicine
Emory University School of Medicine
Atlanta, Georgia

Jean L. Blosser, EdD
Director, Speech and Hearing Center
Professor
School of Communicative Disorders
The University of Akron
Akron, Ohio

Neil Brooks, PhD
Professor of Clinical Psychology
Department of Psychiatry
Gartnaval Royal Hospital
The University of Glasgow
Glasgow, Scotland, United Kingdom

Constance S. Burgess, MS, RN
Consultant
Connie Burgess and Associates
Long Beach, California

Roberta DePompei, PhD, CCC-SP/A
Associate Professor
Department of Communicative Disorders
The University of Akron
Akron, Ohio

Stanley H. Ducharme, PhD
Director, Rehabilitation Psychology
Professor of Rehabilitation Medicine
Boston University School of Medicine
Boston, Massachusetts

Charles J. Durgin, MS
Director of Education and Clinical Training
Community Integrated Programs
NovaCare Comprehensive Rehabilitation
    Services
King of Prussia, Pennsylvania

Timothy J. Feeney, MA
Coordinator of Behavioral Services
New Medico Rehabilitation Center of the
    Capital District
Niskayuna, New York

L. Jeanne Fryer, PhD
Corporate Director of Development and
    Regulatory Affairs
NovaCare Comprehensive Rehabilitation
    Services
King of Prussia, Pennsylvania

Sally E. Guice, MHS
Rehabilitation Consultant
Department of Rehabilitation Counseling
Jennifer Palmer & Co.
Metairie, Louisiana

Patricia L. Kerrigan, BS
Clinical Case Manager
Community Rehabilitation Services of Annapolis
Annapolis, Maryland

Pat Kitchell, MSPA, CCC
Director of Clinical Services
Neurocare, Inc.
Concord, California

Tony M. Lazzaretti
Computer Graphic Designer
North Andover, Massachusetts

Danese D. Malkmus, MA, CCC-SLP
Speech-Language Pathologist
Regional Manager
LINC Case Management Services
San Diego, California

Paul A. Nau, PhD
Director of Residential Services for
    Children & Youth
Bancroft, Inc.
Haddonfield, New Jersey

Gary M. Pace, PhD
Program Director
NeuroCare of Florida
Tampa, Florida

Mary Pepping, PhD
Department of Physical Medicine and
    Rehabilitation
Virginia Mason Clinic
Seattle, Washington

Jack E. Robertson, PhD
President and Chief Executive Officer
Timber Ridge Ranch Neurorehabilitation Center
Benton, Arkansas

Nancy D. Schmidt, MS
Program Administrator for Head Injury Services
New England Rehabilitation Hospital
Woburn, Massachusetts

Pamela Sherron, MEd
Program Manager
Rehabilitation Research and Training Center on
    Supported Employment for the Severely
    Disabled
Virginia Commonwealth University
Richmond, Virginia

Frank R. Sparadeo, PhD, CAS
Clinical Assistant Professor
Brown University School of Medicine
Center for Alcohol and Addiction Studies
Department of Psychiatry
Rhode Island Hospital
Providence, Rhode Island

Beth Urbanczyk, MS
Clinical Discipline Coordinator
Speech/Language Pathology Discipline
New Medico Rehabilitation and Skilled
    Nursing Center of the Capital District
Niskayuna, New York

Paul Wehman, PhD
Professor
Department of Physical Medicine and
    Rehabilitation
Medical College of Virginia
Director
Rehabilitation Research and Training Center on
    Supported Employment for the Severely
    Disabled
Virginia Commonwealth University
Richmond, Virginia

Janet M. Williams, MSW
University of Kansas
Kansas City, Missouri

Mark Ylvisaker, PhD
Assistant Professor
Department of Communication Disorders
College of St. Rose
Albany, New York

Nathan D. Zasler, MD
Executive Medical Director
National NeuroRehabilitation Consortium
Director, Brain Injury Rehabilitation Services
Sheltering Arms Hospital
Director, Concussion Care Center of Virginia
Consultant, NeuroRecovery Program
Metropolitan Hospital
Director, Community Rehabilitation Services
    of Richmond
Co-Director, Richmond Rehabilitation
    Physicians
Richmond, Virginia

Foreword

The field of brain injury rehabilitation has grown at an enormous pace. The number and range of inpatient services has increased, community-based outpatient interventions have become common, and specialist programs have appeared, including coma management, vocational rehabilitation, substance abuse treatment etc. Within all these new developments are individual clinicians trying their best to do the best job for the person with brain injury.

Individual clinicians often face considerable stress because of lack of experience, and the recognition that during their formal training, they received little information about traumatic brain injury. With this situation, the need for staff training and development is obvious, yet it is remarkable that this is the first book to specifically address these issues. The authors have clearly recognized the need for staff development, have identified situations in which training and experience may be lacking, and have proposed practical "how-to" solutions.

A number of different issues are covered, beginning with an excellent chapter dealing with a variety of issues involved in preparing staff to provide quality rehabilitation services. This chapter includes many issues in staff development, support, and training. It serves as a springboard for the rest of the book which covers many central clinical issues (family-centered rehabilitation, ethics, substance abuse, sexuality, the specific issues of residential staff, and many others).

It is invidious to pick out any one chapter in a book of this kind, but the reader's attention is inevitable drawn to the chapter by Schmidt and Kitchell which discusses making an excellent clinician into an equally excellent manager, one of the most difficult rehabilitation issues of all. Clinicians very often fail in making the transition to manager. Often, this is because of poor training and poor support. Schmidt and Kitchell give highly specific guidelines for the training and support necessary to make this transition.

This book will undoubtedly be required reading for managers in neurorehabilitation, for senior clinicians, for aspiring senior clinicians, and for teachers of clinicians. It fills an enormous gap and will not readily go out of date. Congratulations to the authors.

Neil Brooks, PhD
Professor of Clinical Psychology
Department of Psychiatry
Gartnaval Royal Hospital
The University of Glasgow
Glasgow, Scotland, United Kingdom

Preface

The impact of acquired brain injury on a person and his or her family presents substantial challenges to these individuals as well as to everyone involved in providing assistance. In terms of rehabilitation, service quality is directly linked, if not determined, by staff knowledge and performance. Many rehabilitation staff as well as personnel working in other support systems (e.g. schools, community agencies, etc.), however, have not been trained to address the needs of these individuals. This is of great concern as it may result in inadequate care and treatment provided to people in need of quality support, advice, and guidance.

Consequently, persons with brain injury may be missing valuable opportunities to get the type and level of service that will allow them to make a successful adaptation to the injury. Staff training and enhanced systems development is a critical investment for increasing service quality. Although this investment is essential if we are going to achieve outcomes efficiently and efficaciously, accomplishing these goals is not easy. To get results requires clinical knowledge and experience, ongoing training and support, creativity and insight, flexibility, leadership, and a proactive orientation.

Training staff in state-of-the-art clinical and management practices is further complicated by the rapid changes present in today's health care and human service environment. Since many changes are expected to continue for the foreseeable future staff will need to learn and use practical strategies to adapt and grow. In many ways this requires staff to develop a new way of thinking and a new set of skills that go well beyond discipline-specific training emphasized in professional training programs.

FOCUS ON THE FUTURE

This book encompasses many of the philosophical changes that have been influencing clinical services. It also considers how current trends in health care financing and delivery will impact the provision of rehabilitation and other valuable support services. The book is designed to provide staff with skills to improve current practices and strategies for shaping both their own professional development and the future of the field.

Over the past decade there have been tremendous gains in clinical knowledge leading to the development of increasingly sophisticated clinical programs. Although this provides an excellent foundation upon which to build, in many ways new demands and needs have emerged. Due in part to an increased emphasis on client- and family-centered rehabilitation, different environments where rehabilitation is provided, changing reimbursement practices, greater accountability and efficiency pressures, and customer satisfaction expectations, many traditional ways of practicing are no longer feasible, and in some cases, no longer desirable.

Staff are now required to broaden their focus to issues and trends outside the immediate clinical environment and look more intensively at social, financial, family, legal, community, and ethical issues. These issues not only impact individual staff members but also have a dramatic influence on the way organizations are designed and operated. Particular challenges within the field include the dissemination and utilization of existing knowledge to practitioners, designing services that are meaningful to the consumer, offering treatment that will have lasting value, and providing advocacy for creating social change (e.g. preserving and expanding societies' commitment to assist people with brain injury, fostering acceptance for persons with disabilities, etc.).

This text is structured to provide practical advice on how to address many of these complex issues that face all people working in the field of brain injury rehabilitation. Philosophical and humanistic perspectives are provided along with clinical techniques that can be used to achieve positive outcomes. A central focus of the content is reviewing strategies for designing responsive clinical, educational, and management models that are more sensitive to diverse client, family, and staff needs. Suggestions are also offered for improving overall program integration—including clinicians, managers, and support staff, as well as significant parties outside of the treatment setting.

The book is divided into three parts. Part I addresses issues relating to principles and methods of staff development. This includes reviewing barriers to offering staff development programs in addition to providing strategies for the design and implementation of staff training and support initiatives. A number of clinical, management, and ethical principles are also addressed throughout this section.

Part II includes 11 chapters devoted to a wide variety of approaches to clinical practice and staff development. The approaches include both specialized areas of clinical practice and general rehabilitation issues such as working with families and effective communication. Part III addresses a number of management issues related to both staff development and program leadership. This includes strategies for training clinicians to become managers, methods for effectively supporting case management, and a detailed overview of how to direct and manage change.

Each of the chapters begins with a list of learning objectives. It is important to note that each chapter addresses a common set of themes. These include responsiveness to consumers, developing clinical skills to enhance quality and improve outcomes, building teams and networks of support, systems development, creating a positive organizational culture, and achieving standards of excellence. The issues addressed here are relevant to all points on the rehabilitation continuum as well as for providing assistance many years postinjury.

APPLICATION

We hope that this book will result in training initiatives that enhance staff skills in a number of clinical areas, offer techniques for strengthening teamwork and collaboration, provide greater insights for personal and professional growth, and outline methods for building rehabilitation services that are responsive to consumers needs. We also hope that the training process is designed to recognize the important and valuable work that staff already perform.

In some cases it will be important for the reader to extract the key principles and the most relevant material and to find ways to adapt and apply this information to his or her particular setting. This is important because rehabilitation services are currently being offered in many different environments and by people with a wide range of educational and experiential backgrounds. This trend is already well underway as evidenced by the evolution of many specialized alternative care settings, changing reimbursement patterns that shape access to services, and the increasing numbers of people with brain injury that receive services from nonspecialized support systems.

Another critical factor, given the specialized nature of many of the chapters, will be for staff to carefully examine their own capabilities in addressing complex clinical and staff issues. We strongly encourage staff to develop networks of support to gain access to expertise and resources that may not be available within their particular organization. Furthermore, while we address numerous clinical, staff training, and organizational issues, we realize that there are many different perspectives and approaches available that are not covered. We tried to select those issues that frequently present the greatest challenges to staff and organizations in their efforts to provide effective services.

Finally, it should be noted that this book offers a number of nontraditional approaches and, in some cases, controversial ideas and opinions (including clinical and management issues). As editors we did not discourage contributors from expressing views that they have found useful in meeting the demands of this field. As a result the reader will have exposure to stimulating, insightful, thought-provoking, and sometimes controversial issues. This material has been included to challenge each of us to look more closely at what we do. It is included within an ethic of open communication and critical thinking as well as with the recognition that there is continual need for empirical research and scientific evidence to support the many aspects of rehabilitation.

It is our belief that as we continue to work together to develop high-quality, innovative, and effective rehabilitation services we will be able to reduce the substantial human and economic hardships associated with acquired brain injury.

The authors wish to stress that all references to persons with brain injury and their families, whether they be references to single individuals or groups, are conveyed with the full understanding that each individual served is a unique person with special qualities that need to be understood and highlighted for rehabilitation to be maximally effective.

Acknowledgments

Completing a project of this nature requires a total team effort from many exceptional individuals. We would like to recognize a number of people who made this book possible.

First we acknowledge the hard work and commitment of all the contributors. When this book was first conceived we sought out contributors who demonstrate a high level of clinical expertise, a clear understanding of staff needs, and a vision for developing high quality rehabilitation services. The individuals who contributed to this book exemplify each of these qualities and we gratefully thank them for their personal commitment to this project. Without their involvement and dedication this book would not have come to pass.

Included in this group is Tony Lazzaretti and Mr. Clyde Shover. Over the past several years Tony has been an exceptional teacher and leader in helping others understand the impact of brain injury as well as the strategies one can use to adapt to this significant change in life. His art work, displayed throughout the book, illustrates many of the emotions and challenges that are often present after sustaining a serious injury. Tony's drawings are included in the first-person account at the beginning of the book and the title

page for Part I. On the title page in Part II you will also find a photograph of a wood sculpture that he completed during rehabilitation. On the title page in Part III, you will see the drawing that Mr. Shover completed for his son Mike. This drawing was initially found at Mike's bedside in an acute rehabilitation hospital and was reproduced by Mr. Shover for inclusion in this book. Taken together, the art in this book has been included to help illustrate the substantial personal and family challenges associated with rehabilitation and we thank each of these individuals for allowing us to share their material.

We also acknowledge the many individuals and families affected by brain injury who, with great patience and wisdom, have taught professionals what is helpful and what is not. Their feedback and accomplishments have provided us with invaluable knowledge in shaping the philosophical, clinical, and humanistic aspects of providing assistance. Furthermore, we also recognize all rehabilitation staff and the many people in the community who work closely with people with brain injury and their families on a day-to-day basis. This book was inspired by the importance of this work and the fact that it is this *partnership* with families and survivor's that helps to facilitate a successful adaptation to brain injury.

Throughout this project Neil Brooks, PhD, has provided immensely valuable assistance and guidance. His careful review of the manuscript, clinical expertise, continued enthusiasm, commitment to excellence, and willingness to challenge us each step of the way enabled us to both improve the material and to stay excited about this project when we grew tired. Thank you for finding time in your busy schedule to help us with this book.

We also make a special acknowledgement to Sheldon Berrol, MD, who was involved in the beginning stages of this project. Dr. Berrol's immediate support of the idea for this book enabled us to move ahead with the project. He was a guide, a friend, a source of inspiration and joy.

He made each individual he encountered feel special by his ability to be totally receptive to that person, in that situation, at that moment, thus encouraging individuals to be the best that they can be. It is in this spirit that this book was conceived.

Our ongoing association with Aspen Publishers has also been most helpful and rewarding. We thank Loretta Stock for her continual support and wisdom, Barbara Priest for her commitment to editorial quality, and all the other talented staff who have provided assistance throughout.

Finally, C.D. offers his deepest gratitude to Kathy, Alison, and Christopher, who have offered unrelenting support and understanding for the substantial amount of time that needed to be spent on this project.

A Personal Perspective on the Value of Rehabilitation

Tony Lazzaretti

My brain injury deprived me of my individual freedom. I was injured in 1983 and as a result experienced restrictions in my abilities that led to feelings of confinement that I had never experienced prior to my injury. Reaching my highest potential was a constant battle. My efforts to return to college without understanding the impact of my injury led to failures. I could not understand why these failures continued, given the effort that I put forth and my less-demanding academic workload. I felt under a great deal of emotional stress because I was lost as to how I could overcome these obstacles in a way that would allow me to achieve my goals.

Attaining goals is important to me. Prior to my injury I was my high school class president and an All-American swimmer. At the time of my injury I had received a swimming scholarship to the University of Hawaii. I was enrolled in the School of Architecture and my goal for the future was to work in the field of architectural design. I was at a crossroad in my life. Although swimming had been an area of great success and brought much personal satisfaction, my scholarship was now more of a vehicle to assist me with my career objectives.

A PICTURE IS WORTH A THOUSAND WORDS

The four illustrations that follow were drawn at different points throughout my rehabilitation. Art, primarily drawings and sculpture, offered me a great outlet for expression and gave me a constructive way to use my free time. Each drawing illustrates the pressures that are present in learning to adapt to the changes that occur after brain injury. A brief description of the challenges that I was facing when these illustrations were drawn is discussed as well.

Hospital Setting

From July 1985 to December 1985 I participated in a hospital program. This was not a specialized brain injury rehabilitation program, but a hospital that served people with psychological problems. This was the only treatment setting that my insurance company would approve, but it was also my only opportunity for professional support at the time, so I took it. While I was in the hospital I began to see that my problems were not psychologically-based, they were the result of the problems caused by my brain injury. This was not understood by the hospital staff and I felt trapped and scared. It became clear to me that I had problems that I would need to learn to live with—I recognized that the problems could not be erased.

Rehabilitation Underway

I entered a specialized brain injury rehabilitation program in June of 1986. Within the first few weeks I began to feel more relaxed. I began to see that I was not the only person facing similar challenges. Experiences, difficulties, frustrations, and suggestions were shared and, over time, answers came quicker. Dealing with the problems was not necessarily easier, but I did feel more calm because I could explore the injury with other survivors and with professionals who were familiar with brain injury. I felt less isolated and less trapped.

Rehabilitation Concluding

As I moved forward with my rehabilitation I recognized that "balancing the ball" was easier than before. I had supportive opportunities to work collaboratively with therapists out in the real world. These initiatives were focused on goals that I identified as being important to my future. Continued contact with other people with brain injury helped to increase my insight and to give me a better perspective on how to compensate for problems and how to use the support of others where necessary. I became more sure of my abilities and limitations and did not feel that I had to experiment to be aware of them.

Day of Discharge

My last day of rehabilitation was a very happy one. To show my appreciation I placed this illustration in the local newspaper on my day of discharge. I had learned to smile—something I had not done in four years. I learned to focus on possibilities, not on lost opportunities. I also had

clear strategies to move forward with my life, strategies to use myself and to access support from others. My heart was able to slow down, my fingers were able to be calm, I was able to lean back, relax, and laugh with a friend.

THE VALUE OF REHABILITATION

After my injury it took me a long time to realize that I had to set new goals and establish a new direction in my life. My career thoughts were changed, my living situation and social life were disrupted, my modes of learning were in the past, and I had to begin a new form of self-appreciation because my self-esteem was sliding away. Learning that my life could not continue as it was before my injury was, initially, a "cell-locking" experience.

Rehabilitation gave me a foundation to move forward with my life. This was critical because I did not want to keep hitting stop signs in the same patterns that I had been since my injury. I did not need strict answers but I did need help from others to find the correct strategies to reach greater independence. Of particular importance was identifying specific problems (impairments) that were creating difficulties in many other areas. I refer to this as catching the problem at the top of the pyramid so that the person can get a handle on problems before they get too big. After becoming more aware of where my difficulties were coming from, I was better able to accept my situation and compensate for my problems.

Although there were times during rehabilitation that the benefits of what we were doing were unclear, it is hard to imagine how people with brain injury can adjust without specialized assistance. I feel strongly that support systems need to be geared to address the unique problems associated with brain injury. This includes having staff that are familiar with the problems of brain injury and how to best assist people in this situation. In this way, the person with a brain injury can work with professionals to help build support, identify strategies, and to focus on the problems that are creating the most difficulty. For me, I also found it essential to learn from and get support from other people who were facing similar challenges. To this day I continue to stay in contact with a number of survivors I met during my rehabilitation.

There is another critical benefit of rehabilitation that needs to be emphasized. In my own experience and in my observations of others I recognize how easy it is to fall into negative patterns after brain injury. The value of rehabilitation is also found because the process helps people address problems that will most likely have a lifelong impact. Therefore, rehabilitation can not only prevent the person from experiencing failures and taking steps backward, but it can lead to a better form of acceptance and self-appreciation.

Since my injury I have continued to achieve greater levels of personal freedom. I have completed my Associate of Arts degree in Commercial Art, and from that point received a Certifi-

cate in Computer Graphic Design from Northeastern University. I have my own apartment and work as an apprentice in a graphic arts business with advanced computer equipment. I have returned to competitive swimming, and I work as a coach for a youth swimming program (this has also put a smile on my face).

It feels good to not be in the position of always needing help and to have more balance in my relationships with friends and family. The ongoing support of my family, as well as the experiences described above, have both been absolutely critical for positive changes to occur. It is hoped that this information presented, both in written and in visual form, helps to sensitize others to the challenge of adapting to brain injury, the importance of quality staff guidance, and the critical need to make appropriate services available to all persons that may potentially benefit.

1–PSYCHIATRIC HOSPITAL

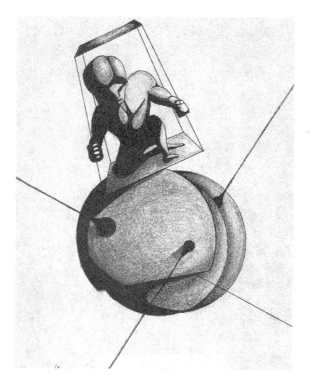

3–REHABILITATION CONCLUDING

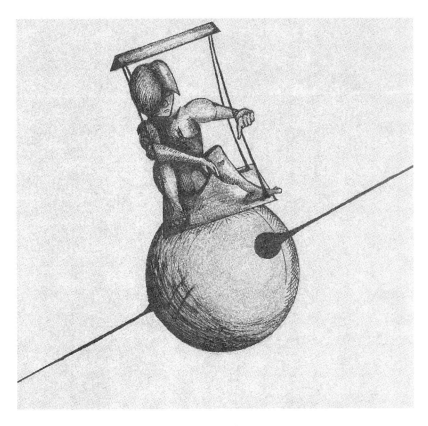

2–REHABILITATION UNDERWAY

4–DAY OF DISCHARGE

Part I

Principles and Methods of Staff Development

Preparing Staff to Provide Quality Rehabilitation Services: Problems and Proposed Solutions

1

Charles J. Durgin

OBJECTIVES

Upon completion of this chapter, the reader will be able to:

1. describe the importance of offering staff training and support in rehabilitation settings
2. identify organizational barriers to conducting staff development programs
3. describe the three levels of the systems view of human performance (i.e., organizational development principles)
4. identify staff training methodology, including how to:
    - conduct a needs analysis
    - perform a training analysis and strategic planning
    - establish learning objectives
    - implement effective instructional delivery
    - evaluate training programs
5. outline the value of using intervention models to help staff understand the process of rehabilitation
6. identify strategies for increasing staff and program effectiveness in the field of rehabilitation, including:
    - improving management practices
    - developing a consumer/family-centered approach to treatment (via first-person accounts)
    - disseminating and utilizing existing knowledge
    - shifting the focus of training content to help staff meet the contemporary demands of providing clinical service

Preparing Staff to Provide Quality Rehabilitation Services

> Undoubtedly, the single most influential factor in transforming the quality of existing programs for people with . . . disabilities is personnel. When . . . staff have mastered the knowledge and competencies important to their role and accept that their learning is unfinished, and further, when they operate from a set of values consistent with the importance of the individual student or client, then 'best practices' come within reach. (Snell, 1990, p.9)

Without question the most significant factor influencing the quality of services offered to persons with brain injury and their families is staff expertise. Most staff, however, enter the field without any formal training or experience in addressing the unique needs of persons with acquired brain injury. This pathway into the field, which most of us experienced first hand at one point in our career, brings with it great learning opportunities as well as challenges.

Working in the field of brain injury rehabilitation is highly demanding. It includes addressing the substantial clinical challenges (Gans, 1983; Prigatano, 1989) as well as the ongoing systems pressures present within virtually all rehabilitation settings throughout the care continuum (McMahon, Shaw, & Mahaffey, 1988; Mullins, 1989). These factors, through their combined and cumulative effects, place great pressures on all levels of staff, both personally and professionally. This is of great concern in that service quality and clinical success lie within staff's capacity to understand and respond to the unique needs of each survivor and family. Consequently, failure to address staff development needs will directly compromise the effectiveness of the services offered. Service providers, in part because of the rapid growth of the field, have not had an impressive record of preparing and supporting staff for the challenges they face.

The basic premise of this chapter is that there needs to be a fundamental and radical shift in the ideas and methods used to prepare staff to provide quality rehabilitation services. The focus of this change includes the need to empower staff

with the skills as well as the autonomy to accomplish clinical objectives that are valued by consumers. This shift, which perhaps is more necessary in action than in ideology, has direct implications for staff education and training, systems development, management practices, and professional ethics. The need for these changes is based on many factors that affect rehabilitation staff and the systems in which they work, most particularly the interplay of complex philosophical, clinical, social, and economic changes that are currently operative and are expected to continue. This chapter reviews strategies that can be used to help staff reach greater levels of clinical and managerial effectiveness in addition to greater levels of personal satisfaction in meeting the challenges that this field presents.

BARRIERS TO OFFERING QUALITY STAFF DEVELOPMENT PROGRAMS

Planning and evaluating training programs for health care professionals involve a complex analysis of needs and requires a set of highly practical decisions that must be made to implement a successful program of learning (Mazmanian, Martin, & Kreutzer, 1991). There are a number of barriers that prevent the establishment and maintenance of effective staff development programs and supports in rehabilitation settings. These barriers generally consist of problems associated with a lack of administrative support or limited training expertise available to conduct progressive training activities.

Despite the fact that most professionals have a strong training ethic, many rehabilitation programs lack the resources or expertise to develop, implement, and evaluate instructional programs according to advanced training methodologies. Training expertise is critical to design effective training programs, to evaluate learning systematically, and to analyze the cost-benefit outcome of training initiatives.

Many service-driven organizations, both in the field of human services and in private industry, view training as a fundamental and essential component of operations. Interestingly, the leading organizations in private industry have been the ones to pioneer effective staff training and organizational development methodologies (Wieck, 1979). Within the field of brain injury rehabilitation these advances have been slow to be adopted.

Unfortunately, many organizational leaders view education and training as an extra or fringe benefit that can be offered when economic times are good, and these are the first to be cut or eliminated when financial pressures increase. This practice of training only when times are good (or when margins are high) is not universal. A number of dramatic precedents have already been set by service organizations that successfully instituted expensive training programs designed to improve service quality to pull them out of financial hard times (Albrecht, 1992; Carlzon, 1987). In some cases organizations have actually increased their financial commitment to training when other sectors of the work force have been reduced. This is in many ways a logical response in that staff in these circumstances need more support and expertise not only to adjust to changes but to maintain (and possibly achieve) service quality.

As a matter of principle it is important to avoid rigidly holding staff supports hostage to bottom line financial performance. This management practice is a narrow view of how to help labor-intensive service organizations improve the quality and range of services offered. After all, it is service quality that ultimately paves the way to achieving rehabilitation outcomes and building financial stability. Many leaders in the field of organizational development stress the need to keep staff involved in education and training programs not only to improve performance but also to foster renewed motivation and greater levels of personal creativity (Peters, 1982).

Beyond administrative support, a lack of training expertise available to oversee and conduct training activities is a common barrier to effective staff development programs. This gap in expertise often results in training programs that target only technical skills and procedural knowledge, thereby missing the full value of what well conceived and effectively implemented training programs can accomplish. This is often characteristic of top-down training initiatives that fail to consider the full spectrum of human resource needs, the implications of change, and the psychological pressures of providing rehabilitation services. Planful staff development programs that study problems in detail and include training participants in the planning process are typically much more useful, relevant, and cost effective.

Furthermore, programs of learning that aggressively involve participants from the outset are often those that inspire staff, help staff rejuvenate, facilitate improved teamwork, establish a greater sense of mutual purpose, help identify role priorities, stimulate more self-directed problem solving, and define more efficient pathways to addressing work responsibilities. Such training initiatives are grounded in or directly related to practical problems on the service level as opposed to being quick-fix reactions that fail to see the big picture or consist of a subjective response to a problem that may not be a concern for all involved.

It is also critical to recognize that training programs that are designed with direct input from service recipients are better able to respond to the needs of those who participate in the rehabilitation process. Engaging consumers in helping define areas to change and improve is an important element of building staff skills and clinical programs. Consumers typically hold a perspective of service value that not only is unique to their individual needs but is generally defined differently and often much more broadly than the perspective held by professionals and organizations. If this perspective is not incorporated into the assessment of staff training and program needs, the training programs developed will not address areas of need consistent with the service mission.

Problems such as those mentioned above can result in a lack of support for staff training and unrealistic expectations as to what training by itself can accomplish. Recognizing and clearly defining these barriers will enable staff to develop strategies to access the support needed for training and to design successful programs of learning tailored to their organization's unique needs. Other common barriers to offering quality staff development programs and supports include:

- poor training history within the organization as a result of negative past experiences (i.e., excessive staff turnover creating disincentives for investing in staff or failure to achieve the desired results of prior training initiatives)
- staff's inability to develop training proposals that include detailed implementation strategies and specify the projected return on investment
- expectations that training can cure organizational problems without a knowledge of how the performance system can block staff effectiveness
- overly centralized power structures that control training programs and resources without facilitating on-line ownership and staff ability to self-direct
- use of generic training packages that cannot be shaped to different program models or regions of the country, individual trainee differences, and the varied human resources that are needed to support implementation
- lack of training models available in the literature that describe how to design and implement training activities for rehabilitation staff

Training initiatives need not be costly endeavors. Some of the most effective training programs originate from the implementation of well designed learning experiences in the natural work environment. Given that these initiatives do not depend on significant amounts of financial support, these programs of learning are often the most flexible and offer promising long-term benefits.

BASIC TRAINING CONCEPTS

Attitudes, Knowledge, and Skills

The target areas of staff development initiatives typically fall within three interrelated areas of human performance: attitudes, knowledge, and skills.

Attitudes influence staff's desire, willingness, and motivation to perform at work. Attitudes have a direct impact on the tasks staff choose to carry out as well as the manner in which they are performed. Frequently within the field of human services, it is these emotional, value-laden, and psychological issues that inhibit staff's ability to contribute to their full potential and in many cases to follow team recommendations. For example, a staff person may know how to facilitate the use of a journal for memory compensation. If that person believes that this goal is unrealistic, however, he or she is less likely to put forth the effort necessary to achieve positive training results. Basic attitudes about the ability of persons with brain injury to learn, their rate of learning, and their right to make choices and take risks are examples of attitudinal issues that affect staff actions.

Another aspect of attitudes commonly addressed in training is supporting the organizational mission. If staff do not understand, support, and value the goals of the program, they are less likely to put forth a strong commitment. In general, simply setting standards and performance expectations will not serve to develop and maintain effective staff motivation.

Knowledge simply refers to staff's ability to understand how they are to perform the specific tasks that they are assigned at work. The assumption is that if given the proper input, support, and resources the staff will know what they need to do to carry out their responsibilities effectively.

Skills refer to being able to apply one's knowledge in a performance situation. For example, staff may understand the recommended procedures to redirect an agitated client but may lack the confidence to follow the intervention. In this case the staff person has the knowledge and motivation to help but requires skills training to be able to follow the intervention selected.

When one is designing training programs, it is critical to consider the attitudes, knowledge, and skills necessary to help staff achieve success. Historically, training programs have focused primarily on increasing staff knowledge through lectures, presentations, and discussions. The more progressive and successful training initiatives address how staff attitudes affect motivation and effort and provide direct training in the natural work environment, where performance-based skills can be taught and evaluated.

There is extensive literature on the various strategies for effective staff training and systems development. For those persons who are heavily involved in staff development activities, a careful review of the many resources that discuss this topic in great detail is recommended (Caffarella, 1988; Gilbert, 1978; Knowles, 1980; Mager, 1984; Sork, 1990; Spencer, 1986; Sullivan, Wircenski, Arnold, & Sarkees, 1990). Some of the key concepts are addressed in this chapter.

Training Definitions

The terms used in discussing the process of staff training are often used interchangeably and can be confusing. For our purposes, we will use the following definitions.

Orientation typically refers to a preservice review of the individual's role, the purpose and philosophy of the organization, how he or she will interface with other program components, and an overview of the needs of those served. The purpose of orientation is to set a foundation for a new staff member to become more familiar with his or her role within the context of the rehabilitation program or system.

Education, by definition, includes formal learning experiences (course work, conferences, workshops, seminars, etc.) that are designed to provide knowledge-based learning experiences. These learning experiences may be designed to prepare the individual for current or future responsibilities.

Training refers to the instruction and acquisition of short-term learning objectives, namely the attitudes, knowledge, and skills to be applied directly on the job. Although all areas of staff development are valuable and share similar elements, the primary focus of this chapter is training principles and methodology.

THE SYSTEMS VIEW OF HUMAN PERFORMANCE

Rummler and Brache (1988) stress that most attempts to improve staff performance within organizations are doomed to failure right from the start. After many years of experience in the field of human resource development, these investigators recognized the substantial limitations of traditional training approaches in enhancing staff performance. Traditional approaches (i.e., in-services, workshops, and lectures) may improve knowledge and skills in the training environment, but once staff are back on the job the implementation of newly acquired skills often does not occur. The investigators stress:

> Any time we try to improve an individual's output solely by changing the input of knowledge or information or skills to that individual, we are making the naive assumption that the person exists in a performance vacuum, isolated from and immune to the rest of the organization. We are ignoring the performance environment. That environment—that "system"—has an enormous impact on the way people do their jobs and on the results the organization achieves. (Rummler & Brache, 1988, p. 45)

After studying the barriers to staff effectiveness in the natural work environment, Rummler and Brache (1993) recommended using a systems view of human performance to evaluate problems. This approach has three interrelated levels that examine the environmental and organizational context in which staff are expected to perform: the individual job level, the process level, and the organizational level. Figure 1-1 illustrates the individual job level of analysis.

The investigators stress that the achievement of consistent performance by each individual staff member is a function of the variables shown in Figure 1-1, namely knowledge/skill, individual capacity, task support, performance specifications, consequences, and feedback. Staff effectiveness is a function of all six of these variables, and a gap in one or more areas will have a direct and negative impact on the others. In this respect it is important to note that performance is rarely changed substantially or permanently by an adjustment in any single variable (Nowlen, 1988).

The model shown in Figure 1-1 is designed to offer a framework to evaluate performance problems and can be applied to any position. When one uses this framework to analyze vari-

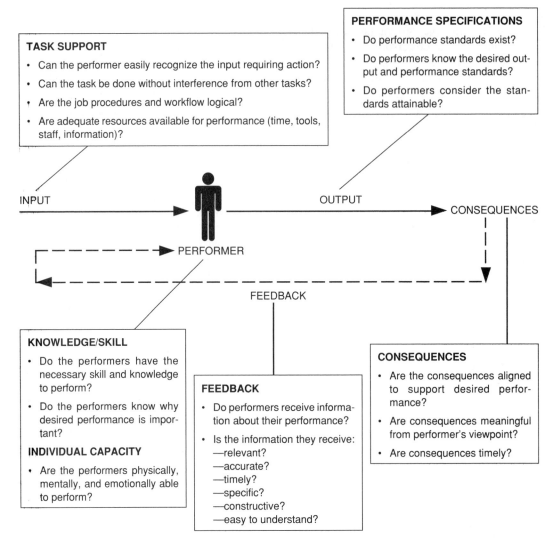

PERFORMANCE SPECIFICATIONS
- Do performance standards exist?
- Do performers know the desired output and performance standards?
- Do performers consider the standards attainable?

TASK SUPPORT
- Can the performer easily recognize the input requiring action?
- Can the task be done without interference from other tasks?
- Are the job procedures and workflow logical?
- Are adequate resources available for performance (time, tools, staff, information)?

INPUT   OUTPUT   CONSEQUENCES

PERFORMER

FEEDBACK

KNOWLEDGE/SKILL
- Do the performers have the necessary skill and knowledge to perform?
- Do the performers know why desired performance is important?

INDIVIDUAL CAPACITY
- Are the performers physically, mentally, and emotionally able to perform?

FEEDBACK
- Do performers receive information about their performance?
- Is the information they receive:
  —relevant?
  —accurate?
  —timely?
  —specific?
  —constructive?
  —easy to understand?

CONSEQUENCES
- Are the consequences aligned to support desired performance?
- Are consequences meaningful from performer's viewpoint?
- Are consequences timely?

Figure 1-1 Troubleshooting the human performance system. *Source:* Copyright © 1983, The Rummler-Brache Group.

ous roles and positions within rehabilitation settings, the barriers to staff performance become quickly apparent.

Rehabilitation staff are working in a new field with constantly evolving clinical knowledge and as a result still face many problems that do not have any clear answers. Additionally, many staff members are asked to perform multiple roles (clinical, management, committee work, etc.), staff turnover creates repeated changes that need to be managed, and most treatment programs are

in the process of designing and redesigning their clinical service models in addition to developing their unique organizational infrastructure. These individual and organizational variables clearly affect each staff member's capacity to perform and grow.

The second level, the process level of analysis, is based on the premise that each individual's performance within the organization is dependent on input and support from other program sectors. This level stresses that every organization is defined by a set of processes that need to defined carefully and linked together to create an efficient flow of information from one program sector to another. These integrated processes or systems encompass the multifaceted interactions of the various program components. The critical distinction between the process level and the individual level is that the former evaluates the full range and scope of program operations to ensure that efficient and effective procedures are being utilized.

The third level of analysis is the organizational level. This is the broadest level of evaluation and examines how well the organization, in its component parts and as a whole, adapts to the demands and pressures of the external world (e.g., the social, economic, political, and legislative climate). Clearly, numerous external variables have a direct impact on rehabilitation providers in all service areas. These socioeconomic issues, particularly those that affect the consumer and his or her family, must be clearly understood and addressed for human service programs to be successful clinically (Biklen, 1988; Durgin, Rath, & Dales, 1991) and financially (Sherman, 1993). The organizational level of analysis monitors the diverse issues and pressures to which programs need to respond (although not necessarily conform), ensures that the internal activities are relevant and valued by consumers, and evaluates the quality and outcome of services provided.

The systems view of human performance offers a comprehensive framework for organizations to use when evaluating problems and shifts the focus of the training analysis and intervention to a broader context. The use of this methodology helps ensure that responses to performance expectations will be focused on attacking the problem and not the person. This is consistent with trends in progressive hospital and rehabilitation systems, which are creating departments responsible for training and organizational development as opposed to focusing more narrowly on education and training. This evolution is in direct response to the enormous complexities of running and working in these organizations and the interdependence of each program sector with the others.

PRINCIPLES AND METHODS OF STAFF DEVELOPMENT

The goal of this section is to provide a basic overview of the training technology that can be used to increase staff effectiveness. As reviewed above, efforts to improve staff performance must be analyzed within the context of the total work environment. To this end, training methodology, when applied correctly, can assess both systems needs and specific content areas that staff need to learn. Ideally, attention to all levels of organizational development is an ongoing process that helps steer the organization, the training activities, and the specific program areas that are in need of further support. Although the various steps involved in the training process are highly interrelated, the major components are reviewed below.

Needs Analysis

The purpose of the needs analysis is to define performance problems, essentially the discrepancy between what is occurring and what is desired. The needs analysis is designed to evaluate whether the problems are systems based (as reviewed above), have to do with staff abilities (i.e., attitudes, knowledge, and skills), or are some combination of these variables.

Data are collected to evaluate the context of the problems identified and the role that training can play in improving the situation. The model in Figure 1-1 can help identify training needs as opposed to systems problems that require a more comprehensive approach to improve staff performance and organizational effectiveness. In many cases the needs analysis will indicate that, given the magnitude of the presenting problems and in light of other organizational needs, recommendations will be offered for performance enhancement and monitoring without the commitment of resources for training.

Data collection methods for the needs analysis can include direct observation, staff questionnaires, documentation audits, customer satisfaction surveys, and interviews of various parties within the performance system. The use of direct observation in combination with the other more formal and structured tools will generally offer the most complete and accurate picture of the problems. The importance of conducting a thorough and detailed needs analysis cannot be overemphasized. This process not only determines the need for training but also sets the empirical foundation for all other training components to follow (Gordon, 1991).

Training Analysis and Planning Considerations

A detailed review of instructional content and administrative resources is a fundamental component of training. Many training programs fail not only because of the misidentification of specific barriers to performance but also through attempts to implement training programs that are too lengthy, complex, or costly. In the field of human services, where it is difficult to free up staff for training, logistical problems more so than cost frequently determine the level of success that training initiatives achieve.

Consequently, it is important that the instructional methodologies under consideration not be restricted to the traditional models of staff training (lectures, workshops, films, etc.). Learning experiences and structured training opportunities need to be available to staff as a matter of course throughout the day and week. This essentially involves establishing training objectives, methodologies, and evaluation processes that can be incorporated easily into the ongoing activities of staff at all levels within the organization. A number of these training models and strategies are reviewed throughout this book.

This nontraditional approach to training is resource efficient in a number of ways. It encourages staff at all levels throughout the organization to develop and conduct training activities without depending on formal training sessions (or initiatives) to enhance staff performance or to offer staff support. This approach can also improve the relevance of the training in that the instruction is provided in the natural work environment, thereby improving the potential for skill acquisition, maintenance, and generalization.

Incorporating training activities into the fabric of the day, with the inclusion of specific performance-based goals, also enables more skills to be taught compared to models that depend more heavily on administrative support (providing the time for training, money, etc.). These approaches also tend to be less like the centralized, top-down initiatives that may be distant from the problems and therefore the solutions.

Establishing Learning Objectives

The information collected from the needs analysis and training analysis is reviewed carefully to identify the goals of training, in other words, what the participants are expected to learn and the anticipated benefits of such intervention. This phase consists of defining the scope of the training as well as the specific attitudes, knowledge, and skills that are being targeted.

Each objective should be behaviorally specific (i.e., conditions, behavior, and criteria) to focus the instructional process and to ensure that the impact of training can be evaluated objectively. When one is choosing learning objectives, it is especially important to verify that the training participants have the prerequisite skills and experience to benefit from the level of training being offered. Knox (1985) stresses that learner participation and motivation is enhanced when the instructional level is not perceived as trivial or as so complex that it is overwhelming.

Instructional Design and Delivery

Once learning objectives are clearly identified, the next phase of preparation consists of determining the best method of instruction.

Adult Learning Theory

Although there is not complete agreement in the literature regarding the empirical evidence for commonly cited adult learning principles, most professional educators suggest that the guidelines for teaching adults are useful when one is conducting training. Most adult learning theories suggest that:

- content relevance is needed
- learner motivation is assumed to be high
- active participation is recommended
- variety facilitates learning
- emotional sensitivity is present in the learner role
- there is a strong need for positive reinforcement
- recognition of participants as individuals is important

Instructional Approaches

With the objectives identified, learning principles in mind, and administrative resources defined, the next step is to plan the optimal approach for instructional delivery. A basic overview of instructional delivery methods is outlined in Table 1-1. Although there is overlap between some of the instructional strategies identified, the fine distinctions between these methods are not reviewed in this chapter.

In general, training programs that maximize participation, engage learners in the direct practice of the targeted skills, provide training and feedback opportunities in the natural work setting, and create a comfortable and nonthreatening learning environment are the most successful. There are two instructional strategies that merit further discussion, however: self-evaluation and modeling.

Self-evaluation opportunities are useful in that they facilitate self-directed learning and effort on the part of the learner. Training programs that incorporate self-evaluation measures not only assist the learner in focusing on competency and skill development but also offer the instructor or facilitator the opportunity to see how the performers rate their own skills. These rating and self-assessment measures can assist supervisors and trainers in selecting the best approach for offering feedback, given that they already have an understanding of how the trainees view their own performance.

Table 1-1 Instructional Delivery Methods

Method	Examples of Instructional Content
Modeling	Running team conferences Diffusing agitation
Demonstration	Use of adaptive equipment Casting and splinting
Role playing	Resolving team conflicts Responding to family concerns
Focused discussions	Values clarification (substance use, sexuality, empowerment) Ethical dilemmas
Video tapes	Teaching compensatory strategies Assessment techniques
Peer reviews	Reviewing reports and treatment plans Sharing data-based approaches to measuring treatment gains
Simulated practice	Observation/documentation exercises Safety techniques for managing aggression
Lectures	Brain-behavior relationships Family member presentations to increase staff sensitivity
Case studies	Facilitating self-awareness Use of naturalistic supports in the workplace
Debriefing incidents	Crisis intervention Communication/systems breakdowns
Direct skills practice and coaching (natural work setting)	Transferring and ambulation assistance Communication skills

Modeling is often sited as an effective approach to training. There are, however, potential negative consequences of modeling if the benefits and drawbacks are not fully understood. For example, negative effects of modeling often occur when an experienced and confident staff member steps into a conflict situation, takes control while others move aside, and then proceeds to manage the crisis to complete perfection. Scenarios such as this often result in decreased confidence among staff and counterproductive attributional conclusions (i.e., "I'm not able to handle tough situations at work, and the rescuer is"). These situations often result in failure to define clearly the specific techniques that lead to success and other approaches to consider if the first attempt does not work (i.e., knowledge). Perhaps most important, the person modeling the intervention has not enabled potential learners to try out their skills for future use.

Frequently the most valuable educational experience that results from modeling is when the intervention chosen is totally unsuccessful and even embarrassing (this will help get the word around). Mistakes offer valuable learning experiences, further substantiate that everyone is allowed to make mistakes regardless of level of experience, and encourage staff to be willing to take the risks necessary to increase their skills and confidence. Although it is not suggested that mistakes be made intentionally to stimulate learning, it is recommended that staff collaborate on difficult intervention dilemmas to build a sense of team and to increase staff's ability to problem solve when they must manage conflicts on their own.

Role playing of both negative and positive responses to managing problems during simulated training sessions, however, is an effective approach to facilitating learning. This training approach is accomplished easily if one takes the following steps:

1. Identify specific problems that are likely to be addressed at work (resolving a team conflict, managing a behavioral incident, generating meaningful documentation, etc.).
2. Ask staff to role play the incident by using an incorrect response first (staff are asked to use exaggerated responses during role playing to highlight the incident and subsequent breakdowns).
3. Ask participants to debrief what went wrong with the staff actions selected (it is also important that the persons doing the role play report their experience and observations as well).
4. Repeat the same role playing situation, but this time ask staff to manage the problem in the most effective manner possible (this is followed by another debriefing session identifying the positive staff interventions

and reviewing other options that were not attempted).

This training approach offers staff the opportunity to practice applied skills in simulated situations that otherwise would be hard to capture during the work day and allows staff to identify and practice the skills that they must master to be successful. When these training sessions are facilitated properly, they can be fun as well as highly educational.

Beyond the instructional methodologies reviewed above, there are also curriculum design options from which staff can select depending on training needs and resources. These include train-the-trainer models, self-instructional curricula and competency-based learning programs.

Evaluation

Evaluation can include direct measures of the attitudes, knowledge, and skills targeted for training as well as measures to evaluate the training process. The most commonly used tests to measure training effectiveness are knowledge-based and performance-based tests.

Attitudinal measures can be assessed by direct questionnaires, ratings, and interviews similar to those used during the needs assessment. Measurement of attitudes is discussed in greater detail later.

Knowledge-based tests are typically used to evaluate training by comparing pretest performance with posttest results. Knowledge-based tests often use multiple choice, short answer, matching, and true/false measures. Frequently this is where training ends, with the assumption that the knowledge acquired will be generalized to work situations.

Performance-based tests assess trainee learning in simulated activities or in the actual work environment where observable behaviors can be measured. Some training models start with knowledge-based training, and follow-up measures are taken in the natural work environment. Others focus training and evaluation efforts in the actual environment where the skills are going to be performed.

USE OF CLINICAL INTERVENTION MODELS TO SUPPORT STAFF PERFORMANCE

A number of leading clinical investigators in the field have recommended posting a clear treatment model in the rehabilitation setting (Ben-Yishay et al., 1985; Prigatano, 1987). Although the importance of using well defined treatment models has been emphasized for years, many rehabilitation settings still do not work from basic models to help guide intervention. Ideally, such models offer the persons served and the staff alike a description of the goals of intervention. This information can function as an easy to follow guide to help all individuals understand the process of adaptation and the sequence of goals that are expected to be addressed as rehabilitation progresses.

Table 1-2 illustrates a modification of the Tunnel of Rehabilitation, originally developed by Ben-Yishay et al. (1985). This model is a condensed version of the original that breaks down each major step in the rehabilitation process into behaviors that most people can understand, incorporates psychotherapeutic concepts

important to making a successful adjustment (Prigatano, 1987), and is posted throughout the treatment setting (Table 1-2 is being used in a number of community-integrated programs).

This visual reference serves to guide staff in using consistent and meaningful language when providing treatment, helps staff provide reinforcement for the specific gains that are made, can be used to help diffuse confrontations by placing conflicts within the context of the process of rehabilitation, and offers a model to help all parties maintain a perspective on the presenting problems as well as progress. Many programs post their models artistically to capture the attention of consumers and staff alike (e.g., Dr. Ben-Yishay uses an illustration of a person running over seven hurdles, which symbolize each step of his treatment model from start to finish).

A number of other treatment models have appeared in the literature to help guide clinical intervention. These include selecting a particular type of teaching approach given the presenting neuropsychological strengths and weaknesses (Barco, Crosson, Bolesta, Werts, & Stout, 1990; Gross & Schutz, 1986), training community mobility skills (Cullity, Jackson, & Shaw, 1991),

Table 1-2 Goals of Rehabilitation

Steps	Engagement	Awareness	Compensation	Adjustment
Behaviors	Attendance Participation Seek out feedback Open to discussing problems Willingness to listen and to try out staff suggestions	Recognize strengths and acquired problems Learn about head injury Evaluate the impact of the injury on yourself and others Recognize the need to change your approach to solving problems Include important people in the rehabilitation process	Use new strategies to solve problems Identify both self-initiated strategies and how to get support from others Demonstrate improved self-control in all settings Avoid getting stuck on problems	Acceptance I'm okay and so are others Tolerate support and feedback from others "Forgiveness" and "letting go" are critical for a successful adjustment

This model is designed to help clients and staff understand the general goals of rehabilitation. It is intended only as a guide given that everyone's injury, personality, and rate of progress are different. This model is largely based on research by Dr. Ben-Yishay at New York University.

treating postconcussional syndrome (Gordon, 1990), shifting the clinical emphasis to empower the consumer with more control and input into the rehabilitation process (DeJong, 1979; O'Hara & Harrell, 1991), and offering family support (Rosenthal & Young, 1988).

In most cases the models currently available in the literature need to be modified to fit with the resources, philosophy, and needs of the persons served to be applicable to each rehabilitation setting. Although these models can be helpful, they are only one tool for rehabilitation. Staff must be careful to base rehabilitation efforts on the needs and desires of each individual relative to their point of recovery and available resources and to use treatment models only as a reference where appropriate.

FUTURE CONSIDERATIONS TO ENHANCE STAFF EFFECTIVENESS

Improving Management Practices—Toward a Service Management Model

Service management developed within private industry as an outgrowth of the changing economy (i.e., the shift from manufacturing to a greater emphasis on the service industries). Since its inception, this management philosophy has grown in acceptance as well as sophistication.

Service management, by definition, is a total organizational commitment that makes quality of service the number one responsibility of every person in the organization. Service quality and value in this paradigm are defined by the consumer and not by those who deliver the services. In his book about methods to reform service organizations' traditional management practices, Albrecht (1992) defines service management as "an overall approach, a philosophy, a management model, and a set of methods and tools that can transform an organization into a service-oriented, customer-driven business" (p. 22).

Within the field of rehabilitation and health care in general, service management in the purest sense is a new area for some and an evolving concept for many. Clearly, all human service organizations have a service mission. The stated service mission of the organization, however, whether written or delivered verbally, does not guarantee that the needed management supports will be present to allow staff to be truly responsive to the needs of the consumer. Perhaps more important, it does not guarantee that management has a significant investment in and direct accountability for supporting the areas of clinical services that ultimately affect outcome.

Often there is a large discrepancy between the organization's stated mission and the management support or clinical autonomy needed to make service quality a reality. Some of the distinctive characteristics of the service management model presented by Albrecht (1992) are discussed below.

Turning the Pyramid Upside-Down

Traditional management models place administrators and senior management staff at the top of the pyramid. As one moves down the pyramid (i.e., along lines of authority or on the organizational chart), one typically finds middle managers, department heads, clinical staff, and various support personnel. Service recipients interface with the organization predominantly at the bottom of the pyramid. The service management model constitutes a dramatic reversal of this structure and essentially turns the pyramid upside-down.

This model essentially places the needs of the service recipient first and shifts management priorities to supporting the individuals in the organization who offer direct services to the consumer. Although this inversion does not change the need for management systems (setting goals, prioritizing, making decisions, providing leadership, etc.), it does shift the way that managers relate to staff across all organizational levels. Inherent in this process is offering direct service staff more control and autonomy in their work.

The traditional top-down flow of demands generated from above is realigned to have management focus on what they can do to help staff achieve greater work efficiency and responsiveness to consumers. Greater support and attention to the needs at this level of the organization will in turn lead to greater creativity and innovation consistent with the service mission. Organizations that provide this level of responsiveness will in turn be more clinically and financially successful in that their services will be in touch with genuine consumer needs. Management functions in effect become a service consisting of a greater emphasis on leadership (as opposed to management) directed at empowering staff to achieve and maintain clinical quality.

Wall-to-Wall Training

Shifting to a service management model requires a total commitment from all levels of the organization. Unless all staff embrace the concept and get the support to operationalize the organizational changes, transitional problems are likely to ensue. The most successful service organizations implement staff training initiatives as one of the fundamental steps to strengthen the service culture.

Although the service management model may appear to be an ivory tower concept, comprehensive staff training, if conducted properly and followed up with the needed supports, can be an effective vehicle to create a unifying service culture within organizations.

Quality of Work Life for All Staff

Experts in the field of vocational psychology have long stressed the need to shift from developing theories of work adjustment to the identification and refinement of instruments that provide direct measures of staff abilities and needs (Lofquist & Dawis, 1969). Consistent with this view, Albrecht (1992) stresses that assessing staff attitudes (and needs) is as important as measuring consumer needs if program leaders are to be effective in improving service delivery. He suggests that measuring quality of work life is an effective strategy to assess the program culture and should at a minimum address the following questions:

- Are staff involved in a job worth doing?
- Are working conditions safe and secure?

- Is there adequate pay and benefits?
- Is job security a concern?
- Is competent supervision provided?
- Is feedback on job performance given?
- Do staff have the opportunity to learn and grow on the job?
- Can staff get ahead on merit?
- Does work offer a positive environment and social climate?
- Is there justice and fair play?

Developing rating scales for these items and other known areas of need can be useful measures to understand and address staff needs. Analysis of these data and appropriate action can result in program changes that are ultimately more responsive to staff needs. Another useful activity is simply to ask staff to list the five most frustrating and reinforcing aspects of their jobs along with suggestions as to how their work can be more effective and satisfying. These data can then be used to develop individualized staff development plans not only to remove some of the barriers to their performance but, as important, to enhance and maximize the rewarding aspects of their work.

Strategic Planning to Avoid Quick-Fix Expectations

A central component of service management is strategic planning. This process enables management staff to facilitate the development of specific objectives and monitoring procedures in key performance areas designed to improve both service delivery and the service culture. Objectives that serve as blueprints for development are prioritized, and follow-up plans are outlined for staff to follow. This program development and change process ideally consists of self-empowered groups on and across all organizational levels that set out to improve specific areas of need. Tracking progress toward these objectives assists staff in recognizing program development priorities and in maintaining a perspective on the progress that is being made because this is easy to lose sight of during day-to-day activities.

The service management model is an excellent one to implement. It is, however, not without complications in its application to brain injury rehabilitation programs. The model is designed to provide a strong unifying framework that sets the clear expectation that consumer needs are the center of focus of all staff. Unless this ethic and value system is practiced at all levels within the organization, there will probably be mixed messages and confusion, particularly at the middle management level.

Additionally, rehabilitation providers are frequently in the position of offering services to customers who may have diametrically opposed goals if not openly adversarial attitudes (e.g., when cost containment pressures are directly contrary to strong clinical recommendations and consumer or family wishes). Guidelines for addressing and tracking these most complex problems are reviewed in Chapter 15.

Although there are complications with any management model in rehabilitation, the fundamental shift toward keeping service quality a universal responsibility will ultimately empower clinical staff to be increasingly responsive to consumer needs. Adherence to this philosophy and approach to management will also enable staff to more confidently address ethical and moral problems that may surface, such as conflicts of interest between consumer needs and organizational goals.

The Power and Value of First-Person Accounts

> After listening to a presentation on cognitive problems after brain injury, the father of a 19-year-old survivor approached the presenter. With an intense look, yet showing little emotion, he stated simply, "You know a lot about what happens to the head, but now can you tell me what happens to the heart?"

First-person accounts are in many ways the best vehicle for staff to increase their sensitivity to and awareness of the needs of persons affected by brain injury. These accounts typically offer staff the vital knowledge they need to understand more clearly the impact of this type of injury and how they can best assist within the context of their role (Sachs, 1991). Fortunately, the professional litera-

ture has recently placed increased emphasis on including highly valuable information and insights from those persons who have been directly affected by a disability (Seligman & Seligman, 1988; Williams & Kay, 1991).

Beyond the professional literature, many detailed personal accounts have been initiated by consumers themselves (Gauer, 1991; Talbert, 1991). These contributions to the field and, in effect, to society include articles and books (published and unpublished), personal presentations, and other valuable artistic and cultural media (i.e., paintings, drawings, poems, films, and specialty journals). A review of some of the titles of these initiatives, such as *Building Satellites is Easier* (Marsh, 1992) and *Why Did It Happen on a School Day?* (Cameron et al, 1993), immediately reinforces the notion that rehabilitation professionals cannot grasp the extraordinary, unique, and personal consequences of brain injury without paying close attention to each individual and family.

The message here is simple: People working in the field need regular opportunities to learn from those who have been most affected by brain injury. This not only helps staff develop a greater awareness of the needs of people with brain injury over time but also serves to remind experienced staff to avoid making generalizations as to what individuals and families need. Additionally, such accounts can be useful to staff by helping them see the value and importance of their role in the rehabilitation process without losing sight of the fact that family members provide the major source of support to most survivors over the course of a lifetime (Brooks, Campsie, Symington, Beattie, & McKinlay, 1987; Jacobs, 1985; Kozloff, 1987).

First-person accounts also serve to illustrate the inspiring accomplishments made by people with disabilities and to define further the valuable partnerships that develop between consumers and professionals (Mahanes, 1985; Turnbull & Turnbull, 1990). Without question, many consumers and family members alike have provided exceptional examples to professionals of how one can overcome what seem to be insurmountable odds to improve one's life after brain injury. Consequently, people with brain injuries and their families need to play a significant training role in shaping staff attitudes, knowledge, and skills. This training, in combination with building a consumer- and family-centered service culture, will ensure that staff efforts remain focused on the most critical aspects of adaptation for each person served.

Within this general arena there is a highly neglected aspect of research that, once studied, will broaden our understanding of the full impact of a disability on the person and family. This neglected area of scientific investigation includes the failure of clinicians and investigators alike to look more closely at the positive contributions that persons with disabilities make to others. Rectifying this requires a recognition of the unique qualities of each individual separate from his or her acquired problems as well as an understanding of how the changes associated with a traumatic event can result in personal growth opportunities for many (Murray-Seegert, 1989; Sachs, 1985).

In reviewing the professional literature, Turnbull and Turnbull (1986) identified two types of negative biases: the tendency to make negative generalizations, and the tendency to make a negative interpretation to explain unexpected positive results. The investigators expressed concern about these findings and stated, "If actions are the by-product of values, what does a negative focus imply about our interpretation of the meaning of disability?" (p. 110). They suggested that assessment tools and studies need to be developed that allow staff to accentuate the positive aspects of each individual's circumstance.

Commitment to Dissemination and Utilization

Training and organizational development needs vary significantly at different points on the continuum of rehabilitation services. This not only is the result of the different technical skills required at different points of recovery, ranging from acute medical intervention to community integration, but also is directly influenced by the size and structure of each organization. Consequently, one cannot generalize about the optimal strategies to prepare staff and design rehabilitation programs.

One can safely say, however, that there is presently a great need to develop training programs for staff that focus on the dissemination and utilization of existing knowledge. This is particularly important because the exponential growth of the field has outstripped our clinical and scientific knowledge base to the extent that many staff are providing services without adequate preparation (Rosenthal, 1992).

Existing clinical knowledge is of limited benefit unless we can create service delivery systems that enable staff to access and use the most current techniques. As this is accomplished, the level of expertise within programs will increase greatly. This result not only will accelerate staff development via the team process but will help ensure that quality services are provided to consumers. This is particularly important given the limited time that consumers and families have in which to make the best use of their resources. A number of training methodologies and staff support systems designed to increase staff skills are reviewed in this chapter and throughout this book.

Furthermore, there continues to be the need for ongoing research to evaluate scientifically the effectiveness of the many clinical interventions commonly used. Research is also needed to identify new clinical approaches and organizational design alternatives. It is critical to note, however, that advances in organizational development should not imply mere institutional growth.

Organizational development within this context refers to devising ways for rehabilitation services to be well integrated with natural, existing, yet underdeveloped community resources (DeJong, Batavia, & Williams, 1990). This approach to program development, which in effect aims to reduce the consumer's dependency on time-limited rehabilitation services, will assist consumers in living more independently and for longer periods of time in the real world (Durgin, Cullity, & Devine, 1991). To accomplish these objectives efficiently, we need to look beyond the specialized literature in the field of brain injury rehabilitation and review other innovative human service initiatives designed to serve people with other types of disabilities who face similar challenges.

Shifting the Orientation of Staff Development Initiatives

Clinical service settings are dynamic environments that are constantly changing (philosophical orientations, needs of the clients and families, reimbursement changes, organizational structure, etc.). In this light, it is crucial to recognize that staff's effectiveness, and in many ways professional self-esteem, is determined by their ability to have their knowledge and recommendations favorably impact in a number of different areas (many of which are slow and resistant to change). This includes a positive contribution to the person with brain injury, his or her family and support system, the clinical team, the rehabilitation program itself, the willingness of financial sponsors to sanction treatment as valuable and necessary, employers, the community at large, and so forth.

Consequently, if training programs are to be maximally effective; if they are to offer staff inspiration for their valuable work and the skills to meet their daily challenges, they must be able to target content areas that are well beyond discipline-specific technical skills. Training and sup-

port programs for staff must focus on the key barriers that impact on staff performance and systems effectiveness. Only in this way can we prepare staff, as individuals and as working teams, to meet the current demands of providing brain injury rehabilitation in our health care environment.

Racino (1991) has stressed that a number of changes need to be made in personnel preparation if staff are to be effective service providers in today's human service environments. Her recommendations are outlined in Table 1-3 and are directed toward preparing staff to assist persons with disabilities return to community living. The shifts in training that she recommends are in direct response to the many diverse changes in the field and the demands that these changes place on staff. Exhibit 1-1 outlines a combination of non-traditional and often underutilized training topics used in rehabilitation settings that are consistent with this need to shift our orientation to staff development. These content areas should also be considered for training in order to increase staff's ability to meet the contemporary and future demands of providing effective clinical services.

CONCLUSION

In the field of brain injury rehabilitation there are inseparable links among clinical quality, staff training, organizational development, pro-

---

Table 1-3 Shifting the Emphasis of Staff Training

Away From	*Toward*
Primary skills-based training	Values-based training
Group training	Individualized curriculum designs
Trainer-trainee model	Facilitator-learner model
Technical focus	Accessing and using support
Rigid personnel roles	Flexible and changeable personnel roles
Teaching others how to intervene (i.e., expert model)	Greater emphasis on how to approach problems, issues, and challenges
Service categories and disabilities	The lives of individual people
Expert opinion in competency development	Identification of important areas by people with disabilities, their families, and practitioners
Human service focus	Cross-disciplinary and public focus
Research in institutional and semicontrolled environments	Longitudinal studies of people living in community settings
Service orientation	Life and community orientation

Exhibit 1-1 Underutilized and Nontraditional Training Topics for Helping Staff Meet Contemporary Service Delivery Demands

Understanding the value of other clinical and personal perspectives

Motivating and reinforcing others to become invested in helping people with disabilities

Addressing ethical problems

Understanding the basics of learning theory and using data-based instructional technologies to measure progress across settings

Leadership and management training

Operating as a change agent in social systems as well as organizations

Advocacy strategies

Creating interdependence through identifying and accessing existing community supports and resources

Conflict management and negotiation skills

Social action models that discuss methods of systematically addressing complex problems

Teaching other adults to carry out interventions and recommendations (professionals, support staff, family members, etc.)

Conducting evaluations that are less deficit focused and place a greater emphasis on identifying and capitalizing on the personal qualities and strengths of those served

Identifying strategies to define consumer-specific reimbursement variables that will affect the scope and duration of the services being offered

Recognizing the positive contributions that persons with disabilities make to others

Outcome research and cost-benefit analysis of rehabilitation to help staff maintain a perspective on treatment

Strategies to empower, inspire, and motivate service recipients

Strategies for clinical and legal risk analysis

Maintaining a stable and enhanced sense of professional identity within the context of transdisciplinary teamwork

Explicit strategies to maintain personal energy, enthusiasm, and commitment

Team-building strategies

Role releasing and overcoming value conflicts in work with survivors, families, and other rehabilitation staff

Understanding the behavioral components of health

Strategies for networking with other rehabilitation programs and professionals

Understanding the context of rehabilitation within the field of health care and the general social and economic climate

Basic clinical research skills (such as single case study designs)

gram management, and external socioeconomic forces. Given that the field is expected to undergo further changes and developments, the interrelationships of these areas will be constantly evolving and continually tested. To meet these challenges, we must recognize that much of our growth in the field is not dependent on a particular domain of expertise but on our capacity to listen carefully and respond to those whom we serve. This includes recognizing our strengths and limitations, operating from a positive set of values and high standards, and supporting the identification of and access to meaningful supports for consumers and staff alike. This in many ways requires staff to broaden their vision of how they contribute, both within their roles and as individuals, to the rehabilitation process.

If staff are to grow and thrive within their roles, they must gain insight into how the demands of rehabilitation require many different kinds of support, technical knowledge, and personal skills. Interestingly, many of the personal qualities that we encourage and teach throughout rehabilitation—perseverance, creativity, risk taking, experimentation, humility, realistic expectations, interdependence, courage, and so forth—are those qualities that we as professionals need to use as well. Staff need well designed training experiences and support on an ongoing basis if they are going to gain this insight and increase their skills in critical development areas.

While we are addressing these challenges, we should never sell ourselves short of what has been accomplished in the field. Nor should we lose sight of the fact that more needs to be done to help many people with brain injury and their families access even the most basic resources to aid in their adaptation to this change. As we move forward we must help each other recognize that we have more to learn, much to give, and a lot to celebrate.

REFERENCES

Albrecht, K. (1992). *At America's service*. New York: Warner.

Barco, P.P., Crosson, B., Bolesta, M.M., Werts, D., & Stout, R. (1990). Training awareness and compensation in postacute head injury rehabilitation. In J.S. Kreutzer & P.H. Wehman (Eds.), *Cognitive rehabilitation for per-*

sons with traumatic brain injury: A functional approach. (pp. 129–146). Baltimore: Brookes.

Ben-Yishay, Y., Rattok, J., Lakin, P., Piasetsky, E., Ross, B., Silver, S., Zide, E., & Ezrachi, I. (1985). Neuropsychological rehabilitation: Quest for a holistic approach. Seminars in Neurology, 5, 252–277.

Biklen, D. (1988). The myth of clinical judgement. Journal of Social Issues, 44, 127–140.

Brooks, N., Campsie, L., Symington, C., Beattie, A., & McKinlay, W. (1987). The effects of severe head injury on patient and relative within seven years of injury. Journal of Head Trauma Rehabilitation, 2, 1–13.

Caffarella, R.S. (1988). Program development and evaluation resource book for trainers. New York: Wiley.

Cameron, B., Brylski, P., Dansiken, M., Felton, J., Hayes, L., & Kitchner, D. (1993). Why did it happen on a schoolday? My families' experience with brain injury. Catonsville, MD: Maryland Head Injury Foundation.

Carlzon, J. (1987). Moments of truth. Cambridge, MA: Ballinger.

Cullity, L., Jackson, J., & Shaw, L. (1991). Community skills training. In B.T. McMahon & L. Shaw (Eds.); Work worth doing: Advances in brain injury rehabilitation. (pp. 307–344). Orlando, FL: Deuteuch.

DeJong, G. (1979). Independent living: From social movement to analytical paradigm. Archives of Physical Medicine and Rehabilitation, 60, 435–456.

DeJong, G., Batavia, A.I., & Williams, J.M. (1990). Who is responsible for the lifelong well-being of a person with a head injury? Journal of Head Trauma Rehabilitation, 5, 9–22.

Durgin, C.J., Cullity, L., & Devine, P. (1991). Programming for skill maintenance and generalization. In B.T. McMahon & L. Shaw (Eds.), Work worth doing: Advances in brain injury rehabilitation (pp. 349–371). Orlando, FL: Deuteuch.

Durgin, C.J., Rath, B., & Dales, E. (1991). The cost of caring: Balancing the human and economic factors when justifying the cost of brain injury rehabilitation. Continuing Care, 10, 21–30.

Gans, J.S. (1983). Hate in the rehabilitation setting. Archives of Physical Medicine and Rehabilitation, 64, 176–179.

Gauer, J. (1991). A traumatic brain injury survivor talks to professionals. (Cassette Recording No. STR 2-91). Richmond, VA: Rehabilitation Research and Training Center on Severe Traumatic Brain Injury, Virginia Commonwealth University.

Gilbert, T.F. (1978). Human competence: Engineering worthy performance. New York: McGraw-Hill.

Gordon, B. (1990). Postconcussional syndrome. In R.T. Johnson (Ed.), Current therapy in neurological disease—3. Philadelphia: Decker.

Gordon, J. (1991). Measuring the "goodness" of training. Training, 28, 19–25.

Gross, Y., & Schutz, L.E. (1986). Intervention models in neuropsychology. In B.P. Uzzell & Y. Gross (Eds.), Clinical neuropsychology of intervention. (pp. 179–204). Boston: Martinus-Nijhoff.

Jacobs, H.E. (1985). The Los Angeles head injury survey: Procedures and initial findings. Archives of Physical Medicine and Rehabilitation, 69, 425–431.

Knowles, M.S. (1980). The modern practice of adult education. New York: Cambridge University Press.

Knox, A.B. (1985). Adult learning and proficiency. In D. Kleiber & M. Maehr, (Eds.), Advances in motivation and achievement: Vol. 4. Motivation in adulthood (pp. 251–295). Greenwich, CT: JAI.

Kozloff, R. (1987). Networks of social support and outcome from severe head injury. Journal of Head Trauma Rehabilitation, 2, 14–23.

Lofquist, L.H., & Dawis, R.V. (1969). Adjustment to work: A psychological view of man's problems in a work-oriented society. New York: Appleton-Century-Crofts.

Mager, R.F. (1984). Measuring instructional results. Belmont, CA: Lake.

Mahanes, F. (1985). A child's courage, a doctor's devotion. White Hall, VA: Betterway.

Marsh, P. (1992). Building satellites is easier. Unpublished manuscript.

Mazmanian, P.E., Martin, K.O., & Kreutzer, J.K. (1991). Professional development and educational program planning in cognitive rehabilitation. In J.K. Kreutzer & P. Weyman (Eds.), Cognitive rehabilitation for persons with traumatic brain injury. (pp. 35–51). Baltimore: Brookes.

McMahon, B.T., Shaw, L.R., & Mahaffey, D.P. (1988). Career opportunities and professional preparation in head injury rehabilitation. Rehabilitation Counseling Bulletin, 31, 345–355.

Mullins, L.L. (1989). Hate revisited: Power, envy, and greed in the rehabilitation setting. Archives of Physical Medicine and Rehabilitation, 70, 740–744.

Murray-Seegert, C. (1989). Nasty girls, thugs, and humans like us: Social relations between severely disabled and nondisabled students in high school. Baltimore: Brookes.

Nowlen, P.M. (1988). A new approach to continuing education for business and the professions: The performance model. New York: Macmillan.

O'Hara, C., & Harrell, M. (1991). Rehabilitation with brain injury survivors: An empowerment approach. Gaithersburg, MD: Aspen.

Peters, T. (1982). In search of excellence. New York: Harper & Row.

Prigatano, G.P. (1987). Neuropsychological rehabilitation for work reentry. Paper presented at the Postgraduate Course on Rehabilitation of the Brain Injured Adult and Child, Williamsburg, VA.

Prigatano, G.P. (1989). Bring it up in the milieu: Towards effective brain injury rehabilitation interaction. Rehabilitation Psychology, 2, 135–144.

Racino, J.A. (1991). Preparing personnel to work in community support services. In A.P. Kaiser & C.M. McWhorter (Eds.), *Preparing personnel to work with persons with severe disabilities*. Baltimore: Brookes.

Rosenthal, M. (1992). Ethics and brain injury: The time has arrived. *Journal of Head Trauma Rehabilitation, 6.*

Rosenthal, M., & Young, T. (1988). Effective family interventions after traumatic brain injury: Theory and practice. *Journal of Head Trauma Rehabilitation, 3,* 42–52.

Rummler, G.A., & Brache, A.P. (1988). The systems view of human performance. *Training, 25,* 45–53.

Rummler, G.A., & Brache, A.P. (1993). *Troubleshooting the human performance system*. Warren, NJ: Rummler-Brache Group.

Sachs, P.R. (1985). Beyond support: Traumatic head injury as a growth experience for families. *Rehabilitation Nursing, 10,* 21–23.

Sachs, P.R. (1991). *Treating families of brain-injury survivors*. New York: Springer.

Seligman, M., & Seligman, P.A. (1988). *Ordinary families, special children: A systems approach to childhood disability*. New York: Guilford.

Sherman, V.C. (1993). *Creating the new American hospital: A time for greatness*. San Francisco: Jossey-Bass.

Snell, M.E. (1990). Building our capacity to meet the needs of persons with severe disabilities: Problems and proposed solutions. In A.P. Kaiser & C.M. McWhorter (Eds.), *Preparing personnel to work with persons with severe disabilities.* (pp. 9–23). Baltimore: Brookes.

Sork, T.J. (1990). Theoretical foundations of education program planning. *Journal of Continuing Education in the Health Professions, 10,* 73–83.

Spencer, L.M. (1986). *Calculating human resource costs and benefits*. New York: Wiley.

Sullivan, R.L., Wircenski, J.L., Arnold, S.S., & Sarkees, M.D. (1990). *The trainer's guide: A practical manual for the design, delivery, and evaluation of training*. Gaithersburg, MD: Aspen.

Talbert, B. (1991). Living with a head injury. *Journal of Cognitive Rehabilitation.* [Special issue].

Turnbull, A.P., & Turnbull, H.R. (1986). Stepping back from early intervention: An ethical perspective. *Journal of the Division of Early Childhood, 10,* 106–117.

Turnbull, A.P., & Turnbull, H.R. (1990). *Families, professionals, and exceptionality: A special partnership*. Columbus, OH: Merrill.

Wieck, C. (1979). Training and development of staff: Lessons from business and industry. *Education Unlimited, 1,* 6–13.

Williams, J.M., & Kay, T. (1991). *Head injury: A family matter*. Baltimore: Brookes.

Ethical Issues in Staff Development

John D. Banja

2

OBJECTIVES

Upon completion of this chapter, the reader will be able to:

1. recognize the role of decision making within the evolution of a rehabilitation consumer's identity as a person with a disability
2. explain four ways that the mere presence of an institutionalized or formal program of care may have negative or injurious effects on rehabilitation consumers
3. discuss how rehabilitation is especially prey to controversies and dilemmas over whose version of rightness or goodness ought to prevail in medical and life-care planning
4. describe how traumatic brain injury (TBI) rehabilitation may be especially challenged by ethical dilemmas over allocating medical resources as allocational criteria are influenced by evolving technology, clinical standards, and an eroding economic base to finance TBI care
5. illustrate how staff development might evolve with respect to guidelines or principles that are routinely encountered in professional ethics

Ethical Issues in Staff Development

Issues pertinent to staff development in the delivery of TBI services are as varied as they are complex, partly as a result of the enormously broad spectrum of clinical, social, and economic concerns precipitated by this type of injury. Despite this complexity, however, the notion of staff development in TBI necessitates a coherent understanding of what that development is intended to achieve and why such an achievement is significant and valuable. In other words, a plan of staff development, no matter how intricate its parts, must ultimately be able to explain why TBI staff development is necessary, why its goals are valuable and meritorious, what is the good that staff development ultimately accomplishes and for whom, and how its goals can be realized efficiently and evaluated fairly.

Most of the chapters in this text are concerned with clinical training and organizational aspects of staff development, but a chapter on ethics allows an examination of those valuative issues on which the staff development construct ultimately rests and that permeate specific moments of the staff development process. To gain a focus on those valuative issues, we might begin by pointing out the obvious: TBI staff development issues from a health care and rehabilitation perspective. Because the overarching goal of that care is to advance the welfare of consumers of TBI services, the goals of TBI staff development must be ethically justifiable. That is, a theory of staff development must articulate a conception of goodness or welfare pertaining to the competence, professional relationships, and service delivery of individuals who care for persons with TBI.

It is all too easy, however, to believe that remedying ethical problems or being ethical only requires a good conscience, authentic moral sincerity, or the moral courage to resist the temptation to do wrong. Furthermore, if ethics simply refers to doing good, then this definition embraces events otherwise too trivial to merit serious attention, such as when a therapist tells a client where to go for subsequent therapy or when the therapist accommodates a client's request for a drink of water. If ethics, however, is

to refer to an important aspect of the delivery of rehabilitative care and staff development, its import must transcend mundane situations that are straightforwardly or unproblematically good, courteous, or beneficial.

Only a cursory glance at the literature on medical ethics is needed to show that, when professional discussions turn to ethics in health care, they invariably do so because doing what is right in a given situation has become unclear. That is, given the situation at hand, it is no longer obvious what is the right thing to do or wherein welfare or goodness consists. Somehow, the problematic situation presents a no win situation in which each of the available courses of action or remedies seems unfavorable or distasteful and common sense is at a loss to decide confidently which course of action to pursue. Indeed, deliberations over ethical dilemmas in health care are largely efforts to sort out and clarify seemingly contradictory rights, duties, obligations, virtues, valuative beliefs, and so forth that inform but collectively seem to impede our view as to the right course of action (Francoeur, 1983).

Scholars and commentators over the last decade or so have sought to clarify the nature of these problems by analyzing bioethical or moral dilemmas in health care as conflicts of rights or duties. (In health care ethics, rights usually pertain to certain expectations or entitlements that health care consumers can expect from health providers. Duties, on the other hand, usually refer to those acts or behaviors that are demanded of health care professionals in their meeting a professional standard of care.) Principal among these rights or duties as they figure in bioethical dilemmas are the following four (Beauchamp & Childress, 1989):

1. *autonomy,* meaning the right of a client to be self-determining and to participate in decisions over his or her welfare, even to the extent of refusing unwanted treatment; correlatively, autonomy betokens the health professional's duty to respect a client's right to be free from coercion and manipulation and to respect the client's

right to determine what shall count as benefits and burdens while he or she is undergoing care

2. *nonmaleficence,* meaning the right of persons not to be harmed or, correlatively, the duty of the health provider to do no harm (*primum non nocere*)

3. *beneficence,* meaning the right of health care consumers to anticipate that the provider will actively pursue measures to secure their welfare; correlatively, the duty of the provider to advocate for the client's welfare and to assist in realizing that welfare

4. *justice,* meaning the right of persons to expect fair and just treatment; correlatively, the duty of the health provider to treat clients justly and to provide them what they are owed without prejudice or discrimination

Interestingly, much of what is called clinical or applied ethics concerns clashes or confusions over the rights or duties as described above. For example, am I acting morally or perversely by securing a sexual surrogate for the client with TBI? Should I endorse or oppose my client's intention to drive an automobile if I am uncertain about the risks that his or her driving would pose? Should clients be summarily discharged from rehabilitation when their reimbursement is exhausted even if their functional potential has not nearly been reached?

The guiding concern of this chapter is TBI staff development, which will be broadly interpreted to embrace the professional identity and growth of individuals in health care as qualified by their moral relationships with clients, intimate others of clients, other professional staff, and society at large. The following pages proceed with an examination of the four principles mentioned above—autonomy, nonmaleficence, beneficence, and justice—as they relate to staff development. The goal of this examination is to show why professionals treating persons with TBI cannot ignore how their professional growth and identity are influenced by certain inherently ethical dimensions in TBI care.

AUTONOMY

Our society evolved from a political insistence on individual liberty and freedom. Indeed, our political heritage is that of a liberal democracy that jealously guards the right of citizens to be self-determining (Calvert, 1991; Hospers, 1990; Rorty, 1990). This right is not absolute because granting everyone unlimited freedom to do as he or she pleases would create a hopelessly chaotic social order whose only mainstays would be anarchy and terror. To the extent, however, that individual expressions of liberty and freedom do not imperil and jeopardize others, our society grants citizens a prima facie right to exercise that liberty, even if doing so invites personal risk. For a governing body to restrict expressions of individual liberty, it must show a compelling state interest (i.e., it must demonstrate how one's behavior jeopardizes others or the general welfare). Thus our society condones boxing but in most states refuses motorcyclists the right to ride without helmets. Presumably, the gravity of the risks inherent in the former do not violate an acceptable social standard and are consented to, are assumed by, and apply only to the boxers; unhelmeted motorcyclists, however, pose an excessive risk of harm to anyone around them should they be struck in the head while riding and subsequently lose control of the cycle (*People v. Kohrig,* 1986).

Individuals entering into a medical setting and commencing a health care relationship with a professional obviously do not lose their right to personal liberty and freedom. Yet the peculiarity of the health care relationship often compromises the expression of autonomy.

The delivery of health care, whether short-term, rehabilitative, or long-term, has historically tended to be paternalistic (Jonsen, Siegler, & Winslade, 1986). Health professionals are trained and become skilled in understanding the nature and process of disease and the available courses of treatment. They become familiar with and skilled in administering treatment interventions, just as they become familiar with what to anticipate in most treatment scenarios. Indeed, staff development largely revolves around the evolution and augmentation of the professional's knowledge and skills as well as the ways in which various staff responsibilities should interdigitate in realizing health care goals.

Clients, on the other hand, are often ignorant of their ailments, may be frightened about their plight, and frequently have made a considerable psychological investment in trusting and therefore relying on the professional's skill and ability to alleviate their discomforts or improve their well being. Given the orientations of the client and the provider, it is easy to understand how the professional can assume control of the relationship by way of determining and then launching a program of care. Nevertheless, it is extremely important for health providers engaged in the process of staff development to recognize that the individuality and personhood of anyone largely derive from the choices and decisions that he or she makes. Consequently, to deprive individuals of their capacity to make choices is to deprive them of their personhood and personal dignity (Agich, 1990; Barrett, 1962).

Rehabilitationists, especially those in TBI, are more than a little familiar with the way in which they assume a proactive and assertive role in implementing therapeutic programs for clients. Yet fundamental and typical differences occur in their relationships with clients in comparison with what occurs in acute, nonrehabilitative care settings.

The autonomy of clients and the preservation of their capacity to make decisions and choices in acute, nonrehabilitative care largely involve the informed consent construct, wherein clients are informed of their conditions, the treatments being contemplated, the risks associated with the treatments, and other sorts of material information. The goal of this information is to allow clients to decide whether such treatment is really in their best interests and even to refuse it if they so choose. As such, client autonomy and the right of self-determination in acute settings is preserved (Rosoff, 1981).

TBI rehabilitation, however, frequently and commonly witnesses an entirely different client-provider relationship, wherein the client's injury has robbed him or her of precisely that decision-making autonomy. If an individual's autonomy and identity are largely a function of the deci-

sions and choices he or she makes, then serious impairments of an individual's ability to formulate choices and judgments will simultaneously affect that individual's autonomy (Caplan, Callahan, & Haas, 1987). This situation is all too familiar in TBI. Clients or their families remark that the client's personality is changed or is no longer present. Customary attitudes, preferences, habits, dispositions, and so on are not what they once were. Indeed, health providers are familiar with claims that their clients have become different persons or different selves. They cannot remember, understand, or process information. Their ability to interact with others and to exhibit acceptable social behaviors has been seriously damaged (Lezak, 1978). These fundamental changes in the way persons with serious TBI behave can present the injured self as only a pale reflection of the former, premorbid self. The client is not functioning autonomously because he or she is unable to determine and integrate his or her choices and decisions into meaningful and coherent patterns. The client loses his or her self by losing precisely those cognitive skills (memory, understanding, reasoning, insight, etc.) on which the self relies in maintaining a comprehensible and meaningful engagement with the world.

A fundamental ethical and legal consideration that must be impressed on TBI treatment staff is how a client's loss of autonomy affects the staff's responsibility for the client's welfare. An irony in TBI rehabilitation is that providers must be wary of serious harms befalling seriously cognitively or behaviorally impaired clients because such clients, being nonautonomous selves, will not be held responsible for the consequences of their actions. Should serious harm occur to the client, the provider who has been entrusted with that client's care may very well be held accountable (King, 1986). On the other hand, the ideal rehabilitation outcome will be one that advances the client toward a return of decisional and functional capacity and a proportional restoration of the client's autonomy. That restoration inevitably implies the client's assuming responsibility for his or her actions and decisions, which in turn requires the provider's gradually relinquishing the protective orientation he or she may have assumed initially toward the client.

If rehabilitation can be said to be an art, this is certainly one of its finer moments. Where clients exhibit significant potential for improved functional behaviors, thinking, and self-understanding, the professional must gradually withdraw his or her paternalistic impulses to allow room for the clients's increasing independence and autonomy. Yet the professional must also temper that withdrawal with a sensitivity to the degree of risk that accompanies those increments in the client's progress toward autonomy. That is, the rehabilitation provider must exercise professional judgment in determining when the client is reasonably ready to assume responsibility for his or her decisions or behaviors. The professional's role, behavior, and expectations—in other words, his or her overall relationship with the client—cannot be static or fixed but must evolve and change as the rehabilitation process moves toward higher levels of functional restoration and independence.

From a vantage point that asks about the ethical foundations or ethical locus of staff development, the ultimate comprehension of that development will target the return of autonomy to clients as its ideal goal. The principal ethical repercussions of this targeting for staff development consist of the following: Staff development as it relates to realizing therapeutic outcomes should not ultimately be driven by some predetermined, professionally articulated vision of what is good for the client, but rather by a client-centered perspective that appreciates how the client would construe his or her individuality, uniqueness and personal dignity. For some clients, this personal dignity will translate into robust self-reliance. For others, personal dignity and individuality will mean their capturing a self that they can accommodate, especially in their interpersonal relationships. For all clients, however, the attainment of authentic autonomy will entail their ability to engage the world in an uncoerced, relatively productive, and personal way, a way that they find meaningful and over which they would wish to exert ownership (O'Hara & Harrell, 1991a).

In the rehabilitation setting, an obvious way to allow clients to express their individuality and dignity is to engage them in decisions regarding their care. This is precisely an area, however, where persons with TBI frequently fault their therapists for assuming too paternalistic an attitude that disallows sharing in decisions. As Debbie, a woman with TBI, urged providers:

> Allow patients to have more say so, more control over what we're doing, be more involved, and have more power over our lives. . . . We need encouragement. Therapists didn't need to keep telling me the negatives and that I wasn't going to get better. Learning I have rights and can be angry and take care of myself, and hearing a doctor give me hope for the first time are what has helped (O'Hara & Harrell, 1991b).

Brandon, another TBI survivor, had this to say:

> Don't make me feel like you are this big person, and I'm the nobody. When doctors tell me what is going on or give me reports, I can understand. I can fight a monster I can see but if I can't see it I can't fight it. You need to let me be part of my treatment (O'Hara & Harrell, 1991b).

The health provider might reply that perhaps neither of these clients realized the extent of risk that they would have assumed in being allowed more say so and more control and that their being allowed that liberty would have put the provider's liability at unreasonable risk. Although there may be considerable truth in such claims, the frequency with which statements such as Debbie's and Brandon's are heard from TBI survivors, combined with the enormous mass of literature attesting to the ways in which health providers simply assume that they are singularly empowered to make decisions for clients, gives substantial credibility to Debbie's and Brandon's criticisms (O'Hara & Harrell, 1991a). Besides, if no room existed within the rehabilitation spectrum of care to encourage individuals such as Debbie and Brandon to assume responsibility for themselves, then rehabilitation's touting the ideals of independence but disallowing expressions of independence is a callous hypocrisy.

Not only must the rehabilitation process reasonably elicit clients' choices and decisions to evoke a sense of empowerment from them, it should ideally facilitate the reconstruction of clients' identities. If a person's uniqueness and individuality issue from his or her choices, then the hallowed notion of independence that rehabilitation has proclaimed throughout its history must ultimately mean establishing or reawakening a rehabilitation consumer's capacity to engage the world in a way congruent with that person's being (Banja, 1988). For that to occur, however, the person's likes, dislikes, preferences, habits, attitudes, values, beliefs, skills, and so forth must be reasonably constant and fairly transparent to him or her. Otherwise, clients' decisions and actions might be utterly incoherent or at odds with their identity.

Understandably, rehabilitationists often conceive of independence as only physical nondependence, such as one's not having to depend on others to accomplish one's activities of daily living. Real independence, however, connotes one's capacity and desire to express who one is, to express one's uniqueness, plans, and life projects. Staff development theory must recognize that the rehabilitation environment will be one of the first arenas wherein clients may want to express that uniqueness and individuality. As such, staff should be keenly sensitive to those expressions and not regard them as instances of noncompliance when they seem to contradict or oppose the treatment plan. Rather, they may be the client's first attempts to reclaim his or her dignity, assertiveness, and sense of control.

Some rehabilitation providers may find these suggestions presumptuous, unrealistic, or unethical. They will ask about those clients with TBI who are so seriously injured that even a marginal return to the former self (i.e., even a marginal return of cognitive or practical behavioral functioning) is unlikely. They may ask about those clients whose behavior has been so impaired from injury that restoring the most rudimentary social graces would constitute a singular success. They may argue with the idea of restoring the client's self with this sort of challenge: "Before injury, the client engaged in substance abuse, excessive risk-taking, and grossly destructive interpersonal relations. Is this the sort of autonomous self I am supposed to restore?"

In response to these challenges, we must recognize that the concept of staff development has thus far been examined only from the standpoint of the principle of autonomy. Autonomy and what it means to function autonomously, however, are remarkably complex notions admitting of an array of ethical, psychological, and sociopolitical connotations (Collopy, 1988). Indeed, remarks thus far may seem to suggest that only clients have autonomy, not their providers. What about autonomy issues pertinent to the treating professionals? Are we to understand that professionals are not at liberty to have some input in the form and content of their own development and the nature of services that they will provide to clients? Must professionals genuflect before their clients' autonomy when expressions of that autonomy will predictably lead to disaster? These issues are discussed below.

NONMALEFICENCE

Hippocrates admonishes physicians above all to do no harm. Examples of health professionals doing harm are odious even to contemplate because they represent a noxious abdication from the professional's socially entrusted responsibilities. Indeed, outright examples of such harm smack of criminal acts, such as when health providers defraud clients, exhaust their financial resources, sexually abuse them, or intentionally injure them.

The duty of nonmaleficence is a categorical injunction never to use clients as means to some end but always to treat them as ends in themselves (Ramsey, 1970). This injunction is precisely congruent with our ultimate goal of restoring a client's dignity, autonomy and independence.

Most health providers would be taken aback by the thought that their therapeutic presence in the recovery of a person with TBI constitutes a danger. McKnight (1989), however, has insightfully discussed the iatrogenic dimensions of health care delivery systems and makes compelling points that seem relevant for TBI staff development.

First, McKnight (1989) points out that the very existence of a care system (such as exists for persons with TBI) not only is an institution-alized response to the existence of some disease or injury but also depends on the incidence of that disease or injury for its own perpetuation. TBI delivery services (as well as any other health care delivery system) are therefore para-sitic on the clinical phenomena they are disposed to treat and, indeed, grow and develop propor-tionally with that syndrome's exerting a toll on the social and economic welfare of citizens. It is well known that clinical syndromes that begin to develop high visibility can witness their associ-ated care systems evolve a life of their own that subsequently risks those systems losing a vision of their original intent. Professional groups, about which more will be said later, begin to de-velop in such ways that their members inevitably depend on those systems for their livelihood. Commercial industries spring up around them. By virtue of their availability and publicity, cer-tain treatment strategies or interventions that were developed for specific purposes become widely, albeit sometimes problematically, used. Thus TBI has itself seen questions raised about costs associated with the use of computerized tomography and the utility of certain other thera-pies. Inevitably, sophisticated bodies of knowl-edge and commercial interests develop in response to the utilization of these treatments, but only recently have we begun to ask serious questions about the morality of their excessive use (Easterbrook, 1987).

To the extent that a service delivery system becomes an end in itself and loses sight of the needs of those persons whom it was intended to serve, that delivery system runs the danger of creating false needs or of advocating treatments or therapies simply because they are available, irrespective of whether the client actually needs them. As one person with TBI remarked, "I was fitted to every program; the program wasn't fit-ted to me" (O'Hara & Harrell, 1991b).

Another iatrogenic dimension of service de-livery systems is that they are frequently costly and often depend on the largesse of government or private insurance. Consequently, a moral ob-ligation exists for health professionals to show that monies spent for services could not be better spent elsewhere. Economic issues are discussed

at greater length later, but it is worth noting that the mere existence of a service is hardly an index of its worth. McKnight (1989) wonders whether monies that underwrite the operating costs of certain service providers might not be better spent by being shifted either into the private sec-tor or directly into the pockets of disabled per-sons themselves. Would more disabled persons, for instance, seek employment if greater mon-etary incentives existed for their doing so, and would it be ethical to create those monetary in-centives by shifting funds from governmentally subsidized programs into other economic sec-tors? Could programs faced with the threat of losing their funding successfully argue that their disappearance would ultimately be more harm-ful to society's disabled citizens than could be balanced by the opportunities that such eco-nomic reapportionment would create?

Furthermore, is it not the case that any health care delivery program runs the risk of creating dependencies among its clients who access that service? The most obvious program candidate in this regard is the social welfare system, although psychotherapy has often experienced a similar accusation. Suspicions run high that certain pro-grams become a permanent substitute for the goal that the program is supposed to realize for the client. Governmentally subsidized welfare becomes a substitute for gainfully employed earnings, and psychotherapeutic sessions be-come a substitute for the client's embarking on a responsible and productive engagement with his or her responsibilities, other human beings, and the world at large.

A fourth iatrogenic hazard of delivery sys-tems that McKnight (1989) discusses is their need for formal labeling and bureaucratic strati-fication of the persons whom they serve. The in-jurious consequences of labeling have long been recognized, and professional caregivers must be acutely sensitive to those possibilities. A person's identity may be overwhelmed by the labels used in reference to his or her need for ser-vices, such as when we speak of persons with TBI as being behaviorally disordered, incompe-tent, or inappropriate.

If the duty of nonmaleficence is doing no harm, then TBI professionals should be wary of certain subtle forms of disrespect or affronts to clients' dignity. One person with TBI complained about nurses who talked behind his back as though he was not there or who referred to him in the third person instead of acknowledging him directly (O'Hara & Harrell, 1991b). Moreover, language should not be used with clients that they do not understand. For example, when a client of limited education and understanding inquired of his physician about the pain in his shoulder, the physician tersely responded that the pain was caused by the shoulder's subluxation.

A most interesting component of nonmaleficence is the phenomenon of countertransference, which may be understood as the health professional's allowing his or her real relationship with clients to be distorted by unconscious forces. Psychiatric theory holds that, although negative or nonproductive countertransference is not an intentional harm, its consequences could certainly have a deleterious effect on the provider-client relationship (Stein, 1985). Suffice it to say that health professionals need to scrutinize their negative feelings about clients, especially when those feelings are thwarting the therapeutic relationship. If a program of therapy with a particular client is not going well and the relationship seems to be deteriorating, the professional ought to ask "What am I doing wrong?" This is not to imply that clients have no responsibility for their recovery. It is to imply, however, that because the relationship between the rehabilitation provider and the client is a therapeutic one rather than a purely contractual one, the provider should interpret unfavorable moments in that relationship psychodynamically. The therapist's impulse to find fault, to blame, to express anger, and so forth may derive from the impaired dynamics of the relationship rather than represent a reasonable response to the client's failings. In short, blaming clients for noncompliance might actually express the provider's way of coping with his or her own inability to deal with whatever is obstructing the client's cooperation. Although such behavior carries different moral connotations from a more intentionally malevolent act toward a patient, such as using the time-out room as a punitive measure, negative countertransference can seri-

ously erode the client-provider relationship and therefore is an important matter of consideration in staff development.

BENEFICENCE

The topic of beneficence vividly introduces the previously mentioned clashes in values that are so representative of dilemmas in health care ethics. The reason is that beneficence connotes the health provider's taking active steps to do good for clients. Because health care has become so complicated by technologic, legal, economic, sociopolitical, and scientific developments, however, the meaning of doing good has become less and less clear. In the field of TBI, for example, was the discontinuation of Nancy Cruzan's nasogastric feeding and her resulting death a greater good than insisting that her feedings be maintained so that she would continue to live (Gibbs, 1990)? Is a greater good achieved by spending tens of thousands of dollars on various postacute, vocationally oriented rehabilitation interventions than by spending those same monies on coma stimulation programs or on research programs aimed at preventing TBI? Further complicating the determination of beneficence is the fact that our society, in the name of autonomy and liberty, condones risk taking. Thus, in the name of liberty and privacy, Americans protect the right to pursue various risk-laden behaviors—from boxing, hang gliding, and car racing to overt abuse of their physical welfare (smoking, alcoholism, overeating, etc.)—as the political legacy of the founders' vision of life in a liberal democracy (Hospers, 1990).

This insistence on accommodating autonomous action, even if it threatens serious personal harm, presents considerable problems for health professionals, who as mentioned above are entrusted with their clients' welfare. The sociopolitical philosophy that condones autonomous action despite its risk presupposes that such risky behavior is transparent to and freely chosen by the actor. The familiar professional experience in TBI settings, however, is the client's frequently having little or no idea of the nature and consequences of his or her act, thus necessitating that the responsibilities for the outcome of that act revert to his or her caretakers. This less than optimal ability to function autonomously entails a number of problems for the TBI professional who is concerned about acting beneficently.

The first is determining whether the client can reliably manage any spheres or domains of decision making or can competently execute functional behaviors such as are involved in activities of daily living. As noted previously, staff development theory must recognize that health providers have no right to usurp a client's freedoms and liberties so long as the client is able to exercise those freedoms and liberties in a way that invites no unreasonable or unintended harm to the client or to others. Consequently, an early task is to identify just what types of (cognitive or functional) behaviors the client is able to execute and then to accommodate those behaviors accordingly (Nolan, 1984).

This suggestion is analogous with the current statutory and judicial trend in creating limited guardianships, whereby the limitations might be temporal (i.e., for a certain period of time at the end of which the guardian must reapply for continued guardianship) or restricted in scope (Hommel, Wang, & Bergman, 1990). Limiting the scope of guardianship means recognizing that an individual might not be able to manage his or her finances but is able to make out a will and to raise a family. This trend is in contrast to the way guardianship laws have historically developed. Because guardianship laws in many states derived from protecting persons with congenital encephalopathies or with irreversible psychiatric disorders, those laws tended to assume that the individual was globally incompetent and that the guardian or proxy decision maker would need to make any and all decisions for his or her ward (Anderson & Fearey, 1989). The more contemporary, enlightened approach of limited guardianship betokens an appreciation of the idea of selective incompetence, which leaves open the possibility of islands or domains of competent function or decision making.

In the abstract, the notion of selective incompetence is appealing, but given the practical exigencies of TBI care, its ideals may be difficult to realize. The first problem is for the staff to come

to some agreement about whether the client can exercise autonomous decisions over some domain. This may be difficult. Consider, for example, John, a client who refuses to participate in cognitive therapy because he finds doing so humiliating. Is such a refusal a competent one, and, if so, should it be honored? Determining whether an individual is competent to make such a refusal may invite a catch-22 situation because the client may be receiving cognitive therapy precisely because of impaired decision making. The therapist may argue that a refusal of cognitive therapy, given John's present diminished competence, cannot be honored until he has advanced to a higher level of insight regarding the degree of his impairment. But this, the therapist may argue, can only occur through more therapy. To discontinue therapy now, the therapist claims, is professionally irresponsible, will deprive John of the opportunity to make considerable improvements in his overall decision making abilities, and will thwart John's efforts to lead an independent life. John, however, claims that the therapy up to now has caused him enormous anguish and that, although he acknowledges his cognitive impairments, he nevertheless knows when he finds an experience psychologically intolerable. What, then, is the more beneficent act: to acquiesce to this client's refusal of the therapy and accept the resulting functional limitations, or to employ some manipulative or coercive strategy to ensure a participation that may lead to considerable improvement?

A straightforward legal analysis might find that, given the bare facts mentioned above, John's wishes to discontinue the therapy ought to be accommodated. So long as his abhorrence of cognitive therapy is consistent and his justification of that abhorrence is basically reasonable or understandable, an insistence that the therapy continue appears sadistic. An important consideration in making such a determination, however, is whether John truly realizes the consequences of his refusal. How would he respond to a well-calculated clinical judgment predicting that, without cognitive rehabilitation, he will not be able to live independently, will have relatively poor vocational potential (and thus a poor earning potential), will experience a diminished social life, and will be constantly frustrated in his inability to make even relatively simple day-to-day decisions? The individual who is cognitively unable to understand or appreciate the impact of those consequences, especially in terms of being unable to compare their burdensomeness against the burdensomeness of continuing with the therapy, might be deemed incompetent to refuse the therapy (Roth, Meisel, & Lidz, 1977).

On the other hand, presumably competent individuals make appallingly bad decisions all the time, such as the individual who blissfully enters into a predictably bad marriage or a predictably dangerous business alliance. If we allow persons without obvious neurological impairments to make poor decisions, why should we not extend the same right to the neurologically impaired?

A response to this question is that our allowance of predictably poor decisions by people who should have known better is significantly conditioned by the notion that such persons ought to be able to manage or cope with the consequences of their decisions. The individual who is blind to the reality of the marriage he or she is entering will presumably have the resources to terminate it once it becomes intolerable and, one hopes, to learn by that mistake. The individual who makes poor business decisions needs to show his or her creditors initially that he or she could summon the resources to pay off whatever debts might accrue or to nullify them should the business decision go sour. But persons with serious brain injuries, whose preferences and desires may create serious, inextricable liabilities for themselves and others, have a much more problematic right to realizing those preferences and desires.

Suppose that Mary has sustained a serious brain injury that has profoundly compromised her ability to live independently. Although she demands the right to live by herself, the last three occasions on which she has done so have ended in disaster. Her decision making is such that she cannot plan a simple meal, cannt hold a job for more than a week, and, on each occasion that she has tried to live independently, has ended up having to prostitute herself to survive.

Although Mary demands to be left alone, what would beneficence demand be done for her?

Despite Mary's insistence on privacy and the unpleasant repercussions that would arise from a health provider's resisting that insistence, a strong moral argument could be made that Mary is simply not responsible or capable enough to protect her own interests and that some sort of paternalistic, welfare-oriented intervention is required. At the very least, Mary's prostituting herself to survive is compelling evidence that, paradoxically, she cannot live unless she places herself at extreme risk to her life (i.e., of being infected with human immunodeficiency virus and, hence, possibly infecting others). The fact that Mary would not voluntarily choose prostitution as a livelihood if she were able to participate in socially acceptable employment provides additional weight to the argument that a beneficent approach to Mary's situation would mandate some type and degree of paternalistic supervision of her behavior, decisions, and lifestyle. The sadness of Mary's situation consists in the predictable struggle that would ensue between Mary and her caretakers over determining an allowable degree of infringement on her privacy. The relevance of cases such as Mary's to staff development consists in their alerting professionals to the need to anticipate situations that resist an easy answer about how much latitude staff ought to be allowed in gainsaying or interfering with their clients' decisions and preferences, even though such interference appears justified.

Unlike issues over determining how society's welfare might be advanced (i.e., greater support for education, housing, medical research, etc.), client care dilemmas involving beneficence frequently reduce to whether the client is competent to make those decisions, what burdens might accrue to the health provider or some third party if the client's wishes are accommodated, and, if the client is not competent to engage in rational decision making, who the surrogate decision maker ought to be and what the scope of his or her authority ought to include. It is important to note, however, that what may superficially appear as problems over whose vision of goodness or welfare ought to prevail may obscure a more complex psychological agenda. Consider the following statement from a person with TBI:

> Professionals need to learn to see and refer to their clients as "customers" realizing that ultimately their most important task is to reinforce and build self-esteem. *Nothing*—from physical health to advanced cognitive ability—can really take place unless self-esteem is intact. . . . The customer should have the final say as to whether or not (s)he will participate in any particular practice, including behavior modification. Lastly, the customer needs to know (s)he has the right to leave treatment at any time. (S)he still retains his/her civil rights (O'Hara & Harrell, 1991b).

Within the context of beneficence, this statement is problematic from the standpoint of determining whether the particular customer with TBI actually is competent to make such decisions and refusals. Yet the wisdom and significance of this statement for staff development consist in its targeting the primacy of self-esteem in the provider-client relationship.

Providers should recognize that a major dimension of their self-esteem consists in the client's engaging them for care. Having the opportunity to exercise their skills gives providers the self-satisfaction of realizing their professional training and reinforces their feelings of self-worth. Clients, on the other hand, also need to identify a quid pro quo, which in nonrehabilitative, acute care environments is generally the anticipation of cure or significant relief from symptoms. In rehabilitation, however, where independence rather than cure is the goal, clients need to be able to muster a fundamental accommodation to the idea of rehabilitation and must believe that they can meaningfully participate in and gain from their therapeutic regimen. In contrast to clients in the nonrehabilitative environment, who place their trust in a surgeon's skills or the success probability of some sophisticated intervention, rehabilitation clients quickly become aware of the effort and commitment they must exert to realize their functional goals. To the extent, therefore, that the client feels depressed, despairing, hopeless, disenabled, and

abused, he or she will be psychologically distanced from the rehabilitation program and may very well resist its objectives.

Within the context of beneficence, such resistance may seem to express itself in treatment refusals, which are often interpreted as dilemmas over whose decisions will prevail as to the client's care. Yet the real rather than the apparent issue may not at all be some theoretical or philosophical calculation of goodness or rightness but the client's unexpressed although desperate need to acquire some feeling of control over his or her destiny, a feeling that has profoundly dissipated since the onset of the client's disability (Caplan et al., 1987). Just as the provider's negative countertransference may result from the provider's not having his or her unexpressed needs met in therapy, so too may the client's unexpressed needs precipitate a maladaptive reaction to treatment in the form of resistance or noncompliance to what would otherwise seem to be in his or her best interests (i.e., participating in therapy).

It is interesting and illuminating to note how the above quotation juxtaposes the notions of self-esteem with decision making. The point is not that clients are inherently hostile to their providers and quick to disagree with them. The point, which has extremely significant repercussions for beneficence, is that until the rehabilitation client can identify a sense or locus of goodness or worth within himself or herself the therapist's pleadings about the goodness or value of some therapy may fall on deaf ears.

Two fairly recent court cases illustrate this phenomenon. In one, a 29-year-old woman who had become quadriplegic from progressive cerebral palsy asked for legal sanction to discontinue her nasogastric feeding (*Bouvia v. Superior Court [Glenchur]*, 1986). Her health care providers balked at her request, claiming that she was depressed (and therefore incompetent to make such a refusal). They also claimed that complying with such a request ran contrary to Hippocratic ideals and provided an opportunity for a homicide suit. In another case, a 35-year-old man who had been quadriplegic for 4 years from a motorcycle accident demanded that his artificial ventilation (on which he was dependent) be discontinued so that he might be allowed to die (*State of Georgia v. McAfee,* 1989).

The courts granted both requests for basically the same reasons. In each case the court found the individuals to be of sufficient mental capacity to realize the consequences of their requests and ruled that competent adults have a nearly absolute right to refuse unwanted treatment, even when that treatment is of a life-prolonging variety. Yet once the judicial decisions were handed down, neither of the appellants carried through their previously stated intentions of having their life-prolonging treatments withheld.

One can only surmise that, although both these persons may have had honest intentions about seeking court authorization to have their life-prolonging treatments discontinued, the affirmations of empowerment that they experienced vis-à-vis the judicial rulings were perhaps sufficient to alter their negativity toward continued survival and their health care providers' values. It is an extremely plausible interpretation that the empowerment they accrued through the legal rulings was an affirmation of their sense of self, personal dignity, and authority over others. Armed with that self-affirmation, neither individual proceeded to resist the treatment ministrations of their respective health providers but, as it were, came to agree with them that continued life and the therapies associated with continuing that life were beneficent or appropriate choices.

To the extent, therefore, that a program of rehabilitation and a theory of staff development aim to achieve unassailably beneficent goals for clients (such as independence and functional restoration) but forget about clients' fundamental feelings of dignity and self-worth, the program and the theory lose their ultimate grasp of what beneficence in rehabilitation is about, namely, that persons ought to receive rehabilitation because as human beings they can claim a right to a life as free as possible from the handicapping effects of a disability. First, therefore, is the basic, fundamental recognition of their personhood—the fact that they are persons with disabilities, not disabled persons (Research and Training Center, 1987). Respect for others and its subsequent demonstrations ought not to materialize in response to a good outcome resulting from those efforts. Ultimately, beneficence reminds us that acknowledging those individuals' inherent dignity and self-worth precedes any therapeutic effort.

JUSTICE

Sooner or later, a theory of staff development must examine what the health care professional owes his or her clients. The reason is that staff development will evolve its professional identity as a derivative of the professional-client relationship. That relationship, however, must admit of certain qualifications in the form of limitations on the expectations to which the participating parties agree. Without such explicit qualifications, an opportunity would be created for significant misunderstandings as to where such parties' reciprocal rights and duties would begin and end. The question that is entertained in this section is how a theory of staff development ought to contemplate the duty of staff to allocate care to clients.

It is taken for granted that health care providers will not allocate care whose nature and scope exceed their skills and competencies (Banja, 1985). Obviously, a physical therapist ought not to perform psychotherapy, and a neuropsychologist ought not to perform orthopedic bracing or casting. Just as obviously, a minimal entitlement of health care consumers is that whoever is deemed most qualified to perform psychotherapy or bracing or casting ought to deliver those services according to a reasonable professional standard. Indeed, an essential element of any medical malpractice action is the plaintiff's showing that the provider failed to meet the professional standard of care (King, 1986).

Although the nature of one's professional training places constraints on the care that he or she will offer clients, the contemporary worry over the allocation of care principally revolves around sustaining an economic infrastructure adequate to pay for it. The most obvious area in which staff development is ethically affected by economic limitations is the quality of care that is afforded to health care consumers. That quality of care is affected by a host of economic factors, such as the ability of the employer to attract skilled professionals by offering competitive or attractive salaries, the therapeutic equipment and technology to which staff have access, the degree to which staff enjoy the economic resources to attend continuing education courses to improve their skills, and, of course, the length of stay that the client's reimbursement source authorizes.

It seems fair to say that ability to pay is today's principal form of rationing rehabilitation or, for that matter, any health care service (Callahan, 1990; Consumer Reports, 1990). It is profoundly clear that a recently injured individual with serious TBI who has only Medicaid insurance will not receive anywhere near the extent of rehabilitation as his or her counterpart residing in a state with unlimited no fault coverage for catastrophic accidents. On the other hand, even if society decides that everyone with TBI is entitled to minimal access to rehabilitation, one might argue that not everyone with TBI needs rehabilitation because certain persons would not benefit from it (Haas, 1988). Memory retraining for a permanently unconscious client would be as wasteful an allocation of a professional service as driver's training for someone with profound, irreversible visual-perceptual deficits.

Our moral intuitions, especially as they derive from a sense of equity and fairness, suggest that the degree of rehabilitation one receives ought to be congruent with the degree of rehabilitation potential one exhibits. Is ability to pay, therefore, a moral principle on which rehabilitation ought to be distributed? The answer depends on how one morally comprehends rehabilitation or, for that matter, any type of health care. That is, if one regards health care as a right or entitlement that is due to anyone with reasonable medical need, then ability to pay seems an inherently discriminatory method of health care allocation that ought not to be tolerated in a society that boasts a moral obligation to further the welfare of its citizens (Outka, 1981). On the other hand, if health care is regarded as a commodity to be bought and sold according to something like free market principles, then ability to pay would seem a reasonable way to determine its distribution, especially in a capitalistic, entrepreneurially driven, liberal democracy such as our own.

Because health care is so basic a need and is so important a requisite for living a meaningful life, most individuals, as indicated by the polls, favor a universal system of access to health care (Blendon & Donelan, 1990). Yet our society has thus far been singularly unsuccessful in determining how that universal access would be subsidized and what would count as a reasonable allocation of care, usually discussed as a reasonable minimum of care, that such universal access would include (Callahan, 1991). Consequently, we continue for the most part to evolve a system of care that is currently beset with enormous pressures to curtail costs and to allocate care according to a fixed, prospective method of reimbursement.

TBI staff development ought to consider seriously the moral impact of the current third party reimbursement system on the professional role. Those dimensions generally comprise four domains of health care considerations: admission to care, care for the sickest, length of stay, and discharge (Dougherty, 1989).

Briefly, if rehabilitation potential and rehabilitation outcomes, especially in TBI care, fluctuate according to a host of factors (e.g., the nature and gravity of the brain insult, the client's age, the presence and acuity of comorbidities, the presence and degree of family support, socioeconomic circumstances, and premorbid intelligence and health status), then rehabilitation facilities may very well assume a conservative position on admitting clients with meager reimbursement resources whose rehabilitation prognosis portends a lengthy and costly stay. Some facilities may yield to a financial imperative and deny the admission of such clients, or, if admission is authorized, the facility may limit the scope of the client's program of care (e.g., restricting the number and/or duration of therapies or the client's length of stay). Facilities may be especially anxious about expediting the discharge of clients with meager reimbursement because locating a discharge site might prove extremely difficult. Indeed, where no discharge site is readily identified, the host facility may face a serious, perhaps devastating, financial loss if the client has to stay and consume expensive but nonreimbursed services.

If TBI staff development, therefore, targets quality care as one of its principal aims, it is important to reflect on the ethical ramifications of how ability to pay affects the realization of that quality and whether rehabilitation services can be delivered in an egalitarian spirit if that allocation is so dependent on the idiosyncracies of a client's insurance plan. From a distributive justice perspective, ability to pay seems particularly repulsive in rehabilitation in view of the enormous disparity in care that different reimbursement levels entail and how restricted access to rehabilitation negatively affects functional outcomes. Indeed, consider the reverse of inadequate reimbursement: What are the ethical ramifications of admitting TBI clients who happen to have an extremely generous reimbursement source? Will staff be tempted to overtreat if they know the client's insurance will pay? Would facilities resist discharging TBI clients if it were known that their insurance would continue to pay for services for however long the facility chose to provide them?

Ethical approaches to remediating the unfairness of undertreating or overtreating clients as a function of health care insurance seem to require at least a scientific understanding of rehabilitation potential and rehabilitation outcome. In the ideal case, treatments would be allocated according to a client's rehabilitation potential and therapeutic progress and would be terminated when that potential has been actualized. Determining rehabilitation potential in an objective, consensually agreed upon manner, however, does not appear to have been realized presently because of the enormous complexity of the holistic context that rehabilitation addresses, the multifactoral nature of phenomena affecting rehabilitation progress and outcome, and the economic considerations affecting the client's ability to pay (Frey, 1990; Haas, 1988). Furthermore, discussions of the quality of rehabilitation outcomes are enormously contentious and value laden. Consider the following remark by Jennett (1984, p. 12):

> How often have I read that a patient has made "a remarkable recovery," only to find him hemiplegic, dysphasic and dependent. Such a judgment is likely to come from those who were familiar with how desperately ill the patient once was, lying in a coma in the intensive care unit. But

compared with his former self, it seems reasonable to ask who is kidding whom?

As long as rehabilitation potential and outcome remain indeterminate and subjectively defined, rehabilitation will be hampered in justifying client care decisions over admissions, length of stay, and intensity of therapy. Having a consensually validated mechanism to justify the claim that a client has truly reached functional potential will expedite discharge and result in cost savings. Eliminating redundant or nonuseful rehabilitation care (and its associated reimbursement) may create greater financial opportunities for access to rehabilitation for individuals who otherwise might be deprived of rehabilitation because of economic insufficiency.

Maintaining quality care in a cost-constraint environment is surely one of the most pressing moral problems of the contemporary era of health care. If the moral backbone of TBI staff development inheres in the client-provider relationship, then staff development needs to assess its evolution within the present economic climate of health care. Crucial to that assessment will be whether the future of cost constraints will seriously jeopardize rehabilitation's traditional caring paradigm, its team approach to client care, and the holistic understanding of the client's needs that rehabilitation has traditionally espoused, in short, whether contemporary cost constraints will force rehabilitation to abandon its historical identity.

STAFF DEVELOPMENT AND PROFESSIONAL ETHICS

In his book *Professional Ethics,* Bayles (1981) lists a number of characteristics of professionals that include extensive training, an intellectual component of the professional's skills, licensure or certification, membership in professional organizations, and a reasonable degree of freedom for that profession to evolve. Most important, however, in any group's boast that it is a profession is its members providing an important service to society.

Fortune tellers, phrenologists, and warlocks would probably be pleased to be called professionals, but their claim to performing an important social service is dubious. Groups, however, that combine an element of intense training (to master a body of knowledge) with the provision of an inarguably valuable service to the community have a relatively unproblematic claim to being called professionals. The reasons are that the social need for the service is uncontroversial and that the service requires sophisticated skills to deliver. Indeed, this combination of social need and requisite skill is so acutely focused among certain professions that society requires their members to be licensed or certified to protect itself from incompetents. This protection via licensure or certification also extends to the profession itself by way of protecting its high standards from being compromised by quacks or charlatans.

If professional groups primarily exist to protect society and to enhance society's welfare, then an immoral professional is one who violates that social trust. An individual acts unprofessionally (and unethically) when he or she jeopardizes society's interests or subordinates those interests to his or her own. Thus we are disgusted when we learn of the engineering construction firm that uses cheap and faulty materials, by the physician who bills insurance companies for services that were never delivered, and by the accountant who diverts assets from a company into his or her own pocket. Such actions represent precisely the opposite of what a professional is supposed to do: advance the welfare of the consumers of that service, not take advantage of them (Bayles, 1981).

The relevance of these observations for TBI staff development consists largely in our recognizing that consumers of TBI services can easily fall prey to fraud and abuse. Because consumers of TBI services can be cognitively or psychologically devastated by the onset of injury or can be simply unable to evaluate the quality of care that a particular provider or facility offers, it is relatively easy for caretakers to go unscathed despite utterly duplicitous behavior. In the presence of serious TBI, neither clients nor their families can be expected to be smart shoppers or to hold providers to anything authentically resembling moral accountability.

As a start, then, one would expect that ethical TBI professionals will hold themselves to a reasonable degree of legal and moral accountability in that they would not exploit or victimize their consumers. We should also expect that any theory of staff development would acknowledge and recommend those widely held social virtues such as respect for human dignity, promise keeping, confidentiality, truthfulness, fidelity, fairness, and so forth. Clearly, no theory of staff development could disregard these habits of the heart because they constitute the links in the chain of the client-provider relationship. Leaving aside, then, these more obvious legal and moral expectations that society anticipates from health care providers, what more problematic challenges provide definition for an ethical agenda for the future of TBI staff development?

Perhaps the first is for TBI staff to develop a sense of team or collective moral conscience. This idea has been discussed elsewhere, so that here we only briefly examine some of its elements (Purtilo, 1988). The idea of developing a team conscience issues from the centrality of the team concept in rehabilitation and the notion that decisions reflecting valuative issues should involve orchestrating the team's collective reflection and effort just as those involving clinical issues do. TBI staff development that wishes to pursue this idea should recognize that ethical dilemmas in medicine require considerable thought and expertise that does not occur without serious study, reflection, and practice. Many individuals seem to reject the idea that expertise in ethical insight and decision making requires any special training. Nevertheless, inherent in the development of the team conscience should be the team's acquiring expertise about how ethical dilemmas commonly arise, becoming familiar with ethical decision-making paradigms, developing a common ethical vocabulary, becoming skilled in identifying the ethical elements in a given dilemma or problematic situation, and developing a keen recognition of the client's constitutional rights and liberties (Thomasma, 1982). These items could well serve as an ethics curriculum for staff development activities.

If the TBI team conscience issues from the realization that individual health care providers might have to subordinate their moral subjectivity to a broader comprehension of objectivity and ethical accountability, then team members have an analogous obligation to define the limits of their professional skills and expertise among themselves to allocate care in the most professional and least costly way. This proposal is acutely relevant to the goals of TBI staff development because rehabilitation seems presently in the midst of assessing a number of clinical models, such as the multidisciplinay, interdisciplinary, and intradisciplinary paradigms of care (Lyth, 1992). The goal of whichever model is utilized is, of course, to deliver the most expeditious and competent care possible. Inherently problematic in the team model, however, are questions about whether the team model succeeds better than a more fragmented or discrete allocation of therapeutic interventions and, even if it does, which team members ought to be doing what.

What are commonly referred to in medicine as turf battles frequently reflect the reimbursement anxieties of whoever is waging the battle. Couched in the rhetoric of better training, better outcomes, and cost effectiveness, turf battles are frequently suspected of reducing principally to fears over losing revenues to rival service providers. Ethics would seem to require that, so long as clinical skills are equivalent among various professionals and clients receive comparable levels of care regardless of who provides the service, fair market value should determine which professional group would most often perform the treatment. The ethical question, therefore, consists in determining ways to adjudicate rival claims over the quality of services delivered by different TBI professionals.

Intertwined with the question of which professional group is most qualified to perform a given treatment, however, are issues of the advisability of the treatment itself. Regardless of whether neuropsychologists, speech pathologists, or occupational therapists are best qualified to do coma stimulation, a fundamental question arises as to the value of coma stimulation itself. Furthermore, questions about treatment efficacy include not only coma stimulation but many other modalities common in TBI, such as psychotropic medications, sophisticated but costly radiologic tests, cognitive retraining strategies, and various other treatment modalities (Cope, 1989; DeJong & Batavia, 1989).

The impact of turf battles and controversies over treatment efficacy demonstrates an ethical imperative in TBI staff development to conduct outcome research. Neither claims over which health care provider can deliver the safest and most capable treatment nor claims over which treatments are advisable and which are not will make much headway without supporting scientific data. In the absence of scientific justification, both types of claims will appear as self-serving professional rhetoric aimed to ensure the economic well-being of the arguer. Consequently, if TBI staff development is to evolve with confidence in the area of quality of care that staff deliver, internecine conflicts must be resolved fairly and objectively. Otherwise, staff development will be fraught with suspicion and hostility as rival groups jockey for position. Such behavior makes for strikingly poor public relations and doubtlessly erodes public confidence in the integrity of the warring factions.

A final ethical consideration regarding the future of TBI staff development is the responsibility of TBI professionals toward the general community of persons with a disability and the cause of disability (e.g., disability prevention and disability rights). Rehabilitation professionals are uniquely qualified to inform other health care providers, civic groups, social organizations, and the general lay community about the nature of disability, its toll on human life, its management, and ways to dilute its impact on persons with disabilities, their immediate caretakers, and the community in which they live. The issue this raises for staff development is operationalizing the notion that rehabilitation and its associated challenges do not end when the client and his or her family leave the rehabilitation facility. Correlatively, the expertise of rehabilitation providers and their professional growth ought not to be viewed as confined to their immediate work environments but could extend to the cause and ideology of disability. An important mission for the future of staff development is considering the moral obligations of the TBI profession toward disabled persons in general and in diminishing the overall impact of TBI on society. The horror and indescribable pain and misery that the onset of serious TBI exerts on the lives of millions of Americans plead for alleviation. Consequently, because TBI is as much a social as a clinical phenomenon, a dimension of TBI staff development should include the evolution of a social conscience and role.

CONCLUSION

This chapter has largely focused on how the nature and direction of staff development is affected by ethical considerations over the client-provider relationship. Unlike contractual relationships, wherein the terms of authority are rather clearly delineated, the client-provider relationship in TBI is fraught with inconsistencies and uncertainty because of the inevitable uniqueness of the participants and the enormous challenges that are posed by the frequently poor functional capacities that persons with serious TBI manifest.

A central argument of this chapter is that TBI staff development must organize and direct itself according to a client-centered perspective that melds the most salient skills inherent in successful living with the client's uniqueness and individuality. Competent therapists will succeed in facilitating the former with their clients. Great therapists, however, will also evoke the latter.

The onset of serious TBI is one of life's great tragedies. An inspiration for staff development, however, should issue from the possibility of the therapeutic relationship's culminating in the client's reclaiming a meaningful life. Given the uncertainties and challenges that such reclamation poses, few health care disciplines present their practitioners with so formidable a challenge. When the therapeutic relationship succeeds, few disciplines are so rewarding.

REFERENCES

Agich, G.J. (1990). Reassessing autonomy in long term care. *Hastings Center Report, 20*, 12–17.

Anderson, T., & Fearey, M.S. (1989). Legal guardianship in traumatic brain injury rehabilitation: Ethical implications. *Journal of Head Trauma Rehabilitation, 4*, 57–64.

Banja, J. (1985). Whistleblowing in physical therapy. *Physical Therapy, 65*, 1683–1686.

Banja, J. (1988). Independence and rehabilitation: A philosophic perspective. *Archives of Physical Medicine and Rehabilitation, 69*, 381–382.

Barrett, W. (1962). *Irrational man*. Garden City, NY: Anchor.

Bayles, M.D. (1981). *Professional ethics*. Belmont, CA: Wadsworth.

Beauchamp, T.L., & Childress, J.F. (1989). *Principles of biomedical ethics* (3rd ed.). New York: Oxford University Press.

Blendon, R.J., & Donelan, K. (1990). The public and the emerging debate over national health insurance. *New England Journal of Medicine, 323*, 208–212.

Bouvia v. Superior Court (Glenchur), 225 Cal. Rptr. 297 (Cal. App. 2 Dist. 1986).

Callahan, D. (1990). Rationing medical progress: The way to affordable health care. *New England Journal of Medicine, 322*, 1810–1813.

Callahan, D. (1991). Medical futility, medical necessity: The problem-without-a-name. *Hastings Center Report, 21*, 30–35.

Calvert, R.E. (1991). *The constitution of the people*. Lawrence, KS: University of Kansas.

Caplan, A.L., Callahan, D., & Haas, J. (1987). Ethical and policy issues in rehabilitation medicine. *Hastings Center Report, 17*, 1–20.

Collopy, B.J. (1988). Autonomy in long-term care: Some crucial distinctions. *Gerontologist, 28*, 10–17.

Consumer Reports. (1990, August). The crisis in health insurance. *Consumer Reports, 55*, 533–549.

Cope, N. (1989). Legal and ethical issues in the psychopharmacologic treatment of traumatic brain injury. *Journal of Head Trauma Rehabilitation, 4*, 13–22.

DeJong, G., & Batavia, A. (1989). Societal duty and resource allocation for persons with severe traumatic brain injury. *Journal of Head Trauma Rehabilitation, 4*, 1–12.

Dougherty, C.J. (1989). Ethical perspectives on prospective payment. *Hastings Center Report, 19*, 5–11.

Easterbrook, G. (1987, January 26). The revolution in medicine. *Newsweek*, pp. 40–74.

Francoeur, R.T. (1983). *Biomedical ethics: A guide to decision making*. New York: Wiley.

Frey, W.R. (1990). Quality assurance in rehabilitation. *Archives of Physical Medicine and Rehabilitation, 71*, 529–530.

Gibbs, N. (1990, March 19). Love and let die. *Time*, pp. 62–71.

Haas, J.F. (1988). Admission to rehabilitation centers: Selection of patients. *Archives of Physical Medicine and Rehabilitation, 69*, 329–332.

Hommel, P.A., Wang, L., & Bergman, J.A. (1990). Trends in guardianship reform: Implications for the medical and legal professions. *Law, Medicine and Health Care, 18,* 213–226.

Hospers, J. (1990). The libertarian manifesto. In E.D. Klemke, A.D. Kline, & R. Hollinger (Eds.), *Philosophy—The basic issues* (3rd ed., pp. 528–535). New York: St. Martin's.

Jennett, B.(1984, September 12). *Third annual Hemphill lecture.* Chicago: Rehabilitation Institute of Chicago.

Jonsen, A.R., Siegler, M., & Winslade, W.J. (1986). *Clinical ethics* (2nd ed.). New York: Macmillan.

King, J.H. (1986). *The law of medical malpractice* (2nd ed.). St. Paul, MN.:West.

Lezak, M.D. (1978). Living with the characteriologically altered brain-injured patient. *Journal of Clinical Psychiatry, 39,* 592–598.

Lyth, J.R. (1992). Models of the team approach. In G.F. Fletcher, J.D. Banja, B.B. Jann, & S.L. Wolf (Eds.), *Rehabilitation medicine: Contemporary clinical perspectives* (pp. 225–242). Philadelphia: Lea & Febiger.

McKnight, J.L. (1989). Do no harm: Policy options that meet human needs. *Social Policy, 20,* 5–15.

Nolan, B.S. (1984). Functional evaluation of the elderly in guardianship proceedings. *Law, Medicine and Health Care, 12,* 210–221.

O'Hara, C., & Harrell, M. (1991a). *Rehabilitation with brain injury survivors: An empowerment approach.* Gaithersburg, MD: Aspen.

O'Hara, C., & Harrell, M. (1991b). *Survivor empowerment surveys.* Unpublished manuscript.

Outka, G. (1981). Social justice and equal access to health care. In T.A. Mappes & J.S. Zembaty (Eds.), *Biomedical ethics* (pp. 523–531). New York: McGraw-Hill.

People v. Kohrig, 498 N.E.2d 1158 (Ill. 1986).

Purtilo, R. (1988). Ethical issues in team work: The context of rehabilitation. *Archives of Physical Medicine and Rehabilitation, 69,* 318–322.

Ramsey, P. (1970). *The patient as person.* New Haven, CT: Yale University Press.

Research and Training Center on Independent Living. (1987). *Guidelines for reporting and writing about people with disabilities.* Lawrence, KS: Author.

Rorty, R. (1990). The priority of democracy to philosophy. In A. Malachowski (Ed.), *Reading Rorty* (pp. 279–302). Oxford, England: Blackwell Scientific.

Rosoff, A.J. (1981). *Informed consent: A guide for health care providers.* Gaithersburg, MD: Aspen.

Roth, L.H., Meisel, A., & Lidz, C.W. (1977). Test of competency to consent to treatment. *American Journal of Psychiatry, 134,* 279–284.

State of Georgia v. McAfee, 385 S.E.2d 651 (Ga. 1989).

Stein, H. (1985). *The psychodynamics of medical practice: Unconscious factors in patient care.* Berkeley: University of California Press.

Thomasma, D. (1982). Moral education in interdisciplinary teams. *Surgical Technologist, 2,* 15–19.

Considerations in Resolving Ethical Dilemmas

1. What is the ethical dilemma at issue? Can it be explained in terms of clashes or conflicts among values or rights? Here are some general parameters:

    - *autonomy:* Is the client's right to be heard respected? Are the client's civil rights imperiled by the way the decision-making process is being managed? Does the client have decisional capacity? Might the fact that the client has a brain injury be used against him or her to justify overriding what would otherwise be an acceptable decision or preference?

    - *nonmaleficence:* Is any outright or immediate harm threatened by the situation at hand or by the outcomes of the modes of action being contemplated? If harm is an inevitable outcome of any available strategy, will the ultimate decision pose the least amount of harm?

    - *beneficence:* How does one define goodness in the particular case at hand? How can one accomplish the most good? What reasons are there to think that the client's version of goodness is unacceptable?

    - *justice:* Is the locus of decision-making power fair and just? Whose version of goodness ought to prevail? Why? Might decisions be made in a prejudicial or biased manner? Is the right of all relevant parties to engage in the ethical decision-making process acknowledged, and is the input of all relevant parties evaluated fairly and objectively?

2. Has objective information been obtained? How much is known with certainty? How much is reasonable to believe? How much is sheer guesswork or speculation? How much speculation over the consequences ensuing from the various resolutional strategies is reasonable?

3. Do all parties understand the ethical language being used and agree on the ethical principles at stake? Might concrete examples or references to actual cases be used to clarify points at issue?

4. Will the decision makers be willing to have the decisional process and outcome serve as a precedent? If faced with a future dilemma similar to the one they now face, will they be willing to decide it in the same way?

5. Is the reasoning of the decision makers logical, objective, fair to facts, and consistent, or is it partisan, subjective, and ideologically biased to the point where it risks corrupting the interests of fairness and justice?

6. Are there professional standards or norms that might be useful to consider in resolving the dilemma? Would the decision makers be willing to exhibit the major elements of their decisional approach as emblematic of such standards?

Part II

Staff Development and Clinical Intervention

Training Staff for Family-Centered Rehabilitation: Future Directions in Program Planning

Janet M. Williams

3

OBJECTIVES

Upon completion of this chapter, the reader will be able to:

1. describe the differences between the current delivery of services for people with head injuries and family-centered rehabilitation
2. understand the basic challenges in making a shift to family-centered rehabilitation
3. define the difference between family support and family services
4. identify approaches to developing supports and services with families that can be integrated into existing rehabilitation programs
5. develop a plan to train staff in working with families

Training Staff for Family-Centered Rehabilitation

This chapter discusses ways for staff to interact with families so that together they can bring about family-centered rehabilitation. The current delivery of services for people with head injuries is reviewed, and a new direction that will lead to family-centered rehabilitation is described.

The greatest challenge in bringing about family-centered rehabilitation is promoting a philosophy that sees families and professionals as equal experts in the process of supporting the self-sufficiency of individuals with head injuries. This chapter attempts to clarify the philosophical base needed and suggests some specific techniques that can be used to help professionals and families understand the changes necessary to bring about family-centered rehabilitation.

The chapter presents seven challenges in family-centered rehabilitation. Strategies are suggested to promote thinking and discussion about the best ways to train professionals. As strategies, they follow the philosophy of family centered rehabilitation because they allow the person who implements the training to choose or creatively tailor training that meets the needs of the person with head injury.

Four basic value assumptions about families, professionals, and the role of rehabilitation serve as a basis for this chapter. First, a person who has experienced a head injury is part of a family. Thus the use of the word *family* includes the person who has experienced head injury. Family members are those people whom the person considers family (Williams, 1991c). Second, families are already competent or have the capacity to become competent if the proper supports are in place (Dunst, Trivette, Gordon, & Pletcher, 1989). Third, every person is assumed to have the right to live in a home in the community with whatever supports are necessary (Racino, 1990). Out-of-home services are temporary and necessary only while the person moves toward self-sufficiency in his or her own home. Fourth, the professional is a facilitator who generates the resources and solutions needed by families to live in their own homes in the community. Professionals provide a range of resources or solutions

that allow families to make decisions that best address their needs in each situation. These values transcend all aspects of a rehabilitation program and serve as a basis from which all supports and services are developed.

CURRENT DELIVERY OF SERVICE

The current system for people with head injuries separates a person from his or her family for extended periods of time (Williams, 1991a). Services are provided within an established framework, and people with head injuries and their families are forced to accommodate to that framework (Turnbull & Turnbull, 1991). These services are called a continuum, and families often find themselves beginning at one point and arriving at another based on the availability of services that are provided, not necessarily the needs of the person. Professionals are experts who work with an individual to achieve his or her goals. Friends, social activities, and community life are often put on hold until a person gets "better". Once a person has completed specific goals, or when funding runs out, he or she is returned to the family or community.

Families are forced to work within the continuum, which begins to rule their day-to-day life. Visits must be arranged, schedules changed, and accommodations made for the family to have some type of involvement in facility programming. Participation is defined by the program, and distance from the site of the program may interfere with a family's ability to be involved.

This peripheral involvement by families has often led to their inability to control what happens in their own lives. Families are forced to interact with a large number of professionals who surround the separated family member. This interaction is often identified as a source of stress for both families and professionals (Carney, 1991).

The current system of service delivery and the consequent tension in the interaction between families and professionals have led many people to question the notion of a continuum (Conde-luci, 1991; McMahon & Shaw, 1991; Williams, 1991a). This inquiry has generated a more challenging direction for the field: toward family-centered rehabilitation.

FAMILY-CENTERED REHABILITATION

A revolution is occurring in rehabilitation (Williams & Kay, 1991). Services are no longer at the center of daily life for families involved in rehabilitation; rather, families are at the center, and services are only one aspect of a family's life. The revolution has created a whole new way for professionals and families alike to think and act. The language of rehabilitation changes, so that now we talk about families involving professionals and an array of services supporting a family's life. A person's social network of relationships, church, and community stays with the person, and needed services are tailored to support, not supplant, the family. Likewise, funding follows the person, not vice versa.

Family-centered rehabilitation keeps the focus of rehabilitation on functional skills that a person can use to keep or acquire his or her own definition of a meaningful life. The main goal is to use common sense and practical approaches that address vocational, social/recreational, residential, and educational services to teach the essential skills of living in the community for the person and family.

The challenge to staff is to respond to this revolution. Staff become one of many equally important members in a family's life. They support the family as family members adjust to new roles as parent, spouse, sibling, or child of someone with a disability. At the same time, professionals continue to support people with head injury in making their own decisions. They are no longer experts who are all-knowing but rather have the role of knowledgeable people with skills to provide information about specific aspects of a family's life.

Ten philosophical principles underlie family-centered rehabilitation. Each should be considered and implemented in programs.

1. People with head injuries and their families know themselves best.
2. Services must promote self-sufficiency of persons with head injuries. Self-sufficiency means learning not only to do for oneself but how and when to rely on others.
3. Medical services should only be provided for medical issues.
4. Hope is an essential fuel for the future.
5. Rehabilitation should be based upon the needs, not the finances, of a person.
6. People with head injuries and their families should always know their financial status with services. They should know the dollar amount of the insurance coverage and the dollar cost of the service. No family should ever be surprised with the news that their funding has run out.
7. All services should be functional. That is, all activities should have a function that makes sense. People should learn to cook in their own kitchens and control behavior in their own homes.
8. The only services that should be provided in a program should be the ones that cannot be provided in the community. Also, only those services that need to be specialized should be. Using comprehensive services for extended amounts of time may prevent a person from becoming fully integrated into the community.
9. Programs should provide a combination of paid services as well as assistance and strategies in developing informal supports. Informal supports may be relatives, friends, and community members. It is important to try to mobilize these resources early on.
10. Every person should live in his or her own home as soon as possible after a head injury.

For staff this means that family and professional interactions change. The philosophy of self-sufficiency drives the program, and staff are no longer in charge. Some principles are attitudinal in nature and are difficult to quantify. Others are more concrete. The next section focuses on changes needed in professional and family interaction to bring about these qualitative and quantitative changes. Challenges are identified and strategies given that can be developed to bring about positive relationships that support families and professionals in their work together.

FACTORS IN FAMILY AND PROFESSIONAL INTERACTIONS

The extended and serious nature of head injury forces families and professionals to interact over longer and more intense periods than ever before (Hostler, 1991). The initial interaction places professionals in the role of experts whose responsibility it is to save the person's life. The family is a passive recipient of information provided by the experts. This expert role is renegotiated over time depending on a number of factors, which may include a professional's attitudes about the competency of a family in making decisions, how information is presented to families, the balance between hope and reality, the nature of reimbursement and medical programs, the style of the professional and family, and the knowledge base each has about the consequences of head injury. The combination of factors forces families and professionals to interact in different ways.

Challenge 1

Family Decision Making

> The nurse disliked my looking at my son's medical charts, which were normally left in the ICU [intensive care unit] room, and removed them, allowing my fears to wheel freely, without any data to ground myself on or to hold me steady. (Andrea Ramsey, mother of Damon, personal communication, June 1991)

There has been little research about professional attitudes toward family decision making. Families relate differing views that range from negative to positive professional attitudes toward a family's ability to make decisions

(Kramer, 1991; Turnbull & Turnbull, 1985). The negative attitudes may result in the withholding of information and the limiting of choices provided to families in the decision-making process. The positive attitudes may result in the provision of information and support for choices that families need to make. Moving from an expert knowledge of what is best to a family decision-making process is a great challenge.

Initially families learn to rely on professionals, and over time professionals begin to ask families to make decisions. Confusion may occur. The confusion for families may arise in the role change. Professionals, who in a medical situation may have been experts, are now offering information to allow families to make choices. The family may interpret this as a lack of professional knowledge or expertise rather than as a desire to involve families more in the decision-making process. Professionals may think that the family is resistant to making decisions when in reality the family has not understood the role change. The challenge is to promote positive attitudes that see families as competent to make decisions while providing support for them to do so.

Strategy: Promote Positive Attitudes about Family Decisions in All Team and Family Interactions

This attitude shift is one of the most difficult to establish, implement, and monitor, especially in programs where professionals significantly outnumber families on a day-to-day basis. Ideally, all meetings about an individual should include the person and family. In reality, this is not always possible. In team conferences it is important for someone to take the place of the family and to advocate for their viewpoint. Creating a situation "as if" the family were present may give greater insight to the needs of the family.

Families should never be categorized or labeled, and all negative talk about families should be eliminated from programs. Families do the best they can with what they have. If someone on the team does not believe that to be true, it must be addressed directly with the family. Programs owe it to families to discuss concerns about the family with the family. In most situations, families have good reasons for behavior to which a professional is objecting, and clear, immediate communication may clarify the reasons. For example, families are often labeled as uncaring if they do not visit frequently. If a discussion is held with the family, it may be revealed that only a certain number of work absences are allowed and that loss of the job means loss of insurance that is funding services.

Families have been labeled for too long, and the list of examples is endless. The labeling must stop, and professionals must concentrate on open, honest, and clear communication with families.

Challenge 2

How Information Is Presented

Families remember how information is provided far longer than the content of what was provided. For example, when asked about the most helpful professional who worked with their family after head injury, Mike and June Davis, parents of Todd, named "the second neurosurgeon who took over while the primary neurosurgeon was on vacation for a period of time . . . we became very close to him. He would come day or night to the hospital and just take the time to talk to us initially and try to console us in any way that he could" (personal communication, June 1991). The interaction took place more than 11 years ago, and the Davises still remember the manner in which the surgeon spoke to them.

The initial delivery of information may set the tone for future encounters with professionals (Williams, 1991b). If the family is given information filled with inaccurate negative predictions, they may begin to feel that any information provided by professionals is devised to dash hopes for the best possible future. In some instances families refer back to the initial "doom and gloom" predictions they heard from the neurosurgeon as proof positive that information delivered by a professional will be wrong again.

In addition, professionals may communicate to families in the everyday technical language they are accustomed to using with their professional colleagues. If a family is unfamiliar with technical terms, they may be hesitant to ask questions for fear of appearing incompetent. As questions go unanswered, the family begins to lose touch with what is going on with the person. The challenge is to provide information in an open and honest way without jargon and negative predictions for the future.

Strategy: Eliminate the Use of Technical Jargon and Negative Predictions in the Provision of Rehabilitation Services

> [Professionals] need to be reminded regularly that if the people they are talking to do not understand what they are saying most of the time, it is indicative of a lack of specialized training and experience with what is happening to them for the first time. It does not indicate a lack of intelligence. (Andrea Ramsey, mother of Damon, personal communication, June 1991)

A major emphasis of rehabilitation is preparing a person and family for the time when professional services are not available or necessary in their lives. Jargon and technical language have no place in a family's everyday life and should be eliminated from the everyday life of rehabilitation. *Ambulating* means "walking" and *right upper extremity* means "right arm," no matter how a person walks or uses his or her arm.

Professionals should spend time listing all the jargon used in rehabilitation and substituting everyday language. The language should then be operationalized in the program, not written up in a glossary for families. Glossaries, when presented, may provide a bridge, but to eliminate the gap a common language should be adopted that makes translation unnecessary.

Strategy: Build in Time for All Staff to Get to Know Families

"One of the most important aspects of personnel preparation is helping people to understand the process of getting to know other people" (Racino, 1990, p. 210). When professionals are getting to know families, three areas should be highlighted: getting to know the best way and the best time to talk with families about different information; knowing which professionals are important to the family; and finding a setting in which both families and professionals feel comfortable sharing information.

The manner in which information is presented and the type of information a family wants vary from family to family and situation to situation. Some families prefer and interact best one to one or in small group situations. Others are not intimidated by the large groups often characteristic of team conferences. Some families want and read everything they can get about how the brain functions, whereas others may prefer to know about issues such as financial planning, support strategies, and other psychosocial issues. Each time professionals have information for a family, they should always ask the family's preference about who should be there to receive the information and how the information should be presented. Additionally, professionals should make written, video, and audio material available to families that covers a range of topics beyond brain functioning.

Not every professional in rehabilitation has a role or good rapport with every family. Often a family gets to know a professional who helps with an area that is vitally important to them. For example, if walking is a major goal toward which a person is working, the physical therapist may become important in that person's life. The physical therapist has ongoing interaction with the family and may become a primary support for the family. Rather than refer the family to the social worker, who may not have an ongoing relationship with the family, the therapist will enlist the social worker's help in understanding how and when to support the family. This may mean taking time to listen to the person's and family's concerns about what walking or not walking means to them in their everyday life. Alternatively, it may mean advising the family about options they could consider in helping with physical therapy when the therapist is not present.

The setting in which families and professionals interact may have great bearing on how they get to know one another. Rehabilitation hospitals and programs are not natural places in which most families would choose to interact with professionals. It is important that professionals take the time to get out of the hospital or program to places where families are more comfortable. Such places may include the family's home, a local restaurant, or other community establishment. Any time that information is to be shared or time is to be spent with families, the comfort of the place should be considered.

A great technique for preparing personnel to get to know families is to have a staff member spend a full day with a person and family outside the rehabilitation milieu. Ideally, the person will be someone who has completed rehabilitation and is living in the community. With this experience, staff can develop an appreciation of the everyday challenges and joys of the person and family. The fact that real adaptation occurs outside a hospital or program will be better understood. The family's story of obstacles they have overcome and others they have yet to conquer gives a wider perspective beyond billable hours and adaptive equipment.

Challenge 3

The Balance Between Hope and Reality

> Teaching people the importance of *hope* as a *fuel* for the family to use for energy during the terrible demands of the hospital and post-acute time [is crucial]. . . . Families want and need both hope *AND* good "spin" put on the situation because they have to live with it and work with it so *it has to be tolerable*. (Phebe Whitehead, mother of Lucy, personal communication, June 1991).

Professionals and families have long grappled with the dilemma of striking the proper balance between hope and reality. Families have leaned more toward hope and professionals more toward reality. The problem seems to be that people believe that more hope means less reality, and vice versa. Is this necessarily true?

In her book *Positive Illusions,* Taylor (1989) examines how, in the face of adversity, the healthy mind can create positive illusions that help with coping. Taylor argues, on the basis of her research, that mental and physical well-being can actually be enhanced by unrealistic optimism.

In day-to-day reality, professionals may be fearful of promoting unrealistic expectations. They may tend to overplay this concern by being negative in their predictions for the future, believing that any better outcome will be a cause for the family to rejoice.

Strategy: Open Discussions Between Staff and Families about Hope

Professionals and families should talk directly with one another about their view of hope and the role hope plays in providing fuel for the family to get through situations. If optimistic predictions are not realized, how will the family deal with disappointment? If each person reflects on personal expectations that were not borne out, he or she will probably realize that we all cope well with disappointments from time to time. The challenge is for each family and professional to work together to discover the comfortable balance of hope and reality in each situation.

Challenge 4

The Nature of Reimbursement and Medical Programs

The severity of a person's head injury and the source of funding often determine how long a person will be involved in medical model programs. The longer a person is medically unstable, the more a family must rely on experts. The experts have the explicit role of saving the person's life and delivering care.

Once a person is medically stable, the boundaries for the provision of medical services become blurred. In part, financing that only pays for medically necessary services may add to the gray area where medical services stop and supportive services begin. Services that may not ordinarily be deemed medically necessary may be defined in a medical way to allow reimbursement for their provision. The combination of medically necessary services and services defined as such for reimbursement adds to a family's reliance on professionals as experts.

Both factors prolong the family's and professional's role of protecting the person who has experienced head injury, the family as the natural protector of kin and the professional as the knowledgeable provider of services. The continued emphasis on rehabilitation may reinforce the urge to learn to do everything for oneself (sometimes called independence, which actually means learning who to rely on for help in certain aspects of everyday life). Meanwhile, the person with head injury begins to express choices as the family and professional continue to define boundaries of protection and control. The challenge is to remain focused on the goal of working to give control back to the person as a contributing member of the family and community.

Joseph Maurer (1991), brother of Ed, expressed the challenge this way: "This, I find, is the great sibling conundrum: How much is enough [in rehabilitation, communication, intervention], and when do you simply embrace what is and live?"

Strategy: Do Not Do Anything in an Institution That Can Be Done in the Community

Currently, people with head injury are taken from their community into a world that forces them to eat, sleep, and drink rehabilitation, deficits, problems, and a constant message to accept what has happened. The message to accept is particularly ironic given that the person is immersed in a world that constantly reminds him or her of head injury.

More and more programs profess to provide comprehensive services, including swimming pools, classrooms, and beauty parlors. People are kept from the community for extended amounts of time, and their neighbors at home think they are too sick to live in the community.

Whenever possible we must base the rehabilitation plan on where we expect the person with a head injury will end up living and working and design our system of support to get the person there as soon as possible. Professionals need to work with people first-hand in communities and homes, teaching them to cook in their own kitchens and to change their behaviors in their own homes. Use the community pool, public schools, and local beauty parlors. Facilitate the use of generic community services as soon as possible so that people with head injury can have more interaction with others and through this process can better understand the consequences of living in the community.

Strategy: Go Beyond Private Funding Sources

The overreliance on comprehensive programs has caused providers to focus on private insurers for package deals of rehabilitation. This all or nothing funding has created a dichotomy of those who are served (the haves) and those who are not served (the have nots). Everyone, at some time, becomes a member of the have nots.

More creative, blended packages of private and public sources are necessary. Public sources include such innovative programs as Medicaid waivers (now available in Kansas) designed to support community life for people with head injuries (Beals, personal communication, 1991). Also, vocational rehabilitation offices in many states have begun to pay for supported employment.

Looking at every possible source of funding is a time-consuming process and is not an option for many people who want community-based rather than facility-based rehabilitation. Time must be spent on this search while a person is still working with professionals on personal future planning. This planning begins with a person's needs and tailors funding around the needs once they have been identified. All resources and options are identified, and a plan is developed to research availability of and eligibility for the resources.

Challenge 5

Family and Professional Style

> The least helpful professional . . . was the neurologist at the acute rehabilitation cen-

ter. He had no desire to work with us. He was the most arrogant, argumentative and self righteous person I have ever met. It was his way or nothing. . . . I could go on, but I must preface the negative with the thought that for every callous professional we met and worked with, we met twenty five who truly cared. (Diane Coffey, mother of Meredith, personal communication, June 1991)

> In my experience it appears that families tend to gravitate to professionals who are supportive and honest. (Bev Whitlock, mother of Barb, personal communication, June 1991)

The style of a professional or a family varies. Some professionals are personable and friendly, taking a personal interest in many aspects of a family. Others provide information related to their specific role and seldom extend their efforts beyond those boundaries. Some families are personable and friendly, searching for knowledgeable professionals who also take a personal interest in their lives. Others want specific information and do not view the professional as an ally. The combination of possible styles can result in a spectrum ranging from a caring relationship to a strictly business relationship.

Because rehabilitation is about facilitating relationships, it is desirable for professionals to strive for a personally caring relationship. Nevertheless, policies, no matter how well written, can only mandate that a professional care *for* another person in a certain way, not care *about* another person. Consequently, the challenge for the rehabilitation team leader is to evaluate relationships and facilitate learning on the basis of the perspectives of those in the relationship, both family members and professional staff.

Strategy: Evaluate the Quality of Family and Professional Relationships on the Basis of Reports from the People in the Relationship

Ongoing evaluation of relationships is a qualitative challenge. All feedback is important and must allow families and staff to remain confident that information shared will not have a negative effect on those who are currently using services. Questionnaires and interviews can be administered at specific intervals to get feedback. Advisory groups or focus groups that meet specifically to discuss how staff and services can be more responsive to families are another possible option. The groups can consist of people who previously used or are currently using services. Staff most knowledgeable about the services should also be involved. The key is to remain family-centered and to provide a blend of services and supports that works for the entire family. For example, relatives may say they cannot visit as often as they would like because child care is difficult to obtain. Because visits are important for all family members, especially the person in rehabilitation, the staff should discuss how they can better support families in finding child care.

Challenge 6

Knowledge about Head Injury

Most of the literature developed for families and professionals focuses on the biological or psychosocial effects of head injury on the injured person (DeBoskey & Morin, 1989; Hutchison & Hutchison, 1983; Swiercinsky, Price & Leaf, 1987). Effects of head injury on the family system have been traditionally considered the domain of social workers and psychologists. Yet every person working in a rehabilitation program interacts with families. There are few resources that explain family functioning to all professionals. Even fewer resources exist with which families can educate themselves about their own natural reactions to head injury. Without this education, it is difficult for professionals to know how to support families and for families to know when and how to seek support.

Because every professional has a role in interacting with and supporting families, all professionals must understand how family systems operate. Professionals and families need to know how the head injury and the subsequent need for different services affect the family system. A professional who focuses strictly on the person

with head injury and not on the entire family system risks defining the person as a problem that must be fixed and may fail to strike a balance between the person's and family's competencies and the ability of the community to support those strengths and needs. The challenge is to provide information to all disciplines and families about the effect of a head injury on families and how families can effectively use supports and services for their own needs.

Strategy: Develop Innovative Strategies to Incorporate Education about Family Dynamics and the Effects of the Service Delivery System on Families after Head Injury

Education about families is ongoing, includes people with head injuries and their families, and gives a perspective of families over time. Ongoing education in the form of inservices and one-to-one interactions is conducted by all staff who have a commitment to seeing families as systems that change over time as a result of different experiences in their lives. Written material about how family systems function and how people respond to significant loss and change in their lives is shared with all staff. People with head injuries and families are always involved in designing and conducting inservices programs. Personal stories are powerful reminders to staff that people overcome tremendous odds and find the resources to continue. Additionally, people who are long past rehabilitation are included. Staff have the constant reminder that their time in a family's life is relatively short given the many years the family has ahead. The reminder recommits professionals to helping families learn how to get the resources they need when the professional is no longer available.

Challenge 7

Eliminating the Gap Between Paid Services and a Person's Natural Support Network

Once a family experiences such a significant life-altering trauma, it is difficult for them to resume their usual activities. The family's focus is the person with head injury. Furthermore, families are sent through a continuum of services and seldom have time to establish long-term and lasting relationships with professionals or other families. Many families travel great distances to see their relative, and it is difficult for them to maintain social ties while also devoting energy to the rehabilitation program. Further complicating the family's dilemma is the fact that rehabilitation focuses on the individual with the head injury rather than the family. Not much attention is paid to overall family needs. If the long-term needs of the person and family are truly the focus of rehabilitation, steps must be taken to ensure that personal support is available while formal services are in place.

Strategy: Support and Include a Family's Informal Network from Day One

Knowing that families may experience social isolation and loss of support from extended family and friends, professionals can begin early to help the family maintain these important ties. There are strategies to keep extended family and friends up to date on a person's progress. For example, a system of communicating with family and friends can be set up. A family can take all the get-well cards and notes a person receives early after the injury and create a family mailing list. The family can write updates on a person's progress and send them to the people on the mailing list. The updates serve several purposes at once. Families find that their interaction with friends becomes easier over time because people begin to understand the consequences of the head injury. Extended family and friends begin to understand that learning to swallow can lead to taking out the breathing tube and the possibility of vocalization. An increase in range of motion of a person's legs can be significant because it could lead to the person's standing or putting weight on the feet and legs. Sharing and discussing this information with family and the support system will enable professionals to better understand how others perceive the situation. Finally, when future resources are needed, friends will have been informed all along and will know

what support they can give. Many times friends will say that they want to help but do not know how. The updates provide concrete ways to help.

Another strategy is to have staff go home with a person to answer questions that family and friends may have. If this is done over time, family and friends can work together to alter their roles in a person's life. For example, initially family and friends may be available for transportation, and later they may help find job possibilities for the person with head injury. These are only two of many creative strategies that professionals can use to keep natural helping networks in place.

SERVICES AND SUPPORTS FOR FAMILIES

The interaction in a family-centered approach changes how we ask about what families need. In a continuum approach we ask, "What *services* does your family need while the person with head injury is in rehabilitation?" Programs logically provide things such as temporary housing near the center, longer visiting hours, and support groups so that families can talk about their challenges. Although this compartmentalized approach has its useful functions, it misses the basic ingredients that many families need.

To get at what a family really needs we must begin to ask, "What *supports* your family?" (J. O'Brien, personal communication, 1990). Families will then begin to talk about needing professionals who care about them, needing to have phone calls returned promptly, and needing to have friends and extended family available. A combination of services and supports is necessary to meet the challenges of family-centered rehabilitation.

CONCLUSION

In summary, there are nine critical strategies that can bring about family supports that meet the challenges in family and professional interaction:

1. Promote positive attitudes about family decisions in all team and family interactions.

2. Eliminate the use of technical jargon and negative predictions in the provision of rehabilitation services.

3. Build in time for all staff to get to know families.

4. Talk about the balance between hope and reality.

5. Do not do anything in an institution that can be done in the community in order to give control back to the person with head injury.

6. Go beyond private funding sources.

7. Evaluate the quality of family and professional relationships on the basis of reports from the people in the relationships.

8. Develop innovative strategies to incorporate education about family dynamics and the effects of the service delivery system on families after head injury.

9. Support and include the family's informal network from day one.

The strategies address both attitude changes and concrete ways to bring about family-centered rehabilitation. The shift described is time consuming and takes staff outside the walls of an institution and, most likely, beyond their discipline-specific training. Current conveniences may have to give way to creative strategies for supporting a person and family where they live their lives. Funding for these services is also a greater challenge. Services that meet a person's needs more completely bring about better outcomes, however, and everyone is more satisfied.

The initial focus of the options is the interaction between families and professionals. The most desirable family and professional interaction limits the prolonged use of medical model programs that promote experts and supports families in becoming competent decision makers. Additionally, interaction leads to a caring relationship that provides information about the consequences of head injury to the person and his or her family. Furthermore, rehabilitation efforts strive toward combining formal (paid) and informal (unpaid) supports and services. If services and supports are available early on, the medical model will be present only to stabilize a person's medical condition, and professional services will become only one of many aspects of a person's life after head injury.

ACKNOWLEDGMENT

The author expresses special thanks to Diane Coffey, Mike and June Davis, Evelyn Esposito, Joseph Maurer, Andrea Ramsey, Phebe Whitehead, and Bev Whitlock for sharing their own experiences with professionals.

REFERENCES

Carney, I.H. (1991). Working with families. In F.P. Orlove & D. Sobsey (Eds.), *Educating children with multiple disabilities: A transdisciplinary approach* (pp. 407–430) (2nd ed.). Baltimore: Brookes.

Condeluci, A. (1991). *Interdependence: The route to community*. Orlando, FL: Deutsch.

DeBoskey, D.S., & Morin, K. (1989). *Head injury: A guide for families*. Houston: HDI.

Dunst, C.J., Trivette, C.M., Gordon, N.J., & Pletcher, L.L. (1989). Building and mobilizing informal family support networks. In G.H.S. Singer & L.K. Irvin (Eds.), *Support for caregiving families* (pp. 121–141). Baltimore: Brookes.

Hostler, S.L. (1991, June). *Family-centered care*. Paper presented at conference, Rehabilitation and the Pediatric Puzzle; Chattanooga, TN.

Hutchison, R., & Hutchison, T. (1983). *Head injury: A booklet for families*. Houston, TX: Texas Head Injury Association.

Kramer, J. (1991). Special issues for a parent. In J.M. Williams & T. Kay (Eds.), *Head injury: A family matter* (pp. 9–18). Baltimore: Brookes.

Maurer, J. (1991). Special issues for a sibling. In J.M. Williams & T. Kay (Eds.), *Head injury: A family matter* (pp. 29–33). Baltimore: Brookes.

McMahon, B.T., & Shaw, L.R. (Eds). (1991). *Work worth doing*. Orlando, FL: Deutsch.

Racino, J.A. (1990). Preparing personnel to work in community support services. In A.P. Kaiser & C.M. McWhorter (Eds.), *Preparing personnel to work with persons with severe disabilities* (pp. 203–226). Baltimore: Brookes.

Swiercinsky, D.P., Price, T.L., & Leaf, E.L. (1987). *Traumatic head injury: Cause, consequence and challenge*. Kansas City, KS: Head Injury Association of Kansas and Greater Kansas City.

Taylor, S. (1989). *Positive illusions. Creative self-deception and the healthy mind*. New York: Basic Books.

Turnbull, H.R., & Turnbull, A.P. (1985). *Parents speak out: Then and now*. Columbus, OH: Merrill.

Turnbull, A.P., & Turnbull, H.R. (1991). Understanding families from a systems perspective. In J.M. Williams & T. Kay (Eds.), *Head injury: A family matter* (pp. 37–64). Baltimore: Brookes.

Williams, J.M. (1991a, May). *Creating community: Whose lift is it anyway?* Keynote presentation at the New York State Head Injury Association's Annual Conference, Binghamton, N.Y.

Williams, J.M. (1991b). Family reaction to head injury. In J.M. Williams & T. Kay (Eds.), *Head injury: A family matter* (pp. 81–100). Baltimore: Brookes.

Williams, J.M. (1991c). Family support. In J.M. Williams & T. Kay (Eds.), *Head injury: A family matter* (pp. 299–312). Baltimore: Brookes.

Williams, J.M., & Kay, T. (1991). *Head injury: A family matter*. Baltimore: Brookes.

Developing a Positive Communication Culture for Rehabilitation: Communication Training for Staff and Family Members

4

Mark Ylvisaker
Timothy J. Feeney
Beth Urbanczyk

OBJECTIVES

Upon completion of this chapter, the reader will be able to:

1. describe common patterns of communication recovery after severe traumatic brain injury.
2. develop a conceptual framework for understanding the relationship between behavioral challenges and communication challenges.
3. describe a positive culture for rehabilitation and the role of communication within that culture
4. define a set of communicative competencies that are the targets of communication training for staff, family members, and friends
5. describe a communication training program that includes inservice training as well as ongoing supervision and situational coaching

Developing a Positive Communication Culture for Rehabilitation

This chapter has four fundamental premises: (1) In brain injury rehabilitation, there is nothing more critical than a therapeutic environment in which communication among clients, family members, staff, and other significant individuals is as effective and satisfying as it can be. (2) In establishing such an environment, all staff (professional and nonprofessional), family members, and friends play the same important role and ideally possess the same interactive competencies. (3) Behavioral issues and communication issues are essentially indistinguishable. That is, behaviors that are considered undesirable or inappropriate often play an important role in the individual's communication system. Even challenging behaviors that are not *deliberately* communicative may easily become so if staff or family members' responses to them are not well conceived (e.g., if staff unintentionally reinforce negative communication behaviors). Furthermore, techniques for managing these behaviors are components of staff and family members' communication systems. (4) Equipping individuals with needed communication skills requires far more than an hour or two, or even a day or two, of pedagogical instruction. Rather, the critical aspects of training are situational coaching combined with an institutional culture and administrative philosophy that value and reward effectiveness in communication.

Consistent with these premises, the chapter explores the importance of a social-environmental approach to traumatic brain injury (TBI) rehabilitation that highlights the value of positive communication and presents a comprehensive approach to teaching communicative competencies to staff and family members and to friends. The authors of the chapter represent the fields of speech-language pathology and behavioral psychology, two of the many professions with a critical interest in communication. Developing this chapter in an interdisciplinary manner is consistent with our conviction that the goal of establishing and maintaining an optimal communication environment in rehabilitation is not the responsibility of one profession alone. The communication themes under examination in this chapter extend to all interactions throughout the rehabilitation program and are of equal importance to all rehabilitation professionals.

The humanistic principles of rehabilitation highlighted in this chapter are consistent with a philosophy of rehabilitation that emphasizes efficient pursuit of specific behavioral objectives. After TBI, functional improvement from behavioral and communicative perspectives is in large measure a result of the communication skills and behaviors of important people in the environment.

PHILOSOPHY OF SOCIAL-ENVIRONMENTAL INTERVENTION

Communication and Stages of Recovery

Although any combination of functions can be spared or impaired by severe TBI, people with brain injury have come to be considered a separate disability group because at any stage of recovery there tends to be some degree of personal fragmentation, cognitive weakness, and difficulty with self-regulation and social interaction. These are the themes that are not only most pervasive in TBI but also most troubling for family, friends, employers, teachers, and others (Brooks, McKinlay, Symington, Beattie, & Campsie, 1987; Oddy, 1984; Thomsen, 1984; Wood, 1984). Improvement after severe TBI follows a fairly predictable course with respect to cognitive and behavioral functions (Lehr, 1990). Depending upon the nature and severity of the injury, sensory and motor deficits may also be present at any stage of cognitive recovery, adding to the challenge of reestablishing effective and satisfying communication.

After a severe injury, individuals may progress through a large number of distinguishable cognitive and behavioral stages. Considering these individuals as a whole from the perspective of rehabilitation services, we have found it useful to divide recovery into three general stages. The first includes gradual emergence from coma and is usually considered the stimulation stage of rehabilitation. The second includes the stages in which individuals are alert but experience confusion, disorientation, and substantial difficulty with inhibition, initiation, or both. During these stages, rehabilitation from a cognitive and behavioral perspective focuses on environmental structure and support for recovery of adaptive and purposeful behavior, antecedent management of behavioral dyscontrol, and facilitation of basic communication routines and interactive competencies. In the late stages, many individuals move beyond confusion and regain the capacity to engage in purposeful, planned behavior in nonroutine environments despite possibly significant residual cognitive and self-regulatory challenges. The overall goal of cognitive and behavioral rehabilitation during this late stage of recovery is to help individuals acquire the cognitive and communicative competencies and compensatory strategies that they need to succeed in their academic, vocational, social, and living environments.

Early Stages of Recovery

The early stages of recovery, characterized by gradual emergence from coma, minimal responsiveness to environmental events, and minimal communication (Levels 1 through 3 on the Rancho Los Amigos Hospital [RLA] Levels of Cognitive Functioning [Hagen, 1981]), typically occur in an acute care hospital or acute rehabilitation setting. Comprehension ranges from no recognition of people, things, or events and no comprehension of language to consistent recognition of common objects and familiar people and comprehension of simple and contextually supported acts of communication. Expressive communication ranges from none to reflexive communication acts (e.g., crying out and withdrawing) to a deliberate use of eye gaze, reaching, and other gestures to express wants and needs.

Communication challenges and problems frequently observed in staff, family members, and friends during this stage of the individual's recovery include the following:

- failing to talk to the injured individual
- failing to communicate nonverbally with the individual

- failing to prepare the individual for nursing or therapy procedures with natural gestures and physical prompts combined with simple verbal cues
- failing to use physical contact during nursing and therapy procedures to communicate security and acceptance
- failing to notice, interpret, or respond to the individual's natural communication gestures
- failing to prompt communication gestures in appropriate contexts
- attempting to establish yes/no communication before the individual is cognitively ready
- talking about the individual as though he or she were not present
- creating an environment that is overstimulating and confusing
- misinterpreting negative behavior as intentionally communicative

Middle Stages of Recovery

The middle stages of cognitive and behavioral recovery (RLA Levels 4 through 6) are defined by rapidly increasing alertness and responsiveness to environmental events combined with some degree (from severe to mild) of confusion, disorientation, and lack of self-control. Information is processed superficially, and learning is often extremely inefficient.

Comprehension of language may be adequate for normal interaction, particularly if language is supported by context. Nevertheless, comprehension tends to deteriorate rapidly with increases in length, complexity, and amount of information presented; with increases in the rate at which communication partners speak; with increases in environmental interference; and with decreases in contextual support. Expressive communication often includes perseveration, confabulation, bizarre or contextually inappropriate language, and disorganized or tangential language. Grammar may be acceptable, but most individuals at this stage struggle to find the correct words to express their thoughts. Some rarely initiate interaction, whereas others demonstrate little ability to inhibit expression of their thoughts and feelings. Disinhibition may result in offensive (often sexually offensive) language.

Staff, family members, and friends may find interaction with injured individuals during this stage stressful. Common communication pitfalls observed in staff, family, and friends include:

- trying to communicate in a confusing environment
- saying too much or too little
- failing to provide nonverbal cues to make comprehension easier
- failing to provide sufficient routine and regularity for individuals to feel oriented and secure
- taking inappropriate or aggressive language personally
- becoming frustrated and expressing frustration when the injured individual forgets a task, wanders, or fails to comply
- ridiculing bizarre utterances
- failing to decipher the communicative intent underlying unusual or aggressive behavior
- failing to provide choices
- not understanding or using the individual's expressive communication system if other than speech
- expecting that an individual who is capable of using a nonverbal system will initiate functional communication with the system and transfer its use to other contexts
- labeling people by their behavior (e.g., "the screamer" or "the hitter")

Late Stages of Recovery

Despite the resolution of obvious confusion and the return of goal-directed behavior, individuals in the late stages (RLA Levels 7 to 8 and beyond) may continue to process information slowly and inefficiently; become confused by large, nonroutine tasks or distracting environments; and struggle to find the correct words to express their thoughts. Many individuals with

TBI whose cognitive recovery is fairly good continue to express themselves in a rambling, disorganized, and therefore confusing manner and to interact in a way that is disinhibited and therefore irritating or offensive to conversation partners. Others may be inactive communicators because of (organically based) reduced initiation, depression and withdrawal, or some combination of these factors. Many of the residual challenges following closed head injury are associated with frontal lobe damage (Ylvisaker, 1992). The physical aspects of speech production may have returned to normal limits or may be severely impaired. Furthermore, these injury-related issues may compound preexisting personality quirks or communicative weakness.

Although communication with individuals at this stage of recovery is far easier and more satisfying than at earlier stages, common communication problems continue to be observed in the interaction of staff, families, and friends with individuals with TBI. These include:

- speaking too fast or saying too much
- overcompensating by speaking too slowly and simply, speaking for the individual, or in other ways infantilizing the individual capable of interacting at a higher level
- not giving injured individuals the opportunity to communicate
- failing to provide natural consequences for communication successes or failures
- failing to encourage new strategies (e.g., word finding strategies or alternative communication systems if the individual is unable to speak intelligibly)
- failing to encourage new communication strategies in natural environments
- addressing the individual in a patronizing and disrespectful manner

Summary

In this discussion of stages of communication recovery after TBI, we have deliberately highlighted the issues, challenges, or deficits on the communication partner side of the communication equation. Effectiveness of communication and rate of communication recovery are not simply consequences of impairments in the individual with TBI or the individual's response to specific communication intervention (Hartley, 1990). On the contrary, the understanding and communicative skill of staff, family members, and friends contribute critically to effective interaction and to the individual's recovery of communication skills (Ylvisaker, Feeney, & Urbanczyk, 1993). On the other hand, if staff, family, and friends are ineffective communicators, the best outcome is that life during the individual's recovery will be less pleasant and more confusing than it need be. More likely, behavioral problems will be exacerbated and ultimate communication compromised. Frustration during these stages easily leads to a pattern of social disengagement that can result in anger, isolation, loneliness, depression, and substance abuse.

Communication Culture

A community's culture is defined in large part by the values shared by members of the community, the means of communicating those values, shared explanations of noteworthy events, roles and expectations for people that are related to the values of the culture, and means for rewarding conduct consistent with the community's values. A rehabilitation program that recognizes the pervasive importance of effective and positive communication must, in effect, create a communication culture, attending to all the components of a true culture.

Values in a Communication Culture

It is often said that the goal of rehabilitation is independence, suggesting in its most extreme interpretation that an individual sustaining himself or herself alone on a desert island would represent the ultimate success in rehabilitation. Clearly this is not a compelling vision, nor is it a vision capable of driving humanistic and socially embedded rehabilitation efforts. A life that lacks satisfying interaction with other human beings is a life that few of us would choose.

Close family ties, friendships, and collegial relationships at school or work are considered by most people critical components of a satisfying life and are sustained by skill and interest in communication. It is not surprising that family members, friends, and employers alike assert that it is the personality changes after brain injury—changes in style, facility, and interest in communicating—that are the most stressful and most likely to interfere with successful reintegration (Brooks & McKinlay, 1983; Lezak, 1987; Oddy, 1984; Prigatano, 1986; Thomsen, 1984).

Communication is not simply the ability to talk and use language to give and receive messages (Burke, 1990; Gordon, 1991). There are many superb communicators who are unable to talk and many completely incompetent communicators whose speech and language skills are unassailable. Rather, communication encompasses a wide range of skills and behaviors, verbal and nonverbal, that enable one to have a desired impact on the thoughts, feelings, and activity of other people and also to have one's own thoughts, feelings, and activity influenced by others (Carr & Durand, 1985b; Donnellan, Mirenda, Mesaros, & Fassbender, 1984; Durand & Carr, 1991; Ylvisaker, Feeney, & Urbanczyk, 1992). For example, the behaviors used by a physical therapist or nurse to calm an agitated patient and thereby to make treatments possible are communicative competencies that are critical to that individual's successfully doing his or her job. The behaviors used by all staff to communicate to families that they are respected and essential members of the rehabilitation team are communicative competencies that frequently make an enormous difference in rehabilitation outcomes. The behaviors used by staff to communicate professional respect to their peers and to bolster institutional morale are communicative competencies that similarly contribute to the overall effectiveness of a rehabilitation program.

Later in this chapter we list communicative competencies that are particularly important for staff to possess. The current points are that communication pervades the life and activity of a rehabilitation facility and that skilled communication is a most valued asset for anybody in this environment. Well trained staff and family members are empowered to set the tone for a facility and thereby to reduce their vulnerability to the challenges and crises that are an inevitable component of this type of rehabilitation. It is a most welcome coincidence that one of the few controllable aspects of life in a TBI rehabilitation program is also one of the most important.

Means of Communicating Values in a Communication Culture

Important values of a culture are communicated in various ways. They tend to be learned at home; reinforced in the educational system; embodied in games, songs, sports, and other cultural manifestations; preached from the pulpit; and, if all else fails, maintained by the stick of law enforcement. Rehabilitation programs often relegate communication values to isolated therapy sessions for clients and to infrequent and short training sessions for staff (Bogdan, Taylor, DeGrande, & Haynes, 1974). Beyond this, communicative effectiveness is commonly left to chance or to the natural gifts of the individuals in the environment (Dunst, Johanson, Trivette, & Hamby, 1991). Clearly these are not communities that value communication or comprehend its pervasive impact on the health and effectiveness of the program.

Adopting a communication culture in a rehabilitation facility entails a total environmental focus on communication skill and recovery in clients and a deliberate and comprehensive program to develop communicative competencies in staff, family members, and other significant individuals (Bernstein, 1982; Reid & Whitman, 1983; Wetzel & Hoschouer, 1984). This chapter describes such a program.

Shared Explanations in a Communication Culture

Cultures often highlight community explanations for important events. For example, religions generally feature their unique explanation of the world's origin and of natural events. A rehabilitation facility with a communication culture analogously looks to communication themes in explaining important events within the program. For example, family members who are hostile and alienated from staff are not written off as intolerable or crazy people. Rather, their emotional response to professionals is considered a natural consequence of often inappropriate and alienating staff interaction at an extremely vulnerable time in the life of the family (Kreutzer, Zasler, Camplair, & Leininger, 1990; Lezak, 1988; Williams & Kay, 1991). Similarly, clients who behave in ways that are inappropriate or intolerable are assumed to be communicating something important about themselves or their reaction to their immediate situation, even if there is no reason to believe that the communication is intentional (Feeney & Urbanczyk, in press). "What is he trying to tell us?" and "How can we make this easier for him?" are questions that come first to mind when one is dealing with stressful situations involving either clients or family members in a rehabilitation program with a communication culture. This heuristic principle, "Look for the communicative intent and/or the communicative impact of unconventional behavior," has proved to be of great value in working with individuals with severe developmental disabilities as well as with TBI (Burke, 1990; Carr, 1988; Carr & Durand, 1985a, 1985b; Donnellan et al., 1984; Gordon, 1991; LaVigna & Donnellan, 1986; Schuler, 1980; Ylvisaker, Feeney, & Urbanczyk, in press; Ylvisaker, Szekeres, Haarbauer-Krupa, Urbanczyk, & Feeney, in press).

Roles and Expectations in a Communication Culture

In a fundamental way, all staff (professional and nonprofessional), family members, friends, and other visitors have the same role to play in establishing a positive communication culture. For individuals who are fragmented and confused, an act of communication is either satisfying and therapeutic or unsatisfying, frustrating, and confusing not because of the occupation or status of the communication partner but because of aspects of the interaction. Therefore, all individuals in the environment should receive the help they may need to improve their communicative competencies. Ideally, training sessions combine staff at all levels with family members and others to underscore the fundamental point that everybody in the environment contributes equally to the creation of a positive communication culture (Slama & Bannerman, 1983). This helps overcome the natural divisions among people in a rehabilitation program, divisions that predictably detract from the goal of rehabilitation.

A facility does, however, have supervisory authority over staff and not over family and visitors. This enables the program managers to underscore officially the importance of communicative competencies by including them as components of staff members' job descriptions (Hollander, Plutchik, & Horner, 1973). For example, physical therapists are expected to be competent in neuromuscular facilitation and inhibition, mobility evaluations and wheelchair training, and much more. In addition, their job descriptions make clear that they are expected to interact with patients in a way that contributes to their intervention and conveys respect. Furthermore, they are expected to interact with families in a way that is clear and instructive and, above all, in a way that shows respect for the family member and encourages positive engagement with the program. We discuss the job description aspect of a communication culture later.

Rewards in a Communication Culture

Connected with expected staff competencies is the issue of reward. Managers within a rehabilitation program with a communication culture highlight communication skills in performance evaluations and consider mastery of communication competencies a valid basis for commendation and for whatever merit awards are available (Montegar, Reid, Madsen, & Ewell, 1977).

Social-Environmental Intervention

Middle Stages of Recovery

The most critical period of recovery from a social-environmental perspective is that domi-nated by alertness combined with some degree of confusion and disinhibition (RLA Levels 4 through 6). From a cognitive and behavioral perspective, the overarching rehabilitation goal is to increase orientation, sense of routine, adaptive behavior within a well understood environmental structure, and effective processing of increasingly complex information. Activities, including communication, that enable the individual to experience success and that encourage gradual expansion of cognitive skills and behavioral self-regulation are at the heart of this stage of rehabilitation. These activities can take place anywhere, at any time, and with anybody. For example, the interaction that the individual has before bed time with a family member, at dinner with a friend, and early in the morning with the person who washes the floors may be the most therapeutic events of the day. Conversely, any interaction at any time with any person can be confusing and fragmenting, can trigger a strong emotional or behavioral reaction, and can set in motion a sequence of events that results in the individual learning and habituating behaviors that might create further obstacles to recovery.

That is, each interaction has the potential to give the individual an experience of success, to decrease frustration, to reduce confusion, and to direct attention positively to productive and orienting targets. Inappropriately managed communication, on the other hand, can increase confusion, sense of failure, and frustration. Furthermore, unskilled interaction on the part of staff and family members easily reinforces undesirable behavior, turning behavior that initially is purely impulsive or the product of confusion into a learned response that becomes progressively harder to modify.

Therefore, the environment must be designed to decrease confusion, to increase orientation, and to increase adaptive, goal-directed behavior. Social-environmental intervention includes consistency in time, schedule, place, and staff; therapy and down-time activities that are carefully designed to be engaging and ensure success; expectations regarding the individual's level of performance that are accurate and consistent among staff and family members; and communication patterns within the environment that ensure satisfying and successful communication. The individuals most critical to the success of a social-environmental approach to rehabilitation for confused patients include family members, friends, and direct care staff.

Late Stages of Recovery

After recovery of adequate orientation to the environment and to routines, of reasonably goal-directed behavior, and of self-regulatory skills strong enough to enable the individual to function appropriately in most familiar contexts, the level of environmental support outlined in the previous section becomes unnecessary. More important, it now becomes crucial to decrease systematically environmental support and to re-introduce real-world forms of unpredictability, stress, and challenge. Thus, although the orientation has changed, the importance of a social-environmental approach to rehabilitation remains.

With respect to communication, it becomes increasingly important to heighten the naturalness of communication and the demand for processing efficiency. This may require the client's deliberate use of strategies to negotiate successfully difficult interactions. If expressive or receptive language strategies are needed, transfer to natural settings is critical. This process of transfer engages the communicative competencies of family and staff alike. Competencies needed by staff and families at this stage differ in point of detail from those needed during the confused stages of recovery, but the general philosophy of a therapeutic communication environment remains.

COMMUNICATION TRAINING

Natural History of Communication Training

Many rehabilitation facilities experience a common and natural progression in their attempts to create a thriving communication culture. Details of this history may differ considerably, but it is instructive to consider the internal logic that drives the progression.

Stage 1: The 45-Minute Inservice for Direct Care Staff

Training often begins with one staff member, often a speech-language pathologist, being asked to do a brief inservice for direct care staff on communicating with individuals who are confused, nonspeaking, aphasic, explosive, or otherwise communicatively impaired. Typically the training is straight pedagogy; that is, the trainees receive information about communication problems after brain injury, about their relation to cognitive and behavioral issues, and about techniques for communicating effectively with communicatively impaired individuals.

There is certainly value in this information. It soon becomes clear, however, that a rushed lecture squeezed into the already full schedules of busy staff people and focused on information rather than skills is poorly designed to equip staff with new and important competencies (Adams, Tallon, & Rimell, 1980).

Stage 2: The 2-Hour Interactive Inservice for All Staff

This phase begins with clear recognition of two important issues: all staff, not just nursing or other direct care staff, must be skilled communicators if the environment is to be genuinely therapeutic; and communication competencies must be observed and practiced to be understood and internalized. The staff person responsible for the training therefore requests more time and changes the focus of the inservice. Information about communication impairments is reduced to a minimum, and the lion's share of the session is devoted to demonstrating the relevant communicative competencies, live or with videotaped models, and to practicing the competencies through role playing.

This training may look a great deal like the inservice session outlined later in this chapter. Its value lies in the focus on skills rather than information alone. Trainees practice interpreting interactive events from various points of view and interacting under various adverse circumstances. The trainer's role is to sensitize, motivate, and coach more than it is to convey information.

This type of training is certainly better suited to the goal of developing communicative competencies than the pedagogical session of stage 1. The net result of effectively implemented interactive training sessions is often disappointing, however. Frequently cited reasons for the modest impact on the program's communication culture include the following: (1) Those staff people most in need of the training somehow escape the inservice. (2) Some of the direct care staff need much more coaching than is possible in a single training session. (3) Supervisors have no administrative authority to enforce the competencies. Consequently, there is no mechanism, positive or punitive, to motivate resistive staff to take communication themes seriously. (4) Family members, friends, and other visitors are as important as staff in establishing a communication culture, and they have not yet been included in the training.

Stage 3: Interactive Training for Staff and Family Combined with Administrative Support

Two critical developments occur in stage 3: the communication competencies become institutionalized and sanctioned, and the scope of training extends outward to include family members and other significant individuals.

Administrative support may take several forms. In our facility, the communicative competencies listed in Appendix 4-1 are an important component of the job description of all clinical staff. On the positive side, this means that those staff members who take this role seriously can be commended and rewarded when this aspect of their job is reviewed at the staff performance evaluation. Negatively, it means that those staff who neglect the competencies are subject to whatever sanctions they would experience if they neglected any other important aspect of their job. For all staff, the administrative message is clear: to be an effective staff person in this brain injury rehabilitation program, you must possess a high degree of communicative competency, and you must work as hard at mastering this aspect of your job as you would at mastering any other aspect of your job.

Equally important, family members and friends are encouraged to participate in communication training. This means considerably more than offering helpful suggestions at family conferences or distributing handouts about how to communicate with individuals with communicative impairment. It means providing the same type of training that is offered to staff (Dunst et al., 1991; Jacobs, 1990; Powell, Salzberg, Rule, Levy, & Itzkowitz, 1987; Schreibman, 1988; Twardosz & Nordquist, 1985). In some programs, family members are included with staff in competency-based training sessions. This is particularly important for family members who are frequent visitors to the program because they have many occasions to interact with clients other than their own family member. All family members, however, whether they are regular or infrequent visitors, are important individuals to train because it is they, not staff, who are responsible for maintaining a positive communication culture over the long run.

Communication training for family members is therefore part of any sensible plan for transition to home. It is essential if transfer of communicative and behavioral skills to a natural environment is an issue for the client, which it predictably is for individuals with significant TBI. On the basis of both clinical and research evidence, inclusion of family members in rehabilitation of individuals with acquired brain injury and in habilitation of individuals with developmental disabilities is generally considered an integral part of the rehabilitative or habilitative process (Deaton, 1987; Dunst et al., 1991; Jacobs, 1990; Kreutzer et al., 1990; Lezak, 1988; O'Brien & Mount, 1985; Satanoff, 1991; Savage & Carter, 1991; Schreibman, 1988; Williams & Kay, 1991; Ylvisaker, Szekeres, Henry, Sullivan, & Wheeler, 1987). In addition to their role as members of the rehabilitative team, family members provide necessary information about the individual's personality, learning style, learning history, and communication style, all of which is needed to develop well conceived intervention plans.

Stage 4: Interdisciplinary Competency-Based Training Plus Ongoing Situational Coaching

The stage 3 combination of competency-based training, facility-wide scope of training, and administrative support for communication competencies goes a long way toward creating a positive and effective communication culture. The final lesson to be learned by the maturing rehabilitation program is that staff and family members who are inexperienced in communicating with communicatively and behaviorally impaired individuals and who may not be naturally gifted communicators require ongoing situational coaching to develop an adequate level of competency. At this stage, staff and family members with particularly strong needs for improved competencies receive the type of situational coaching described below.

Furthermore, by this time in the development of a communication culture, it has become clear that there is enormous overlap between training in communication skills and training in behavioral skills. Thus the speech-language pathologist and the behavioral psychologist, and perhaps others, find it natural to integrate their training efforts. The behavioral psychologist is often the most likely candidate to provide situational coaching for staff and family members alike because he or she typically has a schedule that lends itself to this type of work and because the communication issues identified as most in need of immediate attention typically involve behavioral themes. In addition, an efficiently designed communication training program includes peer tutoring as one strategy for communicating client-specific procedures to all the relevant staff members. This is discussed later in the chapter.

Communication Competencies

Appendix 4-1 contains three sets of communication competencies pertaining to staff-client interaction, staff-family interaction, and staff-staff interaction. In each case, the competencies are divided into five categories: (1) the *content* of communication (e.g., topics and levels of concreteness), (2) the *form* of communication (e.g., length and complexity of utterances, word choice,

and the like), (3) the *environment* in which communication occurs (e.g., avoiding distractions and ensuring confidentiality), (4) *encouragement* offered by the communication partner (e.g., inviting and prompting the individual to communicate and encouraging use of the easiest communication modality), and, most important, (5) techniques for communicating *respect* (e.g., giving clients choices and including family members in assessment and rehabilitation planning).

There are more similarities than differences among the three sets of competencies. At a somewhat more general level of analysis, the competencies needed to communicate respectfully and successfully with clients, family, and staff are identical. A facility may wish to capture this important insight in their staff job descriptions by writing only one set of competencies applicable to all three types of communication partner. This strategy has the advantage of emphasizing an inclusionary rather than an "us against them" attitude toward different categories of people in a rehabilitation environment.

In addition to the communication competencies listed in Appendix 4-1, there are communication-*related* competencies that must be stressed in the training program. These include the ability to identify and interpret communicative behavior, to recognize communicative intent in behavior when it is present and to refrain from attributing intent when it is not present, to recognize cognitive deficits and their communicative consequences, and to use communication skills as a component in general behavior management. There is substantial overlap among the competencies discussed in this chapter and those that are the focus of the chapter dealing with behavioral training (Chapter 6). This is as it should be, given the intimate connection between behavior and communication on the one hand and between behavior management and communication training on the other.

General Communication Training Sessions

Inservice training sessions (which are in reality outservice training sessions because they are removed from the context of actual service or interaction with clients) ideally include varied levels and types of staff to be trained. They may also include family members and friends of the clients. Implicit in this inclusion is a message that deserves emphasis, namely that everybody's role and importance are the same with respect to the goal of establishing a positive communication environment. Furthermore, having administrators and management staff trained alongside direct care staff helps underscore the value that the organization attaches to a positive communication environment.

Purposes of the General Training Session

Ultimately the goal of training is to enhance the effectiveness of the rehabilitation program by creating a positive communication environment. The more immediate and modest objectives of the general training session are:

- to ensure that all staff and family members have the same conceptual framework regarding communication and its role in rehabilitation
- to ensure that all staff and family members understand the connections among cognitive deficits, communication challenges, and behavior after brain injury
- to improve staff and family members' ability to identify and accurately interpret acts of communication, particularly when they are indirect and the true message is not obvious; this includes the communication acts of staff and family members as well as those of clients
- to equip staff and family members with important communication competencies, or at least to begin a process that will continue with situational coaching
- to sensitize staff and family members to the profound impact of cognitive and communicative impairment and to the value of a positive communication culture;
- to motivate all staff and family members to work together toward the goal of establishing a communication culture

Trainer

Individuals ideally suited for the role of communication trainer are knowledgeable in communication, cognition, and behavior after TBI; possess unbridled enthusiasm for and commitment to the goal of establishing a positive communication environment; are good actors because role playing is an essential component of the training; are genuinely respectful of all staff and family members and have earned the respect of the individuals being trained; and are able to create a training environment in which people feel comfortable letting their hair down and practicing various interactive skills. We have effectively teamed speech-language pathologists and behavioral psychologists as trainers, but other combinations of professionals are certainly possible.

Levels of Training

The focus of the inservice session should be general issues in communication and behavior and general communicative competencies rather than communication or behavioral issues that are specific to individual clients. It is natural and common for staff and family members to raise client-specific issues at the training sessions. Flexible trainers can transform these questions and observations into general themes that fit the focus and goals of the session. Issues specific to individual clients are best managed in customized, situational training or coaching sessions.

Outline of the General Training Session

Exhibit 4-1 contains an outline of a 3- to 4-hour general training session. There is nothing divinely inspired about the details of this course outline. Rehabilitation programs with different levels of intervention (e.g., acute or postacute rehabilitation and pediatric or adult clients), with varied staff and family competencies and needs, and at different points in their evolution of a communication culture will inevitably have different emphases in their training. The critical issues that cut across all these differences are an understanding of and a motivation to create a communication culture; a clear understanding of the intimate relations among cognitive, behavioral, and communicative themes; and an understanding that this training is a first step, to be followed by additional situational coaching as needed and by administrative practices de-

Exhibit 4-1 Outline of a General Communication Training Session

I. Introduction: Motivation
   A. Social-environmental approach: The trainer explains the importance of a social-environmental approach to brain injury rehabilitation and the role of communication in that approach.
   B. Roles: The trainer explains everybody's role in this approach and highlights the importance of family members and direct care staff, that is, those individuals who interact most frequently with the clients. The trainer makes clear that everybody's role is the same with respect to establishing a communication environment.
   C. Payoff: The trainer highlights the payoffs that flow from a positive communication environment:
      1. fewer problematic behavioral issues
      2. better outcomes for clients
      3. more satisfying interactions among staff, family members, and clients
II. Introduction: Content
   A. Communication
      1. Communication is pervasive. Communication is not limited to speech and language. Every behavior or absence of behavior is potentially communicative.
      Exercises:
         a. Given one simple message (e.g., "I am hungry"), the group lists 15 or more distinct behaviors that could communicate that message. *The point:* Any behavior, or absence of behavior, can communicate in the right context.
         b. Given a single behavior (e.g., persistent screaming), the group lists 15 or more messages that this behavior might communicate and the contextual evidence that might help in deciphering the message. *The point:* A given behavior might have many possible meanings. If we are committed to a positive communication culture, we will work hard to interpret correctly the communicative intent of the behaviors we observe.
      2. Communication is powerful. The trainer highlights the many functions or purposes served by communicative behavior (with or without language) and the extraordinary frustration associated with communication deficits.
      3. Communication is important. A positive communication culture contributes in many ways to recovery and to everybody's quality of life. The trainer highlights the components of a positive communication culture.
      4. Communication problems after TBI are common. The trainer briefly highlights the variety of communication challenges that individuals are likely to experience at various stages of recovery after TBI.
   B. Relation between cognition and communication
      1. Brainstorm: How would severe confusion and disorientation manifest themselves in communication in this environment?
      2. Brainstorm: How would cognitive disorganization manifest itself in communication in this environment?
      3. Brainstorm: How would weak attention and memory manifest themselves in communication in this environment?
   C. Relation between behavior and communication
      1. Brainstorm: How would severe disinhibition manifest itself in communication in this environment?
      2. Brainstorm: How would impaired initiation manifest itself in communication in this environment?
      3. Brainstorm: How can miscommunication or inappropriate staff communication create behavior problems? Staff-family interaction problems?
      4. Brainstorm: How can effective communication prevent behavior problems? Staff-family interaction problems?
III. Initial competency training
   A. Communicative competencies
      1. The trainer introduces the five categories of communicative competence: *content* of communication, *form* of communication, *environment* for communication, techniques for the *encouragement* of communication, and techniques for communicating *respect.*
      2. The trainer discusses the implications of these general areas of competence for staff-client, staff-family, and staff-staff interaction.
   B. General outline of competency training
      1. Identifying positive and negative aspects of communication and explaining communication breakdowns
         a. Select an important communication competency and context.

continues

Exhibit 4-1 continued

> b. Provide an exaggerated negative model, that is, one in which the communicative competency is not present and negative consequences are clear. This can be done with video taped or role play models. An exaggerated negative model is used for two reasons. (1) It can be funny and attention grabbing. (2) Starting with positive models often communicates that there is only one way to negotiate a given communication task. In fact, there are many, depending on one's communication style.
> c. Practice interpreting the communication in the model. Practice explaining the communication breakdown from cognitive and behavioral perspectives and from the perspective of failures at both the giving and the receiving end of the communication.
> d. Continue this practice (i.e., identifying positive and negative aspects of communication and explaining communication breakdowns) until all the group members have had an opportunity to contribute and feel comfortable with the process.
>
> 2. Practicing positive alternatives
>   a. After viewing and discussing a negative model of interaction, list a number of positive alternatives to the unsuccessful interaction.
>   b. Practice these alternatives. The larger group must be divided into dyads or small groups for this practice. The trainers should move among the groups, providing suggestions, encouragement, and other coaching assistance. The trainer's goal is the trainee's acquisition of the targeted competencies within the context of the individual's preexisting communication style. The training will be resisted and ultimately unsuccessful if the implicit demand is that staff and family members fundamentally revise their manner of relating to other people.
>   c. Dyads that are particularly good at illustrating a particular competency can be asked to role play the competency for the entire group.
>   d. Dyads or small groups can also be asked to create their own negative model of a new competency and subsequently a positive alternative. Facility with both types of role play indicates clear mastery of the competency in question.
>   e. This supervised practice should continue for the duration of the training session.
>
> IV. Summary: The trainer should close by highlighting the forest in the trees: a vision of a positive communication culture and its benefits for clients, family members, and staff.

signed to institutionalize the positive aspects of a communication culture.

Relatively little time should be devoted to the introductory presentation of information. Even critical information about the nature of communication and the relations among communication, cognition, and behavior can be presented briefly in the introduction and explored later in greater depth during the role playing portion of the training. Appendix 4-2 includes several vignettes that could be considered models for the development of role plays or videos to be used in the general training session.

Coaching

It is not easy to communicate effectively with individuals with significant cognitive, communicative, or behavioral deficits. Therefore, it is unrealistic to expect that a general training session, however well conceived and effectively conducted, can bring about a substantial and enduring improvement in the competence of staff and in the communication culture generally. To be sure, there are individuals who are naturally gifted in communication and require little instruction or coaching. The group for which a communication training program is designed, however, includes individuals who require considerable coaching after the general training session has laid a solid foundation.

Coaching can take two quite different forms: (1) video analysis and one-on-one role playing, and (2) training in vivo.

Video Analysis and Role Playing

Clinically unobtrusive but effective coaching can be structured around the video analysis of an inexperienced staff or family member's interaction with a client. Spontaneous, naturally occurring interaction is videotaped and is reviewed by the staff or family member together with a coach, a person who has demonstrated competence in communicating with the client in question and who is capable of communicating in a nonthreatening manner with the trainee. This may or may not be the same individual who is responsible for the general training session. The video review is guided by the coach and includes highlighting those behaviors that are positive and effective. The review is followed by role playing of positive alternatives to interaction that was deemed problematic. Subsequent video feedback can be used for additional skills acquisition or for reinforcement. The effectiveness of video feedback has also been demonstrated in the training of individuals with disabilities and their peers by Keith-Dunlap and colleagues (1992), Booth and Fairbank (1984), and Walther and Beate (1991).

Training in Vivo

Guided observation. The first stage of training in vivo consists of a trainee and coach observing interaction between the client and any communication partner in a natural context. The coach identifies for the trainee specific behaviors of both the client and the communication partner. It may be useful to reemphasize for the trainee the point that all behavior has a communicative function. This is followed by identification and discussion of the effects of the behaviors or possible effects of alternative behaviors in this context. The focus remains the behavior of both partners in the communication and the effects of those behaviors. The trainee's competence at this stage is demonstrated by adequate verbal identification of communication behaviors and their effects.

Coached interaction. The coach prepares the trainee before a natural interaction with the client. They agree that the coach will intervene in the interaction only if the trainee signals a need for help. In this case, the coach enters the interaction, models appropriate interaction, and leaves. Whether

the coach intervenes or not, the interaction is followed by discussion (possibly including videotape review) of the interaction. The discussion highlights what worked, what did not work, and alternatives to what did not work.

Follow-along coaching. After the trainee has demonstrated competence at both levels, the coach assumes the role of resource person, problem solver, and intermittent observer. Initially this role may be structured with planned sessions between coach and trainee. The ideal evolution of this training results in the trainee demonstrating that he or she no longer needs coaching sessions and is ready to assume a coaching role for less experienced persons.

Peer Training and Communication

After a communication culture is fairly well established and most staff members have an adequate level of interactive competence, specific techniques for interacting effectively with particularly challenging clients can be passed from staff member to staff member, much as one communicates by means of a chain letter. Typically, the communication strategy is determined by the treatment team and is then passed on to key members of the direct care staff with the instruction to ensure that colleagues are briefed in the procedure. The speech-language pathologist or behavioral psychologist then probes the staff to determine whether the chain of peer training was, in fact, completed. Peer training is one mechanism for promoting staff ownership of the culture generally and of individual treatment plans specifically (Bernstein, 1982; Bogdan et al., 1974; Wetzel & Hoschouer, 1984).

Evaluation

Evaluating the effectiveness of the training in relation to communication behaviors of staff and family members has two parts. Most important, trainers and supervisors observe the staff or family member interacting in challenging real-world contexts. Success of the training program ultimately stands or falls with the level of skill observed in such situations. If communicative competencies become components of all job descriptions, then evaluation of performance is built into the ongoing supervisory process; the training therefore is more likely to be taken seriously, and its effects are more likely to persist.

The information component of the training can be evaluated with a paper and pencil pretest and posttest. Although this means of evaluation is insensitive to the acquisition of competencies, it is nevertheless important to ensure that the basic conceptual framework and language are in place. Paper and pencil tests are well suited to this task. Appendix 4-3 includes an illustration of one such pretest and posttest.

EFFECTIVENESS OF COMMUNICATION TRAINING IN TBI REHABILITATION

We are aware of no published reports of studies that evaluated the effects of communication training on staff and family members' communication behavior or ultimately on the outcome of the clients served by the head injury rehabilitation program. The source of our conviction regarding the value of the training outlined in this chapter is our combined clinical experience over many years of working in head injury rehabilitation centers together with years of comparable experience and research in the field of developmental disabilities (Adams et al., 1980; Bernstein, 1982; Reid & Whitman, 1983; Slama & Bannerman, 1983; Twardosz & Nordquist, 1985; Wetzel & Hoschouer, 1984). This body of research supports our clinical belief that the goals of training are best accomplished by means of role playing and modeling combined with ongoing coaching and support in vivo.

CASE ILLUSTRATIONS

N.H.

N.H. is a 13-year-old boy who sustained severe brain injury when he was hit by a car at the age of 10. Early recovery was slow and frustrating. After 10 months of hospitalization and acute

rehabilitation, he was at Level 5 (confused and inappropriate) on the RLA Scale of Cognitive Recovery. He was quadriplegic and in a wheelchair, had severe expressive aphasia that virtually eliminated symbolic communication, and had begun to demonstrate self-injurious behavior (e.g., hitting his head with a closed fist). His parents removed him from the rehabilitation center because of a conflict over treatment issues. During the following 2 years, N.H. was introduced to three different educational settings. In each case, he was removed because of behavioral difficulties. The self-injurious behavior continued to escalate in frequency and intensity.

N.H. reentered an inpatient brain injury rehabilitation facility at age 13, 3 years after the injury. Behavioral-communicative analysis of the self-injurious behavior suggested that it primarily served an escape-avoidance function but that on occasion it seemed intended to express a need for attention and interaction. The primary goal of the inpatient admission was to reduce the self-injurious behavior by substituting a functional equivalent that would be effective and also acceptable to staff and family. This by itself would enable N.H. to return to school, which would be extremely beneficial to him and to his family.

Given the communicative function of the challenging behavior, the speech-language pathologist, behavioral psychologist, and parents worked together to develop a system of manual signs and natural gestures that could be taught as replacements for the self-injurious behavior. Communication training for staff and family included traditional inservice presentations related to the target behaviors and procedures for teaching the alternative communicative behaviors. More important, teaching occurred in vivo at a number of levels. Guided observation and observed interaction combined with video feedback were used initially to evaluate the effectiveness of the intervention procedures for N.H. Subsequently, the same strategies were used to evaluate the skills of staff and family members and to continue the coaching process until adequate mastery was achieved. These staff and family teaching strategies were used in the rehabilitation facility and also at home and in N.H.'s school (after his reentry) to ensure that interaction with N.H. was consistent and therapeutic in all critical settings. A year after discharge, N.H. continued to be enrolled in a special education class in his community school and was reported to be making slow but steady progress in communication and other skills.

L.R.

L.R. sustained a severe closed head injury in an automobile accident at age 19. His stage of recovery characterized by confusion and agitation was prolonged. During this stage he expressed frustration by hitting others, breaking glass, and attempting to ingest noxious substances. As his confusion cleared, his dysarthria persisted. Presumably resulting in part from his inability to communicate intelligibly with speech, he continued to express anger or frustration with physically aggressive acts and gestures.

L.R., the behavioral psychologist, and the speech-language pathologist met on several occasions and agreed on a plan for identifying sources of frustration and learning a communication act (a generally understood finger gesture) that could be the functional equivalent of aggression. In addition, L.R. learned techniques of cued relaxation. Because many people consider the symbolically aggressive communication act unacceptable, a large component of family and staff training was counseling them to relate appropriately to the gesture because the alternative was physical aggression.

Staff and family training consisted of general orientation through inservice pedagogy with subsequent teaching and coaching in vivo. Furthermore, because components of the program changed over time, chained training (staff passing information and skills or techniques to other staff) was an important component of staff training. After staff and family acceptance of the communication program for L.R., his physical aggression was eliminated.

CONCLUSION

The forest to be seen within the trees of training detail in this chapter is a vision of a commu-

nity of people that is dominated by a positive communication culture. The community includes all the people who live, work, and visit in a rehabilitation facility. The benefits of this culture include generally improved quality of life for family members, clients, and staff alike; greater ease in dealing with difficult behavioral issues; and improved outcomes in relation to a critical goal of brain injury rehabilitation, namely effective and personally satisfying social interaction.

REFERENCES

Adams, G.L., Tallon, R.J., & Rimell, P.A. (1980). A comparison of lecture versus role-playing in the training of the use of positive reinforcement. *Journal of Organizational Behavior Management, 2,* 205–212.

Bernstein, G.S. (1982). Training behavior change agents: A conceptual review. *Behavior Therapy, 13,* 1–23.

Bogdan, R., Taylor, S., DeGrande, B., & Haynes, S. (1974). Let them eat programs: Attendants' perspectives and programming. *Journal of Health and Social Behavior, 15,* 142–151.

Booth, S.R., & Fairbank, D.W. (1984). Videotape feedback as a behavior management technique. *Behavioral disorders, 9,* 55–59.

Brooks, D.N., & McKinlay, W. (1983). Personality and behavioral change after severe blunt head injury—A relative's view. *Journal of Neurology, Neurosurgery, and Psychiatry, 46,* 336–344.

Brooks, N., McKinlay, W., Symington, C., Beattie, A., & Campsie, L. (1987). Return to work within the first seven years of severe head injury. *Brain Injury, 1,* 5–19.

Burke, G.M. (1990). Unconventional behavior: A communicative interpretation in individuals with severe disabilities. *Topics in Language Disorders, 10,* 75–85.

Carr, E.G. (1988). Functional equivalence as a mechanism of response generalization. In R. Horner, G. Dunlop, & R.L. Koegel (Eds.), *Generalization and maintenance.* Baltimore: Brookes.

Carr, E.G., & Durand, V.M. (1985a). Reducing behavior problems through functional communication training. *Journal of Applied Behavior Analysis, 18,* 111–126.

Carr, E.G., & Durand, V.M. (1985b). The social-communicative basis of severe behavior problems in children. In S. Reiss & R. Bootzin (Eds.), *Theoretical issues in behavior therapy* (pp. 219–254). New York: Academic Press.

Deaton, A.V. (1987). *Pediatric head trauma: A guide for families.* New Kent, VA: Cumberland Hospital.

Donnellan, A.M., Mirenda, P.L., Mesaros, R.A., & Fassbender, L.L. (1984). Analyzing the communicative functions of aberrant behavior. *Journal of the Association for the Severely Handicapped, 9,* 201–212.

Dunst, C.J., Johanson, X.X., Trivette, C.M., & Hamby, D. (1991). Family oriented early intervention policies and practices: Family centered or not? *Exceptional Children, 58,* 115–126.

Durand, V.M., & Carr, E.G. (1991). Functional communication training to reduce challenging behavior: Maintenance and application in new settings. *Journal of Applied Behavior Analysis, 24,* 251–264.

Feeney, T.J., & Urbanczyk, B. (in press). Language as behavior or, the myth of maladaptive behavior. In G. Wolcott & R.C. Savage (Eds.), *Educational programming for children and young adults with acquired brain injury.* Austin, TX: Pro-Ed.

Gordon, N. (1991). The relationship between language and behavior. *Developmental Medicine and Child Neurology, 33,* 86–89.

Hagen, C. (1981). Language disorders secondary to closed head injury: Diagnosis and treatment. *Topics in Language Disorders, 1,* 73–87.

Hartley, L.L. (1990). Assessment of functional communication. In D.E. Tupper & K.D. Cicerone (Eds.), *The neuropsychology of everyday life: Assessment and basic competencies* (pp. 125–168). Boston: Kluwer Academic.

Hollander, M., Plutchik, R., & Horner, V. (1973). Interaction of patient and attendant reinforcement programs: The "piggyback" effect. *Journal of Consulting and Clinical Psychology, 41,* 43–47.

Jacobs, H.E. (1990). A rationale for family involvement in long-term traumatic head injury rehabilitation. In D.E. Tupper & K.D. Cicerone (Eds.), *The neuropsychology of everyday life.* Boston: Kluwer Academic.

Keith-Dunlap, L., Dunlap, G., Clarke, S., Childs, K.E., White, R.L., & Stewart, M.P. (1992). Effects of a videotape feedback package on the peer interactions of children with serious behavioral and emotional challenges. *Journal of Applied Behavior Analysis, 25,* 355–364.

Kreutzer, J.S., Zasler, N.D., Camplair, P.S., & Leininger, B.E. (1990). A practical guide to family intervention following adult traumatic brain injury. In J.S. Kreutzer & P. Wehman (Eds.), *Community integration following traumatic brain injury.* Baltimore: Brookes.

LaVigna, G.W., & Donnellan, A.M. (1986). *Alternatives to punishment: Solving behavior problems with non-aversive strategies.* New York: Irvington.

Lehr, E. (1990). *Psychological management of traumatic brain injuries in children and adolescents.* Gaithersburg, MD: Aspen.

Lezak, M.D. (1987). Relationships between personality disorders, social disturbances, and physical disability following traumatic brain injury. *Journal of Head Trauma Rehabilitation, 2,* 57–69.

Lezak, M.D. (1988). Brain damage is a family affair. *Journal of Clinical and Experimental Neuropsychology, 10,* 111–123.

Montegar, C.A., Reid, D.H., Madsen, C.H., & Ewell, M.D. (1977). Increasing institutional staff to resident interactions through inservice training and supervisor approval. *Behavioral Therapy, 8,* 533–540.

O'Brien, J., & Mount, B. (1985). *Design for accomplishment.* Lithonia, GA: Responsive Systems Associates.

Oddy, M. (1984). Head injury and social adjustment. In N. Brooks (Ed.), *Closed head injury: Psychological, social, and family consequences* (pp. 108–192). New York: Oxford University Press.

Powell, T., Salzberg, C., Rule, S., Levy, S., & Itzkowitz, J. (1987). Teaching mentally retarded children to play with their siblings using parents as trainers. *Education and Treatment of Children, 6,* 343–362.

Prigatano, G.P. (1986). *Neuropsychological rehabilitation after brain injury.* Baltimore: Johns Hopkins University Press.

Reid, D.H., & Whitman, T.L. (1983). Behavioral staff management in institutions: A critical review of effectiveness and acceptability. *Analysis and Intervention in Developmental Disabilities, 3,* 131–149.

Satanoff, N.D., (1991). Effective behavior management of the head injured patient: A holistic approach. *Journal of Head Injury, 2,* 22–25.

Savage, R.C., & Carter, R.R. (1991). Family and return to school. In J.M. Williams & T. Kay (Eds.), *Head injury: A family matter.* Baltimore: Brookes.

Schreibman, L. (1988). Parent training as a means of facilitating generalization in autistic children. In R.H. Horner, G., Dunlap, & R.L. Koegel (Eds.), *Generalization and maintenance: Life style changes in applied settings.* Baltimore: Brookes.

Schuler, A.L. (1980, August). *Communicative intent and aberrant behavior.* Paper presented at the Council on Exceptional Children Topical Conference on the Severely Emotionally Disturbed, Minneapolis, MN.

Slama, K.M., & Bannerman, D.J. (1983). Implementing and maintaining a behavioral treatment system in an institutional setting. *Analysis and Intervention in Developmental Disabilities, 3,* 171–191.

Thomsen, I.V. (1984). Late outcome of very severe blunt head trauma: A 10–15 year second follow-up. *Journal of Neurology, Neurosurgery, and Psychiatry, 47,* 264.

Twardosz, S., & Nordquist, V.M. (1985). Parent training. In M. Nersen & V.B. Van Hesselt (Eds.), *Behavior therapy with children and adolescents: A clinical approach* (pp. 75–105). New York: Wiley.

Walther, M., & Beate, D. (1991). The effect of videotape feedback on the on-task behavior of a student with emotional/behavioral disorders. *Education and Treatment of Children, 14,* 53–60.

Wetzel, R.J., & Hoschouer, R.L. (1984). *Residential teaching communities: Program development and staff training for developmentally disabled persons.* Dallas: Scott, Foresman.

Williams, J.M., & Kay, T. (1991). *Head injury: A family matter.* Baltimore: Brookes.

Wood, R. (1984). Behavior disorders following severe head injury: Their presentation and psychological management. In N. Brooks (Ed.), *Closed head injury: Psychological, social, and family consequences* (pp. 195–219). New York: Oxford University Press.

Ylvisaker, M. (1992). Communication outcome following traumatic brain injury. *Seminars in Speech and Language, 13,* 239–251.

Ylvisaker, M. (in press). Communication outcome in children and adolescents with traumatic brain injury. *Journal of Neuropsychological Rehabilitation.*

Ylvisaker, M., Feeney, T.J., & Urbanczyk, B. (1993). A social-environmental approach to communication and behavior after traumatic brain injury. *Seminars in Speech and Language, 14,* 74–87.

Ylvisaker, M., & Hough, S.F. (1981, October). *Reestablishing communication with children with head injuries.* Workshop presented at Pediatric Head Injury: Innovative Approaches to Intervention, Pittsburgh, PA.

Ylvisaker, M., Szekeres, S., Haarbauer-Krupa, J., Urbanczyk, B., & Feeney, T.J. (in press). Speech and language intervention. In G. Wolcott & R.C. Savage (Eds.), *Educational programming for children and young adults with acquired brain injury.* Austin, TX: Pro-Ed.

Ylvisaker, M., Szekeres, S., Henry, K., Sullivan, D., & Wheeler, P. (1987). Topics in cognitive rehabilitation therapy. In M. Ylvisaker & E.M. Gobble (Eds.), *Community re-entry for head injured adults.* Austin, TX: Pro-Ed.

Ylvisaker, M., Urbanczyk, B., & Feeney, T.J. (1992). Social skills following traumatic brain injury. *Seminars in Speech and Language, 13,* 308–321.

Rehabilitation Staff Communicative Competencies

COMMUNICATING WITH CLIENTS

Content

The staff member will:

1. talk comfortably with the client about topics of interest to him or her
2. use vocabulary that is meaningful
3. use vocabulary that is adequately concrete yet respectful of the client's age
4. give information needed to keep the client oriented

Form

The staff member will:

1. use gestures, writing, and physical prompts if necessary
2. use a natural tone of voice and inflection
3. repeat information if necessary

4. use short sentences if necessary to ensure the client's understanding
5. give adequate processing time between messages
6. use simple grammar if necessary
7. speak clearly

Encouragement

The staff member will:

1. initiate topics of interest to the client
2. use appropriate prompts to encourage communication
3. give the client time to respond
4. give the client words if he or she is struggling
5. respond to the client's verbal and nonverbal communication
6. encourage nonverbal communication
7. offer choices whenever possible
8. seek confirmation of the client's understanding

The authors express their appreciation to Gary Kozick, MSW, for his assistance.

9. reinforce (e.g., through additional conversation time or praise) successful communication attempts
10. avoid ridiculing, teasing, or punishing inappropriate or unsuccessful communication

Environment

The staff member will:

1. minimize distractions
2. maintain the client's attention when communicating (e.g., redirect as necessary, use the client's name, or touch the client to gain attention if appropriate)
3. interact in a familiar setting
4. control the number of people present

Respect

The staff member will:

1. actively encourage the client's participation in treatment planning at whatever level he or she is capable of such participation
2. not talk about the client in his or her presence
3. avoid a condescending style (e.g., baby talk) and condescending words (e.g., *sweetie* or *honey*)
4. communicate respect directly (e.g., "I am sure that it is difficult for an intelligent adult like yourself to accept some of our rules")
5. use polite requests rather than abrupt commands
6. choose an appropriate time and place to discuss personal issues
7. pay attention to the client's emotional state and communicate that his or her feelings are understood and are appropriate
8. never punish, ridicule, or demean a client's atypical behavior
9. use humor that is appropriate and meaningful to the client

COMMUNICATING WITH FAMILY MEMBERS

Content

The staff member will:

1. actively invite family members to identify their own concerns and interests rather than make assumptions about their concerns and interests
2. actively seek information from family members about the client that will be useful for the treatment team
3. provide information to families that will help them stay informed about their family member's care
4. clearly explain facility programs, treatment regimens, staff roles, family roles in rehabilitation, and other related matters

Form

The staff member will:

1. use meaningful vocabulary and avoid jargon

2. speak clearly and use natural inflection
3. use illustrations and repetition as needed to ensure comprehension
4. communicate openness, warmth, flexibility, and humor (if appropriate)
5. use techniques of active listening
6. use effective and encouraging coaching techniques during family training

Encouragement

The staff member will:

1. actively invite family members' participation in assessment, goal setting, and intervention
2. actively invite expressions of concern and family problem solving around treatment issues
3. act on family recommendations unless they are harmful to the client

4. be available to family members to discuss their concerns

Environment

The staff member will:

1. minimize distractions and interruptions during interaction with family members
2. use a private setting to discuss confidential or personal issues

Respect

The staff member will:

1. take family members' questions and rec-ommendations seriously and act on them unless they are contraindicated by the client's needs
2. avoid a condescending or self-righteous manner in communicating with families
3. communicate genuine interest in and con-cern for family members' issues
4. respond promptly to family letters or calls
5. avoid ridiculing or devaluing a family member's behavior
6. respect racial, cultural, ethnic, and reli-gious differences
7. respect the family's right to self-determi-nation (freedom of choice)

COMMUNICATING WITH OTHER STAFF

Content

The staff member will:

1. provide other staff with information that is relevant, useful, reliable, and accurate
2. ask relevant questions of other staff (in-cluding supervisors) regarding clients, policies, treatment, and other issues
3. describe minor concerns to supervisors be-fore they become major concerns

Form

The staff member will:

1. speak clearly and concisely, avoiding pro-fessional jargon
2. use natural inflection and tone of voice
3. avoid defensive responses, particularly in connection with professional turf issues
4. demonstrate initiative and at the same time patience, flexibility, and a cooperative atti-tude in interdisciplinary discussions
5. be supportive of colleagues
6. maintain perspective and a sense of humor, particularly during times of stress

7. give instructions to all levels of staff in a respectful manner

Encouragement

The staff member will:

1. initiate interaction with other staff
2. initiate problem-solving discussions, ac-tively seeking others' opinions
3. actively seek out whatever guidance is necessary
4. use techniques of active listening
5. make time for communication with other staff
6. make expectations of others clear
7. maintain active communication during stressful times
8. freely admit mistakes

Environment

The staff member will:

1. choose the correct time and place to dis-cuss issues, particularly confidential issues

2. be respectful of other staff members' needs for work time and quiet in a busy workplace

Respect

The staff member will:

1. treat all staff with respect, fairness, and courtesy regardless of academic degrees, professional training, or level of employment

2. assume that all staff members' time with clients is important

3. take others' opinions seriously

Appendix 4-2

Sample Vignettes for Role Planing in Staff Communication Training

NOTES TO THE TRAINER

During competency-based communication training, vignettes such as these can be shown on video or role played live. They are designed to present exaggerated negative models of communication. The rationale for using negative models is presented in the text.

When the vignette is completed, trainees identify as many communication or behavior management errors as possible, explain why the staff communication is inappropriate, describe the cognitive and communicative characteristics of the patient that make the staff communication inappropriate, brainstorm about positive alternatives to these negative models, and practice positive alternatives with trainer coaching.

The three vignettes that follow are merely illustrations. After two or three vignettes have been presented by the trainer, the trainees can create and act out their own scripts using the same procedure, given a small set of communicative competencies to be violated in the vignette.

VIGNETTE 1: THE KNOW-IT-ALL THERAPIST

Main Points

One should include alert clients in problem solving; avoid talking about clients in their presence, at least without permission to do so; avoid blaming clients; speak respectfully to other staff; and avoid jargon.

Script

A nursing assistant (NA) pushes an alert but physically impaired patient in a wheelchair into a physical therapist's (PT's) office.

NA: Excuse me, but Jane's got a problem with the footrest of her wheelchair. Her foot constantly comes off and then she complains. It's driving us crazy.

PT (checking the footrest and not greeting or paying attention to Jane): Well, Jane can't seem to follow simple rules, can she? I've told her a hundred times to keep her foot on the footrest. She doesn't know what's good for her. But, you know—you probably won't understand this—she does have significant hypertonus in her lowers and dorsiflexion contractures that interfere with optimal positioning.

Jane (trying to interrupt): Excuse me, but it's very uncomfortable.

PT (to Jane): Don't interrupt! We don't have all day! (to the NA): I think I'll have to just Velcro this foot down. It might hurt, but she has it coming to her for all the fuss that she has caused. It's not as though I was looking for more things to do today. This place is a zoo . . . mutter, mutter . . . (PT walks off).

Positive Alternative

The NA invites Jane to explain the problem; the PT invites Jane to give any information that she thinks is relevant; the PT invites Jane to join in the problem solving; and, if the NA and PT need to discuss Jane, they ask her in advance for her permission to discuss her situation.

VIGNETTE 2: ORIENTATION GROUP

Main Points

One should give disoriented clients personally meaningful information that promotes orientation, avoid quizzing clients, respectfully help clients who have difficulty expressing themselves, communicate understanding of emotions, and encourage nonverbal communication strategies.

Script

A therapist is conducting a morning orientation session for four disoriented clients.

Therapist: All right guys. Let's try to get you ready for the day. Here we go. What's the date? (pause) C'mon, what's the date today?

Ted (struggling): Wed . . . Wednesday.

Therapist: I didn't ask for the day, I asked for the date. John, you tell me.

John: I think, March. . . .

Therapist: No, you're way off. I can't believe you guys don't know this simple stuff. Get with the program here! Don't you read the newspaper? You better find this stuff out. Okay, who's the Assistant Foreign Minister of Iraq? Mary, do you know?

Mary: I want to go home.

Therapist: Enough already with this "I want to go home" stuff (mimicking Mary's speech). I get sick of hearing you guys talking about home all the time. You're not going to get out of here at this rate. Besides, you should be grateful for all the help we give you. Bill, who is your OT?

Bill: I don't know.

Therapist: I can't believe you don't know your OT. You see her every day.

Bill: She's . . . ah, ah got . . . (gestures long hair).

Therapist: Bill, I asked for her name. How can you be oriented without names?

Bill (getting up to leave): Go to hell.

Positive Alternative

The therapist gives meaningful orientation information to the clients, reminds them of ways in which they can find the information (e.g., by looking in their log books or by asking other clients), encourages gestured answers, and indicates understanding of the strong desire to get home.

VIGNETTE 3: THE OUTBURST

Main Points

The way staff approach and interact with clients can either trigger or prevent behavioral outbursts; clients who lack cognitive and behavioral flexibility must be dealt with flexibly by staff.

Script

A nurse enters an easily agitated client's room to draw blood. The client had not anticipated this. He is lying in bed watching TV.

Nurse: Jim, I need blood. Give me your arm.

Jim: Wait til this show is done.

Nurse: I can't wait. I'm busy. I have to do it now. (The nurse turns off the TV.)

Jim (becoming upset): Turn that on! Get out of my face! Nobody told me about blood. Leave me alone! Leave me alone! I'm getting out of this damn place! (He throws a magazine at the nurse.)

Positive Alternative

The nurse knocks on the door, apologizes for the intrusion, and explains the unexpected need for blood; explains that it will only take a minute; possibly waits for a commercial; possibly gives options (e.g., draws blood during a commercial or after the show); possibly makes a few minutes of pleasant conversation about the show; and does not approach physically without permission.

Staff Training Competencies: Communication and Behavior Pretest and Posttest

Date: _____

Name: _____

Job Title: _____

Pretest _____ Posttest _____

1–4: Choose the statement that *does not* fit:

1. When talking with a person with TBI, one should:
   A. talk about issues of interest to the individual with TBI.
   B. give information to promote the individual's orientation.
   C. not be concerned about vocabulary or content.
   D. communicate in a manner that is understandable to the individual with TBI.
2. When talking with a person with TBI, one should:
   A. use whatever form of communication is necessary to ensure that the individual understands.
   B. repeat the information as often as needed.
   C. talk clearly to ensure that the individual understands.
   D. talk loudly to ensure that the individual understands.
3. Communication and behavior are:
   A. separate and different.
   B. often the same.
   C. interdependent.
4. When communicating with families, one should:
   A. invite family members to indicate what issues are of concern to them.
   B. listen to families and include them in treatment decisions.
   C. limit the information given to families to ensure that they do not get confused.
   D. give as much information as necessary to ensure that they do not get confused.

5. Which is *not* true?
    A. Safety is of the utmost importance when managing a person demonstrating challenging behaviors.
    B. Behavior management cannot be used as a technique for behavior change.
    C. When intervening in a behavioral incident, one should use the least restrictive means necessary to ensure everyone's safety.
    D. Physical and pharmacological management of behaviors may be effective therapeutic techniques.
    E. The behavior response team is available to assist with behavioral crises.
6. Name five physical factors to consider when intervening in a behavioral crisis.

    _____   _____

    _____   _____

    _____

7. Name five psychological factors to consider when intervening in a behavioral crisis:

    _____   _____

    _____   _____

    _____

Multiple Choice

Choose the answer that *best* completes the sentence.

8. _____ behaviors should be ignored whenever possible.
    A. positive
    B. cooperative
    C. negative
    D. recumbent
9. Which of the following is *not* a right of an individual receiving treatment?
    A. Respectful treatment
    B. A safe environment
    C. Aggressive behavior
    D. Confidentiality
10. Which of the following is *not* a technique for fostering a good self-image?
    A. Punishing
    B. Praising effort
    C. Modeling positive behaviors
    D. Practicing positive behaviors
11. Often an individual's negative behavior is a way to _____ with others.
    A. walk
    B. attend
    C. communicate
    D. confide
12. Decreasing _____ can increase a person's feeling of safety. This can be accomplished by _____.
    A. noise/turning off the TV.
    B. attention/turning on the TV.
    C. lighting/changing the TV.
    D. room temperature/moving the TV.

13. You can demonstrate respect for patients and their families by considering your choice of _____.
    A. TV shows
    B. hairstyles
    C. language
    D. restaurants

14. A person with TBI shoud be given choices _____.
    A. whenever possible
    B. only in therapy sessions
    C. when the rehabilitation team has determined that he or she is capable of making them
    D. after a few months of therapy

15. Praising, giving positive reinforcement, and encouragement give someone the _____ to do it again.
    A. duty
    B. behavior
    C. coordination
    D. incentive

16. Choose the *best* statement from the following:
    A. Negative behavior has a communicative function.
    B. People engage in negative behavior because they like it.
    C. People who engage in negative behavior are spoiled.
    D. All persons with TBI demonstrate negative behavior when they cannot communicate with speech or alternative communication.

17. Antecedents are events that occur _____.
    A. before a challenging behavior
    B. during a challenging behavior
    C. after a challenging behavior

18. Nonaversive teaching allows people with TBI to _____.
    A. learn how to get away with things
    B. develop alternative methods of communication
    C. hurt as many people as they want as often as they want
    D. scare me

19. Many changes in behaviors take place after TBI, but they are often not _____ and _____.
    A. fun/enjoyable
    B. purposeful/premeditated
    C. interesting/exciting
    D. believable/fulfilling

20. It is important to communicate with clients by using _____.
    A. slang
    B. a childlike voice
    C. a loud voice
    D. age-appropriate language

21. Redirection is _____.
    A. what you do when someone asks you how to get to the facility from the highway
    B. providing an alternative behavior
    C. not B
    D. the appropriate manner in which to give instruction to any client

22. Which of the following does *not* describe a manner of *nonjudgmental* communication?
    A. reassuring
    B. understanding
    C. humor
    D. reprimanding
23. Which of the following people are responsible for promoting improved communication in patients?
    A. behavior staff
    B. nursing staff
    C. speech-language pathologists
    D. administrative staff
    E. all of the above

True or False

T	F	When working with people who are agitated, it is a good idea to remind them of the negative consequences that will occur if they continue to misbehave.
T	F	When interacting with an individual who is upset, it is best to have one person at a time talk with the individual.
T	F	When someone is agitated, it is best to reduce the demands on him or her until he or she is calm.
T	F	When an individual is displaying a challenging behavior, it is appropriate for staff verbally to reprimand him or her.
T	F	Empathy is an effective way to demonstrate that you are listening and trying to understand a person's feelings.
T	F	Aversive approaches to behavior management reduce challenging behaviors better and longer than nonaversive approaches.
T	F	Dealing with behavior problems is not part of your job.
T	F	Behavior is communication.
T	F	Communication is behavior.

Transference and Countertransference Issues in Brain Injury Rehabilitation: Implications for Staff Training

Mary Pepping

5

OBJECTIVES

Upon completion of this chapter, the reader will be able to:

1. identify the specific features of consultant Robert M. Wienecke, MD's model of transference and countertransference as it is used by staff and patients in therapy
2. understand the nature of the masochism (as it is defined in this model) that occurs in human psychological development and fuels these transference and countertransference issues
3. develop an appreciation of the importance of early experience and emotional bonding in humans as the foundation for later issues in rehabilitation (and, one might add, in life)
4. understand the degree to which this early experience, or programming, occurs outside of conscious awareness yet continues to exert profound effects upon later life perception and behavior
5. recognize the common preinjury levels of masochism (e.g., unhealthy aspects of programming) that occur among people with brain injury, as well as among staff
6. provide practical definitions and case examples of these and other features of the model, including the terms *transference, countertransference, masochism, health, bonding, best-interest behavior,* and *fairness*
7. define the ways in which staff of all disciplines can be trained to understand and employ this model effectively in their work

Transference and Countertransference Issues in Brain Injury Rehabilitation

This particular chapter is really the work of two people: the author named in the chapter by-line and a silent author who is very much present in this discussion. It is the vision of Robert M. Wienecke, MD, both as an active, practicing psychiatrist and as a theorist, that provides the foundation for what is written here. Liberal use is made throughout this chapter of his terminology, his particular definitions of psychological concepts, and his perspectives and observations about human behavior. All conceptual credit for the model provided here goes to him.

There are many theories of human behavior and many psychological approaches to treatment. This chapter provides a detailed look at a particular model and its applications to treatment. In this process, terms such as *masochism* and *sadomasochism* are used; these have a unique set of definitions in this context that do not involve whips, chains, or the Marquis de Sade. Also, although this model was initially developed in a psychotherapeutic practice that did not involve people with brain injury, its utility and applications to a rehabilitation population of clients and staff were clear to all concerned.

HISTORY

This application began in the late 1970s in Oklahoma City, when a unique working relationship was forged between psychologist George Prigatano and psychiatrist Wienecke. Their discussions began as over-the-kitchen-table exchanges of information from the realms of neuropsychology, brain anatomy, and function; theories of initial bonding and programming; rehabilitation issues and practices; theories of John Rosen; and more. Both were interested in the biological and intrapsychic underpinnings of human behavior and in how these factors might be further affected by acquired brain injury.

Those initial kitchen discussions led to an ongoing series of monthly meetings between Wienecke and the staff of the Presbyterian Hospital Section of Neuropsychology. Those meetings continue.

As Wienecke shared his ideas and models regarding the biological and experiential determinants of human behavior and the staff detailed their day-to-day interactions with the program participants, applications of the model for both staff and patients became increasingly (and sometimes uncomfortably) clear (Wienecke, 1989).

CLINICAL IMPORTANCE

This general topic (transference, countertransference, and Wienecke's theory of masochism as it relates to these) is clinically important for a number of reasons:

1. It is too easy in any kind of therapy to get caught in unproductive and unhealthy struggles between patients and therapists.
2. Increasing financial and program pressures for good outcomes that must often be achieved with less time and less money than one would like, and sometimes by relatively inexperienced staff, all heighten the potential for adversarial relationships between, and among, staff and patients (e.g., "Why aren't they getting better faster when we are working so hard to help them" or "Team B has easier patients than we do, that's why their outcome statistics look so good").
3. The intensity of brain injury rehabilitation work (which is due in part to the compromise in cognitive, personality, behavioral, and motor abilities, which is further compounded by reason 4 below) can create an atmosphere of struggle and confusion that has the potential to be maladaptive for all (Prigatano, Pepping, & Klonoff, 1986).
4. Individuals with brain injury are more likely than the average person to have important preinjury adjustment issues, which will complicate the therapeutic alliance needed for optimal rehabilitation.
5. Therapists as a group have more than the average amount of early maladaptive pro-

gramming themselves. It tends to take the form of helping other people, which is a laudable goal but too often grounded in a combination of healthy and unhealthy early formative experiences. The unhealthy programming is likely to have a negative impact on rehabilitation efforts.

TRANSFERENCE AND COUNTERTRANSFERENCE ISSUES

If we want to help staff and clients function as effectively as possible given all the potential pitfalls, staff in particular need to be aware of the issues that create such transference and countertransference tendencies and how to address them successfully for all concerned.

Health is defined in this model as successful interdependency, which involves (1) accurate perception, (2) the capacity for best-interest behavior, and (3) the optimal blend of independent achievement and dependent connection with others. More will be said about these specific components later; suffice it to say that we all strive to achieve this kind of health, and most of us are not completely there. The relative degree of our unhealthy (e.g., masochistic, pain-seeking, "not having") compared to healthy behaviors and perceptions, and our awareness of these will determine to a large degree how successful we can be in any given interaction, be it rehabilitation oriented or otherwise.

In most people with acquired brain injury, the amount of preinjury psychopathology is a major determinant of the amount of postinjury psychopathology and of the rehabilitation problems faced by the therapist. Those preinjury issues are of course compounded by the nature and severity of insult to the brain and its integration. The therapist's tasks in this context include teaching the patient specific ways to overcome the limitations imposed or aggravated by the injury and dealing effectively with resistances to that effort.

Resistances are partly related to organically based impairments of awareness, cognition, emotion, and motor/sensory changes. They are also affected by the grief, depression, shame, and other psychological reactions that are a normal part of coming to grips with a profound loss or change in the self. In the long run, however, the most formidable base of resistance is the one we see in all psychotherapy patients; that is, the powerful tendency to continue to perceive oneself in relationship to the world, and relating to that world, in ways learned in infancy and early childhood. This tendency is further complicated by the fact that much of our early learning, bonding, and programming occurs outside of conscious awareness.

Perhaps a few more words about bonding and resistance will help clarify this point. All mammal infants have a powerful instinct to be with their mothers. You do not have to teach a baby monkey to hold onto its mother's belly. In humans, the molding to the mother's being is more psychological than physical. In addition, it is not just mother per se but the overall early environment with which the child is interacting that exerts such important influences upon psychic development (Broussard & Hartner, 1970, 1971; Broussard, 1976).

Therefore, birth trauma, early life-threatening experiences, painful illnesses, and early deprivation of physical contact are all significantly formative events in the programming of an individual's perceptions and relationship patterns. The early rearing person, usually the mother, is typically the most significant element in the totality of significant elements. Her perceptual states and her ensuing behavioral patterns are usually the greatest determinants of what an individual learns about relating, loving, and meaning in life as well as what he or she needs, deserves, and can expect. Once the bonding is established to this early reality, resistance exists; that is, the individual resists being taken away from his or her source of survival as he or she has come to know it, even if that source is pernicious, destructive, or more subtly unfair (Rosen, 1953; Searles, 1965).

Resistance in therapy is a special case of the general resistance to being taken away from how we have learned to perceive and relate; that is, we seek the mother we know and unconsciously wish to remain bonded to her. In therapy, we resist change because it too represents a being taken away from a particular way of being. Therefore, if an individual is programmed early in life to relate in conflict and pain, to be deprived or depreciated, or to lack what is fair, then that person will continue to set up conflict and pain as a way of relating and living. This programmed pattern of conflict, pain, and confusion can also be called masochism.

Yet exactly how does this particular way of being, this masochism, this failure of initial communication, the bonding to pain, to all-or-none, get established? Don't most parents love their children, and don't they try to do the best they know how in raising them? The answer of course is yes, parents love their children, and they love them the way that they (the parents) were taught to love, with whatever degree of health and pathology that involved.

When infantile and early childhood needs are not met adequately, there follows a sense of loss. That sense of loss leads to feelings of hurt and anger. Anger generates an impulse to hurt back, to retaliate against the parent figures one loves and needs. Anxiety and primitive guilt derive from the impulse to hurt Momma, to hurt Daddy. The child is then driven to be hurt in return, to atone through suffering for these unacceptable and potentially dangerous impulses; that is, if we anger or alienate the mother we need for survival, we are at risk. The guilt-driven impulse to atone through suffering contributes powerfully to the generation of sadomasochistic sequences and depression. The sadomasochistic sequence involves doing something provocative to stimulate hurt and anger in others. Retaliation follows.

This sequence of emotion, impulse, provocation, and retaliation occurs outside of conscious awareness. Most individuals only tune in consciously with the perception of an unprovoked attack by others. This perception leads to the final position in this sequence, which is the only completely conscious part: "Poor me" or "Look how I am abandoned" or "Look how poorly I am being treated by others." A vicious cycle frequently ensues in which the masochist then feels justified in punishing the other person through suffering and guilt induction: "Look how terrible you are, how badly you treat me when I haven't done anything to you."

In outline form, this process flows as follows (the first nine aspects of the process occur outside of conscious awareness):

1. The infant or young child's important needs are not met.

2. This leads to a sense of loss.

3. Loss leads to hurt and anger.

4. Hurt and anger lead to the impulse to hurt someone you love and need.

5. This impulse produces anxiety and primitive guilt.

6. The anxiety and guilt lead to a desire to be hurt, to atone through suffering.

7. This leads to sadomasochistic behavior (i.e., the giving and getting of pain) and possibly depression.

8. This sadomasochistic program leads to doing something provocative to stimulate hurt and anger in others (or picking someone who will hurt us, or perceiving that others are hurting us when they are not).

9. This behavior of ours leads to retaliation from the environment.

10. We respond to this retaliation without any conscious awareness of the role our own anger and provocation have played in setting these retaliatory events in motion.

11. This leads to a final "Poor me, look how I am abandoned, look how poorly and unfairly I am treated."

12. It can also lead to punishing the other person(s): "Look how terrible you are, you treat me so bad."

Among people with brain injury, that level of masochism is often found to be operating before the injury in ways that relate clearly to the etiology of the injury. When motor vehicles, falls, or gunshot wounds are involved, the pure accident is a fairly rare occurrence. Often, a pattern where a person behaves repeatedly not in his or her best interest can be seen. These behaviors typically involve taking dangerous physical or social risks and behaving provocatively to others.

The role of the masochism, the program, in the etiology of the injury is not, nor should it be, the primary focus of our rehabilitation efforts. Sometimes, later in the therapy, the question of masochism and injury etiology is addressed, usually if the patient brings it up. For example, after weeks of working on various issues and understanding the role that early programming can play in present behavior, the client may draw the conclusion that he or she was not functioning in a best-interest fashion at the time of the accident. From this new perspective, the person can look back and see that getting drunk and careening down a twisting road outside of town was not simply having fun but courting disaster in a way that was potentially profoundly self-destructive. At that point in time, it is important to acknowledge that various factors contributed to the accident, one of them probably being the programming to not have what is fair, to be in pain, and then to look for ways to identify and promote healthy behavior in day-to-day life from this point forward.

In a rehabilitation setting, what is critically important is that the staff observe and identify the old conflictual and self-defeating patterns that each individual patient presents in light of his or her day-to-day behavior in treatment and at home. As evidence accumulates during rehabilitation, the therapist needs to help the person see the role that his or her programming (i.e., masochism) plays in keeping these problematic behaviors or perceptions alive and hurtful to self and others (Prigatano, et al., 1986).

The manner in which this feedback is provided is important. As a supervisor of Wienecke's once noted, confrontation involves pointing out what a person is doing; interpretation involves pointing out why he or she does it. In our experience, interpretation works better as a therapy tool for establishing solid and long-term change and for reducing somewhat the likelihood of immediate opposition or resistance. The sandwich technique is another valuable tool in this process, providing people with a genuine identification of their strengths and accomplishments while allowing some constructive criticism, which is followed by

a round of applause or further recognition of their efforts to get healthy.

In striving to be optimum therapists, and realizing that early experience and programming exert a profound influence on current behavior and perception, what should we do with this perspective, this understanding? We propose the following pragmatic steps:

1. Really learn about and understand the nature of the programming, the tenacity of the bonding to early life experience, and the instinctual basis for this bonding.

2. Learn equally well about what is healthy and what is fair, kind, and in one's best interest from general ideas and principles through specific applications in one's areas of work, communicating with others, personal relationships, sexuality, finances, time management, and so forth.

3. Practice, practice, and practice some more.

We practice getting from point 1 to 2, and we expect to get lost, get discouraged, want to give up, and feel overwhelmed (what better way for our early programming to win a final victory over the forces for health and change than to convince the healthy part of us that positive and lasting change is impossible). We manage this practice by getting up again after we fall, not judging ourselves or others harshly, finding our bearings again, and making further attempts to be calm and on target instead of disorganized, enraged, frenzied, or despairing. Therapists are an interesting group of individuals who have often had more than the average amount of programming to be masochistic themselves. Our programming sounds something like this: (1) renounce self, (2) take care of mother (later others), (3) resent it, and (4) fail. To whatever degree our own interdependency with our early environment was unsuccessful, we will have trouble perceiving reality accurately and therefore have trouble giving any particular stimulus the response it deserves (i.e., neither overreacting nor underreacting).

For example, perhaps a client in the program says something to us that is demeaning or reflects a lack of appreciation for our efforts on his or her behalf. If we come from a family environment where appreciation was an important unmet need, we are more likely than the average person to react with intense feelings of anger, resentment, or discouragement to such comments. This is often true even if we do not express our feelings directly; the emotional reactions can still occur, accumulate, and affect our own behavior and treatment efforts.

COUNTERTRANSFERENCE

Countertransference problems in psychotherapy and rehabilitation occur when the therapist has inaccurate perceptions as to what to expect from his or her patient. Transference is defined here as any emotion and accompanying impulse based in past programming or life experience but inappropriately projected onto the therapist by the client. Countertransference is this same phenomenon but with the reaction or projection directed toward the client by the therapist. Some examples may help clarify these points.

A person comes to therapy who has longstanding difficulties with self-esteem and identity as an attractive or appealing person to others and a history of poor relationships with both parents, who were caring but harsh. With the added implications now of a brain injury, all these issues are brought even more powerfully than usual to the foreground. The client perceives the therapist as harsh and critical no matter how kindly and supportively the therapist provides feedback, both positive and negative. This set of perceptions is the client's transference reaction to the therapist. As the treatment program proceeds, this client becomes more and more depressed, self-abnegatory, and immobilized.

Meanwhile, although the therapist recognizes that some overreaction may be occurring, the therapist brings his or her own set of issues to this therapeutic interaction. This may include the general paradigm mentioned earlier (e.g., renounce self, take care of others, resent it, and fail). More specifically, if this therapist comes from a home where either or both parents handled stress by becoming depressed, withdrawn, or nonfunctional at times, there is likely to be a strong emotional reaction on the part of the therapist to this client. To the degree that this emotional reaction is more intense than the situation really warrants, we are looking at a countertransference reaction.

Part of what makes team approaches to rehabilitation so important is that the various members of the team can learn over time what their own and other staff members' important issues are with respect to countertransference potential. We can all help each other, and the clients, perceive accurately and behave in a best-interest fashion. When we know what is going on, why, and what to do about it in a healthy way, everyone is on the road to recovery.

Part of why it is so easy to get caught in these transference and countertransference situations might be explained as follows: Whenever we relate to someone who is not fully mature, which is pretty much all the time because none of us is completely mature, we are thrown into the position of being parents of a sort. When this happens, we have a number of choices before us. We can get out immediately, leaving the baby on someone else's doorstep, so to speak. If we stay engaged, then there are probably three additional options:

1. Pursue the illusion of trying to be the perfect parent (or therapist), which of course requires perfect children or patients to affirm us.

2. Operate "in a twit," that is, not really understanding what is going on; feeling inadequate to the task at hand; feeling guilty, anxious, resentful, and retaliatory (the "take care of mother, resent it, fail" script).

3. Develop the good parent option. This option is characterized by knowing what is going on in the process of therapy or rehabilitation, by taking care of ourselves, and by being emotionally strong. From this position of strength, we are then able to function therapeutically as good parents by nurturing, teaching, protecting, and limit setting. In a word, we are prepared to foster health with appropriate levels of independent achievement and dependent connection and closeness.

MAJOR CHALLENGES

One of the major challenges to us as therapists, as parents, and as friends is knowing what is going on and not losing sight of the limitations and resistances of our clients. If we do not keep a clear mind and focus, we will become caught up in the confusion that is the handmaiden of masochism (a term coined by Wienecke). Because confusion per se is also the hallmark of brain injury (a favorite comment of Prigatano's), we are simultaneously faced with two great opportunities for confusion and for losing track of the important issues. Add the third possibility, that our own masochism may be stimulated by the stress of our work to become fully operational, and one can begin to appreciate why the intensive kinds of rehabilitation efforts required to assist people with brain injury are so challenging for staff and patients alike (Pepping & Roueche, 1991).

Sometimes, when the work is particularly difficult, it is easy to fall into the trap of blaming the client (or ourselves) for not being motivated, not really wanting to get better, or not trying hard enough. In the Wienecke model presented here, the part of the client that is neither too impaired by the bonding to pain (we bond to the healthy parts of our formative experiences too) nor too impaired by the brain injury absolutely wants what is in his or her best interest, that is, what is fair. We all need to remember that, by definition, the child part of each of us (client and staff alike) also wants to stay in those early, unconsciously acquired patterns of relating, which involved some suffering way of being. Therefore, the concept of want is relevant only as a way of expressing whether the health-seeking or pain-seeking component of the person is at that point in time more dominant.

If as therapists we can learn that we will teach the best we can and that clients will learn the best they can, it is easier not to overexpect, not to be emotionally overactivated, and not to burn out. The practical applications of this model occur as we do our evaluations, set specific therapy goals that are appropriate to the client's strengths and weaknesses, begin teaching compensatory techniques and strategies, meeting with families, and teaching a bit about patterns of behavior and how these things affect us all. Then, when resistance (i.e., the little kid part clinging desperately to the familiar) interferes with the client's ability to learn from us and to accomplish needed goals, we are able to shift our focus temporarily from the identified rehabilitation goal. We can use the opportunity to help our patients see how those old patterns may be limiting and hurting them, preventing their moves toward health, independence, and successful relating to others.

RESISTANCE AND EXPLANATION

The process of resistance and explanation is a repetitive one, and gains are slow under any circumstances, especially when memory and thinking limitations are added in, but progress, when it does occur, is based on a fairly solid foundation. Over time, Wienecke has developed a number of mnemonic devices that succinctly capture many of the important features of this model, which greatly assists with learning and application among individuals with either neurologic or psychiatric difficulties. One such mnemonic is the three Ps: *p*ick, *p*rovoke, and *p*erceive. Given the programming to be in confusion, conflict, and pain with others, we can always find (pick) someone to treat us badly, or we can aggravate (provoke) someone into treating us unfairly, or we can develop such a distorted view of reality (perceive) that we perceive ourselves as socially, emotionally, or physically injured by others to a greater degree than is true. Within the perceive mode, we can also dwell on past injury or anticipate unduly some future injustice.

To the extent that our clients are programmed to fail and be failed, they will to that extent perceive us as the failing parent and try to provoke us (usually unconsciously) into feeling, thinking, and behaving as this parent to whom they are bonded. As therapists, our choice of career (i.e., to help others) is not sheer coincidence, so that our own degree of programming to fail and be failed is often greater than average. Thus when we are recipients of this negative transference from the client, it may stimulate us over the line into a countertransference type of distortion. In the example used earlier of the depressed and self-abnegatory client and the therapist whose early programming included parents with these same tendencies, the therapist may become angry at the client because the client is depressed and not snapping out of it as soon as the therapist would like. The client's depression may be triggering feelings in the therapist of helplessness or badness for not doing more, or it may tap into painful and partly unconscious feelings of the therapist. These might include some unresolved, hurtful reminders of what it was like to be raised by, or be around, parents who were so demoralized that they could not meet many of their children's important emotional needs.

It is our job as therapists to stay out of these countertransference distortions, to realize that we are being tested, and to try to continue to be the good parent. The good parent not only teaches, nurtures, protects, and sets limits but also avoids the D-E-D triad: We do not *d*epreciate, *e*xploit, or unduly *d*eprive the people we are trying to help. These factors can operate in subtle ways and do not often take the form of major, obvious, and awful attacks on the client's integrity (although that too can happen).

What is more likely to arise is a set of subtle guilt- or shame-inducing statements or behaviors that emanate from us as therapists, or we may consistently avoid contact with a particular client (e.g., depriving them of our relating and input). In other instances we might convey a sense of disappointment in a client's behavior (e.g., he or she has let us down or made our life more difficult). This does not mean that our emotional reactions should be denied or buried or that feedback of a critical nature should not be given to clients. It suggests that our manner of doing this needs to focus on acknowledging and explaining anger, hurt, or frustration. Explaining is the only healthy way we know of expressing hurtful impulses. Sometimes these explanations can also find form in the visual arts, poetry and prose, or musical expression.

Some further discussion of the value of explanation is warranted. We all experience strong emotions, and those emotions are accompanied by impulses. The impulses that accompany love are to relate well and to feel good. The impulses that accompany anger are to hurt or lash out.

Anger and the impulse to hurt, especially because that impulse is frequently acted out, interfere with functioning well and feeling good together.

This impulse to hurt can be acted out against others or against self. This can be done in physical, social, or verbal ways. Physical acting out is the most serious and can include in its extreme forms murder and suicide. It also includes maiming, causing physical pain without maiming, and threatening to inflict physical pain. Social pain is perpetrated by taking something away from self or others, such as presence, cooperation, communication, love making, money, freedom, reputation, and so on. Verbal hurtfulness when directed at the self includes bad thoughts, self-denigrating comments, and the like; when directed at others, verbal hurtfulness usually involves some form of depreciating. Although as adults we may be able to moderate the potentially damaging impact of words, for children words really do hurt and damage and have a more serious impact upon development.

Explaining, or teaching by talking about how we feel, is the primary healthy way of expressing hurtful impulses. One can talk about the reality of the feeling, the impulse to hurt that is present, and the perceived reason for the feeling without inflicting damage upon another. It is not in our best interest to continue getting drawn back into the giving and getting of pain, for which we have all been programmed to some degree by our early environment, with angry reprisals, stony silences, or abandonment.

There may also come those points in therapy, or in friendships and family relationships, where the degree of masochism in the other person is so profound that in spite of all of our best efforts there may not be a way at that time to find some middle ground, some rapprochement. Explaining, kindness, respect, and calmness would also be strongly indicated here to assist the person to find or consider some other source of support and to set a limit that may involve leaving the relationship. At those points in time, we need to look carefully at whether we have really been hurt, whether we are really in jeopardy, and whether it is truly not in our best interest to continue in the relationship. Have we set up unrealistic expectations for ourselves as therapists, and is it our narcissism (in this case, our particular definition of what it means to be an effective and successful therapist) that has been wounded? Talking these kinds of issues over with colleagues and supervisors is invaluable to further our own movement toward health and fairness to self and others.

Until we are well taught and well experienced in recognizing transference and countertransference, these situations rarely feel like transference issues. Instead, we usually feel genuinely put upon, justifiably angry or disappointed, and even entitled to a certain degree of depriving or depreciating of others (sometimes masked in humor or forgetting to do certain things).

DEPENDENCE

Another major issue for us as therapists is the issue of dependence, which in and of itself has been known to stir up great controversy when psychotherapeutic models for change (such as this one) are presented. In particular, it is in the context of brain injury rehabilitation that the goals of independence are often so vociferously stated. After all, isn't that what we are trying to promote and obtain with all this effort? The *Zeitgeist* itself is demanding that language changes occur (e.g., replace the term *patient* or *client* with *consumer*). As a culture, and as a specialty, we are not comfortable with the notion of anything less than complete freedom and independence; we recognize that this less than complete state exists, but it is almost universally viewed as a less than desirable option.

The issue of dependency, from a Wienecke model perspective, is an issue that is commonly and greatly misunderstood. To whatever degree people are masochistic, the source of that programming is childhood dependency, which has been unsuccessful to a proportional degree. Almost any mix of deprivation, depreciation, and exploitation can be responsible for that unsuccessful programming. How often we hear from patients or clients a stated reluctance to get too dependent, and how often young therapists are admonished not to foster dependency.

Yet it is the very essence of therapy for the therapist to be the example, the how-to, the permission, the bridge to the attainment of a successful dependency. Therapy does foster dependency, which is part of (re-)creating the successful interdependency the person needs to be healthy but may not have experienced in early life. It is this corrective emotional experience that occurs within the bounds of good therapy, be it occupational, physical, speech, vocational, leisure, psychological, medical, nursing, or social work, that lays the groundwork for significant and lasting change. The essence of therapy, of this new learning, is experiential, and it is in this process of relating and being in healthy relationship to others that all of us are able to heal some of the early wounds and to grow to more successful integration of self with others.

A few final comments about the features of the Wienecke model are in order before moving into its day-to-day applications in rehabilitation efforts. The first of these comments deals with the concepts of request, demand, and power struggle.

REQUEST, DEMAND, AND POWER STRUGGLE

The difference between a request and a demand is that with a request there is no consequence, but with a demand there are the consequences of noncompliance. As therapists and good determinists (i.e., we hold that people are doing the best they can, given their individual history and perception, and that their choices need to be understood within this context), it is best to keep our demands as minimal as possible and to stay out of power struggles unless we can answer each of the following questions in the affirmative:

1. Is the issue important enough to make a demand, to create a power struggle?
2. Can we win the power struggle (i.e., can the healthy part of us effectively get the healthy part of the patient to follow what we perceive to be in his or her best interest)?
3. Is the cost of winning reasonable?

Another idea for us all to consider is that in any relationship we always have three options: We can stay and suffer, we can stay and make things better, or we can get out. Some of the discussion earlier with respect to transference and countertransference issues also applies here; that is, what is the reality of the current situation, and how much of the pain is being generated by an unholy combination of everyone's past programming? Perhaps it goes without saying that we generally recommend the stay and make things better option unless it is in our best interest to leave. It is never in our best interest to stay and suffer, not in the way these terms are defined in this model.

RESISTANCE LEVELS

Finally, when we see clients (or ourselves) being resistant, it is helpful to think of these resistances as emanating from three separate levels of consciousness. Level 1 (as defined below) is most accessible to consciousness and also the least powerful, but still a powerful enough, source of resistance. Level 3 is always totally unconscious until it is brought to awareness in therapy and is the most powerful component of resistance. Level 2 is vaguely in awareness before therapy and is fairly easily brought to awareness via therapy. This level is intermediate in the power of its contribution to resistance. In treatment, these levels of resistance can be succinctly stated as follows: level 1, "Don't know how to behave healthily"; level 2, "Afraid of failing when trying to behave healthily"; and level 3, "Afraid of succeeding when trying to be healthy."

To expand upon these brief definitions, at level 1 of resistance the client or staff person who has been taught with faulty early models may have trouble determining in advance what are the healthy and unhealthy paths to take. He or she does not know exactly how to get better, to do better, or to be healthier. This difficulty can be further complicated when a person with brain injury has suffered alterations in judgment or planning, when impulsivity is organically mediated, and so forth. People at this level of difficulty might benefit greatly from specific instruction in how to behave more effectively and fairly with multiple opportunities for practice and supportive feedback.

With the level 2 type of resistance, we typically encounter the client or staff person who expects, on the basis of early experience, to be deprived, depreciated, and exploited. These individuals are understandably afraid of needing, trusting, and depending, even though the rehabilitation environment in which they now find themselves may have great potential for fairly meeting their needs. They do not want to risk yet another expected, painful failure, getting their hopes up and then not having their needs met just as they have experienced in the past. Thus there is a reluctance, a resistance, to try for successful interdependency, even though the actual chances of achieving this may be quite good given a supportive therapeutic alliance.

With level 3 of resistance, the person is powerfully and instinctually bonded to his or her first love (i.e., early ways of relating and being loved, which included a significant degree of pain and not a whole lot of fairness). Thus there is the primitive fear and guilt mentioned earlier regarding being successful, having fairness, and having needs met in a healthy way. By being successful in love and interdependency, the person is not being true to his or her original programming to be in pain and to be unsuccessful. Thus if one is successful, one loses mother (i.e., the early unconscious programming to be bonded to pain) and suffers anxiety; by becoming healthy, one is also abandoning mother and suffers guilt.

You may be able to see examples of level 3 resistance operating when you see people doing really well at getting better and then, right on the verge of some important achievement, success, or breakthrough, managing to bungle the situation. We see this sometimes in the relationship patterns of our friends (or selves), where after a series of abusive or painful relationships a person finally meets someone truly nice (having gotten the pick masochism under control). After the initial happiness and glow, however, we watch this friend systematically drive the new, healthy partner away via provocative behavior or misperception of the partner's intentions and actions.

It is certainly possible to alter the programming and to be healthier; it is also a long and careful process. In our work as therapists, we may be able, in the time that we have with our clients, only to begin to lay the foundation of this new way of being. Sometimes a seed is planted, even though we cannot see the results of our efforts or the patient's efforts at that time.

It is important to proceed realistically in the framework of what is, to expect fairly of self and others, and to recognize that everyone is doing the best that he or she can. We can all continue to learn, to support each other in this process, to be gentle, and to have fun. We would also do well to remind each other from time to time that masochists cannot take yes for an answer.

Again and again, in our work with clients, in training interdisciplinary staff, and in addressing our own individual blend of health and masochism, it behooves us to repeat the following broad principles: People are doing the best they can in light of their own experience, judgment, and perception; and we are here to help patients learn to how to make decisions that are in their best interest.

Best-interest decisions are defined here as those that promote health on all levels and take into account the physical, social, and emotional impact of a particular course of action. This includes impact upon the individual in question as well as upon others. A fair balance is sought between personal needs and the needs of others by following what one might term the 50-50 model (as contrasted with the all-or-nothing approach). For many people, the perception of what is fair can be quite clouded by the illusion of perfection, by the notion that there is such a thing as perfect love, perfect fulfillment, or perfect fairness. By insisting upon, or clinging to, such an extreme notion of fairness, the person is unwittingly (and unconsciously) remaining committed to failure, to not having the good things that can ensue from a middle-ground (i.e., healthy) position.

It is also critical for us to make the distinction between what we may have the right to do in any given situation and what may be in our best interest to do. These two realities are not always identical. If someone accidently steps on your toe and mashes it painfully, you have the right to be angry and to push the person off your foot. Yet it may not be in your best interest to shove someone who has unwittingly inflicted some pain with no intent to harm you. It is probably in your best interest to yell "ouch!" so that the person knows what has happened but not to retaliate.

STAFF INTERVENTION

So, how does all this translate into specific interventions for staff? Good therapists, like good parents, need to know what is going on, take care of themselves, and operate from a position of strength. Knowing what is going on and operating from a position of strength both include:

- developing a good foundation of knowledge in your area of specialty
- continuing to augment that basic foundation with new learning, both academic (e.g., with conferences, workshops, and courses) and experiential
- being aware of the possible differences between the content of what someone says or does (i.e., the overt message) and the process by which it is said or done (e.g., the covert message)
- learning as much as you can about your own countertransference tendencies and the transference issues of your particular clients
- knowing what you are doing with clients (i.e., what are clients' major issues and obstacles to becoming healthy and productive, and how do your treatment plans, and the team's plans, dovetail with this reality?)
- operating from a position of cooperation, information sharing, and agreement as a team regarding goals for treatment, methods of delivery, and time frame
- negotiating fairly at critical times on critical matters with an eye toward 50-50, avoiding the illusion of perfection
- promoting the health of clients and staff by being willing to teach, nurture, protect, and set limits as needed

The need to take care of ourselves reminds us as therapists to be alert to our own physical and mental health needs. This may involve asking for help at times from other staff, making sure we are not setting unrealistic goals for ourselves or others, and learning how to nurture ourselves and each other with praise, recognition, and appreciation. Sometimes taking care of self includes admitting when we have reached the limits of what we know how to do, or are able to do, in any given situation.

Reviewing our own lists of personal leisure time activities, checking to see when was the last time we actually relaxed for longer than 5 minutes, and making other such queries can prove quite instructive. Eating properly, exercising for stress relief and cardiovascular fitness, and leaving some unstructured time open for fun are all ways in which we take care of ourselves. Although none of this is news to any experienced therapist, the degree to which these supports are actually implemented in our daily lives can be amazingly low. There we are, teaching relaxation or meditation or biofeedback techniques to our patients, when we have yet to incorporate these activities in our own routines.

Another way that we take care of ourselves has to do with our position within the institutions where we may be working. Are we speaking up if conditions or expectations are unrealistic and therefore unfair? Are we choosing to stay and suffer or to get out when staying and making it better might actually be a viable alternative? Conversely, are we continuing to stay and trying to make it better when all the available evidence over a significant period of time suggests that it is not in our best interest to remain? When people (e.g., staff) operate in an environment where they are deprived, depreciated, or exploited, even if this is done in subtle ways, energy to provide successful rehabilitation is sapped. Sometimes the distinctions among "perfect tit fantasies" (e.g., perfect milk, perfect nurturing, and perfect satisfaction), healthy 50-50 compromising, and undue deprivation are difficult to delineate when we are living them.

Two additional ways, therefore, for staff to take care of themselves are (1) obtaining the services of an outside consultant, who may be able to see more clearly and easily than we do over time the nature of the agreements, tacit or otherwise, within our departments and institutions and the ways in which we may be participating in not having; and (2) getting into individual psychotherapy as a means for further support, enlightenment, and growth.

Individual psychotherapy among rehabilitation staff is still too often viewed as the place of last resort for burned-out staff or for therapists who may be going through a period of personal upheaval but would otherwise never consider (and, of course, never need) such assistance. If you would like to develop a particularly compelling feeling for what your clients experience, in addition to promoting your own growth, allow yourself to be on the receiving end of the interpretation-intervention alliance.

HOW TO PROCEED

Given that we are struggling honestly with all the above, how do we proceed with our clients? Following the good parent/good therapist model espoused by Wienecke, we would move to the step of teaching our clients (in the teach, nurture, protect, and limit set model noted earlier).

We teach by:

- helping clients be aware and appreciative of their residual strengths and difficulties
- informing them compassionately and appropriately about their interpersonal impact upon others
- instructing them in the use of compensatory techniques
- educating their families, friends, and providers about brain injury, its effects, how to manage, and so forth
- allowing for some review of the importance of early experience as it affects behavior now
- modeling and monitoring appropriate work behavior and whatever level of productivity and independence is viable

In the course of a given day, we also have multiple opportunities for nurturing patients.

These include:

- providing consistent praise and recognition
- maximizing chances of success on tasks
- maximizing chances for appropriate levels of feedback and awareness
- charting progress to remind clients of their accomplishments
- discussing feelings and frustrations with compassion, and giving guidance as to the appropriate time, place, and manner of discussion (the latter also overlaps with our teaching function)
- providing emotional support for families via group and individual meetings
- keeping the insurance or funding providers informed and allied with the rehabilitation effort
- admitting our own strengths and weaknesses as appropriate and pertinent to the treatment effort
- generating peer group support and recognition of patient and family efforts
- celebrating birthdays, important anniversaries such as the date of the accident, and other milestone events in clients' lives
- using humor to reduce anxiety and tension and to generate a sense of rapport and shared humanity

Protecting our clients is not always easy, and it is often easy to err on the side of overprotection. Again, striking the balance between individual achievement and dependent connection that represents health or successful interdependency is a challenge. Sometimes the choices are clear, as when someone is acutely suicidal. Most of the time, however, the issues are more subtle and in some ways more difficult. Some of the ways in which we protect include:

- establishing a realistic rate of information delivery to our patients, neither overwhelming them with too much or too complex information nor underestimating their abilities and readiness for more
- leaving clients and their families room to stand (i.e., allowing for important differences of opinion and trying to work in areas of mutual agreement initially; this attempt to negotiate can also be a form of nurturing); as a protective device, we need to respect each individual's readiness to hear certain painful facts and his or her ability to cope at that point in time
- being aware of our own countertransference tendencies and learning how to operate from a position of awareness, compassion, and strength so that we do not unintentionally deprive, depreciate, or exploit our patients; this can take many forms on our part, such as being overly reactive to provocative, limiting, or potentially frustrating behaviors
- consistently using the sandwich technique in delivering feedback (i.e., prefacing constructive criticism with a genuine compliment or acknowledgment of the client's achievements thus far, delivering the possibly painful information as supportively as possible, and finishing this brief presentation with a final compliment or acknowledgment)
- being prepared to be an effective advocate for the client with all providers and in legal circumstances as these may arise, maintaining a position of fairness toward all concerned
- identifying a formal ally or advocate for each client among the team members; this primary therapist will function as a main source of information, support, helpfulness, guidance, and negotiating skills, on occasion operating as mediator between the client and family, the client and other team members, and so forth
- paying close attention to team dynamics and the ways in which the team may operate as a dysfunctional family; sometimes this takes the form of staff members working out their own unconscious issues indirectly and unhealthily, for example by promoting acting out behavior on the part of a particular patient by sabotaging other therapists' treatment efforts, or by getting drawn into adversarial relationships with the client's family

Taking the precepts of the Wienecke model into the realm of limit setting can include the following activities and approaches:

- identify clearly, and post, the basic requirements and parameters of participation in your rehabilitation program or activities; this can apply to residential, postacute outpatient, and community/home health models of service delivery
- be consistent and fair with rules, regulations, and personal limits, and be clear with the client, family, and provider about these
- provide consistent and timely feedback, working hard to strike the balance between too much and too little
- make few demands (per Wienecke's request versus demand model)
- make your requests as fairly as possible with appropriate contingencies that are clearly outlined for all concerned (the client, the family, the team, and, as pertinent, the provider, your administrator, and so forth)
- do not tolerate extended periods of acting out behavior that are destructive, demeaning, depreciating, or exploitive; make use of time out, behavioral analysis, and strategies; model and reinforce appropriate behaviors, broken down into the most usable components, given the abilities and constraints of each client; confront these problems in the appropriate context with an eye to safety and effectiveness for all concerned
- learn to set fair limits with other staff, administrators, and providers; do not suffer in silence if something is unfair or unrealistic but rather speak up, try to operate from a position of knowledge and fairness, make constructive suggestions, and be prepared for less than perfection

CASE EXAMPLE

The following is a composite case drawn from the experiences of several different clients and staff over time; real names are not used.

Sam was a young man who sustained a severe head injury in a motor vehicle accident; he had been drinking at the time and also had multiple other injuries. He was 26 years of age. Before the accident, he had had a number of adjustment difficulties, including problems with drugs and alcohol. His father, to whom Sam had been quite attached, was killed in a freak accident when Sam was 3; his mother had her hands full with the loss of her young husband and several small children to raise alone.

Sam had trouble in school, dropped out of high school, worked in the auto mechanic trade, and also did some construction. About 6 months before his accident, he and his long-time girlfriend broke up because of Sam's repeated infidelities and drug and alcohol problems.

In the program, Sam was angry and withdrawn in groups, inappropriately joked about sexual matters, and frequently stormed out of group and individual sessions. He reported both verbally and behaviorally that he did not like what was being said to him or to others in treatment or how it was being said. Neither could he see the applicability of any of "this rehabilitation mumbo-jumbo"; he had come to the program because he wanted our help in obtaining a job, and were we assisting him with this? According to Sam, the answer was "no".

Cognitively, Sam had significant frontal temporal injuries with the attendant problems of impulsivity, distractibility, disorganization, short-term memory difficulties, and some impairment of abstract reasoning skills. There was also some suggestion that he may have had some form of learning disability before his accident; he had never done well with reading or spelling, although he had always been relatively good at spatial and mechanical tasks.

Family support included his mother, who was worn out from her own situation; now, with the added strain of Sam's behavioral dyscontrol (shouting, sarcastic remarks, and temper outbursts), she was relieved to hand him over to the rehabilitation team. It was clear that she loved Sam very much, but her own adversarial nature combined with her son's antiauthority streak made for some difficult interactions.

Holding fast to the notion that people are doing the best they know how in light of their experience and perception helped us tremendously as a team. Early on, we were able to nurture Sam's mother and to support all the healthy things she had done, not only now but throughout Sam's life, in a way that allowed her to feel recognized (probably for the first time) and not blamed for his circumstances.

This recognition took place in the weekly relatives' group, where Sam's primary therapist made sure that Sam's mother had an opportunity, and an invitation, to tell her story; her day-to-day existence was grueling, and she seldom spoke of it to others. This nurturing also occurred in individual meetings between the primary therapist and Sam's mother. Attempts were made in individual therapy with Sam to teach him how to support and compliment his mother as best-interest behavior for him. Overtly, we were not sure whether these compliments ever saw the light of day; but over time Sam's mothers reported an improvement in his behavior and consideration at home.

Meanwhile, back at the program, Sam and the staff were driving each other crazy. His disruptive behavior in groups, his provocative stance on everything from when the breaks should be between sessions to the flavor of the coffee, and his tendency to mutter under his breath (particularly in the presence of female staff) were aggravating and unnerving at times. He seemed to enjoy playing at being angry, which was sometimes difficult to distinguish from his true rage reactions, especially in the early days of treatment.

Anytime Sam encountered a difficulty on a given task, which was frequently (as a result of his deficits, his 5 years of postinjury maladaptive coping mechanisms, as well as those accumulated before the injury), he would start yelling in a loud voice; swear; become increasingly agitated; make a profane or threatening remark; become completely silent and refuse to look at anyone or speak (eyes closed, arms crossed, etc.); make a sarcastic, critical comment to another client or staff member; threaten to leave the room; leave the room with a lot of commotion; stick his head back in the door to get in some final yell or comment; or all the above.

At this point, Sam would march upstairs (six flights; one of his strengths was his willingness to work on issues related to physical endurance,

strength, and physique development) to George Prigatano's office and lodge a loud and vociferous complaint with the secretaries, people in the waiting room, and Dr. Prigatano.

Even though Dr. Prigatano knew his team well and by now knew Sam pretty well too, he began to question us more closely during our staffing meetings about what we were or were not doing with Sam to help him manage his behavior. The dynamics of the team at that point included a lot of respect for Dr. Prigatano but a fair degree of frustration with the overall situation. Sam was a handful, Dr. Prigatano was taking a 6-month sabbatical from his usual rehabilitation program participation to complete a book, and we felt that Sam was undercutting our efforts by going to the top (literally and figuratively with that six-story climb). We also felt that we were bearing the brunt of Sam's behavior for 6 hours a day and being unfairly criticized by Dr. Prigatano (who was not there) for not doing a better job (our interpretation was a perfect job) with this client. All in all, the situation was a hotbed of transference, countertransference, and staff team dynamics issues.

At one of our monthly meetings with Dr. Wienecke, we decided to bring up Sam's case. In the process of discussing Sam and how difficult it was for us to reach him and help him, many other important issues not entirely related to Sam surfaced. These included the team's fears, resentment, and strong desire to do well during this first instance of being on our own (i.e., the first time in our experience that Dr. Prigatano was not there to lead us). Dr. Prigatano's own worry and guilt about leaving us as well as some irritation that we were not preventing Sam from disrupting time that was supposed to be quiet and productive for him were also playing a role. Add to this Sam's unerring instincts for creating chaos, based upon his early programming, and our tendencies as therapists to renounce self, take care of others, resent it, and fail, and we had a perfect recipe for some destructive transference and countertransference perceptions and behaviors.

By being reminded of these facts and being equipped with a good understanding of masochism and how it can operate, we were able to set up some basic and consistent limits for Sam. For example, if he felt, or we felt, that he was not able to participate in groups by being reasonably quiet and appropriate, he would take a time out and come back in 10 minutes or for the next therapy session. Dr. Prigatano began to redirect Sam to the program staff to resolve complaints rather than get drawn into them himself. We began to compliment Sam on his physical prowess and accomplishments in physical therapy and also to use a little gentle sarcasm back; those two avenues (i.e., the physical and jokes) were the only two ways initially that Sam was able to let himself be nurtured and recognized.

By the end of the program, Sam was still voicing loud complaints about our foibles and limitations but in a more teasing manner. He still had trouble with managing his temper but used exercise more and more as an outlet. He also made one close friend in the program, an easy going man who liked Sam, was about the same age, had the same work background, and had also sustained injuries severe enough to prohibit full-time competitive employment. At graduation, Sam made it clear that he was delighted to be rid of us and that he no longer had to see our ugly faces; he was fond of reciting the song lyrics that end with "no more teachers' dirty looks!"

For a year, we heard nothing from Sam. He did not respond to our invitations to attend our 6-month graduation celebrations, nor did he respond to calls about follow-up. His mother mentioned that he was not working but that he was trying to be productive. A year and half later, without warning, Sam appeared at the graduation celebration and continued to attend faithfully for many subsequent gatherings. He had quit drinking and drug use, had been running in local races, and had implemented a schedule of daily activities (we decided that he really was listening to at least some of the strategies we taught when we thought he was ignoring us). He was getting along better with family and was able to acknowledge his role in driving away the girlfriend whom he had loved. In overheard comments to other clients, it was clear Sam also acknowledged his role in his accident and his self-destructive behavior. He was not presenting these ideas in highbrow or complex psychologi-

cal jargon; he was putting them in terms anyone could understand. Many of these ideas had been presented again and again to Sam by his primary therapist (who was not a psychologist but was well versed in the theories of masochism and best-interest behavior). The ideas seemed to have relatively little effect upon Sam's overt behavior at the time.

Today, Sam is still not as productive from a work standpoint as we had hoped he might be. Yet, judging from his overall level of psychosocial adjustment now, it is fair to say that he, and we, have done well in the face of difficult circumstances. Just as we allowed ourselves to be good enough therapists, doing the best we knew how, so Sam became clearly a good enough rehabilitation graduate.

There are a million Sams in the annals, and halls, of rehabilitation, each of them unique and most of them teachable and reachable with this model. There are thousands of examples of client behavior that serve the overt purpose of trying to get better or pointing out staff deficiencies as a way to improve the overall rehabilitation product but serve the covert purpose of staying unconsciously bonded to pain. Therapists not only are not immune to this behavior but are particularly sensitive to statements that suggest that we are not taking perfect care of our responsibilities.

CONCLUSION

This chapter has been an attempt to show one model's view of some basic principles of human psychological development and how these principles are not only items of historical interest but a critical part of current reality. When the particular aspects of reality reviewed in this chapter are well understood, chances for optimal therapeutic intervention, particularly in a brain injury rehabilitation context, are enhanced. Therapist growth and satisfaction are also increased, and the likelihood of 50-50 fairness for all is enhanced.

Attention to these kinds of transference and countertransference issues and the use of a model such as this may well contribute to the long-term retention of good, experienced staff as well as assist with the day-to-day feelings of fatigue and frustration found among therapists at all levels of expertise. Equipping new therapists, or therapists new to the intensive nature of brain injury rehabilitation, with a model such as the one developed by Wienecke might improve their efficacy and reduce the distress that can too often be an important source of work and personal stress. It would be extremely interesting to design a staff training study with these issues in mind. Ultimately, for both clients and staff alike, each person can come away with a more informed, more moderate (i.e., fair), and more practical way of understanding why we sometimes behave in ways that seem so unproductive when we may have access to (but be programmed against) healthy alternatives.

REFERENCES

Broussard, E.R. (1976). Neonatal prediction and outcome at 10/11 years. *Child Psychiatry and Human Development.*

Broussard, E.R., & Hartner, M.S.S. (1971). Further considerations regarding maternal perception of the first-born. *Exceptional infant: Studies in abnormalities.* New York: Bruner/Mazel.

Broussard, E.R., & Hartner, M.S.S. (1970). Maternal perception of the neonate as related to development. *Child Psychiatry and Human Development.*

Pepping, M., & Roueche, J.R. (1991). Psychosocial consequences of significant brain injury. In D.E. Tupper & K.D. Cicerone (Eds.), *The neuropsychology of everyday life: Issues in development and rehabilitation* (pp. 215–256). Norwell, MA: Kluwer Academic.

Prigatano, G.P. (1986). *Neuropsychological rehabilitation after brain injury.* Baltimore: Johns Hopkins University Press.

Prigatano, G.P., Pepping, M., & Klonoff, P. (1986). Cognitive, personality and psychosocial factors in neuropsychological assessment of brain-injured patients. In B.P. Uzzell & Y. Gross (Eds.), *Clinical neuropsychology of intervention* (pp. 135–166). Boston: Martinus-Nijhoff.

Rosen, J. (1953). The survival function of schizophrenia. *Bulletin of the Menninger Clinic, 14.*

Searles, H.F. (1965). Sexual processes in schizophrenia. *Collected papers on schizophrenia and related subjects.* New York: International Universities Press.

Wienecke, R.M. (1989). *Patient and staff interactions and managing problems of countertransference.* Paper presented at the Barrow Neurological Institute and Menninger Clinic–Phoenix Conference on Psychotherapeutic Interventions after Brain Injury, Phoenix, AZ.

Behavior Analysis in Brain Injury Rehabilitation: Training Staff to Develop, Implement, and Evaluate Behavior Change Programs

6

Gary M. Pace
Paul A. Nau

OBJECTIVES

Upon completion of this chapter, the reader will be able to:

1. identify the principles of behavior change
2. demonstrate the value of behavior analysis in rehabilitation
3. articulate training procedures that will assist rehabilitation staff in acquiring the principles necessary to design, implement, and evaluate effective behavior change programs
4. provide examples of data-based evaluation systems that can be used to determine treatment effectiveness
5. identify program development strategies that will increase staff's ability to implement behavioral programs

Behavior Analysis in Brain Injury Rehabilitation

Of all problems facing individuals with head injury, changes in behavior are often the most debilitating (Harlow, 1848; Slater & Roth, 1969; Wood, 1984) and represent one of the major barriers to community reentry. The problem behaviors most commonly associated with traumatic brain injury include disruptive outbursts, physical aggression, noncompliance, lethargy, the blunting of social skills, and loss of activities of daily living. A methodology known as behavior analysis has been demonstrated to help staff manage effectively many of these behaviors. For example, behavioral technologies have been demonstrated to improve ambulation, independent dressing, cooperation, attentiveness, and speech production (Wood, 1987) in persons with head injury. Behavioral methodologies have been successfully applied to acute (Howard, 1988), community reentry (Hogan, 1988), and day treatment settings (Wood, 1988).

Behavior change after traumatic brain injury may be caused and/or maintained by many factors. During the early phase of recovery some behavior changes may be the result of memory deficits and disorientation. Even the most docile person would be likely to become noncompliant, verbally abusive, or even physically aggressive if a stranger approached and, with no warning, began making requests or assisting him or her in daily hygiene activities. This problem may be particularly frustrating and potentially dangerous for staff, because the individual with head injury can fade in and out of disorientation, often with no apparent warning. Under these conditions, staff who routinely and patiently orient their clients and explain what is expected can often avoid problems.

On the other hand, behavior problems can also result from decreased communication skills. We recently worked with an 18-year-old man who, before his accident, was described as intelligent, athletic, charming, and popular. An automobile accident and subsequent head injury, however, left him with severe cognitive deficits, labored and often inarticulate speech, and an unsteady gait. This young man presented with severe physical aggression and disruptive outbursts. For him, these behaviors appeared to function as a means of communication. Property destruction and physical aggression can function

as effective ways of gaining immediate and focused attention from others. The attention may be negative, but, to an individual accustomed to frequent attention from others and now finding himself or herself without ways of obtaining it in a more socially acceptable manner, negative attention may prove to be a satisfying substitute (Pace, Capriotti, & Nau, 1988). Faced with attention-motivated disruptive behaviors, staff can anticipate positive behavior change only in a situation where new, appropriate attention-getting behaviors replace the disruptive ones.

Similarly, disruptive behaviors may be motivated by their ability to allow one to escape or avoid unpleasant activities (Iwata, Pace, Kalsher, Cowdery, & Cataldo, 1990). Noncompliance, lethargy, and disruptive behavior can significantly interfere with a survivor's rehabilitation by interrupting or preventing necessary treatment. This in turn may prevent the survivor's acceptance into a less restrictive rehabilitation setting or a more normalized living situation. Working with a noncompliant and verbally abusive individual may result in behaviorally unsophisticated staff concluding that the person is not ready for rehabilitation. If escape from or avoidance of therapy is a primary source of motivation, however, it is likely that some individuals will arrange it so that they are never ready for rehabilitation. Alternatively, escape-motivated disruptive behaviors have been successfully treated when people with head injury are taught that they cannot escape or avoid participation in a critically important therapy by engaging in noncompliant or disruptive behaviors (Lucia, Darling, Pace, & Nau, 1989). Situations like these pose complex clinical and ethical dilemmas for staff. When faced with what appears to be escape-motivated behavior, staff often need to make difficult judgments as to the best course of action to address serious behavior problems. Many factors, such as a client's rights, his or her psychological status, communication abilities, level of self-control, and capacity to make sound judgments, all need to be carefully considered. Environmental factors also need consideration to ensure that the treatment setting is the most appropriate environment to maximize the individual's adaptation to brain injury. Addressing issues such as this may involve an analysis of the risks and benefits of providing in-patient, day, or home-based intervention.

These examples serve to illustrate the fact that there is no single treatment or approach to address the behavior problems commonly associated with head injury. That is, there is no single treatment to increase motivation or decrease disruptive behavior in all individuals with head injury. To manage behavior effectively, one must first understand the motivation of the person and then design a specific, individualized, comprehensive treatment plan. For example, ignoring an individual's verbal outbursts may result in a decrease in this behavior in an attention-motivated client but would probably increase the undesirable behavior in an individual who engages in the behavior to escape or avoid undesireable situations. This scenario is even more complicated when one considers behaviors with multiple sources of motivation.

This chapter explores the principles of behavior analysis and offers strategies to help staff effectively apply behavioral methodologies to enhance rehabilitative outcomes. It is critical to emphasize at the outset of this chapter that all behavior change programs must examine multiple factors that impact on behavior. In addition to those mentioned earlier, staff must also evaluate the individual's pre-injury functioning (e.g., cognitive abilities, coping style, interpersonal skills, and interests) as well as the neurobehavioral and neuropsychological impact of acquired brain injury. This data provides a foundation upon which to analyze behavior and develop treatment plans that are responsive to the many variables that influence human learning and performance.

THE PRINCIPLES OF BEHAVIOR CHANGE

What is Behavior Analysis?

Behavior analysis represents a practical and effective method for understanding and, ultimately, changing behavior. The foundation of behavior analysis is based on the fact that behavior is affected by its consequences (Skinner, 1938). More than 50 years of research, both in the laboratory and in the field, have clearly supported this conclusion (Skinner, 1953; Ulrich, Stachnik, & Mabry, 1966, 1970; Vollmer & Iwata, 1991). The implication for head injury rehabilitation is that problem behaviors associated

with traumatic head injury may occur because of their consequences; that is, they produce something the survivor wants, or they allow him or her to escape or avoid something unpleasant.

A second distinguishing characteristic of behavior analysis is the premise that behavior can be maintained by idiosyncratic variables (Carr, 1977). In other words, the sources of motivation that are maintaining the behavior can vary from individual to individual. Accordingly, in conducting a behavior analysis, one attempts to identify the variable or variables maintaining the behavior in question (target behavior). Knowledge of the current sources of motivation has important implications for changing behavior. Once the rehabilitation professional has identified why a behavior occurs, an undesirable behavior can often be changed by removing its source of motivation and, simultaneously, providing that consequence for a desirable behavior. For example, if an individual dislikes an important occupational therapy exercise and can escape it (even occasionally) through noncompliance, one would predict that the disruptive behavior will continue to occur. If the consequence of the target behavior can be changed (i.e., verbal abuse no longer terminates therapy) and the individual is provided an opportunity to terminate therapy by completing specific exercises, however, the behavioral science literature predicts that the target behavior will initially increase and then dramatically decrease.

As the term implies, the focus of behavior analysis is behavior. The behavior analyst is concerned with what people do, rather than what they say they do. It is of little practical value, for example, that a person says, or believes, that he or she can independently prepare a meal; what is of consequence is whether the person can demonstrate safe and efficient meal preparation. Because overt behavior represents the data of the behavior analyst, reliable measurement and observation are of primary importance. As mentioned above, once a behavior has been defined objectively, it can be evaluated and a subsequent plan for remediation developed.

Taken together, then, a behavior analysis represents a systematic approach to understanding and changing the debilitating behaviors associated with brain injury. The following represents the specific steps of a behavior analysis.

Conducting a Behavior Analysis

Identification of Target Behaviors

In our experience, the single most common explanation for unsuccessful behavior change programs is the absence of clearly defined target behaviors. How can one hope to change behaviors in the absence of agreement about, or understanding of, what the target behavior is? Even a target behavior as seemingly obvious as physical aggression can have different interpretations. To a nurse working at the client's bedside, being repeatedly grabbed and hit by the client may be viewed as physical aggression. To the speech pathologist, however, who is working to increase functional communication, these behaviors may represent the client's first attempts at communication, which should be encouraged. The nurse and the speech pathologist would probably agree on the goals of increasing functional communication and decreasing physical aggression; in this example, however, these behaviors are not clearly defined, so that the likelihood of achieving either goal is greatly decreased.

Implicit in any discussion of target behaviors is the notion of consistency. As the above example illustrates, little meaningful behavior change is likely to occur without consistent implementation across all staff and settings. One of the most common responses to behavior change programs is, "I tried that and it didn't work." This response usually refers to isolated efforts by individual staff rather than a consistent and systematic implementation of the procedure.

To reiterate, step one of a behavior analysis is to define clearly and operationally the behaviors to be changed and to ensure that all staff understand the targeted behaviors and goals.

Establishment of a Data System

Once staff agree on target behaviors, they are ready to measure them. As discussed above, objective information (data) is critical to the systematic analysis of behavior. As is discussed in more detail later in the chapter, data systems do not need to be complicated. In fact, the simplest ones are usually the most effective.

Functional Analysis

A functional analysis describes the process of identifying the variable or variables maintaining a behavior. The information derived from this process has important implications for the development of subsequent treatment programs. Although the potential sources of motivation of the behaviors associated with head injury are individualized and therefore virtually limitless, some general sources of motivation are commonly found. Disruptive or noncompliant behaviors are often used as a method of gaining something desirable (e.g., special privileges, staff attention, desired objects, etc.) or avoiding or escaping unpleasant situations such as environmental demands or even social contact (Baumeister & Rollings, 1976).

A functional analysis can be formal (Iwata, Dorsey, Slifer, Bauman, & Richman, 1982; Mace & Knight, 1986), where behavior is observed during specifically arranged conditions, or it can be informal. Informal functional analysis may consist of staff attempting to identify maintaining variables by informally observing the client under various conditions. For example, staff may observe high rates of noncompliance with one particular staff member. In the course of conducting a functional analysis, one would attempt to identify the relationship between the client's noncompliant behavior and the staff member's behavior. That is, what is it about this staff member's behavior that elicits or maintains the target behavior? This type of informal functional analysis can be helpful in identifying the current social or environmental variables maintaining a target behavior.

Heretofore in our discussion of a behavioral analysis, we have focused on the consequences of the target behavior. A functional analysis may also reveal strategies to prevent behavior problems. Certain conditions (e.g., people, places, sounds, etc.), as a function of learned associations or physiological changes, may produce certain behaviors. For example, in the course of recovery a person with head injury may have experienced pain and frustration during physical therapy. Accordingly, this person may have come to associate the sights, sounds, and demands of physical therapy with pain and frustration and therefore may engage in noncompliance during physical therapy. Once a functional analysis identifies the specific components of physical therapy that are associated with the target behavior, an individualized treatment program that gradually introduces the patient to physical therapy will probably be successful (Ivancic & Pace, 1991).

Other antecedents often found to increase behavior problems after a brain injury include noise, fatigue, overstimulation, and unexpected changes.

Implementation of Treatment

As argued throughout the chapter, implementation of treatment procedures should be individualized and based on the results of a functional analysis. Accordingly, a list of specific interventions to treat specific behaviors is not presented. Nevertheless, there are general treatment strategies with which all staff working with persons with head injury should be familiar.

As mentioned earlier, for many individuals attention represents a potent source of motivation. Staff attention, even negative attention (e.g., reprimands, looks of disappointment or frustration, etc.), can maintain disruptive, noncompliant, or helpless behaviors. On the other hand, staff recognition of cooperative behavior not only can help increase the person's self-esteem but can greatly increase compliance and motivation in working toward goals. In general, it is important to ensure that the client does not gain anything (e.g., receiving extra attention or avoiding reasonable environmental demands) by engaging in disruptive, noncompliant, or helpless behaviors.

Additionally, all behavior reduction treatment procedures should include a positive component. That is, never take a source of motivation away from a client. Simply change the consequence. For example, if a functional analysis reveals that a client is engaging in noncompliant behavior so that a preferred staff member will talk to him or her, rearrange the contingency so that the preferred staff member interacts with the client only after he or she has complied with the

expectation. Simply removing the interaction with staff not only is unethical (removing what may be one of the few remaining pleasant activities for the client) but will certainly render the behavior change program less effective. The behavioral science literature is replete with examples of how positive programs providing recognition and pleasurable events contingent on prosocial behaviors can avoid the demonstration of disruptive behaviors (Horner, 1980; Iwata et al., 1982). The establishment of positive programming focusing on reestablishing, increasing, or maintaining prosocial behaviors is clearly one of the major contributions of a behavior analysis and the most critical element of any effective behavior change program.

Evaluation

Once the target behavior has been operationally defined, data has been collected, potential sources of motivation have been identified (functional analysis), and a corresponding treatment has been implemented, one must evaluate the treatment. Evaluation is necessary to determine whether the treatment is effective. It is not enough simply to change a behavior. In a behavior analysis, it is important to identify specifically the aspects of the rehabilitation environment responsible for the change. Because behavioral treatments are individualized, the experimental designs used to evaluate them are likewise varied and individualized. An almost infinite number of experimental design options are available within a behavior analysis (Sidman, 1960). No attempt will be made here to catalog all of them. Rather, the goal is to delineate the underlying rationale of single-subject designs and to present the major design options.

Single-subject designs are used to evaluate behavior change. To accomplish this, data collected before treatment implementation (baseline) are compared to data collected after treatment. Figure 6-1 shows the frequency of aggressive incidents per day in the 18-year-old man with head injury described earlier in this chapter. This figure reveals that during baseline (first 4 days) the client engaged in four to six aggressive incidents per day. Because an informal functional analysis suggested that he was physically aggressive to gain staff attention, treatment consisted of removing him from the opportunity for staff attention (time out) when he aggressed and lavishing him with staff attention for cooperation in the absence of aggression (Pace et al., 1988). Figure 6-1 shows that, by the end of treatment, his physical aggression was reduced to a near zero rate. Staff and family concluded that his behavior was significantly improved. During treatment, he began participating in group therapies for the first time since his accident.

Clearly, a change in this client's aggressive behavior occurred, but does this evaluation allow staff to conclude that the treatment was responsible for the change? Regrettably, the answer is no. This design, or evaluation, does not control for the effects of variables extraneous to the intervention (e.g., changes in therapy, family contact, cognitive changes in the client, etc.) that

may have occurred at the same time the behavior program was implemented and therefore may have been responsible for the observed change in behavior. Although these alternative explanations may be unlikely, they remain a barrier to concluding unequivocally that the observed decrease in aggression was related to the implementation of the treatment protocol.

Reversal designs. Alternatively, consider the experimental design presented in Figure 6-2, which represents data from a 50-year-old man with head injury who frequently engaged in explosive bouts of yelling. A functional analysis revealed that yelling was most likely to occur when the client was prompted to respond during physical, occupational, or vocational therapies and when he was approached suddenly by others (Nau, Capriotti, & Pace, 1988). Treatment consisted of instructing him to move to a corner of the room contingent upon yelling and giving him a short break from work for compliance in the

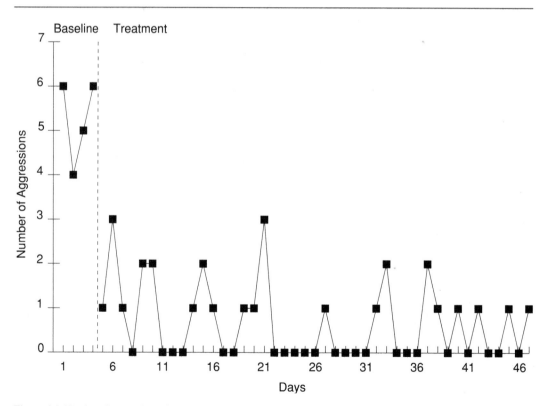

Figure 6-1 Number of aggressive episodes across baseline and treatment conditions

absence of the target behavior. Figure 6-2 indicates that yelling occurred during an average of 17% of the time during the initial baseline and decreased to an average of 1% of the time during the initial treatment. Yelling increased to original levels during the second baseline and decreased again after the reintroduction of the treatment.

Note that the first two phases of this design (baseline followed by treatment) are identical to the phases of the design described earlier (see Figure 6-1). This design, however, allows a clearer evaluation of the effects of the treatment because the first two phases are repeated. This design, called a reversal design (Baer, Wolf, & Risley, 1968), acquires its strength by repeated demonstrations of the effects of the treatment on the tar-

get behavior. The effectiveness of the treatment protocol is unambiguously demonstrated in Figure 6-2 by the dramatic decrease in yelling that occurred whenever the treatment was in effect and the corresponding increase in the target behavior when the treatment was withdrawn.

Multiple-baseline designs. Reversal designs do have limitations (Kazdin, 1982). For example, behaviors such as increased range of motion, ambulation, and independence cannot be reversed. Additionally, it is undesirable to reverse some behaviors, such as physical aggression or self-injurious behavior, that may present a danger to the client or staff. Accordingly, a multiple-baseline design can be used to demonstrate the effects of an intervention by showing

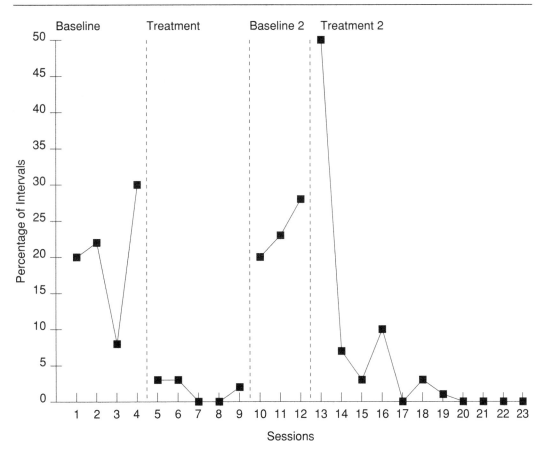

Figure 6-2 Percentage of continuous 30-second intervals in which yelling occurred across repeated baseline and treatment conditions

that the behavior changes occur only when treatment is introduced. Multiple-baseline designs can be implemented across individuals, situations, settings, or time.

Figure 6-3 represents an example of a multiple-baseline design. This figure shows the total minutes of hand pronation across two settings: speech and education. The client was a 14-year-old girl with brain injury. It was clinically rec-

ommended that she maintain her left hand in pronation (target behavior). As Figure 6-3 indicates (baseline condition), however, she rarely complied with this request. Even repeated instructions from therapists did not result in increased compliance (Figure 6-3, top, instruction only). Introduction of a program where she earned extra privileges contingent on increasing the target behavior, however, did produce in-

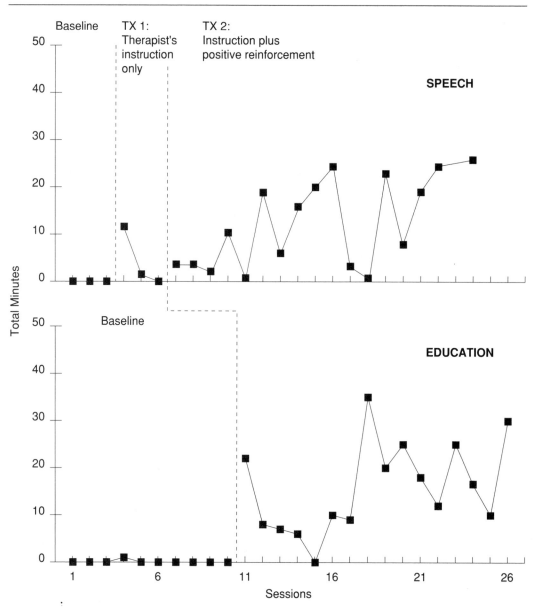

Figure 6-3 Total minutes of hand pronation across baseline and treatment conditions in both speech and education classes

creases in pronation, first during speech and then during education (Lucia et al., 1989). This design clearly demonstrates the effects of the treatment intervention because, in both speech and education, the rate of pronation increased only when the treatment was introduced.

Changing criterion design. Another common single-subject design is called the changing criterion design. In this design, the effectiveness of a treatment is demonstrated by showing gradual changes throughout the treatment phase. An illustration of a changing criterion design appears in Figure 6-4, which shows the disruptive behavior of a 15-year-old boy with head injury. This individual frequently produced annoying sounds during academic classes. These sounds reliably disrupted the class and often escalated into more serious problems, such as profanity and physical aggression. Staff recording the behavior hypothesized that it was maintained by the response of classmates. Subsequent to unsuccessful efforts to teach the other children with behavioral problems in the class to ignore the sounds, however, staff concluded that the primary source of motivation could not be eliminated. Alternatively, staff attempted to design a program whereby the most desirable activities (e.g., group activities, access to video games, outings with preferred staff, etc.) were contingent upon cooperative class behavior and the absence of disruptive sounds.

The top graph in Figure 6-4 reveals that during baseline the target behavior occurred an average of eight times a day. Because this behavior was of long standing and apparently quite resistant to change, we wanted to ensure initial success and contact with the positive consequences of appropriate behavior. Accordingly, we initially only required the client to decrease his frequency of annoying sounds to five times a day to have access to his most preferred activities. Because his baseline rate was eight times a day, a decrease to five times a day was relatively easy and virtually ensured that he would be successful and would begin to learn the positive consequences of appropriate behavior. Figure 6-4 indicates that, during this phase of treatment, the client earned his preferred activities every day but one (session 16). Once his behavior stabilized, the accepted number

of disruptive behaviors was gradually reduced to three and eventually to one per day (Barber, Tenenbaum, Berger, Quinn, & Nau, 1989). The success of this treatment is demonstrated by the observation that the client's behavior changed as the criterion changed. That is, the frequency of the target behavior generally corresponded to the criterion for access to preferred activities.

Figure 6-4 also demonstrates another commonly encountered positive side effect associated with behavior analysis. Many individuals with head injury present with several target behaviors. Accordingly, rehabilitation staff may attempt to implement several behavioral interventions simultaneously. This strategy often results in excessive demands being placed on staff for the implementation of the interventions and may result in poor consistency and monitoring of the program. An alternative strategy is to focus on only one or two behaviors at a time. This allows staff to focus their resources and therefore increases the likelihood of successful behavior change. Furthermore, the behavioral science literature has repeatedly demonstrated that disruptive behaviors covary. Therefore, if one target behavior changes, the others often follow (Russo, Cataldo, & Cushing, 1981), even if no specific intervention is in effect for the other behaviors.

As illustrated in Figure 6-4, in addition to the annoying sounds this client engaged in several other disruptive, noncompliant, and dangerous behaviors. Those behaviors were operationally defined and their frequency was recorded, but no intervention was in effect. Figure 6-4 reveals that they appeared to covary with the annoying sounds and decreased to much lower levels as the target behaviors decreased even though no consequence was in effect.

TRAINING STAFF TO EMPLOY BEHAVIORAL PRINCIPLES

Organization and Selection of Staff

Effective implementation of behavioral procedures requires a high degree of organization and the cooperation of staff at several levels. This is

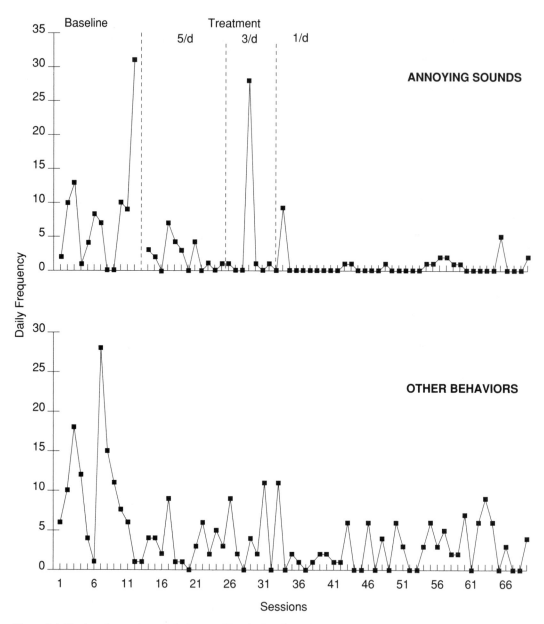

Figure 6-4 Number of annoying sounds (top graph) and other disruptive, noncompliant, and dangerous behaviors (bottom graph) across baseline and treatment conditions

because behavioral treatment of problem behavior involves changing the way the environment responds to the client's behavior. If the changes in the client's behavior are to be significant, the environment must be programmed to respond consistently in all cases and across a wide range of changing conditions. The following is an over-

view of how staff may be structured to meet the behavior needs of persons with head injury.

Behavior Analysts

Usually the overall supervision of behavioral programming is the responsibility of a behavior analyst who holds a master's degree or PhD from a program in applied behavior analysis and has completed a clinical internship or some other supervised clinical training. To ensure that those individuals functioning as behavior analysts possess the necessary skills, some states (for example, Florida) have established minimum training and competency standards. In these states the Department of Professional Regulation or a similar governing body tests and certifies individuals as behavior analysts.

The behavior analyst is responsible for conducting the initial evaluation, specifying the target behaviors and designing an observation system, conducting or supervising a functional analysis, designing a behavioral treatment, and evaluating the treatment effects. The behavior analyst works with the treatment team to obtain necessary client information and to prioritize team goals. The behavior analyst is also responsible for training and monitoring the performance of direct care staff, although he or she may work through an intermediary, such as a behavioral assistant.

The behavior analyst often acts as a consultant to other allied health professionals who have the basic skills to design behavioral programs to change a client's behavior. In these cases, the behavior analyst can help develop procedures for data collection, staff training, and program evaluation. In cases in which restrictive or aversive procedures are being considered, the input of the behavior analyst is essential to ensure that the proposed procedures are appropriate and that proper safeguards exist to avoid undesirable side effects.

Behavioral Assistants or Trainers

The behavioral assistant or trainer serves as an intermediary between the behavior analyst and direct care staff. The behavioral assistant should have a bachelor's degree from a program in applied behavior analysis, but direct work experience may be an appropriate substitute. Under the direction of the behavior analyst, the behavioral assistant transcribes and graphs data, trains direct care staff, and conducts follow-up observation and training. Additional responsibilities

may include making initial observations of clients' behavior, piloting implementation of prospective techniques, and, in some cases, developing simple behavior programs. Behavioral assistants are especially useful where case loads are high or behavior problems are severe.

Direct Care Staff

Direct care staff implement prescribed behavior program steps and record data on behavior and as such are the direct link between the behavioral clinician and the person with head injury. Direct care staff must be familiar with their client's individualized behavior programs. They must also be familiar with the basic techniques of behavior analysis, such as how to define behavior, how to record direct observational data, and how to implement the basic behavioral treatment procedures common to most programs.

Components of Staff Training

Training should be organized around the basic steps of applied behavior analysis discussed previously: define the target behavior, observe and collect data, provide consequences for the behavior to facilitate learning, and evaluate and review the program.

Defining Behavior and Collecting Data

Observation and data collection take place during all phases of behavioral programming from assessment through treatment and program evaluation. Changes in the data across time must reflect changes in the client's behavior and not changes in the definitions of behavior or changes in the data collection system. Consequently, staff observations must remain accurate and consistent during the entire course of treatment. This is done by training staff to describe behavior objectively, establishing standard systems for data collection, and implementing ongoing quality assurance and retraining procedures.

Training Observers to Define Behavior Objectively

The first step in training staff to define behavior objectively is to teach them the distinction between behavioral and nonbehavioral descriptions of behavior. Behavioral descriptions are concerned with an action that can be seen or heard by others. Examples include hitting, swearing, brushing teeth, and so forth. Nonbehavioral descriptions usually try to go beyond the action that took place and include some sort of interpretation about how the client is presumed to have felt or why the client is presumed to have behaved in a particular way.

A simple training exercise is to present staff with a list of terms. The staff must determine whether each term is a behavioral or a non-behavioral description of behavior. For example, the list *angry, yelling, crying, sad, dishonest, lying, friendly,* and *smiling* would be sorted as follows:

Nonbehavioral Term	Behavioral Term
Angry	Yelling
Sad	Crying
Dishonest	Lying
Friendly	Smiling

Once staff members can accurately sort behavioral from nonbehavioral terms, trainers can test their understanding of these distinctions by acting out incidents and having the staff provide behavioral descriptions of what happened. Trainers should review these descriptions and provide the staff with corrective feedback. Staff who make errors should continue to observe and describe incidents until their descriptions are consistent.

The precision and reliability of staff observation can be greatly increased by establishing standard behavioral definitions. Standard definitions can be adopted on a facilitywide basis or on a client-by-client basis, depending on the circumstances. The following is an example of a standard definition:

> *Physical aggression:* Any action that causes physical harm, or has the potential for causing physical harm, to another person. Examples include hitting, kicking, pinching, biting, punching, tripping, shoving, or throwing objects at someone.

When training staff to use standard definitions, trainers should first discuss the definitions with the staff and then act out different scenarios while the staff watch. Staff should then attempt to identify whether the behavior in question occurred. For example, if one trainer throws a pencil at another trainer, staff should identify that physical aggression took place. If the trainer throws a pencil at the floor, however, staff should identify that physical aggression did not take place.

Establishing Systems for Data Collection

As mentioned previously, reliable and consistent measurement of behavior requires systematic procedures for data collection. Observational data can be collected in several ways. The behavior specialist usually chooses the type of data collection to be employed, which often varies on a case-by-case basis.

Frequency. The most basic way to measure behavior is to have staff count the number of times that the behavior occurs within a given period of time. For example, if one is interested in reducing aggression, one might count the number of times each day that the person with head injury hits, kicks, or throws objects at other people. If one is interested in increasing participation in therapy, one may count the number of times that the person makes comments in group discussion and answers questions posed by the therapist. Exhibit 6-1 illustrates a data sheet that can be used in recording frequency data.

Interval sampling. In interval sampling, each observation period (each day, each class period, etc.) is divided into a series of discrete time intervals. Observers then record whether a behavior occurs during each interval. For example, to collect data on appropriate eye contact during conversation, one might observe the client for 15 minutes and then record whether eye contact occurred during that time, without recording the actual number of times the behavior occurred. Then the process would be repeated for the next 15 minutes, this continuing for the remainder of the observation session. Results would be expressed in terms of the number or percentage of 15-minute intervals during which eye contact occurred.

Interval sampling procedures are particularly useful when one is measuring such things as

Exhibit 6-1 Behavioral Data Sheet for Recording Frequency Data

Client: Bill Brown

Date:_____

Aggression:

Verbal Abuse:

Special instructions and definitions:

Make a check mark each time the behavior occurs.

Aggression = hitting, kicking, pinching, biting, punching, tripping, shoving, or throwing objects at others or engaging in any other act that is potentially harmful to others.

Verbal abuse = yelling, screaming, swearing, ridiculing, or threatening others.

swearing, tantrums, appropriate social interactions, off-task behavior, and other types of behavior where it might be difficult to define precisely when one behavior ends and another begins. For example, which client swears the most: One who utters a sentence containing four inappropriate words, or one who utters a sentence containing three inappropriate words? What if the three inappropriate words are uttered in three separate sentences? Interval sampling procedures solve this definitional problem by considering all three of these cases equal as long as they all occur within the same time interval. Exhibit 6-2 illustrates a data sheet that can be used in interval sampling.

Other measurement techniques. In activities of daily living training, where the main interest is in increasing the client's independence, a task is usually divided into a number of discrete steps that the client must perform. For example, getting dressed can be divided into separate steps of putting on underwear, shirt, pants, socks, and so

forth. One can then record whether the client completed each step of the task independently or whether prompting was required. Data are graphed in terms of the number or percentage of task steps completed independently. Exhibit 6-3 illustrates a data sheet used in activities of daily living training. Task analysis can be developed for any trainable skill.

Often, when one is measuring behavior such as having a tantrum, sleeping, working at a task, or watching television, it is best to measure the duration of the activity rather than its frequency. Other examples of specialized behavioral measures include weighing food before and after a meal to measure the amount eaten, counting the number of items assembled to measure work productivity, and measuring body weight to assess compliance with a diet.

Making data systems easy to use. Data collection systems must be easy to use and not so complicated or time consuming that they make it impossible for staff to attend to their other responsibilities. Recently, several electronic data collection devices have been developed to make data recording and analysis simple and quick. These systems may be too expensive for use in many settings, however. In most cases, behavioral observations are recorded with pencil and paper.

Data sheets should be prepared in advance and standardized as much as possible to reduce training time. Instructions should be brief and simple. Writing time should be minimized by having staff make check marks or circle alternatives rather than write prose descriptions of behavior. Portability is important in settings where clients move from place to place, and in these cases data sheets should be pocket-size so that staff need not carry clipboards or notebooks, which can be put down and lost as the day progresses. The examples in Exhibits 6-1, 6-2, and 6-3 illustrate many of these points.

Maintaining the Accuracy of Observers

Data collection requires ongoing maintenance and quality assurance procedures to ensure continued accuracy. The standard method for as-

Exhibit 6-2 Behavioral Data Sheet for Interval Sampling

Client: Bill Brown   Date:_____

Time	Aggression	Verbal Abuse	Comments
9:00 a.m.			
9:15 a.m.			
9:30 a.m.			
9:45 a.m.			
10:00 a.m.			
10:15 a.m.			
10:30 a.m.			
10:45 a.m.			
11:00 a.m.			
11:15 a.m.			
11:30 a.m.			
11:45 a.m.			
12:00 p.m.			
12:15 p.m.			
12:30 p.m.			
12:45 p.m.			
1:00 p.m.			
1:15 p.m.			
1:30 p.m.			
1:45 p.m.			
2:00 p.m.			
2:15 p.m.			
2:30 p.m.			
2:45 p.m.			
3:00 p.m.			
3:15 p.m.			
3:30 p.m.			
3:45 p.m.			
4:00 p.m.			
4:15 p.m.			
4:30 p.m.			
4:45 p.m.			
5:00 p.m.			

Special Instructions/Definitions:

Make a check mark if the behavior occurs within the 15-minute interval. Make a 0 if the behavior does not occur within the 15-minute interval.

Aggression = hitting, kicking, pinching, biting, punching, tripping, shoving, or throwing objects at others or engaging in any other act that is potentially harmful to others.

Verbal abuse = yelling, screaming, swearing, ridiculing, or threatening others.

sessing the accuracy of behavioral observations is to measure interobserver agreement. This consists of having a second person, usually the behavioral assistant or the behavior specialist, observe the client and record data at the same time as the assigned staff. Once the observations are complete, the two data sheets are compared and scored.

When frequeny data are collected, percentage interobserver agreement is calculated by dividing the lower recorded frequency by the higher recorded frequency and multiplying by 100. For

Exhibit 6-3 Behavioral Data Sheet for Recording Morning Activities of Daily Living Sequence

Client: Bill Brown   Date:_____   Staff:_____

Instructions: Use the following procedure for each step of the activities of daily living sequence:

1. **Wait 30 s to allow Bill to start the step independently.** Don't speak or gesture. If he completes the step without prompting, praise him and check **"I"** below.

2. If he does not complete the step after #1, prompt him once, **with a gesture,** to complete the step. Give him 15 s to *start* the step. If he completes the step after this prompt, praise him and score **"G"** below.

3. If he does not complete the step after #2, prompt him once, **verbally,** to complete the step. Give him 15 s to *start* the step. If he completes the step after this prompt, praise him and score **"V"** below.

4. If he does not complete the step after #3, physically guide him through the beginning movement of the step (e.g., put your hand on his and guide it to his head to begin washing his hair). *Do not verbally prompt* him during this stage. **Help him to begin only,** *do not guide him through the entire movement.* Score **"P"** if you use a physical prompt.

	I	G	V	P	Comments
Time at start:_____					
Get towel and washcloth	____	____	____	____	
Get undressed	____	____	____	____	
Enter shower	____	____	____	____	
Turn on water	____	____	____	____	
Wash face and neck	____	____	____	____	
Wash arms and armpits	____	____	____	____	
Wash chest and stomach	____	____	____	____	
Wash genitals	____	____	____	____	
Wash back and buttocks	____	____	____	____	
Wash legs and feet	____	____	____	____	
Rinse body	____	____	____	____	
Shampoo hair	____	____	____	____	
Rinse hair	____	____	____	____	
Turn off water	____	____	____	____	
Towel dry	____	____	____	____	
Get deodorant	____	____	____	____	
Apply deodorant	____	____	____	____	
Time at end:_____					

example, if staff observe 15 instances of target behavior during an observation session and the behavior assistant observes 18 instances, the percentage interobserver agreement would be 83% ([15/18] × 100). For interval recording procedures, percentage interobserver agreement is calculated by counting the number of observation intervals in which the two observers agreed in their observations and the number of intervals in which the two observers disagreed. Percentage interobserver agreement equals the number of agreements divided by the sum of agreements and disagreements all multiplied by 100.

Measures of interobserver agreement should be made as frequently as possible, and if agreement is less than 80% retraining should be implemented. Feedback should always be given to staff after interobserver agreement has been measured. Learning that interobserver agreement is greater than 80% can be positive for staff and may increase the accuracy of their subsequent recordings.

Several other procedures can be implemented on a frequent, ongoing basis to maintain the integrity and accuracy of behavioral data collection. For example, behavioral assistants and supervisory staff should conduct frequent checks to ensure that staff are carrying the data collection sheets assigned to them and that the sheets are completed in a timely fashion. Three common errors are often found. First, staff often cannot find the appropriate data sheets for the clients assigned to them either because they have lost the sheets during the course of their shift or because the sheets were never issued to them in the first place. Second, data sheets are often found to be blank, even though most of the shift has passed and a considerable amount of behavior has occurred. In these cases staff members are often relying on their memories and are waiting for the end of their shift before recording their data, thus jeopardizing accuracy. Third, data sheets are often found to be filled out ahead of time before any behavior has occurred.

Finally, formal inservices must be conducted on a regular, frequent basis. Each data sheet should have a specified renewal date (maximum, 3 months), after which direct care staff will not record data unless a formal inservice is conducted by the behavior specialist or assistant. Informal training should also be conducted daily. One useful and enjoyable exercise is to have trainers role play a client's behavior and then ask the staff to record the behavior that they have just seen. At the end of the drill, the trainer can provide the staff with corrective feedback about their performance.

Program Implementation Skills

Implementation of behavioral treatment poses even greater challenges for staff training. To ensure the consistency that is necessary if behavioral programming is to be successful, training must eventually be given to all persons who come in contact with the client, including direct care staff, clinical team members, case managers, and family members. Moreover, because behavior programs are individualized, each staff member must be familiar with, and able to implement, several different behavior programs at any time.

Training can be greatly simplified, however, if staff receive good basic training during their initial orientation. Most behavior programs have some basic elements and techniques that they share in common with all other behavior programs. If staff are familiar with these basic techniques, only a minimal amount of training may be necessary before a new program is implemented. Furthermore, when complex and unique behavior programs become necessary, training can be focused more effectively on novel program elements.

Basic Skills for Direct Care Staff

Praising. As indicated earlier, virtually all behavior programs specify delivery of some form of positive reinforcement whenever desirable behavior occurs. An event is defined as a positive reinforcer if it increases the likelihood of the behavior that it follows. Praise is the most basic and common form of positive reinforcement, and consequently it is of the utmost importance that direct care staff be capable of praising clients appropriately and effectively.

To be most effective, praise should be immediate. That is, praise should occur as soon as possible after the desired behavior is observed. Staff must understand that, if they delay praising a client, the client may do something undesirable in the meantime. Once this happens, the opportunity to strengthen the desired behavior is lost.

The quality of praise is also extremely important, and different clients respond best to different types of praise. Children often respond best when praise is exuberant and somewhat silly. Praise to children should also include a specific description of what the child did to deserve the praise (e.g., "Johnny, you combed your hair! Great work!"). A different approach may be needed when one is praising adults and adolescents, who sometimes find overly enthusiastic and specific praise to be patronizing and offensive. In these cases, praise is more effective if it is delivered in a matter-of-fact and subtle manner (e.g., "Jennifer, what have you done with your hair? That looks very nice."). Simply saying "Thanks" or "Right" is often the best way to praise some adults.

Other reinforcement techniques. Social attention and individualized activities with staff are other commonly employed forms of reinforcement for people with head injury. In many cases, the most effective reinforcer for such an individual is the opportunity to engage in a normal one-on-one activity with another person. Typical activities include conversation, gossiping, playing cards, going out to eat, taking a walk, and the like. Staff should be encouraged to be on the lookout for activities such as these that can be used to increase desirable behaviors as well as to enhance the quality of their clients' lives. Staff should strive to be as natural and sociable as they would be with others outside of work.

Ignoring. Ignoring is an important component of many programs designed to treat clients who behave inappropriately to gain attention from others. These programs, which are designed to teach clients appropriate ways to obtain attention, are usually composed of two major components. In the main component, staff praise or otherwise attend to the client when he or she is engaged in a desired behavior. In the ignoring component, staff refrain from providing attention to the client when he or she is engaged in an undesired behavior.

Ignoring is a difficult skill to master. When a person with head injury does something he or she should not, most staff have a natural tendency to intervene in some way, either by asking the person to stop, or by reprimanding the person, or by counseling the person. Consequently, staff training should include the identification of techniques that staff can employ while ignoring undesirable behaviors. These techniques include continuing a conversation or activity already in progress, terminating or avoiding eye contact, or leaving the area.

Some behavior programs will prescribe that staff ignore an undesirable behavior, whereas other programs will prescribe that staff withdraw attention. It is important that all staff understand the difference between these two procedures. In ignoring, activities go on as usual, with no special attention being paid when the client engages in the undesired behavior. For example, if a client and a staff member are talking to each other and the client makes a sexually suggestive statement, the staff member would ignore the behavior by continuing with the conversation as if nothing inappropriate had been said. What is important is that the client is not asked to stop making sexual remarks and is not reprimanded in any way.

Withdrawing attention is a more active procedure, in which the staff person immediately terminates involvement with the client when he or she engages in an undesirable behavior. In the above example, when the client makes a sexually suggestive statement, the staff person would immediately stop talking to the client and begin talking to another client, start some other activity such as reading a magazine, or perhaps even leave the room.

Prompting procedures. Often the main goal of head injury rehabilitation is to train clients to decrease their dependence on prompting by others. This takes considerable skill and experience. Many new staff members prompt their clients too frequently, probably in the belief that they are being helpful and providing useful instruction. Their clients, having never been given the opportunity to do things on their own, become increasingly dependent on others rather than increasingly independent.

Training clients to become less dependent on prompts involves a gradual and systematic reduction in prompting, a process called fading. The fading procedure employed varies from client to client and is usually accompanied by a task analysis of the skills being trained (see Exhibit 6-3). The following represents the basic training steps that staff should use to maximize their clients' independence.

1. *No prompting.* Before prompting the client to complete a task step, staff should allow the client time to begin the step independently.

2. *Gestural prompt.* The first prompt to the client should be a simple gesture, such as pointing to the object that the client is to

use or pointing in the direction in which the client is to go.

3. *Verbal prompt.* If the client does not respond to the gestural prompt, staff should provide a verbal prompt. Verbal prompts may be nonspecific (e.g., "What should you do next?") or specific (e.g., "Time to put on your shirt").

4. *Physical prompt.* If the client does not respond to the verbal prompt, the final step of prompting often involves physically guiding the client to begin the task. For example, staff may guide the client's hands to pick up a spoon and begin eating or to pick up a shirt and begin putting it on. It is important for staff to provide only as much physical assistance as is necessary and to terminate the physical prompt as soon as the client begins to move independently.

Physical management. Occasionally, people with head injury behave so aggressively that they may injure themselves or others or damage property, and in these cases staff may be required to use physical means to bring the behavior under immediate control. It is imperative that physical management procedures be used only when they are absolutely necessary and that the procedures are unlikely to cause injury or harm to the client. All staff should complete a course in aggression management with a curriculum approved by their licensing authority and taught by a certified instructor. Although most aggression management procedures make use of behavioral principles, aggression management is not a substitute for an individualized behavior program. The course should be taught by an instructor familiar with the causes of behavior problems after acquired brain injury as well as the unique prevention and deescalation strategies that can be used to successfully intervene.

Presentation Formats

The written format of the behavior program is extremely important in ensuring consistency and quality in program implementation. Written copies of the program serve as training tools and

as ready references during the implementation of the program steps. Consistency and accuracy of implementation can suffer if the written description of the behavioral procedures is unclear, if the essential steps are hidden within paragraphs of unnecessary verbiage, or if the program cannot be reviewed at a glance during an emergency.

Exhibit 6-4 is one format for presenting behavior programs to direct care staff. It illustrates several important features. First, the print is large, which makes it easier for several staff members to read the program at one time. Large print also makes it easier to read the program from several feet away, which can be an advantage in emergencies.

Second, the text generally consists of brief, simple instructions telling the staff member what to do in each circumstance. When multiple steps are involved, steps are listed in sequence and numbered accordingly.

Finally, the entire document is organized into three main sections: antecedents, behavioral definitions, and program steps to be followed. This organization allows staff to locate quickly those portions of the program that are of immediate importance. For example, to find out what steps to follow if the client has an outburst, the staff need only find *outburst* in the middle column of behavioral definitions and then read the instructions listed in the column on the right.

Initial Training

Whenever a new behavior program is implemented or an existing program is changed, the behavior specialist or the trainer should conduct a formal inservice for all relevant staff. It is essential that staff not only read and review the program but practice the program steps as well.

Each training session should follow a standard agenda. First, the trainer should distribute written copies of the program to each staff member and review the program steps while staff members read along. This review should also include information about why the program steps are being implemented and what the effects of the program should be. Once this review is complete, the trainer should demonstrate how to

Exhibit 6-4 Behavior Program Summary

		Client: Bill Brown
Special considerations and reminders: Outbursts may occur during any conversation, including phone calls.		**General program goals:** Decrease outbursts

During these conditions/times:	When Bill engages in these behaviors:	Respond by doing this:
Telephone calls	*Outburst:* yelling, swearing, or making threatening or abusive remarks	1. Say "Bill, I can't listen to this, I've got to go. Good-bye." 2. Hang up immediately. 3. If Bill calls back, say "I'm not ready to talk to you; I'll need at least an hour. Good-bye."
In person	*Outburst:* see above	1. Say "I need to leave." 2. Leave immediately. Keep going until you are outside normal conversation range. 3. Return only after Bill has been calm for 2 minutes.
Any time	*Appropriate conversation:* any questions, small talk, gossip, or other conversation that does not include yelling, swearing, or verbal attacks	1. Answer questions and talk freely. 2. Be warm, friendly, and polite. 3. When the conversation is over, tell Bill that you enjoyed taking with him.

implement the program by using an assistant who plays the role of the client.

The next step of each inservice should be for all staff to practice the program steps just demonstrated, pairing off if necessary so that one member of the pair can play the role of the client. During practice, trainers should observe the staff and provide corrective feedback on their performance. By the end of the practice session, each staff member should be able to recite the steps of the program and demonstrate program implementation without error. Staff who fail to do this should receive further training.

Evaluating and Maintaining the Effectiveness of Behavior Programs

Once the behavior program is written and staff are trained to implement it, the major clini-

cal focus is evaluation of program effectiveness and maintenance of program integrity.

Evaluating Program Effectiveness

Behavioral programs must be monitored on a daily basis. Each morning, the behavior specialist should review and graph the data collected during the previous day. This practice provides the opportunity to uncover any problems with data collection or program implementation and to investigate any discrepancies while the events of the previous day are still easily recalled. Daily review also allows the behavior specialist to make changes in the behavior program quickly.

The emphasis of behavior analysis on the collection and evaluation of observable data means that behavior programming lends itself well to group review and decision making. In settings where there are a number of behavioral specialists, weekly meetings should be scheduled in which each client's behavioral programming is discussed. All cases managed by the behavioral specialists should be reviewed on a regular rotating schedule. Discussion of each client should begin with an introductory summary from the clinician assigned to the case, including an overview of the referring behavior problems, a discussion of the client's reinforcers and the conditions that maintain the current problem behaviors, a description of treatments implemented to date, and an updated review of the data with presentation of graphs. Once the introduction is completed, the behavior specialists can discuss whether the current program is effective, what program steps need to be implemented next, and what steps may need to be implemented later if the new program is unsuccessful. When the behavior program is well designed, the discussion of each client can often be limited to 10 or 15 minutes.

In large and small rehabilitation settings, it is critical for all staff (direct care staff, case managers, and clinicians) meet regularly to discuss behavioral issues regularly. These meetings, which include all members of the rehabilitation team, provide useful information about potential reinforcers, problem behaviors that may be of growing concern, and difficulties that staff are experiencing in implementing the current program. Participating in these meetings will give all team members a better understanding of the rationale behind the current behavior program as well as an opportunity to plan for the future. This process may improve staff skills in implementing the program and allow staff to become better advocates for the program when they discuss it with others.

Maintaining Program Effectiveness

Maintaining staff performance at high levels is always challenging. Working with clients who have serious behavior problems can be especially demanding. People with head injury can be stressful and sometimes dangerous to work with, and most behavior programs do not produce immediate results. Consequently, staff burn-out is often high.

Selection of appropriate targets and interventions. A program that is poorly designed will be poorly maintained. One element of good design is an understanding of direct care staff and the many demands that are placed on them. Direct care staff are usually required to work with a number of clients at once, and each client may have several different programs written for him or her, including programs for self-care, health maintenance, mobility, memory, and so forth. Many behavior programs require more time to implement than staff have available given their other duties. Other behavior programs may require more staff members than are available or require staff members to demonstrate skills in which they have not been trained. To avoid this behavioral specialists need to work closely with all members of the rehabilitation team before designing a behavior program. In doing so, they will gain a better understanding of the amount of time and number of staff available for program implementation (Green, Reid, Perkins, & Gardner, 1991). Direct care staff often have more direct knowledge of the client than anyone else and are excellent sources of crucial behavioral information, such as the circumstances under which a given behavior occurs, the ways in which other clients and staff respond to the behavior, and so forth.

Feedback to staff. Giving feedback to staff has been shown to be an effective method for improving staff performance and maintaining improvements over time (DeVries, Burnette, & Redmon, 1991; Joyce & Nau, 1989; Panyan, Boozer, & Morris, 1970; Parsons, Cash, & Reid, 1989; Sulzer-Azaroff & deSantamaria, 1980). For example, staff can be provided with feedback regarding the number of behavior programs implemented each day, the frequency with which they are observed praising their clients or otherwise interacting with them appropriately, or the accuracy of their program implementation as determined by supervisors or other observers. Feedback can be provided to individuals or to groups. Performance data for the group (living unit, shift, or treatment team) can be posted, printed in a staff newsletter, or merely reviewed with the staff during regular staff or team meetings.

Feedback on program effectiveness. Feedback on program effectiveness is an excellent way to motivate staff to maintain their performance at high levels. Most staff are rewarded by knowing that they are helping their clients. Staff who can see that the behavior program is effective will be motivated to be more consistent and may persuade doubting staff members to begin adopting the procedures themselves.

Perhaps the easiest way to provide feedback to staff is to post the behavioral data in the form of graphs. Graphs can be posted in staff rooms and updated on a weekly basis, thereby providing staff immediate and frequent feedback. Graphs can also be presented at regular staff meetings, such as during the shift report, where the behavior specialist or the trainer can draw attention to recent developments or provide special recognition to staff members who have performed in an exemplary manner.

Regular inservice. Without frequent practice and feedback, even well learned skills may deteriorate. Consequently, once initial training is complete, periodic inservice is necessary to maintain the skills that staff have already learned. Formal group inservice is one way that program implementation skills can be reviewed and improved. The advantage of such training sessions is that, with several staff in attendance, staff members can pair up with each other and role play the procedures. The training should follow the same format as that used during the original training as discussed earlier in this chapter. In some settings, policy dictates that follow-up inservices be held at regular intervals if a behavior program is to remain in force.

Another useful method for maintaining program skills is to conduct brief drills in which trainers meet with staff on a one-to-one basis and ask them to demonstrate a particular procedure. This is similar to the procedure described above for maintaining data collection skills. For example, the trainer might imitate one of the problem behaviors normally exhibited by a client and then ask a staff member to implement the appropriate consequence as indicated in the behavior program. If the staff member makes an error, the trainer can model the proper procedure

and then have the staff member practice until the correct consequence is implemented. Because a drill such as this may take as little as 5 to 10 minutes to complete, the trainer will be able to have some training contact with every member of the team on a weekly basis. These drills are excellent indicators of staff knowledge and skills.

Other reinforcers for staff. Although performance feedback often results in changes in behavior, further improvement often requires additional techniques. To augment the effects of feedback, tangible reinforcers may also be provided to staff as determined by their performance. Examples of these reinforcers are certificates of recognition, promotions, bonuses, and extra days off (Green et al., 1991; Iwata, Bailey, Brown, Foshee, & Alpern, 1976).

A Collaborative Relationship Among All Team Members

The techniques and programs that staff are asked to implement must meet their needs as well as the needs of the clients whom they serve. Otherwise, the techniques will not be functional for them and will not be maintained. The needs of staff vary from person to person and setting to setting but include being able to complete the assigned tasks in the time allowed, seeing clients improve while they are under one's care, working in a safe environment, having opportunities for professional advancement, and maintaining some measure of control and input in one's job.

Anyone wishing to design treatments that will be adopted by staff must form a collaborative relationship with his or her co-workers so that all staff are involved in the development of service delivery throughout all stages. This should include selection of target behaviors, design of an intervention plan, and evaluation of program effectiveness (Fawcett, 1991). Programs that are designed in a collaborative fashion will better meet the needs of staff as well as the needs of clients. When this is done, all members of the treatment team can develop a consistency of purpose and action that will guarantee that quality service delivery will be maintained in all settings (Lubeck & Davis, 1991).

CONCLUSION

We have presented a methodology for understanding and ultimately changing the behaviors associated with traumatic head injury. Despite considerable evidence to the contrary, many rehabilitation professionals continue to view behavior analysis as a collection of procedures used to eliminate undesirable behaviors. As has been pointed out, however, a primary focus of behavior analysis is to establish or strengthen behaviors that may compete with or take the place of disruptive behaviors. The behaviorists' emphasis on individualized treatment, skill building, accountability, and client success makes behavior analysis a valuable and compatible methodology for rehabilitation settings.

REFERENCES

Baer, D.M., Wolf, M.M., & Risley, T.R. (1968). Some current dimensions of applied behavior analysis. *Journal of Applied Behavior Analysis, 1*, 91–97.

Barber, R., Tenenbaum, H.A., Berger, S., Quinn, J., & Nau, P.A. (1989). *Reducing the inappropriate verbal behavior of a head injured adolescent during a speech therapy group.* Paper presented at the 15th Annual Convention of the Association for Behavior Analysis, Milwaukee, WI.

Baumeister, A.A., & Rollings, J.P. (1976). Self-injurious behavior. In N.R. Ellis (Ed.), *International review of research in mental retardation.* New York: Academic Press.

Carr, E.G. (1977). The motivation of self-injurious behavior: A review of some hypotheses. *Psychological Bulletin, 84*, 800–816.

DeVries, J.E., Burnett, M.M., & Redmon, W.K. (1991) AIDS prevention: Improving nurses' compliance with glove wearing through performance feedback. *Journal of Applied Behavior Analysis, 24*, 705–711.

Fawcett, S.B. (1991). Some values guiding community research and action. *Journal of Applied Behavior Analysis, 24*, 621–636.

Green, C.W., Reid, D.H., Perkins, L.I., & Gardner, S.M. (1991). Increasing habilitative services for persons with profound handicaps: An application of structural analysis to staff management. *Journal of Applied Behavior Analysis, 24*, 459–471.

Harlow, J.M. (1848). Passage of an iron through the head. *New England Journal of Medicine, 39*, 389–39.

Hogan, R.T. (1988). Behavior management for community reintegration. *Journal of Head Trauma Rehabilitation, 3*, 62–77.

Horner, R.D. (1980). The effects of an environmental "enrichment" program on the behavior of institutionalized profoundly retarded children. *Journal of Applied Behavior Analysis, 13*, 473–491.

Howard, M.E. (1988). Behavior management in the acute care rehabilitation setting. *Journal of Head Trauma Rehabilitation, 3*, 14–22.

Ivancic, M., & Pace, G.M. (1991). *Systematic stimulus fading to reduce obscenity in a brain injured man.* Paper presented at the 11th Annual Convention of the Florida Association for Behavior Analysis, Sarasota, FL.

Iwata, B.A., Bailey, J.S., Brown, K.M., Foshee, T.J., & Alpern, M. (1976). A performance-based lottery to improve residential care and training by institutional staff. *Journal of Applied Behavior Analysis, 9*, 417–431.

Iwata, B.A., Dorsey, M.F., Slifer, K.J., Bauman, K.E., & Richman, G.S. (1982). Towards a functional analysis of self-injury. *Analysis and Intervention in Developmental Disabilities, 3*, 1–20.

Iwata, B.A., Pace, G.M., Kalsher, M.J., Cowdery, G.E., & Cataldo, M.F. (1990). Experimental analysis and extinction of self-injurious escape behavior. *Journal of Applied Behavior Analysis, 23*, 11–27.

Joyce, J., & Nau, P.A. (1989). *Performance management in a residential brain injury program.* Paper presented at the 15th Annual Convention of the Association for Behavior Analysis, Milwaukee, WI.

Kazdin, A.E. (1982). *Single case research designs: Methods for clinical and applied settings.* New York: Oxford University Press.

Lubeck, R.C., & Davis, P.K. (1991). W. E. Deming's 14 points for quality: Can they be applied to rehabilitation? *Journal of Rehabilitation Administration, 15*, 216–223.

Lucia, T., Darling, J.A., Pace, G.M., & Nau, P.A. (1989). *A comparison of standard occupational therapy techniques and behavioral task analysis in training bathing and dressing skills.* Paper presented at the 15th Annual Convention of the Association for Behavior Analysis, Milwaukee, WI.

Mace, F.C., & Knight, D. (1986). Functional analysis and treatment of severe pica. *Journal of Applied Behavior Analysis, 19*, 411–416.

Nau, P.A., Capriotti, R., & Pace, G.M. (1988). *Head injury rehabilitation.* Paper presented at the 14th Annual Convention of the Association for Behavior Analysis, Nashville, TN.

Pace, G.M., Capriotti, R.M., & Nau, P. (1988). *Treatment of aggression in a head injured client.* Paper presented at the 8th Annual Convention of the Florida Association for Behavior Analysis, Orlando, FL.

Panyan, M., Boozer, H., & Morris, N. (1970). Feedback to attendants as a reinforcer for applying operant techniques. *Journal of Applied Behavior Analysis, 3*, 1–4.

Parsons, M.B., Cash, V.B., & Reid, D.H. (1989). Improving residential treatment services: Implementation and norm-referenced evaluation of a comprehensive management system. *Journal of Applied Behavior Analysis, 22,* 143–156.

Russo, D.C., Cataldo, M.F., & Cushing, P.J. (1981). Compliance training and behavioral covariation in the treatment of multiple behavior problems. *Journal of Applied Behavior Analysis, 14,* 209–222.

Sidman, M. (1960). *Tactics of scientific research.* New York: Basic Books.

Skinner, B.F. (1938). *The behavior of organisms.* New York: Appleton-Century-Crofts.

Skinner, B.F. (1953). *Science and human behavior.* New York: Macmillan.

Slater, E., & Roth, M. (1969). *Clinical psychiatry* (3rd ed.). Baltimore: Williams & Wilkins.

Sulzer-Azaroff, B., & de Santamaria, M.C. (1980). Industrial safety hazard reduction through performance feedback. *Journal of Applied Behavior Analysis, 13,* 287–295.

Ulrich, R., Stachnik, T., & Mabry, J. (Eds.). (1966). *Control of human behavior* (Vol. 1). Glenview, IL: Scott, Foresman.

Ulrich, R., Stachnik, T., & Mabry, J. (Eds.). (1970). *Control of human behavior* (Vol. 2). Glenview, IL: Scott, Foresman.

Vollmer, T.R., & Iwata, B.A. (1991). Establishing operations and reinforcement effects. *Journal of Applied Behavior Analysis, 24,* 279–291.

Wood, R. (1984). Behavior disorders following severe brain injury: Their presentation and psychological management. In N. Brooks (Ed.), *Closed head injury: Psychological, social, and family consequences* (pp. 195–219). London: Oxford University Press.

Wood, R. (1987). *Brain injury rehabilitation.* Gaithersburg, MD: Aspen.

Wood, R. (1988). Management of behavior disorders in a day treatment setting. *Journal of Head Trauma Rehabilitation, 3,* 53–61.

Preparing Personnel for Implementation of Supported Employment Services

Paul Wehman
Pamela Sherron

7

OBJECTIVES

Upon completion of this chapter, the reader will be able to:

1. understand supported employment in its characteristics, model types, and guidelines for choosing it as a service option
2. identify the steps involved in implementing the individual placement model
3. justify the need for consumer involvement during model implementation
4. define the attitudinal, knowledge, and skill competencies needed by supported employment staff who work with individuals who have sustained traumatic brain injury
5. describe a number of supported employment educational and skills training opportunities

Preparing Personnel for Implementation of Supported Employment Services

Traumatic brain injury has become recognized as a national problem of epidemic proportions. Improvements in medical intervention and pharmacological advancements have resulted in a dramatic increase in the number of persons surviving traumatic brain injury. Annually, approximately 400,000 to 500,000 persons sustain a traumatic brain injury, and anywhere from 44,000 to 90,000 of these injuries will be categorized as severe (Goodall, Groah, Sherron, Kreutzer, & Wehman, 1991). In recent years an increased number of persons have been surviving head injuries that fall within the severe category (Wehman & Goodall, 1990). Individuals who survive severe brain injury will probably exhibit cognitive, physical, and psychosocial impairments that will adversely affect their quality of life by reducing their opportunities for employment and other activities of daily living (Brooks, McKinlay, Symington, Beattie, & Campsie, 1987; Cope & Hall, 1982; Wehman, Kreutzer, Stonnington, et al., 1988).

The medical costs for persons after brain injury are substantial; estimates are $6 billion in direct costs (Goodall et al., 1991). Because a significant proportion of survivors are young adults who are either just beginning or have yet to begin their careers, brain injury frequently results in long-term economic hardship on survivors, their families, and ultimately society. Annually, approximately $22 billion in indirect costs such as lost wages from unemployment is accrued (Goodall et al., 1991).

The estimated percentage of individuals with traumatic brain injury who will enter or reenter the competitive work force generally falls below 30% (Brooks et al., 1987). Brooks and colleagues (1987) completed an analysis of employment status within the first 7 years after head injury. The investigators followed 98 individuals and found a preinjury employment rate of 86%. During the first 4 years after injury the employment rate was 27%, and within 5 years 30% of the sample was unemployed. The investigators indicated that there was not a significant change in work status for the sample between 2 and 5 years after injury. As expected, cognitive impairments, behavior dysfunction, and personality problems were significant contributors to unemployment. Significant cognitive impairments included deficits in attention, communication, and memory.

Kay, Ezrachi, and Cavallo (1986) summarized 46 outcome studies. In one of these studies, Peck, Fulton, Cohen, Warren, and Antonello (1984) investigated vocational outcome in a group of 60 people with severe head injury from the Richmond, VA metropolitan area. On the average, 3.5 years had elapsed since injury, and 82% of the participants were between 16 and 40 years of age. Most of the participants (87%) had not resumed preinjury vocational levels. Of those persons who were working, 35% were employed in menial or sheltered workshop settings; more than half the sample (52%) was unemployed. Issues that related to vocational adjustment included attention and concentration, ability to process information, physical ability, and motor coordination. Difficulties with memory and depression were reported by 88% and 78% of the participants, respectively. Approximately 56% reported that they depended on their spouse or significant others as a primary source of income, and 27% of the sample received disability compensation. The conclusion was that diminished status is not unusual even years after the head injury.

Investigators have also reported that many who returned to work were not able to maintain employment for any substantial length of time (Wehman, Kreutzer, West, et al., 1989). Recently an exploratory analysis of the reasons why 38 individuals in the supported employment program terminated their employment was conducted (Sale, West, Sherron, & Wehman, 1991). The reasons for job separation, in order of frequency reported, were issues related to the employment setting or interpersonal relationship problems, mental health problems including criminal activity or other problems, and economic layoffs. Results revealed that, excluding layoffs, more than 75% of the separations involved more than one reason. These findings underscore the difficulties that individuals with severe brain injuries experience in attempting to return to gainful employment.

Recently a service strategy known as supported employment, first conceptualized for individuals with mental retardation and other developmental disabilities, has been utilized with persons with severe traumatic brain injury. Supported employment is a process that provides intensive, individualized vocational assistance to persons with disabilities (Wehman & Kreutzer, 1990). Over the past 20 years, research has revealed that individuals with severe disabilities are able to become productive members of the nation's work force (Wehman & Kregel, 1985). Thousands of individuals who had been denied access to vocational services in the past because they were deemed unemployable or not ready are now earning an income, contributing to the national economy, and becoming more self-sufficient. Acceptance of individuals into supported employment programs, however, traditionally takes place only after they have been unsuccessful with other rehabilitation vocational placement approaches. In these instances the individuals have been unable to gain or maintain any competitive job for an extended period of time.

The supported employment approach has the advantage of providing professional staff support at the point of placement in the work environment. An employment specialist focuses exclusively on an individual client, known as the consumer, at the worksite, where training and support are provided until individual performance meets employer standards.

Outcome reports from supported employment projects for persons with severe traumatic brain injury have been cautiously optimistic. A supported employment program at Virginia Commonwealth University's Medical College of Virginia, which began in October of 1986, reports that 59 persons with traumatic brain injury have been placed into 78 jobs, with a retention rate of 67% after 6 months of employment (Goodall et al., 1991).

The degree to which program staff can be effective in implementing supported employment efforts will be greatly affected by their general knowledge and understanding of the approach, philosophy, and values of supported employ-

ment and their mastery of technical skills. This chapter provides an overview of the supported employment concept; outlines two staffing configurations; describes the possible skills, knowledge, and training needed by staff to implement effective supported employment services for persons with traumatic brain injury; and discusses training delivery methods.

OVERVIEW OF SUPPORTED EMPLOYMENT

> Supported employment is a vocational service delivery approach and is defined by the 1986 Rehabilitation Act as "Competitive work in an integrated setting—(a) for individuals with severe handicaps for whom competitive employment has not traditionally occurred, or (b) for individuals for whom competitive employment has been interrupted or intermittent as a result of a severe disability and who because of their handicap need ongoing support services to perform such work." (Federal Register, 1987, p. 30551)

Supported employment is paid employment in community-based work settings for persons with severe disabilities who would be denied an opportunity to work without ongoing and permanent support at the job site. The hallmarks of this model are the placement of individuals without regard for prior job skills training and the commitment of professional staff to assist individuals in overcoming job difficulties as long as they are employed. Only in recent years has supported employment begun to become a familiar placement option in the vocational rehabilitation community.

Characteristics

Key features that characterize a supported employment approach include the following:

- *Real work for real pay:* The individual placed in employment must earn a wage and work an average of 20 hours per week. Most persons are paid at least minimum wage, but provisions can be made for commensurate pay.

- *Integration:* Co-workers are predominantly nondisabled, and the opportunity exists for the individual to interact with nondisabled individuals. Small group placements should not exceed eight persons with severe disability.

- *Ongoing support:* Services continue to meet the needs of the individual and the employer after the individual has learned the job and met production standards. The quantity and intensity of the services will fluctuate over time and are determined on an individual basis. Services may include additional intervention at the employment site as well as opportunities for job-related supports in the community. A minimum of two contacts per month are provided to the individual and are essential for the individual to maintain employment. Time-limited services that provide placement, training, and periodic follow-up are considered transitional employment, not supported employment.

- *Persons with severe disability:* Supported employment is an option for people with severe physical disabilities, visual impairments, long-term mental illness, or traumatic brain injury if they require ongoing support and could not maintain employment independently.

Traditional Vocational Rehabilitation Approaches Compared to the Supported Employment Approach

Vocational rehabilitation practices are being influenced dramatically by the use of the supported work model. Traditional practices are being scrutinized by professionals as well as significant others and clients, who are questioning the applicability and merit of other approaches. The emphasis is shifting from getting a person ready to work in a clinical or mock employment setting to getting him or her ready to work at work. The supported employment model differs from traditional return-to-work approaches, as illustrated in Table 7-1.

Types of Supported Employment

As more individuals with different disabilities have attempted to acquire or return to employment, variations of the supported employment model have evolved. Two features of these models that are critical to the implementation of supported employment are individualization and client involvement. Supported employment should be a consumer-driven approach and individualized to maximize personal strengths and abilities. As adults, all program participants bring extensive background experience from their personal and professional lives. Service providers should solicit client input and encourage participation in all phases of model implementation. The best supported employment programs have developed processes to ensure that consumer input occurs (Sale, 1991b).

There are currently four primary service delivery models: individual placement, enclave, mobile work crew, and the small business option (Griffin & Revell, 1991).

1. *Individual placement:* The person is placed in a community-based job. Community-based jobs are real work for real pay. Placement is in an environment with nondisabled co-workers for the current rate of pay, not subminimum wage. One-to-one job skills training is provided by an employment specialist. As the person becomes proficient at performing the job duties, the employment specialist gradually fades from the work site. Monthly ongoing communication to ensure employer and client satisfaction is provided.

2. *Enclave:* A small group of individuals, usually three to eight, works at a community-based organization. An employment specialist usually provides permanent support and supervision for the individuals.

3. *Mobile work crews:* This approach is similar to an enclave. Ongoing supervision is provided for three to eight workers with disabilities. The mobile crew is not based at one employment site but travels through the community providing contract ser-

Table 7-1 Comparison of Traditional Activities of Vocational and Supported Employment

Program Feature	Traditional Models	Supported Employment
Intake and consumer assessment	Assessment by means of evaluations and records that may be outdated Exploration of current vocational interests via standardized assessment	Assessment with information from direct observation Informal exploration of current interests
Job development and placement	Assistance given to consumer in locating a job opportunity	Individualized and consumer-specific development of jobs Participation of consumer in placement efforts Thorough analysis of job skills and requirements before placement Interests and current or acquirable abilities matched to job requirements Communication facilitated with employer, co-workers, and significant others Travel arrangements and training provided if needed
Job site training	Employer provides training Trained staff provide one-to-one on-site skills and production training	Trained staff provide one-to-one on-site skills and production training Trained staff design and implement adaptations, modifications, and compensatory strategies Additional advocacy and empowerment provided to ensure adjustment and success
Ongoing assessment and follow-along	Brief or infrequent follow-up checks performed to assess work performance Case management needs often go unaddressed Follow-up provided on a time-limited basis with specific information or data collected about work performance	Consumer's performance monitored on an ongoing basis through data collection techniques and case management needs assessment Regular job-site visitations, phone calls, and supervisor and consumer evaluations provided

Source: From "Traumatic Brain Injury: Supported Employment and Compensatory Strategies for Enhancing Vocational Outcomes" by J.S. Kreutzer and M.V. Morton in *Vocational Rehabilitation and Supported Employment,* P. Wehman and M.S. Moon (Eds.), 1988, Baltimore, MD: Paul H. Brookes Publishing Co. Copyright 1988 by Paul H. Brookes Publishing Co. Adapted by permission.

vices. Contractual work may include groundskeeping, window washing, and office maintenance services.

4. *Small business:* This option entails employment of five to eight persons with disabilities in addition to nondisabled workers in a small community-based business. The business may manufacture a product or deliver a service.

The best approach is the individual placement model. This model is the least stigmatizing, most integrated, and most normalized. Persons should only be considered candidates for group options when repeated individual placements have not yielded success. Individuals involved in group models should be assessed on a continual basis for the potential of participating in the individual placement approach. To date, the Virginia Commonwealth University Supported Employment Program has utilized the individual placement approach with all program participants.

Guidelines for Using Supported Employment

When one is determining whether supported employment is an appropriate placement option, the following should be considered (Griffin & Revell, 1991):

- Can the individual *independently* transfer the skills learned in the preemployment training setting to a work setting? If not, then supported employment is an appropriate service to consider.
- Will the person be able to meet job requirements in a reasonable amount of time without creating undue hardship for the employer? If not, then supported employment services are appropriate.
- Has the individual frequently been terminated from employment? If yes, then there may be a need for support services on the job site.
- Has the person participated in work readiness programs for long periods of time without becoming employed? If yes, then supported employment should be considered.
- Does the individual require specialized employment services to gain and maintain employment? If yes, then supported employment services should be considered.

INDIVIDUAL PLACEMENT MODEL

Exhibit 7-1 lists the activities conducted by an employment specialist during implementation of this supported work model.

Consumer Assessment

The first phase of the individual placement model of supported employment is consumer assessment. The employment specialist collects information from various sources regarding the individual (consumer) who has been referred to the supported employment program. A visit to the individual's home is scheduled as one part of the assessment process. This allows the employment specialist an opportunity to explain the type of service being offered and what the individual can expect from participation in the supported employment program. In addition, during the home visit the employment specialist can learn about the individual's vocational interests and abilities as well as obtain insight into the dynamics of the family system.

Neuropsychological and medical evaluations, questionnaires completed by family members, educational records, and past employment records are also reviewed to form an initial impression of the individual. A situational assessment may be arranged and can provide the employment specialist with more information about and insights into the individual's interests, abilities, personality, and learning potential. A situational assessment involves the use of a real work setting to assess the aforementioned areas in addition to responses to training techniques. The information collected is analyzed to determine a direction for job placement.

Job Development

Job development involves identifying appropriate employment opportunities in the community. Usually, the activity occurs simultaneously with or after the consumer assessment. The employment specialist seeks positions with qualities that are in line with the consumer's expressed interests and abilities. Job openings are discovered from numerous sources such as state and local government listings, the classified sections of newspapers, help wanted signs, and cold calls. The consumer may choose to participate in the process by initiating contact with prospective employers or informing the employment specialist of leads and ideas for job placement.

Once a potential job is identified, the employment specialist contacts the employer for an appointment. The major goals of the specialist's

Exhibit 7-1 Activities Conducted by the Employment Specialist During Supported Employment Model Implementation

Intake and consumer assessment
Consumer assessment is the process of gathering information about current interests and the adaptable abilities of the individuals in the program.
- Conduct interviews with the consumer, significant others, previous employers, and so forth.
- Explain the program and what services to expect to the consumer and significant others.
- Explore expectations and perceptions of potential problems in returning to work.
- Review records from various sources such as educational and vocational training, past employment, medical records, and neuropsychological reports.
- Observe the consumer in a number of settings to learn more about his or her interests and abilities.
- Learn about behaviors by going to public places with the consumer (e.g., a mall, park, coffee shop).
- Establish rapport and develop the relationship.

Job development
Job development is the process of identifying and analyzing appropriate employment opportunities for individuals with severe disabilities.
- Identify positions through classified ads, job listings, networking, and the like.
- Develop resumes.
- Present the model to employers with emphasis on the functional abilities of the consumer.
- Complete the job analysis by observing, shadowing workers, and working in the position.

Job placement
Job placement occurs when information collected during consumer assessment is successfully matched to the requirements of an available job.
- Consider consumer characteristics in relation to job duties, financial requirements, hours, transportation, and physical/cognitive demands.
- Arrange a job interview.
- Ensure travel arrangements to and from through family members, public transportation, co-workers, specialized transportation, or travel training.
- Identify work-related purchases such as uniforms, alarm clock, and the like.
- Communicate with significant others regarding the job placement, hours of employment, effects on benefits, and so forth.
- Coordinate the Targeted Job Tax Credit, if appropriate, with the rehabilitation counselor.
- Notify the Social Security Administration in writing and ensure that a family member will follow up.

Job site training
Job site training involves a number of activities to ensure job retention.
- Familiarize the consumer with the job environment and orient him or her with map or repetition if needed.
- Facilitate communication/integration by assisting the consumer with developing rapport with co-workers and supervisors; encourage the supervisor to give instruction/feedback.
- Ensure task completion whenever possible.
- Train in job skill acquisition/production.
- Enhance skill acquisition and production, implement compensatory strategies, adaptations, and modifications based on job requirements and input from the consumer.

Ongoing support and follow-along
Follow-along is the process of being updated on the consumer's current job performance and support service needs.
- Implement a follow-along schedule and gradually decrease intervention time at the job site.
- Monitor performance by taking data periodically, reviewing supervisor evaluations, checking with the employer and co-workers, and so forth.
- Facilitate ongoing communication with co-workers, supervisors, and family members.
- Address problems that may affect retention such as interpersonal conflicts, decline in job performance, tardiness/absence from work, and the like.
- Provide additional intervention as indicated by management or data collection techniques, such as training for new job duties and behavior intervention.
- Continue to identify case management needs and refer to resources such as transportation, substance abuse intervention, money management supports, and the like.

presentation are to explain the concept and advantages of the supported employment program for the employer and to identify appropriate job opportunities within the company. Effective job development is vital to the success of the supported employment program. If the employment specialist has poor skills in this area, placement delays will result. Exhibit 7-2 presents an outline of a typical employer presentation and some tips that may be useful during a contact.

Job Placement

Upon presenting the supported employment concept, if a job opening exists the employment

Exhibit 7-2 Job Development Guidelines and Tips

Establish rapport
- Engage the employer in a few moments of small talk before delivering the actual presentation. If the employer appears ready to get down to business, however, take the cue and move on to the purpose of the visit.

Introduce the agency
- Establish the credibility of your program by providing information about your agency's mission and role as a supported employment provider.
- Describe how your agency fits into the range of services for someone with a traumatic brain injury so that the employer can see the entire picture.

Identify the population
- Describe persons with traumatic brain injuries in realistic but nonstigmatizing terms.
- Identify the common causes of most brain injuries.
- Give brief examples, in functional terms, of impairments that may result from brain injury. Emphasize, however, that each individual brings a unique combination of experiences, strengths, interests, and support needs to an employment situation.
- Cite placements that the program has made and (if permission has been granted) provide names of employers who are willing to serve as references to prospective employers.

Explain the supported employment model
- Find out what an employer may already know about supported employment.
- Explain that a detailed analysis of the requirements of a job is performed during job development; emphasize that a job placement will not be pursued unless an appropriate candidate for the job opening is identified.
- Establish the role of the employment specialist in accompanying the new employee to the job site, at no cost to the employer, to provide training and support. Inform the employer that the employment specialist will actually contribute to the completion of job duties, if applicable, while the individual develops the speed and endurance necessary for completing the job.
- State that a large part of the employment specialist's time is often spent in helping develop and implement compensatory strategies, such as checklists or diagrams, to assist the individual in learning independently to perform the job.
- Explain that the employment specialist begins to fade gradually and systematically from the job site when the individual is able to perform the job independently and to the employer's satisfaction. Stress that the employment specialist continues to monitor the individual's performance for as along as he or she is employed.

Appeal to vested interests
- Inform the employer of any financial incentives, such as the Targeted Jobs Tax Credit, that are available to businesses for hiring persons with disabilities.
- Mention that research indicates that workers with disabilities are, as a group, motivated and dependable and tend to stay in jobs longer than workers without disabilities.

Wrap-up
- Answer any questions that the employer has before closing the presentation.
- Be prepared to overcome concerns or reservations that the employer may have.

Source: Reprinted from *Supported Employment Services for Individuals with Traumatic Brain Injury: A Guide for Service Providers* by P. Goodall et al. with permission of Virginia Commonwealth University Rehabilitation Research and Training Center, © 1991.

specialist may request a job description and arrange a time to observe or even shadow an employee currently working in that position. The job requirements are analyzed and assessed in terms of numerous factors, including production levels, co-worker interaction, and communication skills. The purpose of a job analysis is to collect detailed information about the job that can be compared with consumer assessment information to make a placement decision.

If the individual's skills match the requirements of the position and the individual is interested in the position, the employment specialist arranges a job interview. The employment specialist usually participates in the interview to clarify the role of supported employment services and provide support to the individual.

Job Site Training

During job site training, the focus is providing job skills training and supporting the new employee. A task analysis is prepared that reflects the most efficient way for the worker to perform the job and provides guidelines for training in a particular job skill. Consistent prompts that enhance learning and natural environmental cues should be used. The employment specialist also spends time designing, developing, and implementing job site adaptations and modifications. Once job site training data are collected and self and employer reports indicate that the individual has become proficient at performing the job duties, the employment specialist begins systematically to fade his or her presence when that particular duty is being performed. Eventually the employment specialist will fade completely from the employment site.

Ongoing Support and Follow-Along

The final phase of the supported employment model is ongoing support and follow-along. As a proactive measure, the employment specialist monitors the individual's work performance throughout employment. Data are collected during periodic job site visits and through com-

munications with the supervisor and co-workers. Individuals also fill out a self-evaluation form that provides the employment specialist with insight into their perception of current job performance.

Case Study

Supported employment involves many interrelated skills, competencies and activities. The case study presented here illustrates these interrelationships (Booth, 1991).

C.P. is a 28-year-old man who experienced a traumatic brain injury as a result of an automobile accident. Before his injury, C.P. had no apparent psychiatric problems, but there were reports by C.P. and his family of alcohol and substance abuse. C.P. reported drinking once or twice a week and had also been arrested for driving while intoxicated. C.P. also reported frequent use of marijuana as well as occasional use of hashish, methamphetamine, and cocaine. Because of a lack of sufficient information regarding C.P.'s family history, no inferences as to the relative stability of the family environment could be made.

C.P. reportedly made Cs and Ds in high school and was held back in the sixth grade. At the time of C.P.'s accident, he was a full-time student and was employed part time as a gas station attendant. Before his injury, C.P. had also worked as a security guard but had been fired for being too young for the job requirements. During his preinjury employment period, his average earnings were around minimum wage. C.P.'s vocational interests during high school included mechanics and electronics.

At age 17, C.P. was involved in an automobile accident. Allegedly, a car ran a red light and hit the car in which C.P. was a passenger. There was evidence suggesting that the occupants of both vehicles had been drinking alcohol. C.P. was in a coma for 3 months and remained hospitalized for an additional 9 months while undergoing extensive rehabilitation. As a result of the head injury, C.P. has a severe gait impairment. Initially he was confined to a wheelchair, and eventually he progressed to walking with the aid of a cane. Presently, C.P. walks slowly and has poor balance but refuses to use assistive devices.

At age 25, C.P. participated in a work-hardening program to explore his vocational goals. When counselors identified a substance abuse problem, and after he failed several times to comply with program policies, it was recommended that C.P. receive inpatient treatment. At this point, C.P. discharged himself from the program as a result of his limited insights regarding his addiction to marijuana and his unwillingness to work with authority figures.

Neuropsychological assessment of C.P. revealed significant deficits in the areas of immediate and sustained attention and concentration, spelling, immediate and delayed auditory memory, delayed visual memory, remote memory, and bilateral speed and dexterity. Vocationally, it was assumed that C.P. would perform work slowly and would probably forget instructions and important information. It was also assumed that C.P.'s performance and self-esteem would probably benefit most by structure, frequent feedback, and extra time for task completion. C.P. often demonstrated impulsive behavior or inappropriate interpersonal behavior. In accordance with this, C.P. required assistance to anticipate the natural negative consequences of his actions by means of a problem-solving approach.

C.P. was referred to the Supported Employment Program at Virginia Commonwealth University in February 1990. At that time, C.P. was unemployed and at risk of losing his apartment. C.P.'s expressed interest in working with machines and his desire to work without supervision led us to a confidential document shredder position in a local bank. Initially, C.P. earned $5.00 an hour and worked 27 hours a week. Because the job was part time, it had no benefits. The bank was located approximately 6 miles from C.P.'s home, and he was able to transport himself to and from work independently. C.P.'s duties consisted of two major tasks: shredding paper with a semi-industrial shredder and compacting the paper into bales.

C.P. reached skills acquisition on the task of shredding in 6 days and on baling in 19 days. He mastered the job-related duties of machine maintenance and signing in and out in 8 and 25 days, respectively. Approximately 3 weeks into training, the employment specialist was able to begin fading and subsequently decreased active intervention to 20% at the end of week 6.

Presenting issues during the skills acquisition phase were limited to labeling hidden controls on the machinery and substituting a flat-bed dolly for the traditional upright dolly. The flat-bed dolly allowed C.P. to flip the bale into a horizontal position, which enabled him to handle the weight of the bale. A rope was attached to the dolly so that, when it was empty, C.P. could easily pull it where he needed it rather than carry it, which threw off his balance. These modifications not only enhanced his ability to perform the work but also had a positive impact on production.

Throughout the course of C.P.'s employment, production continued to be a concern. Initially, a schedule aided in defining the appropriate work speed for C.P. to maintain to meet production. In addition to this, the employment specialist also helped C.P. chart his daily production on a graph. By doing so, C.P. was able to visualize his daily performance and his target objective. Both concepts were modified to meet C.P.'s needs as he became more independent in his position. C.P. currently tracks his own production on a grid designed to monitor performance over a 2-week period. He makes a check mark for every bale completed during the day on the appropriate grid row, and the end result is a bar graph illustrating cumulative production daily and weekly. Furthermore, the employment specialist is able to track production peaks and valleys without daily visits to the site. The course of the graph also signals changes in C.P.'s lifestyle and the onset of substance abuse problems.

Case management consumes much of the time that the employment specialist spends with C.P. C.P. currently has substance abuse problems, which are being handled jointly by the employment specialist and a substance abuse counselor. He is still in the process of denial but continues to participate in the counseling. C.P.'s long-term relationship with his girlfriend also proved to be a source of constant issues. During the term of his employment, C.P. was arrested twice, once on the bank premises, for domestic abusive behaviors. Both the girlfriend and C.P. participated in counseling but were unable to modify their behaviors toward one another. As a result of his last arrest, it was recommended that C.P. end his relationship with his girlfriend and pursue other interests. Since then, C.P. has purchased a house and is living alone. The impact on his work performance to date has been positive.

C.P. has now been employed for 11 months, and his hours have been increased to 32 per week. To date he has earned approximately $6,000.00. His supervisor's evaluations continue to remain positive, although at times they declined from excellent to satisfied. The employer remains supportive of C.P. and has described the declines in C.P.'s evaluations as occurring during periods when C.P. was undergoing many interpersonal problems related to his girlfriend.

STAFFING

The multitude and variety of residual deficits that may result from a traumatic brain injury require that service personnel have a broad knowledge base in several areas. Depending upon the staffing patterns, the employment specialist may find himself or herself in a number of roles, which may include marketer, job site trainer, counselor, case manager, and advocate.

Type of Staffing

The staffing pattern of a supported employment program will depend upon a number of factors, which include program size and the qualifications and experience of staff. The best staffing configuration will ultimately be the one that allows the organization to reach its primary goal of successfully assisting individuals with disability to gain and maintain employment. The two basic configurations for staffing are holistic and partitioned. There are pros and cons associated with each approach (Table 7-2).

In the holistic configuration, the employment specialist directs all aspects of model implementation and is responsible for placement, training, and job retention activities. Generally, a second-

---

Table 7-2 Pros and Cons of Holistic and Partitioned Staffing Patterns

Staffing Pattern	Pros	Cons
Holistic	Vested and committed to client placement Greater likelihood of successful job match Empathy among co-workers who provide different services Continuity for program participants and employers Decreased burn-out of staff as a result of variety of duties	More difficult to recruit staff because of the need for flexibility and greater variety of skills Job may be too demanding for salary offered
Partitioned	Easier to hire staff with skills in one or two areas (e.g., marketing or human services) Staff can become expert in an area Potentially less time delay between placements	Variable pay scale for staff may create the notion of role importance Staff may get bored by performing repetitive roles Requires dependence on other staff and more effective communication Requires more staff (i.e., one to four job trainers to keep one job placement specialist busy) Devaluing of job trainer activity because of professional, businesslike demeanor of job developer

ary staff person will also be involved to ensure continuity of service if the primary staff person is unavailable.

In the partitioned configuration personnel are responsible for implementing activities specific to a particular program component. For example, some staff perform job placement activities, and others provide on the job training and follow-along services. Also, some partitioned patterns may further delineate responsibilities and limit staff to providing only job site training, job placement activities, or follow-along activities.

Job Description

Either configuration will require a thorough job description for staff recruitment. An organization's job description will always be evolving and changing. Before every recruitment, the program manager should review the existing description to individualize it to the program's current needs and practices. The program's job descriptions should include a general description of the job, an outline of specific responsibilities and duties, the minimum qualifications and requirements, and information about salary range and benefits. Exhibit 7-3 is a sample job description for staff recruitment in the holistic configuration.

PREPARATION OF SUPPORTED EMPLOYMENT PERSONNEL

Need for an Interdisciplinary Team

Although the goal of rehabilitation is to return the individual to a functioning level of independence, the clinical and supported employment models of service provision are different in several ways. For instance, the clinical model looks to remediate the underlying cause of dysfunction, whereas a supported employment model takes a behavioral approach to intervention. This is directed at changing behaviors that are observable and measurable. Clinical interventions are generally geared to improving a specific dys-

function. Supported employment is holistic in nature and focuses primarily on providing interventions that assist the individual in maintaining employment. This often will include interventions that are based on case management needs so that the potential for adverse effects on employment retention will be minimized.

The likelihood of successful vocational rehabilitation for persons with traumatic brain injury can be enhanced by utilizing an interdisciplinary team approach. Key members of the treatment team may include the client and significant others; employment specialist; neuropsychologist; physiatrist; occupational, speech, and physical therapists; social worker; and rehabilitation counselor. Through interdisciplinary collaboration, the team can communicate frequently and set mutual treatment goals for recovery. Once the individual's goal of being employed is reached, team members can continue to work together in an advisory fashion. Thus the contributions of related service staff can be valuable. It may be the case, however, that supported employment program staff do not have access to some team members.

The skills and knowledge that supported employment staff may need will also depend upon the accessibility of other disciplines for input and problem solving on individual cases. It will also rely upon the ability of the medical professionals to present information in understandable and functional terms that will transfer to the client's activities of daily living. It is important for a supported employment program to give continuous feedback to medical personnel and evaluators to improve the interpretability of all the information provided.

Supported Employment Curriculum

Few secondary education curricula are designed to prepare the employment specialist with the kinds of knowledge and skills they need to fulfill their roles in supported employment. Employment specialists enter the field with various educational backgrounds and work experiences. Many staff may not have a college degree or formal education in providing services to people with

Exhibit 7-3 Sample Job Description for Staff Recruitment in the Holistic Configuration

General Description

The employment specialist is involved in all aspects of community-based vocational placement, training, and follow-along for persons with severe disabilities. The successful candidate will meet with potential employers in an attempt to secure employment opportunities. Also, he or she will provide one-to-one training for job skills while, in most cases, ensuring that the job duties are completed to the employer's required standards. In addition, he or she will maintain ongoing contact with the employer after job training has been accomplished. The employment specialist will work as part of a team and will interact frequently with clients and encourage their ongoing participation in program implementation. Last, the employment specialist will participate in interagency case meetings.

Specific Duties and Responsibilities

Intake and consumer assessment. The employment specialist will obtain assessment and evaluation information. This may include reviewing evaluations from other professionals or agencies, interpreting reports, interviewing persons knowledgeable about the consumer, and making direct observations. The employment specialist will ensure that the consumer understands how employment will affect benefits status.

Job development. The employment specialist will complete marketing activities by presenting the program to prospective employers until appropriate job opportunities have been secured. This will include a thorough analysis of the job duties and environmental characteristics.

Job placement. The employment specialist will provide guidance and leadership in various activities, which include but are not limited to assisting with the completion of an application, providing support during the interview, and making recommendations about accepting job offers. He or she will also assist with initial planning for work (i.e., transportation arrangements, uniform, etc.).

Job site training. The employment specialist, in most cases, will provide one-to-one training until the consumer can maintain job performance without regular assistance. Job site training duties may include development and implementation of behavioral programming strategies, employer and co-worker advocacy, and precise and detailed data collection on work performance.

Ongoing support and follow-along. The employment specialist will maintain contact, at a minimum of twice a month, with the consumer, employer, and others as needed to facilitate job retention. The employment specialist will be available to assist in resolving any hindrances to continued employment.

Other. The employment specialist will perform other related duties, including but not limited to participation in agency meetings, development of materials, coordination of case management services as necessary, and maintenance of accurate consumer records and documentation.

Qualifications

In addition to excellent oral and written communication skills, effective interpersonal skills, knowledge of vocational issues and strategies as they relate to persons with disabilities, and the ability to work with a high degree of independence, the following specific qualifications apply.

Education and experience. The applicant must have completed a bachelor's degree, preferably in special education, psychology, business, or a closely related field. Experience with persons with disabilities, preferably in direct training activities. Extensive and successful vocational training experience may be considered in lieu of a college degree.

Transportation. The applicant must possess a valid driver's license and have his or her own reliable transportation.

Other. The applicant must be able to work in a number of service, manufacturing, and professional settings and maintain a flexible schedule.

Salary and Benefits

Salary. $23,000 to $29,000.

Benefits. Continued educational opportunities, two weeks paid vacation and one week sick leave annually.

disabilities. A regional survey revealed that of 234 employment specialists 60% held an undergraduate degree. The majority (96%) indicated that they had received some training but desired additional technical assistance in a number of areas, including those specific to the disabled population being served (Everson & Brooke, 1990).

Sale (1990) states that supported employment curricula should include foundation, core, and specialty areas (the last of these is discussed in detail below). He suggests that the foundation courses include content related to competencies in philosophical, historical, ethical, and legal issues related to persons with disabilities. The core area should include information about implementation of the supported employment model and may include strategies for marketing, consumer assessment techniques, job placement activities, job site training, and follow-along interventions. Specific emphasis on the application of behavioral analysis and behavioral change strategies should be provided. Case management and advocacy should also be a content area in the core curriculum. Supported employment personnel should become familiar with ways to access and coordinate community resources. Last, ways to become an effective advocate should be explored. Advocacy should emphasize techniques to facilitate rapport, communication, and support from co-workers, supervisors, and other community service providers.

Specialty Area

After training in the foundation and core curricula, learners should receive area specialty training in traumatic brain injury to develop skills related to this specific consumer population. Within this specialty area three major realms of information should be covered: an overview of traumatic brain injury, advanced implementation strategies for supported employment for individuals with traumatic brain injuries, and case management for individuals with traumatic brain injury.

Mastering information in the specialty area will assist direct service staff in becoming more

accomplished at providing quality supported employment services for persons with traumatic brain injury. This specialty area will prepare staff for concerns unique to the population with traumatic brain injury, for example issues that may arise during model implementation (e.g., criminal history, substance abuse, and physical and cognitive deficits). Appendix 7-1 provides a list of resource centers where a trainer may obtain additional information about supported employment and traumatic brain injury. Also, national and local head injury foundations will have much useful information.

Overview of Traumatic Brain Injury

First, the learner should receive an overview of traumatic brain injury to become familiar with basic concepts and information (Table 7-3). Specifically, in this section the learner should become acquainted with the incidence and prevalence of traumatic brain injury and its many etiologies. Also included in the traumatic brain injury overview is content related to the normal anatomy and physiology of the brain and central nervous system, daily functioning after injury, and family systems. The learner should become versed in the continuum of care (from injury through acute care to community integration) for persons with traumatic brain injury, with particular attention being given to medical and neuropsychological components. This information is often novel to supported employment specialists who do not have a medical background.

Implementation of Supported Employment for Persons with Traumatic Brain Injury

Next, supported employment model implementation specific to persons with traumatic brain injury should be provided. Table 7-4 describes the suggested purposes, learning objectives, and subject content for this area, which covers the specific knowledge and skills needed to provide supported employment for this population. Critical factors such as family and marital stability, substance abuse, and the like must be examined during consumer assessment to facili-

Table 7-3 Overview of Traumatic Brain Injury

Purpose	*Learning Objectives*	*Subject Content Areas*

To examine the extent of traumatic brain injury in the United States	Define traumatic brain injury as written by the National Head Injury Foundation
	
	State, in order of most frequent occurrence, the major causes of traumatic brain injury
	
	Describe the characteristics of persons who sustain traumatic brain injury, including sex, age, educational, economic, and vocational background and experiences
	
	Compare and contrast the costs of services in traumatic brain injury with those of other disabling conditions, such as muscular dystrophy and spinal cord injury
		I. Definition of traumatic brain injury
		II. Incidence
		  A. Scope of problem
		  B. Causes of traumatic brain injury
		III. Demographics
		IV. Comparison of occurrence and cost with those of other disabling conditions

To know how the unimpaired nervous system functions	On a diagram, label the parts of the brain and write the primary functions of each: include medulla, reticular formation, cerebrum, thalamus, hypothalamus, corpus callosum, pituitary gland, cerebellum, spinal cord, brain stem, frontal lobe, temporal lobe, language area, and parietal lobe
	
	List and describe the purposes of the parts of a neuron (dendrite, soma, and axon)
	
	Discuss the division of the peripheral nervous system (somatic and autonomic)
	
	State how visual fields and optic tract are associated with certain areas of the brain
		I. Functional neuroanatomy and the nervous system
		  A. Central nervous system
		    1. The brain
		      a. Divisions
		      b. Functions
		      c. Ventricular system
		    2. Spinal cord
		    3. Neurons
		      a. Parts
		      b. Purpose
		  B. Peripheral nervous system
		    1. Somatic
		    2. Autonomic
		      a. Sympathetic
		      b. Parasympathetic
		  C. Sensory systems

To understand how an injury to the head can lead to diffuse and secondary brain damage	Compare and contrast an open with a closed head injury
	
	Identify and describe the range of severity in traumatic brain injury
	
	Describe the types of primary damage to the brain, including diffuse axonal injury and skull fracture
	
	List the causes of secondary brain damage
	
	Distinguish among the three types of hematoma
	
	Explain why increased intracranial pressure is of importance
	
	Define brain edema
	
	Define hypoxia
	
	Discuss two neurological conditions that can result in functional deterioration after traumatic brain injury
		I. Types of injury
		  A. Decelerating
		  B. Accelerating
		  C. Penetrating
		II. Severity
		  A. Primary damage
		    1. Diffuse
		    2. Concussive
		    3. Coup-contrecoup
		  B. Secondary damage
		    1. Hematomas
		    2. Hypoxia
		  C. Neurological
		    1. Posttraumatic epilepsy

continues

Table 7-3 continued

Purpose	Learning Objectives	Subject Content Areas
To become aware of the service delivery system and the role of professionals who attend to persons with traumatic brain injury	Describe the role of the neurosurgeon in the acute care setting	I. Acute hospital care
	Explain the uses of computed tomography and magnetic resonance imaging in diagnosing traumatic brain injury	A. Neurosurgeon
		B. Coma
	Describe the course of recovery for a person with a severe traumatic brain injury as outlined by the Ranchos Los Amigos Hospital	1. Glasgow Coma Score
		2. Ranchos Los Amigos scale
To become familiar with the role of the physiatrist and the need for long-term follow-up services	Compare and contrast posttraumatic and retrograde amnesia	II. Postacute care
		A. Continuum of care
	Describe the process used in calculating a Glasgow Coma Score	B. Roles of service providers
	When given a series of Glasgow Coma Scores over time, determine whether a person with brain injury is improving	1. Physiatrist
		2. Speech therapy
To know the specialty and medical terminologies often used in medical evaluations and reports		3. Physical therapy
	When given a range of Glasgow Coma Scores, identify the degree of traumatic brain injury as mild, moderate, or severe	4. Occupational therapy
		5. Social work
	Discuss the role of the rehabilitation team by indicating the major players and stating their roles in assisting the person in the recovery process	6. Vocational counselor
		C. Specialty area terminology
	Define the role of the physiatrist	
	Define the following specialty terminology:	
	• *Speech:* anomia, confabulation, aphasia, disarthria, verbosity parapnasis, perseveration prosody, sequencing skills, pragmatic language	
	• *Physical:* ataxia, motor weakness, fine and gross motor, apraxia	
	• *Sensory:* perceptual, dyslexia, finger agnosia, agnosia, neglect, hemianopsia, diplopia, perceptual scanning	
	• *Behavior:* initiative, motivation, frustration tolerance, response control	
To understand the types of medical issues and physical disabilities that may result from traumatic brain injury	Discuss types of medical and physical disability that may result from traumatic brain injury and state possible medical interventions	I. Types of medical/physical issues resulting from traumatic brain injury
	Discuss the complexity involved in isolating physical performance from cognitive or psychological influences when assessing an individual with traumatic brain injury	A. Visual
		1. Field deficits
		2. Blindness
		3. Color vision problem
	State the risk factors for posttraumatic epilepsy	4. Sensitivity to light
	List the steps one should follow if an individual experiences a seizure	5. Blind spots
		6. Double vision
	Describe the components of a functional medical evaluation	B. Audiovestibular
		1. Sensorineural hearing loss
	Discuss the usefulness of visual, sleep, substance abuse, and driving evaluations	2. Conductive hearing loss
		3. Vestibular dysfunction, dizziness
		4. Balance

Table 7-3 continued

Purpose	Learning Objectives	Subject Content Areas

		C. Oropharyngeal
		   1. Communication with vocal cord dysfunction
		   2. Dysphonia
		   3. Swallowing difficulty
		   4. Dysphagia
		D. Communication
		   1. Dysphasia
		   2. Dysprosody
		   3. Dysarthria
		   4. Oromotor dyspraxia
		E. Bowel and bladder
		   1. Urinary urgency
		   2. Incontinence
		F. Posttraumatic epilepsy
		II. Evaluation
		   A. General medical
		   B. Visual
		   C. Sleep
		   D. Substance abuse
		   E. Driving

To know the types of cognitive deficits that may result from traumatic brain injury
To become familiar with formal and informal ways to assess cognitive function
To acquire a skill for functional interpretation of neuropsychological test results
	State the types of services a neuropsychologist may provide to individuals with traumatic brain injury
	Explain what a neuropsychological evaluation can provide and what records may be reviewed before results are reported
	List questions that may be useful to ask a neuropsychologist before the evaluation so that he/she can assist in providing useful functional information for the return to work plan
	When given a series of test scores, interpret the results presented as percentiles or normalized scores
	When provided with neuropsychological measurements, recognizes the possible tests used to measure specific skills
	Explain the limitations of a neuropsychological evaluation
	Describe informal methods of assessment for memory, attention, motor skills, communication, visual perception, judgment, problem solving, and social skills
	Discuss the implications for functional use of neuropsychological tests
		I. Neuropsychologist
		II. Cognitive assessments
		   A. Formal
		   B. Informal
		   C. Functional interpretations
		III. Counseling options
		IV. Functional manifestations and neuropsychological issues
		   A. Arithmetic
		     1. Computation (written)
		     2. Reasoning (oral)
		   B. Attention and concentration
		     1. Immediate
		     2. Sustained
		   C. Language
		     1. Word finding
		     2. Oral fluency
		     3. Auditory comprehension
		     4. Handwriting accuracy
		   D. Spelling
		   E. Reading accuracy and comprehension

continues

Table 7-3 continued

Purpose	Learning Objectives	Subject Content Areas
		F. Learning and memory 　1. Auditory memory 　2. Visual memory 　3. Remote memory/ fund of information G. Motor 　1. Right- and left-handed motor speed/dexterity 　2. Grip strength 　3. Bilateral coordination H. Reasoning 　1. Common sense, judgment of safety 　2. Logical deductive reasoning 　3. Hypothesis testing I. Visual skills 　1. Perception 　2. Construction J. Qualitative aspects of performance 　1. Error recognition 　2. Error correction 　3. Mental flexibility 　4. Organization 　5. Planning 　6. Rate of information processing K. Executive deficits
To create an awareness of the psychosocial issues that may result from traumatic brain injury	Explain psychosocial issues that individuals with traumatic brain injury may experience Discuss how to recognize the symptoms of psychosocial problems Describe strategies that may be used in managing psychosocial issues	I. Identification A. Depression B. Aggressive behavior C. Dysfunctional family systems D. Impaired self-awareness E. Substance abuse F. Lack of friendship II. Managing psychosocial issues
To develop an understanding of the impact of traumatic brain injury on a family system	After reviewing current literature, cite several studies of parent, spouse, and offspring perspectives and interpret the findings in terms of the impact that traumatic brain injury has on significant others and family systems Describe how the family system/environment to which a person is returning can positively or adversely affect the extent of ongoing improvement	I. Impact of traumatic brain injury on family system A. Coping B. Adjusting II. Special needs of family members III. Family assessment and interview

Table 7-3 Continued

Purpose	Learning Objectives	Subject Content Areas
	Identify ways to determine when it is necessary to refer the individual to a professional to address the special needs of parents, spouse, and children	IV. Family dynamics A. Preinjury B. Postinjury V. Family counseling VI. Family resources
	Discuss some of the problems that significant others may face and some possible advice that can be given to them	
	Describe the components of an approach that may be used when assessing a family's needs and developing rehabilitation strategies	
	Explain how exploration of preinjury family dynamics can be useful during vocational planning and implementation	
	Identify local resources to which family members may be referred (e.g., medical, psychological, recreational, financial, legal, and respite services)	

tate effective job placement. In addition, and unlike supported employment for many other populations, implementation of supported employment for persons with traumatic brain injury may require more intensive job seeking and acquisition skills. Resume preparation, career guidance, and consumer participation in job development are emphasized in this subject area. Job site training issues such as the need for job site adaptations or modifications and compensatory strategies are included in this area as well. Strategies for job retention such as proactive and ongoing follow-along methods and general vocational and therapeutic counseling techniques should also be delineated.

Case Management

Traumatic brain injury requires substantial coordination of services and resources. Table 7-5 describes fully the content matter related to effective case management services for people with traumatic brain injury. There is often a paucity of services available at the local and state levels. This subject area should therefore identify existing resources and strategies for developing new resources for individuals and their families. This may include unconventional uses of private and public fiscal resources, redefinition of traditional roles of related service personnel, and initiation of new programs.

Educational and Skills Training Opportunities

Opportunities for training are provided through college and nondegree programs. Descriptions of each approach for personnel preparation are provided below.

College Preparatory

In the late 1980s, the Department of Education funded several master's-level programs to prepare supported employment personnel (e.g., Virginia Commonwealth University, the University of Illinois, and the University of Oregon). These programs generally were designed to prepare advanced supported employment specialists or program managers. Most of the programs still exist. Commonly a 39- to 42-credit hour program consisting of general education or rehabilitation principles, applied behavioral analysis and instruction, and business administration courses is offered at the master's level.

There has been continuing discussion about the need for an employment specialist to have a master's degree. The consensus now is that a master's degree is not required (nor is it supported financially by rehabilitation agencies). Currently, efforts are underway to develop and demonstrate the effectiveness of bachelor's and community college degree programs (e.g., in

Table 7-4 Implementation of Supported Employment for Persons with Traumatic Brain Injury

Purpose	Learning Objectives	Subject Content Areas

To develop a general knowledge of skills needed to implement intake and assessment procedures for persons with traumatic brain injury returning to new or former employment	List 8 critical factors that may be examined for effective case planning and for each factor state 2 questions that may determine whether a consumer is at risk in the area
	Define consumer assessment activities by identifying 3 approaches that can be used to gather information and formulate a vocational goal
	Contrast assessment activities utilized in return to new or former employment
	Describe each component of a functional resume and discuss its usefulness to program participants
		I. Intake process
		  A. Critical factors
		  B. Records review
		II. Assessment
		  A. Home visit
		  B. Situational assessments
		  C. Medical evaluation
		  D. Neuropsychological evaluation
		  E. Other assessment methods
		III. Developing vocational goals
		  A. Functional resume
		  B. Career guidance

To develop a general knowledge of job development activities with emphasis on consumer participation and skills needed to locate community-based employment opportunities for persons with traumatic brain injury	Define job development by stating the 3 primary activities involved in the process
	Describe procedures for performing job market screening and development of a marketing plan
	State 10 ways to identify job vacancies
	Show a knowledge of helpful hints for making telephone contact by viewing a videotape of a conversation and critiquing it
	Demonstrate the ability to communicate effectively with an employer by participating in a role play that follows the framework for conducting a presentation and providing rebuttals to difficult employer questions
		I. Job development
		  A. Job market screening
		  B. Marketing strategies
		  C. Employer contact
		    1. Types
		    2. Presentation
		II. Consumer initiated job development

To develop a general knowledge of job placement techniques and skills associated with performing job analysis and placing a person with traumatic brain injury in new employment or assist with return to former employment	When given tools used to record job analysis information, demonstrate the ability to complete each
	List 9 of 12 critical issues to consider at job placement and for each give at least 2 considerations
	Describe guidelines that an employment specialist may use before, during, and after a consumer job interview
	Discuss techniques used with persons who continually refuse job opportunities
	Demonstrate the ability to hold a preemployment conference by role playing the process and completing the contract
	State activities that should be performed to ensure a successful first day of work
		I. Job preplacement activities
		  A. Job analysis
		  B. Critical issues to consider
		  C. Job interview
		II. Job postplacement activities
		  A. Preemployment conference
		  B. Preparation for first day at work
		III. Return to former employment
		  A. Role of employment specialist
		  B. Establishing training criteria
		  C. Legal issues

Table 7-4 continued

Purpose	Learning Objectives	Subject Content Areas

To develop a general knowledge of job site training strategies with emphasis on consumer involvement in selection and data collection techniques that may be implemented to ensure that an individual with traumatic brain injury learns job tasks and meets production standards
 	
To become familiar with the application of rehabilitation engineering at employment sites
 	
To become aware of strategies to use when attempting to resolve behaviors that may impede successful employment
 	
To understand when to fade from a job site
 	
To become familiar with and acquire a skill for consumer advocacy
	Demonstrate the ability to write a task analysis and record data
	Show an ability to assess, design, and implement a program to increase an individual's production level
	Discuss the need for and ways to determine individual training techniques used during job site training
	Describe techniques/strategies that may be used to enhance learning for persons with various cognitive impairments
	Demonstrate an ability to implement compensatory strategies (adaptation, modification, and job restriction) by responding to case scenarios that outline potential issues and suggest resolutions
	Describe guidelines used when developing compensatory strategies
	Evaluate at least 5 sets of job site training data and determine whether and what kind of intervention may be required
	Describe behaviors that may impede successful employment and strategies that may be used to resolve the problem behavior
	Demonstrate the ability to collect and analyze behavior data
	When given a case scenario, design a behavioral contract
	Describe how to determine when the employment specialist may begin to fade from training activities
	When given job site training data, develop and define a schedule for fading off the job site
	When provided with individual case scenarios, express ways that an employment specialist could advocate
		I. Job site skills acquisition training
		  A. Task analysis
		  B. Systematic instruction
		  C. Reinforcement
		  D. Data collection
		II. Production training
		  A. Determining rate
		  B. Increasing rate
		III. General training techniques
		  A. Approaches to alleviate cognitive dysfunction
		  B. Use of compensatory strategies, adaptations, and modifications
		IV. Behavioral counseling
		  A. Strategies to succeed
		  B. Data collection
		  C. Contracting
		V. Fading techniques
		VI. Advocacy

To develop a general knowledge of follow-along activities and skills needed to identify job retention issues and implement potential resolutions	State areas that may require ongoing assessment
	Recognize considerations to take into account when determining the level of follow-along
	Describe formal and informal methods of providing follow-along services
	When given issues that may arise during follow-along, describe data collection techniques with emphasis on issues to investigate and possible strategies to use
	Discuss the need for providing proactive follow-along/job retention services
	State the activities that an employment specialist should complete at separation from employment
	Describe the purpose of the exit interview
		I. Follow-along areas of ongoing assessment
		II. Determining levels of intervention
		III. Methods
		  A. Formal
		  B. Informal
		IV. Issues to investigate
		  A. Data collection
		  B. Strategies
		V. Separation

continues

Table 7-4 continued

Purpose	Learning Objectives	Subject Content Areas
To become aware of general counseling techniques	Demonstrate the ability to counsel individuals with traumatic brain injury State what steps to follow in case of suicide threat Describe signs that may indicate that an individual should be referred for professional counseling	I. Counseling II. Referral to professional counseling

Utah and North Carolina). The content of these undergraduate programs generally mirrors that proposed above with the exception of the specialty area.

Nondegree Training Programs

By far, the majority of supported employment personnel hold no supported employment degree. As a result of the diverse backgrounds of incumbent personnel, nondegree programs such as 1- to 3-day workshops, video and audio teleconferences, and 1- to 2-week course institutes are the most commonly utilized approaches to training.

Workshops lasting 1 to 3 days bring personnel together to participate in lectures, discussions, small group activities, and clinical experiences.

Table 7-5 Case Management

Purpose	Learning Objectives	Subject Content Areas

To become aware of community resources to which persons with traumatic brain injury may be referred	Analyze information collected during intake/assessment in an effort to uncover needs for services and to determine the need for referral to community resources
	List and describe the roles of agencies and organizations that may be able to meet individual case management needs
	Describe effective methods for coordinating services
	Describe the types of scenarios that may arise and develop a list of resources that may be needed during crisis management
	Discuss how to organize efforts to promote systems change to improve service delivery and create new resources
	Describe creative funding methods that may be used for provision of services
		I. Needs assessment
		II. Identification of resources
		  A. National Head Injury Foundation
		  B. Adult protective services
		  C. Centers for independent living
		  D. Medical
		  E. Vocational
		  F. Residential
		  G. Recreational
		  H. Financial
		  I. Transportation
		  J. Education
		  K. Counseling
		  L. Other
		III. Coordination of services
		IV. Crisis management
		V. Legislation
		VI. Creative funding
		  A. Plan to achieve self-support
		  B. Private foundations
		  C. Third party payers
		  D. Interagency funding coalitions
		  E. Other

These short, intense sessions can bring together various knowledgeable instructors and a diverse student group, thus supporting the sharing of regional ideas and approaches. A typical agenda and needs assessment for such a workshop is shown in Exhibits 7-4 and 7-5. These workshops can lay a foundation for more intensive skill training.

Longer training programs are generally formatted as course institutes, where participants come together for a week or longer. The advantage of institutes is that they provide much more of an opportunity for meaningful, hands-on experience to support theoretical material. For example, usually institute participants work with a supported employment provider and actually

Exhibit 7-4 Supported Employment Training Program in Traumatic Brain Injury

Program Description

This 3-day training program is designed for rehabilitation professionals (program managers, employment specialists, rehabilitation counselors, and case managers) who want to learn about supported employment services for persons with traumatic brain injury. Nationally recognized experts will present detailed instruction in how to implement the individual placement model of supported employment, job placement, and job site trianing as well as the role of compensatory strategies on the job site, interpreting a neuropsychological assessment, case management issues, and the impact of substance abuse on employment. Didactic lectures, case studies, and small group activities will be used. Opportunities to problem solve and network with other supported employment service providers will be encouraged.

Program Agenda

Day One
Overview

8:00–8:30 a.m.	Registration (coffee and bakeries)
8:30–9:00 a.m.	Introduction/needs assessment
9:00–9:45 a.m.	Past, present, and future: Supported employment for persons with traumatic brain injury
9:45–10:30 a.m.	Overview of traumatic brain injury
10:45–11:15 a.m.	Traumatic brain injury and vocational rehabilitation
11:15–11:45 a.m.	Funding limitations in traumatic brain injury: Can rehabilitation professionals effect policy change?
11:45 a.m.	Lunch (on your own)

Assessment

1:15–1:45 p.m.	Medical evaluations for employment that are relevant to the real world
1:45–2:45 p.m.	Cognitive, emotional, and behavioral assessment: Tips from a neuropsychologist
3:00–4:30 p.m.	Setting up and conducting situational assessments (case study activity)
4:30 p.m.	Wrap-up

Day Two
Implementation

9:00–10:45 a.m.	Job development and job placement
11:00–12:00 p.m.	Job site training: Job restructuring, assistive technology, and compensatory strategies
12:00 p.m.	Lunch (on your own)
1:30–3:00 p.m.	Job site training (case study activity)
3:15–4:00 p.m.	Follow-along: Issues and solutions
4:00–5:00 p.m.	Psychosocial issues that affect employment: Family, substance abuse, criminal behavior
5:00–6:30 p.m.	RECEPTION

Day Three
Issues

9:00–10:30 a.m.	Case management/advocacy: What are the limits of a job coach?
10:45–11:30 a.m.	Consumer feedback panel
11:30–12:00 p.m.	Closing activity
12:00 p.m.	Wrap-up/evaluation

Source: Workshop Agenda, Presented by Rehabilitation Research & Training Center on Severe Traumatic Brain Injury, Medical College of Virginia in conjunction with Rehabilitation Research & Training Center on Supported Employment, Virginia Commonwealth University, and the Association for Persons in Supported Employment, Richmond, VA.

Exhibit 7-5 Needs Assessment for Traumatic Brain Injury Training

Name: _____ Employer: _____
　　　　　　　　　　　(Optional)　　　　　　　　　　　　　　　　　　　　　　　(Optional)
Position: _____ Length of Employment: _____
Length of time involved in implementing supported employment: _____
State your areas of expertise in model implementation: _____
_____

Briefly describe your experience implementing supported employment for persons who have traumatic brain injury:
_____
_____

Please state three questions or issues you would like to have addressed during the training:
_____
_____
_____

Read the following training content areas and rate your knowledge/experience in each.
1 = No knowledge/experience, 2 = Some knowledge/experience, 3 = Very knowledgeable/experienced/no training desired

I.   Overview of Traumatic Brain Injury

The extent of traumatic brain injury in the United States

1	2	3
No knowledge	Some knowledge	Very knowledgeable/no training desired

How the unimpaired nervous system functions

1	2	3
No knowledge	Some knowledge	Very knowledgeable/no training desired

How an injury to the head can lead to diffuse and secondary brain damage

1	2	3
No knowledge	Some knowledge	Very knowledgeable/no training desired

Awareness of the service delivery system and the role of professionals that attend to patients who sustain traumatic brain injury

1	2	3
No knowledge	Some knowledge	Very knowledgeable/no training desired

Familiarity with the role of physiatrist and the need for long term follow-up services

1	2	3
No knowledge	Some knowledge	Very knowledgeable/no training desired

Specialty and medical terminology often used in medical evaluations and reports

1	2	3
No knowledge	Some knowledge	Very knowledgeable/no training desired

What types of medical issues and physical disabilities may result from traumatic brain injury

1	2	3
No knowledge	Some knowledge	Very knowledgeable/no training desired

Types of cognitive deficits that may result from traumatic brain injury

1	2	3
No knowledge	Some knowledge	Very knowledgeable/no training desired

Familiarity with formal and informal ways to assess cognitive function

1	2	3
No knowledge	Some knowledge	Very knowledgeable/no training desired

A skill for functional interpretation of neuropsychological test results

1	2	3
No knowledge	Some knowledge	Very knowledgeable/no training desired

Types of cognitive deficits that may result from traumatic brain injury

1	2	3
No knowledge	Some knowledge	Very knowledgeable/no training desired

Exhibit 7-5 continued

Awareness of the psychosocial issues that may result from traumatic brain injury

1	2	3
No knowledge	Some knowledge	Very knowledgeable/no training desired

Understanding of the impact traumatic brain injury has on a family system

1	2	3
No knowledge	Some knowledge	Very knowledgeable/no training desired

II. Implementation of Supported Employment for Persons with Traumatic Brain Injury

Skills needed to implement intake and assessment procedures for persons with traumatic brain injury

1	2	3
No knowledge	Some knowledge	Very knowledgeable/no training desired

Developing a general knowledge of skills needed to implement intake and assessment procedures for persons returning to former employment following traumatic brain injury

1	2	3
No knowledge	Some knowledge	Very knowledgeable/no training desired

Implementation of job development activities with emphasis on consumer participation and skills needed to locate community-based employment opportunities for persons with traumatic brain injury

1	2	3
No knowledge	Some knowledge	Very knowledgeable/no training desired

Job placement techniques and skills associated with performing job analysis and placing a person with traumatic brain injury

1	2	3
No knowledge	Some knowledge	Very knowledgeable/no training desired

Job placement techniques and skills associated with performing job analysis and returning a person with traumatic brain injury back to former employment

1	2	3
No knowledge	Some knowledge	Very knowledgeable/no training desired

Job site training strategies, with emphasis on consumer involvement in selection and data collection techniques that may be implemented to ensure an individual with traumatic brain injury learns jobs tasks and meets production standards

1	2	3
No knowledge	Some knowledge	Very knowledgeable/no training desired

Familiarity with the application of rehabilitation engineering at employment sites

1	2	3
No knowledge	Some knowledge	Very knowledgeable/no training desired

Strategies to use when attempting to resolve behaviors which may impede successful employment

1	2	3
No knowledge	Some knowledge	Very knowledgeable/no training desired

Fading from a job site

1	2	3
No knowledge	Some knowledge	Very knowledgeable/no training desired

Acquiring a skill for consumer advocacy

1	2	3
No knowledge	Some knowledge	Very knowledgeable/no training desired

Implementing follow-along activities and skills needed to identify job retention issues and implement potential resolution

1	2	3
No knowledge	Some knowledge	Very knowledgeable/no training desired

III. Case Management

Awareness of community resources to which persons who sustain traumatic brain injury may be referred

1	2	3
No knowledge	Some knowledge	Very knowledgeable/no training desired

Exhibit 7-5 continued

Awareness of the role of the employment specialist in case management

1	2	3
No knowledge	Some knowledge	Very knowledgeable/no training desired

During training which instructional style do you prefer?

_____ Lecture

_____ Lecture with visual media (slides, video, and overheads)

_____ Lecture with visual media and group activities

_____ Other (please describe) _____

Why would you be motivated to attend a 2-day training session on implementing supported employment for individuals who sustained traumatic brain injury?

_____

_____

_____

_____

implement the components of the supported employment model.

Face-to-face workshops and institutes are valuable and a preferred method of training but have inherent logistical and fiscal problems associated with them. Participants must often leave their home communities and workstations, incur travel and per diem expenses, and lose the benefit of learning with their local peers. Audio and video teleconferencing provides an alternative to face-to-face training. Typically, a national or regional organization sponsors either ad hoc or sequenced televised instruction, which is viewed in multiple sites across the country. Most often these telecasts are live and interactive, allowing the students to ask questions and discuss their views on presented topics. One such program, the Supported Employment Telecourse Network (SET NET) at Virginia Commonwealth University, has been performing this type of training since 1988. Although this methodology can be very cost effective, disadvantages include the inability of the televising institution to ensure quality practice at receiving locations. Additionally, because the number of people trained at once can exceed 1,000, the variability of needs presents special instruction challenges. The instruction provided via the television, however, can be integrated with on-site and clinical training to reinforce the principles learned.

Clinical Experiences

Regardless of the type of training, it is imperative that didactic information be supported with hands-on experience. Learners should be paired with other experienced employment staff so that knowledge can be developed into practiced skills. For example, learners should have the opportunity to meet with real employers under actual job development conditions while they are under the tutelage of seasoned personnel. Likewise, job site training skills should first be performed with the assistance of someone who has trained individuals on a variety of job sites.

CONCLUSION

Supported employment emerged because there were thousands of people with severe mental disabilities who were viewed as incapable of working by most service providers and in many cases, advocates. Their options in life were to be in day programs, adult activity centers, or sheltered workshops, to stay at home, or perhaps even live in institutions. In the mid to late 1970s, a number of professionals began to experiment with different ways of providing services. The reason for this experimentation was primarily to meet a need. The need was for people to realize that all persons have the right to obtain competitive employment, earn a decent wage, and develop a "real work" history. The roots of supported employment are deeply entwined in an individual's interests, choices, and need for inclusion. These roots are what has made supported employment one of the most popular and sustainable programs in the United States.

A major focus of supported employment is to use a proactive approach to problem resolution in an attempt to increase job retention. For example, job placement procedures are currently being modified to take a more in-depth look at a number of factors in the employment setting, such as a change in task criteria, employment culture, and client aspirations and preferences. Careful attention to these factors will provide a more thorough method of job analysis. This approach, combined with continued employer education and building naturalistic supports at work, will improve retention rates. Consumer assessment activities are also being modified in an effort to better define the characteristics of the type of job each consumer prefers. In addition, it is not unusual for an individual to have a myriad of case management issues present upon referral (e.g., substance abuse, an unstable housing situation, etc.) that the employment specialist must address. It is believed that further support and resource development outside the workplace will significantly improve retention rates as well.

Another complication is that program participants are often referred to vocational services many years post-injury, and at this point there is usually little if any possibility of returning to former employment. In such instances positive and optimistic attitudes toward effective inpatient and outpatient referral processes may provide greater opportunities for returning to the pre-injury employment situation. It should also be noted that the majority of program participants are young males with a normal life expectancy, so it is only natural that their employment preferences and aspirations will change over time. Services and funding must be available for future changes in employment status that are likely to occur.

Outcome reports from the VCU/MCV supported employment project for persons with TBI have been optimistic. These reports have generally indicated that participants have achieved employment earnings and work hours comparable to their pre-injury status (Wehman, Kreutzer, West et al., 1990). Frequent work-related problems and job separations have occurred (Sale et al., 1991), however participants who have continued involvement with the program have generally maintained stability in the workforce and most have become reemployed following job loss (Wehman, Kreutzer, West et al., 1989; Wehman et al., 1989). Programs should continue to develop, implement, and test the effectiveness of a variety of job placement and retention strategies. Future programs and research should strive to refine the current models to meet the unique challenges posed by traumatic brain injury.

REFERENCES

Booth, M. (1991). C.P. Case Study. Unpublished manuscript.

Brooks, N., McKinlay, W., Symington, C., Beattie, A., & Campsie, L. (1987). Return to work within the first seven years after head injury. *Brain Injury, 1*, 5–19.

Cope, N., & Hall, K. (1982). Head injury rehabilitation—Benefit of early intervention. *Archives of Physical Medicine and Rehabilitation, 63*, 433–437.

Everson, J.M., & Brooke, V. (1990). Training job coaches to serve employees with multiple and low-incidence disabilities: Implications for the 1990s. *Rehabilitation Education, 4*, 287–300.

Federal Register. (1987, August 14). Washington, DC: U.S. Government Printing Office.

Goodall, P., Groah, C., Sherron, P., Kreutzer, J., & Wehman, P. (1991). *Supported employment services for individuals with traumatic brain injury: A guide for service providers.* Richmond, VA: Virginia Commonwealth University Rehabilitation Research and Training Center on Supported Employment.

Griffin, S.L., & Revell, W.G. (1991). *Rehabilitation counselor: Desk top guide to supported employment* (pp. 38–41). Richmond, VA: Virginia Commonwealth University Rehabilitation Research and Training Center on Supported Employment.

Kay, T., Ezrachi, O., & Cavallo, M. (1986). *Annotated bibliography of research on vocational outcome following head trauma.* New York: New York University Head Trauma Center.

Peck, G., Fulton, C., Cohen, C., Warren, J.R., & Antonello, J. (1984). Neuropsychological, physical and psychological factors affecting long-term vocational outcomes following severe head injury. Paper presented at the annual meeting of the International Neuropsychological Society, Houston, TX.

Sale, P. (1990). Preparation of supported employment personnel. In A.P. Kaiser & C.M. McWhorter (Eds.), *Preparing personnel to work with persons with severe disabilities* (pp. xx–xx). Baltimore: Brookes.

Sale, P. (1991a). *Preferred characteristics of job site intervention.* Unpublished manuscript.

Sale, P. (1991b). Staffing and recruiting for supported employment. In P. Wehman, P. Sale, & W. Parent (Eds.), *Supported employment* (pp. 263–283). Stoneham, MA: Andover Medical.

Sale, P., West, M., Sherron, P., & Wehman, P. (1991). Exploratory analysis of job separations from supported employment for persons with traumatic brain injury. *Journal of Head Trauma Rehabilitation, 6*(3), 1–11.

Wehman, P., & Goodall, P. (1990). Return to work: Critical issues in employment. In P. Wehman & J.S. Kreutzer (Eds.), *Vocational rehabilitation for persons with traumatic brain injury* (pp. 1–16). Gaithersburg, MD: Aspen.

Wehman, P., & Kregel, J. (1985). A supported work approach to competitive employment of individuals with moderate and severe handicaps. *Journal of the Association for Persons with Severe Handicaps, 10,* 3–11.

Wehman, P., & Kreutzer, J.S. (1990). *Vocational rehabilitation for persons with traumatic brain injury.* Gaithersburg, MD: Aspen.

Wehman, P., Kreutzer, J., Sale, P., Morton, M., Diambra, J., & West, M. (1989). Cognitive impairment and remediation: Implications for employment following traumatic brain injury. *Journal of Head Trauma Rehabilitation, 4*(3), 66–75.

Wehman, P., Kreutzer, J., West, M., Sherron, P., Zasler, N., Groah, C., Stonnington, H., Burns, C., & Sale, P. (1990). Return to work for persons with traumatic brain injury: A supported employment approach. *Archives of Physical Medicine and Rehabilitation, 71*(13), 1047–1052.

Wehman, P., Kreutzer, J.S., Stonnington, H.H., Wood, W., Sherron, P., Diambra, J., Fry, R., & Groah, C. (1988). Supported employment for persons with traumatic brain injury: A preliminary report. *Journal of Head Trauma Rehabilitation, 3,* 82–94.

Wehman, P., Kreutzer, J., West, M., Sherron, P., Diambra, J., Fry, R., Groah, C., Sale, P., & Killam, S. (1989). Employment outcomes of persons following traumatic brain injury: Preinjury, postinjury, and supported employment. *Brain Injury, 3,* 397–412.

Resources for Information about Supported Employment and Traumatic Brain Injury

Research and Training Center on Improving Supported Employment Outcomes for Individuals with Developmental and Other Severe Disabilities
    Virginia Commonwealth University
    School of Education
    MCV Box 568
    Richmond, VA 23284
    Objective: To improve employment outcomes for individuals with developmental and other severe disabilities

Research and Training Center on Severe Traumatic Brain Injury
    Virginia Commonwealth University
    Medical College of Virginia
    Box 568 MCV Station
    Richmond, VA 23298
    Objective: To generate data to develop a program for delivery of innovative services to individuals with severe brain injury

A Comprehensive Model of Research and Rehabilitation for the Traumatically Brain Injured
    Virginia Commonwealth University
    Medical College of Virginia
    Box 568 MCV Station
    Richmond, VA 23298
    Objective: To establish a new database and evaluate new techniques for rehabilitation of persons with brain injuries

Model Project for Comprehensive Rehabilitation Services to Individuals with Traumatic Brain Injury
    Mt. Sinai Medical Center
    School of Medicine
    One Gustave L. Levy Place
    New York, NY 10029
    Objective: To propose a model system for rehabilitation services for persons with traumatic brain injury

Southeastern Michigan Traumatic Brain Injury
System
  Wayne State University Medical Center
  Rehabilitation Institute of Detroit
  Detroit, MI 48202
  Objective: To demonstrate and evaluate a
model service delivery system for individuals
with traumatic brain injury

Medical Research and Training Center in
Traumatic Brain Injury
  University of Washington
  Department of Rehabilitation Medicine
  BB919 Health Science Building
  Seattle, WA 98195
  Objective: To establish a rehabilitation
research and training center in traumatic brain
injury

Research and Training Center on Head Injury
and Stroke
  New York University Medical Center
  Department of Physical Medicine
  400 East 34th Street
  New York, NY 10016
  Objective: To provide a rehabilitation
research and training center for head trauma
and stroke

Research and Training Center for Community
Integration of Persons with Traumatic Brain
Injury

State University of New York (SUNY)/
  Buffalo
  197 Farber Hall
  3435 Main Street
  Buffalo, NY 14214
  Objective: To establish a research and
training center on community integration of
persons with traumatic brain injury

Research and Training Center in Improving the
Management of Rehabilitation Information
Systems
  West Virginia University
  West Virginia Division of Rehabilitation
    Services
  Charleston, WV 25305
  Objective: To develop a program for needs
analysis, program development, and training in
rehabilitation technology

Model Family-Professional Partnership
Interventions for Childhood Traumatic Brain
Injury
  New York State Head Injury Association
  Office of the Executive Director
  194 Washington Avenue
  Albany, NY 12210
  Objective: To model family-professional
partnership interventions for childhood
traumatic brain injury

Training and Development of Residential Staff in Community Integrated Programs

8

Charles J. Durgin

Nancy D. Schmidt

Patricia L. Kerrigan

OBJECTIVES

After completing this chapter, the reader will be able to:

1. define the importance of the residential staff member's role in the rehabilitation process
2. identify psychological barriers that can impede residential staff performance
3. specify organizational and support system variables that present barriers to staff effectiveness
4. describe training and organizational development strategies that can be used to improve staff attitudes, knowledge, and skills
5. outline the benefits of using a competency-based training model with residential staff
6. identify competency areas that can be used to develop a training curriculum for application in community integrated programs

Training and Development of Residential Staff in Community Integrated Programs

Many human service agencies have come to rely on staff who are not professionally trained to enhance the range and quality of services offered. These staff members historically have been referred to as paraprofessionals and typically perform a number of roles critical to the success of treatment programs.

Paraprofessionals are used extensively in the field of rehabilitation and are assigned a wide variety of responsibilities and job titles (e.g., Life Skills Teacher, Residential Counselor, Daily Living Technician, Clinical Assistant, etc.). Although the primary focus of this chapter is on enhancing residential staff performance, the training principles and methods outlined are applicable to all program staff.

This chapter discusses the critical role that residential staff play in community integrated programs, analyzes staff development and performance barriers that residential staff commonly face, discusses training and program development strategies that can remove barriers to staff performance, and reviews a competency-based training model for helping residential staff improve their job performance as well as their overall job satisfaction.

STAFF ROLES

In their discussion of the use of paraprofessionals in rehabilitation counseling, Crisler and Young (1987) suggest that paraprofessionals may differ from professionally trained staff in a number of dimensions. For example, compared to their professional counterparts, paraprofessionals typically have less formal training and credentialing, receive less compensation, and are assumed to perform less complex tasks. Furthermore, a common role distinction made in the literature between professional and paraprofessional staff is as follows. The professional ensures a complete evaluation, synthesizes and integrates data, and evaluates the effectiveness of interventions on the basis of relevant theory. The paraprofessional primarily performs clearly defined tasks that are based on his or her experience level under the direction of a professionally trained staff member (Auvenshine, 1971; Wright & Fraser, 1976).

It is not unusual for experienced paraprofessional staff eventually to play significant clinical, administrative, management, and leadership roles in the daily operations of rehabilitation facilities. This includes staff who over time acquire credentials through formal education in addition to those who develop valuable skills through their personal dedication and experience. Nevertheless, most paraprofessional staff working in rehabilitation programs do not achieve on this level or make this type of personal commitment. They frequently contribute to the organization for a relatively short period of time and then move on to another position or return to school.

Consequently, the training model chosen needs to support skill development for persons who are content to view their position more as an interesting job or a work opportunity as well as for those who are on a well defined career path. For those staff with a high degree of internal motivation and with human service career aspirations, training will offer focus, resources, and direction to supplement their initiative. For all participants, the training offers structure and support to ensure that they develop the knowledge and skills necessary to be effective in their roles.

TERMINOLOGY AND ORGANIZATIONAL STATUS

The terminology used to describe staff working in rehabilitation is often confusing. To eliminate this confusion, in this chapter we make the following distinctions. Those individuals who have received formal professional training in a specific discipline (e.g., neuropsychology, physical therapy, occupational therapy, vocational counseling, etc.) are referred to as clinical staff. As a group these individuals provide the majority of their services in day treatment and community settings during traditional work hours. Residential staff are referred to as such and are defined as those individuals who for the most part have not completed professional training and are primarily involved in supporting the residential and community integration services provided outside the clinical day.

This choice of terminology is in no way meant to imply that residential staff do not play a significant role in helping clients achieve clinical objectives. On the contrary, residential staff are crucial to the successful delivery of comprehensive services to persons with brain injury. It is, however, our preference to avoid whenever possible use of the terms *professional* and *paraprofessional* to distinguish between these two groups because the connotations of the term *paraprofessional* may to some extent diminish the perceived importance of support staff in rehabilitation. We wish to advocate a program ethic that recognizes the positive and valued contributions of all persons involved in the diverse operations of rehabilitation programs.

RESIDENTIAL TREATMENT AND THE THERAPEUTIC MILIEU

The most successful rehabilitation programs integrate treatment, intervention, and support into a larger service delivery model. This level of integration is particularly important for servicing people with acquired cognitive impairments. These individuals often are confused, misjudge their own abilities, are under a high degree of psychological stress, and may need to relearn basic living tasks and to develop skills for adaptive community living (work, school, shopping, etc.). The structure and support of the residential environment, which is one critical component of the therapeutic milieu, can offer a great deal of assistance to clients in these and other critical areas of rehabilitation.

Milieu therapy encompasses all aspects of treatment from the physical environment to client, family, staff, and community contacts. Milieu treatment is both complex and dynamic in nature. The structure and tone of the treatment setting are constantly changing given the needs of the clients and the experience levels and clinical biases of the staff.

To be responsive to changing clinical needs, the treatment setting requires a high degree of communication among all staff members at all points in time. Staff, in collaboration with clients and families, need to define explicitly the priority treatment goals and to review progress systematically across all settings. Care must be taken to ensure that all clients receive individualized treatment that is based on their unique needs. Central to making this treatment approach work successfully is having each staff member gain an understanding of the various disciplines and how each individual staff member brings valuable skills and perspectives to the therapeutic process.

If the rehabilitation program is to create a potent learning environment, it is critical that the service delivery model be formally designed to provide a high degree of staff collaboration throughout all program components. This can be facilitated through ongoing strategic planning sessions, integrated documentation systems, cotreatment, team meetings, training, supervisory supports, and effective policy and procedure development. Clinical continuity will help provide the client with an environment that offers consistent feedback and support from all staff and will ensure that treatment efforts are directed toward the most critical areas that present the greatest barriers to successful community living.

There are many characteristics of the residential staff role that make it an important one within the rehabilitation process. For example, residential staff routinely observe clients in a wide variety of settings (residence, clinic, community, work, etc.). Carefully observing client functioning in these settings is critical because people with brain injury frequently respond differently in situations that provide various levels of structure, stimulation, and stress.

Defining these performance variations and providing training in these settings are crucial if we are truly working to help clients adapt to the demands of the real world. Residential staff in many ways are in the best position to describe behavioral inconsistencies and to implement interventions to assist the individual in compensating for problems. As illustrated in Figure 8-1, direct involvement of residential staff with clients encompasses all aspects of the clients' lives, including interpersonal relationships, community contacts, and the performance of the functional living skills that clients need to become more self-sufficient.

Compared to other program personnel, residential staff have more continuous contact hours with clients. Although demanding, this experience has a number of clinical benefits. It provides the opportunity to:

- evaluate the level of supervision needed for clients to be safe at home and in the community
- determine the expected level of assistance that clients need to perform specific life skills tasks (use of adaptive equipment, memory aids, task sheets, etc.)
- assess adaptive behaviors that are difficult to evaluate in structured day programs (fatigue, use of free time, initiation, ability to

self-medicate, social judgment, emotional and behavioral control, etc.)

- evaluate the anticipated burden on family members in light of clients' presenting problems
- assess the ability of clients to learn and generalize the skills being taught in various settings and situations

Sustained contact over time in less formal clinical environments also provides the opportunity for residential staff to develop a strong therapeutic relationship with clients. This can be a valuable source of support to clients and families as they strive to adjust to the demands that brain injury places on the family system. A positive therapeutic rapport can develop only if the relationship between client and staff is professionally healthy. Staff therefore must provide support and encouragement to the family, maintain professional boundaries, and act within the scope of their role within the organization.

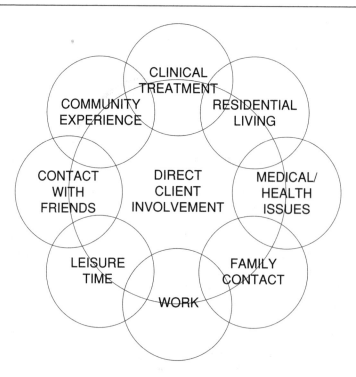

Figure 8-1 Direct involvement of residential staff with clients encompasses all aspects of clients' lives

When staff step outside their role in these areas, it can create problems for all involved.

From a clinical perspective, it is also important to recognize that it is often easier for clients to understand the impact of their injury when they experience problems in their day-to-day living. This may include burning dinner, losing personal belongings, getting lost in the community, being unable to sleep, experiencing repeated interpersonal conflicts, and eating excessively, to name a few. Acquired problems frequently are easier for clients to understand in these situations than when they are simply discussed in the abstract, as often occurs during the clinical day.

The skilled residential staff member, with direction and support from the clinical team, can help the client connect the relevance of the clinical focus with real life experiences. A central element of this staff collaboration is formal communication and documentation systems that ensure that the observations made by residential staff are clearly known to the clinical staff. This permits clinicians to steer clinical treatment toward the most functional problems faced by the client.

It is well known that many people who have sustained a serious brain injury will not be able to resume their previous lifestyle. Often the greatest accomplishments take place in areas such as improving social skills and community mobility, making productive use of free time, tolerating help from others when needed, and restoring a sense of self that allows clients to move forward with their lives. Prigatano (1989a) has suggested that neuropsychological recovery needs to include normalized human experiences such as work, love, and play for the client to be able to establish a sense of direction and identity. A structured and well designed residential setting, when integrated with other program and community support systems, has tremendous potential to help clients achieve greater levels of personal competence and self-satisfaction.

Consequently, residential staff play a core role in helping people with brain injury achieve their treatment objectives. Failure to adequately train and support staff within this arena not only will result in a less effective treatment model but

may cause services to be fragmented and disjointed across settings. If this occurs, the program may in effect intensify the frustrations that clients experience and compromise the ability of the program to address individuals' primary barriers to successful community living.

WORKING IN RESIDENTIAL TREATMENT SETTINGS: THE REALITIES

If programs are to develop and retain quality residential staff, the rewards and demands inherent in the position must be recognized. Furthermore, unless one has had the personal experience of working as a residential staff person, it is difficult to appreciate fully the demands of the role.

Appendix 8-1 outlines the results of a survey of 30 residential staff members working in community-based rehabilitation programs (Durgin, Bouchard, & Jones, 1988). Staff were asked about the rewards and demands of working with persons with brain injury by means of an open-ended questionnaire and direct interviews. Appendix 8-1 lists the statements most commonly reported in the categories of rewards and demands.

The primary rewards reported by staff included the following:

- effectively helping others (making a contribution)
- being a part of the team (connectedness to the total program)
- learning on the job (improving skills, opportunities for advancement)
- receiving recognition for providing a valued service (acknowledgment by clients, families, peers, and senior program staff)

The reported demands of the position covered many broad areas of the role:

- dealing with role conflicts (confusion, overload, competing priorities)
- addressing cognitive and behavioral problems of clients (resistance, communication

problems, interpersonal conflicts, behavior management difficulties)

- coping with the psychological demands of the role (client, staff, and organizational stressors)

To illustrate further the demands of the role, Exhibit 8-1 presents segments from incident reports generated by residential staff. This information highlights the difficulties that residential staff face when responding to complex clinical and organizational problems.

The rewards and demands of residential work create a most challenging balance for staff to manage. How do these experiences make staff feel on the job? In many cases, it makes them highly emotional and in need of direction and support from others. Discussed below are common feelings and emotions reported by residential staff.

Strategies to provide staff support as well as to improve technical skills performance are re-

viewed throughout the remainder of this chapter. Ultimately, both areas of staff development— teaching specific skills and providing ongoing staff support—need to be addressed to achieve and maintain optimal staff effectiveness. Understanding staff emotions and the psychological barriers to effective job performance that may result from them will enable senior program staff to develop rehabilitation programs and leadership styles that will remove some of these barriers.

PSYCHOLOGICAL IMPACT OF RESIDENTIAL WORK

Fear

Staff fear in the rehabilitation setting is frequently present yet often goes unaddressed. Perhaps more than for any other emotion, it is difficult for staff to discuss their fear openly. If

Exhibit 8-1 Incident Report Segments

9:00 p.m.—Tom called the apartment and was slurring. He rambled on about "empowerment" and then admitted to being drunk ("I have a buzz on"). He asked that I not report our conversation to the clinicians. After a few minutes I tried to get him to give me a phone number where he could be reached in case of an emergency, and he told me, "Don't worry, I'll be back tomorrow . . . sometime."

2:15 a.m.—I woke Jim to use the bathroom (as scheduled). . . . He left the bathroom and walked into the living room naked and asked for his Sunday morning cigarette. . . . I said he could have his cigarette if he put his shorts on (he did). . . . When he returned he sat on the couch and asked if he could "mess around" with me. I said "NO". . . . (15 minutes later) . . . he came out of his room and took his towel off in front of me . . . and tried to touch me. . . . I stated that this is unacceptable behavior. (30 minutes later) Jim returned from his room (again naked) . . . started rubbing himself and I told him to go to bed. . . . He said "Only if you touch it. I'll go to bed only if you touch it."

8:15 a.m.—Sue (client) was knocking on the bathroom door stating that Lisa (client) had been in there long enough. . . . Lisa left the bathroom and proceeded to their bedroom and locked that door. . . . Sue then knocked on the bedroom door to get something and heard Lisa mumbling "bitch" underneath her breath. The door opened and Sue threw an object at Lisa with a lot of force and Lisa screamed . . . (redirection worked). At 8:25 a.m. both clients were overheard making threats to one another using soft voices. . . . Sue stated "You die . . . tonight you die. . . ." I had a 3-minute talk with Lisa to help her relax . . . then we all got in the van and went to the rehabilitation center.

7:55 p.m.—Bill was in the process of changing his shirt when he called me in his room. He asked me to look at the "bumps" on his shoulder, indicating that he had not noticed this before. Bill became increasing aggravated at this discovery, stating that he was upset with his body. He picked up a hairbrush and started hitting his shoulder, stating that he would "fix the bumps by breaking them." I moved my arm in the way to block the impact and Bill discontinued striking himself. I cued him to relax but on the way out of the bedroom he started repeatedly slamming his shoulder up against the wall. This continued until redirection helped to remove him from the area and to settle down.

Note: the names and some details in these reports have been changed to protect confidentiality.

senior staff make a practice of openly expressing their own fears and concerns, this will often provide an opening for others to discuss sensitive issues. For this to occur, program leaders need to have a strong sense of security in the context of their own abilities and limitations as well as a true understanding of how difficult residential work can be.

Staff fear can have many sources, such as fear of:

- physical injury
- being personally offended by what clients say or do
- reprimands by clients, family members, or management
- not acting in a manner that is consistent with helping clients
- rejection by clients
- making mistakes that are highly visible to others
- working with newly admitted clients who are not well known to staff
- the disability itself

Fear shapes staff actions and can ultimately lead to an unhealthy avoidance of problems. For example, one residential staff member reported that she routinely walked a half-mile out of her way to avoid the possibility of walking by a wheelchair-bound client who often directed profanity toward staff. Fears such as this will often surface in the program in a number of ways, such as an increase in the number of sick days taken, avoidance of taking clients on community outings to prevent public incidents, and staff turnover.

Additionally, most residential staff are women, and their clients often are young men. Understandably, female staff are often concerned about managing sexual advances and behavioral problems in settings without immediate staff back-up. These concerns can result in psychological barriers that may lead to inconsistencies in how staff respond to clients as well as an overall reluctance among staff to speak up about sensitive clinical issues and staff conflicts.

Sadness, Frustration, and Anger

Staff often become discouraged as they grow to be more aware of the serious consequences of brain injury and the limits of their ability to change some of these realities. Most staff have a genuine investment in the clients' well being and will often feel a sense of loss when they see the discrepancy between the clients' goals and abilities.

The psychosocial repercussions of brain injury, which include dependency, egocentricity, irritability, and the frequent need for attention (Lezak, 1988), place substantial pressures on staff as well. Working with people who display these behavioral and interpersonal problems can be draining and eventually may result in high levels of staff frustration and anger.

Poor relationships with clinical team members and management can be an additional source of frustration. If there is a lack of recognition and support, residential staff often feel (and in fact are) set up for failure when asked to work effectively with clients and families while being held accountable for managing diverse residential and community activities (e.g., supporting activities of daily living, maintaining a pleasant and safe environment, transporting clients, etc.).

Reluctance

In many ways residential staff need to be assertive enough to manage groups of clients (many of whom may be impulsive and resistant to feedback) and to have enough guts to disagree with professional staff, who may have long titles and impressive letters after their names. Any one of the emotions discussed above can result in staff reluctance to express their concerns, observations, feelings, opinions, and needs.

Unless supervisors and managers establish a program culture that values staff feedback and trains staff to view conflict as common, expected, and a valuable opportunity to solve problems, many significant clinical and staff difficulties will go unaddressed. Not only does there need to be an explicit value system of open communication and mutual accountability, but it is also critical that the formal organizational structure of the program provide opportunities for staff to discuss problems and to learn strategies to manage stressful situations.

Failure to encourage open communication and to provide regular opportunities to manage conflict will probably create adversarial relationships throughout the treatment setting. Residential staff, like all staff, need frequent opportunities to discuss problems, to process why clients act the way they do, to understand the ramifications of acquired cognitive problems, to learn how to intervene, and to develop a better overall perspective of how they can best assist within the limitations of their role (Gans, 1987; Prigatano, 1989b).

Even with a support ethic active within the program, residential staff observations and opinions still need to be solicited routinely. Many staff will not be assertive, secure, or confident enough to raise issues or to disagree with professionally trained staff. Actively soliciting input from residential staff will help minimize difficult situations such as those that arise when staff avoid communicating that clinical interventions are not working or when they fail to seek clarity when they are confused as to how to implement suggested treatment plans.

Hopefulness, Satisfaction, and Happiness

A significant part of coping for all people working in human service professions is recognizing how one's efforts ultimately make an important contribution. When clients improve and when staff feel as though they have played an effective helping role, the hard work pays off.

More than any other factor, if staff are to feel a sense of job satisfaction they need first to develop realistic expectations of themselves, their peers, and clients and families. Helping staff develop realistic expectations and recognize the vital role that they play is an ongoing process. These issues need to be addressed routinely throughout the week and during special events such as discharge parties, when the therapeutic community comes together to recognize the accomplishments of those served.

Although Appendix 8-1 identifies a number of experiences that staff find rewarding, staff satisfaction is an individual matter. Staff often have unique interests and talents (e.g., music, arts, recreational interests, etc.) that not only can be rewarding for them to offer others but can be immensely beneficial to clients. Furthermore, many programs have residential staff play an advocacy role (see Appendix 8-2), so that they have more meaningful client-centered responsibilities after they have gained some initial experience.

BARRIERS TO RESIDENTIAL STAFF PERFORMANCE

Selection Problems and Considerations

When consulting with community programs, it is always easy to stress the importance of being highly selective in filling residential staff positions. After all, this is the first step to ensuring a top quality residential team. In running community programs, however, it seems that during the interview process one of the dominant concerns is how soon the candidate can start. The following are considerations for screening and hiring that can improve the selection process.

Whenever possible, candidates should be screened by the residential director and asked to return for a more intensive interview. Ideally, during the second interview the candidate should be given the opportunity to meet representatives from the clinical, residential, and management areas; spend time with clients and staff in the day program and residence; and learn more details about the role itself. Direct observations of the candidate's interpersonal skills and comfort level with clients are essential.

An aggressive reference check should be made through contacting at least three previous employers. If the candidate has prior experience in human services, references should be requested from the agency. Personal characteristics to investigate are reliability, ability to get along with others, flexibility, stamina, ability to manage stressful situations, and openness to feedback. Interpersonal skills and willingness to learn may be more important than experience.

The "Hire and Hope" Method of Staff Development

Perhaps the only staff development approach that is less methodologically sound than the "train and hope" approach (Stokes & Baer, 1977) is the "hire and hope" approach; that is, hire staff and hope that they and the clients alike survive without major incidents. Unless basic training and support systems are provided, clinical quality suffers. Clinical and liability risks increase substantially as well. Although most program managers have a strong staff development ethic, due in part to the limited resources to which they have access many fail operationally to offer meaningful assistance to direct care staff.

Poor Role Definition

When asked about the most difficult aspect of his job, one residential staff member stated, "Never knowing from one day to the next, or one moment to the next, what I was going to be asked to do." This lack of role clarity, in combination with concerns of role overload and role conflict, is a known formula for staff burn-out (Burke, 1985).

Consequently, staff need a clear understanding of their role expectations and how they are supposed to interface with other program components. This is best provided by a number of written supports, such as a detailed job description, a specific outline of the competencies that need to be mastered, and clear guidelines to follow when performing specific tasks.

Knowledge Level of Professional Staff

Professional staff are often in the position of training and supporting residential staff. In an early review of the responsibilities that professionally trained staff have in working with para-

professionals, Allen (1973) made a number of suggestions that still warrant attention today (Crisler & Young, 1987). Allen stressed that professionals are responsible for:

- ensuring the quality of the service programs to which paraprofessional staff contribute
- clearly defining the role of the paraprofessional, including specific tasks, expectations, and limitations
- training, teaching, and supervising paraprofessionals
- assisting in the development and maintenance of a job market for paraprofessional staff
- seeing that adequate financial compensation is provided for the contributions that paraprofessionals make
- maintaining an awareness of the legal liability of paraprofessionals in the provision of services and the legal implications of the use of paraprofessionals

Providing this level of support is at least a duel challenge for many clinical and management staff. Not only are professional staff striving to learn more themselves given their limited training in the field of brain injury rehabilitation, but many have not been trained to teach and supervise staff effectively.

In many ways, if residential staff are to improve their skills significantly, professional staff themselves often need training to be able to understand the purpose and process of providing comprehensive services to persons with acquired brain injury, to recognize residential staff contributions to the overall program (including the scope and limitations of the role), to detect signs of ineffective staff performance, to implement training methods that facilitate staff learning, and to design databased monitoring and feedback systems that track staff's ability to follow clinical recommendations.

Providing training in these areas is important. It is also important, however, that residential staff have opportunities to develop their role and identity within the rehabilitation program given the support, guidance, and supervision of experienced staff. Residential staff should be encouraged to develop ownership in identifying their needs for training and support and to formulate strategies for improving service quality.

Poor Integration of Residential, Clinical, and Managerial Operations

A consistent problem cited in the rehabilitation literature is the lack of training programs to teach all levels of program staff—residential, clinical, and management—to work together effectively within the context of the organizational structure (Crisler & Young, 1987; Delworth, 1974; Feild & Gatewood, 1976). To help overcome these barriers, training at all levels needs to encompass strategies for staff to work with other program sectors and interests. Furthermore, the organizational structure should be designed to anticipate these problems and to engineer systems to enhance integration where this is critical to ongoing program operations.

For example, the residential director should be a member of the management team and should be included in all major clinical and administrative decisions whenever possible. This presence will help all staff understand the implications of program decisions and changes. Well designed documentation systems need to flow through the various sectors of the program, ensuring that the right type of information gets to those who need it. To guarantee optimal systems functioning and to provide motivation for staff to adhere to documentation protocols, it is critical to use follow-up mechanisms in responding to priority concerns.

It is not unusual to hear residential staff complain, for example, that they faithfully write incident reports or document observations in residential charts without ever receiving formal acknowledgment that this information has been reviewed. Follow-up calls, notes, and official response forms are essential to complete the cycle of communication. This practice can prevent residential staff from feeling that their efforts are unimportant and inconsequential in clinical services and program operations.

Another method to facilitate integration is to select quality improvement elements that monitor the communication and documentation systems identified as priorities for better systems functioning. This may include quality improvement elements such as requiring clinician sign-offs on residential documentation, monitoring residential staffs' access to treatment plans, and tracking incident report follow-up procedures, to name a few.

To help build and maintain effective clinical-residential bridges, many residential programs require clinical staff to work shifts that extend into the evening or weekend. If this structure is implemented properly, with all staff understanding the purpose behind it, improved staff consistency can result. Clinical staff working these shifts can also help clients see the connection between day and residential programming and can develop treatment goals that are based on observations made in functional settings. When clinical staff work these shifts, it is important that they recognize that they are there not just to work with clients but to build a sense of "team" in addition to strengthening the skills of the residential staff.

To address issues such as this, many programs establish a clinical-residential task force. This group consists of clinical and residential staff who meet on an ongoing basis to evaluate and develop strategies to improve staff efficiency and program integration. The task force works as a change agent to improve the service model, to enhance the program's ability to respond to those persons currently being served, and to identify ongoing training needs that, once addressed, will increase staff effectiveness.

Leadership and Supervisory Gaps

Many programs find it difficult to establish a residential service model that offers adequate on-line supervision to direct care staff. Frequently, residential staff are spending long hours with clients who have challenging needs without having easy access to support.

To address such problems, some programs have worked to build a staffing infrastructure that can offer more direct assistance. This may include shift coordinators, weekend managers, and residential supervisors. These individuals typically oversee residential services and provide training, support, and ongoing supervision.

These positions are often filled with people who advance from within the program, are familiar with the multiple demands of the role, and know how to get things accomplished within the organization. Some programs hire professionally trained staff to fill these positions (occupational therapists, social workers, behavioral specialists, etc.) to strengthen the services offered and to improve staff supervision.

Effective leadership and direct supervision in the residential setting are critical given the rapid pace of change that is often characteristic of rehabilitation programs. This support can help the program adjust and respond to the ever changing needs of the individuals in treatment, to the clinical issues brought on by new admissions, and to the staffing changes that are inevitable over time. Modeling, giving direct praise and reinforcement for positive staff actions, and offering corrective feedback can help educate as well as motivate staff to increase their skills and maintain their performance level. Ongoing leadership themes that need priority attention include helping staff maintain a therapeutic relationship with clients and family members, fostering a sense of identity among residential staff individually and collectively, facilitating a strong commitment to team work throughout the facility, helping staff keep sight of the meaning of their role, and setting realistic expectations in all areas.

Perhaps Crisler and Young (1987) best summarize the performance barriers that residential staff face. In reviewing the efficacy research and historical use of paraprofessionals, they state:

> Rehabilitation agencies, both public and private, have used paraprofessionals to provide services to disabled clients. Although there have been some successful programs, in many cases problems arose because of (1) inadequate definition of the purpose for which paraprofessionals were hired and the roles they were to play; (2) insufficient training and supervision; (3) the tendency of professionals to assign [them] excessive . . . responsibility . . . or to assign them only routine, repetitive tasks; and (4) inadequate opportunity for advancement. . . . The paraprofessional has been essentially on a dead end street, working at low pay with inadequate train-

ing and supervision and without much possibility for climbing a career ladder. (Crisler & Young, 1987, p. 446)

IN SEARCH OF A PRACTICAL TRAINING MODEL

The training model discussed in this chapter is currently being piloted in six community integrated programs for persons with acquired brain injury. This model is based in part on lessons learned from the implementation of three other staff development programs. The major components of these three training initiatives are reviewed briefly to help the reader better understand the needs and principles on which the training approach is based.

It is anticipated that this conceptual information will assist those interested in developing similar staff development programs in their own treatment facilities. As is emphasized in Chapter 1, all staff development initiatives need to be designed within the context of each program's philosophy, clinical and managerial strengths and weaknesses, and access to resources that affect training efforts.

Example 1

Dillon, Durgin, Kearse, and Lombardo (1981) developed a comprehensive training program for graduate level special education interns. Upon entering the graduate program, each intern had immediate teaching responsibilities and needed to acquire a number of clinical competencies in a short period of time. Much like staff in rehabilitation settings, the interns were in a position of providing direct services after a brief orientation.

Supervisors, on the other hand, needed to devise a system to offer adequate guidance to all interns and a procedure for identifying those who either needed immediate help or may not have been suited for the profession. Such a system was vital because poor staff performance quickly had a negative impact on the quality of services offered.

To address these problems, a competency-based training system was developed. It included a flexible and paced educational curriculum that outlined precisely the knowledge and skills that the interns needed to learn on a month-by-month basis. All staff competencies were prioritized and sequenced according to the developmental learning process that was expected to take place. In this way, high-achieving and experienced interns could use the competency-based curriculum to self-direct their professional development without intensive supervision at every step of the process.

On the other hand, the built-in performance evaluations conducted early on and throughout placement facilitated the provision of more intensive supervision for those who needed it the most. This allowed supervisors to use the comprehensive curriculum to track skill acquisition for all staff and provided a structured method for identifying and addressing problems early on in the training process. If necessary, specific competencies could be reintroduced over time to focus the interns' attention on critical skill areas that needed more work.

Another important characteristic of this training program was that all interns participated in extensive self-evaluation in all the competency areas selected. This enabled supervisors to understand each intern's self-assessment before developing a plan to offer feedback. It is important to note that the approach used was, by design, a positive and reinforcing staff development system. The large number of competencies reviewed provided many opportunities for supervisors to praise interns for their accomplishments.

The problems faced by clinical supervisors and student interns in this example in many ways mirror the difficulties that residential staff face in moving quickly into a most complex and demanding role, often with limited on-line supervision and guidance.

Example 2

The May Institute is an internationally known, award-winning residential treatment program for children with severe communication and behavioral problems. This program has developed a number of highly focused staff development and management systems designed to ensure clinical quality and managerial efficiency (Larsson, Luce, & Christian, 1989; Luce & Christian, in press). Given the intensive needs of the children served, it is not surprising that this program historically has had a strong behavioral treatment orientation. This orientation is reflected in the staff development systems used in this setting as well.

In many ways the model used to train residential staff at The May Institute is similar to that described in the first example. Supervisors conduct monthly reviews of staff performance throughout the first 6 months of employment by means of a sequenced curriculum of staff competencies. If specific competencies are not learned at an acceptable level, they are reintroduced and taught until they are mastered. In fact, by design a number of the priority skills (e.g., behavior management) needed for successful life skills instruction by residential staff are repeated over time for skill reinforcement.

A number of the distinct characteristics of this training curriculum should be noted. Each staff competency is written in specific behavioral terms using a task analysis format to describe precisely each step to be followed. For example, the dispensing medication checklist has 13 steps. This includes basic steps such as washing hands, locking the cabinet, and verifying that the medication container matches the medication tracking sheet. This high level of specificity sets clear expectations for staff and provides a detailed written reference for staff to follow if needed.

New residential staff are taught and evaluated by experienced staff who have already completed training. This procedure spreads the training responsibility among many staff. The training results are documented on a skills checklist, which is then forwarded to the appropriate supervisor. Ratings on the skills checklist for the most part are based on direct observation and direct questioning. For quality assurance measures, all trainers must also successfully complete a separate skills checklist, which ensures that they have the teaching and interpersonal skills necessary to provide effective training to others in need of guidance. The majority of the training is provided in the situations and settings where staff need to perform the targeted skills.

Training is provided on a one-to-one basis and is conducted when the trainer and trainee are both available. This is an efficient approach because it does not require staff to find the time to conduct large group training workshops, where coverage problems may arise. It is the responsibility of the new staff members to see that all competencies are met before the end of the month in which they are due; these due dates begin at the date of hire.

Example 3

Schmidt and Durgin (1989) directed a comprehensive training initiative for more than 300 residential staff working in community integrated programs for persons with acquired brain injury. They developed a 10-module curriculum that was based on an extensive needs analysis. The curriculum included modules written by subject matter experts and consisted of learning exercises to be carried out in the natural work environment in addition to providing teaching methodologies for a total of 20 hours of workshops. All workshops emphasized active participation and direct performance of skills needed on the job (documentation, consulting with clinical staff, role playing of effective communication strategies, etc.).

Experienced and respected residential supervisors and shift coordinators were recruited in each facility to implement the training by means of a facilitator model. Staff facilitators received a salary increase to take on the additional responsibility and participated in a training program themselves to prepare for their role as facilitators. Residential staff also received a salary increase after successfully completing the program. The role of the facilitators was to guide residential staff, most of whom were under their supervision, through the curriculum in accordance with the stipulated training methodologies.

A critical component of this training was structuring experiences that would create a greater level of integration between the residential service area and other program components, namely clinical services and administrative supports. For example, clinical staff were required to help facilitate specific curriculum modules, and residential staff were assigned the task of meeting with various clinical staff during their work day to solicit information about clients (i.e., team building, communication). Curriculum facilitators met with clinical and administrative staff to discuss the training and to review more global residential needs. These integration activities were procedurally defined in the teaching methodologies and created ongoing opportunities for systems development (addressing both program and staff development issues). Exhibit 8-2 lists several of the benefits of this training as reported by residential supervisors.

Two problems with this training approach should be noted. The use of workshops, although reported to be effective by residential supervisors in teaching both knowledge and skills, presented significant logistical difficulties for treatment facilities (e.g., freeing up staff for training). Also, training quality was difficult to maintain when facilitator turnover occurred. On the other hand, the financial incentives, emphasis on program integration, and team-building opportunities facilitated throughout the workshops were all believed to be particular strengths of this training.

Curriculum Design

A competency-based training model designed to incorporate the successful components of the three programs described above and to avoid known traps that frequently lead to problems is outlined below.

Orientation

The orientation process is essentially a preservice educational program that sets the foundation for working with clients. The emphasis is helping new staff members become more familiar with their role; how their role fits within the organization; program policies and procedures; basic characteristics of the individuals served; orienting to the physical environment, staff, and clients; and treatment philosophy.

Exhibit 8-3 is an example of a 3-day orientation schedule. The activities listed are modified ac-

Exhibit 8-2 Reported Benefits of Residential Staff Training

Ability of residential staff to perform general responsibilities increased.

Residential staff awareness as to why residential and community-based interventions are essential components of a comprehensive rehabilitation effort increased.

Posttest (knowledge-based) results indicated that experienced staff demonstrated learning gains at a level equal to that of new staff.

Clinical staff understanding of the value of the residential staff role in the entire rehabilitation process increased.

During direct work with clients, trained staff were observed providing spontaneous assistance and support to untrained staff.

Residential staff's ability to manage conflicts (client and staff) improved.

Staff were prompted to seek out additional information about brain injury rehabilitation.

Morale, confidence, and enthusiasm improved.

Exhibit 8-3 Sample Orientation Schedule for Residential Staff

Day 1   Welcome/ice breaker/trainee introductions
        Brief agency/company overview
        Purpose and mission of the treatment program (within the context of the care continuum)
        Structure and function of the various program elements (clinic, residence, worksites, etc.)
        Program values and beliefs
        Client rights/confidentiality
        Site tour/meeting with program staff
        Review of staff roles and how they interface
        Direct observation of therapy and some opportunities to interact with clients
        Policy and procedure review
        Administrative and personnel issues

Day 2   Initial discussion/questions and answers
        Overview of different types of injuries (traumatic brain injury, stroke, anoxia, etc.)
        Basic brain-behavior relationships
        Consequences of brain injury (sensory, perceptual, cognitive, physical, behavioral, medical, psychological, etc.)
        Review of terminology
        Communicating with clients and building therapeutic relationships
        Team building (team philosophy and how we work together)
        Family needs and involvement

Day 3   A day in the life of a residential staff member (review of role responsibilities on a given shift)
        Documentation standards and expectations
        Emergency procedures (on-call, medical assistance, fire safety, etc.)
        Treatment plan and the treatment team
        Basic behavior management
        Physical management protocols (transferring, ambulation, etc.)
        Orientation to residential training program
        Risk management issues
        Client review

First   Follow-up instruction in the residential setting is conducted by experienced staff (reviewing the critical principles covered during orientation and applying them to the clients currently being served)
three
shifts

cording to the current needs of the clients in the program and the strengths and weaknesses of the staff participating. Suggested materials to facilitate learning include videotapes, organizational flow charts, policy and procedure manuals, sample reports, documentation forms, and easy-to-follow handouts. Although most orientation activities involve the dissemination of information, direct skills practice through role playing and documentation exercises is desirable.

The formal 3-day orientation is followed by three shifts of observing and collaborating with experienced residential staff. New staff gradually take on more responsibility during these shifts and learn how to apply the information presented during orientation to their direct work with clients.

Structural Characteristics and Content Overview

The structure of the curriculum is competency based. A competency-based model offers clarity in role expectations and provides a performance evaluation system to monitor learning as well as ongoing performance. Although there is limited research in this area, some initial findings have indicated that staff prefer this type of on-the-job, task-analyzed instruction to other, more traditional forms of training (Thibadeau et al., 1982).

The primary focus of the curriculum content is enhancing residential staff knowledge and skills and engineering positive integration throughout all relevant program sectors. Helping staff to develop healthy professional attitudes is addressed throughout the training process and through the various support systems discussed earlier. The residential staff training content presented constitutes only one aspect of staff development. Other learning experiences in which all program staff need to participate are not included (e.g., health and safety protocols and other routine inservices).

Table 8-1 describes the characteristics of the curriculum structure and the rationale behind the training design. The conceptual premise on which this model is based has been discussed throughout the chapter. Table 8-2 is an overview of the training content. This includes the training section, skill areas covered, review months, and the primary focus of the competencies addressed.

Training Procedures and Measurements

Training objectives cannot be addressed efficiently if the curriculum is difficult for staff to understand and implement. To be effective, training initiatives need to be well conceived and strategically designed and at the same time practical and easy for staff to follow. This curriculum model follows an implementation plan similar to that of The May Institute.

Experienced staff who have satisfactorily completed training move into a trainer role. The new staff member is responsible for completing training within the time frames established. Most of the skill competencies are taught through a variety of methods that are related to the skills in question, such as verbal explanations, modeling, role playing, simulated practice, staff coaching, videotape reviews, and observation-feedback sessions. The teaching methods are outlined for the trainer so that he or she can facilitate the learning process.

The curriculum overview in Appendix 8-3 and the residential staff competency forms in Appendices 8-2 and 8-4 through 8-6 illustrate the measurement system utilized. A 5-point frequency rating scale is used to measure staff performance for each competency.

The first measure includes a self-evaluation rating completed by the trainee. Once the self-evaluation (SE) is completed, it is followed by the trainer rating (TR). The trainer also uses observation codes (OC). This information specifies the basis on which the trainer made the ratings.

Table 8-1 Curriculum Design Characteristics

Characteristic	Purpose/Benefit
Comprehensive	Covers more than 35 critical skill areas that staff need to address
Integrated	Structures formal communication and collaboration with all program components (clinical, management, etc.)
Behaviorally specific	Avoids use of vague and confusing language (skill areas use task analysis)
Measurement oriented	Performance ratings are based on both observable skills and verbal knowledge
Proactive	Training information is available upon hire and is immediately put to use
Paced instruction	Training content is prioritized and introduced sequentially
Contextual relevance	Knowledge and skill competency is primarily taught during direct work with clients in community and residential settings
Skill reinforcement	Priority skills to be learned are systematically reintroduced to ensure skill mastery and retention
Self-evaluation	Self-evaluation is used to guide supervisory intervention and facilitates self-directed learning
Flexible	Content can be modified and/or expanded to meet the needs of individual staff members
Shared ownership for training	Staff who have achieved skill competency have the opportunity to train new staff
Program development function	Training is structured to ensure that ongoing feedback is provided to clinical and management staff so that the program design can respond to ongoing needs

Table 8-2 Model of a Residential Staff Training Curriculum

Training Section	Skill Area	Review Month(s)	Focus of the Staff Competencies
Team building	Conflict resolution and problem solving	1–4	To practice professional team building and conflict management skills that create a therapeutic environment for clients and a positive work environment for staff
	Staff-to-staff communication	2–5	To demonstrate effective, clear, respectful, and efficient communication among all staff members
	Accessing support from supervisor(s)	1–6	To ensure that staff use strategies to get the support needed, to achieve resolution of problems when they surface, and to maintain a clear perspective on clinical services as well as their own performance
Client services	Understanding brain injury	1–3	To develop a basic understanding of brain function and the nature of the various problems expected after brain injury
	Communication with clients	1–3	To identify and use effective approaches to communicate and interact with clients who have various cognitive/communication problems
	Therapeutic rapport	2–4	To demonstrate the ability to establish a healthy professional relationship with the client and family through maintaining clear boundaries, establishing trust, and providing consistency
	Teaching strategies	3–5	To demonstrate the ability to provide feedback to clients in a manner that facilitates learning and increased independence
	Leisure skills support	3–5	To facilitate leisure skills development and participation through use of program/community resources and by implementing planned activities
	Environmental management	2–5	To create and maintain a safe, risk-free, and comfortable environment for clients to live in (i.e., clean, organized, and secure)
	Supporting clinical services	3–6	To demonstrate the ability to implement, evaluate, and document clinician planned activities consistent with the goals and procedures outlined
	Understanding behavior problems	1–3	To identify premorbid, social, environmental, psychological, and cognitive factors that may lead to behavioral problems
	Behavior intervention techniques	2–4	To use behavior management techniques that prevent problems, reinforce desirable actions, and avoid reinforcing problematic behaviors
	Behavioral crises: philosophy and intervention	1–4	To understand practical strategies for responding to crises and to demonstrate skills specific to prevention, deescalation, management, and follow-up
	Behavioral crises: safety techniques	2–4	To demonstrate the ability to avoid personal injury if an aggressive episode occurs (block hit/kick, escape from hair pull/being grabbed, etc.)
Client services (optional)	Advisor role	4	To advocate the services provided within the residential setting (i.e., to work as a member of the treatment team to help design, implement, monitor, evaluate, and report progress)

Table 8-2 continued

Training Section	Skill Area	Review Month(s)	Focus of the Staff Competencies
	Job coaching	2	To demonstrate the ability to provide support in a work environment consistent with the direction of the vocational specialist
Documentation	Individual charts	2–5	To demonstrate the ability to locate important chart information and to document meaningful observations in a clear and objective fashion
	Incident reports: when to generate	1	To document all client incidents as required and to forward the report to the case manager within the specified time frame
	Incident reports: how to document	2	To provide comprehensive, easy-to-read, descriptive, and timely documentation after a behavioral incident
	Shift change reporting	3–6	To demonstrate the ability to communicate critical issues in written and verbal form to the staff entering a shift (via the shift change report)
	Staff communication log	3–6	To use consistently the staff-to-staff communication log, which includes reading the material, signing off, and recording information as needed
Medical issues	Emergency medical procedures	1–4	To understand when to follow emergency medical procedures and to demonstrate the ability to access program and community medical support systems when needed
	Medication administration	1–3	To keep medications in secure areas as prescribed, to supervise clients in taking medication, to complete required documentation, and to notify on-call staff if an error is identified or suspected
	Seizure management	2–5	To recognize, monitor, and document any seizure activity while providing support to the affected client (as well as to other clients present)
On-call access	On-call: when to use	1	To be able to discriminate when to use the on-call system to access support
	On-call: ability to access support	2	To demonstrate the ability to access the on-call person and to use the alternative support options available if the on-call person cannot be reached
Transportation	Policy review	1	To understand the company policy on providing safe transport (including both personal and company responsibilities) and to recognize general legal/liability matters that pertain to this issue
	Road test	1	To demonstrate the ability to check thoroughly that the vehicle in use is in safe working condition and to demonstrate the ability to drive the vehicle safely
Working with families	Understanding the needs of families	1–4	To demonstrate an understanding of and sensitivity to the broad impact of brain injury on family members and of why rehabilitation staff need to respond to their needs

continued

Table 8-2 continued

Training Section	Skill Area	Review Month(s)	Focus of the Staff Competencies
	Communication with families	2–6	To demonstrate the ability to communicate effectively with families, who have unique needs, concerns, interests, and values
	Responding to family concerns	2–5	To listen to family concerns and criticisms without being defensive and to take immediate action to solve the problem (or to solicit input to determine appropriate action)
Mobility and physical support	Safety awareness	1–4	To understand the various safety risks associated with poor balance, limited strength, fatigue, and impaired judgment as they relate to mobility in the residence and in the community
	Ambulation support, wheelchair use, and transfer guidelines	1–2	To demonstrate the ability to support client movement and overall mobility by using proper body mechanics, following the recommended transfer protocols, providing the required level of supervision, and maintaining a safe physical environment for ambulation/mobility
Professional skills development	General work skills	2–5	To demonstrate the ability to self-manage one's job responsibilities in all situations without prompting and reminders
	Stress management	2–5	To demonstrate the ability to take care of oneself without experiencing burn-out or energy loss leading to attitude, performance, or personal problems
	Advancement	4–6	To take responsibility for advancing one's knowledge and skills through the use of existing program resources and training opportunities and to find ways to make unique contributions to the program/field consistent with one's interests

The observation codes indicate whether the competency was taught through verbal explanation or whether the trainee actually demonstrated the skill rated (either during a training session or in direct work with clients).

Ideally, trainer ratings (i.e., feedback) are provided immediately after observation sessions but can be completed at the 1-month review cycle if necessary. For many competencies the latter is necessary given the scope of the curriculum, which makes it difficult to observe all skills addressed. The reality is that the trainers will not be able to observe directly all skills covered. Assuming that there are limited resources available for training, the only way this problem can be remedied is by drastically reducing the length of the curriculum. This option must be weighed against

the need to offer staff clear and comprehensive guidance with a built-in feedback system designed to review all priority staff development issues.

After reviewing the training process during orientation and after completing the first few residential staff competency forms, staff typically come to feel at ease with the training and review process. Additional goals and comments can be added at the bottom of each form to address the individual needs of each staff member. This training program offers the combined benefits of a teaching curriculum and a performance review system.

CONCLUSION

When rehabilitation programs choose to provide residential services to people with brain injury, they take on a large responsibility. Offering residential services adds a significant level of complexity to the service delivery model and to staff development needs.

Many programs that have attempted to improve services in the residential arena have been discouraged by repeated problems with staff performance and turnover. This experience has often been a disincentive to put more resources into an area that is difficult to change. In many cases failure to strengthen the quality of residential services has been due to a number of factors, including a lack of training provided, an ineffective training methodology, and poor systems integration.

The model reviewed above was designed to minimize the problems historically associated with enhancing residential staff performance. Nevertheless, we are still learning about the merits and drawbacks of this approach. A number of research studies have assessed training programs for support staff working with other disability classifications and have for the most part concluded that clear expectations, direct instruction in the natural work environment, feedback, and accountability are all critical to maximize the results of training. Some of these studies have been able to demonstrate positive clinical gains attributable to staff training with models similar to those reviewed in this chapter (Dyer, Schwartz, & Luce, 1984; Greene, Willis, Levy, & Bailey, 1978; Ivancic, Reid, Iwata, Faw, & Page, 1981; Page, Iwata, & Reid, 1982).

Many questions remain as to how we can help staff acquire, generalize, and maintain their skills. More work needs to be done to identify scientifically how residential staff can increase their ability to respond to the unique needs of people with brain injury and their families. The first step is a commitment by program leaders to offer more direct support and to implement practical training methods that facilitate staff development and enhanced program integration.

ACKNOWLEDGMENT

The authors thank Jerry Southerland for his comments and assistance during the development of this chapter.

REFERENCES

Allen, D.A. (1973). Peer counseling and professional responsibility. *Journal of the American College Health Association, 21,* 339–342.

Auvenshine, C.D. (1971). Support personnel and counseling in vocational rehabilitation. *Rehabilitation Counseling Bulletin, 15,* 166–125.

Burke, J.M. (1985). Relationship between Type A behavior, role stress, job enrichment, and burnout among college counselors (Doctoral dissertation, Texas A&M University). *Dissertation Abstracts International, 46,* 10.

Crisler, J.R., & Young, M.E. (1987). A new perspective on paraprofessionals in rehabilitation counseling. In B. Caplan (Ed.), *Rehabilitation psychology desk reference* (pp. 437–452). Gaithersburg, MD: Aspen.

Delworth, U. (1974). Paraprofessionals as guerrillas: Recommendations for system change. *Personnel and Guidance Journal, 53,* 335–338.

Dillon, J., Durgin, C., Kearse, A., & Lombardo, S. (1981). *Competency sequence review: A model for training special education teachers.* Unpublished manuscript, State University of New York at Albany Graduate School of Educational Psychology, Albany, NY.

Durgin, C., Bouchard, N., & Jones, S. (1988). Life skills counselor role development: The rewards, demands, and challenges. In. N. Schmidt & C. Durgin (Eds.), *Life skills counselor textbook.* New Medico Health Care System Department of Education and Training.

Dyer, K., Schwartz, I.S., & Luce, S.C. (1984). A supervision program for increasing functional activities for severely handicapped students in a residential setting. *Journal of Applied Behavior Analysis, 17,* 249–259.

Feild, H.S., & Gatewood, R. (1976). The paraprofessional and the organization: Some problems of mutual adjustment. *Personnel and Guidance Journal, 55,* 181–185.

Gans, J.S. (1987). Facilitating staff/patient interaction in rehabilitation. In B. Caplan (Ed.), *Rehabilitation psychology desk reference* (pp. 185–218). Gaithersburg, MD: Aspen.

Greene, B.F., Willis, B.S., Levy, R., & Bailey, J.S. (1978). Measuring client gains from staff implemented programs. *Journal of Applied Behavioral Analysis, 11,* 395–412.

Ivancic, M.T., Reid, D.H., Iwata, B.A., Faw, G.D., & Page, T.J. (1981). Evaluating a supervision program for developing and maintaining therapeutic staff-resident interactions during institutional care routines. *14,* 95–107.

Larsson, D.G., Luce, S.C., & Christian, W.P. (1989). Attaining clinical competence at The May Institute. *Behavior Therapist, 12,* 219–222.

Lezak, M.D. (1988). *Psychosocial repercussions of emotional disturbance in head injury.* Paper presented at the Head Injury: An integrated approach to behavioral rehabilitation, Boston, MA.

Luce, S.C., & Christian, W.P. (in press). State-of-the-art programming in Massachusetts: A brief description of The May Institute. In C. Gillberg (Ed.), *Diagnosis and treatment of autism.* New York: Plenum.

Page, T.J., Iwata, B.A., & Reid, D.H. (1982). Pyramidal training: A large-scale application with institutional staff. *Journal of Applied Behavioral Analysis, 15,* 335–351.

Prigatano, G.P. (1989a). Work, love, and play after brain injury. *Bulletin of the Menninger Clinic, 53,* 414–431.

Prigatano, G.P. (1989b). Bring it up in the milieu: Toward effective traumatic brain injury rehabilitation interaction. *Rehabilitation Psychology, 34,* 2.

Schmidt, N., & Durgin, C. (1989). *Developing effective training programs for residential staff in post-acute pro-* *grams.* Paper presented at the 13th Annual Symposium of the National Head Injury Foundation, Chicago, IL.

Stokes, T.F., & Baer, D.M. (1977). An implicit technology of generalization. *Journal of Applied Behavioral Analysis, 10,* 344–367.

Thibadeau, S.F., Butler, K.K., Gruber, B.K., Luce, S.C., Newsom, C.D., Anderson, S.R., & Christian, W.P. (1982). *Competency-based orientation and training of human service personnel.* Paper presented at the Annual Convention of the Association for the Advancement of Behavior Therapy, New York, NY.

Wright, G.N., & Fraser, R.T. (1976). *Improving manpower utilization: The "Rehabilitation Task Force Performance Evaluation Scale."* Madison: University of Wisconsin Rehabilitation Research Institute.

The Rewards and Demands of Residential Work

REWARDS

Seeing clients progress

Having the opportunity to be creative and flexible

Making a difference through my relationship with the client

Working with a team of highly dedicated care givers

Helping clients with their communication difficulties

Helping clients feel that their lives are worthwhile

Learning from other team members

Teaching/job coaching

Receiving positive feedback from families, clients, and staff

Learning about head injury

Helping clients learn to control their behavior

Helping other residential staff

Establishing trust with a client

Feeling that something that I said or did helped

Observing a client leave for a new life in the outside world

Collaborating to develop treatment interventions

Watching a client gain insight into his or her cognitive problems

Helping clients enjoy their leisure time

Helping clients feel more secure

Recognizing more clearly why a client is having a problem

Being involved in a new and challenging field

Having exposure to different human service professions

Having opportunities for personal growth

DEMANDS

Knowing how and when to intervene or give feedback

Finding ways to get more involved/not being underutilized

Not getting angry with clients when they act out

Avoiding burn-out

Keeping track of everything that is going on

Separating my feelings personally and professionally

Standing up for something that I believe in/being assertive

Needing time to learn and do more/prioritizing

Managing clients as a whole group

Being able to diffuse a tense or stressful situation

Talking with clients who are not getting the message

Working with clients who make slow progress

Being short on staff

Wishing for more one-on-one time with clients

Dealing with constant change/role confusion

Managing staff disagreement

Working with clients who are demanding of my time

Being strong emotionally at all times for all clients

Carrying over goals and procedures without enough training

Facilitating/mediating communication among clients

Maintaining my self-control when clients lose theirs

Seeing the resistance of clients who have poor insight

Appendix 8-2

Residential Staff Competencies

TRAINING SECTION: Client Services
SKILL AREA: Residential Advisor Role
REVIEW MONTH(S):   4+

DATE:
TRAINEE:
TRAINER:

SE = Self-evaluation by trainee; OC = Observational code used by the trainer only;
TR = Trainer rating

COMPETENCIES EVALUATED	SE	OC	TR
A) Reads the client's entire chart prior to admission.			
B) Participates in the admission process at the center and assists the client and family to get situated in the residential setting (i.e., clothing, basic orientation to people and the environment, etc.).			
C) Corresponds with the assigned Case Manager on a weekly basis in person or by phone to review progress and any problems.			
D) Completes the Residential Progress Summary and forwards the report to the Case Manager within 2 days before the scheduled team meeting.			
E) Participates in team meetings or identifies a spokesperson to discuss progress as observed by residential staff.			
F) Reads and signs off on each Comprehensive Monthly Report.			
G) Coauthors treatment plans with clinical staff specific to goals that need to be addressed in residential and community settings.			
H) Conducts weekly residential chart audits to evaluate the quality of documentation and to identify any information that needs to be shared with other program staff.			
I) Tracks medication to ensure that there is an ample weekly supply (and notifies the Health Educator or Case Manager within three business days of when the medication is expected to run out).			
J) Ensures that all the current clinical recommendations and treatment guidelines are posted in the staff office for easy access and review.			
K) Reviews the client's and family's needs during weekly staff meetings, in addition to soliciting input from staff about progress and concerns.			

COMMENTS:

Courtesy of Community Rehabilitation Services of Annapolis, Maryland.

Overview of the Residential Staff Training Curriculum

TRAINING PHILOSOPHY

Residential staff members play a vital role in each client's rehabilitation program. They offer a critical link to helping the client understand the purpose and focus of treatment in addition to providing direct training and supervision in real world settings (residence and community). This training curriculum has been developed to help staff learn to address the multiple problems that brain injury presents.

PURPOSE

To provide the opportunity for staff members to receive positive feedback for the many strengths that they have (i.e., validate that they are doing well in key areas) and to provide staff with materials and feedback on areas critical for personal growth and client success. This curriculum is designed to be a highly positive, success-oriented process.

DEVELOPMENT

The curriculum content is based on residential staff input and on training models used in many human services environments (including college and university settings). It is written to be practical, easy to follow, and flexible.

This material is a starting point and will be modified on the basis of the input received (all staff members are encouraged to shape these materials so that they have maximum relevance and utility). Staff members who have used this training system have consistently reported it to be highly beneficial.

TRAINING PROCEDURE

1. The trainee reviews the competencies to be learned on a monthly basis.
2. The trainee meets with a trainer for direct training, an observation session, and to complete the ratings.

3. The outcome of these meetings should be a completed trainee self-evaluation, a trainer rating, and comments about the items reviewed.

4. A copy of the rated competencies should be forwarded to the trainee's direct supervisor at the end of each monthly cycle.

5. Specific competencies can be repeated on the basis of supervisor/trainer input and/or trainee request.

6. It is important to note that the frequency ratings are used in the self-evaluation (SE) and trainer rating (TR) columns on the residential staff competency form.

FREQUENCY RATINGS

5 = Almost all the time (81%–100%)

4 = Frequently (61%–80%)
3 = Sometimes (41%–60%)
2 = Seldom (21%–40%)
1 = Almost none of the time (0%–20%)

OBSERVATION CODES (FOR TRAINER ONLY)

V =   Verbal knowledge*
T =   Skill competence demonstrated during a training session (i.e., simulated practice)
D =   Skill competence demonstrated during direct work with clients, family members, and staff
N/O = Not observed or taught

*When the V (verbal knowledge) code is used by the trainer, no frequency ratings are to be used. Frequency ratings are only used to rate the skills demonstrated by the trainee.

Residential Staff Competencies

TRAINING SECTION: Team Building (for use with all staff)   DATE:
SKILL AREA: Conflict Resolution & Problem Solving   TRAINEE:
REVIEW MONTH(S):   1,4 (+ as needed)   TRAINER:

SE = Self-evaluation by trainee; OC = Observational code used by the trainer only;
TR = Trainer rating

COMPETENCIES EVALUATED	SE	OC	TR
A) Takes the initiative to express concerns openly, understands that problems are expected and a valuable opportunity to improve services/team functioning, and recognizes that staff are encouraged to speak up about sensitive issues.			
B) Takes ownership when solving problems (staff and client) and acts as part of the team effort rather than taking a distant and critical view of others and events.			
C) Willing and open to not getting approval or acceptance for ideas right away.			
D) Points out the positive contributions of others when they are having difficulties and are in need of support.			
E) When a problem occurs, he/she actively seeks out all the facts and information before forming opinions, making judgments, and taking action.			
F) In a supportive manner, makes efforts to understand why other staff may view problems and solutions differently (due to experience, role, educational orientation, stress level, value differences, etc.).			
G) Addresses problems as they surface (not letting critical issues build up).			
H) Takes interpersonal problems to the source (or to the supervisor) rather than to other people.			
I) Refers to others in a respectful way when they are not present.			
J) Makes "I" statements when expressing feelings and concerns.			
K) Flexible, open to compromise, and willing to try out solutions before making judgments.			
L) Takes a resolution-oriented posture when problems arise rather than fixating on the issues (i.e., offers solutions to problems whenever possible).			
M) Recognizes and articulates the positive contributions that can result from conflict.			

COMPETENCIES EVALUATED	SE	OC	TR
N) Maintains a positive balance of offering constructive and supportive comments as well as criticisms (i.e., is not constantly critical and negative).			
O) Uses constructive language (descriptive and noninflammatory language) when discussing problem/conflict situations.			
P) Uses a positive sense of humor in conflict and stressful situations to create a relaxed atmosphere. Humor is used appropriately, not cynically or destructively.			
Q) Does not confuse disagreements with lack of support/respect toward the person forming the opinion (acceptance of others' opinions as well as their styles).			
R) Effectively negotiates responsibility for addressing problems with staff in a manner that results in a clear plan, with the tasks, timelines, and people responsible identified.			
S) Follows through on the agreed plan of action designed to resolve problems.			

COMMENTS:

Courtesy of Community Rehabilitation Services of Annapolis, Maryland.

Residential Staff Competencies

TRAINING SECTION: On-Call Access　　　　　　　DATE:
SKILL AREA:　　　　　When To Access On-Call Staff　TRAINEE:
REVIEW MONTH(S):　1　　　　　　　　　　　　　TRAINER:

SE = Self-evaluation by trainee; OC = Observational code used by the trainer only;
TR = Trainer rating

COMPETENCIES EVALUATED	SE	OC	TR
A) Unplanned departure (i.e., running away or "signing self out" of rehabilitation).			
B) Fall or injury to client, staff, or visitor.			
C) Physical fight, emotional disagreement, or client agitation.			
D) Threats made to leave or to harm self or others.			
E) Significant changes in clients' typical behavior (appearance, speech, cognitive functioning, physical abilities, etc.).			
F) Medical problems.			
G) Medication error or confusion over medication administration.			
H) Staff problem or conflict.			
I) Family complaints or conflict.			
J) Client late from community outing (more than 30 minutes late before 11:00 p.m. and more than 15 minutes late from the expected time of arrival after 11:00 p.m.).			
K) Safety problem (i.e., adaptive equipment, maintenance/property issue).			
L) Sexual actions of concern.			
M) When you as a staff person need support or time to discuss a current or anticipated problem.			
N) When in doubt.			

COMMENTS:

Courtesy of Community Rehabilitation Services of Annapolis, Maryland.

Residential Staff Competencies

TRAINING SECTION:	Documentation	DATE:
SKILL AREA:	Incident Reports: How To Document	TRAINEE:
REVIEW MONTH(S):	2	TRAINER:

SE = Self-evaluation by trainee; OC = Observational code used by the trainer only;
TR = Trainer rating

COMPETENCIES EVALUATED	SE	OC	TR
A) Locates incident reports when needed.			
B) Completes the incident report within 10 minutes of the incident (or at the earliest possible time after the incident).			
C) Completes all sections to be filled out on the incident report form.			
Describes each of the following in specific, descriptive language:			
1) Antecedent—Comprehensive description of the events that were occurring before the incident (i.e., all events that were taking place in the environment).			
2) Behavior—Details the specific words, events, and actions that took place (including all persons present at the time).			
3) Consequences—Description of what occurred after the behavioral incident (What were the responses of those present? Was there any resolution?).			
D) Enters all documentation in a manner that can be easily read by others.			
E) Forwards the incident report to the Staff Communication Log for review by all staff.			

COMMENTS:

Courtesy of Community Rehabilitation Services of Annapolis, Maryland.

Substance Use: A Critical Training Issue for Staff in Brain Injury Rehabilitation

9

Frank R. Sparadeo

OBJECTIVES

Upon completion of this chapter, the reader will be able to:

1. identify problems associated with substance use and traumatic brain injury (TBI)
2. list substance use assessment tools and intervention strategies designed to assist people with brain injury and their families
3. describe the components of a categorization system that can be used to guide treatment efforts
4. specify treatment variables that increase the probability of a successful long-term outcome
5. define staff training and program development strategies that will improve staff skills and confidence when working with people with substance use problems and TBI

Substance Use

The role of alcohol in the occurrence of TBI has been discussed in the literature since the mid-1970s. It was not until 1987, with the development of the National Head Injury Foundation (NHIF) Task Force on Substance Abuse, that the issue of substance use and abuse was brought to the forefront as an important rehabilitation issue. Progress continues to be made. In 1990 an entire issue of the *Journal of Head Trauma Rehabilitation* focused on substance abuse. The number of conference presentations and workshops focusing on TBI and substance abuse has increased dramatically. Addressing the substance abuse issue is a critical component of rehabilitation if we are to assist survivors in improving their chances for long-term success.

BRIEF REVIEW OF THE LITERATURE

It has been established that substance use, and in particular alcohol use, contributes to the incidence of TBI. Several investigators have noted significant blood alcohol levels (BAL) in more than 50% of TBI survivors at the time of injury (Kraus & Nourjah, 1989; Rimel, Giordani, Barth, & Jane, 1982; Sparadeo & Gill, 1989).

The implications of BAL at the time of injury are unclear, but some investigations have demonstrated associated recovery complications after TBI, such as lower levels of consciousness, longer duration of coma, longer periods of agitation, lower cognitive status at discharge, and long-term effects on memory (Brooks, Symington, Beattie, Campsie, Bryden, & McKinley, 1989; Edna, 1982; Sparadeo & Gill, 1989). Consistent with these findings, new data suggest that a history of substance abuse may predict increased behavioral disorders, poorer memory and slower overall TBI recovery in an acute rehabilitation setting (Mishkin & Sparadeo, 1991).

An ongoing and critical issue is the incidence of substance use in the TBI survivor. Kreutzer and colleagues (Kreutzer, Doherty, Harris, & Zasler, 1990) reported an overall level of postinjury alcohol consumption among TBI survivors of 43%. Of these individuals, 20% were moderate to heavy drinkers. Further analysis classified between 8% and 14% of TBI survivors as problem drinkers. Although in comparison to their preinjury drinking TBI survivors on the whole drink less, a large number continue to use alcohol.

The use of alcohol may have a significant negative impact on rehabilitation and long-term outcome (Burke, Weselowski & Guth, 1988; Kreutzer, Marwitz, & Wehman, 1991; Sparadeo & Gill, 1989). The NHIF Task Force on Substance Abuse (which comprises both professionals and survivors) has taken the position that the healthiest recommendation to a TBI survivor is that alcohol and other nonprescribed drugs should be avoided. In other words, the Task Force has advocated an abstinence philosophy. The origin of this philosophy and its continued support derive from the observation that the use of alcohol and illicit drugs increases the probability of such problems as seizures (Kaitz, 1991), worsened cognitive impairments (Karol & Sparadeo, 1990; Solomon & Sparadeo, 1992), poor social functioning (Dunlop, Udvarhelyi, Stedman, O'Connor, Issacs, Puig, & Mather, 1991), another head injury, negative interactions with prescribed medications, and behavioral disorders. In addition to these risks, vocational failure and criminal behavior have also been linked to use of alcohol and other drugs after injury (Kreutzer, Marwitz, & Wehman, 1991).

The literature cited above clearly establishes the need for TBI rehabilitation professionals to attend to the problem of substance use and abuse. Through survey information gathered by the NHIF Task Force in 1988 and again in 1991, it appears that, in general, the field of TBI rehabilitation (as represented by TBI rehabilitation programs) has recognized the problem of substance use and abuse. The NHIF Task Force surveyed 75 rehabilitation facilities across the United States. These facilities admitted that substance use, particularly alcohol use, was a problem for their clients; furthermore, these facilities did not believe that they were being successful in their interventions (Sparadeo, Strauss, & Barth, 1990). Initial information from the follow-up survey conducted in 1991 suggests that there is an increase in the number of facilities recognizing the problem of substance use, that more facilities are integrating substance use interventions into the general TBI rehabilitation process, and that more facilities are expressing confidence in their interventions.

ASSESSMENT AND INTERVENTION

In developing a substance abuse program there are critical decision points that need to be established. These have to do with identification, assessment, and the form of intervention that is utilized.

Assessment and Identification

At the point of contact with the TBI survivor, the rehabilitation program must include in its overall evaluation an assessment of the survivor's history of substance use. It is from this information that a statement can be made regarding the role of substance use in the individual's life and the type of programming that will be necessary to handle this issue. Ultimately the rehabilitation team must make a predictive statement regarding the probability of the client's using substances either during or after formal rehabilitation. Sparadeo, Strauss, and Kapsalis (1992) have suggested employing an identification model that categorizes the client according to low risk for use, high risk for use, and current use. A similar identification format has been suggested by Moore (1992).

Low Risk

The low-risk individual has no previous history of substance abuse or heavy use and is not currently using. This individual also reports no craving or urges for substances, has few if any

triggers (antecedents) for use, has no immediate family member in trouble with substances, and has a relatively intact support system.

High Risk

The high-risk individual has a history of addiction or heavy use or is an individual whose substance use was a central theme in his or her life but who is not currently using. This individual reports cravings or urges for substances and has many triggers; he or she may have one or more family members in trouble with substances. Also, this individual may have a limited support system or a support system that enables him or her to use substances despite obvious associated problems (e.g., poor self-concept, depression, or other significant psychosocial difficulties).

Current User

The current user has experienced a brain injury and has returned to use of substances. In this case the individual must be assessed not for potential use and potential corresponding problems but for the present level of life disruption due to current use and potential life disruption if use continues. This client presents a dilemma because it is known that substance use interferes with cognitive recovery. The TBI rehabilitation program must request abstinence to achieve maximum results. Abstinence requests are much easier to comply with in residential settings compared to outpatient programs. It will be necessary to establish a rule regarding the approach to abstinence violations during the rehabilitation process.

There are no set rules regarding the consequences of abstinence violation in the TBI rehabilitation field. In the substance abuse field, an abstinence violation usually results in discharge from treatment. Such an approach is not practical in TBI rehabilitation. Although abstinence is a goal for the TBI survivor, it must be understood that, even when the TBI survivor desires abstinence and states an understanding of the program rules and risks of continued use, the probability of his or her remaining abstinent is low. A program must understand that achieving abstinence in a TBI survivor will require abstinence skills building. In the absence of abstinence skills, complete adherence to an abstinence rule is unrealistic, although abstinence remains the goal. Abstinence skills building needs to be an essential component of the TBI rehabilitation program.

Further Assessment

An individual who fits the category of current user or high risk for use requires further assessment so that a full description of past and/or present use can be developed. In addition, further categorization is required for users in relation to severity of use (e.g., addiction, problem drinking, heavy social drinking, light social drinking). Kreutzer et al. (1991) have suggested using standard measures such as the Quantity Frequency Variability Index (Cahalan & Cisin, 1968a, 1968b) and the Michigan Alcohol Screening Test (Zung, 1979). Other standard measures also exist, such as the CAGE Questionnaire (Ewing, 1984).

One problem with standard measures is that they do not account for the individual who drinks in a limited way but experiences significant life problems as a result of alcohol use. A helpful tool for delineating the role of alcohol or other drugs in a person's life is the Alcohol Troubled Person Model (Willoughby, 1979). This model states that a person is alcohol troubled if the quality of life has been negatively affected by alcohol (or other drugs) in any one or more of the following life areas: emotional (including cognitive), social (including family), financial (including job or school), and physical. The severity of trouble is measured along a continuum from minimal to moderate (i.e., two life areas affected) to severe (i.e., addiction) to severe and chronic (i.e., significant losses and continuous intoxication).

Standard measures are also problematic in that they do not take into account the functional value of alcohol or other drug use. The functional value is the way in which the individual perceives substance use as helpful in coping with various life situations.

Standard measures also do not usually measure the situational cues (triggers or antecedents) for substance use. Most of the time substance use cues are not present in a rehabilitation setting, and therefore the client stays abstinent easily. Once the client returns to the home environment and is exposed to unanticipated situational cues, the probability of substance use increases dramatically.

Standard measures usually do not take into account the cognitive level of the client. The process of abstaining from substance use is complex and requires self-monitoring strategies as well as memory and decision-making competence.

There are a number of standard measures that are utilized as measures of treatment progress and success as well as initial assessment measures. For example, a pretreatment and posttreatment assessment can be made by means of such measures as the Alcohol Use Inventory (Horn, Wanberg, & Foster, 1987), the Alcohol Expectancy Questionnaire (Brown, Chassin, & Sher, 1987), the Inventory of Drinking Situations (Annis & Davis, 1989), the Situational Confidence Questionnaire (Annis & Davis, 1989), and the Situational Competency Test (Chaney, O'Leary, & Marlatt, 1978). Outlined in Figure 9-1 is an identification model and categorization system that can be used to match the survivor's substance abuse risk level with specific intervention strategies.

Intervention

Assessment and identification lead to a specific intervention. Interventions can be conceptualized on the basis of the differential assessment categories discussed above and illustrated in Figure 9-1. Essentially, approaching both low- and high-risk TBI survivors can be viewed as having an emphasis on prevention, whereas approaching the survivor who is a current user requires a more comprehensive treatment intervention. The components of the interventions differ in content and intensity. The low-risk TBI survivor is often successfully treated with didac-

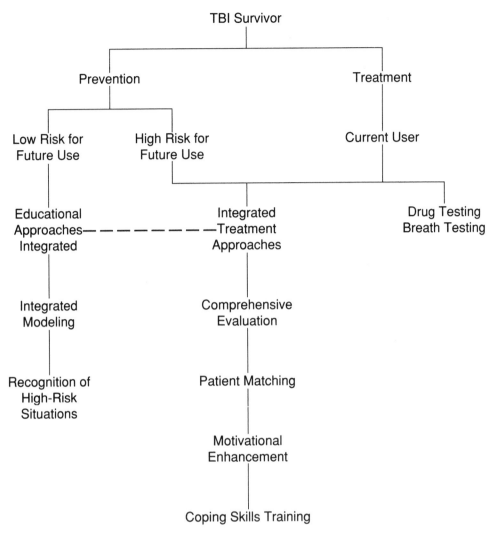

Figure 9-1 TBI survivor substance use categorization system

tic educational programming in combination with abstinence skills building. The high-risk TBI survivor and the current user both require high-intensity programming, as suggested recently by Langley and Kiley (1992). The treatment program has a slight advantage with the high-risk client because he or she is not currently using.

Langley (1991) suggests an integrated team approach to treatment. This integrated approach requires the presence of a clinician who is knowledgeable and trained in substance abuse interventions and the cooperation and interven-

tion of the rest of the TBI rehabilitation team. The term *integrated* refers to the folding in of substance abuse intervention program with the TBI rehabilitation treatment plan. Although a substance abuse counselor is part of the treatment team, implementing the intervention is the responsibility of the entire team.

The complexity of working with the TBI survivor, particularly in regard to developing motivation for abstinence, requires an entire staff effort. TBI survivors typically have impairments in impulse control, self-monitoring, insight, learning, and memory. As a result of these types of impairments, educationally based prevention and intervention programs for substance abuse are often ineffective. Behavioral models have been suggested (Blackerby & Baumgarten, 1990; Langley, 1991), and recently behavior/skills-building models have been developed (Jones, 1992; Langley & Kiley, 1992). The traditional models of substance abuse treatment, with their heavy emphasis on Alcoholics Anonymous type programming and insight, have been difficult to apply to the TBI survivor. First, research on the effectiveness of such programming for the substance abuse population is sparse, and second, there is great reliance in these programs on self-directed problem solving, insight, and didactic education, which, as discussed above, are particular cognitive vulnerabilities of TBI survivors.

The model with the greatest promise for preventing and treating substance abuse in persons with TBI appears to be the Skills Acquisition/Behavioral Model. This model is functionally based, taking into account the many factors that stimulate and maintain substance use and then providing an individually based intervention that focuses on teaching the TBI survivor the skills necessary to maintain abstinence. This is accomplished by helping the TBI survivor develop a lifestyle that is incompatible with substance use. In other words, the model focuses on increasing the occurrence of incompatible target behaviors (effective coping) rather than strictly on reducing substance use directly (Langley & Kiley, 1992).

Recent treatment models (Blackerby & Baumgarten, 1990; Langley, 1991; Langley & Kiley, 1992) have developed a staging approach that proceeds as follows: evaluation and assessment, education, skills training, aftercare planning, and follow-up.

Evaluation and Assessment

All models stress the importance of determining the severity of the substance use problem as well as the severity of the cognitive problems that the individual experiences. Langley (1991) suggests using standard instruments in assessing the centrality of alcohol use in the client's lifestyle and suggests the Alcohol Use Inventory (Horn et al., 1987). The utility of such an instrument is that it assists the treatment team in determining the style of alcohol use, the perceived benefits of alcohol use, and the consequences of alcohol use. This information allows for a better understanding of the reasons for use and therefore better treatment planning. For example, as pointed out by Langley (1991), an individual may use alcohol in anticipation of a reduction in tension level, so that the degree to which the individual now experiences increased tension is directly proportional to the likelihood of his or her drinking. Another important example stated by Langley (1991) is the individual who experienced few serious consequences of drinking before the brain injury. This individual might be less interested in accepting abstinence as a treatment goal. An executive function deficit such as limited self-monitoring and limited ability to benefit from negative feedback is likely to contribute to this individual's reluctance to see abstinence as a goal. Langley (1991) suggests that in these highly reluctant clients it is more useful to focus the treatment approach upon the development of alternative behaviors that are incompatible with drinking, such as physical exercise, rather than use confrontation, which increases anxiety, resentment, and anger.

Knowledge of the client's cognitive impairments and their operative value in maintaining alcohol or other drug use is a critical component of the evaluation process. There is a tendency to oversimplify a client's reluctance to develop abstinence goals by stating that he or she is denying. The issue of denial may be irrelevant. Instead, by analyzing and understanding the degree to which cognitive limitations contribute to substance use as well as understanding specific psychosocial issues that maintain use, and furthermore by understanding the functional utility of use, an educated approach can be developed to reduce the probability of continued substance use.

As a component of comprehensive evaluation, family assessment must also be performed. Substance use may be adaptive for family functioning (Steinglass, Bennett, Wolin, & Reiss, 1987) in situations in which the integrity of the family structure is threatened by the occurrence of brain injury. It is recommended that family assessment become a standard component of the evaluation process. Standard family assessment tools, such as the Family Assessment Device (Epstein, Baldwin, & Bishop, 1983), are available. For a more thorough review of standard family assessment procedures, refer to Bishop and Miller (1988). Families can unknowingly contribute to substance use by not acknowledging potential negative consequences, by their own use, by exposing the survivor to high-risk situations, and by their own reaction to the survivor's head injury. Langley (1991) offers a good example of this last point. Specifically, he points out that alcohol use can have short-term adaptive consequences for a family that is denying the cognitive impairments associated with the brain injury. In other words, the family can attribute the survivor's behavioral and cognitive problems to alcohol use, and therefore the drinking behavior is inadvertently reinforced because it protects the family from experiencing significant anxiety regarding the brain injury and its consequences.

Assessment with Accurate Patient Matching. Patient matching to specific interventions has received much attention recently. It has been established that the success of the intervention is strongly correlated with the accuracy of the match between the patient's problems and corresponding needs and the specific treatments applied. The process of matching heavily relies on the comprehensive assessment and evaluation of the individual. This evaluation process determines the specifics of the intervention to be applied. The application of an intervention begins with a statement of goals by the survivor. Development of the aftercare component of the treatment is also a significant aspect of the patient matching approach. Earlier, a categorical matching system was recommended. The initiation of the patient matching approach requires the clinical team to differentially determine the TBI survivor's presenting level of substance use risk. This level of risk determines the content and intensity of the intervention. It is necessary to continue the evaluation process throughout formal

intervention because a TBI survivor can move from low-risk to high-risk or from high-risk to user. This type of movement requires the treatment team and the TBI survivor to redevelop both goals and intervention.

Education

The fundamental assumption for the development of interventions for substance abuse in the TBI survivor is the need for change. The process of encouraging change requires knowledge that change is necessary. The knowledge base must often be provided by the treatment team and others (e.g., family and friends) so that the client can be brought to the point of awareness. Awareness is the first step toward change (Sparadeo, Barth, & Stout, 1992).

The process of change has been investigated frequently, and Prochaska and DiClemente (1986, 1992) have developed a well researched and respected model of change that points out that the individual must travel through several stages before change can occur. In the precontemplation stage of change a problem exists, but the client is unaware of the problem and therefore sees no reason to change. The educational process is geared to raise the level of awareness to achieve movement from the precontemplation stage to the contemplation stage. The contemplation stage is that point when the client uses the information given and determines that a problem exists and that it may be necessary to change. During the contemplation stage the client is actually ambivalent about the need for change. The continuing educational process points out to the client the results of the comprehensive assessment and describes the role of substances in his or her life and how the continued use of these substances will jeopardize future adjustment to the brain injury.

It is hoped that the client will then move from the contemplation stage to the next stage called determination. This is when the balance tips in favor of change (Miller, 1989). At this point the client is setting goals for change and is committed to change (Sparadeo, Barth, & Stout, 1992). The educational process as it continues through the client's treatment also contributes to the client's movement to the next and most critical stage of change, action. The action stage is that point when the client accepts (Sparadeo, Barth, & Stout, 1992) that he or she must no longer use substances and therefore must participate in treatment and continue to develop treatment objectives toward the ultimate goal of long-term abstinence (maintenance stage).

Educational approaches must be varied and range from formal to fully integrated. Formal educational approaches are usually didactic and occur within group and lecture formats. Integrated education occurs through educational information passed on to the client by every staff member whenever the opportunity arises and also on a planned basis. For example, it is not unusual for a client to have various discussions with his or her physical therapist during treatment. This is a good opportunity for the physical therapist to provide information to the client about the effects of substance use on physical functioning. Similar examples can be developed with all the therapeutic disciplines.

Skills Training

Staying substance free requires the acquisition of specific skills. The process of skills training is occurring from the moment a TBI survivor arrives in the treatment program. When one considers the cognitive and behavioral activities that are required for the client to turn down a drink, it is clear that certain skills are needed for him or her to be successful. The skills training becomes much more focused and meaningful once the client has moved from the contemplation stage of change to the action stage. Langley (1991) and Blackerby and Baumgarten (1990) point out the need for the client to express a desire to change before skills training treatment goals can be developed or reached. In the TBI survivor who is in the precontemplation phase of change, specific skills training is not likely to bring positive results. Instead, the treatment team must continue to provide information and create a need in the TBI survivor. The creation of the need often occurs through positive peer pressure (often in formal groups as well as in informal social situations) and modeling of staff as well as survivor peers.

Langley (1991) divides coping skills training into three subcomponents: problem-solving training, formal instruction and modeling, and other skills training techniques. The specific skills trained are determined by the information gathered in the comprehensive evaluation. The evaluation yields information about the role of substance use, the cues (situational and internal) for substance use, the factors maintaining substance use (expectancies and family issues), the probability of return to use or continued use, and the cognitive strengths and weaknesses of the individual. In general, this process of training in coping skills works well in group circumstances (Blackerby & Baumgarten, 1990; Langley, 1991).

The main objective of problem-solving training is to improve the client's ability to recognize high-risk situations and to respond to those situations in an adaptive, non-substance using manner. This requires the treatment approach to teach the TBI survivor to inhibit impulses, develop alternative responses, and adjust those responses on the basis of feedback (D'Zurilla & Goldfried, 1971). The client's success at learning problem-solving skills is obviously strongly dependent on his or her level of cognitive functioning. Group approaches are helpful in assisting the client to identify common high-risk situations and to role play various solutions to the problem. Through the use of the Inventory of Drinking Situations and the Situational Confidence Questionnaire (Annis & Davis, 1989), a series of situational scenarios can be developed for the TBI survivor and then role played in a hierarchical manner from least to most difficult. Langley and Kiley (1992) point out that the TBI survivor's skillfulness in responding to various scenarios can be measured with the Situational Competency Test (Chaney et al., 1978) and the Adaptive Skills Battery (Jones, Kanfer, & Lanyon, 1982).

Videotaping is also a powerful adjunct to creating good problem-solving skills (Blackerby & Baumgarten, 1990). After a period of training, the client can be asked to identify personal high-risk situations and to share these with the group.

Many TBI survivors have a deficiency in self-awareness. It is essential that self-awareness be addressed in the evaluation, and for clients with

Table 9-1 Self-Statement Based Problem-Solving

Self-Statement	Process
Stop, step back, and think	Problem sensitivity and orientation
What is the problem?	Problem identification and formulation
How can I solve the problem?	Generation of solutions
Which is the best solution?	Decision making
What is my plan of action?	Implementation

limitations the treatment process must provide sensitization. Part of the process of gaining self-awareness is active self-monitoring. This process is initially externalized through recognizing and recording events and eventually becomes internalized as self-awareness.

Langley (1991) suggests an approach to assisting the client in developing problem-solving skills based on a model developed by D'Zurilla and Goldfried (1971). The model uses five simple steps that occur as self-statements and stimulate a problem-solving process (Table 9-1).

Cue cards are often helpful, and in some cases they are a necessary adjunct to the treatment process (Foxx, Martella, & Merchand-Martella, 1989). Langley (1991) suggests that cue cards be faded, along with verbal prompts, as the client learns the technique. There are, however, clients who will require cue cards on an ongoing basis as a result of severe deficits in learning and memory. Clients who experienced anoxia at the time of the brain injury or who have bilateral temporal lobe lesions will often experience significant memory and learning problems, and cue cards may be streamlined over time; they are rarely completely faded, however.

Cue cards (sometimes called sober cards) can be directive (e.g., "Avoid the town common"), metaphorical (e.g., "Straight—sober—success"), instructional (e.g., "Alcohol slows down my recovery"), or indirect (e.g., "Remember to bring my cane"). In the last example (indirect), the client often forgets his or her cane, which leads to leg pain, which cues the use of narcotics.

Another variation on the cue cards is the community passport (Sparadeo, DePasquale, & Beardsly, 1990). In this procedure the TBI survivor who is in a rehabilitation program is asked to apply for a community passport each time he or she leaves the facility. The passport consists of the survivor's name, his or her picture, and a series of standard high-risk situations (e.g., walking past the liquor store on Main Street) and coping response cues. In addition, nonstandard anticipated high-risk situations are written in the passport along with coping response cues that are either self-generated and checked with staff or coached. Upon completion of the passport application process, the survivor carries his or her passport into the community, where it serves as a cue card.

It is one thing to have a solution to a problem prepared. It is another thing actually to carry out the solution plan. Formal instruction, modeling, rehearsing, feedback, and homework are helpful and often necessary to reduce the likelihood of substance use. TBI survivors often demonstrate a disconnection between intent and action as a result of frontal lobe damage. To bridge this gap between intent and action, it is helpful continually to provide opportunities for the client to model problem-solving techniques and to rehearse them as well. Group interventions were discussed above in the context of problem identification and solution planning. This group format is also excellent in providing a forum for rehearsal. Group exercises in real-life circumstances allow the client to model other successful clients as well as staff members in solving naturally occurring problems.

It is often necessary for a client to modify a problem-solving response. The client must first recognize that his or her response requires modification. This occurs through feedback. Feedback is often most powerful when applied in a group format, although it also can be effective in one-on-one circumstances as well. When a client modifies a problem-solving response in reply to feedback, it is important to reinforce the client to ensure the acquisition of this skill. Feedback is most effective when applied in a specific way rather than in a global format (Rose, 1989) and when it is relevant to the client (Langley, 1991).

Skills acquisition does not occur only during formal therapy sessions. It is important for clients to utilize various skills acquisition techniques on their own. This is best accomplished by assigning clients homework that allows for independent practice of various skills building techniques. Langley (1991) points out that homework assignments should challenge but not overwhelm the client's coping abilities, thereby creating the effect of inoculation to stressors.

In addition to coping skills training, it may be necessary to train clients in other techniques that will assist in developing and maintaining sobriety. Langley (1991) points out several procedures that can be utilized on an individual basis. These include covert sensitization (Rimmele, Miller, & Dougher, 1989), which is the pairing of nausea-producing images and drinking images; the community reinforcement approach (Hunt & Azrin, 1973; Sisson & Azrin, 1989), which is a set of behaviorally based treatment procedures; and cue exposure and response prevention, which are procedures to desensitize the individual to anxiety-provoking situations that lead to use of substances. In addition to these specific skills training approaches, it is often helpful to train a client in the process of leisure time utilization. The recreational therapist is trained to assist TBI survivors in developing antidotes to boredom and constructive activity plans. The avoidance of boredom increases the probability of remaining abstinent from alcohol or other drugs.

Aftercare Planning and Follow-Up

The usefulness of an intervention is ultimately determined not only by the progress a client makes during the treatment process but also by the long-term outcome. Long-term outcome is dependent on a number of factors, some of which are beyond the control or influence of the treatment team. Part of the treatment program philosophy is designing the entire intervention around increasing the probability of long-term success. Many of the fundamental approaches to treatment discussed above contribute to increasing the probability of success. Comprehensive assessment and evaluation lead to appropriate matching of treatment plan to treatment needs, and specific skills are necessary to carry on treatment gains beyond the structure of formal treatment. A number of additional factors also contribute to increasing the probability of long-term success. Some of these are program

consistency, interdisciplinary responsibility, family or support system involvement, use of community resources, follow-up contact, and ongoing staff training.

Treatment Program Consistency

Program philosophy and program delivery must be consistent. Consistency must also be reflected among staff members. Intrateam differences can cause inconsistency in the actual delivery of interventions. This sometimes surfaces in the utilization of self-help approaches such as Alcoholics Anonymous or Narcotics Anonymous. Some staff members may support the use of these approaches as a component of the treatment plan, wheras others may feel different. Another problem that often arises is a philosophical split between staff utilizing behavioral approaches and those utilizing interpersonal counseling approaches. One of the implications of philosophical splits between team members is that the client will often manipulate these splits as a way of avoiding or sabotaging his or her own treatment.

Inconsistencies must be recognized and resolved, or the integrity and credibility of the total program will be jeopardized, and clients and their families will become confused. This confusion will contribute to either relapse or poor outcome.

It is possible for programs to reflect a number of approaches within a consistent program format if all staff members respect the value of each other's approaches. Presently, no one knows the correct approach to guaranteeing a successful long-term outcome, so that it is necessary to respect alternative approaches that are ethically sound and generally accepted.

Interdisciplinary Responsibility

It is necessary for all members of the TBI rehabilitation team to learn about substance use, its implications, and the role that each team member can play in working toward the goal of sobriety. If all members of the treatment team are educated about substance abuse, and if all members of the team realize that substance use by a TBI survivor is risky and therefore unhealthy, then each member can develop a specific approach to each client in confronting this issue. The occupational therapist, speech therapist, physical therapist, recreational therapist, and so forth can all contribute to improving the probability of a successful substance abuse intervention. In some cases interventions can be developed specifically to address the issue of substance use (e.g., the recreational therapist leads a trigger identification group to anticipate drinking triggers that may occur on an outing); at other times the issue of substance use can be a coexisting target (e.g., a cognitive rehabilitation approach that integrates a sobriety message while training in problem-solving skills). A fully integrated team exposes the client to a number of situations in which sobriety is emphasized and alternatives to substance use are suggested and encouraged.

Family or Support System Involvement

Family involvement is a critical variable in increasing the probability of long-term successful outcome. Because family involvement is so critical, the issue of substance use must be addressed with the family early in the TBI rehabilitation program (Sparadeo, Strauss, & Kapsalis, 1992). Teaching the family relapse prevention techniques, such as eliminating enabling behaviors, improving communication, increasing positive interchanges, utilizing conflict resolution procedures, and developing behavior change agreements, is essential. It is also important to prepare the family and the client for lapses by explaining the difference between a lapse and a relapse. Familiarizing the family and client with community-based resources will go a long way toward increasing the probability of a good long-term outcome (Sparadeo, Strauss, & Kapsalis, 1992). Not all TBI survivors have intact or supportive families, however, and it is sometimes necessary to solicit the help of other individuals who constitute the client's support system. Whoever is willing to become involved will require the type of training suggested above.

Use of Community Resources

Case managers will find it necessary to become knowledgeable about the substance abuse services available in a client's community and to assist the client in choosing an appropriate aftercare program. This is a difficult process because not all communities have comprehensive networks of services, and often even when the services exist the client will be turned away because of his or her history of TBI. On other occasions a substance abuse program may be willing to admit the TBI survivor but will have little knowledge of the TBI issues that need continued attention. It may be necessary to build bridges between the TBI rehabilitation system and the substance abuse system by offering to provide mutual inservice education programs and ongoing dialog.

Follow-Up Contact

Each client discharged from a TBI or substance abuse program must be contacted regularly after discharge. A client who completes a program has made a significant personal investment in that program and in his or her relationship with the program staff. An absence of follow-up contact is likely to result in disappointment and feelings of abandonment, which increase the probability of substance use. The client must feel comfortable calling and visiting the program. It is sometimes helpful to organize formal reunions of clients at the program facility, where they can interact with staff, peers, and clients currently undergoing treatment. During active rehabilitation it is useful to develop a follow-up plan that includes a review of the projected risk factors with the support system. At the time of follow-up contact these risk factors can be reviewed once again, but with respect to the survivor's success in coping with them, and new risk factors can be added and discussed.

Ongoing Staff Training

A comprehensive staff training program that involves all members of the staff, including administration, program leadership, clinicians, and support staff, increases the probability of long-term successful outcome by providing the staff with confidence as well as skills. Skillful and confident staff not only are directly helpful to the client at the time of treatment in a formal sense but also are good role models for future reference, and they are people who can be trusted should the client seek them out. Staff training should always be considered ongoing. It is helpful, when this area of specialty programming is initiated, to develop a training curriculum that includes regular updates.

STAFF TRAINING

Initial Steps

Addressing the issue of substance abuse within the context of a TBI rehabilitation program is necessary and complex. It is necessary because of the large number of TBI survivors who had a substance abuse problem before their injury, are likely to develop a substance abuse problem after the injury, or are currently experiencing a substance abuse problem. The various options for addressing the substance abuse issue as well as the reactions to those options by staff, family, and clients reflect this complexity. The process of formal program development requires the hurdling of certain barriers. Two of the obvious initial steps in program development are convincing senior management staff of the need for such programming and overcoming resistance from all levels of staff.

Convincing Senior Program Management

Senior program management staff typically consists of the following positions: executive director, program director, associate program director, case manager, the board of directors, discipline directors, and administrators. These individuals are responsible for creating and establishing policy, approving intervention protocols, determining staff levels, conducting program evaluation, supporting programs, and conducting the formal operations of the program. If this group of individuals is not convinced that a substance use protocol needs to be implemented, such programming will only be seen as adjunctive and therefore not critical.

Training of senior program management obviously requires their willingness to participate. There is often resistance by various members of the senior management staff to participating in training programs. Often, time constraints are cited. Most resistance is due to erroneous belief systems (e.g., "Substance abuse does not occur in my facility") and fear (i.e., acknowledgment of the issue of substance abuse will initiate self-examination).

It is also common for program development pressure to come up from the clinical staff to the senior management staff, so that senior management staff training is difficult to initiate because the program concept did not originate with them. It must be demonstrated to senior management staff that substance abuse programming is a response to a clinical need and that outcome is likely to be affected by the integrity of such programming. Rehabilitation programs have a responsibility to the client and family to address issues that are likely to increase the risk of postrehabilitation failure.

Coping with Resistance

There is probably no topic other than sexuality that generates as much fear, ambivalence, and resistance as substance abuse. Much of the fear is due to notions that offering substance abuse services will cause clinical chaos, attract undesirable clients, and upset families. It must be pointed out to staff that more than 50% of all admissions to TBI rehabilitation programs are either active or recently active substance users. It must also be pointed out that without intervention a minimum 40% of the clients admitted to a TBI rehabilitation program are likely to use alcohol either during or after rehabilitation.

Much of the ambivalence regarding substance abuse in general and in relation to training seen among all levels of staff is often due to personal experience with substance use. More than 72% of people in the United States have at least tried marijuana (Shuckitt, 1989). About 80% of all adults in the United States drink alcohol, and more than 90% of teenagers are drinkers by the time they leave high school (Shuckitt, 1989). It is difficult for a rehabilitation professional to advocate abstinence for a client when he or she uses a substance.

There are critical differences among types of substance use that need to be brought to the forefront when one is trying to resolve this ambivalence. It is clear that, although most adults drink, most do not abuse alcohol, develop life problems due to alcohol, or become addicted to alcohol. In other words, most adults are responsible in their drinking. The TBI survivor is often left with cognitive or physical disabilities. The interaction of these disabilities and alcohol is not fully understood, but initial information suggests that alcohol at any level may be harmful to these clients (i.e., it slows down cognitive recovery, has an exaggerated pharmacological effect, magnifies judgment and other cognitive problems, and increases the risk of seizure activity, falls, and accidents). It is important that the staff realize that their responsibility is to counsel TBI survivors on the healthiest life course. The TBI survivor ultimately makes his or her own decision about the use of substances. In view of the multiple risks associated with the use of alcohol and other drugs in the TBI survivor, it is incumbent upon the clinical team to stress abstinence, particularly during the rehabilitation process.

Another issue that feeds ambivalence and increases resistance is personal experience with substance abusers. Almost all adults have had experiences with a substance abuser, perhaps a parent, sibling, other relative, spouse, or good friend. Often, unresolved feelings about these experiences shape an individual's attitudes and behaviors toward people with substance abuse problems. TBI rehabilitation programming, as part of staff training, must bring up this issue and allow staff to discuss it. Sometimes it is necessary to refer a staff member for counseling to assist him or her in resolving this problem. This should be expected, and therefore appropriate resources should be available.

Although resistance can be due to both fear and ambivalence, it occurs for other reasons as well. The simplest explanation of resistance is dislike of change. Whenever a new idea or program is initiated, there is some initial resistance. Experienced program managers and staff resolve this type of resistance through staff training, policy setting, and strategic planning. Often, staff feel unprepared to handle a new clinical program responsibility. Staff training and pro-

gram development must therefore be ongoing, with key staff being fully trained (e.g., certified in substance abuse counseling or formally trained in substance abuse) and experienced to serve as resources for other staff. Developing a substance abuse intervention program without fully trained and experienced key personnel will result in confusion and staff conflicts over sensitive value-based issues. This will lead to the staff feeling insecure, which will build resistance and further contribute to program failure.

Staff Training Curriculum

The development of a comprehensive staff training curriculum on substance abuse requires recognition that the issue of substance abuse affects all staff members. Training must be targeted and designed separately for each staff category, provided on an ongoing basis, and flexible enough to respond to individual staff needs. Sparadeo, Strauss, and Barth (1990) have made suggestions regarding the content of such training, and Blackerby and Baumgarten (1990) have suggested a curriculum that appears to be geared to clinical staff. The following discussion reviews the rationale for substance abuse staff training for each of the major staff categories typically in place at a TBI rehabilitation program (see also Appendix 9-1).

Senior Program Management Staff (Nonclinical)

Often, administrators or executive directors have limited clinical training. A curriculum for this group must demonstrate the ubiquitous nature of substance abuse, the fact that more than 50% of TBI survivors were under the influence of alcohol or other drugs at the time of injury, and the fact that of that group at least 50% were clearly substance abusers before injury. It must also be demonstrated that ignoring substance abuse issues will contribute to poor outcomes for TBI survivors and that substance abuse is likely to be a problem for at least 10% of the staff. This last point is rarely discussed in staff training, but it is obviously important to the issue of program consistency. Furthermore, staff substance abuse problems are costly to the program. The cost is experienced in poor work habits, work-related injuries, absenteeism, tardiness, and unhealthy influence on clients. Finally, a staff training curriculum for administrators must emphasize the need for comprehensive training for the entire staff and must stress the need for the facility to establish formal procedures to address this area of service.

Senior Program Management (Clinical)

The clinical senior program management staff usually consists of the program director, associate program directors, and clinical specialty directors or coordinators. A staff training curriculum for this group of staff must emphasize the need for programming. This is accomplished by reviewing the epidemiological literature on TBI and substance abuse as well as reviewing the substance abuse treatment literature. Before the development of an actual treatment program, policies must be developed that address a number of important issues: assessment and evaluation of all clients for substance abuse identification, the use of substances in the facility, the use of drug testing and breath testing in the facility, and protocols for aftercare and follow-up. This policy development begins within the context of staff training by reviewing policies developed in other programs and by discussing the implications of these policies and the facility's ability to implement the same or similar policies.

Once policy development training is underway, program development issues must also be addressed within the context of staff training. This is accomplished by reviewing the structure and success of existing programs, treatment options and models, self-help approaches, and the degree to which all disciplines contribute to treatment. It is often helpful to suggest the development of a program development team, which would consist mainly of clinicians; on such a team, however, it is important to include at least one member of each of the major staff categories, and consideration should be given to including a survivor or family member to help define clinical efficacy.

The issue of staff use of substances must also be addressed within the context of this training. Development of a policy regarding assisting troubled staff is a must if a substance abuse program is to develop for clients. Senior program management staff must confront personal issues and concerns regarding substance use as well as their own staff's issues. This must be addressed early in staff training in a sensitive and informative way. It is often the case that during staff training on substance abuse a number of staff members will identify themselves as troubled and request a referral. It is helpful to have this in place before staff training continues on to the majority of staff (i.e., clinicians and support staff).

As is the case in the training of nonclinical senior program management staff, it is important to emphasize to the clinical senior management staff the importance of comprehensive training for all staff. It is also important to include the clinical program leadership staff in all aspects of the clinical training.

Clinical Staff

The most extensive training must occur with the clinical staff because they will be delivering the bulk of the intervention for each client. There are numerous topics to cover in a curriculum for clinical staff training and a significant amount of content. The implementation of such a comprehensive training program will require time, but once the program has been completed the benefit will be much more efficient interventions with TBI survivors who have substance use issues.

The most difficult training topic to address is personal issues. The difficulty with substance abuse interventions, particularly those that promote abstinence, is that they are often administered by people who use alcohol. As discussed above, this often sets up internal conflict in those clinicians being asked to learn about substance abuse interventions and to apply these interventions. Through staff training and experience, this problem can be handled by reviewing attitudes, e.g., providing information, destroying misconceptions, clarifying values, and resolving internal conflicts. It is not uncommon after these training sessions for at least one or two staff members to be referred for counseling to assist them in resolving their internal conflicts. Ultimately, in addition to providing that base for skills development, staff training seeks to normalize value differences among staff to avoid team conflicts.

Other important topics for the clinical staff to address in staff training are as follows: assessment and evaluation, self-help models, barriers to successful interventions, intervention models, integrating substance abuse issues into the TBI rehabilitation program, maintaining change, aftercare, and follow-up.

Support Staff

When a staff training program is established, the support staff are often left out. This is unfortunate because the support staff have a high level of involvement with clients. Often, clients confide in these staff members more than in the clinical staff. These important interactions vary in quality and effect. Staff interactions with clients who are confronting a substance abuse problem require consistency and sensitivity. A staff member who is ambivalent, unaware, or unsupportive of the goals of substance abuse interventions in a client will be unprepared to deal with a situation in which a client is seeking support for a planned return to substance use or support in hiding current substance use. Crisis protocols must be developed and shared with the support staff for effective management of such issues.

When a client has a sudden personality or behavioral change, it is often indicative of a return to use of substances (or at least contemplation of return to use). Often, this change is first recognized by support staff. These staff need to realize that they are also part of the treatment team and that their observations are valuable to the entire treatment team. A major component of a training program for support staff is assisting them in developing communication skills and strategies in relation to both clinical staff and clients.

Incorporating support staff into staff training on substance abuse requires establishing the need for the training. The need is established by presenting the facts and figures on the role of substance abuse in our society and more specifi-

cally in the occurrence and rehabilitation of TBI. Finally, just as all other staff must confront personal issues regarding substance abuse, so too must the support staff.

CONCLUSION

Professionals are increasingly recognizing the need to confront the issue of substance use and abuse within the field of brain injury rehabilitation. Many TBI programs have now developed substance abuse education and intervention programs for their clients. The need to respond to the problem of substance abuse is creating a surge in program development, but few treatment models have been described in the rehabilitation literature, and none has produced any outcome data as of this writing. The most promising model appears to be the skills-based prevention and treatment model (Langley, 1991; Langley & Kiley, 1992). The probability of successful interventions can be increased by comprehensive evaluation and treatment matching, program consistency, integrative treatment approaches, family and support system involvement, use of community resources, aftercare and follow-up contact, and ongoing staff training. The response to program development needs begins with comprehensive staff training. Staff training must be geared to the entire staff including both clinical and nonclinical senior management staff, clinical staff, and support staff. Staff training must take into account conflicting belief systems, resistance, and personal issues related to substance abuse. Ultimately staff training will improve the level of knowledge regarding substance abuse in relation to TBI rehabilitation, normalize value differences among staff, reduce or avoid staff conflict regarding the issue of substance use, improve the facility's skill level in intervening, and improve the probability of successful rehabilitation in the TBI survivor.

ACKNOWLEDGMENT

The author acknowledges the State of Massachusetts Statewide Head Injury Program Substance Abuse Task Force for giving input and allowing the time to complete this chapter. Special thanks to Debra Kamen, Director of SHIP and to Dr. Fran LaVecchio.

REFERENCES

Annis, H.M., & Davis, C.S. (1989). Relapse prevention. In R.K. Hester & W.R Miller (Eds.). *Handbook of alcoholism treatment approaches* (pp. 170–182). New York: Pergamon.

Bishop, D.M., & Miller, I.W. (1988). Traumatic brain injury: Empirical family assessment techniques. *Journal of Head Trauma Rehabilitation, 3,* 16–30.

Blackerby, W.F., & Baumgarten, A. (1990). A model treatment program for the head-injured substance abuser: Preliminary findings. *Journal of Head Trauma Rehabilitation, 5,* 47–59.

Brooks, N., Symington, C., Beattie, A. (1989). Alcohol and other predictors of recovery after severe head injury. *Brain Injury, 3,* 235–246.

Brooks, N., Symington, C., Beattie, A., Campsie, L., Bryden, J., & McKinlay, W. (1989). Alcohol ad other predictors of recovery after severe head injury. *Brain Injury, 3,* 235–246.

Brown, S.A., Chassin L., & Sher, K.J. (1987). The Alcohol Expectancy Questionnaire: An instrument for the assessment of adolescent and adult expectancies. *Journal of Studies on Alcohol, 48,* 483–491.

Burke, W.H., Weselowski, M.D., & Guth, W.L. (1988). Comprehensive head injury rehabilitation: An outcome evaluation. *Brain Injury, 2,* 313–322.

Cahalan, D., & Cisin, I. (1968a). American drinking practices: Summary of findings from a national probability sample: I. Extent of drinking by population subgroups. *Quarterly Journal of Studies on Alcohol, 29,* 130–151.

Cahalan, D. & Cisin, I. (1968). American drinking practices: Summary of findings from a national probability sample: II. Measurement of massed versus spaced drinking. *Quarterly Journal of Studies on Alcohol, 29,* 642–656.

Chaney, E.F., O'Leary, M.R., & Marlatt, G.A. (1978). Skill training with alcoholics. *Journal of Consulting and Clinical Psychology, 46,* 1092–1104.

Dunlop, T.W., Udvarhelyi, G.B., Stedman, A.F., O'Connor, J.M., Isaacs, M.L., Puig, J.G., & Mather, J.H. (1991). Comparison of patients with behavioral deterioration during the first year after traumatic brain injury. *The Journal of Neuropsychiatry and Clinical Neurosciences, 3,* 150–156.

D'Zurilla, T.J., & Goldfried, M.R. (1971). Problem solving and behavior modification. *Journal of Abnormal Psychology, 78,* 197–226.

Edna, T. (1982). Alcohol influence and head injury. *Acta Chirurgica Scandinavica, 148,* 209–212.

Epstein, N., Baldwin, L., & Bishop S. (1983). The McMaster Family Assessment Device. *Journal of Marital and Family Therapy, 9,* 171–180.

Ewing, J.A. (1984). Detecting alcoholism: The CAGE questionnaire. *Journal of the American Medical Association, 252,* 1905–1907.

Foxx, R.M., Martella, R.C., & Merchand-Martella, N.E. (1989). The acquisition, maintenance, and generalization of problem solving skills by closed head injured adults. *Behavior Therapy, 20,* 61–76.

Horn, J.L., Wanberg, K.W. & Foster, F.M. (1987). *Guide to the Alcohol Use Inventory.* Minneapolis, MN: National Computer Systems.

Hunt, G.M., & Azrin, H.H. (1973). A community-reinforcement approach to resocializing alcoholics in the community. *Journal of Studies on Alcohol, 43,* 1115–1123.

Jones, G.A. (1992). Substance abuse treatment for persons with brain injuries. *NeuroRehabilitation: An Interdisciplinary Journal, 2,* 27–34.

Jones, S.L., Kanfer, R., & Lanyon, R.I. (1982). Skill training with alcoholics: A clinical extension. *Addictive Behaviors, 7,* 285–290.

Kaitz, S. (1991, Summer). Integrated treatment: Safety net for survival. *Headlines,* 11–14.

Karol, R., & Sparadeo, F.R. (1990). *Alcohol, drugs and brain injury: A survivor's workbook.* Lynn, MA: New Medico Head Injury System.

Kraus, J.F., & Nourjah, P. (1989). The epidemiology of mild head injury. In H. Levin, H. Eisenberg, & A. Benton (Eds.). *Mild head injury* (pp. 8–24). New York: Oxford University Press.

Kreutzer, J.S, Doherty, B.A., Harris, J.A., & Zasler, N.D. (1990). Alcohol use among persons with traumatic brain injury. *Journal of Head Trauma Rehabilitation, 5,* 9–20.

Kreutzer, J.S., Marwitz, J.H., & Wehman, P.H. (1991). Substance abuse assessment and treatment in vocational rehabilitation for persons with brain injury. *Journal of Head Trauma Rehabilitation, 6,* 12–23.

Kreutzer, J.S., Wehman, P., Harris, J., Burns, C., & Young, H. (1991). Substance abuse and crime patterns among persons with traumatic brain injury referred for supported employment. *Brain Injury, 5*(2), 177–187.

Langley, M.J. (1991). Preventing post-injury alcohol related problems: A behavioral approach. In B.T. McMahon & L.R. Shaw (Eds.). *Work worth doing: Advances in brain injury rehabilitation.* Orlando, FL: Deutsch.

Langley, M.J., & Kiley, D.J. (1992). Prevention of substance abuse in persons with neurologic disabilities. *NeuroRehabilitation: An Interdisciplinary Journal, 2,* 52–64.

Miller, W.R. (1989). Increasing motivation for change. In R.K. Hester & W.R. Miller (Eds.). *Handbook of alcoholism treatment approaches* (pp. 67–80). New York: Pergamon.

Mishkin, D., & Sparadeo, F.R. (1991, December). *Effects of pre-injury alcohol use on acute TBI rehabilitation.* Paper presented at the Annual Meeting of the National Head Injury Foundation, Los Angeles, CA.

Moore, D. (1992). Substance abuse assessment and diagnosis in medical rehabilitation. *NeuroRehabilitation: An Interdisciplinary Journal, 2,* 7–15.

Prochaska, J.O., & DiClemente, C.C. (1992). In search of how people change: Applications to addictive behaviors. *American Psychologist, 47*(9), 1102–1114.

Prochaska, J.O., & DiClemente, C.C. (1986). Toward a comprehensive model of change. In W.R. Miller & N. Heather (Eds.). *Treating addictive behaviors: Process of change* (pp. 3–27). New York: Plenum.

Rimel, R., Giordani, B., Barth, J., & Jane, J. (1982). Moderate head injury: Completing the clinical spectrum of brain trauma. *Neurosurgery, 11,* 344–351.

Rimmele, C.T., Miller, W.R., & Dougher, M.J. (1989). Aversion therapies. In R.K. Hester & W.R. Miller (Eds.). *Handbook of alcoholism treatment approaches* (pp. 128–140). New York: Pergamon.

Rose, S.D. (1989). Coping skill training in groups. *International Journal of Group Psychotherapy, 39,* 59–78.

Salcido, R., & Costich, J.F. (in press). Recurrent traumatic brain injury. *Brain Injury.*

Sisson, R., & Azrin, N. (1989). The community reinforcement approach. In R.K. Hester & W.R. Miller (Eds.). *Handbook of alcoholism treatment approaches* (pp. 242–258). New York: Pergamon.

Solomon, D., & Sparadeo, F.R. (1992). Effects of substance use on persons with traumatic brain injury. *NeuroRehabilitation: An Interdisciplinary Journal, 2,* 16–26.

Sparadeo, F.R., Barth, J.T., & Stout. (1992). Addiction and traumatic brain injury. In C.E. Stout, J.L. Levitt, & D.H. Ruben (Eds.). *Handbook for assessing and treating addictive disorders.* New York: Greenwood Press.

Sparadeo, F.R., DePasquale, M., & Beardsly, J. (1990, November). *Substance abuse, brain injury and rehabilitation.* Paper presented at the Annual Meeting of the National Head Injury Foundation, New Orleans, LA.

Sparadeo, F.R., & Gill, D. (1989). Effects of prior alcohol use on head injury recovery. *Journal of Head Trauma Rehabilitation, 4,* 75–82.

Sparadeo, F.R., Strauss, D., & Barth, J.T. (1990). The incidence, impact and treatment of substance abuse in head trauma rehabilitation. *Journal of Head Trauma Rehabilitation, 5,* 1–8.

Sparadeo, F.R., Strauss, D., & Kapsalis, K. (1992). Substance abuse, brain injury and family adjustment. *NeuroRehabilitation: An Interdisciplinary Journal, 2,* 65–73.

Steinglass, P., Bennett, L.A., Wolin, S.J., & Reiss, D. (1987). *The alcoholic family.* New York: Basic.

Willoughby, A. (1980). The alcohol troubled person: Known and unknown. Chicago: Nelson Hall.

Zung, B. (1979). Psychometric properties of the MAST and two briefer versions. *Journal of Studies on Alcohol, 40,* 845–850.

Staff Training Curriculum: Substance Abuse and TBI

Topic	Content
Clinical staff	
Statement of need	Literature review to include the topics of substance abuse in general, the effects of various drugs of abuse on cognitive and behavioral functioning, substance abuse and brain injury, and the effects of substance abuse on brain injury outcome
Personal issues	Review of misconceptions and stereotypes Attitude review, change, and development Values clarification Availability of referral for staff
Assessment and evaluation	Review of standard measures Applying standard measures to the TBI population: problems and adjustments Review of interview techniques Differential diagnosis Taking into account collateral psychiatric diagnoses Integrating cognitive and psychosocial assessment with the substance abuse assessment Review of the concept of client matching and its appropriateness
Treatment planning	Integration of assessment and evaluation in the development of the treatment plan Matching treatment approach to the specific needs of the client
Barriers to successful intervention	Defensiveness (e.g., denial, rationalization) Substance use expectancies Boredom

Topic	*Content*
	Family issues
	Friends and acquaintances
	Emotional factors (depression, poor self-image, anxiety)
	Cognitive impairment
Models of intervention	Behavioral skills acquisition
	Interpersonal model
	Change theory
	Group interventions
	Self-help approaches
Overview of self-help models	Alcoholics Anonymous
	Narcotics Anonymous
	Others
Integrating substance abuse treatment and prevention into the TBI treatment plan	Unique role of physical therapist, occupational therapist, speech therapist, recreational therapist, psychologist, social worker, nurse, physiatrist, and other rehabilitation specialists
	Overlapping roles of all staff members
	Understanding the need for a team approach
	Anticipating barriers
	Understanding the important role of the family and/or significant others
The role of the family	Assessing family functioning
	Integrating the family into the intervention process
Maintaining change	Relapse prevention
	Understanding substance use expectancies
	Understanding situational cues for substance use
	Understanding situational confidence levels for maintaining sobriety
	Family support
	Group process
	Anticipating triggers
	Preparing for lapse
	Understanding situational cues
	Understanding situational confidence levels for maintaining sobriety
Aftercare	Family training
	Support system training
	Utilization of community-based substance abuse resources
	Follow-up programming
Crisis intervention	Determining the basis of the crisis
	Determining the first thing to do
	Rewarding partial success
	Distinguishing between lapse and relapse
	"To discharge or not"
	"To detox or not"

Topic	Content
	Postcrisis analysis
	Reviewing factors leading to the crisis
	Reviewing and adjusting the treatment plan

Senior program management staff (nonclinical)

Need for programming	Review of the literature on substance abuse and TBI, particularly information about the incidence of the problem of substance abuse among TBI survivors as well as the incidence of substance use after rehabilitation
	Review of the effects of drugs abuse on behavioral and cognitive functioning
	Discussion of the impact of substance use on long-term outcome
Staff issues	The cost of substance use/abuse among staff and clients
	Anticipation of assisting staff with their own substance use issues once identified
Staff training	Demonstration of the ongoing need for staff training regarding substance use/abuse at all staff levels (clinical staff, senior program management staff, and support staff)

Senior program management staff (clinical)

Need for programming	Review of epidemiological literature on TBI as well as literature on factors contributing to failure after TBI
	Review of substance abuse and head injury literature
	Review of substance abuse treatment literature
Clinical training	Participation in the clinical staff training program (described above)
Policy development	Standardizing assessment and evaluation procedures
	Development of minimum standards for addressing the issue of substance use/abuse in the TBI program
	Development of protocols for addressing the issue of substance use at the program site
	Development of protocols for addressing substance use by a client while involved in active rehabilitation
	Development of a protocol for the use of drug testing and breath testing
	Addressing aftercare and follow-up needs of the clients programmatically
	Development of a policy and procedure for addressing substance use/abuse by staff, to include referral for staff requesting assistance
Program development	Review of treatment program models
	Review of self-help models

Topic	Content
	Review of integrated treatment versus categorical treatment options
	Review of the pros and cons of hiring a specialist in substance abuse to coordinate substance abuse prevention and intervention and to conduct ongoing training

Support staff

Topic	Content
Establish need	Review of facts and figures regarding TBI and substance abuse
	Review of the effects of drugs of abuse on cognitive and behavioral functioning
Personal issues	Values clarification
	Attitude review, change, and development
	Availability of personal assistance if needed
Communication	The role of support staff in the treatment process
	Specific communication pitfalls and approaches
	Communication options with the clinical staff
Observation	Reporting of personality or behavioral change among clients
	Maintaining objectivity and avoiding judgment
Crises	Techniques for avoiding crises
	Developing an intervention plan
	Participation in clinical staff training on crisis intervention

Beyond the Management of Sexual Problems: Creating a Therapeutic Environment for Addressing Sexuality Issues

10

Stanley H. Ducharme

OBJECTIVES

Upon completion of this chapter, the reader will be able to:

1. describe how traumatic head injury affects sexuality and sexual functioning
2. identify the most common barriers to sexual adjustment in the rehabilitation setting
3. outline the staff competencies needed to effectively address areas of sexuality
4. state the various educational modalities available for staff training and for clients in the areas of sexuality
5. identify program development strategies that will assist rehabilitation programs to become more responsive to clients' emotional recovery and sexual health

Beyond the Management of Sexual Problems

Over the past decade there has been an increasing awareness and acceptance of the fact that issues of sexuality are an important consideration of the rehabilitation program. Today, most major rehabilitation facilities include sexual education programs, counseling for clients on these issues, and periodic training programs for staff members. This is in sharp contrast to studies of 15 years ago that indicated that only approximately 50% of rehabilitation clients received any information about areas related to sexual health (Bregman & Hadley, 1976).

Unfortunately, in brain injury rehabilitation the focus of sexuality training has not been on providing information and education to clients. Neither has it been the development of a therapeutic milieu that encourages psychological growth and a reaffirmation of one's sexuality. Instead, what has been more widely recognized is a desire in the rehabilitation community for information about the management of hypersexual disorders and inappropriate sexual behavior. It has only been recently that isolated case studies have utilized a more positive approach that focuses on development of social skills and a redirecting of stimulus control (Zencius, Wesolowski, Burke, & Hough, 1990).

This is a welcome change from an approach to sexual problems that has been restrictive in nature and punitive toward the development of sexual identity. There is a risk in labeling male or female clients as sexually inappropriate or as sexually acting out. When clients are categorized as such, there is a danger that they will be denied sexual information or education. In these clients, there is often an unspoken fear that education about sexuality will intensify their acting out and make them less manageable during their rehabilitation program. These clients are frequently labeled as troublemakers and are isolated from ongoing social interaction, where important interpersonal skills may be learned. For a man with a disability, these labels of being sexually inappropriate can easily intensify feelings of identity confusion, emasculation, inadequacy, and shame. For women, feelings of vulnerability, humiliation, and victimization are not uncommon. For both men

and women, this type of experience can inhibit the development of self-esteem and interpersonal expression (Ducharme, 1991).

Often, this behaviorally oriented and restrictive approach to sexuality is reflective of anxieties on the part of the staff. It is certainly not unusual for staff members to be uncomfortable with issues of sexuality and unsure as to how such issues should be dealt with among their clients. In fact, Gill (1988) reported that the majority of staff members in her study felt uncomfortable with the topic of sexuality and that only 9% of staff regularly included the topic in their rehabilitation plans.

This chapter discusses the nature of sexual dysfunction after head injury and typical barriers to sexual adjustment that are often observed in head injury rehabilitation programs. In addition, the chapter reviews treatment and educational modalities currently being used in centers throughout the country.

From the outset, it is critical to note that institutional support and commitment to sexual health among clients is a primary consideration. It is the supportive, nurturing, and caring attitude of the administration that will ultimately filter down through staff members to the clients, their partners, and their families. Institutional recognition that sexuality is an important component of the rehabilitation program will ultimately result in an educated staff and a healthy therapeutic environment for clients, where relatedness, interpersonal consideration, and self-respect are validated.

It has been said that sexuality, broadly defined, is the most important part of rehabilitation because of its relationship to self-esteem, body image, interpersonal attachment, and motivation (Sha'ked, 1978). Although this may be an overstatement, traditional definitions of mental health also highlight its importance. Freud, for example, defined mental health as the ability to love and to work. To the extent that the person with a disability can learn to value his or her new sexual abilities (as opposed to trying to regain the same sexual life as before) and establish some method of communication, he or she will achieve a satisfying sexual adjustment. People with head injury who achieve success in sexual functioning frequently do so because of increased communication and a willingness to experiment with developing romance and intimacy as well as technique. They are secure enough to realize that not every experiment will work, and they value nongenital erogenous zones (Glass & Padrone, 1978).

Especially important is the development of skills in communication and intimacy. The need for specific and open communication between sexually involved partners is essential for a satisfactory relationship. This is even more true after the onset of head injury (Renshaw, 1978). If communication skills are not learned during the rehabilitation process, there is a danger that essential communication regarding sexuality may never be established after discharge. If staff do not discuss sexuality with clients, spouses, and appropriate family members during rehabilitation, questions and concerns about intimacy may remain in secrecy and not discussed. If the institution does not sanction the importance of intimate relationships and sexual health, we can hardly expect that the client and his or her partner can feel positive in this critical area of human nature.

In much the same respect, this openness about sexuality must also translate to specific learning strategies, in the rehabilitation setting. The ability to form intimate relationships requires training in a broad range of areas relevant to head injury. For example, it may be important to teach a person with a head injury about the various types of relationships, such as those with professional colleagues, friends, lovers, and family members. Not all relationships with members of the preferred gender need be sexual (it also may be necessary to teach the staff that not all sexual relationships need be loving relationships). Finally, to enhance the development of intimacy for people with head injury, specific behaviors need to be taught. These may include sharing feelings and experiences, touching, accepting others, recognizing others' needs, trusting, and developing communication and listening skills. All these are critical skills if one is to achieve sexual satisfaction in a sustained intimate relationship.

Although the focus of this chapter is areas of a specific sexual nature, it is also important not to ignore the more emotional issues such as sharing of feelings, caring for others, and respecting individual differences. Concerns such as these are at the core of a sexuality training program and should never be ignored in the educational process. In much the same respect, however, it is also important to realize that people with head injury, like all of us, have sexual needs and drives that also must be addressed whether or not they occur within the context of a loving, caring relationship.

THE EFFECTS OF BRAIN INJURY ON SEXUALITY

It has only been recently that investigators have begun to concern themselves with the impact of head injury on sexual functioning. This lack of attention is surprising considering that it has been reported that up to 50% of individuals with head injury have some type of sexuality disturbance after their injury (Blackerby, 1988). This is probably a low estimate because sexual dysfunctions often are not acknowledged or discovered until the individual has been discharged from acute rehabilitation and has returned to the community. In addition, psychological issues secondary to head injury can certainly impair functioning, disrupt communication, and alter sex drive. Considering the multitude of systems involved in head injury (physical, cognitive, and emotional), it is probably safe to assume that virtually all individuals with head injury must undergo certain adjustments in the sexual realm.

Although psychological considerations need to be addressed in all discussions regarding sexuality, basic physical information is equally important. Often an open, sensitive discussion regarding topics such as sensation, birth control, lubrication, and erections can be supportive. Such topics are usually on the minds of most partners, and of most clients, later in rehabilitation, but anxiety prevents a thorough discussion with appropriate health care professionals.

Physical changes after head injury tend to be minimal except when the spinal cord has been involved in the injury. In these cases, there are typical losses in erection and ejaculation, mobility, sensation, and fertility for men. For women, there is a loss of lubrication, disruptions in menstruation, decreases in sensation, and limitations in mobility. Fertility in women remains unchanged once menstruation has resumed 6 to 12 months after injury. For people of both sexes, there are accompanying changes in bladder and bowel functioning. Although the type of sexual dysfunction is clearly unique to each individual, there is most often a combination of alterations. When the client sustains head injury alone, it is rare that he or she will experience difficulty with lubrication, erection, ejaculation, and sensation (Berrol, 1981).

The literature on sexuality and head injury is sparse and occasionally contradictory. Anecdotal reports are more common that group studies. Bond (1984) noted that sex drive may increase (frank disinhibition is frequently described), decrease, or disappear. A decade earlier, Weinstein (1974) remarked on this variability, stating that brain damage affects the way in which sexuality is expressed in social contexts. Weinstein argued that the sexual behavior of people with brain injury is not inherently abnormal but only seems so by virtue of the situations in which it occurs. Berrol (1981) asserted that the most common sexual consequences of head injury are loss of libido, distractibility, and an impoverished fantasy life. For example, a person with a head injury may be unable mentally to create a romantic mood and setting that will enhance the quality of the love making. He stated that impotence in the man with head injury rarely has a physical cause. Ronsenbaum and Najenson (1976) studied 10 patients with severe brain injury and their spouses 1 year after onset. They found that sexual difficulties had an interpersonal basis; spouses avoided intimacy with their partners, who no longer resembled the men or women they had married. McKinlay, Brooks, Bond, Martinage, and Marshall (1981) found that nearly half the spouses of severely injured clients described alterations in their partner's sexual behavior at 3, 6, and 12 months after injury. Fifty percent of the married patients studied by Mikula and Rudin (1983) reported sexual difficulties.

Although residual physical disabilities may impose some limitations upon sexual activity, it is the cognitive and behavioral sequelae—impulsivity, irritability, self-centeredness, lability, rigidity, impaired social judgment, concrete thinking, memory loss, and attentional deficits—that generally have the more profound effects (Lezak, 1978). Information derived from a neuropsychological evaluation may offer insight into the patient's information-processing skills and style and may provide guidelines for the diagnosis and treatment of sexual dysfunction (Ducharme, 1988).

If, as the literature seems to suggest, sexual dysfunction after head injury rarely has a physical basis, supportive counseling for both patient and partner would seem indispensable. Partners must understand the effect of neuropsychological deficits on emotional and sexual behavior. They must learn, for example, that the client's inattentive behavior does not signal rejection but rather an organic distractibility that may ultimately be resistant to treatment. Recognition of issues such as this is critical if the relationship is to remain healthy and satisfying.

Wood (1984) notes that much of the disinhibited sexuality found in the person with head injury is linked to frontal lobe involvement. Lesions in this region typically produce impulsivity, loss of insight, and impaired social judgment, and these deficits compel a poor prognosis, particularly if no postacute rehabilitation is provided, where these types of gains may be made.

These functions have a serious impact on the ability to form and maintain a sexual relationship even when there is no impairment in the physical ability to perform sexual acts. In addition, the psychological adjustment reaction common to all disabilities may reduce sexual drive or impair performance at least initially, In general, the more severe the cerebral damage, the more serious the impairments in personal, social, and sexual functioning (Price, 1985).

The few reports on marital stability after head injury are contradictory. One long-term follow-up study (Panting & Merry, 1972) found a 40% divorce rate, whereas another study (Walker, 1972) reported a rate of only 11%, less than half the prevailing rate for men in the United States.

Mikula and Rudin (1983) found a divorce rate of 15% among their group of clients with head injury, who were studied at least 6 months after injury. These investigators noted a tendency for marital difficulties to be more common in the later years after injury. Among their married clients, 75% reported experiencing marital difficulties. It is important to keep in mind that the population with head injury contains a disproportionate number of individuals with premorbid histories of social maladjustment, drug abuse, and the like (Rimel & Jane, 1983). Within this group an elevated incidence of divorce might be obtained, even in the absence of head injury. Further study of this issue is needed.

BARRIERS THAT MAY INTERFERE WITH ADDRESSING SEXUAL CONCERNS

As health care providers, we have a primary responsibility to separate our own values and attitudes from the feelings of the client. From the outset, it is important to remember that feelings and values are neither negative nor positive. Our feelings are simply a part of who we are as individuals. It is not unusual for staff members to have high expectations of themselves. They believe that they should like all their clients and that they should be able to "cure" the people with whom they work. Such high expectations lead to feelings of guilt, frustration, and disappointment. These feelings can also create barriers that can seriously impede the sexual rehabilitation process. Such feelings do not necessarily need to be changed. Rather, they need to be kept in check so as not to interfere with professional duties and responsibility. Some of the more common reactions of staff are discussed below.

Anxiety about Sexual Topics

Generally, all people have a certain degree of discomfort or anxiety about sexual topics. Early in life, we learn that sexuality is personal and private, and we operate from this premise throughout most of our lives. Even discussions about sex with partners and close friends can be difficult and embarrassing. It is no wonder, therefore, that such a focus on sexuality with clients can be anxiety provoking. Putting this anxiety aside is a process that requires education, practice, and time. Often simply acknowledging the anxiety to the other person will be helpful in reducing tension and embarrassment for all parties.

Lack of Objectivity

As children, we often learn about sexuality in the context of secrecy and shame. We are often taught by our parents, clergy, friends, or teachers that certain sexual acts are right or wrong. For example, we may have been told that masturbation is bad, that oral sex is dirty, that sex before marriage is wrong, or that sex should only occur in the bedroom, at night, and with the lights off. Again, with so many values attached to our sexuality, it is often difficult to remain objective and nonjudgmental with clients. Value judgments can be destructive and harmful to the psychological growth of our clients. They also tend to inhibit open discussion about sexuality and to perpetuate the clients' feelings of inadequacy and helplessness.

Overprotection of Clients

Most health care professionals enter rehabilitation because of their desire to help others and to work with other people. When confronted with a client with a severe disability, these good intentions can easily become misdirected into a sense of denial and overprotection. Overprotection tends to infantalize clients and to foster feelings of dependency. At times, these feelings may slow the clients' growth and may manifest themselves in the misconception that sex education and counseling are not relevant for the client.

Anger toward Clients

Another typical reaction to the client may be anger. Although at times feelings of anger from the staff may be appropriate for a number of reasons, excessive anger may be destructive and harmful. Anger may result from a number of situations that arise in the work setting. It may result from clients not progressing quickly enough or from stress and burn-out. Anger from the staff can be directed in an openly hostile manner, or it can be more subtle, manifesting in a passive-aggressive fashion. At other times, it can result in overly restrictive limit setting or verbal attacks on the client. Any of these ultimately will hurt the client-staff relationship and the client's self-esteem.

Fear of Inappropriate Sexual Behavior

Many professionals believe that people with head injury are no longer sexual beings. Others believe that any sex education will result in an increase in inappropriate behavior or hypersexuality. Both views are erroneous. There are certainly sexual behaviors that are harmful, dangerous, or inappropriate. These might include assaults on staff or fellow clients, public masturbation, or activity that creates problem pregnancies. Sex education, however, does not intensify these behaviors. In fact, lack of information can lead to acting out or testing of limits. Inappropriate sexual behavior should be dealt with by direct feedback and redirecting to more socially acceptable behavior that is less dangerous to the client. This will facilitate the client's adjustment.

Attachments to Clients

For young staff members, empathy and identification with young clients may be difficult and stressful. Romantic feelings, overprotection, and feelings of pity can interfere with objectivity. Subsequently, the rehabilitation process can be threatened. For people with head injury, overly close emotional attachments can be confusing and frightening. Such feelings on the part of staff will only encourage sexual acting out and increase inappropriate sexual behavior.

In the area of sexual rehabilitation especially, clear boundaries, limit setting, and direct communication are essential. When staff-client attachments are unhealthy and overly strong, education about sexuality easily becomes embarrassing or anxiety provoking. In such cases, informal consultation with a colleague or a supportive supervisor can help restore the balance and professional role that will ultimately benefit the client.

Problems Perceived by Staff

For staff members, a number of studies have suggested that inadequate comfort level and training are major problems encountered on a daily basis in rehabilitation settings (Davis & Schneider, 1990; Gill, 1988). In this regard, Davis and Schneider (1990) reported that staff problems most frequently noted in their study were staff attitudes, discomforts, and biases (35%); inadequate education and training (30%); and insufficient or inappropriate facility regulations (12%). To address these problems, staff members surveyed suggested increasing education and training and developing a formal sexuality program. A summary of staff competencies and knowledge areas is listed in Exhibit 10-1.

Medlar and Medlar (1990) have pointed out that this need for further education is especially true in the nursing profession. Payne (1986) has identified nurses as less knowledgeable and more conservative in their attitudes than other health care providers. As is true for other professionals, dealing with the sexuality of clients confronts nurses with their own sexual values, beliefs, and identities. They may not have had the opportunity to work through and clarify their own attitudes. Subsequently, as for all professions, these values can interfere with an effective treatment approach in the area of sexual rehabilitation. Again, the basic need is for training and values clarification.

It is interesting to speculate about why administrators are so reluctant to provide these essential skills and guidelines for staff members who deal with these issues on a daily basis. It is just as important to address all components of sexual behavior and functioning as it is to improve skills in mobility, self-care, communication, and

Exhibit 10-1 Staff Competencies in Addressing Areas of Sexuality

---

Staff values: The staff members will be aware of their own values and attitudes so as not to impose them on the client. Staff will be aware of:

- how their religious beliefs influence their sexual attitudes
- their attitudes toward masturbation, oral sex, and alternative forms of sexual expression
- their attitudes regarding homosexuality
- their reaction to sexually explicit language
- their reaction to sexual behavior among partners who are not in a loving relationship
- their emotional reaction to the occasional disfiguring qualities of head injury
- their own feelings of attachment, anger, frustration, pity, and love toward the people with whom they are working

Staff knowledge: The staff members will have knowledge about the impact of head injury on sexual function and intimacy. Staff will know:

- the physical changes in sexual functioning resulting from the head injury
- the cognitive and perceptual difficulties that affect the development of intimacy and sexual satisfaction
- the emotional sequalae and adjustment issues that affect intimacy and sexuality
- the partner's emotional reactions and feelings toward the person with head injury

Staff skills: The staff members will have the skills to promote healthy sexual development after the injury. Staff will:

- be able to give permission and recognition that sexual issues are relevant to the rehabilitation process
- be able to provide information and suggestions to promote sexual satisfaction
- provide training in communication and social skills that encompass intimacy
- facilitate emotional and sexual adjustment through counseling, role playing, and empathic listening
- provide referral for specific sexual problems when deemed necessary or appropriate
- promote an atmosphere where caring for others, dignity, and mutual respect are encouraged

---

vocational reentry (Mardorsky & Dixon, 1983). Yet, perhaps because of administrators' own biases, potential legal ramifications, or inadequate resources, these areas are left to the discretion of individual staff members. In such cases, the task is often assigned to another person or discipline that may be perceived as knowledgeable in this function. Typically, this might be the physician or psychologist. In reality, often clients are discharged from the program with no one having spoken with them about this important aspect of their lives. It is no wonder, therefore, that many clients remain sexually inactive long after injury.

CREATING A THERAPEUTIC ENVIRONMENT

Developing a positive environment that will foster clients' development and sexual growth involves a number of areas. Program development should always begin with a general needs assessment. A simple assessment questionnaire should include level of training in human sexuality, attitudes and feelings, knowledge of issues, and experience in working with clients on these concerns (Medlar, Faria, Unger, Kidder, & McGrath, 1986). It is advisable to respect staff confidentiality in the assessment process and to develop a sense of respect and trust early in the training process. Whenever possible, the program needs assessment should include clients, partners, and family members as well as staff.

Once the needs assessment has been completed, a specific intervention may be implemented. Strategies may include consultation with an educational specialist in this area, individual and group psychotherapy programs, an inservice education program, attitude change workshops, and the development of an institutional sexuality committee to oversee policy development as well as educational and therapeutic programs (Ducharme & Gill, 1990).

When Should Services Be Provided and By Whom?

The newly disabled client's concerns regarding sexuality may be voiced at any time. It is not unusual for clients seen after coma to ask questions about the sexual consequences of their conditions. Other clients, however, avoid the topic entirely, silently drawing their own, often erroneous, conclusions. The staff's receptiveness to questions about sexuality can serve as a cue to the client that it is a legitimate domain of concern in rehabilitation.

If clients themselves do not raise the topic of sexuality, staff members can and should let them know that there are professionals available to discuss this area. Merely stating that most people have questions about sexuality can open the door to further discussion and education. In so doing, staff members counter the misconception that people with disabilities are asexual beings. It is advisable to broach this subject before the client's first overnight pass because this is usually his or her first opportunity since the onset of the disability to engage in sexual activity.

Sexuality is not the exclusive province of physicians or mental health workers, although in practice these groups often have primary responsibility. Ideally, all rehabilitation staff should be able to discuss, at least to some extent, the area of sexuality and disability. It could be argued that the appropriate staff member to discuss sexuality with any given client is that person whom the client identifies as the one with whom he or she feels most comfortable talking about this sensitive subject. Thus all staff members need to be equipped to handle initial inquiries and to dispel misconceptions.

In a therapeutic environment, all staff members have a role and a responsibility in providing information about sexuality. For example, physical therapists can provide education in the areas of positioning and sexual mobility. Occupational therapists can provide expertise in adapting vibrators and sexual toys. Important aspects such as placing a condom on the penis, inserting a diaphragm, masturbation techniques, and undressing should all be dealt with in occupational or other therapies. Speech pathologists can provide assistance in sexual communication, body language, and subtle expressions of affection. Finally, recreational therapists can provide training in social skills, interpersonal relationships, and utilizing feedback from others.

These activities of daily living should be addressed in weekly team meetings along with mobility and other traditional components of rehabilitation. These skills require practice and can only be developed with the cooperation and integration of all disciplines. If they raise anxiety on the part of the staff, then they will be avoided, and at best information in this area will be given in an environment of shame and secrecy. Ultimately, the message conveyed is that sexuality is not a legitimate rehabilitation concern and should not be dealt with in the rehabilitation setting. This will quickly halt the emotional growth of the client.

Of course, sexual education and counseling must be offered with the client's background, attitudes, and current emotional state in mind. Otherwise the process may cause undue anxiety, perhaps foreclosing on the possibility that the client will pursue the subject at a later time. Many clients cannot tolerate discussion about sexuality at an early phase; the purpose of initial conversations, therefore, may be simply to sanction later inquiries. If however, all members of the team are addressing sexuality in their individual disciplines, the topic will take on an air of appropriateness and normalcy. Feelings of embarrassment will soon dissipate.

Professional Roles

The PLISSIT model of professional roles developed by Annon (1974) provides a useful framework for discussing the various phases of intervention. Four successively more sophisticated levels of intervention are postulated: permission, limited information, specific suggestions, and intensive therapy. With this model, clinicians can readily identify their own level of competence and determine whether they possess the requisite intervention skills in particular cases.

The first level of intervention, giving permission, may require no more than raising the topic of sexuality to let the client know that this is a legitimate area of interest. Professional sanction alone may relieve some anxiety and encourage clients to think, experiment, and inquire. At the second level of intervention, clients are given specific facts regarding the sexual consequences of their conditions. Doing so corrects misconceptions and prevents future problems. For example, men with spinal cord injury should be informed about the effects of cord injury on erectile ability and fertility. In cases of head injury, discussion might center on changes in level of desire. It is usually advisable to include the client's partner in teaching sessions.

All members of the rehabilitation team should be able to provide these two levels of intervention. At succeeding levels, however, the staff member comes to function more as a counselor than an educator. Thus more sophisticated interventions should be conducted by those with specific training and expertise.

At the next level, specific technical suggestions are offered to the client and partner. A necessary prologue is the taking of a sexual history to determine the client's premorbid sexual practices and beliefs. Of course, one must also be familiar with the disability itself and its impact on sexual functioning. Finally, it is vital that the staff member be aware of the client's emotional status and the psychological significance of the subject of sex. Examples of specific suggestions include advice about positioning, contraceptive measures, bowel and bladder management, and techniques for sustaining erection. Suggestions may also be provided concerning social skills that are related to sexuality, such as ways of meeting new people, effective communication, and assertiveness.

Clients with more complex sexual dysfunctions may require the fourth level of intervention: intensive therapy (which should be provided by professionals with advanced training in the various modalities of sexual counseling). Rehabilitation staff members are obligated to assist in the referral of such clients to suitable therapists. Certainly, rehabilitation professionals with appropriate training may assume this role (Ducharme, 1988). Typical problems that may require intensive therapy might range from preexisting psychiatric issues to an involved history of sexual abuse or trauma. In such cases, the sexual adjustment may be complicated by personality issues that will need to be addressed before education in sexual health is provided. In other cases, marital conflict, interpersonal difficulties, or preexisting sexual dysfunction will need to be resolved if intimacy is to be achieved after discharge. For some people, intimacy may be a new experience that requires preparation over a long period of time.

Sexual History

Early in the rehabilitation program, a sexual history should be taken from the client and, if possible, from the partner. A good sexual history defines expectations, needs, and behavior. It also identifies problems and misconceptions as well as areas requiring education, counseling, and reassurance in relation to sexual issues (Zasler & Horn, 1990).

The language of the interview should be neither too technical nor too causal. In practice, many clients present with some anxiety about sexual topics, and language used by the interviewer can help create an atmosphere of permission to discuss the topic as well as to be explicit about sexual matters. Examples of terms that carry a pejorative connotation are *frigidity* and *impotence*. Although these terms may accurately reflect true feelings, the terms *nonorgasmic* and *erection problems* are more accurate and carry less stigmatizing meanings. The interviewer models a sensitive and matter-of-fact attitude while listening carefully to the attitudes expressed by the client's language.

A sexual history should include an assessment of preinjury sexual functioning so that all preexisting difficulties can be identified. The client and partner should be interviewed regarding sexual intercourse as well as other sexual activities practiced, such as oralgenital sex, anal sex, and masturbation. Details about which partner initiates sexual activity and the frequency of their intimacy should also be discussed. It is also important to clarify sexual preferences at the outset of the interview and that heterosexuality never be automatically assumed. Both client and partner should always be given the opportunity to ask questions throughout the session as well as at the end. In fact, it is often helpful for the interviewer to speak with the couple at a later time to inquire about whether additional questions arose after the history-taking session ended.

If significant sexual problems are uncovered during the rehabilitation process, referral to a qualified sex therapist might be indicated. In cases such as these, a detailed history will be obtained regarding the client's sexual difficulties. These are comprehensive assessments, requiring at least 2 to 3 hours of interview time, that include questions regarding early childhood learning about affection, trust, and the nature of interpersonal relationships; the emotional climate in which one was raised; religious values and attitudes; sexual learning history; dating behavior; adjustment in previous relationships; extramarital relationships; development and quality of the present relationship; communication; lifestyle issues; children; definition of the presenting complaints; current sexual repertoire; attempts at solving the problem; traumatic sexual experiences; goals for treatment; and resistance to change.

Opinions vary regarding when to address sexual adjustment. The initial sexual history might be conducted as soon as the client's medical condition has stabilized to the point of ensuring survival. At the other extreme, the topic might be reserved until close to the time of discharge from the rehabilitation setting. Those who wait until the client brings it up may find that the topic is never addressed because of the client's concerns that the subject is taboo. A useful rule of thumb, then, is to integrate this topic into the total rehabilitation program, raising it along with other aspects of client education and allowing clients to decline detailed inquiry if they so desire. Some clients will not be ready to address their own sexual adjustment in depth until years after the onset of the disabling condition, but the permission to discuss the issue that is conveyed by sexual history questions can be extremely valuable in promoting later adjustment.

Sexual Counseling

Turning now to a consideration of sexual adjustment after traumatic head injury, the same principles as those for adjustment in general apply. The losses need to be mourned so that the remaining strengths can be developed and nurtured. Everyone has some ability to function sexually, some repertoire of behavior that can communicate sexual feelings. Frequently, however, clients go through a period of reduced sexual drive or performance. Choosing celibacy is not always a sign of giving up and must be considered a viable option if it is agreeable to the

client and his or her partner. Substantial numbers of clients, however, fail to resume an active sex life owing to fear, misinformation, or problems of adjustment. Others go through a period of sexual acting out. The partner's adjustment may depend on the client's cognitive level of functioning after head injury. Issues such as impulsivity, poor judgment, and emotional liability may play a role.

It is important to emphasize that the adjustment process is a result of the combined emotional and cognitive issues after the head injury. An overreliance on the psychological areas can lead to inappropriate treatment planning, poor therapeutic rapport with the client, and character judgments of the client. On the other hand, an overreliance on the cognitive areas and neglect of the psychological realm can lead to a lack of empathy, poor adjustment of the client, and social withdrawal of the client after discharge. Again, the integration of emotional, cognitive, and behavioral issues is a balance that must be maintained.

Those who do resume sexual relations are advised to keep separate the roles of caretaker and partner to preserve intimacy, which is diluted when one spouse is perceived as needy and helpless compared with the other. The process of sexual adjustment and the balancing of the roles can be facilitated by providing information and counseling.

Traumatic head injury creates an intense narcissistic wound that involves a major mobilization of defenses. Typically there is an initial period of regression that reawakens early separation-individuation phenomena as well as earlier struggles concerning sexual identity (Ducharme & Ducharme, 1984). Thus psychological problems that may have occurred early in life, such as abuse or abandonment, may complicate the adjustment process. A significant number of rehabilitation clients are adolescents and young adults in the process of disengaging from their families and asserting their independence. For these individuals, emotional rehabilitation, and sexual adjustment in particular, is complicated by both preinjury and postinjury psychosocial factors.

With time, the individual with a head injury begins the task, necessary for long-term psychological well being, of incorporating a new body image into his or her self-concept. To achieve this task, issues of sexual identity, sexual function, and intimate relationships must be addressed specifically. Sexual functioning involves both the ability to sustain intimacy and a prescribed series of genital behaviors. Similarly, when studying the impact of disability on client adjustment, the health care professional must consider the client's entire lifestyle including his or her health, diagnosis, status, relationships, vocation, role, self-esteem, body image, independence, intellectual capacity, and ability to communicate. If a client's status, appearance, or mobility is not standard according to cultural prescriptions, the client may suffer and conclude that he or she is not only disabled but also handicapped. In these cases, individuals gradually incorporate society's view of them as inferior or inadequate. Health care practitioners can combat societal stereotypes and discrimination by focusing on the abilities that the client retains after illness or injury. In sexual rehabilitation the emphasis that succeeds is the one on remaining strengths; in this way clients may learn to value themselves again.

Several basic premises guide the practitioner who delivers health care services to people with disabilities. There is no one right way to express sexuality. Everyone who acts in a responsible way has a right to make choices about sexual expression. For the rehabilitation staff member, the critical factor is to validate and support the choices being made by the client.

A common fear expressed by the people with a disability is increased vulnerability to physical and sexual assault. Conditions that result in cognitive impairment, weakness, and balance or mobility problems increase the risk of being vulnerable. Programs of self-defense and programs to assist victims of assault have been instituted. Psychotherapy and prevention may assist clients in planning ways to reduce their vulnerability and in feeling and acting competent and powerful (Stuart & Stuart, 1981).

For staff to understand the client's sexual adjustment, it is essential that they get a clear picture of the relationship context in which this adjustment occurs. The impact of head injury on the psychological status of the client and family is part of that context. When a referral is made to treat clients with sexual problems, the therapist needs to assess the couple's readiness for sex therapy on the basis of whether the relationship itself is stable and whether the partners are ready and able to negotiate and resolve disputes. Only then can the sensitive issues of sexual intimacy be addressed. If there are more basic issues that need to be resolved, sex therapy is postponed.

One example of a more basic problem is alcohol or drug abuse. Kaplan (1983) categorically states that this is a contraindication for sex therapy, and some practitioners will refuse to treat a couple with an active substance abuse problem. The reason is not only the impact of drugs on psychological functioning but also the pathological interpersonal and family relationships that are present in substance-abusing clients. A referral for family treatment of these problems is a prerequisite to formal work on sexual issues if any long-lasting progress is to be achieved.

However important it is to view the client as part of a social context encompassing partner, family, friends, co-workers, neighbors, and even the hospital milieu, there are a number of psychotherapeutic issues that need to be addressed by the person to promote psychosocial and sexual functioning. The issues of identity, dependency, self-esteem, and values are among the major concerns that the client needs to face in the course of his or her adjustment to disability. Identity refers to questions of who one is, was, and can become in the face of altered cognitive and physical capacities as well as who one is as a sexual person. Dependency involves not only the issue of increased reliance on others for help subsequent to disability but also much broader emotional issues about personal power and locus of control. In the sexual context, lack of resolution of this issue contributes to serious relationship conflict and inability to take responsibility for one's own sexual needs and behavior. Self-esteem, referring to body image as well as an accurate but compassionate evaluation of oneself, is seriously challenged by head injury. Self-esteem is necessary for optimum sexual functioning and is more a matter of attitude than of attributes. The issue of values includes ethical principles of behavior, the meaning of life and of the disability, and deeper spiritual considerations. Sexual values guide behavior, and an awareness of one's value promotes healthier and more honest choices.

Because of the personal nature of these issues, and individual therapy format is recommended; this may precede or accompany couple's therapy if indicated. It is also the treatment of choice for single parents (who have a right to sexual information and counseling) or those in relationships in which the partner is unwilling to participate in the therapy.

Couple's Therapy

In cases where cognition, memory, and other neuropsychological functions permit, couple's therapy can be helpful to the person with head injury and his or her partner. The initial stage of therapy with couples in sexual rehabilitation involves the establishment of therapeutic rapport. The couple must come to understand that the therapist will not take sides but is the agent of change for the relationship. In the first session, the couple begins to trust the therapist and to receive validation of their feelings and permission to be open about their sexual issues. The next stage of the process is a thorough assessment of their physical, psychological, interpersonal, and sexual strengths and weaknesses. This information is gathered from interview, psychological and medical testing, a review of the records, and input from other team members who work with the client and the partner. The process of the interview requires a nonjudgmental stance and open-ended questions to put the couple at ease and to promote the most accurate and open reporting. The content of the assessment is described above.

The next stage of therapy is to integrate these data into an individualized treatment plan. It is helpful to provide feedback to the couple about how the therapist conceptualizes the problem and how the course of treatment will be responsive to the problems they have reported and to their goals. The central issues are addressed first, and it is important to build in early success so as to motivate the couple to continue to work in a step-by-step, gradual way toward change. Engaging the couple actively in the planning and

review of the treatment empowers them and fits the interventions to their unique needs.

Another role of the therapist is to provide education and information relative to the sexual changes encountered. Many therapists include a course of systematic relaxation training that eliminates any contribution of anxiety to the sexual dysfunction and that is compatible with learning increased awareness and consciousness of feelings and sensations. The couple is instructed to experiment at home with new behaviors and new attitudes, again in a gradual, nonthreatening way, thereby increasing the effectiveness of their sexual technique and building a teamness between the partners to replace the common pretreatment adversarial stance between them (Ducharme, 1988).

In brief, the principles of sexual adjustment counseling are the same for able-bodied and disabled clients. Relax, go slow, get information, experiment, and communicate. When head injury has occurred, however, the issues often become more complex. Cognitive, neuropsychological, and behavioral problems need to be dealt with for both the client and the spouse. Behavior therapy approaches may be indicated, and education for the noninjured partner will be critical. Communication has typically broken down, and there may be pressure to perform for both partners. Depression, lifestyle changes, and frustration must be acknowledged and dealt with in the context of the relationship. Once this has been accomplished, the opening of communication and nonpressured sexual experimentation should help restore a satisfying intimate relationship and a balance of power in the relationship.

Group Therapy

Traditional group therapy assumes that there will be sufficient duration of a stable and somewhat homogeneous group membership to allow the development of group cohesiveness, which is the matrix for change in the group setting. This may take up to 6 months to establish before significant work can begin. These characteristics of group therapy are impractical in most inpatient settings, and even if outpatient follow-up is provided group membership is often variable. In addition, the range of severity of brain injury often makes groups especially difficult to conduct. In spite of the difficulties, there have been reports of success in conveying information about sexual issues in a short-term group format (Berkman & Macaluso, 1984).

With outpatients, a more generalized support group can play an important role in facilitating adjustment to injury. These groups can also include the topic of sexuality among the many other issues that they address. The advantage of including sex as an ongoing topic in the group, or even of focusing specifically on the topic for the short periods in the context of a continuing group, is that there is much more opportunity for members to express their feelings and concerns (as opposed to being recipients of sexual information, as in the educational groups). Group members set the agenda rather than having it detailed to them. In general, the role of the group leader is to create a warm, nonthreatening environment that promotes sharing of information about sexuality in a confidential and non-judgmental manner (Mayers, 1978).

Another type of group is the self-help group. These are often coordinated through organizations such as the National Head Injury Foundation. This type of group is formed by clients, or in some cases by families, to provide peer support, to assist in problem solving, and to fill a need that is frequently unfilled by health care providers. The main advantage of this format is that responsibility for behavior change is placed directly in the hands of the clients instead of the clients being helped (the latter of which connotes helplessness). Although discussion in these groups is not focused specifically on sexual topics, interpersonal issues are clearly a large component of the issues they cover.

INSTITUTIONAL APPROACHES

Values Clarification

The Sexual Attitude Reassessment (SAR) seminar has gained widespread acceptance as a means of educating both rehabilitation staff members and people with a disability. It has also been widely used in the general public. This program was developed by the National Sex Forum in San Francisco and was modified by Cole (1973) for use in rehabilitation centers. The seminar uses explicit sexual material to demythologize and desensationalize sexual behavior and attitudes. In doing so, the program accomplishes its goals of aiding professionals in understanding and accepting their own sexuality as well as the sexuality of others. This is a first step toward acquiring the skills needed to provide sexual counseling to people with head injury.

The 2-day program uses a multimedia presentation to cover a number of topics, such as masturbation, fantasy, homosexuality, and relationships. At strategic points through the workshop, participants, usually a mix of people with disabilities and rehabilitation staff, meet in small groups to examine and share their attitudes and feelings about the material presented. Although the programs have been found to be effective, current funding problems and other issues have made it difficult for the SAR programs to continue in many locations. Adaptations and modifications of the SAR program, however, can generally be arranged for the unique needs of a particular institution.

Inservice Education

Although it is always important to process feelings in programs such as the SAR, specific information must be taught to a full range of staff members. An ongoing lecture series is often helpful in this regard. These lectures can be grouped in a series given in a time-limited format, or they can be scheduled over a larger period of time. These too should end with ample time for processing of feelings and reactions. This is especially true if explicit media are used to supplement the material being presented. Printed material, handouts, and references are also helpful for those individuals who might want to deepen their understanding of the topic area.

The needs assessment, discussed earlier in this chapter, should provide the basis for developing the education program. It is hoped that staff will have indicated topics that they would like discussed that may be unique to the setting. These topics might include anatomy and physiology, effect of head injury on sexual functioning, effects of medications, treatment options such as penile implants, counseling techniques, and professional roles (Exhibit 10-2).

Most often, inservice education programs will raise concerns about staff-client interaction. This is usually the primary area of staff anxiety, and sensitive discussion is usually welcomed and appreciated. In addition, training in behavior modification principles can be helpful. This should be geared specifically toward sexual areas, and theories such as reinforcement schedules should be reviewed for the staff. It is also important to discuss why sexual acting out may occur so that staff members can appreciate the client, which can easily not happen in the rush to develop a behavioral program. Finally, issues such as limit setting and client-staff boundaries should be discussed and emphasized. A review of these topics will almost certainly lead to discussions of specific cases and incidents that have occurred within the facility. Ample time should be devoted to this discussion because this might well be the critical feature of the educational program.

An evaluation component should be built into the program to assess the extent to which the behavioral objectives have been met. This evaluation mechanism will help define topics for future education programs and the needs of the staff. It will also provide information as to which teaching methods have been most effective. In general, the programs should be varied and should include a number of methods such as media, lectures, case presentations, and discussions. Many facilities have found it effective to bring in former clients or partners who feel comfortable discussing their sexual adjustment and answering questions from the staff.

Consultation

An outside consultant is often helpful in the development of an institutional sexuality program. The consultant can also advocate for the needs of the client and staff on the basis of their familiarity with other programs and settings. Often the consultant serves as a catalyst in organizing staff members to address sexual issues.

In many settings, the consultant serves as a resource person who can respond to staff questions about sexual issues. The staff may feel more comfortable addressing these questions to an outsider rather than to a supervisor or fellow staff member. Ultimately, the consultant can help staff members learn how to handle specific situations that might arise. This person serves as a model for openness, sensitivity, and permission giving regarding sexuality. By his or her presence, this person validates the importance of sexual issues and acknowledges the need to address these issues in the treatment program.

Sexuality Committee

The development of a sexuality committee within a facility is often the method of choice for addressing sexual areas. Administrative support of the committee is essential. Ideally, a member of the program administration should also serve as a member of the sexuality committee. This validates the importance of the committee and provides a sense of safety, recognition, and administrative approval. Usually, the committee is composed of interdisciplinary staff members who have interest and expertise in sexuality issues. The development of facility policy, procedures, and guidelines is the first task and perhaps one of the most important.

Exhibit 10-2 General Topic Areas for Inservice Education Curricula

Anatomy and physiology
Effect of head injury on sexual functioning
Sexuality across the life span
Effects of medications
Cognitive changes and expression of sexuality
Emotional and personality considerations
Treatment options
Administrative and policy issues
Counseling techniques
Roles of various disciplines
Sexually transmitted diseases

Most institutions are seeking recommendations and guidelines in this area, so that comprehensive training and client treatment programs can be implemented. Administrators are frequently all too aware of the importance of this topic but lack the understanding necessary to address this area with both staff and clients. Many are fearful of the potential legal implications of these issues and believe that legal consultation is necessary throughout the process. Once they are reassured that it is better to address these issues than to avoid them, most are eager to implement programs with an overall view toward sexual health. Rehabilitation staff members can then address sexuality, self-esteem, and body image as activities of daily living considerations in client care (Cole, 1991).

Additional responsibilities of the committee will be to establish policies and procedures regarding the most sensitive sexual issues that arise within the institution or program. It is essential that the committee institute policies on such matters as whether to provide a privacy room for clients and partners, public and private masturbation, partner sexual activity, dissemination of birth control information and supplies, prevention of sexual assault, prevention of sexually transmitted diseases, and institutional policies relating to the relationship between clients and staff members (Ducharme & Gill, 1990).

Another area that must be addressed by the committee is the issue of surrogate partners. This possibility is often raised to staff members by clients and occasionally by families as well. The topic is a controversial one and has therapeutic, moral, legal, and ethical considerations that must be addressed by the administration. Unfortunately, many facilities ignore the need to develop policy on this and other issues. This leaves the staff member unsupported and relying only on his or her own experience to assist the client in these delicate matters. When there is no formal policy on these matters, clients and appropriate family members should make their own decisions on the basis of their personal needs and values. Even when there is policy, the pros and cons should be explained so that clients can make their own decisions once they have left the program. These are personal decisions that

exceed the authority of the therapist and must be made by the client and appropriate friends and family members.

All the above issues are potentially explosive within a head injury facility. As for other areas of rehabilitation, a consistent approach among staff members is essential for the client's well being. Therefore, staff education and ongoing dialog are critical in each of these areas as programs are developed and implemented. The committee cannot work in isolation from the facility but must move steadfastly and slowly toward an environment of positive sexual growth. Resistances are common and will occur at every juncture. Personal values, religious beliefs, and a false sense of protecting the clients will thwart the easing of restrictions. It is much easier to maintain a restrictive, controlled, and punitive environment than an open, nurturing atmosphere where clients are involved in the decision-making process.

Institutions, like individuals, move along a developmental continuum. Changes tend to occur slowly and in an orderly and progressive fashion. Sexual health and the therapeutic environment that nurtures sexuality must also be developed slowly. There are certain prerequisites. The facility should have adequate staffing, administrative support, positive morale, and a staff that is free from burn-out and committed to quality client care. When these are present, programs that foster sexual health can be introduced gradually and will evolve naturally within the facility. Above all else, a positive therapeutic environment is created by staff who empower their clients through warmth, sensitivity, and genuine respect for the individual.

CONCLUSION

The last decade has seen vast changes in the field of sexuality and disability. Most important, professionals have come to recognize the prevalence of sexual concerns among their clients and their own obligation to address this area, despite the difficulties involved. There is a growing consensus that sexual teaching and sexual counseling are vital components in the rehabilitation of individuals with disability. Further research, however, must demonstrate their efficacy. The availability of written material about sexuality has facilitated this process and has encouraged rehabilitation staff to demand these services for their clients. For head injury survivors, however, much of the material about sexuality has tended to focus on behavioral programs. The goal has often been to eliminate inappropriate sexual acting out. Although no doubt important, this focus has been restrictive and overly negative. It tends to discourage positive sexual development. It can be destructive not only to the clients but also to their partners.

For clients in hospitals or rehabilitation centers, there are multiple restrictions on the rights of sexual expression. Clients must be allowed to retain their rights as long as they do not infringe on the rights of others. Health practitioners must achieve a balance between protecting the rights, dignity, and privacy of hospitalized clients and providing a safe, secure environment. To that end, rehabilitation staff have a responsibility to provide sex education relevant to head injury, to accept displays of affection among clients, to allow privacy for masturbation, and to provide private visitor rooms for clients and their partners. As staff attitudes are retrained away from control and imposing restrictive values, a therapeutic environment that fosters self-esteem and sexual growth will begin to unfold.

Rehabilitation and health professionals have made considerable progress in addressing issues of sexuality with their clients. With head injury survivors, however, this progress has been somewhat slower and more complex. Misconceptions regarding the sexuality of people with head injury continue to exist, especially in inpatient settings and postacute programs. Fears, negative attitudes, and reluctance on the part of health providers in addressing these issues create undue restrictions, social isolation, and shame among those with head injury. Self-esteem and quality of life are ultimately affected.

People with head injury have the capacity for and the right to sexual expression and intimate relationships. As health professionals, we have the obligation to ensure such rights through teaching, counseling, and providing health care in this critical area of human development. It is by this attention to and validation of head injury survivors as people that the therapeutic environment is created.

ADDITIONAL RESOURCES

American Association of Sex Educators,
   Counselors and Therapists
435 North Michigan Avenue, Suite 1717
Chicago, IL 60611
(312) 644-0828

National Task Force on Sexuality and Disability
American Congress of Rehabilitation Medicine
5700 Old Orchard Road, First Floor
Skokie, IL 60077
(708) 966-0095

Coalition on Sexuality and Disability, Inc.
122 East 23rd Street
New York, NY 10010
(212) 242-3900

National Head Injury Foundation
1776 Massachusetts Avenue, NW, Suite 100
Washington, DC 20036
(202) 296-8850

Sexuality and Disability Training Center
Boston University Medical Center
88 East Newton Street
Boston, MA 02118
(617) 638-7358

Sexuality and Disability Training Center
University of Michigan Medical Center
1500 East Medical Center Drive
Ann Arbor, MI 48109
(313) 936-7067

Journal of Sexuality and Disability
Human Sciences Press
233 Spring Street
New York, NY 10013
(212) 620-8000

REFERENCES

Annon, J.S. (1974). *The behavioral treatment of sexual problems* (Vol. 1). Honolulu: Enabling Systems.

Berkman, A.H., & Macaluso, E. (1984). *A sex counseling program in groups in a hospital setting.* Paper presented at the AASECT/SSS Combines Annual meeting, Boston, MA.

Berrol, S. (1981). Issues of sexuality in head injured adults. *Medical Aspects of Human Sexuality, 15,* 15–16.

Blackerby, W.F. (1988). Head injured rehabilitation: Sexuality after TBI. *Professional series on traumatic brain injury.* Houston: HDI.

Bond, M. (1984). The psychiatry of closed head injury. In N. Brooks (Ed.), *Closed head injury: Psychological, social and family consequences* (pp. 148–178). Oxford: Oxford University Press.

Bregman, S., & Hadley, R. (1976). Sexual adjustment and feminine attractiveness among spinal cord injured women. *Archives of Physical Medicine and Rehabilitation, 57,* 448–450.

Cole, T. (1973). A new program of sex education and counseling for spinal cord injured adults and health professionals. *Paraplegia, 2,* 111–124.

Cole, S. (1991). Introductory statement. *Sexuality and Disability, 9,* 3–6.

Davis, D.L., & Schneider, L.K. (1990). Ramifications of traumatic brain injury for sexuality. *Journal of Head Trauma Rehabilitation, 5,* 31–37.

Ducharme, S. (1988). Sexuality and physical disability. In Caplan (Ed.), *Rehabilitation psychology desk reference* (pp. 419–435). Gaithersburg, MD: Aspen.

Ducharme, S. (1991). From the editor. *Sexuality and Disability, 9,* 3.

Ducharme, S., & Ducharme, J. (1984). Psychological adjustment to spinal cord injury. In Krueger (Ed.), *Emotional rehabilitation of physical trauma and disability,* (pp. 149–156). New York: Spectrum.

Ducharme, S., & Gill, K. (1990). Sexual values, training and professional roles. *Journal of Head Trauma Rehabilitation, 5,* 38–45.

Gill, K. (1988). *Staff needs assessment data.* Unpublished manuscript.

Glass, D., & Padrone, F. (1978). Sexual adjustment and the handicapped. *Journal of Rehabilitation, 44,* 43–47.

Kaplan, H.S. (1983). *The evaluation of sexual disorders: Psychological and medical aspects.* New York: Bruner/Mazel.

Lezak, M.D. (1978). Living with the characterologically brain injured patient. *Journal of Clinical Psychiatry, 39,* 592–598.

Mardorsky, J., & Dixon, T. (1983). Rehabilitation aspects of human sexuality. *Western Journal of Medicine, 139,* 174–176.

Mayers, K.S. (1978). Sexual and social concerns of the disabled: A group counseling approach. *Sexuality and Disability, 1,* 100–111.

McKinlay, W.W., Brooks, D.N., Bond, M.R., Martinage, D., & Marshall, M. (1981). The short term outcome of severe blunt head injury as reported by relatives of the head injured persons. *Journal of Neurology, Neurosurgery and Psychiatry, 46,* 527–533.

Medlar, T., Faria, J., Unger, L., Kidder, R., & McGrath, N. (1986). *Sexuality and the whole person: Development of a program for use in head injury rehabilitation.* Paper presented at the Braintree Hospital Seventh Annual Head Injury Conference, Braintree, MA.

Medlar, T., & Medlar, J. (1990). Nursing management of sexuality issues. *Journal of Head Trauma Rehabilitation, 5,* 46–51.

Mikula, J., & Rudin, J. (1983). *Outcome of severe head injury patients after head injury rehabilitation.* Paper presented at the meeting of the American Congress of Rehabilitation Medicine, San Diego, CA.

Panting, A., & Merry, P.H. (1972). The long term rehabilitation of severe head injuries with particular reference to the need for social and medical support for the patient's family. *Rehabilitation, 38,* 33.

Payne, T. (1986). Sexuality of nurses: Correlations of knowledge, attitudes and behavior. *Nursing research. 25,* 286–289.

Price, J.R. (1985). Promoting sexual wellness in head injured patients. *Rehabilitation Nursing,* 12–13.

Renshaw, D.C. (1978). Impotence in diabetics. In J. Lopiccolo (Ed.), *Handbook of sex therapy.* New York: Plenum.

Rimel, R.W., & Jane, J.A. (1983). Characteristics of the head injured patient. In M. Rosenthal, E. Griffith, M. Bond, & J. Miller (Eds.), *Rehabilitation of the head injured adult* (pp. 9–21). Philadelphia: Davis.

Rosenbaum, M., & Najenson, T. (1976). Changes in life patterns and symptoms of low mood as reported by wives of severely brain injured soldiers. *Journal of Consulting and Clinical Psychology, 44,* 881–888.

Sha'ked, A. (1978). *Human sexuality in physical and mental illnesses and disabilities: An annotated bibliography.* Bloomington, IN: Indiana University Press.

Stuart, C., & Stuart, V. (1981). Sexual assault: Disabled perspective. *Sexuality and Disability, 4,* 246–253.

Walker, A.E. (1972). Long term evaluation of the social and family adjustment to head injuries. *Scandinavian Journal of Rehabilitation Medicine, 4,* 5–8.

Weinstein, E.A. (1974). Sexual disturbances after brain injury. *Medical Aspects of Human Sexuality, 8,* 10–31.

Wood, R.L. (1984). Behavioral disorders following severe brain injury: Their presentations and psychological management. In Brooks (Ed.), *Closed head injury: Psychological, social and family consequences.* (pp. 195–219). London: Oxford University Press.

Zasler, N., & Horn, L. (1990). Rehabilitative management of sexual dysfunction. *Journal of Head Trauma Rehabilitation, 5,* 14–25.

Zencius, A., Wesolowski, M.D., Burke, W., & Hough, S. (1990). Managing hypersexual disorders in brain-injured clients. *Brain Injury, 4,* 175–181.

Professional Training and Development for Pediatric Rehabilitation

11

Roberta DePompei

Jean L. Blosser

OBJECTIVES

Upon completion of this chapter, the reader will be able to:

1. identify characteristics of the child or adolescent who has sustained a traumatic brain injury (TBI)
2. define barriers that may interfere with the development of comprehensive programming for children and adolescents with TBI and their families
3. suggest methods of professional training and development (PT&D) that can lead to collaborative problem solving based on the needs of children and adolescents with TBI and the environments to which they will return
4. outline treatment strategies that focus on developing individualized and functional treatment plans, structuring the environment and training significant persons in the environment, and directing the professional's role in implementing treatment
5. specify target competencies, objectives, and important topics for discussion in implementing PT&D programs to prepare professionals to serve children and adolescents with TBI effectively
6. identify specific procedures for involving family and peers in comprehensive planning and treatment

Professional Training and Development for Pediatric Rehabilitation

Each year approximately 1 million children and adolescents sustain central nervous system injuries as a result of falls, motor vehicle accidents, sports injuries, or abuse. It is difficult to ascertain accurate statistics on the number of children and adolescents who sustain TBI because there have been no systematic guidelines presented to trauma centers, rehabilitation facilities, or school systems that provide uniform methods of record keeping.

Various studies have reported some statistics that can be taken as indicators, however. The National Center for Health Statistics (1982) reports that TBI is the leading cause of death and disability in children between the ages of 1 and 14 years. Kraus, Fife, Cox, Ramstein, and Conroy (1986) report that the majority of injuries (about 85%) are mild, with many children not experiencing loss of consciousness. Of the estimated 1 million who are injured annually, approximately 165,000 may require postinjury hospitalization, and about 18,000 to 20,000 will be categorized as having a moderate to severe injury (Kalsbeek, McLauren, Harris, & Miller, 1980; Savage, 1991; Waaland & Kreutzer, 1988).

With additional interest in children and adolescents with brain injury, departments of special education, community trauma centers, state offices of head injury, and families who advocate, more accurate numbers should be forthcoming in the next decade. Regardless of the specific numbers, there are certainly enough individuals affected by this serious disability to generate concern among rehabilitation and education professionals.

TBI is especially of concern when a developing child or adolescent is injured. The injuries can manifest as impairments that can affect physical, cognitive-communicative, social, emotional and behavioral development. Children and adolescents possess the potential to participate over many years as active members of families, schools, workplaces, and communities. Because the effects of the injury can have an impact on lifelong learning and living, professionals who find themselves in a position of working with these individuals have many challenges in developing and implementing effective treatment programs.

Children and adolescents present such diverse and complex needs that current program planning frequently falters. Although acute care and rehabilitation facilities are often successful in the treatment of individual impairment areas, the carryover into functional, independent learning and living situations may not be as successful as all would like. Traditional client-centered approaches that focus primarily on remediating specific target skills fall short of providing the type of overall planning and programming needed because they are too narrow in scope and nonfunctional by design.

Effective programming for children and adolescents requires a proactive approach. This includes the anticipation of problems that are likely to occur because of the acquired impairments and psychological changes in addition to considering the environments to which the child or adolescent is likely to return. This framework focuses on helping professionals be prepared to develop a range of treatment alternatives. It also plans for the challenging situations that individuals with TBI may encounter when returning to home, school, work, and community. This approach leads to programming that is relevant to the child's or adolescent's individual needs; acknowledges the importance of family, teachers, peers, and community members; and facilitates reintegration.

The development of such comprehensive programming is often blocked by inadvertent obstacles. Blosser and DePompei (1991, 1992) have identified five major barriers that frequently interfere with adequate program development that can be considered comprehensive and functional in terms of the needs of the child or adolescent. These obstacles were identified through a national survey of more than 1,500 professionals in hospitals, rehabilitation facilities, and school systems; anecdotal reports by professionals and families; and direct observations of numerous children reintegrating into the school environment. They include:

1. the child's or adolescent's impairments as a result of TBI and the impact of those impairments on learning capabilities
2. inadequate networking among rehabilitation professionals, education professionals, family members, and community support systems
3. lack of organizational readiness and capability to serve youth with TBI
4. professionals' inadequate understanding of the unique problems of these individuals and their lack of readiness to provide service
5. families' and peers' understanding and expectations for the rehabilitation, reintegration, implementation, and maintenance process

As a result of barriers such as these, the child's or adolescent's potential for benefiting maximally from treatment and planned reintegration into home, school, work, and community is reduced. The remainder of this chapter supports a plan for PT&D that prepares professionals to identify solutions to the barriers outlined above. It explores the need for preparing professionals in various fields to work with children and adolescents who have sustained TBI with a vision of achieving the best possible return to the child's or adolescent's functional world.

There are several assumptions that will guide the proposed PT&D approach. These assumptions are central to our philosophy of staff training and program development. They are what we will call fixed stars. Wrenn (1992) tells us of the inhabitants of a remote village some 75 years ago who saw Halley's comet, a frightening light in the sky, coming closer each night. They were frightened and believed it might be the end of the world. A pastor noted their fear, but he saw something else in the sky. He said to them, "I see what you all see, a bright moving star coming closer to us each night. I also see all the other stars in the heavens just where they have been night after night. These thousands of stars are not getting any closer, they are almost station-

ary. So look beyond the threatening moving star to the steady fixed stars and you won't be so frightened by the bright one" (p. 701).

Working with children and adolescents with TBI is a new experience for many professionals. As they learn about the needs of these individuals and the hard work it takes to plan appropriate rehabilitation and reintegration, some are prone to believe that there is too much to learn and not enough time to become proficient in yet another specialty area. This feeling of being overwhelmed prevents the professional from reaching back to the wealth of information he or she possesses about assessment, treatment, and understanding of individuals with disabilities and their families that can be adapted. There are fixed stars in the professional's understanding of disabilities and his or her armamentarium of treatment approaches that will make the job easier. They are essential in our format for working with the challenges presented after brain injury and establish the basis for all programming suggestions that follow.

- The main goal of any programming is to help the child or adolescent to function as independently as possible in various situations and environments.
- The combination of acquired impairments can be unusual and unique. Most of the characteristics are observable in other special populations, however, and although there are differences there are also similarities.
- Professionals may not know the unique problems associated with TBI, but they are adaptive, creative, and well founded in techniques that can aid them with these individuals.
- Strategies need to be relevant to the needs and capabilities of the individual with TBI and his or her family.
- Families and peers will ultimately play more important roles than any professionals, and therefore they need to be prepared to do so.

If we keep our eyes on the fixed stars, the task before us will be less overwhelming. What follows is a discussion of barriers that interfere with program development, the impact of each, and the proposed solutions that can be brought about through PT&D.

BARRIER 1: IMPAIRMENTS RESULTING FROM TBI AND THEIR EFFECT ON THE PERFORMANCE AND ADAPTATION OF THE CHILD OR ADOLESCENT

Impact

A number of problems can affect learning, performance, and adjustment in youth with TBI. The impairments can be responsible for lack of expected performance in specific situations that arise in home, school, community, or work.

Proposed PT&D Solutions

In developing a PT&D program, issues that professionals will need to consider in terms of this barrier include impairments that result from the injury and the characteristic behaviors that can appear, the developmental issues, the impact of the injury on living and learning, the development of programming based on the strengths and needs of the individual, and the assessment and development of treatment plans based on the supports and demands present in the environment to which the child or adolescent will return.

Areas Affected by TBI

In pediatric TBI, various physical, social, behavioral, cognitive, communicative, and emotional problems can result. For the person with a brain injury to perform successfully in the home, school, community, or work, these areas of need must be identified and treated. Because every TBI is unique in terms of the characteristic behaviors and impairments that may emerge, careful attention to the characteristics of the particular individual being evaluated and treated is important. Professional staff need a clear understanding of all possible skills areas that can af-

fect the functioning of the child or adolescent. Various investigators (Begali, 1987; Blosser & DePompei, 1992; Cohen, 1986, 1991; DePompei & Blosser, 1987, 1991a, 1991b; Lehr & Savage, 1990; Nierenberg, 1992; Savage, 1991; Telzrow, 1987; Tyler, 1990; Ylvisaker, 1985; Ylvisaker & Sezekeres, 1986) have outlined characteristic behaviors that may be observed in children or adolescents with TBI, and the reader is referred to these sources for detailed descriptions. Exhibit 11-1 is a compilation of the various consequences of brain injury that have been reported in youth with TBI.

It should be noted that any of the characteristics listed in Exhibit 11-1 can be identified in children or adolescents with a variety of different handicapping conditions. There are indeed similarities between the characteristics of individuals with brain injury and children with other disabilities. These commonalities can be used as a basis for discussion of treatment strategies with professionals who do not understand TBI but who have extensive experience working with other types of disabilities. The development of programming for the child or adolescent with TBI can rely on some techniques that have worked with other disabilities. Selecting the appropriate strategies and applying them to the special needs of the person with a brain injury are essential.

There are also unique differences in people with brain injury that must be understood. According to Begali (1987), Blosser and DePompei (1991a, 1991b), Lehr (1990), Lehr and Savage (1990), and Ylvisaker, Hartwig, and Stevens (1991), it is the extremes of the behavior as well as the unusual combinations of characteristics that set people with brain injury apart. Exhibit 11-2 lists some of the notable differences that can be expected.

Developmental Issues

One of the primary issues that must be addressed in PT&D programs for treatment of youth is the fact that the person being treated is not a little adult. Children and adolescents, by virtue of their age, are in periods of rapid change that affect physical as well as intellectual (cogni-

Exhibit 11-1 Types of Impairments in Individuals with TBI

The following characteristics can occur in an individual with a head injury. They can occur in a number of combinations, and no two individuals will demonstrate the same patterns.

Medical:

Complications may include
—Seizures   —Pain
—Bowel and bladder control   —Orthopedic

Sensory:

Consider that there may be difficulty with
—Vision   —Hearing
—Smell   —Taste
—Touch   —Kinesthesia

Physical:

Look for impairments in
—Mobility   —Hearing
—Strength   —Balance
—Coordination   —Skilled motor activities
—Endurance

Perceptual-motor:

Think about involvement in
—Visual neglect   —Motor speed
—Visual field cuts   —Motor sequencing
—Motor apraxia

Cognitive-communication:

Observe for problems with
—Articulation   —Language
—Tangential speech   —Abstraction
—Hyperverbal speech   —Reading comprehension
—Confabulations   —Writing
—Anomia (word finding)

Cognitive:

Watch for difficulty in
—Memory (both short- and long-term)   —Egocentric thinking
—Thought processes   —Inability to anticipate and plan for the
—Conceptual skills   future
—Problem solving   —Inability to plan action to meet desired
—Attention   goals
—Concentration   —Self-regulation difficulties
—Self-awareness of abilities

Behavior:

Be aware that brain injury may account for
—Impulsivity   —Denial
—Poor judgment   —Depression
—Disinhibition   —Emotional lability
—Dependency   —Apathy
—Anger outbursts   —Lethargy
—Poor motivation

Social:

Sensitize yourself to know that the survivor may
—Not learn from peers   —Be bossy and argumentative
—Not learn from social situations   —Demonstrate poor responsibility and
—Withdraw   dependency
—Distract in noisy surroundings   —Misperceive social actions and events
—Become lost even in familiar   —Be easily influenced by others
  surroundings

Other behaviors that may be displayed include:
—Loneliness   —Unrealistic plans for the future
—Restlessness   —Sexually inappropriate behaviors
—Stubbornness   —Hypersensitivity to noise or confusion
—Mood changes without reason   —Reluctance to seek assistance when
—Perseveration   needed

Source: From "Strategies for Helping Head Injured Children Successfully Return to School" by R. DePompei and J. Blosser, 1987, *Language, Speech, and Hearing Services in Schools, 18,* p. 293. Copyright 1987 by American Speech-Language-Hearing Association. Adapted by permission.

Exhibit 11-2 Differentiating Characteristics of Traumatic Brain Injury and Other Types of Disabilities

The student with traumatic brain injury is not a "peer" of other students with handicaps. The learning handicap has been acquired. Following are some of the characteristics of these students making them different from individuals with other disabilities. Educators and other professionals must be aware of these differences and their effect on learning in order to appropriately plan for class placement and participation. The student with TBI typically has:

—a previous successful experience in academic and social settings
—a pre-morbid self concept of being normal
—discrepancies in ability levels
—inconsistent patterns of performance
—variability and fluctuation in the recovery process resulting in unpredictable and unexpected spurts of progress
—more extreme problems with generalizing, integrating, or structuring information
—poor judgment and loss of emotional control which may make the student appear to be emotionally disturbed at times
—cognitive deficits which are present as in other handicaps but are uneven in extent of damage and rate of recovery
—combinations of acquired problems resulting from the TBI which are unique and do not fall into usual categories of disabilities
—inappropriate behaviors which may be more exaggerated (more impulsive, more distractible, more emotional, more difficulty with memory, information processing, organization, and flexibility)
—a learning style which requires utilization of a variety of compensatory and adaptive strategies
—some high level skills which may be intact, making it difficult to understand why the student will have problems performing lower level tasks
—a previously learned base of information which assists relearning rapidly

tion, learning, and personality) development. Well into their teen years, they are in the process of learning how to learn and how to interact with situations and people in their environment. There are three important developmental factors to be considered when a child or adolescent sustains TBI: long-term effects, which can be cumulative as the child or adolescent develops; delayed onset of the deficits; and differences in each developmental stage (newborn through adolescence).

Long-Term Effects

The injury can interfere with long-term capacity to develop. Therefore, the possible cumulative impact of deficits must be considered. For example, if we are to put faith in the words of Piaget (Furth, 1970; Gruber & Vonech, 1977), we must recognize that the child moves through a series of cognitive stages that influence what cognitive skills would be expected to be present at a particular age level. A child of six years may be expected to develop vocabulary and to add factual information that will aid in the learning of new information in the future. Because of the injury, vocabulary development and retention of facts may be limited, thus hampering new learning. As the child progresses through school, demands on these learning processes increase, and the child may begin to falter. It may take years to recognize a deficit such as this. Professionals who assess and treat children and adolescents need to keep this possible cumulative developmental problem in mind when establishing both short-term and long-term program goals.

Delayed Onset of Deficits

According to Lehr and Savage (1990), "Unique to pediatric traumatic brain injury is the possibility of delayed onset of deficits. Since an injury may affect parts of the brain that are in the process of developing or not expected to be fully functioning for a long period of time after injury, it is possible for injury effects to not be apparent for even many years after onset" (p. 302). Savage (1991) points out that a child in elementary school may look fine during the first several years after injury. It is when additional demands of deductive reasoning, organization, or interpretation of written material are introduced in the upper grades that the child, now an adolescent, falls apart. Because so much time has passed between the injury and the onset of problems, parents and educators may not realize the connection between the earlier TBI and the lack of performance years later. The child's or adolescent's coping abilities and sense of identity may also change throughout different developmental stages or as new problems surface.

Consequently, learning style, performance capabilities, and emotional adjustment all need to be monitored over time.

Age Variability

There are few empirical data available regarding the various age levels from infancy to adolescence in terms of the impact that TBI may have on each developmental stage. Lehr and Savage (1990) provide an excellent description of infancy, preschool, elementary, and teenage levels and how TBI may affect each developmental stage. They define the physical, emotional, and cognitive development and possible impact of TBI on each. The reader is referred to this resource for detailed information.

Several points about children and adolescents in various stages of development should be emphasized.

- The vast majority of children younger than 5 years will return home after hospitalization. Even when it appears that no problems have resulted from the TBI, families of young children should be encouraged to stimulate them for language, learning, and exploration through play so that valuable developmental time is not lost.

- There is wide variability in preschool children's development that is considered normal. It should not be assumed that all suspected developmental delays are a result of the TBI.

- Even though they appear to be fine after injury, children and adolescents should be reevaluated annually through all developmental years because problems can appear at later stages.

- PT&D programs must emphasize follow-through with community agencies or school districts so that assessments and recommendations can be completed and monitored over extended periods.

- Parents should be informed of the possibility that, as the child develops and there are additional cognitive, social, and psychological demands, problems related to the

TBI could emerge years after the injury. They should be given resources for obtaining assistance whenever they have concerns about this issue.

Impact of the Impairments on School, Home, Community, and Work

It is the combination of developmental issues and the impact of the TBI that challenges the professional who provides treatment for the child or adolescent with TBI. In addition, understanding how the injury will affect the child's or adolescent's performance in the home, school, community, or work is important.

Every environment into which the child or adolescent reintegrates will pose demands that will challenge his or her performance capabilities. The child's or adolescent's ability to meet the challenge of various environments depends on the nature of the individual's impairments, personality, language skills, and temperament. All behaviors will occur within a social or learning context that involves friends, teachers, family, or community members.

Many professionals who evaluate children or adolescents with TBI are quite adept at determining the deficit areas. Their reports reflect the physical, cognitive, communicative, and emotional impairments that are present. What may be lacking, however, is the application of these deficit areas to functional, social, and learning situations to which the child or adolescent will return. For example, a report to a teacher may list specific problems such as delayed processing and slowed response time. This piece of information would be more useful if it were stated in terms of how the delayed processing might appear in a classroom. The report could state that the child will take a longer time to sort out a teacher's question, formulate a response, and actually give that response. This would allow the teacher who receives the report to understand the impairment within the learning context in which it may occur and to develop alternative plans for dealing with the problem.

By describing the impairment and behaviors that can result, a picture of how a child may perform in a real life situation may begin to emerge. Problem areas may also be anticipated. Treatment can focus on developing reasonable compensations for the individual within a given situation. Also, people within the environment can propose alternative ways of handling the situation so that the child or adolescent can be more successful.

PT&D Issues for Assessment and Treatment of the Individual with TBI

PT&D training programs should include information about the assessment and treatment needs of the child or adolescent with TBI. Comprehensive programming should regard evaluation and treatment planning for the individual as ongoing and always changing because the child or adolescent will often undergo alterations in behaviors, strengths, and needs. The ultimate goal of assessment and treatment should be the best possible reintegration into functional situations within home, school, community, and work.

Assessment Issues

PT&D training programs should emphasize the importance of both formal and informal assessment of the strengths and needs of the child or adolescent. Both types of assessment provide valuable information regarding present abilities and potential for developing skills for performance in a number of settings.

Formal assessment is necessary to determine placement issues in some facilities. It provides information about a variety of standardized performance measures that contribute to an understanding of underlying processes that may be impaired. A number of articles have been written about formalized assessment of children and adolescents. The reader is referred to articles by Begali (1987), DePompei and Blosser (1991a, 1991b), Lehr (1990), Rosen and Gerring (1986), Sohlberg and Mateer (1989), Telzrow (1987, 1991), Ylvisaker (1985), and Ylvisaker et al. (1990) for detailed information regarding test domains and specific assessment tools that may

be useful with children with brain injury. As of this writing, there are no tests available that have been developed and normed for pediatric head injury.

Informal assessment procedures provide valuable information for clinical decision making. They can be completed in natural environments rather than in structured one-on-one situations. They can provide information about performance in real-life situations. DePompei and Blosser (1991a, 1991b) suggest a number of informal assessment techniques, including interviews and surveys, direct observation, and experimental manipulation of variables believed to be related to the behavior in question (i.e., work, home, and classroom situations). Milton, Scaglione, Flanagan, Cox, and Rudnick (1991) outline a number of techniques for developing functional assessments based on interests and daily activities of the adolescent with TBI. Additional information about informal assessment is provided by Blosser and DePompei (1991), Kruetzer and Wehman (1991), and Ylvisaker (1985).

Treatment Issues

When planning treatment programs for youth with TBI, agencies should be interested in developing proactive approaches that facilitate individualized adaptation for the environments into which the child or adolescent will reintegrate. Treatment, if it is to be functional, cannot begin and end with component training. Treatment directed toward increasing any underlying process, such as attention or discrimination, without a specific behavior related to a functional task may not be applicable to people with brain injury.

Milton (1988) and Milton et al. (1991) suggest that task analysis (determining the various steps in successful completion of a task) be applied to any number of functional learning situations. This approach to therapy, taking treatment to the environment where the child will be asked to perform and developing compensatory strategies around the task requirement, is an effective approach to achieve performance success.

For a comprehensive review of treatment strategies the reader is referred to Blosser and

DePompei (1992), Beukelman and Yorkson (1991), DePompei and Blosser (1991a, 1991b), Kreutzer and Wehman (1991), Milton (1988), Sohlberg and Mateer (1990), Ylvisaker (1985), Ylvisaker et al. (1991), and Ylvisaker and Sezekeres (1986), all of whom provide a wealth of material from which to plan innovative and proactive programs for children and adolescents with TBI. PT&D programs should maintain reference material for staff regarding this type of treatment planning.

There are a number of additional relevant issues relating to assessment and treatment that PT&D programs should emphasize:

- *Medical history:* Information regarding any prior medical conditions, abuse, or illnesses should be obtained from all sources. Children may have reasons other than the TBI for developmental delays.
- *Developmental history:* Information regarding developmental milestones achieved before the TBI is useful in determining whether other physical, cognitive, communicative, or behavioral problems may have existed.
- *Effects of medication on performance:* Many youth will be taking antiseizure or other medications. Knowledge of the medication prescribed and possible effects on test and skill performance is essential.
- *Educational and work history:* Knowledge of the type of student or worker this individual was before injury is essential for determining his or her potential after injury. It is possible that the person had problems with learning before the injury, so that an inability to perform in school may not be related to the TBI but to preexisting abilities.
- *Test environment:* Optimal results are obtained in a quiet, one-on-one test environment. These results may not describe the child's performance in functional situations, where many distractions are present. Therefore, additional observations in real-life situations are helpful.
- *Timing of the assessment:* Telzrow (1991) suggests that assessments not be given to children or adolescents during periods of rapid growth or alteration. Periods when the child or adolescent is rehearsing new learning or has plateaued may be best for formalized evaluation.
- *Redundancy across agencies:* When discharge from one facility takes place, another agency is often beginning services for this child or adolescent. Assessment often takes place upon both discharge and admission. If agencies jointly determine those tests results that will be pertinent for treatment and placement in the new facility, duplication of testing or administration of tests deemed irrelevant by the new facility can be avoided.
- *Recognition of strengths of the individual:* Professionals are trained to recognize impairments in individuals and to help compensate for them. It is essential that the individual's strengths also be documented. Statements about strengths in the assessment reports are useful in planning treatment and reintegration strategies.
- *Use of family members:* Family members can often provide important clues as to how an individual can be motivated and assessed. Obtaining their insight before and throughout assessment and treatment is important.
- *Use of consumer advocates:* Often, agencies cannot or should not advocate for specific programming or assessment at another facility. There are consumer advocates for children, such as the Coalition for Handicapped Children, that will provide impartial third parties to ensure the best possible services for children and adolescents. They should be regarded as friends and used to help facilitate assessments, planning for transitions, and implementation of treatment programs.

By understanding the unique problems that children and adolescents can exhibit after TBI, the need for age-appropriate and functional assessment and treatment, and the environmental requirements for reintegration, the professional who provides services will be better equipped to develop programs that are appropriate to the individual's needs. PT&D program training must emphasize all these important components.

BARRIER 2: INADEQUATE NETWORKING AMONG REHABILITATION PROFESSIONALS, EDUCATION PROFESSIONALS, FAMILY, AND COMMUNITY

Impact

Effective communication may not take place among professionals at various facilities and with family and friends. This may result in misunderstanding and confusion about the child's or adolescent's strengths and needs, loss of effective planning time, inappropriate placement, and inadequate services.

Proposed PT&D Solutions

When developing a PT&D program, professionals will need to learn to organize plans to collaborate with professionals and families. These plans should include frequent and clear communication, education of individuals regarding available services, early exchange of information, and ongoing mechanisms for sharing ideas.

When working with children and adolescents, the concept of team collaboration is essential to appropriate planning. The two types of collaboration that must take place are: (1) working cooperatively among the facility team itself, and (2) developing active relationships with other community resources to which the child or adolescent will reintegrate.

Facility Team Communication

The team within the facility must be developed with transdisciplinary concepts that allow for common goal setting among all disciplines and team members. This approach consists of having each team member play an active role in setting and addressing the priority outcome goals throughout all environments. Family members and the child or adolescent should be involved in this process whenever possible. Transdisciplinary treatment models also encourage team members to work with the client at the same time on similar activities with different treatment objectives. For example, the physical therapist may work with a child to develop sitting balance while the speech/language pathologist may use sitting balance for posturing for swallowing and feeding. Both work on similar activities to achieve different goals. This level of collaboration among all members of the treatment team facilitates the development of a potent learning environment by setting clear priorities and providing consistency.

In order to achieve maximal transdisciplinary collaboration, the team must develop a philosophy that reflects this team concept. One of the primary stumbling blocks to achieving transdisciplinary treatment is unclear communication among team members. Each discipline has developed a number of professional terms that may not be meaningful to other team members. When in collaborative meetings, the use of descriptions of behaviors or terms not couched in the jargon of a particular profession is most helpful. For example, the speech/language pathologist can explain that a child exhibits severe apraxia of speech with anomia, or the therapist can report, "This child has motor planning problems which make the formulation of words difficult; he may miss the production of a word like 'tornado' by saying 'terneedo.' Also, he has trouble thinking of the names of things and may be unable to name simple objects in the PT or OT therapy room." The second description offers concrete examples that other team members can understand and use within their own treatment sessions.

There are numerous other considerations for team building that are discussed elsewhere in this text. All those suggestions will aid in the development of clearer communication within teams at a particular facility.

Interagency Communication

A second consideration is collaboration with other facilities and agencies where the child or adolescent will receive additional education or treatment. In some cases, transition from one facility to the next is well planned. Unfortunately, where children and adolescents are concerned, there may be poor and ineffective communication among key players in the transition process. Areas where ineffective planning appears include the following:

- Communication between facilities does not occur early enough in the planning process.

- Professionals from one facility do not have adequate information regarding the mission, resources, level of expertise, policies, and procedures of the other agency.

- Family members have not been involved in the transition process and do not know the procedures for acquiring appropriate services.

- Meaningful communication among family and professionals does not take place.

Suggested solutions to these problems include the following:

- *Communicate early with facilities such as the school where the child/adolescent is to return.* Often, treatment agencies do not think about contacting a school district until a child or adolescent is ready for discharge. This contact does not allow the school to adequately prepare for a readmission. As soon as the child or adolescent is admitted to a treatment facility, contact should be made with the school district to which the individual with TBI will return. This contact must be made with the full knowledge and permission of the parent or guardian. The contact can be initiated by either the treating facility, the family, or the school district. Ideally, the school and facility will provide one person each to maintain contact about the progress of the individual and to cooperatively plan for reintegration to school as well as home and community. With Public Law 101-476 and new Commission on Accreditation of Rehabilitation

Facilities (CARF) standards in place, schools and agencies should find it easier to meet these communication requirements.

- *Educate professionals from one facility about the capabilities of others.* One of the concerns expressed by professionals in various settings is that individuals in other settings are not prepared to meet the needs of children and adolescents who demonstrate unique characteristics and behaviors related to TBI. Because learning about brain injury has been challenging for most professionals in therapeutic settings, it is sometimes assumed that professionals in education or community agencies do not understand the needs of these individuals. That assumption is often correct. However, what sometimes results from this assumption is an attitude of one team about the knowledge and capabilities of another team. What may develop are adversarial roles and positions which hamper the transition process and the opportunity for each group of professionals to learn from the other.

Rehabilitation professionals need to learn about school dynamics and procedures as much as education team members need to learn about TBI. There is a certain assumption that there is no need to understand what schools can provide as we who attended school already know the processes that exist. Usually, rehabilitation team members were not involved in any special education or tutoring programs and have little accurate knowledge about these processes. Additionally, major changes in education policies have developed in recent years. Knowledge about the law, as well as local school procedures for children with special needs is essential for all team members. Visits to schools to observe classes and learn procedures are most helpful. The reverse education is also necessary. Teachers and others from school districts should visit hospitals and rehabilitation facilities to learn the processes of rehabilitation that the child is experiencing.

- *Develop networks among facilities that will work.* In order to facilitate communication among various interagency facility teams several approaches are useful.

—Respect each others education and knowledge base. While specific information about TBI may be lacking, most education and community professionals have experience with children with other special needs. Their ideas can often be adapted successfully when they are provided with accurate information regarding the specific nature of the problems experienced by an individual with TBI. An initial attitude of attempting to solve problems together is more successful than any team member trying to insist that only one approach or strategy can be successful. Both sets of teams must use their creativity and set realistic expectations of each other in order to provide a successful transition and to establish functional treatment plans.

—Use clear communication and definitions. The avoidance of jargon and provision of specific examples of how an impairment can affect performance and adjustment in a given situation is the most helpful means of program planning and clear communication.

—Acquire accurate information about laws and admission criteria for education or community programs. The PT&D program should include references to specific due process manuals and guidelines developed by state departments of education and special education divisions regarding their standards for TBI programs. Other community agencies' specific requirements for admission should be accumulated in a manual and available for team use. Additionally, PT&D programs should work to develop a simple pamphlet that outlines the admission policies and treatment procedures for their facility that can be shared with other facilities.

—Develop means of written communication which can be transmitted across families and agencies for follow through. DePompei and Blosser (1987) have developed a checklist for use as a basis for discussion among families and professionals. This is used by rehabilitation personnel to fill in the chart upon discharge, and by education or community staff to rechart at 2 to 3 month intervals. Discussion can then be related to improvement or lack of improvement observed. Charts such as this can be developed or adapted further according to the needs of a specific set of facilities.

Exhibit 11-3 presents a planning worksheet for developing information about the child or adolescent that may be useful for team review and analysis. Information can be supplied by family members, health care professionals, rehabilitation professionals and education team members. The composite picture can be sorted and discussed in team planning meetings. If organized systematically, the information can be used as a guide for periodic ongoing case review. Findings can serve as a framework for further assessment and intervention planning.

Ylvisaker et al. (1991) provide a transition chart from rehabilitation facility to school which is also helpful in completing all the communications necessary for a smooth transition. Additionally, PT&D training programs may want to provide a means for their facility to provide information to schools about how to initiate transition. The checklist in Exhibit 11-4 may be helpful in this regard.

The use of checklists, charts and descriptive reports is one way of providing contacts with agencies that are appropriate to the needs of the individual with TBI. Additionally, provision of information that is relevant to the environments of home, school, community, or work will aid in the networking process. Attention to both intra– and interagency communication continues to be the key to avoiding problems within this barrier.

Exhibit 11-3 Planning Worksheet for Team Review and Analysis

GENERAL STATUS

Each team member should make a statement of his or her observations and impressions of the student's general behavior and status.

MEDICAL STATUS

Area of brain involved: _____

Severity of injury: _____

Extent of motoric involvement: _____

Glasgow Coma Scale: _____

Ranchos Los Amigos Level:

_____ At Discharge

_____ At School Reentry

_____ 3 Months Post Entry

_____ 6 Months Post Entry

_____ 9 Months Post Entry

Seizure Activity: _____

Medication:

Type _____ Dosage _____

Health status at time of reintegration: _____

Potential impact of medical status on intervention:

_____

_____

_____

_____

_____

_____

_____

COGNITIVE-COMMUNICATION STATUS

(Based on test results and observations)

Expressive Language	Receptive Language
Phonology	Orientation
Syntax	Attention
Semantics	Memory
Pragmatics	Association
	Executive Functioning

PSYCHOSOCIAL STATUS

Interpersonal behaviors with family, friends _____

Mood most days _____

Potential impact of psychosocial behavior on intervention

_____

_____

ACADEMIC INFORMATION

Grade level in specific curricular areas (math, reading, language arts, writing)

_____

Strengths and needs in classroom related behaviors (attending, self control, awareness, independence, persistence, organization, problem solving, information processing)

_____

_____

_____

_____

Source: From "A Proactive Model for Treating Communication Disorders in Children and Adolescents with Traumatic Brain Injury" by J. Blosser and R. DePompei, 1992, *Clinics in Communication Disorders, 2*, p. 56. Copyright 1992 by Butterworth-Heinemann. Reprinted by permission.

BARRIER 3: LACK OF ORGANIZATIONAL READINESS AND CAPABILITIES FOR SERVING YOUTH WITH TBI

Impact

Children and adolescents with TBI encounter a diverse range of facilities and programs after sustaining a brain injury. These include hospitals, rehabilitation centers, community-based outpatient programs, school placements, and community agencies. Often the organizational system is not ready to receive and serve the individual. The lack of organizational readiness and capabilities to accept and treat the young person with TBI may result in interrupted, inappropriate, or ineffective services.

Proposed PT&D Solutions

Identification of TBI as a unique situation with individualized intervention needs is still relatively new. Many challenges face organizations providing services to children and adolescents with TBI. Often programs were originally designed to treat adults with TBI or to serve individuals with disabilities other than TBI. Consequently the policies and procedures followed, as well as the service delivery options offered, are unable to respond to the needs of children or adolescents with TBI. To

Exhibit 11-4 Case Management Checklist from the Educator's Point of View

EFFECTIVE REINTEGRATION REQUIRES EFFECTIVE COMMUNICATION AND PLANNING.
PLANNING MUST BE A TWO-WAY PROCESS IN ORDER TO BE EFFECTIVE.

Families may request a child or adolescent with traumatic brain injury be re-enrolled in an educational setting. If the rehabilitation facility has not initiated contact with the school, the following procedures are recommended to educational teams, who can initiate the networking process.

Date Completed	Initials	Reintegration Procedures
		I. PRIOR TO SCHOOL RE-ENTRY A. Determine who will act as the school's liaison and work to establish a relationship with the family and hospital/rehabilitation personnel.
		B. Inform the family of the school's interest in working toward a successful re-entry experience for the student and family.
		1. Follow designated school policies and procedures for obtaining information and making contact/visiting with outside agencies.
		2. Request to meet with persons who have been involved with student prior to the time of re-entry.
		3. Meet to work out a plan for exchanging information, educating one another, and implementing effective re-entry.
		4. Find out all you can about the student. Begin to compile data for later analysis and use.
		C. Learn about the student's present status and jointly determine readiness for school re-entry.
		1. Obtain medical/rehabilitation records.
		2. Gain an understanding of the nature of the student's traumatic brain injury.
		3. Determine the treatment history and progress.
		4. Describe cognitive-communicative status at discharge
		5. Discuss with hospital/rehabilitation personnel their impressions of the student's readiness for returning to school based on the demands of the educational setting.
		6. Obtain samples of the student's work which are representative of the current level of performance.
		7. Identify the physical, cognitive-communicative, psychological, and social behaviors that will intererfe with learning and social activities at school.
		8. Relate this information to the requisite needs for educational success.
		9. Provide information about the school and classroom setting, expectations, routines, classroom materials, peers, etc.
		10. Provide samples of the work the student may be expected to complete upon return to school.

Exhibit 11-4 continued

Date Completed	Initials	
		D. Inform family and rehabilitation professionals about the school's capabilities and readiness to handle the student's return.
		1. Discuss the school system's policies and procedures regarding special education, placement, services and how they might be applied given the: student's present status requisite needs for school success school's capabilities
		2. Invite family and rehabilitation personnel to the school to meet the staff and assess the school situation respective to the student's status, needs, and capabilities.
		3. Make arrangements for pertinent evaluation/assessments to obtain information for placement and educational planning decisions.
		4. Jointly determine barriers which will impact on successful re-entry. Look at the student critically from the perspective of program offerings, personnel, etc. Conduct a search for the most appropriate persons to be involved.
		5. Jointly plan for modifying, eliminating, or reducing the barriers. Establish objectives (for the educators as well as for the student).
		6. Jointly plan the I.E.P.
		7. Make arrangements for placement and/or scheduling special services as indicated.
		8. Implement in-service programs for educators, peers, etc.
		E. Make special considerations when selecting the classroom placement and teachers.
		1. Design instructional objectives so they are functional and relate to the curriculum.
		2. Determine a functional scheduling plan.
		3. Assess socialization characteristics and needs of peers.
		4. Structure the classroom climate and environment for success.
		5. Determine the teacher's willingness to learn and/or level of understanding of exceptional children and brain injury.
		6. Consider other teacher characteristics: Flexibility Acceptance Patience Positive, supportive attitude Comfortable with suggestions from others
		F. Identify contingency plans in the event that the first placement experience is not a good match with the student's needs, abilities, and interests.
		G. Additional comments

continues

Exhibit 11-4 continued

Date Completed	Initials	
		II. AFTER THE RE-ENTRY A. Maintain communication about the student's performance through an organized flow of information.
		1. With the student (document method)
		2. With the family (document method)
		3. With the former rehabilitation personnel (document method)
		4. With other educators involved (teachers, psychologists, special educators, speech-language pathologists, physical therapists, occupational therapists, administrators, etc.) (document method)
		B. Assess the student's performance and success of the re-entry; decide what can be changed, eliminated, increased.
		1. Gather involved personnel and family
		2. Review objectives and performance
		3. Recommend revisions
		C. Develop peer support systems
		1. Encourage peer support (document method)
		2. Encourage socialization (document method)
		3. Provide opportunities for extra-curricular activities (document method)
		D. Additional comments

meet the challenge posed by this barrier, organizations need to identify areas of their programs where lack of readiness is apparent, to understand the implications of federal legislation and accreditation standards, and to take steps to prepare systematically for providing services.

Lack of Organizational Readiness

Developing programs appropriate to the strengths and needs of children and adolescents with TBI can be a challenge to facilities. Organizations need to review carefully their preparedness to work with these individuals and their families. Areas where organizational readiness may be a concern include the following:

- limited interagency and intraagency service coordination

- preconceived notions of how to serve people with brain injury
- discipline-specific decision making regarding treatment
- implementation of disability- or deficit-specific assessment and treatment procedures rather than functional ones
- limited opportunity for family and peer involvement
- restrictions on who interacts with the client as well as how the services are delivered
- restrictions on the scope, duration, quality, and type of services offered
- limited staff preparation to address the needs of children and adolescents with brain injury

In many situations the organizational design may need to be modified. A considerable portion of the PT&D effort will need to focus on making the organizational system ready. To lay the groundwork for pediatric rehabilitation or reintegration, personnel in the organization will need jointly to reconsider the organization's philosophy, mission, and goals.

Procedures for client intake, selection of service delivery options, interagency service coordination, transition to other programs, and the like should be clearly defined. Flexibility and responsiveness should be stressed. Staff need to be involved in this organizational planning process because they will be responsible for carrying out plans. Visits to model programs and discussions with consumers will help staff identify needs and directions for change. Administrators should support efforts to develop organizational readiness by providing educational and inservice opportunities, facilitating self-study, and providing staff with time and resources for this undertaking.

Federal Legislation and Accreditation Standards

Three recent initiatives can provide impetus for developing organizational modifications. These are Public Law 101-476, the new standards for TBI developed by the Commission on Accreditation of Rehabilitation Facilities (CARF), and expanded definitions of mental retardation/developmental disabilities (MR/DD).

Public Law 101-476

In January 1991, the Education for All Handicapped Children Act (Public Law 94-142) was amended, renamed, and reauthorized by Congress. The new act, Public Law 101-476, is referred to as the Individuals with Disabilities Education Act (IDEA). The reauthorized law now includes a special category for students with TBI. At present, state departments of education are developing rules and regulations for provision of services to students with brain injury. This law means that children and adolescents with TBI, if they qualify for special education, must be provided with appropriate education regardless of the severity of their disability. For further information about how an individual state will handle this requirement, contact individual state departments of special education.

CARF Standards

CARF has revised its requirements for individuals with TBI in organizations that they accredit. The new standards became effective July 1, 1992. For the first time, CARF standards are outlined for organizations with a designated pediatric program providing services to children or adolescents with brain injury. Standards define staff make-up and education, provisions for children and adolescents, provisions for family, and coordination of services for school reintegration. The following is an explanation of each of these standards:

- *Staff make-up and education*
  1. Professionals should show evidence of orientation, preservice, and inservice training that addresses needs of siblings and peers, normal childhood development, parenting issues, and skills in working with families. These topics are listed in addition to suggestions for education topics for professionals who treat persons with TBI.
  2. Programs must provide, or make formal arrangements for, the services of an education specialist. Additionally, the services of a pediatrician, if the child is 12 years of age or younger, are required.
  3. Core teams in a pediatric program should include a developmental specialist and a special education liaison.
- *Provisions for the child or adolescent*
  1. Programs should provide space, equipment, furniture, and materials according to the ages and developmental needs of children and adolescents.
  2. Separate areas for beds should be provided for children and adolescents according to their ages and developmental needs and away from adults.
  3. Private areas equipped with age-appropriate materials and furniture should be provided for peer and family visitation.
  4. Assessment must be age-appropriate and developmentally appropriate.

5. Periodic reassessment to monitor cognitive processes until the child or adolescent reaches adulthood should be completed.
6. Consumer satisfaction surveys should be adapted to elicit responses from children.

- *Provision for family*
    1. The family is recognized as a focal point and is to be included in all phases of planning.
    2. Services, as needed, that are to be provided for the family include advocacy training, counseling, education, parent-to-parent interactions, and sibling and peer support.
- *Coordination of services for school reintegration*
    1. Programs should request preonset school records.
    2. Programs should demonstrate familiarity with current federal laws specific to the education of children.
    3. The program should have procedures for cooperative education and training of school and rehabilitation personnel regarding each other's programs, family training in educational issues and procedures, integrated planning, and involvement in the Individualized Education Program planning process.

Additional information about the standards can be obtained from the *Standards Manual for Organizations Serving People with Disabilities* (CARF, 1992).

Expanded Definitions of MR/DD

Several states have undertaken initiatives to develop new definitions of MR/DD. These expanded definitions may provide additional service opportunities for some youth with TBI. For example, in the state of Ohio, the definition of MR/DD now includes functional definitions of developmental delays. This definition states that individuals who were injured before age 22 may be eligible for services (such as therapies and group housing) under MR/DD boards if they have two or more handicapping conditions that interfere with normal life functioning. Although many individuals may not qualify for services, organizations should be aware of the possibilities for providing such services and recommending alternative options.

Summary

To summarize, we recommend that organizations prepare to serve children and adolescents with TBI by taking the following steps. The emphasis will vary depending on the nature of the organization involved and whether they are developing new services or expanding existing programs.

1. Obtain administrative support for expanding services to youth with TBI.
2. Conduct an organizational self-study to determine organizational readiness, attitudes toward serving people with brain injury, staff needs, and resource capabilities and needs (including equipment and space).
3. Incorporate services offered to people with TBI and their families into mission, goal, and objective statements.
4. Strengthen collaborative efforts among professionals within the organization.
5. Form teams to develop policies and procedures as they relate to provision of services.
6. Contact other service delivery agencies in the community (hospitals, rehabilitation centers, and schools) and establish working relationships.
7. Maintain current information (contact persons, addresses, and phone numbers) about advocacy groups at state and national levels.
8. Review legislation and accreditation standards as they relate to service provision to individuals with TBI.
9. Monitor program implementation to determine outcome effectiveness.
10. Strive to improve areas identified as in need of change.

Implementing a service delivery program for children and adolescents with TBI is a challenging task for organizations. To do so effectively, the organizational system has to be ready to handle the diverse needs of this group of individuals. Organizational leaders as well as staff at all levels will need to work together to determine how to incorporate service delivery into existing frameworks. The planning process can be facilitated by conducting an organizational self-study, gathering pertinent information from various sources, involving many persons in the planning stages, monitoring outcomes, and making changes as needed. Much of the preparation can be completed through PT&D strategies.

BARRIER 4: PROFESSIONALS' INADEQUATE UNDERSTANDING OF THE UNIQUE PROBLEMS OF THIS POPULATION AND THEIR UNREADINESS TO PROVIDE SERVICES

Impact

Professionals working with children or adolescents with TBI must have a clear understanding of the nature and consequences of this disability, its impact on psychosocial development and learning processes, and strategies for assessment, treatment, and ongoing management. Many professionals are unprepared to provide adequate services. The lack of professional expertise and preparation is a major stumbling block to successful reintegration.

Proposed PT&D Solutions

Until recently, formal professional training for rehabilitation and education professionals has had a limited focus on the nature and needs of persons with TBI. Practicing professionals acquired the knowledge they possess independently through inservice training, through on-the-job experiences, and by seeking answers and information when problems or questions arose. Although these methods are helpful, they cannot compare to systematically planned, comprehensive personnel training and development approaches that use various adult teaching methods. Emphasis in PT&D programs must be placed on identifying skills and competencies necessary for addressing the needs of people with brain injury and their families, developing awareness of applicable treatment strategies, building collaborative relationships, and determining which educational formats may be the most useful to particular staff members.

Professionals' Skills and Competencies

Appendix 11-1 is a suggested outline of competencies that professionals need to gain to serve youth with TBI adequately. It includes awareness information as well as direct and indirect intervention strategies.

Each professional on the TBI team will bring a specific set of skills and competencies to the situation. PT&D efforts can be maximized if professionals are provided with opportunities to relate what they learn about TBI to what they already know about treating people with other disabilities.

Treatment Strategies

Most professionals employ a wide repertoire of strategies for treatment. When confronted with a difficult or new clinical problem, they often conclude that new treatment strategies are needed. This tendency may be particularly strong in school systems and community agencies that see a relatively low incidence of TBI compared to staff working in rehabilitation settings. This assumption may be erroneous. Instead, it will be most beneficial for professionals to learn to apply strategies that they are already secure in using. In a PT&D curriculum, this can be facilitated by discussing behaviors that people with TBI present and brainstorming ideas for treatment from the group. The expected outcome of this exercise is helping inexperienced staff recognize that they are already familiar with strategies that can be useful in working with people who have sustained brain injury. This process can build staff confidence while at the same time expand their knowledge of effective teaching and management techniques. The following are some teaching strategies that have been found to be successful with students with TBI:

- supplement written instructions with verbal instructions, and vice versa
- present information at a slow rate, allowing adequate time for auditory and visual processing
- avoid abstract language (as well as puns or sarcasm) when delivering important messages
- repeat tasks several times
- define new vocabulary and concepts being introduced
- structure activities by asking W questions (who, what, where, when, and why)
- encourage the use of assistive and augmentative devices such as calculators, computers, assistive listening devices, and augmentative communication devices
- develop systems for organizing assignments and information
- encourage discussion of problems
- structure the treatment environment to encourage practice of functional skills
- implement small-group activities
- encourage self-monitoring and self-correction
- discuss the steps in completing a task before initiating the task
- gain and maintain attention to the task at hand, even if only for a short time
- redirect attention if the child or adolescent becomes distracted or frustrated

Team members should jointly determine the one or two strategies that will be most beneficial to the child or adolescent. All team members should then apply the identified strategies consistently in treatment sessions to achieve maximum benefit. When looking for appropriate intervention strategies it is helpful to describe the individual's behavior in a particular situation, to relate the behavior to a cognitive-communicative deficit resulting from the injury, and then to determine jointly applicable treatment strategies. Table 11-1 illustrates this decision-making effort.

Building Collaborative Efforts

In addition to increasing professionals' understanding of assessment and direct treatment strategies, PT&D curricula should emphasize the concept of team building and the collaborative philosophy. Topics that should be addressed include the following:

- processes for collaboration
- perceived strengths and needs of the staff
- team composition and philosophy
- family members as equal partners
- role definition
- strategies for joint decision making and problem solving
- policies and procedures for teaming
- perspectives on treatment unique to each discipline
- plans for monitoring and improving quality of service delivery
- responsibilities and time lines

Effective programming for children and adolescents with TBI requires a multidisciplinary perspective. In organizing the PT&D efforts, the diverse composition and existing competencies of the training participants must be recognized. Before the content and training format are determine, a needs assessment must be made. Data should be acquired about the participant's current knowledge base, attitudes, learning styles, interest levels, roles in the organization, and perspectives on treatment. In this way, individual group strengths as well as needs and motivation can be determined. Analysis of this information will lead to training programs that are interesting and relevant for all participants. It will also eliminate the potential for presenting redundant information or general information that may not be applicable to their current situations.

Formats for Implementing PT&D Programs

Funding, time constraints, reduced budgets, and conflicting schedules pose problems in implementing PT&D programs. Additionally,

Table 11-1 Cognitive-Communicative Impairments and Recommended Strategies

Environment	Cognitive-Communicative Impairments	Behavior	Cognitive-Communicative Strategy
School	Word retrieval errors.	Answers contain a high use of "this", "that", "those things", "whatchamacallits".	WORD RECALL: Teach the student association skills and to give definitions of words he can not recall.
			Teach memory strategies (rehearsal, association, visualization, etc.).
Home	Difficulty learning new information.	Unable to understand rules for a new card game.	Break information into shorter chunks.
			Provide ample time for responses.
			Restate.
			Teach to ask for repetitions.
Community	Poor problem solving.	Takes purchases to a counter to find no clerk at register; individual can't figure out what to do and leaves the store.	Teach to identify personnel in specific work environments by their clothing, badges, etc.
			Teach to request assistance from other individuals.
Work	Poor ability to abstract, understand humor, sarcasm.	Doesn't "get" the humor or slang used by co-workers.	Introduce "small talk" skills.
			Teach slang, work environment "lingo", puns.

Source: From "A Proactive Model for Treating Communication Disorders in Children and Adolescents with Traumatic Brain Injury" by J. Blosser and R. DePompei, 1992, *Clinics in Communication Disorders, 2,* p. 64. Copyright 1992 by Butterworth-Heinemann. Reprinted by permission.

adults learn well with a number of different approaches. For example, some individuals would be interested in specific lecture presentations, whereas others would prefer to read selected materials independently. Therefore, a number of teaching formats should be employed, including traditional didactic and lecture approaches, audio and video presentations, informal discussion groups, teaching and collaboration in the natural work environment, journal study groups, self-study programs, guest speakers, and question-answer techniques.

The most effective teaching formats will be those that encourage active participation, have a direct relationship to everyday situations that occur on the job, and have a follow-up component to assess skills acquisition and to address further training needs that may arise. See Blosser and DePompei (1991, 1992) for further discussion of issues related to professional training and development.

Professionals are willing to put effort into gaining new knowledge when they are respected for what they already know and when they see how new information can be applied directly. PT&D programming should take into account the types of information that will be considered valuable. Informational sessions should present pertinent information and techniques and employ a number of training formats that can serve to challenge the professional seeking information.

BARRIER 5: LACK OF UNDERSTANDING AND INVOLVEMENT OF FAMILY AND PEERS

Impact

Formalized treatment within the rehabilitative, clinical, or school setting can only set the stage for reintegration. To be successful, the child or adolescent with TBI must be able to interact effectively with many individuals in his or her environment. Significant persons, including family members, co-workers, and friends, need to learn about the nature of TBI and how they can support the child or adolescent. This is particularly important if they are to help facilitate the reintegration process and successful long-term adaptation.

Proposed PT&D Solutions

The current professional literature supports working with family members as equal partners in the rehabilitation process. Most professionals, however, have had little formal training in how to establish meaningful working relationships with family and friends of their clients. Both the professionals and the family members quite often feel uncomfortable about the level of involvement that is possible or the types of activities that can be carried out by people who have not been professionally trained.

There are three major topics that PT&D programs can address to prepare professionals for working with family and friends: understanding families in crisis, encouraging family and friends to replicate intervention strategies away from formal treatment settings, and advocating for their loved one.

Understanding Families in Crisis

DePompei and Zarski (1989) and Williams and Kay (1991) provide excellent overviews of issues related to understanding the needs of families of individuals with TBI. They describe some reactions that might be observed as well as stages of adjustment that families might experience. They also recommend strategies for counseling families and involving them in the reintegration process and beyond.

Before family members and friends can be totally involved in the reintegration process, the professional must understand their perspectives, capabilities, problems, values, and needs. Coping styles can vary from family to family, and the development of an understanding of how to cope in a healthy manner is important to the family and professionals who work with them. A review of the literature on family systems, family dynamics, and home-based intervention can be helpful in facilitating professionals' understanding of pertinent issues.

Skill Generalization and Carryover of Intervention Strategies

Generalization of targeted skills to situations outside the clinical setting is often slow and tedious. Daily stimulation and practice in a number of contexts can help promote continuity. Direct instruction and treatment in the child's or adolescent's natural environment (e.g., home, school, community) will facilitate skill generalization and use of strategies in their own environment. Family members, co-workers, and friends can bring about the needed practice if they are empowered to do so. Clinicians should instruct key persons to use selected strategies and techniques naturally during interactions in the home, school, work, or community setting. Professionals should take the following steps to encourage the replication of strategies:

1. Help others learn to identify the child's or adolescent's problems and strengths and relate these behaviors to specific impairments that may have resulted from the TBI.
2. Teach family members and friends to recognize which of their own interactions and communication styles will facilitate positive responses or create problems.
3. Facilitate their understanding of how to elicit specific types of responses and to

seize opportunities for providing assistance.

4. Teach them how to implement specific treatment strategies and when to implement them.

5. Instruct them in procedures for evaluating success and making changes when necessary.

By using this model as a focus for discussion, PT&D facilitators can help professionals develop systematic procedures for transferring important intervention responsibilities to key persons in the child's or adolescent's life. Blosser and DePompei (1992) provide an explanation of how professionals might teach others to use strategies for improving cognitive-communicative skills. The recommended strategies can be found in Exhibit 11-5.

Preparing the Family for Roles as Partners and Advocates

Preparing families to assume equal and meaningful roles in planning and implementing interventions may be one of the most beneficial contributions that professionals can offer. Ideally, the family should have a working knowledge of the rehabilitation or education program for the child or adolescent. They should be aware of progress and problems at all times. They should be skilled at interpreting medical and clinical reports when they encounter professionals in the future. These skills can be facilitated by consistently incorporating family members into treatment sessions and decision-making meetings.

Throughout rehabilitation and reintegration, professionals can provide family members with information that will help them understand their loved one's problems and needs. The information should not be relayed haphazardly. Decisions need to be made regarding the type of information to be discussed, who will deliver the message, the format for delivery, and the amount of information to be discussed during a particular time. Particular attention needs to be paid to the timing of sharing information that may be too early to address (i.e., long-term implications

Exhibit 11-5 Recommended Interactive Cognitive-Communication Strategies

Monitoring quality of conversations
Giving instructions and directions
Explaining new concepts and vocabulary
Monitoring speech selection
Organizing and sequencing information
Attending to student's behaviors, queries, comments
Supporting verbal communication
Permitting adequate response time
Announcing and clarifying topic of conversation
Making the student aware of others' responses
Reading to the student
Communicating through writing
Reinforcing the student's communication attempts
Requiring and expecting communication
Encouraging responsiveness
Fostering communication through any means possible
Arranging the physical environment for communication
Structuring communication activities
Developing memory skills and compensatory strategies
Practicing higher level thinking and communicating
Welcoming discussion of frustrations, concerns, problems

of the injury) and the family's readiness to discuss sensitive issues. Below is a suggested sequence of information that might be presented at different points during the rehabilitation and reintegration process:

1. *Early stages:* the nature of TBI, answers to medical questions, the recovery process, necessary treatments

2. *Throughout rehabilitation:* the resulting deficits, the impact on performance and adjustment, treatment methods and techniques, management routines, the impact of TBI on the family system and social interactions

3. *Reintegration to home, school, and community:* coping and problem solving, strategies for successful adaptation to various environments, legal and ethical considerations, long-term planning of lifelong management and care

The relationships that families and professionals form can influence the success of the individual's reintegration in either positive or negative ways. Understanding the family's potential to help and mentoring them in the development of positive attitudes and technical skills represent an important role for professionals. Recognizing the family's strengths and anticipating problems and needs are essential in promoting smooth transitions from one situation to the next.

CONCLUSION

This chapter has been developed to assist those who treat, teach, and live with children and adolescents who have sustained TBI. These individuals can provide much support for children and adolescents who will be returning to home, school, community, and work. It is important for these individuals to understand the special problems associated with assessment, treatment, and programming for children and adolescents with TBI. Their contributions will be more effective if they are armed with strategies for helping and the confidence to implement the help when needed. It is hoped that professionals will be challenged to develop PT&D programming that is coordinated and effective, so that the child or adolescent can gain the maximum benefit within the rehabilitation and reintegration process.

REFERENCES

Begali, V. (1987). *Head injury in children and adolescents: A resource and review for school and allied professionals.* Brandon, VT: Clinical Psychology Publishers.

Beukelman, D.R., & Yorkson, K. (1991). *Communication disorders following traumatic brain injury: Management of cognitive, language, and motor impairments.* Austin: Pro-ed.

Blosser, J., & DePompei, R. (1991). Preparing education professionals for meeting the needs of students with traumatic brain injury. *Journal of Head Trauma Rehabilitation, 6,* 73–82.

Blosser, J.L., & DePompei, R. (1992). A proactive model for treating communication disorders in children and adolescents with traumatic brain injury. *Clinics in Communicative Disorders, 2,* 52–65.

Cohen, S. (1986). Educational reintegration and programming for children with head injuries. *Journal of Head Trauma Rehabilitation, 1,* 22–29.

Cohen, S. (1991). Adapting educational programs for students with head injuries. *Journal of Head Trauma Rehabilitation, 6,* 56–63.

Commission on Accreditation of Rehabilitation Facilities (CARF). (1992). *Standards manual for organizations serving people with disabilities.* Tuscon: Author.

DePompei, R., & Blosser, J.L. (1987). Strategies for helping head-injured children successfully return to school. *Language, Speech, and Hearing Services in Schools, 18,* 292–300.

DePompei, R., & Blosser, J.L. (1991a). Families of children with traumatic brain injury as advocates in school reentry. *Neurorehabilitation, 1,* 29–37.

DePompei, R., & Blosser, J.L. (1991b). Functional cognitive-communicative impairments in children and adolescents: Assessment and intervention. In J. Kreutzer & P. Wehman (Eds.), *Cognitive rehabilitation for persons with traumatic brain injury.* Baltimore: Brookes.

DePompei, R., & Zarski, J. (1989). Families, head injury, and cognitive-communicative impairments: Implications for family counseling. *Topics in Language Disorders, 9,* 78–89.

Furth, H. (1970). *Piaget for teachers.* Englewood Cliffs, NJ: Prentice-Hall.

Gruber, H., & Vonech, J.J. (1977). *The essential Piaget.* New York: Basic.

Kalsbeek, W., McLauren, R., Harris, B., & Miller, J.D. (1980). The national head and spinal cord injury survey: Major findings. *Journal of Neurosurgery, 1,* 53.

Kraus, J.F., Fife, D., Cox, P., Ramstein, K., & Conroy, C. (1986). Incidence, severity, and external causes of pediatric head injury. *American Journal of Diseases in Childhood, 140,* 687–693.

Kreutzer, J.S., & Wehman, P.H. (1991). *Cognitive rehabilitation for persons with traumatic brain injury.* Baltimore: Brookes.

Lehr, E. (1990). *Psychological management of traumatic brain injuries in children and adolescents.* Gaithersburg, MD: Aspen.

Lehr, E., & Savage, R. (1990). Community and school integration from a developmental perspective. In J.S. Kreutzer & P. Wehman (Eds.), *Community integration following traumatic brain injury* (pp. 301–309). Baltimore: Brookes.

Milton, S.B. (1988). Management of subtle cognitive communicative deficits. *Journal of Head Trauma Rehabilitation, 3,* 1–11.

Milton, S., Scaglione, C., Flanagan, T., Cox, J.L., & Rudnick, D. (1991). Functional evaluation of adolescent students with traumatic brain injury. *Journal of Head Trauma Rehabilitation, 6,* 35–46.

National Center for Health Statistics. (1982). Advance report, final monthly statistics. *Monthly Vital Statistics Report, 31*(6).

Nierenberg, B. (1992). *Team development in pediatric and adolescent rehabilitation.* Unpublished manuscript, University of Miami School of Medicine, Jackson Memorial Hospital, Miami.

Rosen, C.D., & Gerring, J.P. (1986). *Head trauma: Educational reintegration.* San Diego: College-Hill.

Savage, R. (1991). Identification, classification, and placement issues for students with traumatic brain injuries. *Journal of Head Trauma Rehabilitation, 6,* 1–9.

Sohlberg, M.M., & Mateer, C.A. (1989). The assessment of cognitive-communicative functions in head injury. *Topics in Language Disorders, 9,* 15–33.

Sohlberg, M.M., & Mateer, C.A. (1990). Evaluation and treatment of communication skills. In J.S. Kreutzer and P. Wehman (Eds.), *Community reintegration following traumatic brain injury* (pp. 67–83). Baltimore: Brookes.

Telzrow, C.F. (1987). Management of academic and educational problems in head injury. *Journal of Learning Disabilities, 20,* 536–545.

Telzrow, C. (1991). The school psychologist's perspective on testing students with traumatic head injury. *Journal of Head Trauma Rehabilitation, 6,* 23–34.

Tyler, J.S. (1990). *Traumatic brain injury in school-aged children: A training manual for educational personnel.*

Kansas City, KS: University of Kansas Medical Center, Children's Rehabilitation Unit.

Waaland, P.K., & Kreutzer, J. (1988). Family response to childhood traumatic brain injury. *Journal of Head Trauma Rehabilitation, 8,* 51–63.

Williams, J., & Kay, T. (Eds.). (1991). *Head injury: A family matter.* Baltimore: Brookes.

Wrenn, C.G. (1992). "Fixed stars": A message from the past for our troubled future. *Journal of Counseling and Development, 70,* 701.

Ylvisaker, M. (1985). *Head injury rehabilitation: Children and adolescents.* San Diego: College-Hill.

Ylvisaker, M., Chorazy, A., Cohen, S., Mastrill, J., Molitor, C., Nelson, J., Sezekeres, S., Valko, A., & Jaffe, K. (1990). Rehabilitative assessment following head injury in children. In M. Rosenthal, E. Griffith, M. Bond, & J.D. Miller (Eds.), *Rehabilitation of the adult and child with traumatic brain injury* (2nd ed., pp. 558–584). Philadelphia: Davis.

Ylvisaker, M., Hartwig, P., & Stevens, M. (1991). School reentry following head injury: Managing the transition from hospital to school. *Journal of Head Trauma Rehabilitation, 6,* 10–22.

Ylvisaker, M., & Sezekeres, S. (1986). Management of the patient with closed head injury. In R. Chapey (Ed.), *Language intervention strategies in adult aphasia* (pp. 474–487). Baltimore: Williams & Wilkins.

Competencies, Objectives, and Topics for Professional Training and Development Programs

IDENTIFICATION OF THE NATURE OF TBI

- Target Competencies
  - —Professionals will have a common base of understanding of the nature of TBI and related medical aspects from which to discuss implications for the settings to which the child/adolescent will return.
- Objectives
  - —To increase awareness of the causes, incidence, and significance of TBI.
  - —To understand the demographic, medical, and recovery aspects; ranges of disability; and resulting deficits.
- Topics for Discussion
  - —Causes, incidence, pathophysiology, terminology associated with TBI.
  - —Medical aspects and recovery issues
  - —Severity classification systems
  - —Physical, cognitive, communicative, psychosocial outcomes frequently observed following TBI.
  - —Prognostic factors
  - —Developmental issues

SIMILARITIES AND DIFFERENCES BETWEEN CHILDREN/ ADOLESCENTS WITH TBI AND CHILDREN/ADOLESCENTS WITH OTHER TYPES OF HANDICAPPING CONDITIONS

- Target Competencies
  - —Professionals will understand how this child/adolescent is similar to or different from other child/adolescent populations with which they are familiar.
- Objective
  - —To develop a frame of reference that will enable professionals to compare and contrast what they currently know about students with other handicapping conditions, such as learning disabilities, mental retardation, emotional disorders, behavioral disorders, physical impairments, and other health or learning disabilities with what they are learning about TBI.
- Topics for Discussion
  - —Diversity and variability within the TBI population.

—Individual student's variability in performance and skill levels.

—Premorbid educational, medical, work history, and performance levels.

THE IMPACT OF IMPAIRMENTS RESULTING FROM TBI ON THE CHILD/ADOLESCENT'S PERFORMANCE

* Target Competencies
  —Professionals will associate performance and behaviors observed in environments such as home, school, community with impairments that have resulted from TBI.
* Objectives
  —To identify child/adolescent's performance and behaviors in various environments that are representative of impairments.
  —To relate problems observed in various environments with impairments from the TBI.
* Topics for Discussion
  —Learning problems and behaviors frequently observed in children/adolescents with TBI.
  —Impact of impairments on learning capabilities, emotions, social interactions
  —Response patterns that may be representative of impairments resulting from TBI.

PROGRAM DECISION MAKING INCLUDING POLICY AND ADMINISTRATION

* Target Competencies
  —Professionals will understand the difficulties of fitting the child/adolescent with TBI into the present scheme of educational/vocational programming given the current policies and guidelines under which various agencies must operate.
* Objective
  —To develop criteria for making programming decisions appropriate for meeting

children/adolescents' needs and in agreement with established local, state, and national guidelines and laws.

* Topics for Discussion
  —Educational programming during hospitalization.
  —Networking between rehabilitation professionals and education professionals during hospitalization and rehabilitation, including roles and responsibilities of each discipline.
  —Legal and ethical issues related to children/adolescents' needs.
  —Financial problems and constraints related to meeting children/adolescents' needs.
  —Classification and placement within the current educational framework and under the current educational guidelines.
  —Placement for vocational and community programs within agency guidelines.

PROGRAM DEVELOPMENT INCLUDING ASSESSMENT AND MANAGEMENT STRATEGIES

* Target Competencies
  —Professionals will understand how to develop effective programs based on the unique configuration of strengths and acquired problems presented by the child/adolescent with TBI, including assessment and management strategies.
* Objectives
  —To understand aspects of TBI that need to be considered during the assessment process.
  —To identify assessment techniques applicable to this population.
  —To incorporate assessment outcome data into the individualized education program or home, community, work reintegration plan.
  —To select appropriate teaching strategies, materials, and resources for treatment of the child/adolescent with TBI.

- Topics for Discussion
  - —Skill areas to be assessed.
  - —Functional assessment strategies and methods.
  - —Support services frequently needed by children/adolescents with TBI.
- Guidelines for Making Placement Decisions
  - —Specific instructional strategies and environmental adaptations appropriate for the child/adolescent's needs.
  - —Development of individualized treatment plans for children/adolescents with TBI.

CONSULTATION AND COLLABORATION BETWEEN PROFESSIONALS (REHABILITATION; EDUCATION) AND WITH FAMILIES FOR EFFECTIVE PROGRAM PLANNING

- Target Competencies
  - —Professionals will work cooperatively with other professionals (rehabilitation and education) to plan and implement programs.
  - —Professionals will meaningfully involve family and peers of children/adolescents with TBI in program planning and implementation.
- Objectives
  - —To implement a coordinated team approach to meet, to plan, and to implement

programming for children/adolescents with TBI.

- —To share information and to exchange ideas with interdisciplinary team members and family about program planning and applicable assessment and management strategies.
- —To identify the most common family/ peer issues and situations that interfere with school, vocational, and community reintegration.
- —To identify ethnic and cultural factors that may significantly impact program decision making.
- —To actively involve family in the planning process by seeking their input regarding treatment goals, placement, and teaching methodologies.
- Topics for Discussion
  - —Consultation and collaboration as program approaches to meet the needs of this population.
  - —The roles and responsibilities of various disciplines with regard to children/adolescents with TBI (psychologists, speech-language pathologists, occupational therapists, physical therapists, educators, medical personnel, social workers. etc.).
  - —The impact of TBI on the family.
  - —The impact of TBI on relationships with peers.
  - —Strategies for incorporating family and peers into the planning process and program implementation.

Source: Adapted from "Preparing Education Professionals for Meeting the Needs of Students with Traumatic Brain Injury" by J.L. Blosser and R. DePompei, 1991, *Journal of Head Trauma Rehabilitation, 6,* pp. 73–82. Copyright 1991 by Aspen Publishers, Inc.

A Medical Perspective on Physician Training and Brain Injury Rehabilitation

Nathan D. Zasler

12

OBJECTIVES

Upon completion of this chapter, the reader will be able to:

1. understand staff development issues as they relate to physicians
2. develop a sensitivity to patient and family issues specific to communication, developing a therapeutic rapport, and predicting outcome
3. examine the role of the physician on the interdisciplinary team
4. describe challenges associated with building an effective multidisciplinary clinical continuum of care
5. provide an introspective analysis of some general, albeit controversial, issues in brain injury rehabilitation

A Medical Perspective on Physician Training and Brain Injury Rehabilitation

There are myriad issues relative to the medical perspective on staff development in the field of brain injury rehabilitation. This chapter provides an overview of issues pertinent to physician staff development in brain injury rehabilitation. This includes but is not limited to physician development, training controversies, continuing physician medical education, client and family issues, physician and team interactions, multidisciplinary neuromedical matters, and an array of general rehabilitation tenets. It is hoped that this information will serve as a constructive foundation for further rational introspection about physician-related perspectives regarding this critical area within the field of rehabilitation.

The material in this chapter is based on the premise that a solid neuromedical basis in staff development should serve as a primary cornerstone for high-quality neurorehabilitation of any kind; this is possibly more true in traumatic brain injury (TBI) than in any other subspecialty area. All too often there is inadequate neuromedical expertise on the part of physicians involved in treating survivors of TBI, not just in the realm of rehabilitation but throughout the continuum of medical care. An inadequate physician knowledge base in turn has the potential to adversely affect staff development and clinical skills relative to the wide spectrum of neuromedically related issues that are critical for staff to understand and implement in their daily clinical treatment activities. This problem then produces a domino effect relative to the potential adverse consequences that it has in quality of care rendered to the client and family, chances for clinically significant morbidity, and monetary expenditure on the part of third party payers. Ultimately, a strong neuromedical knowledge base and physician support in staff development helps to drive cutting-edge neurorehabilitation. This specialized quality of care focus will create a stimulating learning and work environment for all, promoting interdisciplinary staff unity and retention.

PHYSICIAN STAFF DEVELOPMENT

Nonphysiatrists

If one examines the roots of medical staff development in brain injury rehabilitation, it is apparent that there has been a lack of training, structured or otherwise, for physicians during all phases of their medical and clinical education. Generally, there are no formal opportunities in college, medical school, or non-physical medicine and rehabilitation (PM&R) residency training programs to master the clinical practice of brain injury rehabilitation. Once physicians become active practitioners, their relative lack of awareness and hands-on experience only presents further obstacles to facilitating appropriate referrals and care for persons after TBI. Practitioners in family practice, internal medicine, emergency medicine, general and trauma surgery, orthopedic surgery, neurology, and neurosurgery are likely to see at least some number of persons with TBI. Although the spectrum of neurological insult severity and functional impairment may range from mild to extremely severe, the neurorehabilitative needs of this population are significant (Kreutzer, Zasler, Wehman, & Devaney, 1992; Sandel, 1989). A clinician who neither recognizes the clinical entity of TBI nor understands the benefits of involving rehabilitation professionals in the ongoing treatment process may only promulgate problems. These problems potentially affect the client, the client's family, and the medical system at large. Additionally, simple matters such as understanding the role of the physiatrist as well as of the interdisciplinary rehabilitation team in the clinical continuum of care could go a long way toward optimizing the potential for timely and appropriate consultation with neurorehabilitation professionals. Ultimately, the end goals should be optimization of client care, minimization of morbidity, and maximization of neurological and functional outcome.

Physiatric Training Issues

Even in PM&R residency training programs there exists a dearth of adequate clinical rotations and experiences in brain injury rehabilitation. Many residencies have no specialized program or unit for clients after TBI and no physiatrist dedicated to this subspecialty area. Given this fact, many graduates of PM&R training programs either receive their brain injury training off site or do not receive any substantial training in this area of rehabilitation at all. It should be noted that there is presently no requirement for training in brain injury rehabilitation for board certification as mandated by the American Board of Physical Medicine and Rehabilitation (American Board, 1992). As a consequence, many graduates enter positions directing brain injury rehabilitation units or programs their first year out of residency training without having sufficient preparation. This phenomenon is to a great extent driven by the supply and demand paradigm. Such trends in hiring practices cannot continue relative to quality of care and accountability implications. Historical trends in other areas of medicine indicate a trend toward fellowship training or dual boarding (e.g., PM&R/neurology, PM&R/neurosurgery, or PM&R/pediatrics) in brain injury rehabilitation. A physician who has completed a 4-year training program in PM&R is generally not qualified to direct patient care or to handle administrative responsibility and program development issues without supervision from a more seasoned clinician.

Specialization Controversies and Training Requirements

Many physiatrists are extremely protective of turf issues regarding neurorehabilitation, insisting that they are the only physicians who can do the job correctly. Ultimately, it is unlikely that there will ever be enough physiatrists with specialized training, or for that matter interest, in TBI care to attend adequately to all persons with TBI. Therefore, it will be necessary in the immediate future to ensure that other neuromedical disciplines receive adequate training in relevant areas (e.g.,

neuropharmacology, neuropsychiatry, neuroorthopedics, etc.) and network more effectively with rehabilitation professionals to care optimally for this special group of clients.

This author feels that physiatrists are the best suited physicians to direct brain injury rehabilitation programs. This statement is based on training and on the philosophical approach of functionally oriented holistic treatment. Physiatrists are by training and interest equipped to work within the structure of an interdisciplinary team model of care (Kreutzer et al., 1992). A well trained physiatrist should have received adequate clinical and administrative experience in dealing with issues germane to brain injury care throughout the clinical continuum and across all levels of brain injury severity. Clinical experience should ideally include adequate training in a number of areas outside the field of physiatry, including but not limited to neuropsychopharmacology, neuropsychiatry, neurology, neurosurgery, neuroorthopedics, neurootology, neuroophthalmology, internal medicine, basic neural sciences, and neuropsychology. Physiatrists working with survivors of TBI must know when outside consultative assistance is required and appropriate, and therefore adequate knowledge of associated medical disciplines is critical. How the rehabilitation physician networks, both medically and personally, with consulting subspecialty physicians can greatly affect the clinical success of a program. Administratively, brain injury physiatrists must be able to direct interdisciplinary teams; supervise clinical programmatic development; deal in a timely and effective manner with staff, family, and client issues; and be able to network with other providers, payers, and the legal community relative to client and general health care issues. Physicians must also possess the administrative skills to advocate on behalf of clients with their own hospital administration and peer review or quality assurance organizations as well as with third party payers, when this becomes necessary.

Continuing Medical Education

Examination of physician staff development models relative to continuing medical education

(CME) in TBI rehabilitation yields an interesting cornucopia of practice alternatives. There is presently no organized system for assurance of CME in brain injury rehabilitation aside from general state requirements for licensure renewal. Given the ongoing growth of the neural sciences in general and brain injury rehabilitation specifically, it is unfortunate that there are not more specific mechanisms in place to ensure that physicians are staying abreast of current treatment practices and issues. The following thoughts and perspectives will provide the reader with a sense of what faces the clinician relative to this important aspect of ongoing physician development and practice.

Educational conferences have always attracted relatively large numbers of clinicians, in part as a result of CME accreditation requirements for state licensure. Historically, this has probably been less true for brain injury rehabilitation physicians than nonrehabilitation physicians. There is, however, probably a trend contrary to this in the last 10 years or so. A significant number of clinicians, physicians, and allied health professionals alike do attend CME accredited courses in brain injury rehabilitation to keep abreast of new developments in the field. A concern about these meetings is the relative lack of new, progressive, and research-based information that is evident at such meetings.

There are many professional meetings now accessible at a national level. One of the challenges for the professional is to decide between staying local or regional and ultimately spending less money or going out-of-town and spending not only time away from practice but more money as well. In general, the quality of speakers and the programmatic content at professional meetings are not always congruent. There are several meetings nationally that historically have gained reputations as high quality meetings relative to the relevance and timeliness of topics covered, the quality of the speakers relative to expertise and speaking skills, and the general program organization. Some of the well respected rehabilitation meetings focusing on brain injury in this country include (in alphabetical order) Braintree, the National Head Injury Foundation, the Santa Clara Valley Medical Center, and the Williamsburg Conference. In general, there seems to be a trend toward more focused meetings (e.g., coma management, mild TBI, etc.) and toward meetings that are designed for more experienced clinicians. There will always be a need for ongoing education of new clinicians, and this obviously should not be ignored by conference planners and coordinators. There is the risk, however, of saturating the TBI conference marketplace and adversely affecting the success of most if not all meetings by diluting attendance. Conference success and attendance have also in part been affected negatively by the present economy and the tendency toward cost containment.

There is presently an explosion of literature in the neural sciences that is potentially both relevant and critical to the physiatrist dealing with survivors of TBI. Books and journals have become a frequently used resource for ongoing physician education. It is neither warranted nor practical to try and keep up with all these publications. Selective reading based on analysis of professional book reviews is recommended for clinicians seeking to broaden their intellectual and clinical knowledge base. It appears that many physicians working in the field of brain injury rehabilitation do not actively read the multidisciplinary medical literature being published on brain injury. Even more disturbing is the fact that many are not able to or do not attempt to keep abreast of the literature in physiatry related to this specialized topic area. Admittedly, it is logistically and practically quite challenging to maintain an active clinical practice and to stay up to date with the cornucopia of medical literature in this specialized field of medical study.

There presently are a few journals that focus on brain injury rehabilitation and related issues. Generally, these publications either take a thematic or a research focus. A busy clinician's time is probably better spent in reading quality thematic material that is practical in nature and reviews recent clinical and research advances in the field. Practically presented information will be much more likely to affect positively clinical care than more esoteric research articles (this does not of course negate by any means the value of methodologically sound research).

Physician and staff interactions obviously serve as a potential mechanism for both ongoing, structured, didactic learning and less formal learning. Clinicians should try to increase their opportunities for interactions with other multidisciplinary neuromedical specialists as well as with therapy staff to maximize educational opportunities for all. Although such programs can be formal educational seminars or lectures, there are multiple other paradigms that can work just as well, including informal client conferences, teaching rounds, and one-on-one discussions. Day-to-day clinical work can and should serve as the basis for most of a practitioner's ongoing continuing education, but this can only be truly effective if the clinician has the motivation and wherewithal to pursue the educational components of these experiences.

CLIENT ISSUES

Developing Rapport

Developing a good rapport with clients is not something one learns by reading this or any other book chapter or article. Instead, as with many of the aspects of medical care, rapport is learned through experience and hands-on work with clients. PM&R, and in particular brain injury rehabilitation, is one of a few medical specialties that truly allows the physician to develop a long-term relationship with clients and a rapport that is seldom equaled in other disciplines. First impressions can go a long way toward building long-lasting rapport between clients and clinicians. Taking the extra time to let clients know that you care about them, in a sense treating each one as if he or she were your only client, helps further facilitate bonding between physician and client. Trying to minimize interruptions during discussions with clients also lets the individual and family know that you are there to address their needs. Any measures that can be taken to fulfill special requests will provide an additional basis for nurturing a trusting relationship.

When a physician develops a good rapport with clients, it not only optimizes the working relationship between these two parties but also enhances the quality of care, compliance with prescribed interventions, and the ability of the client to comprehend the treatment process. Physicians working with survivors of TBI should be more aware of how they come across to clients, in particular their first impression. We must at all times remain attuned to the import that first impressions have relative to setting the stage for building rapport and optimizing the working relationship.

Client Rights Issues

As physicians working with survivors of TBI, we may see persons at times in their lives when they are extremely vulnerable on both an individual basis and a more global societal basis. It is our duty to safeguard each client's individual and civil rights as fellow human beings. All too frequently, we as rehabilitation professionals have lost sight of our commitment as health care professionals to guarantee clients the right of free choice when they have the capability of making the required decisions. If and when they do not have the capacity medically to make independent, sound decisions, then appropriate measures should be taken to safeguard their rights by proceeding through established judicial measures such as guardianship. We should advocate on their behalf and, more important, facilitate their own abilities to advocate for themselves.

As professionals, we should ensure that our facilities have a client rights policy and be well aware of what the policy states to ensure further that client rights are not infringed upon. We must also make sure that clients, as appropriate, and families receive copies of such policies to make them aware of their own inalienable rights (Banja, 1992).

We must also be more aware of respecting the rights of client confidentiality and privacy, which all too often do not receive the attention they deserve in rehabilitation settings. In part, this may be due to a tendency to think that we know best what to do for the client. Our collective attitude may at times be somewhat paternalistic. In part, this attitude may be due to physician training and perspectives on client care as well as our self-perceived role as overseers of client care. Physicians and rehabilitation professionals in general should be more introspective with regard to how providing health care of any kind may desensitize those providing the care to the needs of those receiving it.

Capacity and Competency Issues

Although physicians deal with capacity and competency issues on a daily basis in the field of brain injury rehabilitation, many are unfamiliar with the medical and legal aspects of determining capacity. Additionally, physicians should be familiar with the functional levels of capacity, thereby protecting client rights relative to overly broad rulings regarding capacity. By advocating on behalf of clients and ensuring that the least restrictive environment that optimally guarantees their safety is provided, we can avoid situations that result in restriction of clients' constitutionally protected rights (Koplan, 1990).

Medicolegal Perspectives

Many physicians in our field enter the professional work arena with absolutely no training or experience in the area of medicolegal aspects of health care. As a physician, one is obliged to learn about the ins and outs of the health care system from a medicolegal standpoint whether one likes the idea or not. Understanding the legal components of health care practice will minimize the potential for future negative litigation experiences (Dussault, 1989). Additionally, as a physician with specialized knowledge in the field of brain injury care, one may have the unique opportunity to advocate on behalf of the client and family relative to medicolegal liability or damages. Inherent in treating clients with catastrophic neurotrauma are opportunities for involvement in medicolegal work, plaintiff and defendant cases alike. Physicians who do medicolegal work should learn early on in their careers how to deal effectively with the legal system. Contracts between physician and lawyer specifically delineating fees for service are becoming more and more common. There are, however, no do-it-yourself references on the medicolegal aspects of brain injury rehabilitation. Most professionals learn by trial and error.

FAMILY ISSUES

One of the biggest issues that families find disconcerting during their dealings with reha-

bilitation physicians is the inability to get timely and straightforward information regarding the status of their loved one. Physicians vary tremendously in the time that they commit to talking with families. Many physicians are so busy that they not only do not attend family meetings regularly but also do not invest the time to sit down and talk with families in a comfortable environment. Another concern is that impressions conveyed to families are many times not based on real-world experience and seem to reinforce unrealistic expectations. For example, if a physician has only seen two clients with TBI and concomitant severe hypoxic brain injury and only followed both for less than one year, how does that professional make any statement to a family of a similar individual regarding anticipated problems and outcome? When communicating with families it is critical to maintain a balance between optimism and realism. Our role as physicians should be to inform families to the best of our capability but at the same time never to remove hope. Faith and motivation are clearly two factors that drive clients as well as families to go beyond the boundaries of what professionals may have deemed realistic.

Physicians need to empower families to advocate for their loved one as well as for themselves. By empowering families, we help facilitate the rehabilitation process and further enhance its efficiency. The process of empowerment is facilitated by understanding how families function, ideally from a systems perspective (Turnbull & Turnbull, 1991). Part of empowerment is providing education to families and clients alike. Education may include details regarding injury specifics, associated complications, rehabilitation health care options, medication side effects, prevention issues for subsequent TBI, and disposition alternatives. Educating families is of paramount importance in maximizing compliance with prescribed programs as well as medications. The physician should help guide the family educational experience by providing timely and appropriate neuromedical information. Many times family members may not be ready to hear certain types of information. It is nevertheless the physician's job, and as appropriate the job of other team members, to convey information; sooner or later the family will be able to use this information to assist in their adaptation to this change. Being able to communicate with families in language that they understand and not in medical mumbo-jumbo further facilitates the educational process. As physicians, we become so used to our scientific technical language that we sometimes find it difficult to communicate in a manner that is comprehensible to the family. Being cognizant of how we communicate, rather than just being aware of what we communicate, is essential in helping families gain a better understanding of the specific concerns and recommendations that we are sharing (Williams, 1991).

THE PHYSICIAN AND THE INTERDISCIPLINARY TEAM

Physician Leadership Issues

Typically, we as physicians, regardless of our specialty, see ourselves as the rehabilitation team leader. This concept has its roots in the traditional medical model and may not always be applicable to all phases of the brain injury care continuum. Physicians must be able to see themselves in nonleadership roles and feel comfortable interacting with supervising staff who are typically lower in the traditional line of authority.

For those of us in positions of authority, both physicians and other rehabilitation professionals alike, it is critical to realize that leadership is not something one is given; on the contrary, it is something that one earns and nurtures. An effective leader is one who can work in a synergistic fashion with fellow staff and lead the team toward meeting its collective goals. Leaders are leaders because they develop and maintain a certain level of respect from others in the professional community. Respect is gained first and foremost by being fair and honest with both staff and families. Respect is reinforced with knowledge, personal achievement, approachability, and the ability to demonstrate one's humanistic qualities (Lyth, 1992). Although important, administrative expertise, particularly as it pertains to dealing with staff issues, is generally a leadership quality that most physicians develop after graduation from residency training, if they de-

velop it at all. Physicians and others in leadership positions should not assume that they deserve respect as a team leader by virtue of their educational background or the status of their role within the organization.

Being able to interact with staff in a positive and synergistic fashion is a critical skill for every physician to develop. As well as being a good physician, this skill requires that the physician be diplomatic, particularly with regard to being a people manager. Team decisions should be just that: decisions facilitated through a team decision-making process, not dictated by the team leader or some other administrative body. For the team to see the physician as the team leader, the physician must be part of that team from a functional standpoint. A physician whose only presence on a unit or in a community-based program is to make rounds or see clients when they are sick will not have the same degree of effectiveness as a physician who is more involved. The physician who attends and participates in team rounds, interacts with clients and therapists during therapy sessions, and meets with staff on a regular basis for administrative and planning purposes will ultimately stand in better stead with the team in the role of team leader. Above all, the physician must be willing to listen to what other team members have to say and be able to consolidate the information and come to fair and just decisions. The physician who dictates to fellow staff will not be anywhere near as effective as the physician who listens and attempts to come to mutually acceptable decisions. Having a sense of humor in the workplace also goes a long way toward breaking down some of the communication barriers that may exist between staff and physician.

Physician Role Through the Continuum of Care

The role of the physician on the rehabilitation team may vary somewhat relative to the setting in question. The physician role has historically been more significant in the acute and subacute care settings and less important in postacute settings. Although in a gross sense the perspective that the physician becomes less involved over time is true, there continues to be insufficient appreciation of the role of the neurorehabilitation physician in the postacute setting relative to long-term neuromedical, cognitive-behavioral, and psychosocial aspects of community and vocational reintegration (Zasler, 1989). A rehabilitation physician who continues to be involved with client care will help to optimize the client's integration into the community environment as well as the client's independence.

Maximizing Physician-Team Relations

Physicians who are well versed in what the individual therapy disciplines do and can offer will add an additional dimension to both client care and physician-staff interaction quality. A physician who can intelligently discuss and even debate therapeutic intervention rationale with a therapist will not only facilitate a level of mutual quality control but also encourage critical analysis of treatment plans and goals. The more a physician can directly interact with the therapy staff, whether in rounds, didactics, or therapy sessions, the more the therapy staff will feel positive regarding the level of commitment from the physician. Staff members who feel connected and communicative among themselves and with the physician or medical director are more likely to be retained than staff members who do not. Physician disinvolvement in day-to-day programmatic and treatment issues surely does nothing constructive relative to reinforcing positive team image and retaining valuable staff members.

All too often, staff have little idea as to the extent of the physician's work load and therefore find it difficult to understand why at times he or she is not readily available. Part of developing a sophisticated brain injury rehabilitation team is to sensitize all team members to the roles of their fellow cohorts, including the physician. All new staff should undergo an orientation period, which should include meeting with all supervisory personnel from each discipline area, including the program's medical director.

Physicians should also make a concerted effort to participate in ongoing didactic programs to assist in continuing staff education. A staff that realizes that their medical director is committed to teaching them will not only benefit from this teaching but will also be a more cohesive team as a result of such training. Physicians should also attempt to attend other staff continuing education inservices to keep abreast of ongoing advances within the therapy disciplines as well as to demonstrate to staff a personal commitment to listening to what they have to say.

Working closely with the program clinical director is also of paramount importance in maximizing the efficacy of the physician in his or her role as medical director. A well run program must be facilitated by a strong team leader, who does not necessarily need to be the medical director. The medical director should, however, have the opportunity to provide input into programmatic issues, design, and efficacy assessment. When one divorces the physician from the clinical programmatic issues at hand, regardless of what aspect of the continuum of services is in question, it leaves the team without potentially important neuromedical input.

MULTIDISCIPLINARY MEDICAL ISSUES

Continuum of Clinical Care

As more clinicians have worked in the field of brain injury rehabilitation, we have developed a greater awareness of the benefits of providing services to survivors of TBI in an organized and systematic fashion. We now know that outcomes can be improved, both neurologically and functionally, when rehabilitative issues are addressed from the earliest time after injury and subsequently in an ongoing fashion. Such a continuum not only improves outcome but also apparently controls the costs of caring for this special client population by creating a more efficient and thereby cost-effective system (Mackay, Bernstein, Chapman, Morgan, & Milazzo, 1992; Ragnarsson, Thomas, & Zasler, in press).

Providing a clinical continuum of care from the scene of the accident throughout community reentry is easier said than done in most cases.

Developing a continuum of care requires not only an understanding of the clinical and nonclinical needs of survivors of TBI but also a sensitivity toward how to network effectively across providers to develop the desired continuum.

As a general rule, it is and will be rare to find a single provider, whether for-profit or not-for-profit, who is able to establish and maintain a full service continuum in a community. Providers, particularly for-profit ones, must change their historical mentality of just being out for themselves if we are to grow as a service provider field. The concept of provider networking as advocated here must be pursued aggressively by all service providers to optimize the efficacy of everything that we all do relative to service provision. Typically, for-profit and not-for-profit organizations have had a difficult time networking, mainly as a result of the disparate nature of their mission and the tendency to provide similar services. For-profit businesses must make some level of commitment to meeting the needs of suboptimally funded survivors. By making such compromises, one would hope to narrow the present gap between providers, thereby increasing cooperative provider efforts in meeting survivor needs and filling gaps in the continuum of care.

All too often, providers will not commit to developing a part of the continuum because that particular segment may be perceived as a cost-minus venture. This type of mentality has its roots in the for-profit concept that everything one does must make a profit. Obviously, certain types of service provision will be better reimbursed than others. Providers must realize that they will be successful as long as they can structure their continuum so that the total sum of services being rendered yields a cost-plus outcome. Additionally, by networking with other providers, even ones outside the immediate brain injury rehabilitation field, one can many times develop creative ways of addressing the needs of survivors, particularly in the postacute setting.

It should also be recognized that realistically and logistically speaking it is, at least for now, impossible to expect development of state-of-the-art continuums in every community. There are just not enough professionals, paraprofes-sionals, or funds to meet the needs of every survivor in every community. This apparent impasse can be lessened through several venues. First, educating other health care professionals regarding the need for specialized care for persons with brain injury is of paramount importance. Second, development of a neutral organization to endorse program strengths and weaknesses is critical to serve families and payers as a more objective quality assurance measure (see below). Third, the rehabilitation field must advocate for greater emphasis on recruiting professionals, including physicians, nurses, and therapists, among others, to enter the field of brain injury rehabilitation care and to remain there to help fill the large gaps in the service provider and caregiver network. Fourth, there needs to be a continued effort to effect proservice governmental legislation with regard to funding for needed services in the rehabilitation continuum. Fifth, we must work collectively toward increasing our own awareness of what interventions are most effective in meeting the needs of survivors of TBI.

Coordination of Services

A clinical continuum of care cannot be set up without an awareness of the components required or the coordination necessary to see that the continuum is utilized correctly (Dixon, 1989). From a medical perspective, networking with skilled physiatrists, neurologists, neurosurgeons, neuropsychiatrists, and orthopedic surgeons is of paramount importance. Other medical disciplines that are also of a critical nature in addressing the needs of people with brain injury include, but are not limited to, neurootology, neuroophthalmology, pulmonology, otolaryngology, and endocrinology. Understanding the role of each of these clinicians in the clinical continuum is a basic tenet of development of that continuum. Just as important, each of the physicians from the aforementioned medical specialties must understand his or her own role in the continuum of care.

The lead physician involved in the brain injury rehabilitation continuum must advocate appropriately for affiliations with the necessary consulting and primary medical staff. Such advocacy can only be accomplished if the clinician in question is savvy enough to know the ins and outs of the physician politics within his or her community as well as the bottom-line issues relative to the neuromedical needs that he or she is seeking to fulfill for the continuum being developed. Many times a skilled specialist in a given discipline with experience in brain injury may not be available within the community in question. The best step in such a scenario is to try to find a physician who is willing and able to take the time to learn by networking, by consulting, and by doing. If there is no one who can meet the needs locally in a specific consulting discipline, then efforts should be made to hire a non-local physician to do periodic on-site work or to network with a non-local clinician to whom one can refer clients for specialized testing and care (Ragnarrson et al., in press).

Prediction of Outcome

One of the biggest problems in our field today is the disparate nature of prognoses that are provided across medical disciplines to clients, families, other health care professionals, case managers, and insurance companies. There are various reasons for this problem.

Historically, there will always be some physicians who see the cup half full and others who see it half empty. There are those clinicians who are forever the eternal optimist and those who rarely if ever have anything good to say about anything. It would seem to be to no one's advantage to give either extremely optimistic or extremely pessimistic predictions, particularly when these are often made on inadequate databases. All too often clinicians make predictions that are premature or inaccurate; this is based in part on their desire to tell those requesting this information something and in part on their own internal need to convey their knowledge to others.

Perhaps not surprisingly, many physicians do not have the foggiest idea of the range of potential neurologic or functional outcomes after TBI. Many do not even have an adequate grasp of the

historical as well as the current literature pertaining to outcome predictors, both early and late. Yet there is a large body of literature that provides clinicians with guidelines for prognostication on a multitude of clinical issues ranging from early mortality and morbidity to long-term functional outcome (Jennett, Teasdale, Murray, & Murray, 1992).

In general, it is important not to use the words *always* and *never* when talking with clients and families. Such words, either in the short run or in the long run, have the potential of alienating the client and family from the physician. Clients must have some threads of hope to cling to if they are to maintain an adequate level of motivation to facilitate their ongoing rehabilitation efforts.

We as professionals must bear in mind that overly optimistic as well as overly pessimistic prognostications only serve to hinder client and family confidence in the physician. Of the two, one would rather err on the side of being too conservative. If the client does better than predicted, so much the better. Nonetheless, we should aim for realistic appraisals of prognosis based on the available literature, prognostic clinical parameters, client and family traits, and our own personal clinical experiences.

Clinicians should avoid any seemingly definitive confirmation pertaining to prognosis, neurologically or functionally, until such time as there is no statistically significant chance of further improvement. It is important to remember that there are only a few clinical conditions after TBI for which the prognosis is 100% certain early after the initial insult or within the first 1 or 2 years after injury. Clinicians must remain aware of this fact and take it into consideration when talking with clients and families.

Another factor that sometimes negatively affects early predictions, particularly on the part of nonrehabilitation physicians, is the fact that many of these professionals do not follow survivors of brain injury over the long term. They therefore have little if any perception of what happens either neurologically or functionally 1, 5, and 10 years after injury.

Ultimately, prognoses should be given when requested but should be based in a philosophy of realistic but optimistic appraisal. In general, use of terms such as *never* and *always* should be avoided because there are seldom absolutes relative to predictive validity in our field. Instead, we should strive for presenting a range of outcomes, from the worst potential scenario to the best, with the most likely outcome being somewhere in the middle of that range.

It is also important to realize that it is okay to say that we do not know exactly how well someone is going to do relative to their functional recovery (e.g., whether he or she will ever talk or walk again or whether he or she will always have severe behavioral problems). There has been and probably will continue to be an expectation that the physician can, to some extent, cure or correct presenting problems. Issues regarding prognosis of outcome surely focus our attention on the fallibility of this commonly held belief and our own insecurities regarding these issues.

GENERAL ISSUES

Nomenclature Issues

One of the biggest problems in our field is the continued disparity in nomenclature used across disciplines. This phenomenon is just as frequent within the confines of interdisciplinary rehabilitation as it is relative to crossdisciplinary medical nomenclature dealing with brain injury issues. When three physicians come in a room and examine the same client and each one labels what he or she sees differently, we know that a problems exists. Terms such as *coma, vegetative state,* and *persistent vegetative state* are commonly misused, as are terms such as *brain injury* and *head injury*. If we do not even know what we mean, how can we expect others to understand what we are saying and, more important, continue to support our efforts in both principle and practice?

We need to make a concerted effort to agree on a common nomenclature (Dixon, 1989). The place to start is obviously within our own field. Once we all have agreed, we need to work on educating others as to the rational for the nomenclature change and the preferred terminology.

Defining Outcomes

As rehabilitationists, we have an obligation to assess critically what we are doing relative to interventional efficacy. If we are not using objective, valid, and reliable outcome measures that have been standardized, we are falling quite short of the present and future standard of care within the field. A discussion of what measures to use and when to use them is beyond the scope of this chapter, but it is critical to note that each measure will have inherent liabilities and benefits. Understanding the pros and cons of each measure, their sensitivity, and their specificity is of paramount importance in using them properly (Haffey & Lewis, 1989).

Appropriately used outcome measures, preferably functionally based, can assist clinicians in multiple ways, including assessment of program and interventional efficacy, documentation of rehabilitation course and outcome, and assessment of the need for specific services or interventions. They can also be used as adjuvant discharge or admission criteria for specific programmatic levels.

Standards of Neurorehabilitative Care

Another major problem that our field continues to grapple with is the issue of standardizing and accrediting programs. For more than a decade, the field of TBI rehabilitation went relatively unchecked with regard to program quality assessment, ethics of practice, and program accreditation by an impartial organization. Presently, there are no national protocols in active use in our field for dealing with any aspect of brain injury rehabilitation care. Everyone has different ways of approaching the same clinical problems; sometimes these lead to the same clinical outcomes and sometimes not. Part of the problem stems from the general lack of a consolidated research foundation for the field of rehabilitation at large (Haffey & Lewis, 1989). Another part stems from the historical lack of reciprocity across providers relative to working together to better the state of the field at large. A major agenda item for the field of brain injury rehabilitation over the next two decades should be to work collectively to standardize clinical care being provided to survivors of TBI.

The whole issue of accreditation has really not gotten the attention that it deserves. For example, although the Committee on Accreditation of Rehabilitation Facilities (CARF) standards have significantly improved in recent years, achieving CARF certification really does not differentiate programs that do it great from programs that just do it. The intent of accreditation is to ensure compliance with standards that have originated from peer review as a set of minimal competencies. There is presently no organizational entity that can provide families, case managers, insurance companies, and others with an objective assessment regarding program quality questions. We need to develop methods of assessing and certifying programs relative not just to meeting a minimal criteria but to designating levels of provider expertise. Issues that could be assessed might include delineation of specific admission and discharge criteria; identification of clinicians (physicians and nonphysicians alike) involved with the program, their training, and their levels of expertise; delineation of functional measures utilized in the program; cost-benefit analyses relative to functional outcome; and numbers of clients seen per year. Such a rating system would assist survivors, families, and payers in choosing the best facilities to provide the needed services as opposed to picking facilities that only meet a set of minimum service criteria.

Accountability

Probably the one area that has received the most attention recently in our field is accountability (Dixon, 1989; McMahon, 1991). We should anticipate that this will persist from here on out, not just for the for-profit provider but for everyone, including the physician. We need to realize that we are all being scrutinized by those around us, including survivors, family, payers, the lay community at large, the government, and fellow health care professionals. Inherent in this scrutiny is a need for working collectively to ad-

dress the problematic areas presently facing our profession. We can positively affect the quality of our service, the efficacy of our interventions, and the success of our efforts by remaining keenly aware of the need to be accountable to everyone for what we do. First and foremost, we can attempt to meet this challenge by being accountable to ourselves.

CONCLUSION

This chapter has attempted to provide the reader with an overview of a medical perspective on staff development, including important issues pertinent to the field of brain injury rehabilitation at large. It is hoped that if nothing else has been accomplished but to make the reader think hard on some of the aforementioned issues and to leave the reader with the impression that we collectively have much room for improvement, then it has been largely successful. If, on the other hand, anything read in this chapter positively affects the way that you practice brain injury rehabilitation we have achieved success as a team.

REFERENCES

American Board of Physical Medicine and Rehabilitation. (1992). *Booklet of information*. Rochester, MN: Author.

Banja, J.D. (1992). Ethics in rehabilitation. In G.F. Fletcher, J.D. Banja, B.B. Jann, & S.L. Wolf (Eds.), *Rehabilitation medicine: Contemporary clinical perspectives* (pp. 269–298). Philadelphia: Lea & Febiger.

Dixon, T. (1989). Systems of care for the head-injured. In *PM&R: State of the art reviews—Traumatic brain injury* (pp. 169–181). Philadelphia: Hanley & Belfus.

Dussault, W.L.E. (1989). Legal aspects of head injury. In *PM&R: State of the art reviews—Traumatic brain injury* (pp. 183–192). Philadelphia: Hanley & Belfus.

Haffey, W.J., & Lewis, F.D. (1989). Rehabilitation outcomes following traumatic brain injury. In *PM&R: State of the art reviews—Traumatic brain injury* (pp. 203–218). Philadelphia: Hanley & Belfus.

Jennett, B., Teasdale, G., Murray, G., & Murray, L. (1992). Head injury. In R.W. Evans, D.S. Baskin, & F.M. Yatsu (Eds.), *Prognosis of neurological disorders* (pp. 85–96). New York: Oxford University Press.

Koplan, K.I. (1990). Medicolegal aspects of head injury. In M. Rosenthal, E.R. Griffith, M.R. Bond, & J.D. Miller (Eds.), *Rehabilitation of the adult and child with traumatic brain injury* (pp. 506–515). Philadelphia: Davis.

Kreutzer, J.S., Zasler, N.D., Wehman, P.H., & Devaney, C.W. (1992). Neuromedical and psychosocial aspects of rehabilitation after traumatic brain injury. In G.F. Fletcher, J.D. Banja, B.B. Jann, & S.L. Wolf (Eds.), *Rehabilitation medicine: Contemporary clinical perspectives* (pp. 225–242). Philadelphia: Lea & Febiger.

Lyth, J.R. (1992). Models of the team approach. In G.F. Fletcher, J.D. Banja, B.B. Jann, & S.L. Wolf (Eds.), *Rehabilitation medicine: Contemporary clinical perspectives* (pp. 225–242). Philadelphia: Lea & Febiger.

Mackay, L.E., Bernstein, B.A., Chapman, P.E., Morgan, A.S., & Milazzo, L.S. (1992). Early intervention in severe head injury: Long-term benefits of a formalized program. *Archives of Physical Medicine and Rehabilitation, 73,* 635–641.

McMahon, B.T. (1991). Ethics in business practices. In B.T. McMahon & L.R. Shaw (Eds.), *Work worth doing: Advances in brain injury rehabilitation* (pp. 5–27). Orlando, FL: Deutsch.

Ragnarsson, K.T., Thomas, J.P., & Zasler, N.D. (in press). Description of a model system of traumatic brain injury. *Journal of Head Trauma Rehabilitation.*

Sandel, M.E. (1989). Rehabilitation management in the acute care setting. In *PM&R: State of the art reviews—Traumatic brain injury* (pp. 27–41). Philadelphia: Hanley & Belfus.

Turnbull, A.P., & Turnbull, H.R. (1991). Understanding families from a systems perspective. In J.M. Williams & T. Kay (Eds.), *Head injury: A family matter* (pp. 37–64). Baltimore: Brookes.

Williams, J.M. (1991). Family reaction to head injury. In J.M. Williams & T. Kay (Eds.), *Head injury: A family matter* (pp. 37–64). Baltimore: Brookes.

Zasler, N.D. (1989). The role of the physiatrist in planning work reentry for persons recovering from traumatic brain injury. In P. Wehman & J. Kreutzer (Eds.), *Vocational rehabilitation for persons with traumatic brain injury.* Gaithersburg, MD: Aspen.

Rehabilitation Nursing Education and Practice: Innovative Responses to a Changing Delivery System

13

Constance S. Burgess
Carol Ann Balch

OBJECTIVES

Upon completion of this chapter, the reader will be able to:

1. specify the current marketplace trends that impact on the rehabilitation nurse's role and function
2. identify the specific variables that have been and will continue to be barriers for many rehabilitation nurses to overcome in order to participate fully in the rehabilitation team process
3. describe the various rehabilitation nurses' roles as described in the "differentiated practice" model
4. discuss the impact of the "differentiated practice" model on interdisciplinary team process
5. identify staff development strategies that will improve clinical effectiveness and client outcomes

Rehabilitation Nursing Education and Practice

The demands on today's nurses to provide comprehensive rehabilitative nursing care are markedly different from those of only a few years ago. What once seemed to be a straightforward, task-oriented approach to meeting the nursing needs of a person with brain injury has evolved into a dynamic, multidimensional, holistic, and client-focused approach to performing nursing care assessment, planning, and intervention. Health care in the 1990s is experiencing a process of remarkable transformation that is being driven by multiple forces. Technological advances in treatment and diagnosis of disease conditions, an increasingly aging population with chronic illnesses, a shortage of professional nurses and therapists, more discriminating consumers, and a shifting of greater responsibility for health maintenance toward the individual are but a few of these forces. Perhaps the greatest impact has derived from spiraling health care costs accompanied by a plethora of cost containment measures, which are forcing drastic changes in America's health care treatment systems and professional practice models. An understanding of the new rehabilitation and health care environment is necessary before the educational approach to brain injury or rehabilitation nursing can be discussed. This chapter explores the rehabilitation environment of the 1990s, why nursing can no longer respond in traditional ways, alternative methods to meet the new challenges, and recommendations for training to support staff in meeting these challenges.

OVERVIEW OF THE HEALTH CARE ENVIRONMENT

According to Moccia (1990), there is a growing concensus that the nation's health care system is becoming increasingly inadequate to meet the real health care needs of the American population and that the public is increasingly dissatisfied with the quality and costs of services. This, coupled with the fact that the cost of providing health care has risen more steeply than that of any other human service, has created changes in the methods of both public and private health care financing and of client delivery systems. The pivotal driving force in the delivery of health care is cost containment, resulting in increasingly restrictive national trends in private, third party, and federally regulated reimbursement policies. Restraints on institutional lengths of stay and constrictions on the reimbursement range of health care services have refocused the health care vision on the cost of care. Cost effectiveness strategies have influenced the quality of health care delivery, and evaluation of quality care has become progressively client outcome driven. Patients are discharged from acute care facilities much earlier because of restrictions on lengths of stay, and, increasingly, lower cost health care alternatives are being chosen, including early transfer to extended care and subacute facilities (Ellis & Hartley, 1988). As a result of these changes, the nursing profession has been compelled to define more clearly the standards of practice and to expand and clarify nursing roles in multiple settings. This has been evident in the development of patient care delivery models such as primary nursing, shared governance, and differentiated practice. In addition, these changes have led to an examination of the appropriate levels of educational preparation necessary for nurses to function in each of the roles to meet client needs. Rehabilitation nurses must develop insight into and an understanding of these changes because they create a demand for a dramatically different type of rehabilitative nursing practice and a markedly different type of rehabilitation service delivery.

Economics of Health Care

Consideration of the economics of health care is commonplace for members of the rehabilitation team. The high cost of catastrophic injuries brought cost containment and resource management into the rehabilitation practice setting several years before the advent of managed care. Health care costs in the United States continue to rise at a rate of 10% per year, representing approximately 13% of the Gross National Product. This increase is expected to reach 15% per year by the end of this century (Grace, 1990).

Emerging from this economic crisis is the rise in the use of managed care systems. *Managed care* has become the new buzz word in health care delivery (Knollmueller, 1989). The concept is dominating the health care market, and the phenomenal growth in this model is being attributed to employers, who are the primary buyers of health care insurance, and the insurance companies themselves. Breaking with an old tradition, today's marketplace is controlled by the buyers, not the sellers, of health care services. Buyers are, more than ever before, paying a higher cost for medical insurance. They are investing in systems that can promote appropriate management and utilization of medical, financial, and human resources that produce quality measurable outcomes. This explanation is commonly used as the working definition of managed care. Del Togno-Armanasco, Olwas, and Harter (1989) add an additional perspective: Managed care "is a methodology for organizing patient care through an episode of illness so that specific clinical and *financial* outcomes are achieved within an allotted time frame."

Although reimbursement was once considered the responsibility of the finance department, the advent of managed care has forced the nurse to consider and understand each client's reimbursement picture and to plan his or her care with an eye toward resource management. It is no longer acceptable for the rehabilitation nurse, or team, simply to develop a clinical treatment plan for the client's immediate stay. All goals and care plans must reflect long-term planning beyond the staff's practice setting and must ensure that all the financial resources will not be used up before the client needs them in other settings. Managed care requires the rehabilitation nurse to move faster, to prioritize treatment into those functions that the client must be able to perform to move to the next level of care, and to

plan effectively for those elements that can be handled in the client's next setting.

The managed care environment demands a new accountability by the team not only for effective clinical outcomes but also for efficient management and use of financial resources. These factors are changing the relationship between the client and the nurse. Clients no longer view physicians, nurses, or therapists as omnipotent and unchallengeable. They are holding them accountable for their behavior. They actively pursue information about diagnoses, courses of treatment, and cost of care and are more questioning regarding provider recommendations. In short, many clients are unwilling to relinquish control and insist on participating in all decisions about where, how, and when they will be treated and what it will cost.

Patient Care Settings: Acute to Alternative Care

A second factor influencing rehabilitation nursing and practice began with the implementation of Medicare's prospective payment system in the early 1980s. The institution of diagnosis-related groups (DRGs) has resulted in a decrease in the number of acute hospital admissions and shortened lengths of stay. At about the time that DRGs appeared, brain injury rehabilitation in particular, with feedback from insurance companies about costs, began to develop more cost effective alternatives to acute inpatient rehabilitation programs. DRGs and other cost trends related to the advent of managed care have caused numerous medium and large hospitals and health care centers to increase diversification efforts by instituting alternatives to acute care services. Hospitals are examining the benefits of providing subacute services and long-term care. Long-term care providers are expanding into the rehabilitation arena, and the rehabilitation industry continues to boost its growth through joint ventures or management contracts with acute care hospitals and long-term care companies. Clark and Krentz (1991) state that, although many acute hospitals may be interested in developing long-term care services, individual hospitals are likely to vary significantly in terms of the specific services they ultimately develop. In this context, long-term care refers to an array of programs that range from intermittent ambulatory services such as home care, day treatment, and case management to 24-hour institutional and housing services such as multilevel nursing homes, independent and assisted living programs, respite care, and inpatient hospices.

With shorter lengths of stay in acute care settings, there is a dramatic shift of acuity at lesser levels of care. Rehabilitation nurses in acute, subacute, and postacute programs are faced with sicker clients, many of whom continue to require ongoing management of medical problems while participating in the rehabilitation process. This shift from acute to alternative care settings requires a new set of competencies for the nurse that were not previously addressed in orientation or education programs.

Increased Demand for Professional Nurses

Although the shift of clients to nonacute settings creates additional challenges for the rehabilitation nurse, it also offers unparalleled opportunities for new career expansion. This, coupled with other variables, has led to an increased demand for professional nurses. As rehabilitation services move into the alternative care settings, rehabilitation nurses will be needed in community-based agencies, in the home, and among those living outside society's structures and organizations, such as those who cannot gain access to health care (the uninsured and the homeless). Additionally, technological, demographic, and economic factors are moving all health care services toward community-based delivery systems. With that, whether one accepts the usual or broader definition of health (Moccia, 1990), nursing's expertise will be increasingly in demand and increasingly valued.

The nation, however, is caught up in a nursing shortage. This shortage, like those in the past, has its roots in historical, social, and political issues over which nursing has little control (Ryan, 1990). Nursing shortages have been reported since the 1920s. Before the 1970s these were mostly linked to a disparity between nursing wages and salaries that could be obtained outside the profession. Since the 1970s, shortages have been directly in response to hospital reimbursement. This, coupled with inadequate staffing ratios, lowered job satisfaction, and career opportunities for women in other fields, has no doubt continued to fuel the shortage into the 1990s.

A shortage of trained rehabilitation nurses creates liabilities for physicians, providers, and payers. It jeopardizes the quality of rehabilitation services at a time when all health care will be held accountable and will probably be reimbursed only on the basis of evidence of health care's having met measurable outcomes.

REHABILITATION NURSES' CURRENT REALITY

Rehabilitation Delivery Systems

One variable that influences the preparation of the rehabilitation nurse is the model of clinical service delivery. Most rehabilitation professionals talk about the interdisciplinary process and functioning as a team. It is apparent, however, that a good number of teams still work predominantly in a multidisciplinary model. Clients are admitted to rehabilitation, where they are typically evaluated by each discipline separately and then are written up with physical therapy (PT) goals, occupational therapy (OT) goals, speech/language pathology (SLP) goals, and nursing goals. They are then scheduled for PT, OT, SLP, psychology, and the like for an hour or so at a time. Once a week the team comes together to report on clients' progress. PT reports on lower extremity function, OT on upper extremity function, and so on. PT may say that a client is independent in transfers, and nursing may say that the client still needs assistance. Situations such as this often deteriorate into debates about who is wrong.

When these situations are examined closely, however, it becomes clear that no one is wrong. The difficulty arises because staff have been working on similar problems all week but have rarely (or never) come together to compare notes, and as a result, they sometimes find that they seem to be talking about entirely different clients. They work in systems that situate each discipline in a separate work area (e.g., the PT gym, the OT gym, and the SLP office). Each team member evaluates the client separately, documents his or her findings in one part of the medical record (in cryptic, discipline-specific language that uses many abbreviations), and sets the discipline goals for the client. In this common scenario, no one has had to talk to anyone outside his or her own area.

Inherent in this process is the expectation that nursing will carry through with what the therapists have established for the client during treatment. This is frequently followed by great disappointment and subsequent blaming and conflict among all team members. The cycle repeats itself, often concluding with the identified need for more training for nursing. The reality is that more training for nurses is not the only answer because it is not the only issue. A larger issue is the effectiveness of the service delivery system for rehabilitation.

Rehabilitation sprang up amidst the traditional medical model and in many settings is driven by those traditional beliefs and practices. In many institutions, treatment remains grounded in these practices and is at odds with client and family-centered rehabilitation. Most team members were trained in this model and many have been unsuccessful in moving away from the constraints that traditional models present. Beyond the issue of basic education and preparation for all team members is the belief by many that nurses are the only team members who were not trained in rehabilitation. Melvin (1980) notes that in fact no discipline is trained in an interdisciplinary process in school; rather, each is taught only in its particular modality. Although there has been some improvement in this area in recent years, this approach to professional preparation still continues. Nursing has perhaps the leanest curriculum related to the specialization of rehabilitation, and in most cases nurses must complete postgraduate courses to attain even the required technical knowledge base.

For these factors to be dealt with effectively, there must be a shift in thinking about the true nature of the health care and rehabilitation environments and what needs to change to produce appropriate outcomes. This means a shift in the health care delivery paradigm. It means redefining quality of care from the concept of providing everything that is possible to the concept of providing everything that is required. For rehabilitation it means stepping back from day-to-day operations and identifying those variables that stand in the way of rehabilitation's becoming more efficient. In many instances this requires a major systems reorganization and an administrative design change to eliminate a good deal of tradition, which frequently translates into waste. For nursing it means a radical change from routines, tasks, and acute care planning to early assessment and long-range planning throughout the client's participation in the rehabilitation continuum and reentry into the community.

Most nursing and administrative executives in acute medical-surgical settings are unfamiliar with the clinical process of rehabilitation and how the role requirements of the rehabilitation nurse differ from those in the medical-surgical environment. The medical model focuses on episodic medical incidents with an eye toward cure during short lengths of stay. Nursing is organized around supporting the model with its scheduling structures, assessments, patient monitoring regimens, medication and treatment routines, and diagnostic and therapeutic appointments. The pace is fast, the approach is "doing for the patient," and the goal, beyond wellness, is to get the patient out of the hospital. Staffing is based on census and acuity and is described in acute care terms. Lengths of stay are short, so that there is little time to expand beyond those basic necessary issues. In rehabilitation as well, lengths of stay are reduced far below those of just a few years ago. The time available to deliver the programs is reduced. Nursing systems that maintain their traditional nursing approaches while trying to incorporate rehabilitation education concepts will continue to create conflict that allows little time for creativity and ultimately jeopardizes client outcome.

Organizational Designs

Rehabilitation and brain injury programs located in acute care hospitals often present additional barriers to the rehabilitation nurse and team. The concept of rehabilitation nurses reporting to the vice president of patient services of an acute care medical-surgical hospital is based on maintaining the professional integrity of nursing. For the rehabilitation nurse, this design is inhibiting, distracting, and fundamentally nonsupportive of their role on the interdisciplinary team. To become a specialist in anything, one must concentrate on the area of specialization. In the acute inpatient rehabilitation unit, housed in an acute care hospital and utilizing the traditional nursing reporting structure, the nurse's energy, attention, accountability, and loyalty are divided. Nurses frequently sit on housewide committees that have nothing to do with the business of rehabilitation. Nurses are compelled to follow many of the policies and procedures designed for the medical-surgical patient that may be only slightly modified for rehabilitation. In some instances nurses are even required to dress the same way as acute care nurses, which clearly reflects an illness model and not a rehabilitation wellness approach. All the time spent in responding to medical-surgical issues is time lost for developing high-level, rehabilitation-appropriate policies, standards of care, and client environments that reflect wellness, not "hospital-like" illness. All this leaves little time to analyze fully what the client really needs and the best way to organize the staff to meet those needs. Today's health care environment has little time or tolerance for long-standing tradition. Hospitals will not survive economically if attention is not paid to designing efficient delivery systems that are client and family centered.

Nursing's traditional reporting systems also support the most divisive issue facing rehabilitation teams: discipline territories. What is frequently missing is a structure that allows the rehabilitation nurse to become totally involved in rehabilitation and to be accountable to the team and to clients. With all team members, regardless of discipline, being accountable to the same leader and manager, appropriate planning for client programs, delivery systems, staff education, and case management can be addressed. Common goals can be set and achieved without issues of control interfering and clouding the is-

sues. Decisions can be made in a timely way and acted on without delays. In addition, if a shift in the reporting structure such as under a single rehabilitation vice president is implemented, the vice president of nursing can be more effective than before. A strong consultative role in relation to the rehabilitation nurse manager can focus time and energy appropriately on specific issues relevant to the nurse, include assistance with advanced practice issues, administrative and leadership problems, financial principles, and information regarding the organization's goals and strategies for the future. All these issues are critical to the effective operation of rehabilitation services but do not carry the obstacles of the acute care nursing model. They require both the nurse executive and the rehabilitation nurse manager to function at higher levels, to give up some of the old baggage and control, and to see the bigger picture. It allows each team member to practice in his or her area of expertise with fewer barriers and better outcomes. Rehabilitation nurses will not be able to function as effective team members until they become complete team members.

Nursing's Current Practice

At a time when health care is experiencing cost restraints, expansion of alternative delivery systems, and nursing shortages, the question of nursing's ability to respond must be addressed. Nursing's current organizational structures, variations in educational preparation, and the often indiscriminate assignment of nursing personnel to a broad spectrum of roles are no longer consistent with the complex needs and expectations of the client. This could not be demonstrated better than in the interdisciplinary brain injury team, where the needs of the client and family support systems require the highest level of critical thinking, problem solving, planning, communication, and financial management.

Nurses practicing in brain injury rehabilitation have many similar characteristics. These include:

- limited or no rehabilitation training in formal nursing school education

- a large number of practicing nurses, representing different levels of formal education and training, who have less than a bachelor's degree
- new hires who frequently lack previous experience in rehabilitation or brain injury care
- new hire orientations that frequently focus on acute care technical competencies as opposed to rehabilitation-specific content
- a lack of provider-driven brain injury curricula that mandate demonstrable competencies within a reasonable time (e.g., 3 to 6 months)
- a lack of educational parity between many nurses and their therapy counterparts

This last issue is of particular importance. The differentiation of roles based on formal training is well known in the field of rehabilitation. Take for example the differences between registered PTs and OTs and their AA degree counterparts. Physical Therapy Assistants (PTAs) and Certified Occupational Therapy Assistants (COTAs) are not expected to guide their discipline's activities within the interdisciplinary team. They do not establish the client's plan of care, represent their discipline in the weekly conference, or document the essentials required by licensing, certification, and reimbursement agencies.

As vital members of the rehabilitation team, PTAs and COTAs provide myriad technical services that assist in the overall delivery of care. Their job description defines their scope of practice on the basis of expected competencies that follow their educational programs. The difference between a registered therapist and an AA therapist is clear.

Although this delineation does not exist in nursing, the large number of AA registered nurses representing professional nursing may underscore some of the common beliefs about nursing that are held by the interdisciplinary team. Nurses are often viewed as less empowered than other team members, weaker communicators, and bound by rules and regulations. These attitudes are manifested in practices that limit real therapy to 8 to 5 Monday through Saturday and do not address those client needs that

go beyond such a schedule and are the primary responsibility of the nurse. Another example is client and family education by nursing, which is not routinely scheduled as part of the weekly plan. Nurses and therapists are aware of this tension and are taking a closer look at the contributing factors.

The problem begins with the basic educational preparation of the registered nurse. AA nurses are well grounded in technical and procedural aspects of care. With orientation to the setting, they can be prepared to carry out procedures and programs planned for the client regardless of the discipline designing the activities. Additionally, they are prepared to carry out specific client assessments and to institute care plans surrounding the client's nursing needs. What the AA nurse has yet to experience in the educational process are the areas of leadership, management, in-depth psychosocial theory and practice, research, and advanced client care assessments and planning. Also not addressed at the AA level are the issues of health care administration, business, reimbursement, organizational design, marketplace trends, and problem solving.

The disadvantage to the AA nurse seems clear in concept, and in fact it frequently plays itself out at interdisciplinary planning meetings or conferences. Nurses frequently are perceived as less prepared, less interactive than other team members, and more focused on medical issues than on client goals, which are transdisciplinary in nature. Many struggle with interactive problem solving with their team counterparts, who hold bachelor's, master's, and at times doctoral degrees.

MAKING IT WORK IN THE FUTURE

Changes in Rehabilitation Delivery Systems

The ultimate goal of a sound approach to rehabilitation nursing education is the rehabilitation experience and outcome for the client and family. For successful outcomes to be achieved, the integration of nursing practice, along with the practice of all other disciplines treating the client, into a single model of care is imperative.

Given the economic environment of health care and the new fiscal as well as clinical accountabilities of staff, the ability of a team to assess, plan, and treat clients given the time and financial resources available to the client is truly challenged. This is nowhere more true than in brain injury systems, which are being scrutinized for their effectiveness in light of their costs to the payer.

Although brain injury systems have no doubt been highly visible in developing low-cost levels of care through the continuum of care concept, many have been less successful in deviating from the standard approach to care. Starting over with assessments, goal setting, and care planning at each level of the continuum, along with various therapeutic techniques such as transfers from setting to setting, have added to the frustration of many.

Rehabilitation Planning with Salient Factors

The buyer's response has been to seek new treatment paradigms that are more focused on the individual client, demonstrate an ability on the team's part to manage all the resources throughout the continuum of care, and provide continued, consistent care from one setting to the next. One example of such a model is the salient factors approach to rehabilitation planning.

Several years ago, Rodger Wood (1987), while at Casa Colina Hospital for Rehabilitative Medicine, introduced the concept of salient factors in describing a brain injury model of rehabilitation delivery. The original concept has evolved and now encompasses a broader definition and application among a number of diagnoses.

A salient factor is defined simply as a striking issue. Used in the context of rehabilitation planning, salient factors address the key issues in the client's life that must be addressed for that individual to go home. This approach looks beyond the physical problems and acquired impairments and takes into account all aspects of the client's functioning and future living environment. A salient factors approach addresses the long-term needs and goals of the client from the beginning of the rehabilitation process to plan an appropriate treatment strategy that effectively utilizes and manages the client's resources. This approach is based on the unique needs of each person with brain injury and does not rely on standardized programs designed for everyone being treated with the same diagnosis.

The World Health Organization (WHO) disability classification system has identified three levels that help to explain how a salient factors model can assist the team to become focused on exactly what the client needs to achieve maximum benefit from rehabilitation. The three lev-

Table 13-1 WHO Classification System

Level	Definition	Example 1	Example 2
Impairment	Relates to basic level of involvement	Muscle/nerve damage on the right side	Memory loss
Disability	The functional impact of the impairment	Inability to negotiate stairs, uneven surfaces, and to move around obstacles (i.e., tables, chairs)	Forgets to perform ADLs, gets lost in the community, not able to follow through on verbal directions
Handicap	Social disadvantages that result from the disability	Restricted access to most rooms at home, problems accessing the community, needs 24-hour supervision, risk of long-term institutionalization	Diminished work performance, social acceptance decreases due to appearance and unreliability, accumulative effects affect psychological status

els address the areas of impairment, disability, and handicap (Table 13-1).

Designing rehabilitation goals that address salient factors shifts the intervention process from a traditional approach (e.g., goals that target the treatment and remediation of impairments) to reducing the level of disability caused by the impairments. Rehabilitation efforts that identify the impact of acquired problems on the individual's functional living situation will be able to focus treatment on the most critical areas of need. Reducing the level of disability, whether it is accomplished by client-initiated strategies or environmental adaptation, will diminish the handicapping consequences of the injury at home, school work, or in the community. This approach provides each client with what he or she specifically needs to function in his or her own world.

The salient factors approach can often drive the integration of the interdisciplinary process within the team. By asking the client to identify the five or six things that he or she needs to be able to do to go home, or by applying the same question to the next level of care, the team's energy moves beyond some traditional barriers, such as the establishment of discipline goals, to what the client needs. When team members reinforce all aspects of the client's plan of care, there is a 24-hour learning environment and staff accountability for outcomes. The institution of an interdisciplinary documentation system throughout the continuum supports every aspect of the process. When the initial client assessment after admission is carried out by several team members in close collaboration, redundancy is virtually eliminated, and each team member hears and sees the same things. Everyone can focus on the key issues for clients as judged from where they are going and what it will take to get them there. Staff can share their interpretation of observations and teach one another different aspects of their areas of expertise. Care planning that clearly defines the long-term, discharge, and short-term goals in measurable terms lets staff know the parameters within which they are working and what is expected of them. Additionally, when specific interventions are clearly outlined so that every member of the

team or family who comes in contact with a client uses the exact same technique each time, consistent ongoing training is provided to the client, and confusion as to the right way of doing something is eliminated. With every team member assuming equal accountability for functional outcomes, territories are eliminated, and new awarenesses of staff capabilities are opened.

For example, if a family needs to learn how to transfer a client so that the client can go home, but the family is only available after 7 P.M. each evening, does that mean that the PT must be there or come back to teach them? Not in an interdisciplinary model. The evening nurse can assume that job and thereby becomes accountable to the client and the rest of the team to reach that goal. Likewise, if a client is on a bladder training program and needs to void in the middle of therapy, the therapist can toilet the client by using therapeutic transfer and dressing techniques while at the same time reinforcing the client's bladder training regime. The point is that the client's legs and the transfer do not belong to the PT and the bladder to the nurse. They all belong to the client. *Interdisciplinary* does not mean that the OT designs the bladder program and the PT designs the swallowing care plan. It means that each team member specifically trained in certain aspects of care facilitate the development of the client's care plan in his or her area of expertise and then ensures that the rest of the team is clear about how to reinforce the program and is competent to carry it out.

The true implementation of interdisciplinary rehabilitation practice takes desire, time, facilitation, and constant reinforcement. The investment in these areas at times seems overwhelming. The positive outcomes that result can be an incentive to the staff and can be cost effective to the client and the facility. Team members frequently become more creative and function at higher levels. The benefits to the clients will speak for themselves.

Changes in Nursing Education

The education of the rehabilitation nurse is both simple and complex. On the one hand the technical aspects are fairly straightforward regardless of the complexity of the procedure, protocol, or standing order. All nurses fundamentally use a step-by-step approach that can be learned in various ways (e.g., classroom lectures, demonstrations, and self-learning modules). Many educational approaches have been developed and utilized for rehabilitation nursing education on the basis of adult learning theory, the latest educational techniques, or motivational theory. When delivered by committed, experienced teachers, most of these approaches have worked well. It is a question not of what works but rather of how far the process goes in preparing nurses beyond technical competency and in carrying them into critical thinking, advanced practice, autonomous judgments, and dynamic interdisciplinary interaction.

Basic Professional Nursing Preparation

For more than three decades, various groups nationwide have struggled to reach consensus on standardizing educational preparation for entry into nursing practice. Although this issue remains unresolved, the health care industry continues to labor under the mistaken belief that all registered nurses are alike and therefore continues to expect similar levels of competency. Basic nursing preparation provides the practitioner with the knowledge and skills necessary to enter the practice of nursing. Depending on the type of program selected, the new graduate enters the market with a sound technical orientation or an advanced education that also incorporates leadership and management capabilities, comprehensive assessment, and decision-making and problem-solving skills.

Rehabilitation nursing specialty practice draws upon specialized skills and knowledge required to deal effectively with a broad range of individuals who have disabling conditions. Rehabilitation nursing is practiced within a dynamic relationship involving the client and family, therapists, physicians, payers, and providers. It necessitates an expanded knowledge base and is practiced in an interdisciplinary process that is outcome oriented. Major roles of the rehabilita-

tion nurse are teacher and reinforcer, client advocate, case manager, counselor, researcher, and care giver (Mumma, 1987).

Inherent in these roles is a high level of independence and critical thinking, which separate the bachelor's prepared nurse from the registered nurse with an associate's degree. The bachelor's program graduate possesses an expanded knowledge of the theories and models that guide nursing practice, leading to the development of appropriate nursing diagnoses and comprehensive teaching plans that promote, maintain, or restore health. Priorities are established that focus on the continuing health and functional needs of the client and the appropriate use of human, physical, and financial resources. The bachelor's prepared nurse utilizes his or her knowledge of theories in leadership, decision making, motivation, and management to supervise others and to act as a change agent within the organization.

The nursing expertise and professionalism demanded in today's rehabilitation environment are not matters of more but of different. "Because of the future needs of the community, nurses will need educational preparation that is different from the education of nurses of today" (National Commission on Nursing Implementation Project [NCNIP], 1987, p. 2).

Differentiated Practice in the Rehabilitation Setting

The future supply of nurses and assisting personnel must be planned to guarantee an adequate number of nurses with appropriate qualifications for both general client care and specialized leadership roles. Predictions suggest that the trend toward higher levels of educational preparation for nurses will continue, just as it has for other health care workers. Furthermore, there will be an increased need to retrain and cross-train nurses as nursing services respond to changes in the client population in the health care system.

To facilitate this process of change, a number of nursing organizations have determined that there will be two categories of registered nurses: the professional and the associate nurse. The professional nurse holds a bachelor's or post-graduate degree in nursing, and the associate nurse holds an AA or a diploma in nursing. Although the issue of the experienced AA nurse being supervised by the inexperienced BS nurse has been raised, it is common practice for people with higher educations to move directly into supervisory and leadership roles in business as well as all in other aspects of health care.

The idea of establishing two levels of nursing has been discussed for years, but was formally put forth in 1985 by the NCNIP, which gave the following definition of differentiated practice: "Differentiated practice distinguishes professional and technical nursing roles from the current single role of today's registered nurses. Differentiated practice enables nurses to perform distinct jobs, based on their educational preparation" (NCNIP, 1987). Today in rehabilitation, most licensed registered nurses perform the same job regardless of their educational preparation. "The differentiated practice curricula for ADN and BSN programs builds minimal levels of practice leading to different levels of decision making" (NCNIP, 1987).

There are substantial differences in roles and accountabilities, with the professional nurse assuming the leadership role in all aspects of client care, nursing related activities, and supervision of other nursing staff. The professional nursing role takes into consideration the desired effects of nursing and the role of the other members of the health care team in delivery of cost-prudent, high-quality health care services through assuming the responsibility and authority to:

- provide nursing care services that are flexible to meet the changing needs and demands of consumers, taking into consideration sequencing, frequency, and timing of service delivery
- identify, implement, and monitor strategies of nursing care that promote the best possible consumer outcomes and utilization of available human and financial resources
- promote a dynamic environment that generates a high degree of communication and collegial interaction regarding the delivery and outcomes of client care

- identify and develop policies, protocols, and procedures that govern the services provided by rehabilitation nurses
- contribute to the continued professional competence and development of the nursing staff

The role of the associate nurse is complementary to that of the professional nurse and is operationalized within an established model of care developed by the professional nurse. The associate nurse assists in the delivery of client care and can direct peers and ancillary personnel. Examples of differentiated practice roles in the rehabilitation setting are shown in Table 13-2.

The ratio of associate nurses to professional nurses is an important decision that each unit, program, or organization needs to make on the basis of the clients whom they serve, the treatment models that are in place, and the availability of nursing staff. The relevance of this approach to rehabilitation nursing becomes clear when one is addressing issues such as client assessment and care planning, client and family education, staff education, the client care conference, and other activities that involve an interdisciplinary process. In each of these instances, nursing must be represented by an individual who is able to combine a holistic outlook, logical reasoning, and intuitive thinking with competencies for scientific practice. The professional rehabilitation nurse needs to be able to interpret data and to analyze problems in such a way as to design client-specific, if not innovative, care plans. Nurses must be able to take the long view of the client's needs and goals in light of medical, financial, and human resources and the requirement for further treatment beyond the immediate setting. This ability to envision the future allows the nurse to provide interventions early that will have a measurable impact.

Along with the emphasis on problem-solving abilities, the educational preparation of the professional nurse provides an understanding and appreciation of the various other disciplines and the writing, speaking, and listening skills that are essential requirements for successful dialog, negotiation, and interaction during the client care conference and other activities that involve the interdisciplinary team, payer representatives,

Table 13-2 Differentiated Practice Role of Nurse

Professional Registered Nurse	Associate Registered Nurse
Knowledge and skill is based on nursing science synthesized with other scientific, behavioral and humanistic disciplines.	Knowledge and skill is based on established nursing principles immediately applicable to practice.
Establishes, modifies and improves communication systems of self, patients/families, team and external groups.	Works with established communication systems and modifies own communication with patients/families, team and external groups.
Uses communication system to network with team to modify health care delivery as well as patient plan of care.	Uses established communication systems to implement an effective patient plan of care.
Assesses health status and health potential of patients, families and communities and systematically establishes a data base with or without predesigned assessment tools.	Assists with establishing data base and identifying individual patient problems through the use of established assessment tools, protocols and/or formats.
Identifies and anticipates predictable and unexpected consequences in patient's status.	Identifies deviations from the usual responses to common rehabilitation problems.
Develops plan of care for rehabilitation patients with problems or conditions for which standards of care are not designed.	Develops plan of care based on previously established standards or protocols.
Implements plan of care for patients/families and groups throughout the continuum of care.	Implements plan of care for patients/families and groups in specific, structured clinical setting.
Synthesizes information provided by Associate nurse in team conference and provides critical thinking, problem solving and advance nursing concepts into interdisciplinary patient care planning.	Identifies patient response to interdisciplinary plan of care from nursing perspective in team conference.
Involves supervision, management, and development of nursing staff and team members.	Assigns and directs assisting personnel to implement nursing care.
Collaborates with research team and applies research findings to nursing practice.	Recognizes and participates in the research process and uses the results within the clinical setting.
Participates in the development of nursing and interdisciplinary team standards, protocols and criteria in providing patient care.	Utilizes nursing and interdisciplinary standards, protocols and criteria in providing patient care.
Accountable for own practice within a professional, legal, and ethical framework and promoting responsibility in others.	Accountable for own practice within the established legal and ethical framework.

or other consumers. The professional registered nurse works to enhance interdisciplinary team productivity through a posture that:

- demonstrates a commitment to goals and objectives that transcend self or one's discipline
- unifies the team's actions and promotes synergy and openness
- enhances communication through shared definitions, meanings, and understandings
- holds all team members accountable for their actions and results of their actions

The educational background of the professional nurse also provides for experience in client, family, and community education. Effective teaching requires effective communication skills and the ability to assess learning needs and to translate them into learning objectives that can be documented in terms of measurable outcomes.

Rehabilitation nursing draws upon numerous models that promote a self-directed approach to client, family, and staff education and most often incorporates adult learning theory. Adult learners have their own learning styles, needs, and life experiences. In the rehabilitation setting, the professional nurse develops a plan of client teaching that shifts the nursing role from primary care giver to teacher. This fosters an environment that promotes learning and attainment of the client's goals through a combination of individual and group learning activities, skills practice, discussion, exercises, and demonstration. Numerous studies have documented the long-term benefits of client education (Kruger, 1990). These include shorter lengths of stay, increased compliance and ability for self-directed care, and decreased utilization of health services.

The orientation and ongoing education of other nursing staff is also a function of the professional nurse. Staff development programs require a systematic approach to teaching. According to Carpenito (1987), the teaching and learning process consists of steps that reinforce the concept of nursing process. "Inservice programs that focus on teaching principles help nurses to become more proficient and comfortable with the art of teaching" (Boyd et al., 1991, p. 90). The majority of nurses do not learn the principles or practice of teaching during their formal education, and they are not necessarily born teachers. It becomes mandatory for facility-based education to assume the responsibility for staff preparation to teach clients by means of sound educational techniques, including the ability to measure whether learning has occurred.

A final aspect and benefit is that, once staff are placed in appropriate positions through differentiated practice, mentors and role models more naturally line up for further expansion of education and training.

Basic Orientation for the New Brain Injury Nurse

Beyond the basic issues of nursing education and differentiation of roles are the specialized training needs required for rehabilitation practice. The burden of these training needs currently falls upon the rehabilitation providers, who often find themselves pressed to get the nurse on the unit as soon as possible, with limited resources or well prepared materials for orientation and training, and with limited qualified staff to teach. These factors result in orientation training programs that are superficial and basic, whose content often resembles that of the acute medical-surgical program, and that do not establish a foundation of rehabilitation knowledge or skills on which to build future trainings. Continuing education tends to be fragmented and is not based on progressive, sequential learning steps. It also is not as readily available to nurses who work evenings and nights, when there is less support from the rest of the team and when the client becomes the total responsibility of the nurse. As a result, in many settings a new rehabilitation nurse can be out of orientation, filling a full-time position within 1 to 2 weeks of hire, and without a plan for additional training for several months. Orientation allows for no real understanding of the types of clients to be treated and the complexities of their treatment, such as deviations in behavior, safety, interpreting symptoms, family needs, and knowing how to handle related problems or when to seek immediate help. At the same time, however, the expectation of the nurse is to plan and carry out care successfully. Many do not have a clue as to how to proceed and achieve an outcome, and they fall back on their previous acute care background. For example, a nurse may establish a bladder program without a full understanding of the neuropathology associated with the injury, or he or she may attempt to teach a client some task or content without an understanding of how impaired cognition affects the client's ability to learn and why he or she fails. In addition, when institutional belt tightening is necessary, education is often the first to go. The time for orientation is abbreviated even further, and ongoing education becomes more fragmented and inconsistent.

What is suggested is that the entire educational process be revisited and mapped out with a sequential learning process that looks at the role of the nurse from the viewpint of educational preparation and experience and then builds an ongoing program around the requirements of the nurse's position. Starting with orientation, a determination is made as to those aspects that relate to everyone and those that must be differentiated according to role. Once orientation is complete, educational tracks for differentiated practice are established, with overlaps and differences delineated. Career advancement and promotions are based on the timely, successful completion of appropriate educational modules. Specific time frames should be established for competency, and both the nurse and the institution should be held accountable for seeing that they are offered and completed. An example of what the initial orientation might look like is given in Exhibit 13-1.

Exhibit 13-1 Initial Orientation: Content

Health care and rehabilitation trends in the 1990s
- National health care trends
- Rehabilitation delivery systems
  1. Continuums of care
  2. Reimbursement models
  3. Outcome expectations
- Case management models and expectations
  1. Buyer based
  2. Provider based
- Community-based resources
  1. Clinical
  2. Social
  3. Noncompensated
- Centers of excellence
  1. Concept
  2. Criteria
  3. Locations

Facility-specific information
- Size
  1. Beds
  2. Treatment areas
- Client/payer mix
- Continuum of services
  1. Levels of care provided/settings
  2. Non–facility-based parts of the continuum
- Interdisciplinary team composition and structure
- Model(s) of treatment delivery
  1. Discipline/department
  2. Programmatic
  3. Interdisciplinary
- Staffing models
- Special features and programs

Rehabilitation nursing
- Role of the professional and associate nurse
  1. Communication
  2. Client and family assessment
  3. Client and family care plan development
  4. Care plan implementation
  5. Client and family responses to care
  6. Client team conference responsibilities
  7. Management
  8. Research and development
  9. Practice accountabilities
- CRRN requirements and recommendations

- Client and family education support systems
  1. Materials, supplies, staff, approaches, space
  2. Monitors for client competencies in self-care or self-directed care
- Creating a therapeutic environment
- Client rights/Americans with Disabilities Act
- Ethics

Brain injury services
- Physical environment, general safety policies and procedures
- Overview of unit/program services
  1. Interdisciplinary client programs and protocols
  2. Team structure and functions
  3. Client and family conferences and meetings
  4. Staff meetings
- Paperwork
  1. Admissions, transfers, and discharges
  2. Documentation system and forms
  3. Physician orders
  4. Diagnostic procedures and reports
  5. Special appointments
- Relationships with other services, departments, and programs

Nursing issues with the client with brain injury
- Comprehensive patient assessment*
  1. Head to toe
  2. Neurological/levels of consciousness
- Nursing accountabilities in client management issues
  1. Cognitive impairments
  2. Eating/swallowing
  3. Communication
  4. Skin
  5. Circulation and breathing
  6. Urinary elimination
  7. Bowel elimination
  8. Dressing, bathing, hygiene, feeding
  9. Movement, mobility
  10. Sexuality
  11. Grieving, coping, adapting
  12. Health maintenance
  13. Assessing and care planning for home and community
- Emergency procedures and medical complications
- Neurosensory stimulation techniques

*It is recommended that client assessment be carried out as an interdisciplinary process by the team at one time to avoid duplication of questions to the client and so that everyone hears the same thing and learns from one another.

Once orientation is over, the nurse should know what is expected and available for ongoing learning in the treatment of clients with brain injury. Content should be differentiated on the basis of the nurse's role rather than the typical generic classes for all nurses. Also, a systematic, sequential approach to the educational process will help the nurse progress through a well thought-out program and will control for competency. Although clinical resources and client-family needs will determine the content of the training required, topics might include:

- assessing the client with brain injury
- care of the comatose client
- interdisciplinary care planning
- neuropsychological impairments and functional implications
- neurobehavior intervention strategies
- outcome after brain injury
- characteristics of adult learners
- components of a positive learning environment
- teaching skills

The idea of establishing sequential learning modules is not new to nursing. Many nursing departments have used the method for years, and it is a model that deserves revisiting. It is an approach that can incorporate interdisciplinary education and builds in an evaluation of the learner's knowledge at each step. Learning at each level is based on understanding the content from the previous module. With this method, the nurse does not move on to the next activity until comprehension and competency are demonstrated with the current material. In addition, it should be made clear when the nurse is expected to complete the series. This approach would facilitate strategic coordination and integration of learning programs. For example, clinical competencies associated with learning to care for a comatose client would include support classes in such things as neuroanatomy, deficits resulting from brain injury, assessment of clients with brain injury, interdisciplinary care planning, neurobehavior intervention programs, and so on.

There are many approaches that have been used for years to develop an ongoing education process. Although a specific model is important, it is not nearly as important as the recognition that a program is needed and the presence of commitment to establishing it. A concept that should be considered when one is developing programs of learning is to explicitly define the role of the participants as active learners. What are their responsibilities toward their own education? For example, when self-learning modules are used, a clear definition of goals, objectives, expected clinical competencies, and the time frame in which the module should be completed (e.g., 1 month) holds the nurse accountable to complete the activity. Because the majority of nursing staff work evenings and nights, many presentations are missed. Inservice classes, interdisciplinary presentations, guest speakers, and so on should be videotaped. This is particularly important when staff are accountable for the content and will be asked to integrate it into practice. The really innovative educator will take those tapes and create self-learning modules by writing behavioral objectives, learner activities, and a posttest covering the key points. Brain injury content, such as case studies of real clients with brain injury, should be used when documentation systems are taught, modeling appropriate care planning, interventions, discharge plans, and expected standards of care to reinforce the learning. All interdisciplinary discussions and documentation should include specific brain injury content when appropriate. Every opportunity should be taken to use the tools available in the environment to reinforce learning. By developing these areas, all staff, and especially the evening and night staff along with part-time and per diem nurses, will no longer be playing catch-up for information or having to revert to acute care principles when a rehabilitation approach is available and more appropriate.

CONCLUSION

The demands of today's health care environment are so drastically different that old ways of operating no longer apply. Administrators can no longer operate in isolation from the clinical aspects of care and their requirements for support when making major administrative decisions. Every time education dollars are cut, so is the institution's competitive edge because there is no way to keep up and because future business will be based on cost effective clinical outcomes. Conversely, nurses and other clinical staff can no longer isolate themselves from the financial aspects of operating a program or setting up a client's plan of care. Associate nurses cannot continue to be placed in the position of fully presenting and developing sophisticated client care alternatives without an adequate educational background. It may be that all rehabilitation programs must have a minimum number of staff who are bachelor's or master's prepared or that there must be a nursing care specialist who consults on every client so that advanced practice concepts can be implemented. If neither of these alternatives is available, plans should be made to work toward them. It may mean in the beginning that the nurse manager sits in on all client care conferences to supplement what associate nurses plan.

We are in an age of accountability to employers, clients, and one another. We are absolutely being called upon to bring forth our greatest creativity in the provision of brain injury rehabilitation and to question everything we have done in the past. We are being asked to look at every client individually, to determine his or her specific needs, and to meet them quickly, clearly, and without frills. We are challenged critically to evaluate past practices and to abandon those that are not crucial to the client. This challenge is stimulating to some, frightening to others, and impossible for a few. Regardless of the response, the drive for change will only increase. It is up to every individual working in the health care arena to determine his or her own ability to change, to

move forward into a new way of doing the business of rehabilitation, and to invest energy to respond effectively.

> Today, the man who is the real risk taker is anonymous and non heroic. He is the one trying to make institutions work (Ward, 1955, p. 124).

REFERENCES

Boyd, S., Cleary, B., Coomer, M., Cooper, P., Cosner, D., Summins, N., Decell, K., Kemper, B., Kirsky, V., Sims, S., Van Den Dries, D., & Wingate, L. (1991). Professional nursing roles. The reintegration of patient teaching. *Journal of Nursing Staff Development*, 88–90.

Carpenito, L.J. (1987). *Nursing diagnosis: Application to clinical practice*. Philadelphia: Lippincott.

Clark, C., & Krentz, S. (1991). Planning long term care services: A guide for acute care hospitals. *Topics in Health Care Financing*, 73–82.

Del Togno-Armanasco, V., Olwas, G., & Harter, S. (1989). Developing an integrated nursing case management model. *Nursing Management, 20*, 26–29.

Ellis, J.R., & Hartley, C.L. (1988). *Nursing in today's world: Challenges, issues and trends* (3rd ed.). Philadelphia: Lippincott.

Grace, H.K. (1990). Can health care be contained? In J.C. McCloskey & H.K. Grace (Eds.), *Current issues in nursing* (pp. 380–386). St. Louis: Mosby.

Knollmueller, R. (1989). Case management: What's in a name? *Nursing Management, 20*, 38–42.

Kruger, S. (1990). A review of patient education in nursing. *Journal of Staff Development*, 71–74.

Melvin, J.L. (1980). Interdisciplinary and multidisciplinary activities and ACRM. *Archives of Physical Medicine and Rehabilitation, 61*, 379–380.

Moccia, P. (1990). Towards the future. *Nursing Clinics of North America, 25*, 606–613.

Mumma, C.M. (1987). Rehabilitation nursing specialty practice. *Rehabilitation Nursing: Concepts and Practice, A Core Curriculum, 2*, 13–14.

National Commission on Nursing Implementation Project. (1987). *Second invitational conference.*

Ryan, S. (1990). *Nursing Clinics of North America, 25*, 597–605.

Ward, J.W. (1955, November). *Time*, 124.

Wood, R.L. (1987). *Brain injury rehabilitation: A neurobehavioral approach*. Gaithersburg, MD: Aspen.

Part III

Management Issues and Staff Development

Developing Clinicians into Managers: Effective Training Strategies

Nancy D. Schmidt
Pat Kitchell

14

OBJECTIVES

Upon completion of this chapter, the reader will be able to:

1. state the benefits of preparing and promoting qualified staff into management level positions
2. initiate a process of selecting clinicians for management pursuit
3. develop a plan that outlines the steps for developing clinicians into managers
4. determine effective training methods for developing management skills within key areas of management specialization
5. identify the role and accountability shift that clinicians must address to be effective in management positions

Developing Clinicians into Managers

During the past decade, the evolution of head injury rehabilitation has been fast paced. Clinicians have been faced with expanding case loads, challenging treatment issues, and pressures to produce measurable outcomes within shorter periods of time. Clinicians often see these challenges as site specific rather than industry based and leave their jobs or leave the field. This loss of staff takes a toll on any organization. The shrinkage of the professional work force (Bureau of Labor Statistics, 1990), and the ever growing number of providers of head injury rehabilitation services have resulted in a shortage of experienced professionals to deliver the services that are so readily sold to the consumer.

Rehabilitation care is only as good as the staff who deliver the service, so organizations that provide rehabilitation are prudent to enroll good clinicians and to find compelling reasons for them to build their careers there. Ongoing education and training play a vital role in career building. Continued training is essential for keeping clinicians up to date on treatment techniques and strategies. Providing clinicians with career tracks with advancement potential is another powerful vehicle for growth and promoting the clinician's longevity within an organization.

The most common career advancement that health care offers clinicians is in the area of supervision and management. Good clinicians do not always make good managers, however. Often, the skills required to be an effective clinician are different from the skills required to be an effective manager. Clinicians rarely take business and management courses in their academic preparation. They are often unprepared for the transition to management responsibilities. The health care organization that prepares clinicians for management level responsibilities through education, training, coaching, and mentoring will increase the success of the entire organization. Career building through advancement into management, however, must be well planned and carefully implemented, monitored, and evaluated.

This chapter discusses the rationale behind developing capable clinicians into managers and describes a training process to facilitate a successful transition. Methods for teaching about management and developing new, broader responsibilities are also reviewed.

RATIONALE FOR PROMOTING CLINICIANS INTO MANAGEMENT

Upper management in many organizations asks the following question when a supervisory or management level position is vacant: Should we fill the job from talent within, or should we hire someone outside the organization? There are many issues that will ultimately be considered before the final decision is made, but the most important consideration usually is determining who is most qualified for the job. Unless there is an ongoing process whereby clinicians are educated and trained for management responsibilities, internal staff may fall short of possessing the skills necessary for a management level position. On the other hand, the learning curve for someone hired outside the organization, plus the chance of a new hire not fitting into the organizational culture or producing the desired results, makes hiring outside the organization an expensive risk.

It has been estimated that it costs an organization approximately $20,000. to hire and train someone into a management level position. This can be a positive investment or an expensive loss, depending on the success or failure of the individual. Therefore, developing talent from within the organization for management level positions may be a cost effective strategy. In addition to being cost effective in dollars, promoting staff who have been trained from within the organization enhances organizational stability and continuity of care for the client, and communicates that the career growth of clinicians is important to the organization. All these factors serve to produce a healthy morale within the clinical setting. This may result in higher quality of care for the client and better customer service.

DO GOOD CLINICIANS MAKE EFFECTIVE MANAGERS?

Health care organizations often promote experienced clinicians into a supervisory or management level position on the basis of their professional knowledge, technical skills, seniority, leadership qualities, or expressed interest. The interested individual may have had little or no experience as a manager. The ability to learn the multiple skills of management entirely on one's own is rare. Management requires broad knowledge, mature attitudes, and a wide variety of skills that need to be trained and refined from practice, failures, feedback, and coaching.

Becoming a manager from a clinical background requires a shift in thinking and an alteration in the methods by which work is accomplished. A few of these changes are as follows:

- Primary identification of oneself as a professional therapist must shift to identification as a manager.
- Clinicians are the primary providers delivering clinical results, whereas managers complete their work through other people.
- A clinician's success is measured by how he or she produces specific clinical results, whereas a manager's success is measured by how well he or she has managed a number of resources toward meeting the goals of many clients and the organization.
- Clinicians give input, whereas managers make decisions based on staff input.

The major difference between working as a clinician and working as a manager is that clinicians primarily focus on practical and effective methods of assisting the client toward meeting goals; managers, on the other hand, focus on practical and effective methods of assisting the organization toward meeting its goals. Clinicians accomplish much of their work independently, whereas managers accomplish their work through other people. Clinicians who can understand and align with their organization's goals and mission and can shift from delivering a service to producing a result will find an environment that is conducive to their learning of management skills and responsibilities.

Good clinicians do not become effective managers just because they were good clinicians. For clinicians to ready themselves for management responsibilities, there needs to be a reciprocal investment on the part of management and the clinician. First, management must communicate its goals and mission to the clinical staff. Management must articulate a vision of the organization, of where it has been and where it is going. It is useful for the organization to define a policy on internal management development. When positions arise, a process of selection must occur. Clinicians must determine whether management is their choice for career advancement, and management must determine whether it is able to provide access to education, training, and coaching to develop clinical staff into key management roles and to be clear about what kind of management is needed. Once the selection process has begun, management and the clinician must work out a management self-development plan (MSDP). An MSDP is a behavioral plan whereby the position competencies are defined, the clinician's strengths for management responsibilities are identified, and skills that need to be developed are outlined. Goals and objectives with time frames are agreed upon. A training plan is outlined that addresses the methods for achieving management skills and position competencies. Through this process, good clinicians who are motivated toward management as a career choice may become effective managers.

MANAGEMENT CHARACTERISTICS

Clincians who are considering a career in management are likely to ask themselves whether they have management potential or whether they would enjoy a management position. Likewise, management is often searching for signs of management potential within the staff. In both situations, it is important to remember that managers are not born but trained. Management skills do not just appear or develop automatically. Becoming a skilled manager involves more than just being good with people. In the same way that it took a physical therapist, an architect, or a carpenter to become skilled at his or her trade through skills identification, practice, application, and more practice, it takes training and practice to become skilled as a manager. Management can also be subdivided into categories to include personnel management, project management, and program or systems management. The characteristics listed below are necessary for most managers to be effective within the health care environment and therefore represent a brief checklist for management potential:

- See and relate to the big picture (i.e., look beyond the immediate situation and see how short- and long-term goals interact).
- Maintain a "can do" attitude and encourage results in a realistic and honest manner.
- Separate fact, interpretation, opinion, feeling, and action.
- Communicate concisely, both in verbal and written form.
- Enroll a team in a vision and gain commitment to results.
- Listen and hear the message.
- Listen for commitment and new potential in a speaker's message.
- Learn from feedback and mistakes without becoming inhibited or self-conscious.
- Give direction, feedback, and structure for producing results.
- Manage multiple projects, create a plan, and set and realign priorities.
- Generate a vision of the future without being constrained by reactions to the past.

These characteristics may be developed through training. For some individuals, they were modeled, developed and reinforced in home, school, and early work opportunities. For these individuals, the ability to manage may appear to come naturally. Even when these abilities have been acquired at an early age, however, most managers feel that they need to be more clearly defined, practiced, and enhanced on an ongoing basis.

In addition to the above mentioned characteristics, the organization developing managers from within should articulate the expectations and performance criteria for clinicians and managers. Having these criteria clearly articulated allows clinicians to evaluate whether the target accountabilities will be meaningful and whether the work will be worth their personal investment. By having this clearly defined, clinicians may begin a process of determining for themselves whether the work of management is something they are interested in pursuing and for which they have the aptitude.

THE SELECTION PROCESS

Selecting individuals for management level positions is a two-way process. Clinicians should evaluate whether management is a direction in which they desire to move their career. The organization should define a clear set of expectations about what qualities they look for in individuals whom they wish to move into management positions. The expectations should be articulated through job descriptions for each management position as well as through a list of competencies required for the position.

HOW CLINICIANS MAY BEGIN EXPLORING MANAGEMENT AS A CAREER

In his book *Management Skills for the New Health Care Supervisor,* Umiker (1988) suggests that clinicians ask themselves the following questions as a way of determining whether they are well suited for supervisory or management responsibilities. If most questions are responded to with a yes, clinicians are likely to be happy in a management position (Umiker, 1988, p. 4):

- Do you prefer leading other people to working alone?
- Do you enjoy teaching others how to do things?
- Do you like to chair committees and to moderate meetings?
- Do you like making decisions or solving problems?

- Are you willing to take an unpopular stand?
- Are you regarded as a good listener?
- Do employees frequently seek your advice?
- Are you willing to take the responsibility for the work of others?
- Do you want more responsibility and authority?
- Are you a good planner and organizer?
- Do you like sharing information with others?
- Are you willing to do a reasonable amount of paperwork?
- Are you assertive?
- Do you handle stress well?
- Do you keep up-to-date professionally and technically?

In addition to the clinician asking these questions, he or she should seek feedback from peers and supervisors whom he or she respects with the above questions used as the structure for discussion.

Another aspect of management that should be explored when clinicians are considering a supervisory or management position is the changes that will occur in interpersonal relationships at work and how such a shift might influence one's self-concept. Moving into management often means a shift in relationship with co-workers who are not management. This may be accompanied by anger, resentment, fear, loss, and loneliness. Umiker (1988) points out that becoming a part of management in many organizations means becoming part of "them," especially at times when the manager must enforce policies and guidelines that are unpopular with the rest of the team. A new manager learns to see himself or herself with a new, broader management perspective. This does not automatically put a manager in opposition with the team or other staff members, but it does mean that the manager will be expected to interpret and carry out decisions made by the organization's management. This change in interpersonal relationships may affect one's self-concept, particularly in moments when a difficult decision must be made or when the desire arises to share old collegial discussion. Until the new manager is comfortable with

the management team, he or she may experience conflict with the new identity. This, then, is a key area for coaching and mentoring. As new managers gain experience and become comfortable with their role, their self-confidence will grow and their self-concept gradually adjust to the point where they see themselves as a manager with a clinical background committed to the organization's mission. When this transition goes well, it can put an excellent depth of expertise in key management positions. If it is a bad match, the individual as well as the organization will suffer.

After the clinician and the organization have completed the manager assessment process, both can decide to launch a management development plan that focuses on the job and the person and takes the organization's resources and needs into account.

SKILL ASSESSMENT

The first steps in developing an MSDP are to define management competencies for the job at hand and to ask the clinician to list what he or she believes to be personal strengths and limitations as a manager in the job. This should be the only structure given for the initial assignment. By providing no structure, the supervisor is able to observe the clinician's perception of his or her own skills and limitations as well as the clinician's understanding of management's roles and responsibilities. This information will help the supervisor determine whether the clinician requires basic orientation and education regarding what management is all about. If the clinician's level of information is noticeably deficient, the supervisor might suggest as a first exercise that the clinician speak to supervisors about how they spend their time or assign the clinician a small project to manage to gain some familiarity with the responsibilities of supervision and management.

After the self-assessment has been completed and reviewed, the supervisor may ask the clinician to fill out the following general management skills inventory by rank ordering the activities shown in Exhibit 14-1.

Using these two self-assessment exercises as an initial foundation (e.g., the clinician identifying

Exhibit 14-1 General Management Skills Inventory*

Working with others to complete a job
Working independently to complete a job
Managing the details of an activity
Completing paperwork in an efficient and timely manner
Leading a meeting
Speaking before a group effectively (getting the message across clearly and concisely)
Finding new ways of getting a job done/creativity
Assigning work
Planning ahead: setting goals, objectives, and deadlines
Organizing work: considering what needs to be accomplished and knowing the best way to sequence the steps to completion
Problem solving and decision making
Managing time efficiently
Communicating effectively in writing (reports, memos, etc.)
Directing people and activities
Writing, organizing, and managing a budget
Establishing policies and procedures, standards of performance, and quality assurance systems
Coordinating activities and interfacing with other departments
Implementing decisions with which others do not agree
Managing many projects and activities simultaneously
Resolving conflicts
Managing stress

*The clinician rank orders these activities from 1 to 21; with 1 indicating the activity in which the clinician feels most competent and 21 indicating the activity in which he or she feels least competent.

- fiscal management
- personnel management
- self-management
- leadership
- multiple project management
- systems management

Fiscal management involves organizing and managing a budget as well as being held accountable for financial goals. Personnel management is concerned with the human relations of the workplace: directing people toward completing work, motivating staff, listening, counseling, giving feedback, resolving conflict, building and maintaining morale, teaching and training staff, and ensuring that personnel policies are appropriate to the organization's accreditation and licensing guidelines. Self-management and leadership are about organizing and presenting oneself to guide, coordinate, and facilitate the performance of the team as opposed to hindering teamwork and requires skills such as planning ahead; setting goals, objectives, and deadlines; delegating tasks skillfully; coordinating activities simultaneously; analyzing a situation and formulating a decision; managing stressful situations; and maintaining a vision regarding the future direction of the organization, department, and team members. Multiple project management is about effectively defining and implementing multiple priorities with responsible priority setting and resource allocation within the overall scope of the organization and program plans. Systems management involves effective integration of all previously stated management areas, ensuring that each leader accountable for results is in communication and coordinated action with the others and that projects, plans, and resources fit within the organization's mission, goals, quality standards, and business requirements.

BUILDING A MANAGEMENT SELF-DEVELOPMENT PLAN

After the clinician and mentor have identified skill strengths and gaps within the key areas out-

his or her projected management strengths, limitations, and rank ordering the management skills inventory), a manager can assist the clinician in identifying management strengths and skills gaps. Dialog about the inventory emphasizes a balance of skills that go into management for a wide range of specific positions. A serious deficit in one or more skills areas might lead to problems with successful management, which might require specific prehire training to address deficits or a creative organizational model to account for gaps.

Another way skills may be grouped is as follows:

lined above, the supervisor will begin to assist the clinician in building an MSDP. The plan will clearly identify the targeted result, the actions necessary to achieve the target, and the time frames in which progress will be measured. Clinicians in rehabilitation will be familiar with this process because it does not differ from the process by which treatment or service plans are developed for persons served. Table 14-1 is an example of an MSDP illustrating three of these categories of training.

EVALUATING PROGRESS

The MSDP should cover all areas that the clinician and supervisor mutually agree need strengthening. The plan should include both short- and long-term goals. Progress should be evaluated on an ongoing basis between the clinician and supervisor with at least monthly written reviews. A progress chart such as the one suggested by Umiker (1988, p. 257) may be used. Exhibit 14-2 depicts a sample progress report. It

Table 14-1 Management Self-Development Plan

Category	Behavior/Target Result	Action	Start Date	Finish Date
Self-management	Delegating	1. Review key variables of delegation and accountability with supervisor.	9/30	9/30
	Will hold project accountability; will delegate projects and tasks to produce result on time at criteria for quality	2. Observe supervisor delegating.	10/1	10/15
		3. Role play at supervisor meeting.		10/16
		4. Delegate three tasks by means of techniques rehearsed.	10/20	10/25
		5. Follow-up as planned.	10/25	3/30
Fiscal management	Fiscal report writing	1. Read fiscal reports.	11/10	11/15
	Will write monthly and quarterly financial report with a 95% accuracy with supervisor input	2. Review key characteristics of fiscal report at supervisor meeting.	11/16	11/16
		3. Attend management orientation.	11/20	11/25
		4. Read financial operations manual.	11/25	11/30
		5. Write sample fiscal report and review at supervisor meeting.	11/30	12/5
		6. Prepare quarterly fiscal report with supervisor.	12/6	12/18
Personnel management	Performance appraisals	1. Review personnel policies and procedures manual.	10/5	10/15
	Will write and review appraisals with key reports; appraisals will include target competencies, current status, specific examples of performance, short-term goals, and resources needed	2. Attend management meetings.	10/20	11/25
		3. Review procedure with supervisor at two meetings.	12/5	12/10
		4. Write sample appraisal and review with supervisor.	12/20	1/5
		5. Role play performance appraisal for successful and difficult to supervise staff members.	12/1	1/5
		6. Complete performance appraisals on two staff members.	12/1	1/10
		7. Review appraisal interview and documentation with supervisor.	12/1	1/12

Exhibit 14-2 Management Development Plan: Progress Report

MANAGER NAME: *Joe Smith*

JOB TITLE: *Day Treatment Clinical Services Coordinator: Traumatic Brain Injury*

START DATE: *September 15*

TRAINING COMPLETION DATE: *December 15*

AUDIT DATE: *October 30*

COACH: *Nancy Field*

COMPETENCIES

Key Area: Systems Management

1. Manage staff-to-client ratio to meet clinical outcome, customer service, and budgetary criteria.

BELOW STANDARD				AT STANDARD				ABOVE STANDARD	
1	2	3	4	5	6	7	8	9	10

   STRENGTHS: *Consistently reviews staffing ratio, staff costs to budget targets*

   WEAKNESSES: *Does not consistently make staff adjustments in timely fashion*

   SPECIFIC ACTIONS TO TAKE: *Train in use of week and month projections, explain and model staff scheduling changes*

2. Ensure that all client behavior plans are completed and documented.

BELOW STANDARD				AT STANDARD				ABOVE STANDARD	
1	2	3	4	5	6	7	8	9	10

   STRENGTHS: *Reviews plans with team, makes appropriate suggestions*

   WEAKNESSES: *None*

   SPECIFIC ACTIONS TO TAKE: *None*

NEXT AUDIT DATE:

---

is recommended that progress be measured by both the clinician and the supervisor independently and then compared and discussed at regular supervisory meetings.

THE ROLE OF COACHING, MODELING, AND TRAINING IN DEVELOPING MANAGERS

In addition to tracking progress in management development with a chart such as the one shown in Exhibit 14-2, a supervisory manager who is effective in developing clinicians to take on management responsibilities will use coaching, modeling, ongoing feedback, and direct training as tools for promoting progress. These tools are used to mold and sharpen the skills of future managers.

Coaching

Anyone who has experienced competitive sports through participation or observation knows what coaching is all about. The coach and the player form a partnership committed to the development of the player and optimal performance.

A coach is committed to winning by helping the manager focus on obtaining target results. A coach develops the new manager by doing the following:

- being committed to the manager and verbalizing this commitment
- having a personal stake in the success of the manager
- being willing to take the heat when the manager fails

- being honest and straightforward regarding performance expectations
- being results oriented, not circumstances oriented
- being uncompromising with the details every step of the way
- being committed to the possibility that there are never absolute limits to performance for either the individual or the organization

Modeling

Modeling is when the supervisor demonstrates, through his or her own behavior, skills that the manager in training needs to acquire. There are two kinds of modeling: formal and informal. Formal modeling is when a plan has been written to increase a targeted behavior. For example, the supervisor might say to the manager in training, "I want you to observe how I conduct our upcoming business meeting so that you can begin running these meetings. Watch how I state the purpose, results, measurements, and agenda." In this situation, the effective supervisor will identify specific behaviors that he or she wants to model: "Pay close attention to how I delegate tasks and handle objections. After the meeting, tell me what went well, what was missing, and what you would have done." Formal modeling can be an effective tool in developing a manager when the distinction is made between modeling and emulating. The goal of modeling is to demonstrate or illustrate a skill or process in producing target results. The goal is not to transfer style but content.

Informal modeling is also a powerful tool in developing managers. The old adage, "Do as I say, not as I do," does not carry much weight when one is developing managers. Just as adults who become parents tend to adopt a parenting style modeled after that of their parents, clinicians moving into a management role may adopt a management style similiar to that of their manager. Supervisors therefore should be rigorous in modeling effective management on a daily basis. They should practice what they preach. It is also useful for supervising managers to point out key characteristics of their leadership, management,

and coaching as well as to distinguish target results, approach, style, and variation options for the manager in training to apply.

Education and Training

If one could learn how to be an effective manager by reading a book or taking a course, two things would happen: Businesses would be overcrowded with excellent managers, and management training would become a lucrative business. Although the first event has clearly not happened, the second has. According to Thomas Quick in his recent book *Training Managers So They Can Really Manage* (1991), American corporations will spend approximately $10 billion this year to train their supervisors and managers to manage effectively: "Trainees will sit in classrooms and training courses and listen to multitudes of management theories, concepts, principles, and techniques. But there will be shockingly little learning, considering the enormous investment of money and time" (Quick, 1991, p. 1).

What is the problem with traditional classroom education and training for teaching effective management skills? Is it a waste for health care and rehabilitation organizations to sponsor management training classes or to send their potential managers to a course on management? Quick (1991) points out that the root of the problem is in how adults learn. The traditional education models used in elementary, high school, and college systems are not effective in teaching the adult learner. Three variables must be understood for adult learning to take place as related to management training (Quick, 1991, pp. 2–3): (1) Adult learners must see a reason for learning, one that they consider valuable; (2) management trainees may be unable or unwilling to try applying what was learned in the classroom to the work situation; and (3) feedback and rewards are essential to adult learning and retention.

These three points clearly reveal the value of utilizing an approach to developing managers that is not academically oriented, or classroom based. The MSDP referred to in this chapter incorporates the three principles of adult learning listed above. First, the plan is not initiated unless there has been an agreement between the clinician and the supervisor that developing the clinician's management potential is both their goals. Thus the learner clearly sees the reason and value of learning. Second, the application of the learning is built through the action category of the MSDP (see Table 14-1). There is agreement between supervisor and clinician that action will be taken to build skills and to produce target results. Third, feedback and rewards are built into the plan. Either feedback is scheduled to occur at the next supervisory session, or it occurs immdiately after the action. The reward is explicit: recognition, more responsibility, a promotion and higher salary, and, often more powerfully in the long run, results effectively achieved.

The MSDP is results oriented. It occurs on the job, which reinforces the generalization of the learning. In this way, it is no different from the principles used in effective rehabilitation. The main reason that management training courses fail is the lack of generalization and application of knowledge to the workplace. Identification of weekly and monthly training priorities in combination with supervisor coaching and reinforcement ensures the application of new skills.

MANAGEMENT ORIENTATION

Although developing management skills through classroom instruction has limited effectiveness, an orientation for new management staff plays a valuable role in the health care setting. The purposes of the orientation are to provide the new manager with a statement of the goals and philosophy of the organization, to overview the organization's structure and systems of operation, and to provide a basic overview of the organization's expectation of the manager in the areas of fiscal accountability, personnel management, self-management, leadership, project management, and systems management. These areas were reviewed earlier in the section about how to develop an MSDP.

The management orientation is for orientation, not training. Its primary expectation is not to increase skills; this is done through ongoing training. The goal is educational: to provide an overview of information necessary for the manager to learn about his or her job and about the context in which it will be performed.

The management orientation is for any new manager regardless of his or her experience as a manager with other organizations. Orientation, even if it is provided informally to get management training underway, should occur before the MSDP is constructed between supervisor and manager. It forms a base of knowledge on which management skills can be built. Participation is essential for clinicians such as occupational therapists, physical therapists, speech pathologists, nurses, and other allied health professionals who may have had no business training in their academic preparation. In fact, in some instance, orientation may be used to support selection decisions for a supervisor and potential clinician/manager who may be unsure about a management role. By learning about what is involved in a management position, candidates may better decide whether this type of work is fitting for them.

The management orientation should be provided on a regular basis, depending on the organization's need. The size of the organization and hiring trends will influence the frequency and format of the orientation. Large organizations may offer a class session every 8 to 10 weeks; smaller organizations may find it sufficient to offer a semiannual or quarterly class or less formal orientation procedures that can be accomplished on site with minimal disruption; these may include a series of individual and small group meetings.

Topics to Cover in Management Orientation

Listed below are topics that are often covered in a Management Orientation.

- Overview of the organization
  1. History of the organization
  2. Goals, philosophy, and purpose of the organization
  3. The organization's structure

4. The systems within the organization with which managers interface

5. The organization's standards of conduct for staff

- Personnel management

1. Overview of management's responsibility in personnel management (i.e., clinical supervisor, department head, case manager, senior management)

2. Administrative responsibilities with staff members

3. Improving staff performance through clear and realistic performance expectations

4. Communicating effectively with staff

5. How to give feedback/positive reinforcement, constructive criticism, and discipline

6. The organization's standards for performance appraisals

7. How to develop staff contracts

8. The manager's role in recruitment and hiring

- Fiscal management

1. The manager's role and accountability for fiscal management

2. The organization's fiscal goals

3. Review of the budgetary process

4. How to develop a budget

5. How to manage a budget

6. How to complete financial reports required by the organization

7. Fiscal/operations interaction

- Self-management

1. Knowing your management strengths and limitations

2. Identifying skills gaps and determining how to fill them

3. Organizational skills
   —planning ahead
   —delegating
   —follow-up

4. Problem solving and decision making

5. Time management

6. The role of negotiation in management: How and when to negotiate

- Principles of leadership and management

1. Strategic intent

2. Distinguishing vision, strategy, mission, and tactics

3. Enrolling groups in a vision, mission, or project

4. Identifying and overcoming group barriers to goal achievement

5. How to empower the leadership in groups

6. Breaking through or working with organizational politics

Who Should Teach Management Orientation?

If the organization has a training department, the management orientation will usually be organized and implemented from that department. The most effective training occurs when the training department utilizes managers from the organization to teach the various topics. For example, the organization's most effective fiscal manager may be asked to review the fiscal management materials. The manager who has excellent personnel management skills may be asked to review personnel management. Utilizing successful managers within the organization as teachers enhances the face value of the material being covered. Existing managers will not be teaching from an academic point of view but from a practical, "this is how it really works" perspective. This also helps the new manager meet potential mentors and coaches within the organization. Smaller organizations can provide management orientation by arranging a series of small group discussions with key managers, by phone correspondence, individual meetings, or by videotaped presentations that are followed by group discussions.

Essential Ingredients of Management Orientation and Training

There are three ingredients essential to the success of a management orientation or any training program: (1) It must have senior management support and sponsorship, (2) staff must be given the time away from their daily responsibilities to participate, and (3) links from training to the new manager's specific accountabilities must be clear.

Adequate time must be built into both the trainer's and the trainee's schedule to allow for on-the-job training and supervision to carry out the MSDP. Often, the best laid plans for staff development and training are not fully actualized because adequate time is not allowed for staff participation or because the trainer does not rigorously attend to the details of the training. Because clinicians' time equals money, the rehabilitation organization is sometimes reluctant to commit much time to training efforts. Time not spent in training is often spent in solving problems or results in slowed progress for the organization related to errors, lack of clarity, or lack of knowledge in the new manager.

Of critical importance to the success of management training is senior management support. Clear senior management support communicates openness to learning. Orientation and training should be offered as an opportunity. This invitation, as opposed to obligation, sets a tone of possibility and openness to growth. It creates an opportunity for trainees to contribute to their own growth, to share the depth of their experience, and to maintain competence with new skills development.

STEPS TOWARD DEVELOPING A MANAGER

Table 14-2 outlines the sequence of steps that will be taken to develop consciously and planfully a clinician who will undertake management responsibilities. Table 14-2 demonstrates that becoming an effective manager takes time and preparation; it does not just happen as the result of a promotion. The organization that is willing to take the time and steps necessary for this process will develop a number of managers with unique skills who are well prepared to handle the diverse responsibilities of management.

LEADERSHIP, MANAGEMENT, AND SUPERVISION: THE SAME OR DIFFERENT?

Within management literature, distinctions are often drawn among leadership, management, and supervision. Supervision is typically referred to as overseeing the production of work for a unit of people. In a rehabilitation organization, this might be what a senior clinician does. A physical therapy or occupational therapy supervisor, for example, is the person who supervises a group of clinicians. A shift coordinator and nursing coordinator would also be considered supervisors.

Management is referred to as the process by which multiple units are managed. A manager usually has more than one supervisor reporting to him or her or manages multiple projects. Managers, therefore, often juggle multiple priorities and must manage several activities simultaneously. Within a rehabilitation organization, managers may be department heads, case managers, or program managers.

Leaders are often the people in the organization who are visionary and who have an ability to translate their vision for the direction of the organization in a way that drives the organization's mission. The obvious leaders of an organization are in senior management. They typically have managers who work for them to operationalize the vision and promote the mission of the organization.

There have been long-standing arguments about whether leaders can be managers and managers be leaders. It may be more useful, however, to look at leading, managing, and supervising as distinct skills sets that can be applied in any role. Managing may be referred to as the creation and use of structure to get work done. Supervising may be considered the coaching, directing, and reinforcement of staff producing a result, and leading may be the thought of as seeing and articulating vision and empowering a group to work together toward a goal. Leadership is not a scarce commodity. Good managers evoke and empower leadership from the whole work force to promote team ownership of addressing organizational goals.

Table 14-2 Steps for Developing Managers

Event	Action	Time Frame
Management interest identified	Confirm level of interest by supervisor; management checklist completed	Within 2 weeks
Management characteristics	Supervisor reviews management questionnaire with clinician	Upon initial discussion
Clinician initiates application for management	Clinician completes the self-assessment exercises (e.g., identification of management strengths and limitations and the management skills inventory)	After discussion of questionnaire
Management orientation	Supervisor authorizes attendance at orientation	
Skills inventory complete	Skills level reviewed, strengths and gaps identified	Next supervisor meeting
	Supervisor assigns a project for clinician to manage; gear to skill strength, personal goals, areas of need	Completed in 2 weeks
Trial project completed	Review performance, identify strengths and skills efficiency	Immediately
	Assign project to manage, gear to skills gap	Assigned within 2 weeks
Management orientation completed	Develop MSDP	1–2 weeks
MSDP completed	Follow course of action outlined by plan, monitor closely with regular feedback and frequent training sessions	1 time per week for approximately 3 months

The health care economy is forcing organizations to streamline middle management positions. We cannot afford to have layers of management with rigid boundaries around these three key elements of organizational management. Therefore, supervisors are also managing, managers are leading, and so on. Good supervisors and managers possess leadership abilities. Supervisors, managers, and leaders do not function in a vacuum; they function in the context of their organization and its mission. In rehabilitation today, managers at all levels routinely apply these three skills sets. Rehabilitation managers may be more skilled in one role than another, but they supervise, manage, lead, train, teach, and coach all within any one working day. Therefore, the issue is not whether leaders, managers, and supervisors are more similiar than different in their functions. The issue is that in the 1990s, for an organization to be effective, a manager needs to be able to supervise, lead, manage, teach, and coach. Management principles are similar to those used in individual and group treatment sessions, rehabilitation planning, and achievement of clinical outcomes. New managers who shift their focus of work to staff and organizational activities are more likely to be successful if they are fully educated and trained. Through this process, we are developing not only managers but leaders.

CONCLUSION

As health care and rehabilitation evolve through the 1990s, organizations will feel the impact of managed care and cost control, consumer sophistication, and the drive for measurable outcomes. Quality standards and centers of excellence will be felt by all members of the head injury rehabilitation community. These issues are likely to impact staffing patterns, staff responsibilities, and career advancement within the brain injury rehabilitation industry.

Many professionals will examine management as one option for job security, satisfaction, and growth. It will be useful for organizational leaders strategically to design and implement multiple growth tracks for the most critical resource in rehabilitation: human beings. Advancement into management positions is one of the key options that can help organizations retain staff.

There is a rich literature available to rehabilitationists on management development, organizational development, and training. In this chapter, we have made an effort to touch on key variables relevant to selecting, promoting, and training managers from the clinical staff of allied health professionals. Organizations that choose to invest in developing clinicians into managers will have to design and implement their plans on the basis of organizational resources. Orientation, education, and training, however, will increase the likelihood of success.

The organization may choose to train internally or to use external training resources. Designing and implementing an MSDP and assigning a coach to support the manager in training will reduce the overall time invested in shifting accountabilities to the new manager and will reduce the risk of upset to the new manager, clinical staff, and persons served due to errors and lack of clarity or direction. This approach will also increase the possibility of committed health care professionals applying the strong foundation of clinical experience to the evolving field of traumatic brain injury rehabilitation.

REFERENCES

Bureau of Labor Statistics. (1990). *Projections 2000*. Washington, DC: Office of Economic Growth and Employment Projects.

Quick, T.L. (1991). *Training managers so they can really manage: Confessions of a frustrated trainer*. San Francisco: Jossey-Bass.

Umiker, W.D. (1988). *Management skills for the new health care supervisor*. Gaithersburg, MD: Aspen.

Facility-Based Case Management: Accountability for Outcome, Costs, and Value

15

Danese D. Malkmus

OBJECTIVES

Upon completion of this chapter, the reader will be able to:

1. define the purpose of incorporating management practices into the process of determining and achieving rehabilitation outcomes
2. understand the historical roots of case management
3. specify the accountabilities and functions common to facility-based case management
4. describe guidelines for the selection, training, and retention of facility-based case managers
5. identify generic, consumer-driven, outcome pathway paradigms used in the practice of facility-based case management
6. describe practices employed by facility-based case managers in admission, assessment and evaluation, outcome progression, conferencing, reporting, consumer support, discharge, and follow-up processes

Facility-Based Case Management

THE NEED FOR FACILITY-BASED CASE MANAGEMENT

By definition, rehabilitation programs provide professionally trained and qualified staff to administer assessment, evaluation and service planning, and treatment for service beneficiaries and their families. Staff composition and size may vary according to the organizational mission and areas of outcome that are emphasized. Regardless, within the context of acquired brain injury, the consequent diverse and complex symptoms frequently are addressed through an interdisciplinary team approach.

Internal Management Systems

Inherent within the interdisciplinary team approach is the notion of group consensus as integral to decision making and outcome accountability. The team is empowered, often as an essentially closed, self-driven group, to determine what outcomes will be achieved for a given individual. Service recipients, family members, and financial sponsor representatives may or may not be actively engaged in team membership. Given this consensus approach, accountability for outcome accomplishment, both behavioral and time components, rests on the shoulders of many. Consequently, accountability is widely diffused.

Similarly, rehabilitation programs guide the general operations and practices of their staff through a set of standards articulated in policy and procedure format. It is assumed that, given adequate structure and definition of process, quality service delivery and outcomes will result. This assumption is reinforced by traditional accreditation and quality assessment methodologies, which until recently stressed structure and process rather than outcome and its progression.

External Management Systems

Depending upon the source and type of financial coverage, some form of external oversight or management is likely to be present. It may be prospective, that is to say dependent on the client meeting preadmission criteria or on the particulars of an established contractual relationship between financial sponsor and service provider. It may be retrospective, with reimbursement being dependent on meeting the financial sponsor's criteria after services are delivered and reports are reviewed. It may be concurrent, with oversight and management occurring simultaneously with service delivery. Frequently, it is some combination of these. Direct involvement on behalf of the financial provider may be intensive or virtually nonexistent relative to proactive input and case monitoring. It may be conducted by a professional with extensive experience in brain injury rehabilitation or by one with virtually none. In most cases, quality, defined as excellence in conforming to stated requirements for efficient and effective service delivery and as meeting or exceeding consumer or customer expectations, is of concern to financial providers. Witness their search for centers of excellence to provide the highest quality of services available. They are equally concerned with the rising costs of health care, however. Further, regardless of motivation, philosophy, or manner of benefits management employed, the capability of the program to meet quality standards is key to successful conclusion of a given case and to customer satisfaction.

Single Point Accountability

Essential to ensuring quality, reliable outcome accomplishment, and customer satisfaction is continuous, focused accountability for service delivery practices and their results. Such accountability must extend to all outcomes of service provision. These include the outcomes achieved by the service beneficiary; their costs; the value that the outcomes hold for the client and family; the satisfaction of the client, family, and financial provider; and outcome durability.

Facility-based case management provides a single point of accountability, benefiting both service providers and consumers purchasing or receiving services. As in other case management models it promotes a consumer orientation, balancing data, values, and expectations of all concerned in the process of achieving outcomes and ensuring their durability. Balancing provider and consumer interests on a daily basis also extends to ensuring focused, efficient allocation of resources and management of attendant costs.

Facility-based case management is not a clinical function. It is a management function designed to ensure quality and value through intensive management of data and resources to achieve outcome, cost, and consumer satisfaction objectives. Although not directly revenue producing, effective facility-based case management can reduce or contain costs and can enhance revenues through efficient resource allocation, high outcome reliability, and high consumer satisfaction, resulting in continuing relationships with financial providers.

As previously stated, many service providers have relative equivalence in staffing qualifications, interdisciplinary approaches, standards of practice meeting accreditation and licensing requirements, quality assessment and program evaluation systems, and financial provider interaction requirements. It is the singular accountability and effective management of clinical processes that can distinguish one program from another in terms of quality and excellence. Facility-based case management, at its best, ensures consumer-driven services, effectively managing both clinical services and customer relations to meet consumer needs and expectations.

HISTORICAL ROOTS OF CASE MANAGEMENT

Medical Case Management

Medical case management has provided the general paradigm for facility-based or internal case management models. Its roots were firmly planted in the late 1960s and early 1970s subsequent to increased emphasis upon rehabilitation within the workers compensation and casualty

arenas and passage of the Rehabilitation Act of 1973, the availability of third party financial resources through insurance carriers or self-insured employers, and the failure of the public sector to provide services that resulted in a return to work (Henderson, Bergman, Collard, Souder, & Wallack, 1988). Other influences promoting medical case management systems included pressure placed by employers upon the health insurance industry to contain spiraling premium costs, increasing experimentation with managed care concepts, and data illustrating disproportionate cost influences of relatively few high cost rehabilitation users (Henderson et al., 1988; Moffat, 1991; Papastrat, 1991; Roughan, 1990).

Henderson et al. (1988) define two types of high cost users. The first group includes individuals incurring one episode of treatment for major illness or injury. The second group comprises those with chronic medical conditions resulting in repeated hospitalizations and treatment. Summarizing statistics published between 1982 and 1986, they suggest that 10% of our population accounts for nearly 70% of the total health care expenditures, with the top 5% and 1% being responsible for approximately 50% and 25%, respectively. Key within the high cost, catastrophic illness and injury group is acquired brain injury.

By the 1980s, private sector medical case management was firmly entrenched in the management of high cost cases. At the same time, managed care systems such as health maintenance organizations (HMOs) and preferred provider organizations (PPOs) became the emerging force in private industry's quest to control health care costs.

Although no singular, agreed upon definition of medical case management prevails, it has been defined as a "systematic approach to identifying high cost patients, assessing potential opportunities to coordinate their care, developing treatment plans that improve quality and control costs, and managing patients' outcomes" (Delaney & Acquillina, 1987, p. 31). Capitman, Haskins, and Bernstein (1986) define case management as an "administrative service that directs client movement through a series of phased involvements . . . with the goal of increasing the quality and cost effectiveness of care" (p. 399). Del Togno-Armanasco, Olivas, and Harter (1989) describe it as "a methodology for organizing patient care through an episode of illness so that specific clinical and financial outcomes are achieved within an allotted time frame" (p. 77).

Individualized High Cost Management

Medical case management is distinguished from other practices of benefits administration by the development of customized management plans designed around the needs of the individual client and family identified as high cost on the basis of diagnostic and cost criteria. Representing a cost management strategy, it is directed toward long-term cost containment. Immediate cost savings, however, are achieved through efficient phasing of health and rehabilitation services. Rather than rationing services, medical case management seeks to rationalize a care plan (Henderson et al., 1988) and, in the case of acquired brain injury, to maximize cost differentials related to types and levels of care and services on both short- and long-term bases. As Papastrat (1991) points out, "virtually all well-managed situations share two common factors: appropriate care and reduced costs" (p. 44).

MANAGED CARE SYSTEMS

Managed care describes systems that integrate the financing and delivery of health care services to covered individuals through selected providers. Hughes (1987) indicates that, although the term originally referred to prepaid health care administered within a fixed budget, thus allowing costs to be managed, it now applies to other forms of service delivery and benefits administration.

Managed care systems originated with the advent of HMOs. Rather than paying a predetermined percentage or amount assigned to a specific covered loss, as in traditional indemnified coverage, the HMO assumes both the responsibility and the financial risk for providing a set of specified services during a defined period of

time at a preestablished price. Providers of services share these risks and are incentivized for achieving quality and cost criteria. Common to this approach is the primary care physician, who serves as the gatekeeper or regulator of quality and costs. Service provision is dependent upon gatekeeper authorization.

Hughes (1987) describes four basic HMO models: staff, group, independent practice, and network. A staff model hires physicians individually, paying a salary for services delivered in the HMO facility. In a group model, a set amount per client is paid to a group of physicians to provide a specific range of services. The group determines the compensation and profit sharing for each physician. An independent practice association (IPA) contracts with individual physicians or other service providers who also see patients other than the HMO members. Payment occurs on a modified fee-for-service basis or a capitation basis, wherein, regardless of usage frequency, a per member monthly payment is made in advance of service delivery. A network model describes an IPA consisting of multiple group practices. These pure HMO models have given birth to a number of hybrids and have become more varied in nature as competition among managed care providers has increased.

Friedan and Trasker (1989) describe three hybrid structures of managed care systems. Preferred provider organizations (PPOs), conceived in competitive response to HMOs, are groups of physicians, pharmacists, or medical facilities that contract on a discounted, fee-for-service basis with employers, insurance carriers, or a third party administrator (TPA) to provide services to subscribers, usually at 10% to 20% below usual fees. An increasingly popular hybrid is the point-of-service plan, which is essentially an open-ended HMO or PPO wherein enrollees willing to assume the extra costs may use services outside the network. Another hybrid gaining attention is the exclusive provider organization (EPO). Based upon the PPO structure, EPOs seek effective quality and cost management through selection of a smaller, exclusive number of providers.

All forms of managed care employ a set of tools to approve or deny, monitor, and regulate service delivery usage. This may include explicit provider selection criteria, precertification or preadmission screening, utilization review, and cost-risk sharing incentives. Although the roots of medical case management lie within traditional indemnified and workers' compensation coverage, medical case management is rapidly becoming a primary managed care tool as well (Beresford, 1991; Moffat, 1991). As rehabilitation providers enter contractual relationships as managed care service providers, intimate knowledge of these tools is essential. Also resultant is an increased recognition of the value of internal case management. Like the primary care physician, the facility-based case manager can play an effective gatekeeper role in regulating quality and cost. Efficient movement of service recipients to less costly service delivery modes, focused outcomes and resource allocation resulting in high productivity, and timely service completion are but a few of the mechanisms for managing costs and quality.

FACILITY-BASED CASE MANAGEMENT

To be effective, facility-based case management should operate in concert with the objectives of medical case management and managed care approaches. The facility-based case manager is a consumer surrogate, acting on behalf of service consumers (both direct beneficiaries and their financial sponsors) to achieve negotiated and durable outcomes of value to the consumers, to manage the related costs, and to ensure consumer inclusion and satisfaction with process and outcome. The case manager is not a treater but a professional who integrates clinical experience and management principles into rehabilitation service delivery practices. In fact, the facility-based case manager employs the same practices used by external case managers and other managed care professionals to achieve targeted results efficiently.

The facility-based case manager also must operate in concert with the objectives of the service recipient and the family. In this respect, the case manager performs life events management

under difficult life circumstances that the service recipient would execute if he or she were not faced with the nature and complexities of injury to the brain. Acting as an agent or broker, the case manager contracts for and manages service delivery and outcome achievement on behalf of service beneficiaries.

Finally, the facility-based case manager must integrate the goals and objectives of rehabilitation professionals with those of consumers. Aligning various sets of values, biases, and expectations into appropriate outcome objectives and ensuring a timely, successful conclusion at the least cost represent the essence of facility-based case management.

CASE MANAGEMENT FUNCTIONS

Variations

The specific functions performed by facility-based case managers vary considerably in brain injury rehabilitation. In part, this is related to the youth of internal case management and its ongoing evolution. It also is related to the diversity of settings and services employed, philosophical differences, organizational needs, staffing issues, and variance in reimbursement sources (Dixon, Goll, & Stanton, 1988; Jaffe, 1991).

There are two areas of significant variance: cost management, and direction and coordination of services. These two variances are not merely interwoven; they cannot be separated. Typically, in medical settings physicians provide direction and oversight, and the case manager acts as payer liaison. In nonmedical settings, the case manager often is the primary person driving outcome and its progression, reporting to a nonphysician, clinical director. In small programs, or in the case of a single clinical service provider such as a neuropsychologist or speech-language pathologist, the clinical director or clinician also may act as case manager.

When accountability for process, costs, and results is diffused, costs cannot be regulated. Unless a gatekeeper approach is employed and an individual is identified to regulate costs, effective cost management will not occur. A primary benefit of internal case management lies in the potential for cost management, which sets the stage for enhanced productivity and reliable outcome achievement. As Wulff (1991), a pioneer in internal case management, points out, "the empowered case manager is capable of improving productivity or . . . outcome without increase in cost or decreased cost without decrease in delivery outcome" (p. 127). The case manager can be central to cost savings and satisfactory achievement of results within the context of fixed budgets and fixed price contractual agreements with funding sponsors. For example, Wulff (1991) indicates, given an annual salary of $40,000.00 and a caseload of 8 persons, the per day case manager labor cost is $26.00. Increasing the caseload to 10 persons would reduce the labor cost to $20.80 per day. In either case, the potential savings to service provider and financial sponsor far outweigh the labor costs.

Commonalities

In general, the following functions are representative of those that are likely to be performed in acquired brain injury rehabilitation settings:

- assurance of successful, safe admission of the service recipient into the program
- orientation of the client, family, and financial provider to the program setting and the individualized service program
- assurance of staff responsiveness to client rights, individual preferences, and needs
- consumer-driven direction and coordination of the interdisciplinary team effort in assessment and development of outcome objectives, treatment goals, and an integrated service plan that efficiently allocates resources for effective, timely goal attainment and cost management and that ensures outcomes of high utility and value for consumers
- direction and coordination of interdisciplinary team conferencing to monitor effectiveness and efficiency of the implemented service plan on behalf of the service consumers

- assurance of appropriate documentation of the service plan and outcome progression
- maintenance of effective and timely communication among and between service consumers and service providers
- protection and preservation of funding for successful completion of current outcome objectives and anticipated future service needs
- direction and coordination of discharge planning, resource development, and effective transition of the service beneficiary into the next setting
- strengthening of family capabilities through the sharing of case management practices and tools
- development and implementation of individually designed postservices follow-up to support outcome durability
- accomplishment of targeted functional outcomes within targeted time frames (outcome reliability)
- assurance of consumer satisfaction with both process and outcomes

SELECTION AND TRAINING

Qualifications

In response to workers compensation needs, medical case management traditionally has been performed by nurses, with vocational counselors completing the process when reemployment objectives have been present. Within the context of rehabilitation of persons with acquired brain injury, the internal case manager is required to manage the complexities of multiple and diverse symptoms and professional disciplines, integrating experience, knowledge, data, and resources to achieve negotiated objectives and consumer satisfaction. The facility-based case manager is a generalist whose specific discipline is of little real consequence. Of considerable consequence, however, are personal characteristics and skills.

Characteristics

The facility-based case manager is a graduate of an accredited, professional training program in a medical or allied health field who holds current license, registration, or certification within the given discipline or within the field of case management. Job performance entails interfacing with a vast number of individuals of various backgrounds and interests. These interfaces can be viewed as a resource pool to be employed in managing and achieving outcomes. It is essential that the case manager possess a working knowledge of a substantial number of professional and community settings, and of persons within them, that can serve as resource options.

The effective case manager likes to solve problems, is capable of convincing and motivating others, and likes to make things happen. Essential is the ability to communicate a professional in-charge stance and to engender trust and confidence from professional, community, and consumer groups alike. Requisite is the maturity to stand apart from the interdisciplinary clinical team and to act as a manager for service consumers. A level of maturity also is needed for ego-free, consumer-centered resource management that uses and credits others and their solutions in accomplishing objectives.

Knowledge and Skills

According to Roughan (1990), performance of case management functions demands

> . . . knowledge of the coverage area (workers' compensation, health, etc.), an idea of what constitutes appropriate treatment, and knowledge of the common complications associated with a specific diagnosis and their impact on the recovery process. You must then be able to articulate this information to the appropriate parties, and to negotiate support for a plan that optimizes outcome while managing costs. (p. 45)

The diversity and complexity of issues and resources central to acquired brain injury require an intimate knowledge of brain injury and clinical management options so that internal case management functions can be performed successfully. It is unlikely that one can acquire sufficient knowledge with less than several

years of experience as a practicing clinician in brain injury rehabilitation. This is especially important in light of all else that is to be learned from the outset of job performance.

At the very least, one must possess sufficient knowledge of all involved disciplines so that one can ask the right questions and have confidence in judging what a specific intervention is targeting, in evaluating other means of efficiently addressing a problem and the intended outcome, and in determining reasonable time frames for achieving subcomponents of the outcome and the outcome as a whole. Technical knowledge of rehabilitation service continuums and family systems theory and the ability to interpret laboratory and diagnostic reports are necessary. Knowledge of reimbursement systems is helpful, but the basics can be learned quickly. In reality, each payer representative is a unique customer whose obligation, exposure, needs, and interests must be thoroughly explored.

Management skills needed to perform internal case management functions include strong verbal negotiation capabilities for aligning consumer and professional expectations; for adequately representing consumers in contracting for services, outcomes, and time frames; for preserving or extending funding; for resolving conflicts; and the like. Analytical thinking, cost consciousness, and the ability to integrate vast numbers of data are essential to determining desirable and useful outcomes, designing efficient outcome pathways, phasing and allocating resources, monitoring intervention results, and performing cost-benefit analyses. Prioritization capability is important not only to resource allocation and the staging of outcome goals and objectives but also to the use of time on a daily basis. Flexibility, focus, and perseverance are crucial to shifting activity priorities and meeting nonnegotiable or important deadlines. Although the concept of time management is fallacious, because time itself cannot be managed, effective activity management is essential. The facility-based case manager is in a position of constantly reprioritizing and balancing activities. Finally, it must be stressed that the function is not one of simply managing communications and writing reports. The facility-based case manager must be able to maintain focus upon the dynamics of outcome, process, and cost management.

Training and Support

Given a carefully constructed, well developed case management system, identified and effective selection guidelines, adequate training, and ongoing support systems, facility-based case management can be a powerful tool in managing outcomes and their costs. Basic and ongoing training, incorporating clearly defined objectives with related learning materials and course work, should be standard practice for all organizations employing case managers. Objectives should relate to the capabilities and functions that are identified as critical to practices within the specific rehabilitation setting. Although functions may vary across settings, a number of generic competencies and training needs exist (Table 15-1).

Supplemental educational support might include management training to develop an effective personal management style and to ease the shift from a clinician to a manager role. Another useful support is a glossary of terms covering organizational, legal, financial sponsor, and disability-specific terminology. Resource manuals facilitating access to resources, benefits, and alternative care and treatment settings will minimize research time.

The delivery of training may be the responsibility of one or more persons. Training in the principles, practices, and tools of internal case management may be partially accomplished by using well designed self-instruction materials. These can be useful for several reasons. Once implemented, the time-cost factors related to the individual(s) who might otherwise teach the new case manager are minimized. Training is not dependent upon availability or skill of staff members. When a self-instruction methodology is used, identical expectations and content are presented to each new learner. Self-instruction also places responsibility for learning upon the learner. To ensure satisfactory transfer of knowledge, each learning unit should begin with a set of learner objectives specific to the critical competencies to be developed. The educational material relevant to learner objectives and basic

competencies should follow, the unit concluding with a test that allows the learner to determine knowledge status immediately. Whenever possible, learning and testing should entail practical applications of the information to be learned, incorporating hypothetical cases and situations.

Training in the application of principles and practices should occur simultaneously through the assignment of an on-site mentor for a specified period of time. Other staff should be identified as having strengths in one or more areas to assist new and seasoned case managers, whether within or outside the practice setting.

Supports and Effective Use of Time

Appropriate clerical support will prevent time spent in front of a copy machine or performing other activities that take time away from the important tasks of planning and managing. In using time as a critical resource, it is essential that the case manager recognize that the most effective managers do not operate behind closed doors in an office. It is important to know the service recipient, the family, and the financial sponsor intimately, as well as all environmental influences affecting outcome progression. Such knowledge must be obtained by spending time in the various settings in which the service recipient is and will be involved and by ensuring formal meeting time on a routine, periodic basis with all consumers. Often, with the multitude of demands inherent in the position, the new case manager tends to overschedule, filling in each hour in the appointment book with meetings, paper tasks, and other activities and excluding time in treatment, residential, and community settings. When the telephone rings, or when a service recipient or family encounters unexpected difficulty, the case manager must respond. Consequently, frustration occurs as the case manager falls behind with what was an unrealistic schedule to begin with. Weekly organizing, by prioritizing important goals to accomplish in a given week and allowing ample unscheduled time for people, will permit the daily adapting needed for responding to unanticipated events, relationships, and experiences in a meaningful and effective way (Covey, 1989).

Table 15-1 Facility-Based Case Management Core Training

Competency Area	Learner Content Units
Service provider organization	Organizational mission and philosophy Management and clinical systems Role and functions of case management
Acquired brain injury	Causes, consequences, and interventions Rehabilitation options and cost alternatives
Reimbursement systems	Private and public sector systems External case management Third party administrator organizations Review and appeal processes
Family system impact	Family systems theory Family response to catastrophic injury Family training in disability management
Customer relations	Consumers and sponsors as customers Assessment of consumer expectations for outcome, quality, and value Alignment of consumer expectations
Consumer rights and benefits	Legal rights of the catastrophically injured Community benefits and counsel Support and advocacy organizations
Risk management	Administrative and clinical liability Documenting risk: Risk-benefit analyses Managing risk

Negotiation	Negotiation skills training
	    Group dynamics and leadership role
	    Staff negotiations
	    Consumer/funding sponsor negotiations

Outcome pathways designs	Data acquisition, analysis, and planning Pathway design and resource allocation Consumer inclusion

Quality management	Principles of quality management
	    Standards of practice
	    Customer satisfaction
	    Cost and quality relationships
	    Quality measurement and usage

Report generation	Report formatting and timing
	Report composition
	    Defensibility, auditability, usability, and feasibility
	    Protecting and preserving funding
	    Language and type of funding

Retention

Although the demands upon the facility-based case manager are considerable, they usually are balanced by the excitement of the opportunity to have a profound impact on outcomes, costs, and, ultimately, the life of one or more persons in a positive and satisfactory way. Staff retention depends upon other factors as well. The author surveyed a 25-person case management staff across six program sites. The following were cited as critical factors influencing retention:

- understanding, acceptance, and support of the case management model by clinical staff
- empowerment within the role as a full member of the program management team
- a manageable case load that supports case management objectives
- case load variation rather than specialization

- a job ladder that recognizes enhanced competencies and gives rites of passage for seniority and expertise and opportunity for growth as a manager
- opportunity for participating in activities, projects, and contributions other than routine functions
- reward for meeting outcome and cost management goals, quality standards, and other relevant job performance criteria

ADOPTING A CONCEPTUAL FRAMEWORK

The manner in which outcomes are conceptualized, defined, and accomplished is directly related to the conceptual framework that underlies and supports service delivery. The concept of interdependence is used deliberately in this chapter because it is key to the theme of consumer-driven service delivery. Condeluci (1991) presents an insightful, persuasive analysis of conceptual paradigms that shape existing service delivery systems in rehabilitation. He suggests that independence, generally conceded to be the optimal outcome state by rehabilitation professionals, is but a foundation for the higher, more satisfying objectives of interdependence. As described by Condeluci (1991), use of an interdependence paradigm as a philosophical framework permits a focus upon capacities that not only include skills but define interests, preferences, attributes, and the like. It stresses the importance of relationships beyond the medical and rehabilitation network, focusing upon connectedness with community for service beneficiaries and families. It also views support building as being as important as skills building. Rather than limiting a given person on the basis of the level of skills achieved, the interdependence paradigm integrates community-based supports into the portrait of outcome. The burden, so to speak, no longer rests upon the client alone but is shifted to what ideally is a partnership between service recipient and case manager. Thus the basis for interdependence is established, as is the foundation for achieving an

outcome that is a balance of skills, environments, relationships, and supports.

Finally, the paradigm succeeds in promoting these ideals through consumer empowerment. The notions of consumer rights and consumer control are brought to bear by assuming consumer competency for defining both problems of personal significance and acceptable outcomes of utility and value. This paradigm can serve as a powerful base for shaping both outcome and process, including how outcome is defined in general and how it is individually described for each service beneficiary.

A GENERIC OUTCOME MODEL

Accomplishment of case management accountabilities is facilitated by a generic model illustrating the outcome pathway common to all persons served by the program. In essence, the model describes the set of key actions or activities initiated by the case manager from admission to discharge. A generic or consistent model also supports process and outcome monitoring and identification of best practices for achievement of specific clinical and consumer goals.

Service Delivery Model

The generic client outcome pathway (Figure 15-1) identifies a consistent process for achieving behavioral outcomes for all service recipients. Upon a client's admission into the clinical program, assessment and evaluation of results occur via acquisition of a standard minimum database. Assessment and reporting of findings may be comprehensive, making use of the entire set of database categories and assessment methodologies. When length of stay is quite limited, however, an abbreviated database, focused assessment, and correlated report of findings may be the best use of service recipient and staff time. Determination of comprehensive or focused assessment to build the requisite database for treatment and accomplishment of useful, functional outcomes is based upon factors such as preadmission agreement with one or more

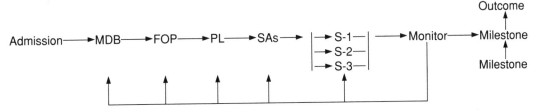

Figure 15-1 Generic client outcome pathway. MDB, minimum database; FOP, functional outcome projection; PL, problem list; SAs, service agreements; S-1, S-2, S-3, services implemented.

consumers, length of stay or dollar limits, specific reimbursable services, and the like.

The case manager uses the database gained from clinical assessment, along with historical and current data regarding personal, familial, social, community, and environmental systems, expressed interests and expectations of all consumers and service providers, and knowledge of funding parameters, to construct a profile of client status, a functional outcome projection, and a problem list. The problem list serves as the basis for setting treatment goals. It is based upon only those problems that, when resolved as specified, permit achievement of the functional outcome projection, not all problems uncovered by assessment. For example, if the service recipient experiences vocational problems but time or reimbursement factors do not permit intervention and achievement of vocational objectives, the problems are noted in an evaluation report but not on the active problem list. Next, one or more milestones signifying major achievements, or changes in status along the pathway to outcome, are defined. Service delivery is then designed for milestone accomplishment. Additional information regarding the design of individual pathways is discussed later in this chapter.

The case manager, acting as an agent or broker on behalf of the service recipient, next contracts with individual clinical staff for specific outcomes that are components of the next milestone to be reached. It is important to note that the contract is for an outcome, not a specific service, treatment modality, or discipline (e.g., physical therapy). It means agreeing upon what the result will be, such as safe ambulation at normal speed without equipment on even and uneven

surfaces, rather than gait training, strengthening, or physical therapy. The service agreement (Exhibit 15-1) is signed before services are initiated. It features a clear statement of the outcome or the expected result of services, the time frame allowed for accomplishment, and checkpoints to be used by the case manager for monitoring outcome progression and reliability in meeting goals and time frames. The process supports accountability, with monitoring occurring continuously until an outcome is achieved.

Service Model

The generic customer service pathway (Figure 15-2) is a model for achievement of service outcomes identified by each consumer group related to a given case. It illustrates the set of actions taken by the case manager for ensuring that consumer needs are defined and met and that customer satisfaction is optimal.

Upon admission of the service recipient, the case manager ensures not only that efficient assessment of client capabilities is completed but that the components of customer satisfaction are equally addressed. Whereas the generic client outcome pathway (Figure 15-1) provides a model for achievement of client-specific behavioral outcomes, the generic customer service pathway describes how service outcomes of importance and value to the client, the family, and the financial sponsor are orchestrated. The case manager first builds a customer service database, assessing needs through structured interaction with each consumer. An essentially equivalent set of questions is answered by each

Exhibit 15-1 Sample Service Agreement

Agreement for Goal Accomplishment

Client: _____ Client Number: _____

Case Manager: _____ Database Category: _____

I. **Pre-Treatment Status** (baseline description of specific behaviors to be addressed in treatment):

_____

_____

II. **Outcome Goal and Criteria** (specific behavior(s) to be achieved, including measurement dimensions and period of time behavior must occur for goal to be met):

_____

_____

III. **Methodology** (summary of methods/approach to be used):

_____

_____

IV. **Time Frames:**

Services will begin on:_____ Services will be completed on:_____

V. **Checkpoints** (time and means of confirming client is progressing toward outcome goal within stated time frame):

Date	Target State to Observe for	On-Course	Off-Course
_____	_____	_____	_____
_____	_____	_____	_____
_____	_____	_____	_____

VI. **Adjustments to Outcome Goal and/or Time Frame** (based on new data or off-course status):

Change		Date
_____		_____
_____		_____

VI. **Status Achieved** (description of outcome):

_____

_____

Status Code: _____ Goal Met _____ Goal Not Met _____ Goal Terminated

Date Status Achieved:_____

VIII.

_____   _____
Signature of Responsible Professional   Signature of Client or Representative

_____   _____
Signature of Clinical Case Manager   Date of Proposal Agreement

Courtesy of Learning Services Corporation, Londonderry, New Hampshire, 1990. Adapted with permission.

---

consumer, allowing the case manager to identify discrepancies in interests, expectations, and priorities among consumers and between consumers and the interdisciplinary team. From the database, the case manager develops a customer need list, which is prescriptive and culminates in a service plan that is based upon the customer service outcomes to be achieved. As in the client outcome pathway, the service plan is imple-mented, with the case manager monitoring consumer satisfaction and making any necessary adjustments until time of discharge.

Pathway Integration

The completed paradigm for outcome achievement is one that integrates the generic client outcome and customer service pathways

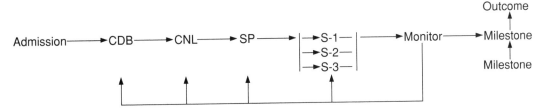

Figure 15-2 Generic customer service pathway. CDB, customer database; CNL, customer needs list; SP, service plan; S-1, S-2, S-3, service plans implemented.

into a single model of discrete activities and processes, bringing equal focus upon the functional and behavioral outcomes achieved by the client and the lasting perceptions that consumers have regarding quality, utility, value, and satisfaction with process and outcome (Figure 15-3). Through unification and analysis of clinical and consumer-specific data, the case manager may creatively individualize the pathway and apply resources efficiently in progressing from milestone to milestone.

ADMISSION PLANNING AND ENTRY

Managing Risk

The facility-based case manager is responsible for ensuring the quality of the admission to the service program. This includes ensuring the safety, health, and well being of the entering client and establishing the appropriate tone for successful progression through the rehabilitation process. Although by nature rehabilitation is a risk business, the greatest risk exists at the time of admission. This is when the least information regarding the client and other consumers is known by the clinical staff. It also is when the client, family, and financial sponsor know little of the program and staff and are often apprehensive. Risks threatening successful admission and completion of the intended clinical program include the following:

- client elopement and unplanned discharge
- the physical safety of the client and others
- the physical health of the client
- the mental health of the client or a family member

- apprehension, confusion, or dissatisfaction felt by one or more consumers

The case manager can best avert these risks through proactive risk analysis and development of a risk management plan before the admission. This is dependent upon acquisition of pertinent data through a thorough preadmission assessment and evaluation.

Preadmission Data Requirements

In addition to demographic data normally acquired before client admission and a global screening evaluation of client mobility, activities of daily living status, vision, hearing, cognition, and communication, it is vital that potential risks be identified, documented, and addressed. General areas for risk data collection include the following:

- summary of injury and significant consequences, including injuries not related to the primary diagnosis, health problems, and psychiatric sequelae
- physical safety, including problems with impulsivity, wandering, mobility, seizures, medication levels, medical conditions, swallowing status, allergic reactions, skin condition, continence, and so forth
- mental status and behavior, including evidence of depression, suicidal ideation, paranoia, denial, hypersexuality, substance abuse, self-injurious behaviors, fire setting or other destructive acts, verbal or physical aggression, noncompliance, and management of emotions in general

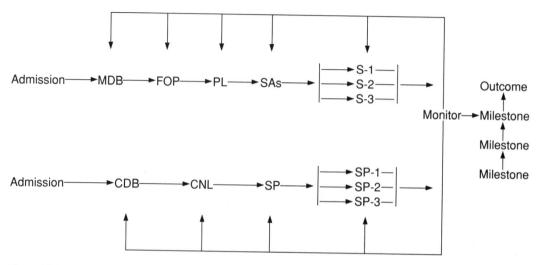

Figure 15-3 Integrated, consumer-driven outcome pathway. The process is iterative. As additional data are acquired and monitoring ensues, resultant adjustments are made. MDB, minimum database; FOP, functional outcome projection; PL, problem list; SAs, service agreements; S-1, S-2, S-3, services implemented; CDB, customer database; CNL, customer needs list; SP, service plan, SP-1, SP-2, SP-3, service plan implemented.

- financial influences upon client-family participation (e.g., a pending or awarded financial settlement)
- consumer expectations for services and their outcomes
- special needs or requirements, including evaluations or consultations beyond those usually provided, previously scheduled outside appointments, special care needs, equipment owned or needed to be ordered, dietary needs, guardianship status, and emotional support needs of the client
- the key family member or other significant family members, their knowledge of acquired brain injury and rehabilitation, cultural issues and needs, concerns regarding admission, anticipated involvement, and emotional support needs
- financial sponsor data, including the knowledge base and experience of the representative, type of funding, contractual agreement with the payer, specific obligation to the insured, ancillary services of the financial provider, precertification requirements, documentation and billing requirements, funding review schedule, length of stay or dollar limits, and types and frequency of contacts desired

DATA ANALYSIS AND PLANNING

Interim Management Strategies

Once the preadmission data are obtained, the case manager needs to perform a thorough review and analysis to identify potential risks and their magnitude to develop an interim management plan to address admission, assessment, and evaluation processes. Risk analysis should pertain to those issues holding the potential to interfere with successful admission, program compliance, and program completion. Once potential risks and their magnitude are identified, the case manager develops and documents an admission risk management plan in conjunction with the interdisciplinary team. Thereafter, risk and its management should be assessed and documented continuously. This includes those risks inherent in activities in which the client may engage while progressing through the program toward greater independence, client resistance to safety precautions, and the like. Use of a risk-benefit analysis format to document responsible consideration and decisions protects the service provider while permitting the recipient the dignity of risk and the potential for accomplishment.

When evidence of self-management problems is identified, such as aggression or noncompliance, or when mental health deterioration is noted, it is advantageous to develop proactive management strategies that support development of a solid foundation for successful outcome achievement. Data may be needed in addition to those normally obtained before admission. These may include behavioral parameters such as the type of behavior exhibited; its frequency, intensity, and duration; precedents and antecedents; and so forth. Previously applied management strategies used by both family members and professionals, and their success, should be determined. Review and recommendations for management by a member of the psychology staff should follow. Although the strategies may be based on minimal, indirect evidence, such proactive practices will ensure that an appropriate tone is established for participation and that the problems are not unattended. Once admission occurs and assessment begins to yield additional data, strategies may be modified and a more sophisticated approach devised.

Preadmission Conference

Before admission, the case manager should conduct a preadmission meeting with the interdisciplinary team. Having reviewed the preadmission data in detail, the case manager can present a snapshot profile of each consumer and his or her needs. The objectives of the conference are as follows:

- to confirm the admission and concurrent arrangements
- to develop an interim management plan until assessment and evaluation are completed
- to develop an appropriate assessment plan and schedule
- to ensure an optimal admission that supports the well being of all consumers and efficient progression toward successful outcomes

- to ensure occurrence of consumer-driven service delivery

During the meeting, the case manager should confirm the date and anticipated time of admission; the family members or others who will be present; special arrangements, such as meals or lodging for the family; and medication, dietary, and equipment needs. Other special requests or needs should be brought to the attention of the team as well. These may include such items as telephone calls, legal representation, and the like. Development of an interim management plan to address risk management and known symptoms requiring immediate intervention should culminate in assignment of responsibility for each need to a member of the team.

The case manager should come to the meeting with an assessment plan. On the basis of the presenting problems, the interests and expectations of the client and family, the obligations and interests of the financial sponsor, and known funding and reimbursement parameters, the case manager should specify the database that needs to be compiled from the assessment. If the client has but 45 days of funding, assessment must be accomplished efficiently and be pertinent to salient functional outcomes that can be accomplished within a 45-day time frame. Further, if a specific discipline or treatment modality is not reimbursable, assessment within that categorical area may be unwarranted. A focused assessment in keeping with parameters for all involved consumers, related to attainable functional outcomes of value and importance to the consumers, and for which outcome justifies cost will benefit consumers and ensure productive use of staff and client time. Given knowledge of the client's health, emotional status, endurance, and assessment needs, an individualized schedule for the first week should be established before admission to ensure productive, efficient use of time from the onset of admission.

Admission

As the professional accountable for the safe and successful entry of the client into the program, the case manager should conduct the actual admission. Regardless of the time of arrival or day of the week, the case manager should greet the arriving client and family, who are likely to be apprehensive and vulnerable at this time. Whenever possible, it also is helpful to contact consumers by telephone before admission to explain what will occur or, should they tour the program before admission, to set aside time to meet and discuss admission and consumer concerns.

Admission is a critical point for all invested in client progression and outcome. A successful admission can set the appropriate tone for what will follow by engendering consumer trust, dispelling apprehensions and discomfort, and creating an atmosphere of hope, promise, and support. It is important that the case manager immediately cultivate a relationship with the client and family as their advocate and agent and that the role is well understood. Of major significance is the review and explanation of client rights, the general guidelines and expectations for all clients, and interactive discussion of assessment and the appointment schedule. All three areas are crucial to providing predictability and consumer empowerment. The last allows consumers to feel in control of their person and destiny, provides assurance of inclusion in the planning and evaluation of services and outcomes, and may prevent a premature discharge. It also sets the stage for a collaborative rehabilitation process that results in empowerment, self-esteem, and the creation of outcomes and supports of value to the consumer.

It is equally important to view admission as a vital point in the program's relationship with the financial sponsor. Although preadmission data may yield sufficient information regarding the minimum needs and expectations of the sponsor, it is quite possible that the case manager will be relating to another person. Regardless, it is vital to confirm the needs, expectations, and financial obligation of the sponsor and to advise the representative of the admission and status of the client and family. A telephone call within 24 hours of admission and subsequent written confirmation of admission, confirmation of individualized financial sponsor needs to be met, the date of the first planning conference, and the schedule of written reports to be generated will support a positive, collaborative relationship.

INDIVIDUALIZED CUSTOMER SERVICE PATHWAY

Upon admission, the case manager should begin the consumer data collection that initiates development of an individualized customer service pathway. This may be accomplished by developing a database that systematically addresses expressed needs across equivalent service categories for client, family, and financial sponsor. Subsequently, the service plan serves as a proactive tool for ensuring consumer satisfaction, preservation of existing funding, negotiation for other appropriate services and their funding, and completion of the intended program.

Table 15-2 provides an overview of topical areas for formulating a questionnaire for data gathering. Once the data are collected, the case manager assesses the data, determines significant discrepancies among consumers or between consumers and staff, develops a service plan to meet the service needs of each consumer and to reduce existing discrepancies in expectations, communicates the service plan to the interdisciplinary team, implements the plan, and monitors consumer satisfaction on the basis of the needs list and service plan at least monthly. The database, needs list, and plan also may be used for measuring satisfaction upon discharge and later follow-up and may be incorporated into the program evaluation system.

INDIVIDUALIZED CLIENT OUTCOME PATHWAY

Integrating and Balancing Interests

The facility-based case manager assumes an integrative function in ensuring that balanced professional and consumer assessment data are interwoven into a set of consumer-relevant, functional outcome objectives and treatment goals. In structuring the assessment process and

Table 15-2 Consumer Database: Service Plan Components

Financial Sponsor	Family	Client

Contractual relationship with claimant
  Financial/legal exposure
  Interpretation of obligation in terms of program
  Review of process, frequency, recourse
	Contractual relationship with sponsor
	  Understanding of contractual exposure
	  Understanding of specific obligation in terms of program
	  Satisfaction level
		Contractual relationship with sponsor
		  Understanding of contractual exposure
		  Understanding of specific obligation in terms of program
		  Satisfaction level

Clinical program expectations
  Behavioral outcomes
  Treatment services
  Length of stay
  Special needs
	Clinical program expectations
	  Behavioral outcomes
	  Treatment services
	  Length of stay
	  Special needs
		Clinical program expectations
		  Behavioral outcomes
		  Treatment services
		  Length of stay
		  Special needs

Service expectations
  Informational needs
  Use of reports for supporting funding
  Language to use/avoid
  Telephone contacts
  Meetings, conferences, agendas
  Special needs
	Service expectations
	  Informational needs
	  Progress reporting
	  Telephone contacts
	  Meetings, conferences, agendas
	  Education and training
	  Special needs
		Service expectations
		  Informational needs
		  Progress reporting
		  Meetings, conferences, agendas
		  Case manager contact
		  Special needs

Satisfaction
  Perceived disability/burden rating*
  Definition of reduced burden
  Definition of satisfaction
  Definition of value and high value
  Service or supports for added value
  Concerns
	Satisfaction
	  Perceived burden self-rating*
	  Definition of reduced burden
	  Definition of satisfaction
	  Definition of value and high value
	  Service or supports for added value
	  Concerns
		Satisfaction
		  Perceived disability self-rating*
		  Definition of reduced disability
		  Definition of satisfaction
		  Definition of value and high value
		  Service or supports for added value
		  Concerns

*Use of a 7-point scale for rating effects of disability and subsequent perception of burden felt by the consumer.

the subsequent use of assessment data in planning client and service outcomes, it may be useful to remind all involved of the totality of data needed for appropriate decision making and of the value of consumer relevancy.

The case manager must ensure that client outcome planning incorporates analysis of the following:

- professionally obtained assessment data defining key problems interfering with achievable client or family states and potentially resolvable through intervention or support

- environments and community relationships in which the client is likely to function and their inherent behavioral requirements

- consumer values, interests, expectancies, and priorities

- the acceptability and value that each potential outcome may have for each consumer

- available funding, definition of reimbursable services, allowable length of stay for outcome accomplishment, and supports within the community system available to the client and family

- cost-benefit of each potential outcome and cost-outcome alternatives both present and future

Consumer Relevancy

In reality, the results of the rehabilitation effort may be viewed as a product (albeit a behavioral, human outcome). Like any other product that a consumer might purchase, it should hold both value and utility for the consumer. It also should be durable. Each member of the interdisciplinary team necessarily brings his or her own beliefs, values, training, experience, and biases to the outcome planning process. The speech-language therapist truly believes that the most human trait and requisite skill constituting quality of life is communication. The occupational therapist believes strongly in the dignity of independent performance of activities of daily living. Examples could be cited for each professional participating on the team. If the client determines that the effort expended for connected, coherent verbalization fails to yield a better result than a telegrammatic but effortless response, however, what will the probable outcome and its durability be? Similarly, if the client achieves independent dressing but requires several hours to dress, and if the client and family seek other uses of that time, what point is there in pursuing that outcome when it has no value or usefulness for the consumer? Outcome planning should begin by asking, "Whose outcome is it?" Effective outcome planning incorporates the consumers who purchase and use the products. They should be informed of the results of assessment and of all parameters used in evaluating results and planning outcomes and should be included in the process of designing the products with which they will go away. It also should be recognized that consumers have the right to negotiate, renegotiate, and refuse components of the outcome and the processes by which they are achieved.

In acting on behalf of the consumers, the case manager needs to ensure not only balanced data and consumer inclusion in outcome planning but also that clinical staff receive support in dealing with rejection of proposed goals and objectives. It is likely that clinicians may encounter ethical dilemmas from time to time within a consumer-driven rehabilitation culture. Each clinician is a primary resource whom the case manager uses to achieve client outcomes. A wise case manager will be sensitive to clinician conflict, provide support, encourage creativity and risk taking, and assist staff members in separating self-worth from consumer acceptability issues.

Cost Influences

Outcome planning also must address the best use of the monies available to the service recipient. In accepting accountability for costs, the case manager should work within a fixed budget with each case. It is helpful, and often eye-opening, to work with real dollar figures to project costs in relationship to specific outcomes. Responsible planning should include cost-benefit analysis but must weigh benefits according to the total value an outcome has for all consumers per individual case. Consideration needs to be given not only to alternative means of allocating time and resources but also to the future needs of the service beneficiary and their funding. Given limited time and comprehensive needs, the case manager may focus upon those problems that cannot be resolved in other, postdischarge settings. In other cases, outcome expectations and the proposed time-dollar commitment may be reduced to preserve funding for future needs. In all cases, the case manager must explore and determine the most efficient route to outcome achievement, ensuring that services are planned and sequenced for high productivity and timely outcome achievement.

Functional Outcome Projection

Integral to outcome planning and the development of individualized outcome pathways is the functional outcome projection. This describes in lay terms precisely how the client will live, the environments and settings of interdependency, what the client will do in those settings, and what supports will be in place to promote optimal client, family, and community interdependence and outcome durability. Although written by the case manager, the functional outcome projection is formulated in concert with the clinical staff after their assessment.

The functional outcome projection is a descriptive tool for projecting outcome in functional terms on the basis of an understanding of the service beneficiary, the family, the community, and financial sponsorship. Consequently, it serves as the basis for functional goal setting. In illustrating postdischarge status, or how the client and family will be connected to one another and the community, the following may serve as categorical headings for subsequent description:

- living setting and supports
- personal daily need satisfaction and supports
- productive activity and supports
- family and community relationships

The functional outcome projection also meets an important need of the financial sponsor. A survey of 50 financial provider representatives, including medical case managers, claims adjusters, and claims managers from the private and public sectors, was conducted by Jones and Evans (1991) to investigate what financial sponsors consider important clinical and service outcomes. The highest ranked service, or provider outcome, was early prediction of expected outcomes. Ranked second and third, respectively, were reliability in achieving projected outcomes and outcome durability.

In illustrating postdischarge client and family life, the case manager has provided the financial sponsor a key for estimating future costs. Consequently, appropriate cash reserves may be set in anticipation of known needs and supports covered by contractual obligation. By attaching costs to outcome states and support needs, cost-benefit analyses and cost savings determinations may be accomplished.

The Problem List

Once the functional outcome projection is formulated and a clear picture of postdischarge life is constructed, the case manager and clinical staff need to define the specific problems illustrated in the database that need to be resolved through treatment or supports to achieve the objectives given in the projection. Often, this is accomplished simultaneously with construction of the projection, with assessment reports including a description of the functional outcomes that the clinician expects to achieve, the interfering problems delineated through assessment, and the proposed goals.

The case manager constructs a complete problem list, or series of problem statements defining all baseline states that will be addressed actively through treatment or support. The list is dynamic in that new data are gathered continuously. These often alter client, family, or community profiles and, thus, the list. A second dynamic aspect of the problem list is its relationship to outcome milestones. The list is directed toward milestone accomplishment. Although the case manager maintains a complete list of problems that may be addressed by the time the client completes treatment, usually on the computer, the active problem list consists only of problems currently under treatment. Other identified problems are placed on hold. Goal statements are not formulated until treatment is initiated because the additional data accumulated in the interim are likely to influence and modify statements written earlier. When problems are resolved to the measurable extent described in the goal statement, they are moved to an inactive, or goals met category.

The problem list of correlated problem and goal statements is documented in a formal report issued to all consumers and within the service agreements serving as outcome contracts between the case manager and the clinical staff. Not only can it be used to direct movement of the client from one milestone to another, but it serves as an index by which interventions and outcome progression may be monitored and efficiently managed.

Problem Statements and Outcome Goals

Problem statements, and statements identifying the goals of intervention, provide not only an index by which intervention is planned, implemented, and monitored but a means by which the process may be objectified. Through specificity of language and measurement criteria, problem and goal statements will support a clear, objective demonstration of progression toward outcome at any point in time that measurement is performed.

In general, the problem statement describes the measured baseline state, defining the behavior or problem to be addressed through treatment. The correlated goal statement defines the specific behavioral state or support to be achieved upon completion of treatment. Essentially, the former states what the client or family cannot accomplish, and the latter states what the individual will be able to accomplish within a given environmental context when intervention is completed and any needed supports are in place. For example, the problem statement may say, "Randy requires physical set-up, five to seven verbal prompts, and up to 45 minutes for completing self-dressing in the residential and home settings." Its counterpart goal statement might then assert that, by a given date, "Randy will initiate and complete self-dressing without set-up or verbal prompts in 15 minutes or less in the residential and home settings for 14 consecutive days."

Statement Composition

Because specificity and objectivity are the hallmarks of well written behavioral statements, problem and goal statements should include the following:

- *the behavior:* an observable, quantifiable behavioral state
- *the conditions:* observational parameters defining where and when the behavior was or will be observed and measured
- *the criteria:* the standard by which achievement will be judged; the acceptable performance level or score

In defining behavioral outcomes, goal statements should address targets that are achievable given the available time and dollar resources. A client may hold potential for further achieve-ment, but the statement should define what actually will be accomplished rather that what could be given additional resources. It should bear a clear relationship to an outcome milestone and to the description of client and family life found in the functional outcome projection.

Barriers to Useful Statements

The choice of language is a crucial determinant of a statement's usefulness. Terminology, frequently global or generic in nature, fails to address the specific, individualized behavior observed. For example, *dysphagia* is a general term indicative of an entire set of discrete behaviors. The actual difficulty experienced by an individual may relate to only one part of the mastication-swallowing process. The clinician may wish to describe a unique aspect of the process, such as moving food from the front to the back of the mouth, mastering a specific food consistency, or swallowing unthickened liquids, to define clearly both problem and target outcome. Similarly, words such as *improved, appropriate,* and *assisted* obscure acceptable performance levels and their measurement. Descriptors such as frequency, rate, duration, amount, latency, accuracy, normative standards, self-report ratings, and the like may be used alone or in combination to ensure specificity. Failure to incorporate the period of time over which the targeted behavioral state must persist for the goal to be met will result in arbitrary judgments and dissension.

Statements incorporating a number of behaviors into a single problem or goal have little usefulness. For example, a client may experience problems with all activities of daily living. The clinician or case manager may thus be inclined to group the actual behaviors demonstrated and targeted into a single statement. Each problem is likely to resolve at a different time, however. For example, proficiency in brushing and flossing the teeth may precede competency in bathing by a number of weeks. Goal achievement should not depend upon accomplishment of the entire set. This fails to substantiate benefit in a timely manner, discouraging the client, family, and funding sponsor. It also may preclude definition of acceptable performance levels or result in a statement of remarkable length once criteria are stated for each component of the global behavioral set.

Table 15-3 presents examples of weakly composed goal statements and preferred versions. The reader is referred to Rush, Rose, and Greenwood (1988), Sulzer-Azaroff and Mayer (1977), and Vargas (1972) for additional instruction in specifying behavioral objectives.

Outcome Milestones

A milestone serves as a significant point or event in the progress toward the functional outcome. Most often, it signifies accomplishment of a set of goals that enables the client and family to enjoy a reduction in their perception of disability and burden. For example, upon reaching a set of goals related to self-care, mobility, self-medication, safety, and peer relationships, the client may function in less restrictive treatment or living settings offering expanded empowerment, choices, and self-governance. At other times, the marker may be accomplishment of a single but significant goal, such as oral feeding.

The purpose of using outcome milestones is to attain focus and economy of effort. Milestone accomplishment is synonymous with accomplishments in living arrangements, meeting personal daily needs, productive activity, and relationships. Although this may not appear to apply in cases of limited client responsiveness, achievements in health status, level of care, and family status also may be addressed within this context.

Efficient resource allocation is achievable when one focuses first upon the functional outcome, next upon the set of milestones, and then

---

Table 15-3 Composing Measurable Goal Statements

Weak	Preferred
Randy's weight is within normal limits.	Randy's body weight will measure within normal limits for age, height, and gender, or 158 to 165 lbs, for 3 consecutive months.
Randy is able to follow complex, multi-step verbal directions.	Randy will follow four- to five-step verbal directions at a compound sentence level when learning and performing tasks in a trial job setting at 90% accuracy for 3 consecutive weeks as measured and reported by the job coach.
Randy is independent in bathing.	Randy will initiate and complete showering in a stall shower with grab bars without verbal prompts, in standing position without loss of balance, in 15 minutes or less for 10 consecutive days.
Randy is independent in ambulating on even surfaces.	Randy will walk up to 200 ft at 80% of normal speed without falling, on even surfaces in and out of his house, without physical assist or stand-by support, for 10 of 10 consecutive trials.
Randy is verbally appropriate.	Randy will demonstrate zero incidence of verbal threats of harm to staff and peers when in physical therapy for 2 consecutive weeks.
Randy has improved his ability to manage his own money.	Randy will perform bank deposits and cash withdrawals, will pay bills by due dates through check writing, and will maintain an accurate checkbook balance ± $10 for 3 consecutive months.
Randy's headaches will not interfere with attending treatment.	Randy will attend 100% of scheduled therapy of no less than 6 hours per treatment day and will report headache discomfort intensity of no greater than 2 on a scale of 1 to 7 at 10:00 A.M. and 3:00 P.M. for 3 consecutive weeks.

upon interfering problems and goals in relationship to the next milestone to be reached. By its very nature, the interdisciplinary team approach may encourage all team members to have and implement goals across the entire course of treatment. The use of milestones discourages this approach, setting a discrete set of goals pertaining to the next milestone and allocating resources and effort economically. It also permits the client, family, and financial sponsor to focus upon a reasonable number of short-term goals, to understand how disability or its manifestations will be reduced through the milestone description, and to feel a sense of accomplishment at periodic intervals as milestone-to-milestone accomplishment ensues.

Pathway Illustration

As shown in Figure 15-4, the individualized outcome pathway may be illustrated for clinical staff and consumers by means of a Gantt chart prepared by the case manager. Moving from week to week horizontally, milestones are placed next to their expected date for accomplishment, culminating in outcome. On the left side of the chart, outcome goals are listed vertically and grouped according to the milestone to which they relate. A bar, or other indicator, is then extended horizontally from each goal to the week targeted for accomplishment. The case manager and others now have a tool for visualizing and regulating process. It is helpful to keep in mind that this is a dynamic tool to which goals and dates are likely to be added, omitted, or altered as the process unfolds.

The Service Agreement

Although the case manager is accountable for the ultimate outcomes of the rehabilitation process, their accomplishment is dependent upon the professional skills and expertise of others. Therefore, the case manager subcontracts with clinical staff to achieve components of the projected functional outcome. The service agreement signifies a contractual relationship between the case man-

ager, who is purchasing the outcome, and the clinician, who provides the services and ensures that the outcome is delivered. As shown in Figure 14-4, the terms of the agreement are clearly specified, including the goal statement describing the outcome, a summary of methodology, the completion date, and clinician-determined checkpoints for tracking movement toward the goal. The concept of contracting for outcomes does not rule out collaborative team effort toward achievement of a single goal. A wise clinician will enlist others for timely goal achievement. In keeping with the concept of single point accountability, however, it does place responsibility for goal achievement upon a specific clinician.

Negotiating Service Agreements

Once the functional outcome projection and milestones are determined in agreement with consumers, service agreement negotiation between the case manager and the interdisciplinary team usually is limited to composition of the goal statement, goal completion dates, and resource allocation, or the timing and sequencing of services. The case manager may suggest rewording of the goal statement to provide clarity, specificity, or applicability to a particular type of funding. Goal completion dates may need adjustment, when possible, for timely milestone accomplishment. By using a Gantt chart for illustration, the case manager also may suggest altering the use or timing of clinical resources to manage time and costs more productively.

Outcome Contracting and Monitoring

The significance of the service agreement lies in the contractual relationship, in keeping with a consumer-driven system of accountability; the nature of the contract, which is for an outcome, not a discipline, service, or mode of intervention; and the creation of a mechanism for monitoring problem resolvement continuously. By using clinician-determined checkpoints, as illustrated in Exhibit 15-1, the case manager monitors outcome progression and, upon detecting

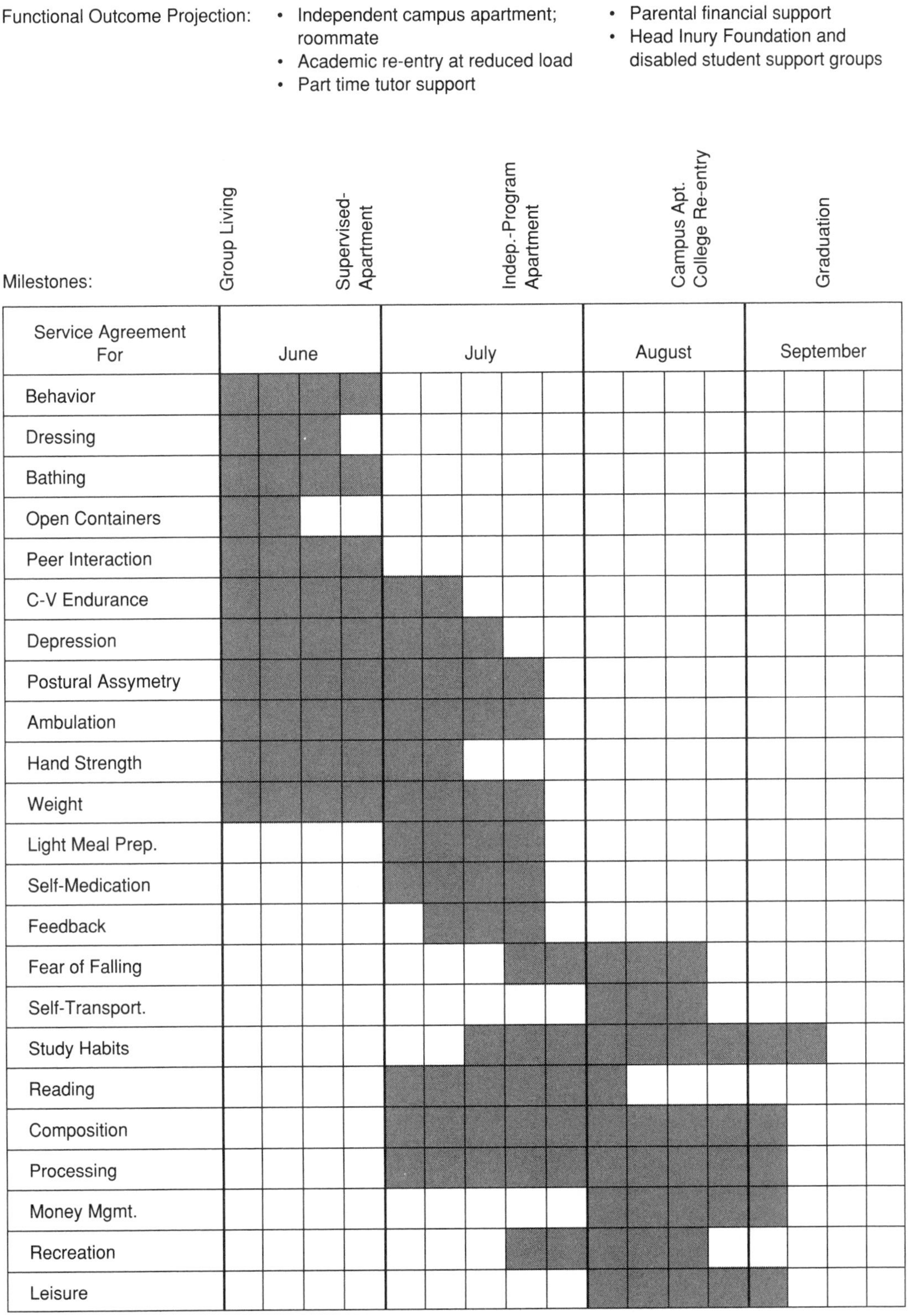

Functional Outcome Projection:
- Independent campus apartment; roommate
- Academic re-entry at reduced load
- Part time tutor support
- Parental financial support
- Head Inury Foundation and disabled student support groups

Milestones: Group Living | Supervised-Apartment | Indep.-Program Apartment | Campus Apt. College Re-entry | Graduation

Service Agreement For	June	July	August	September
Behavior				
Dressing				
Bathing				
Open Containers				
Peer Interaction				
C-V Endurance				
Depression				
Postural Assymetry				
Ambulation				
Hand Strength				
Weight				
Light Meal Prep.				
Self-Medication				
Feedback				
Fear of Falling				
Self-Transport.				
Study Habits				
Reading				
Composition				
Processing				
Money Mgmt.				
Recreation				
Leisure				

Figure 15-4 Gantt illustration: Individualized outcome pathway illustrating timing and sequence of service delivery in relationship to milestone accomplishment.

problems, rapidly corrects them to regain on-course status. Use of the service agreements in case conferences will ensure active monitoring of status and will focus attention on results rather than on process. Every contract need not be addressed every time the case is discussed. Monitoring of intervention results should be primarily directed toward upcoming checkpoints.

REPORTING

Report Design

In serving as the single point of accountability, the facility-based case manager must ensure appropriate documentation and reporting of the service plan and its results. Typically, reporting systems are based upon internal, clinical values, or what the team considers professional.

In reality, documentation and reporting systems must meet both internal criteria, which are based upon organizational need, and external criteria, which are related to consumer need. As illustrated in Table 15-4, these may be summarized as legal defensibility, auditability, useability, and feasibility.

Just as it is useful and, in a consumer-driven system, necessary to ask, "Whose outcome is it?" it is important to ask, "Whose report is it?" when one is designing and implementing the report system. Although financial sponsors require documentation of service delivery results at least monthly to justify their expenditures and consider reports a top service priority, families are less reliant upon documentation in general. Hosack, Malkmus, and Evans (1991) surveyed 35 families, requesting them to rank both clinical and service outcomes according to their importance or value. Although there was strong agreement between the families and providers surveyed by Jones and Evans (1991) about clinical outcomes, families ranked written reports 9th of 10 service outcomes in order of importance. The highest ranked family service item was direct family involvement and communication with the interdisciplinary team pertaining to input, decision making, and feedback (Table 15-5).

The survey by Jones and Evans (1991) also revealed that the 50 financial sponsor respon-

dents managed an average annual case load of 504 cases, each averaging 37 acquired brain injury cases annually. This points to the need to reduce the amount and length of written communication to the minimum necessary. This may be confirmed through dialogue with financial sponsors. The author conduced a survey in 1990 of 15 financial sponsors and referring gatekeepers, who indicated the following report features as desirable:

- a single integrated report rather than separate reports by each discipline
- short, highly focused evaluation reports illustrating real-life problems consequent to injury or affecting disability reduction
- early prediction of client and family outcome and the target completion date
- visual displays providing an overview of problems, goals, and time frames and their current status (e.g., a Gantt or other chart providing an audit trail)
- status reports demonstrating measurable results of intervention per outcome goal and time frame compliance
- a minimum of terminology, with definitions when used
- goals stated in language appropriate to the type of funding provided to justify expenditures and to preserve financial sponsorship (e.g., related to medical necessity for group accident and health coverage or vocationally based and disability reduction goals appropriate to workers' compensation funding)
- evaluation of family and community as resources
- consistency of format within and across programs or facilities

Format and Composition

Although formatting and reporting schedules need to be consistent within and across programs, report flexibility also is needed to meet variances among financial sponsors. As in the process of writing behavioral statements, the use

Table 15-4 Reporting Criteria Guidelines

Criteria	Internal	External
Legal defensibility	Reduces exposure through factual, nonjudgmental documentation of occurrences and client status	Provides factual, nonjudgmental, complete descriptions of occurrences and client status in nonbiased manner
	Supports reimbursement of services rendered	Justifies reimbursement for services rendered
Auditability	Provides for baseline and systematic measurements of client status and outcome progression by staff	Clearly delineates measured client status and progress
	Defines and tracks the individualized client outcome pathway	Indicates major markers of progress toward outcome achievement
	Permits on-site or off-site audit	Permits financial sponsor audit
Useability	Promotes systematic analysis of client data, construction of individualized client pathways, and efficient resource allocation	Supports efficient achievement of client outcomes and cost containment at program and ancillary service levels
	Readily adapts to customers' interests, orientation, defined needs, and funding parameters	Meets common and unique interests and needs of customers/recipients
	Minimizes communication subject to interpretation	Presents data in language commonly understood by all report recipients
Feasibility	Minimizes demands upon staff time without sacrificing completeness and quality	Minimizes demand upon recipients' time for review, analysis, and use

of terminology and obscure language requires close evaluation in light of useability and legal defensibility criteria. All terminology should be directly followed by definition. Adjectives, adverbs, and language suggesting subjective value judgments are best avoided.

CONFERENCING

It is common to find facility-based case managers leading most meetings and conferences. The occurrence of this function points to the benefit of training in group dynamics and leadership functions. Meetings conducted by case managers should be consumer and results oriented. The case manager should endeavor to include all consumers in all group discussions

regarding evaluation results, service planning, and outcome progression. To do otherwise would be discriminatory and exclusionary. Individual meetings, and paper paths between case manager and clinician, can serve as preparation for what might otherwise result in an uncomfortable or negative situation. If the case manager is well prepared, however, entering the meeting with a complete and well communicated intent of what is to be accomplished, and conducts the meeting so as to maintain focus, the presence of consumers should enhance, not detract from, the achievement of desired results.

Avoiding Consumer Conflict

Empowerment of the client and family, and inclusion of the financial sponsor, will serve to

Table 15-5 Priority Rankings for Clinical and Service Outcomes

Clinical Outcomes (Equivalent)		Service Outcomes (Nonequivalent)	
Financial Sponsor Rankings (N = 50)	Family Rankings (N = 35)	Financial Sponsor Rankings (N = 50)	Family Rankings (N = 35)
1. Independence in activities of daily living	1. Independence in activities of daily living	1. Early identification of outcomes	1. Family involvement in decision making and planning
2. Improved living situation	2. Improved communication skills	2. Achievement of agreed upon outcomes	2. Training and experience of program staff
3. Improved communication skills	3. Improved physical mobility	3. Outcome durability	3. Sensitivity, respect, and caring from program staff
4. Improve health status	4. Problem behaviors controlled	4. Outcomes achieved at or below agreed upon cost	4. Intensity of daily treatment services
5. Improved physical mobility	5. Ability to manage own affairs	5. Outcomes achieved within agreed upon time frame	5. Outcomes achieved within agreed upon time frame
6. Client satisfaction with outcomes	6. Reduced need for supervision	6. Ancillary costs kept to a minimum	6. Family education, counseling, and support services
7. Ability to manage own affairs	7. Improved living situation	7. Forecasting of future medical and support costs	7. Financial sponsor involvement
8. Problem behaviors controlled	8. Improved health status	8. Client status follow-up after discharge	8. Availability of medical support services
9. Reduced need for supervision	9. Client satisfaction with outcomes	9. Predictable ancillary costs	9. Written progress/ status reports
10. Reduced need for rehabilitation services	10. Reduced need for rehabilitation	10. Equitable treatment access for all persons in need	10. Access to other families
11. Improved employment status	11. Improved educational status		
12. Reduced need for health care services	12. Improved financial status		
13. Family satisfaction with outcomes	13. Improved employment status		
14. Improved financial status	14. Reduced need for health care services		
15. Improved educational status			

Source: Excerpted from Jones, M., & Evans, R. (1991, February). Rating of outcomes in post-acute rehabilitation for acquired brain injury. *The Case Manager, 2*(1), 44–47 and Hosack, K., Malkmus, D., & Evans, R. Family priorities in post-acute rehabilitation for persons with acquired brain injury. Unpublished material, adapted with permission. Learning Services Corporation, Londonderry, NH (1991).

support outcome accomplishment. The case manager should take care to ensure that adversarial positions with the financial sponsors are avoided, however. This is especially important when the client's family has retained an attorney and when the plaintiff's counsel is present. Although the service recipient has priority of obligation, it is important to keep in mind the position and possible long-term obligation of the financial sponsor. The case manager should inform all professionals attending a meeting of the purpose and results sought from the meeting,

the agenda, who will attend, the relationships, and the need to provide unbiased, factual information that avoids the appearance of collusion or bias toward one consumer over another.

Tracking Outcome

In tracking client outcome progression, the case manager's use of tools such as those illustrated throughout this chapter will support focused meeting time. Clinicians should bring pertinent service agreements to meetings for discussion of checkpoints to be reached in the near future. The customer service plan and results also should be reviewed during discussions of outcome progression, with the case manager actively inquiring and providing information about satisfaction levels at least monthly.

SUPPORTING EXTERNAL CASE MANAGERS

Frequently, the financial sponsor employs or contracts with an external case manager to coordinate care, services, and financial resources for high cost cases. Although the common title *case manager* may suggest similarity of purpose and function, and although similarities indeed exist, the differences between external and facility-based case management are important. If these are not understood and thoughtfully addressed, barriers to successful internal management may arise.

Although both types of case managers are dedicated to the client and family, the external case manager is employed by the insurer, employer, or sponsoring agency. The interests and needs of the client and family must be balanced with those of the financial sponsor. Facility-based case managers, employed by the service provider, often balance even more financial interests. They must accomplish objectives within a relatively short time frame, whereas the external case manager, usually assigned early in the life of the case, often assumes a long-term relationship that is likely to span a number of years.

Both types of case management use people, supports, and dollar resources to accomplish their objectives. The resources and their use may differ, however. For example, the external case manager may be working with both the financial sponsor and a plaintiff's attorney, as is common in workers' compensation cases. At times, questions of liability, related disability, and, thus, justification of sponsorship may arise. The case manager may assemble a team of trusted experts outside the rehabilitation setting to establish the relationships among injury, disability, and consequent liability. At this or other times, the team of ex-

perts may be asked to help develop a life care plan and to be prepared to justify it in a court hearing. This activity usually and properly exists outside the current rehabilitation objective. The facility-based case manager must be sure to know all objectives of the external case manager to respond appropriately throughout the course of service delivery and must ensure that the external case manager understands the differences between case management roles, does not perceive a threat, and that collaborative management occurs. The facility-based case manager should endeavor to enlist the external case manager as a colleague and primary resource for ensuring that outcome objectives are met. In so doing, the objectives, perspectives, and long-term nature of the external case manager's responsibility must be fully considered and incorporated into planning and actions. The facility-based case manager should endeavor to build a relationship of immense trust and to ease the amount of effort needed on the part of the external case manager for a given case.

SUPPORTING THE CLIENT AND FAMILY

Although employed by the service provider organization, the facility-based case manager functions in the pivotal position of driving outcome and process from the consumer's point of view. It is impossible to function apart from the organizational view of mission and means of accomplishment, however. Condeluci (1991) classifies rehabilitation ideologies into medical, educational, economic, and interdependence paradigms. Each projects a view of where the problem and the power to resolve it reside. In the first three paradigms, the problem is within the service recipient. Empowerment is linked to those delivering services. In the interdependence paradigm, Condeluci (1991) argues that the problem lies within the system, its view of disability, its resultant laws and customs, and the resources and supports available. Power is retained by service recipients, who define problems, define outcomes, and drive the process for goal achievement.

It is important to acknowledge that the operative paradigm will necessarily cause a certain set of actions to occur, guiding the self-concepts, expectations, and behaviors of both service providers and consumers. Condeluci's (1991) equation for establishing the bases for problem and power and the goal of reconnecting distanced, disenfranchised persons to relationships and community are in keeping with a yet unmentioned but most important objective of facility-based case management. Although the case manager will be evaluated and judged relative to his or her effectiveness in achievement of clinical outcomes, cost management, and customer satisfaction, success may be measured in an additional way. The case manager has assumed daily advocacy and management functions on behalf of the client and family. Success also occurs when one or more service recipients assume advocacy and management functions and, in effect, replace the case manager.

The facility-based case manager can play a powerful role in supporting role competency enhancement as a bridge to activities relevant to the interdependence paradigm. Possessing a working knowledge of effective advocacy and management practices, the case manager is a teacher by example. Case management tools and practices can be incorporated into client and family education and training. Moreover, interdisciplinary effort can be guided toward role competency enhancement, support building, relationship building, and systems advocacy actions described in Condeluci's (1991) paradigm. As Bush (1989) points out,

> ... if the basic belief system is that the case manager is a facilitator, there to help client/families make decisions and orchestrate resources, then a related set of behaviors will follow. This approach can often set the most positive tone for recovery. (p. 95)

TRANSFERRING MANAGEMENT PRACTICES

Data acquisition, organization and utilization are basic to management. Each case manager employs a system enabling effective resource data access and management. Families, and often clients, also will benefit from similar systems and techniques that facilitate process mastery. One means of promoting enhanced consumer competency is training in case management and advocacy roles and practices.

The use of an information and resource notebook as a catalyst for competency acquisition promotes active learning and supports the concept of consumer competency (Hosack, Malkmus, & Centrella, 1991). Upon admission, the user is given the notebook, with a preprinted index (Exhibit 15-2), introduction, and dividers, and is asked to bring it to all future meetings and events.

Educational objectives, framed by content areas of the notebook, are the basis for training by the case manager and others as applicable. For example, before a case conference, the case manager can instruct a family member on salient note taking, self-advocacy and assertiveness, and the expression of questions, concerns, and needs. After the conference, coevaluation will promote reinforcement of useful practices and interaction. The case manager should ensure that each section is appropriate to individual needs and is used as frequently as possible so that its usefulness is known. The teaching of case management practices also may be incorporated into group, family, and client educational programs.

DISCHARGE PLANNING

The facility-based case manager is accountable not only for outcome reliability, or achieving targeted behavioral outcomes within specified time frames, but for durability, or the staying power of achieved outcomes. Responsible discharge planning is based upon the notion of outcome durability, or what will support or endanger outcome status. Barriers to durable outcomes include the following:

- failure of assessment to focus upon non-client outcome parameters (e.g., ecological systems and relationships)
- failure of outcome research and program evaluation measures to focus sufficiently

Exhibit 15-2 Sample Index: Family Information and Resource Book

I.   Introduction
  • Organizational philosophy
  • Statement of rights
  • Introduction to book
II. Appointment Calendar
III. Communications
  • Record of phone calls, meetings, events
IV. Advocacy
  • Support groups
  • Legislative data
V.   Insurance Information
  • Representatives, addresses, phone numbers
  • Policies
  • Completed forms
  • Correspondence
  • Notes
VI. Medical Information
  • Names, addresses, phone numbers
  • Recent reports, records
  • Key historical data
VII. Legal Information
  • Names, addresses, phone numbers
  • Documents
  • Correspondence
VIII. Educational Materials
  • Articles, references, etc.
  • Notes from educational meetings and other training
IX. Emergency Information
  • Consent for emergency treatment
  • Emergency legal documents: living will, guardianship papers, etc.
  • List of community emergency services, locations, directions, phone numbers

Source: From *Family Reference and Information Guide* by K. Hosack, D. Malkmus, & J. Centrella (1991). Learning Services, Londenderry, NH. Unpublished material, adapted by permission.

upon durability, to measure outcome at the appropriate time or beyond the date of discharge, or to perform and incorporate analysis of nondurable outcomes into programmatic changes
• failure to include consumers (product users) in the processes of assessing, planning, and evaluating resources and supports
• failure to enhance or train consumer competencies crucial to outcome satisfaction and durability

• inadequate postdischarge follow-up
• absence of reimbursement for a professionally guided trial and problem solving within the actual discharge setting before discharge

These, and other consumer-specific barriers to a durable outcome and effective discharge, should be reviewed at every event where outcome and its progression are discussed. If only skills and behaviors are discussed, and if the settings, relationships, and supports to which they must be connected are ignored, nonlinkage will result in outcome breakdown. Ideally, assessment places equal emphasis upon ecological systems and, whenever possible, permits the case manager an opportunity for on-site evaluation. It is interesting to note the fastidious planning given to admission, the time and effort given to assessment and evaluation, and the short amount of time and effort given to discharge, which is an equally important event. Failure to incorporate consumers into the process or to enhance their self-image, coping, and management capabilities will result in a product that, because it was not chosen or of value, will not be used. By the nature of their contractual obligations, many financial sponsors encounter difficulty in supporting a trial run of the discharge plan, although most agree with the benefit of resolving issues before termination of services and reimbursement. Failure to design a thoughtful follow-up plan or to be able to carry it out in light of other, pressing responsibilities may obstruct durability. Finally, were we to measure outcome achievement not on the day of discharge but at least 3 months later and beyond, we might consider and alter both focus and activities.

DISCHARGE TRANSITIONS

Each client is entitled to services delivered in the least restrictive and least costly setting feasible without sacrificing effective, expedient movement toward consumer-acceptable outcomes. Thus it may be determined that the outcomes intended to be accomplished in the present setting may be better accomplished in another setting, resulting in discharge. Responsibility for continuously assessing, evaluating, and facilitating movement of clients into levels of enhanced independence or equally effective, less costly settings rests with the case manager. Guidelines that may be used for such transitions, or service-cost phasing, include the following:

- client ability to manage safely and effectively a proposed transition and/or lessening of professional supports
- risk-benefit analyses (i.e., documentation that the benefits to the client outweigh potential risks)
- financial sponsor acceptability
- client and family acceptability

A second type of discharge transition is completion of the intended program and achievement of the outcome objectives as planned. A third, and undesirable, type of discharge is premature or unplanned discharge. Instances of unplanned discharge may result when:

- medical status deterioration requires services and supports exceeding the mission and capabilities of the current setting
- psychiatric status deterioration places the client or others at risk and the client requires or will benefit from interventions outside the mission and capabilities of the current setting
- physical safety is at risk because of wandering, which cannot be contained even with added person supports, or because reimbursement for additional safety supports cannot be attained
- the client elects to terminate services
- the family elects to terminate services
- the financial sponsor elects to terminate services
- the client is removed by court order
- the service provider elects to terminate services for financial reasons (i.e., inadequate reimbursement)
- the service provider elects to terminate services for cost-benefit reasons (i.e., benefits

attained do not warrant service reimbursement continuation)

The facility-based case manager is accountable for minimizing the occurrence of unplanned discharges. Use of the risk analysis and risk management planning procedures described in the admission section of this chapter supports this function. As a member of the management team, the case manager also should track the type and frequency of this occurrence, note incidence trends, and, along with other staff, endeavor to reduce incidence.

When an unplanned discharge occurs, the case manager should immediately generate a discharge report and notify all concerned parties. The report should offer a concise, nonjudgmental summary of the circumstances of discharge; the current status of the client and family; needs requiring immediate attention, such as health and safety; and recommendations for appropriate, realistic action, including any follow-up or follow-through to be performed by the program staff. Unless otherwise requested, the case manager should devise a reasonable follow-up plan and continue to advocate for the client and family to the extent feasible.

FOLLOW-UP SERVICE

A carefully constructed set of follow-up activities that include scheduled contacts with the client, family, financial sponsor, and community resources can serve as a warranty for promoting outcome durability. The purpose of the plan is to anticipate and avert obstacles to a sustained outcome, not to continue management of the case. The plan should be documented, incorporate others for problem-solving issues that are likely to arise, and have a trigger system to ensure that action occurs as scheduled. It is likely that additional, unscheduled activity will occur. In this respect, the case manager seldom services the number of consumers representing the current case load. When reasonably defined and orchestrated, however, the time given to follow-up is well spent in protecting outcome achievement.

Follow-up findings and action plan results should be documented in such a way as to be incorporated into outcome and program evaluation studies. A brief, written communication to the financial sponsor will document organizational commitment and will support other referrals. The major value of follow-up, however, is in systematically collecting and using data to improve discharge transitioning and outcome durability.

DISCHARGE

As discharge arrives, the case manager needs to ensure that:

- the date and the achievement of agreed upon outcomes are confirmed to all consumers and to the community resources to be accessed after discharge
- all tangible and emotional supports are in place and understood by all parties
- a comprehensive, agreed upon follow-up plan is in place and understood by all parties
- there is a plan for acknowledging and reinforcing consumer and service provider accomplishments

Before admission, the case manager was accountable for ensuring a safe, effective client and family transition into the rehabilitation setting that would set the appropriate tone for the events to follow. Similarly, an appropriate tone must be established as service beneficiaries transition into the next setting. This occurs, in part, from well planned, negotiated follow-up support and, in large part, from competency support and enhancement that have prepared consumers for change. A third key to effective transition is actual closure of the rehabilitation process. Given the effort and achievements of consumer-provider partnerships, discharge should be a time of celebration. It falls upon the case manager to orchestrate individually relevant actions that bring positive closure to service delivery.

The client and family are to be congratulated for their effort and accomplishment. This may occur through ceremony, written communication, or both. The financial sponsor is deserving of formal appreciation and confirmation of the beneficial results of sponsorship. In this light, the discharge report should be designed to underscore goal, outcome, and time frame accomplishment. A cover letter indicating such outcome reliability and expressing appreciation for the opportunity to serve the service beneficiaries will further support appropriate closure. Finally, the interdisciplinary team needs reinforcement for timely outcome achievement and special effort as indicated. These important actions at the closure of service delivery are more than matters of simple etiquette. They are central to good management practices and to the role of facility-based case management.

CONCLUSION

A successful outcome occurs when there is achievement of negotiated outcomes within agreed upon time frames that:

- hold high value for service consumers
- minimize costs to consumers, funding sponsors, and the service provider
- result in high consumer satisfaction with process and outcome
- have a lasting, positive effect for service beneficiaries
- result in reinforcement of the service delivery staff for productivity, reliability, accomplishment, and thus internal satisfaction

As an orchestrator of events, a facilitator of action, and an employer of resources for the benefit of others, the facility-based case manager faces an immense challenge in effectively focusing and integrating data, resources, and activities toward these ends. The role is dynamic, assertive, demanding, and central to ensuring reliable, efficient service delivery. As managed care and consumer values shape the health care system, the role of case management within the service delivery context will continue to be shaped.

Just as the case manager challenges fellow service providers to examine organizational and personal ideologies, the consequent roles thrust upon those served, and the impact of such actions, the case manager must challenge himself or herself. As guardian of consumer-driven service delivery, the case manager's role in process and outcome management is significant. Acknowledgment of the vital linkages among consumers, the interdisciplinary team, and the community is crucial to effective outcome determination and durability. Moreover, facility-based case managers currently engaged in exploring the boundaries and practices of this emerging function and responding to the needs of financial sponsors, service providers, and service recipients have the opportunity to be the architects of their own future. Research into the functions, practices, effects, and cost savings of facility-based case management and into customer satisfaction, definition of best practices, and articulation of such data through professional communications within rehabilitation and financial sponsor arenas will support both need and growth.

REFERENCES

Beresford, L. (1991). Cracking the big case. *Case Manager, 2,* 50–58.

Bush, G. (1989). Catastrophic case management: Thoughts from a teacher/consumer/advocate. *Brain Injury, 3,* 91–100.

Capitman, J., Haskins, B., & Bernstein, J. (1986). Case management approaches in coordinated community-oriented long term care demonstrations. *Gerontologist,* 398–404.

Condeluci, A. (1991). *Interdependence: The route to community.* Orlando, FL: Deutsch.

Covey, S.R. (1989). *The seven habits of highly effective people.* New York: Simon & Schuster.

Dixon, T.P., Goll, S., & Stanton, K.M. (1988). Case management issues and practices in head injury rehabilitation. *Rehabilitation Counseling Bulletin, 31,* 325–343.

Delaney, C., & Acquillina, D. (1987). Case management: Meeting the challenge of high-cost illness. *Employee Benefits Journal,* 31–35.

Del Togno-Armanasco, V., Olivas, G., & Harter, S. (1989). Developing an integrated nursing case management model. *Nursing Management,* 76–81.

Friedan, J., & Trasker, M. (1989). Managed care: It's everywhere, but what is it? *Business and Health,* 22–24.

Henderson, M., Bergman, A., Collard, A., Souder, B., & Wallack, S. (1988). Private-sector medical case management for high-cost illness. *Advances in Health Economics and Health Services Research, 9,* 213–245.

Henderson, M.G., Souder, B.A., Bergman, A., & Collard, A.F. (1988). Private sector initiatives in case management. *Health Care Financing Review,* 89–95.

Hosack, K., Malkmus, D., & Centrella, J. (1991). [Family reference and information guide]. Unpublished manuscript. Londonderry, NH: Learning Services.

Hosack, K., Malkmus, D., & Evans, R.W. (1991). [Family priorities in post-acute rehabilitation of acquired brain injury]. Unpublished raw data.

Hughes, E. (1987). Glossary. *HMO/PPO Trends, 1,* 13–16.

Jaffe, K. (1991). Facility based case managers: The evolution continues. *Case Manager, 2,* 39–42.

Jones, M., & Evans, R.W. (1991). Rating outcomes in post-acute rehabilitation of acquired brain injury. *Case Manager, 2,* 44–47.

Moffat, J. (1991). Case management in a managed care environment. *Case Manager, 2,* 64–72.

Papastrat, L.A. (1991). Saving lives and money, too. *Best's Review,* 44–100.

Roughan, J. (1990). Case management: Definition, process and perspective. *Case Manager, 1,* 40–46.

Rush, F.R., Rose, T., & Greenwood, C.R. (1988). *Introduction to behavioral analysis in special education.* Englewood Cliffs, NJ: Prentice-Hall.

Sulzer-Azaroff, B., & Mayer, G.R. (1977). *Applying behavioral analysis procedures with children and youth.* New York: Holt, Rinehart & Winston.

Vargas, J.S. (1972). *Writing worthwhile behavioral objectives.* New York: Harper & Row.

Wulff, J.J. (1991). Clinical case management. *Journal of Insurance Medicine, 23,* 124–129.

Effective Strategies for Directing and Managing Change in the Rehabilitation Setting

16

Charles V. Arokiasamy

Jack E. Robertson

Sally E. Guice

OBJECTIVES

Upon completion of this chapter, the reader will be able to:

1. develop an understanding of the complex nature of traumatic brain injury rehabilitation
2. define the scope and impact of change within the field of brain injury rehabilitation
3. identify strategies to effect intentional change, manage unanticipated change, and cope with ongoing change
4. describe philosophical, humanistic, and strategic approaches to management that place an emphasis on team work, leadership, staff empowerment, and responsiveness to consumers
5. understand the importance of organizational culture and structure in handling change
6. develop an organizational culture that can make the most positive use of change

Effective Strategies for Directing and Managing Change in the Rehabilitation Setting

Before the Industrial Revolution, permanence, stability, constancy, and set, rigid ways of doing things were important societal values. Ancient practices handed down from generation to generation in the form of tradition or customs were held to be important, if not sacred. In fact, change was more likely to be seen as deviant. In the postindustrial era, however, and a fortiori in the present day of the information age, the tables have been exactly reversed. Change, growth, innovation, and frequent and continuous modification have become the rule of the day. Popular futurists, such as Alvin Toffler in *Future Shock* (1970) and *The Third Wave* (1980) and John Naisbitt in *Megatrends* (1982), and social scientists alike clearly show change to be a predominant value of present society. Change not only is an important value but also is inescapable and accelerating at a faster and faster pace. Children urge their parents to get with the times, and staff members are apt to see their bosses and supervisors as stuck in the mud or out of touch.

Change is becoming so fast and so pervasive that people and organizations have rapidly become forced to engage in such activities as restructuring, long-term forecasting, strategic planning, and developing futuristic think tanks just to survive (Arokiasamy, Leja, Austin, & Rubin, 1988; Riggar, Crimando, Bordieri, Hanley-Maxwell, Benshoff, & Calzaretta, 1989). *Proactive thinking* is now one of the more common buzzwords of the day. People and organizations alike are being dragged into immediate action, which not only serves to quicken the pace of change but also adds to the confusion. Toffler (1970) asserts that individuals or organizations, and even societies, that do not adjust to change and become proactive are likely to be the dinosaurs of the future, moribund and extinct. On the other hand, individuals and organizations that effectively manage and facilitate change are likely to prosper and grow. Brain injury rehabilitation professionals, as will be seen shortly, have also been caught up in the vortex of change. We too have been assailed by rapid change, and have had to respond faster than we might like.

Accelerating change not only forces proactive postures and quick action but also leaves people and systems undergoing current change bewildered and caught in a constant struggle to keep up or drop out. In addition to the stress of one's needing to be proactive to survive, enormous pressure is brought to bear in the process of change, especially at its current ever increasing pace. Evidence of these stressors at both individual and organizational levels can clearly be seen in the increasing rate of stress-related mental, psychological, and emotional dysfunction among individuals and in systems breakdowns at organizational and societal levels. Burnout among rehabilitation workers (Butt & Gerber, 1987; Riggar, Garner, & Hafer, 1984; Riggar, Godley, & Hafer, 1984) and the distress over our education and health care systems provide graphic examples of breakdown at these different levels. Hence just recognizing the need to be proactive does not automatically guarantee success. Individuals and organizations still need to learn how to change and how to adapt to change and how to be successfully proactive.

In light of the above discussion, certain premises become clear: Change is inescapable, change is often stressful and even painful, change is necessary and potentially beneficial, and there are many different types and sources of change. To these may be added the premise that change is precisely what the work of rehabilitation is about. This chapter focuses on the impact of change within brain injury rehabilitation. Specifically, it describes the scope and impact of change in brain injury rehabilitation, establishes the rationale for change, discusses the different types and sources of change to increase understanding of the dynamics of change, and describes strategies to effect, manage, or cope with change, particularly organizational change. Examples and case studies are used to illustrate the various principles and strategies discussed. The reader is encouraged to examine these principles carefully and to find ways to apply the concepts discused to each unique rehabilitation setting.

CHANGE IN TRAUMATIC BRAIN INJURY REHABILITATION

It is not surprising that brain injury rehabilitation has not been able to escape the strong winds of change mentioned earlier. As an industry, it presents an interesting study of societal change. Brain injury rehabilitation deals with change of such variety and at so many levels that change can arguably be said to be one of its hallmark characteristics. Change can come from external societal forces, or it can be generated by developments within the industry, or it can pervade each microcosm of the industry, namely the individual facilities. All three sources of change are examined below.

Change External to the Brain Injury Industry

First, of course, are the ongoing changes of society, among these are technological advances such as the intrusion of the computer into the workplace and rehabilitation practices (Arokiasamy, Benshoff, McLean, & Moss, 1992; Chan, Matkin, Parker, & McCollum, 1988; Crimando & Sawyer, 1983; Growick, 1983; Kagan & Pietron, 1987; Schmitt & Growick, 1985). Other external changes include the geographical and upward mobility of the work force contributing to staff turnover (Emener, Lauth, Renick, & Smits, 1985; Riggar, Hansen, & Crimando, 1987; Toffler, 1970) and the increasing cost of health care, which places restrictions on providing optimum care such as limiting access to and participation in the rehabilitation continuum (Kraft, 1992; *U.S. News and World Report*, 1991). Furthermore, the vagaries of the economy affect individual practitioners and the industry as a whole, and demographic changes including aging and immigration as well as role changes such as more active roles played by women change the composition of the persons who sustain brain injury and require treatment.

In addition to these changes, rehabilitation professionals are accountable to a number of different parties, many of which have different expectations and outcome priorities. This includes the consumer, the funding source, and the rehabilitation facility or system. Each of these presents its own set of changes. Prime examples are the rise of the consumer and civil rights movements (DeJong, 1979; Hahn, 1983, 1985), increased restrictions by funding sources to keep health costs down (Kraft, 1992; Nadelson, 1986; Stout, 1992), and industrywide changes that came about as a result of these trends. In addition, it is helpful to remember that rehabilitation in general (not necessarily brain injury rehabilitation) is a profession that came about as a result of legislative mandate. As such, state and federal legislative changes always remain a possibility. A clear example is the passing of the Americans with Disabilities Act in 1990. What began as the Rehabilitation Act of 1973 to cover state and federal agencies and rehabilitation systems has now extended its purview to the entire American economy, including private for-profit rehabilitation (Field & Norton, 1992; U.S. Equal Employment Opportunity Commission, 1991; West, 1991). Although brain injury rehabilitation, for the most part, developed as a response of the private sector to the particular need to treat people with brain injuries, it is not insulated from legislative mandate. The recent congressional hearings into private brain injury rehabilitation, current considerations of the Traumatic Brain Injury Act of 1992, and increased media publicity should concern anyone in the field. In fact, the genesis of this field within the private sector opens the industry to another set of concerns, such as the health of the economy, the fiscal soundness of the insurance industry, and so on.

Change Within the Brain Injury Industry

Although it is clear that there is much external to brain injury rehabilitation that can cause change and flux, the industry is also exposed to the vicissitudes of internal change. In the first place, the industry itself emerged as a result of medical advances in emergency care of persons with brain injury. More than just emerging, it literally exploded into existence as the survivor rates for brain trauma increased fourfold and facilities to care for these individuals jumped from just 6 before 1980 to more than 700 by 1988 (McMahon & Growick, 1988).

In the face of such explosive need, a whole new field for rehabilitation has had to come into being, developing techniques of care and service delivery at an extremely rapid pace. Suddenly, many different professions and clinical specialists were working together in a wide variety of treatment environments addressing the complex and multifaceted needs of people with acquired brain injury. New service delivery models such as cross-disciplinary, interdisciplinary, and multidisciplinary teams have become pressed into service (Abramson, 1990; Conder et al., 1988; Leland, Lewis, Hinman, & Carrillo, 1988; Prigatano, 1987; Thomas, 1988), and case management functions have taken on roles that are at once unique and innovative (Dixon, Goll, & Stanton, 1988).

Team approaches in rehabilitation were not unique inventions of brain injury rehabilitation. Treatment teams had begun to show up in mental health counseling (Seligman & Ceo, 1986), in treating people with physical disabilities (Carpino & Newman, 1991), in treating people with hemophilia (Carrai & Handford, 1983), in working with children with phenylketonuria (Fisch, Cornley, Eysenbach, & Chang, 1977), and in treating an assortment of other problems such as heart disease, peptic ulcers and bronchial asthma (Aitken & Cay, 1975). The comprehensive nature of the consequences of brain injury, however, moved the team models to their ultimate expression, making them the fundamental base from which to provide rehabilitation. Although professional cooperation and gradual moves to teamwork approaches predated brain injury rehabilitation, this disability, which affected in a startlingly obvious way the entire person and his or her environment—mental, physical, cognitive, emotional, familial, social, sexual, vocational, recreational, financial, and even spiritual (Brooks, 1984; Levin, Benton, & Gossman, 1982; Rimel, Jane, & Bond, 1990; Trieschmann, 1990)—has forced and forged entirely new forms and levels of such cooperation and team work. Brain injury rehabilitation requires far more comprehensive, more varied, and closer cooperation than previously was needed in other areas of human services.

The same impetus, namely the comprehensive nature of this disability, has also added a new twist to another old notion: continuum of care. In brain injury rehabilitation, the treatment baton can be passed through a long line of treatment phases, from the trauma center, to intensive care, to acute rehabilitation, to postacute rehabilitation, to outpatient rehabilitation or day treatment, and finally to community integration (Arnow, Desimone, & Wood, 1987a; 1987b; Burke, 1987; Burke, Wesolowski, & Zencius, 1988; Cervelli, 1990; Deutsch, 1988; Fralish, 1988; Jacisin & VanKirk, 1989; Jacobs, 1989; Johnston & Cervelli, 1989; McKinlay & Pentland, 1987; Thomas, 1988; Uomoto & McLean, 1989). Even at the final stage, there is often continued professional or paraprofessional support (Condeluci, 1988; Karol, 1989). At other times, needs are such that they require long-term supported living (Deutsch & Fralish, 1988).

Brain injury rehabilitation has now achieved recognition as a specialty, one that is unique in its complex, multicomponent nature. Being a new specialty, it remains in much ferment as it searches for more effective and less complex ways to achieve successful outcomes. Each phase of rehabilitation, however, remains an avenue for change, growth, breakdown, or stress. Although not all these avenues of change affect all players in the field equally or simultaneously, the complicated interconnectedness of brain injury rehabilitation makes any serious change in any component cause ripples that affect many, if not most, at some level of intensity or magnitude.

Change Within Each Facility

What has been described thus far are the global or macro changes that affect or can affect brain injury rehabilitation. Change, however, is ever present within each facility or organization as well. Three major sources of these changes are the facility, its staff, the person with brain injury and his or her family. People working in rehabilitation are likely to face changes in administrative policy, clinical practice, staffing, service delivery models, organizational structure, reporting procedures, program evaluation, clinical focus, corporate focus, accountability demands, accreditation standards and job responsibilities, and personnel reorganization in both administrative and clinical areas. Client census and composition add yet another source of change and stress, with each new admission and discharge adding synergistically to the mix. Additionally, staff turnover is a further source of change (Butt & Gerber, 1987). In quite a different vein, change sometimes comes about as a result of the dissonance in private for-profit rehabilitation due to its desire to project itself as the caring profession (Banja, 1990) and its need to fulfill its mission of making a profit (Eisenberg, 1986; Nadelson, 1986). The unresolved tension between these perceived contradictions can lead some individuals to act the beneficent role in good times and suddenly to switch their focus to the bottom line and costs when financial goals are not achieved.

Finally, and perhaps most important, change in brain injury rehabilitation comes from the client. Each client and family presents a new and unique constellation. In addition, most clients and their families have already undergone some of the most profound intrapersonal and interpersonal changes ever imaginable (Brooks, 1984; DePompei, Zarski, & Hall, 1987; Florian, Katz, & Lahav, 1989; Hartman, 1987). Many of these changes affect the people who choose to work with them. Staff can become effected by psychosocial problems such as projection, confusion, retaliation, behavioral variability, emotional lability, denial, resistance, or displaced anger (Florian et al., 1989; Gans, 1983; Graffi & Minnes, 1989; Mullins, 1989; Ridley, 1989; Shaw & McMahon, 1990). Staff can react to these pressures through passive and even active retaliatory actions, such as displaying indifference, anger, frustration, or less caring approaches (Gans, 1983; Mullins, 1989).

Rehabilitation practitioners also know that it is difficult for clients to handle change. Appropriately, then, attempts are made to minimize or structure change appropriately. Paradoxically, change is also the ultimate goal of rehabilitation. Rehabilitation professionals constantly endeavor to achieve the greatest possible positive change in clients and their environment. Staff are also often pulled between developing a service delivery model that is flexible enough to meet individual client needs yet stable and predictable enough to provide a positive work environment for staff.

THE RATIONALE FOR CHANGE

Change Is Inescapable

As we survey this bewildering confluence of change, it may perhaps be tempting to ask, Why bother? Wouldn't it be possible to find a happy, stable medium and to expend our efforts in maintaining a balanced and serene status quo? Wouldn't it be better to stop this race to change before it overcomes us? This brings us of course to our first premise, that change is inescapable (Toffler, 1970, 1980). As has often been repeated, from the earliest of philosophers to their modern day contemporaries, the only thing that is constant is change. It is a given fact of life.

Change is not only inescapable but, according to our second premise, it is often stressful and even painful. The stress and resistance associated with change come from various sources: fear of the unknown; lack of adaptability skills; anxiety over outcome; fear of personal loss of power, position, prestige, responsibility, and even a job; novelty overload; inability to deal with ambiguity; a need for structure; the grind of having to relearn; and insecurity over abandoning the tried and true (Calish & Gamache, 1981; Gibb, 1974; Kirkpatrick, 1986; Toffler, 1970). Such fear and anxiety over change in brain injury rehabilitation lead to inevitable conflicts among groups advocating for particular types of change or no change at all. Paradoxically, some people thrive on change. Evidence of this is seen in many entrepreneurs, who leave a business that they started once the business becomes stable and move on to their next challenge and start a new company (Hyatt, 1991b).

Some recent examples of the changes within brain injury rehabilitation illustrate the pressures that change places on staff. In the last few years brain injury rehabilitation has seen a major industrywide switch from discipline- or department-based treatment to interdisciplinary teams (Prigatano, 1987). Many facilities still trying to adapt to that change continue to struggle with it. Old and revered disciplines such as physical therapy, occupational therapy, speech pathology, and psychology had been used to meeting and working as individual departments. They shared a common history, values, traditions, methods, and even language and were led by clinical supervisors from their own discipline. These departments were splintered and assigned to teams. Suddenly, they are in positions where they must explain to a whole team what they do, how they do it, and why they do it. Instead of answering to a primary clinical supervisor, they frequently answer to a team supervisor, who may have limited education in their area of expertise. In many cases, they answer to both their clinical department head and their team supervisor. Other members of the treatment team can now legitimately intrude onto their professional turf. These professionals are often forced to modify their treatment according to the dictates of the team. Such changes surely came about to enhance holistic and comprehensive treatment and to promote the kind of cross-disciplinary sharing necessitated by the nature of brain injury rehabilitation. Nevertheless, transition was, and still is, not without pain.

Another example of change that continues to rumble in the hallways of treatment is the conflict between those advocating more autonomy and family or client involvement in treatment and those wishing to stick to a more directive, paternalistic style of rehabilitation (Jacobs, 1990; Johnson & Higgins, 1987). This increased emphasis on greater client and family rights, participation, and control continues to leave many rehabilitation staff confused and debating over how much client and family power and autonomy they feel comfortable supporting, where they should draw the line between their professional judgment and client or family rights to determine the best course of treatment, and how

they should reconcile client or family decision making with funding source demands regarding treatment and outcomes. Staff may also face having to discard past ways of relating with clients and families and learn new ways, which sometimes leads to confusion over roles and professional boundaries.

These changes still challenge staff working in brain injury rehabilitation, and the stress from these conflicts continues to affect staff, organizations, and consumers alike. In addition, increases in the availability of specialized rehabilitation programs and changing patterns of reimbursement have resulted in census drops, decreased financial stability of programs, layoffs, shuffling of roles nd responsibilities, and a general rise in insecurity. These are but a few examples of the stress that change has brought to brain injury rehabilitation.

Change Is Necessary and Potentially Beneficial

If change is all this painful, one may be tempted to ask whether change is really necessary. Would it perhaps be better to standardize our procedures so that change becomes unnecessary? In the first place, the premise that change is inescapable makes this question moot. If it is inescapable, it matters not whether it is necessary. The nature of change makes this question worth pursuing, however, because change has the potential to bring much benefit. Although change comes with some risk of adversity, without change there is no growth. In fact, not changing can also bring great risk, and the necessity of change is perhaps better illustrated by looking at the costs of not changing. For brain injury rehabilitation, remaining static in an industry and society that continue to move on results in a number of undesirable consequences (Arokiasamy et al., 1988; Riggar et al., 1989; Weber, 1947). Momentum can be lost; techniques, equipment, organizational process, and even outcomes can become antiquated, compromising quality of care; potential benefits may be passed over; and, worst of all, the facility or industry itself can lose societal support for the valuable services it provides. The temptation to postpone small changes can result in major crises, which bears out the old proverb "a stitch in time saves nine." In brain injury rehabilitation, facilities that stuck to old philosophies and procedures in the face of managed care initiatives and consumer demands soon found themselves facing larger and larger obstacles to overcome.

Resistance to change diverts resources from being used productively to take advantage of change to dealing with conflicts between forces that want to change and those that are opposed to change. Such conflicts result in depressed morale, confusion, loss of focus, destabilization of purpose and mission, loss of revenue, increases in inefficiency, and poor client care. Nobody in brain injury rehabilitation needs to be provided with examples of such clashes between those wanting to maintain the status quo and those who want change, a battle that is often reframed by each of the opposing forces in terms that are deleterious or favorable according to the orientation of each group. Thus those wanting change will use words such as *progress, growth, innovation,* and *updating* while calling the stance of the opposing force inflexible, rigid, out of touch, or fearful of change. In contrast, the proponents of the status quo frequently view themselves as champions of continuity, guardians of stability, and protectors against chaos. Their opponents are considered fickle, faddish, anarchy prone, impulsive, and insensitive. Circumstances such as this can deteriorate into each side ascribing blame to the other, particularly when there is no strong philosophical base from which to guide the resolution of conflict.

The ambivalent nature of change, that is its potential to bring both benefits and losses, makes it important to distinguish between beneficial change and destructive change. Although in general, change is necessary, not all change is desirable. It is at least as important to identify undesirable change and to combat it as it is to promote beneficial change. Thus the industry should not sit back and accept all change. Some change should actually be addressed by putting a stop to it or fighting back (Galvin, 1989). As Nadelson (1986), speaking about rising health care costs, stated, "The physician is asked to limit care while at the same delivering it. The lawyer is not expected to be an advocate and judge simultaneously" (p. 951). Staff should not back itself into a trap of just accepting or coping with change. They must always retain the option to resist or reject change when they find proposed changes irresponsible or unjust. The industry has much to offer society. It should retain its right to ask individuals, groups, and society to change, especially in instances where growing trends compromise its basic mission of providing quality care.

TYPES AND SOURCES OF CHANGE

If one accepts that, although stressful and often painful, change is an inescapable fact of life and that it is necessary, one can move on to strategies of effecting, managing, or coping with change. In fact, these premises make it imperative that organizations and individuals learn to effect, manage, and/or cope with change.

The most critical factor of change is control. Change that is chosen or desired is more readily accepted and managed. As a number of investigators have put it, proactive change is more desirable and likely to succeed than reactive change (Crimando, Riggar, & Bordieri, 1988; Smits, Emener, & Luck, 1981). Moving to a new and desirable job, falling in love and deciding to marry, or going on a long vacation all involve a great deal of change. Because these activities are chosen, however, they lead to little resistance. It is those changes that we cannot control or those factors of even desired change that escape our control that lead to problems.

One of the first steps toward controlling change is understanding it. In this section the nature of change—its types and sources—is described briefly to provide a better understanding of change as it affects us. Furthermore, implementing strategies to effect, manage, and/or cope with change requires some understanding of the various types and sources of change. Different strategies are needed to impact on the different types of change.

Change can be classified according to its nature as modernization, transformation, or survival/adaptation (Schaller, 1972). Others see change as innovation adaptation (Backer, 1986), transformative change (Buckley & Perkins, 1984), individual change (Jackson, 1985), organizational integration (Kilmann, 1984), organizational behavior modification (Luthans, Maciag, & Rosenkrantz, 1983), service/value change (Neufeldt, 1986), individual adaptation (Rogers, 1962), or culture change (Schein, 1985). When one is designing the organization's response to change, it may be important to take into account the nature of the change to devise strategies that are appropriate and effective in addressing that particular type of change. Riggar et al. (1989) have provided an overview that identifies the strategies or mechanisms that accompany each of these different approaches to change. In planning change strategies, one may also want to determine whether the change is internally or externally motivated and whether the change is intentional or has been involuntarily imposed. This is an example of increasing one's understanding of change by studying the characteristics of its source.

Schaller (1972) also mentions another source of change that is not often obvious but may be important to keep in mind. Change can come as a result of indecision. Doing nothing can cause change. This may be seen in brain injury rehabilitation when one fails to take action when a client is engaging in self-destructive behavior patterns, or not stopping a therapist who may be engaging in unethical behavior, or, in the case of management, not providing leadership in the face of obvious need. All such inaction can cause problematic change. Similarly, expectations of change that are not met can also cause change. Staff expecting a promotion or conference travel support and not receiving it can be expected to react negatively. In formulating strategies, the importance of accurately identifying the type of change faced or required is discussed below.

STRATEGIES OF CHANGE

It has already been shown that change is complex and involves various levels, types, and sources. Trying to address change globally or without regard to using an organized approach can only lead to confusion. Frequently in this chapter we have mentioned change from three perspectives: effecting change, managing change, and coping with change. Strategies for effecting change, which implies intentional change, are by necessity going to be different from the strategies needed to cope with change that is ongoing or to manage change that was unanticipated.

All writers of repute in change management (Dalziel & Schoonover, 1988; Drucker, 1986; Lawrence, 1954, 1990; Peters, 1987) strongly emphasize paying attention to the social aspects of change rather than just the technical aspects. Lack of attention to the social aspects of change management is why many change plans get suddenly blind sided by totally unexpected resistance. The repeated advice of these experts is to keep the focus on people (Emener, 1989).

Effecting Change

There have been many models proposed to effect organizational change (Barczak, Smith, & Wilemon, 1987; Conner, 1988; Crimando, Riggar, Bordieri; Hanley-Maxwell, Benshoff, & Calzaretta, 1989; Dalziel & Schoonover, 1988; Egan, 1988; Goodstein & Burke, 1991; Kilmann, 1989; Kissler, 1991; Levy, 1986; London, 1988; Schaller, 1972; Young & Smith, 1988). These various models can be boiled down to six basic steps: (1) determination of the need for change, (2) planning for change, (3) communicating the change, (4) identifying and overcoming resistance, (5) implementing the change, and (6) evaluation. Change suggestions and initiatives, whether they be large or small, should come from staff at all levels within the organization as well as from consumers.

In prescribing strategies for change, one has to be extremely careful that the methods prescribed fit the organizational culture (Bender, Murphy, & Redden, 1990). Hence approaches that recommend participatory management will not fit in an organization that practices Theory X types of directive, hierarchical management styles (McGregor, 1960; Vogenthaler & Riggar, 1985). Furthermore, all who write about organizational change have their own biases regarding appropriate management styles. The authors of this chapter are no exception. Our clear bias is toward participatory management and staff empowerment for these brief reasons. For the most part, brain injury rehabilitation consists of highly educated, dedicated professional staff. To treat such staff as unable to contribute intelligently to management decisions is to invite trouble. Additionally, not to utilize their high motivation and intelligence is a tremendous waste of human resources. Such professionals are usually amenable to collegial approaches to management. Among change managers in rehabilitation and in business, there is almost consensus that participatory management and communication are vital to successful implementation of change (Backer, 1986; Bunker & Wijnberg, 1988; Galvin, 1989; Kanter, 1983; Kilmann, 1984; Lewis & Lewis, 1983). Finally, the gurus of business management clearly advocate participatory management (Drucker, 1986; Lawrence, 1954, 1990; Mayo, 1933, 1945). Examples of the success of participatory management with staff having far less education and training than rehabilitation professionals abound in the business literature (Hyatt, 1991a; Stack, 1992). The reader who is more committed to autocratic styles of management should read the strategies offered here with care before considering, let alone attempting, any implementation.

Determination of the Need for Change

Identification of the Problem. Change only comes about as a result of some dissonance or discomfort. This dissonance can come from a number of sources. A change in the external or internal environment of the organization may have made current practices less effective or counterproductive. For example, shortened lengths of stay demanded by funding sources may lead to the realization that the old way of taking a month for evaluation and working on multiple treatment goals is a luxury that is no longer affordable. Thus an organization may prescribe shorter evaluations and concentrate on high priority treatment goals. Another cause of dissonance can occur when there is a sense of unease between what was desired and what is actually achieved. Thus brain injury rehabilitation, finding department-based treatment to be less effective, switched to the interdisciplinary team model to achieve outcomes closer to what is desired. Dissonance also could arise from perceived contradictions between what is said and what is actually practiced. Hence staff may discover that institutional practices are inconsistent with the information promoted in its literature. A chance visit to another facility may create dissonance when the visitor finds a procedure there being more effective than what is currently used at his or her facility.

Determination of need begins with an examination of what is presently unacceptable or ineffective and what can be gained from change. In other words, it begins with the identification of a problem or a better way of doing things. Before any change can begin, there needs to be careful examination to determine whether a problem really exists. This can be done by checking available data, checking the perceptions of staff other than the one reporting the problem, and checking with the people most affected to see whether a problem exists.

Importance of empirical data. As far as possible the examination of the problem should involve empirical data and not only subjective perceptions. Using program evaluation is one method to gather such information. Two examples from a facility with a sophisticated program evaluation system illustrate the importance of using hard data.

The first example came from upper management's desire to cut costs by reducing the number of staff involved in client and family conferences. Simultaneously, there was also some concern by staff that the presence of large numbers of professionals at these conferences might be intimidating and disempowering to family participants. The number of staff were gradually decreased. Program evaluation data continued to show that satisfaction with these conferences remained high with all constituents: staff, clients, and families alike. In fact, in some instances there were slight increases in satisfaction as the number of staff involved decreased.

Another example grew out of program evaluation data showing some decline in client satisfaction. Again, analysis of these data showed the most dissatisfaction to be centered on one particular team. Data also showed that male clients expressed less satisfaction. It was found that the team in question had a high proportion of male clients. Finally, analysis found that the team in question comprised of younger, inexperienced staff.

The establishment of an efficient data collection, retrieval, and analysis system is so important, not only to determination of need but also to planning, implementation, and later evaluation of change, that it merits some special emphasis here (Attkissen, Hargreave, Horowitz, & Sorenson, 1978; Cronbach, 1982; Dolan, 1982; Posavac & Carey, 1985; Rossi & Freeman, 1982; Salyers, 1989; Walker, 1972). For too many facilities, program evaluation is just a white elephant to meet the needs of the Commission on Accreditation of Rehabilitation Facilities (CARF) or other accreditation bodies instead of a vital source of hard data to be used in support of decision making. Throughout all phases of the change process, the availability of accurate data is crucial. Not only can data aid in proper diagnosis, planning implementation, and evaluation of change; they can sometimes allay fears and reduce stress by providing a clearer perspective and more control. It is precisely the absence of empirical data, whether it be program evaluation or other empirical information, that often makes dealing with change stressful. Guessing at needs and pulling estimates out of thin air are probably prime reasons for the failure of much change implementation.

Use of subjective data. Although empirical data are crucial, subjective perceptions must not be ignored. When such perceptions are contradicted by accurate data, they still need to be pursued to arrive at their causes. New needs for change may surface from such efforts. Again, examination of subjective perceptions should go beyond just the perceptions of the person reporting the problem. Other involved staff need to be questioned, sometimes via anonymous surveys.

Just as important, consumers need to be consulted. One caveat should be noted, however: Just asking people may not provide the data needed. A survey for The White House Office of Consumer Affairs underscores this point. The survey found that 96% of unhappy customers never complain about discourtesy. Of these, however, 91% will not use the business that offended them again. Even more telling was the finding that the average unhappy customer will related his or her story to at least 9 other people and that 13% will tell 20 or more people (Executive Wealth Advisory, 1990).

The following scenario illustrates the importance of consulting with consumers to ensure that changes are responsive to their needs. At a particular facility, the size of monthly client reports sent to independent case managers, funding sources, and families averaged about 40 pages. The reports usually consisted of a compilation of reports by each individual discipline. Often many client data were repeated, with many of the discipline subsections starting with "Mr X is a white male aged 22 who suffered a brain injury from a motor vehicle accident on December 19, 1987. He was seen by. . . ." Some staff began complaining about the reports being an arduous waste of time. One or two claimed that family members had also complained. The reports not only took clinicians' time but overburdened word processing staff and were costly to produce and mail. Staff suggested a 3- to 5-page executive summary written by the case manager to replace current reports. The chief executive officer was adamant that these reports were the only tangible product that the company offered the funding sources and independent case managers. They should therefore be detailed, professional, and impressive. He claimed to know the funding sources and independent case managers better and was convinced that the present format was what they should receive. The chief executive officer also suspected that staff wanted to get out of the work of generating these reports, especially because a number of them were behind on reports.

How would you go about determining whether the report format should be changed? One solution could be to survey the independent case managers, funding sources, and families who receive these reports. The advantage of this approach, especially if kept anonymous, is that it may yield some useful data. The disadvantages include the following: Many of the people receiving these reports tend to be busy people and do not want to be bothered by surveys; in the absence of an alternative format, those surveyed may just respond positively, especially if they have already worked out adaptive ways of getting what they need without reading the entire report; even if those surveyed say they do not like the reports, the facility is now left with the question of how to modify them; and there is overwhelming evidence in psychological literature that there is often a vast discrepancy between what people profess and what they actually do or even how they really feel.

An alternative solution would be to select five or six persons from each of the constituent groups and send them both formats, asking them which they prefer. This way the data are more objective, recipients have alternatives from which to choose, they are required to make a choice rather than just providing opinions, and their responses could suggest actions the facility could take. (It so happens that, when one of the authors was a case manager and gave such a summary to an independent case manager, she was thrilled because the shorter report saved her the task of wading through the 40-page tomes to write her report to the insurance company.)

Determination of need must also take into account what can be gained by change and what will be lost by change. Only when the benefits outweigh the losses should a decision to implement change be made. Again, valid and reliable data are necessary in making these assessments. Finally, some determination should be made of the level of priority this change merits in the list of needs competing for the organization's resources and attention. Changes that entail less cost or are easier and quicker to achieve and changes that bring about greater benefit should receive higher priority.

Planning for Change

Planning for change entails a number of components, many of which are overlapping and will vary in emphasis depending on the size and structure of the organization. This includes: creating a change team, gathering data, engaging sponsor support, breaking down change into smaller steps, involving change agents and the persons likely to be affected by change, developing the change plan, addressing training needs, preparing for change implementation, building an evaluation component, and making the final decision. Each of these steps is discussed below.

Creating a change team. Once the determination to make a change is made, the first step is to create a change team. In putting such a team together, there is often a temptation to get people who would agree with one another. Such a conformist group would lead the organization into trouble and would derail proper implementation of change just as President Kennedy's think tank led him to the Bay of Pigs debacle. In addition to recruiting conformists or like-minded persons, there is a temptation to introduce conformist norms within the team even if pertinent team members were initially recruited. As Yalom (1985), perhaps the most renowned expert on group therapy, repeatedly warns, such norms, once established, are difficult to break. Getting team members who can comfortably challenge each other is vital for successful change management. Differences of opinion should be encouraged rather than suppressed. The terrible tragedy of the explosion of the space shuttle Challenger may have been averted if the whistle blowers at Morton Thiokol had not been suppressed. History is replete with such examples. Staff with dissenting views, however, like proponents of an idea, should be encouraged to back their position with accurate facts and clear logic. Unsupported arguments result in fractious debates and team breakdown.

According to Dalziel and Schoonover (1988), ideally the team should have persons to cover the following six roles: inventor (integrates trends and data to develop the big picture), entrepreneur (instinctively focuses on efficiency and effectiveness and seeks new possibilities and advantages), integrator (forges alliances and gains acceptance of the team and its plan, natural change agents, or persons with influence over staff, are ideal for this role), expert (has responsibility for technical knowledge and skills and explains information in a logical way), manager (simplifies, delegates, assigns priorities, and gets the job done at all costs), and sponsor (provides political support and resources). It is less important who fills each role than that each role is filled. Sometimes one person can play two or three roles.

Gathering data. Among the first tasks of the change team is gathering data. What exactly is the problem? What exactly has to be changed? Why should this particular situation be changed? What can be gained by changing? What will be lost by changing? What will be lost by not changing? Who are the people who will be affected by the change? How will they be affected? Will there be resistance? How strong and in what forms will this resistance be? Once the exact problem and the proposed changes have been identified, the team should decide about the general goal of the change. At this stage, the problem, the change, and the goal can remain general and global.

Most people engaging in planning for change become immediately focused on the present and the future. The past, however, is another important and often ignored source of a particular kind of data that may prove important. As part of gathering data, the change team would be wise to check the archives of their organization and to delve a little into the history of how the organization handled change before. What approaches were used? Which ones succeeded? What mistakes were made? What kinds of resistance and other problems were encountered, and how were they handled? It may prove instructional to interview those involved in past change for advice about what to do and what to avoid, what worked for them and what did not. Just the act of asking these people encourages their involvement and support. The truism that those who ignore history are destined to repeat its mistakes is a truism precisely because it has so often come true. Ignoring history itself is a mistake that keeps getting repeated. Exploration of past efforts will also give the present change planners a sense of the organizational culture and what to expect.

Engaging sponsor support. The next tasks are to engage sponsor support. Can the entire upper management be counted on for support? If not, is there a person in upper management who will champion the change? How strong will sponsor support be? How much are they willing to commit in resources? Frequently, it is upper management that is initiating the change. Even in such cases, there needs to be some clarity it terms of how far they are willing to go and how much they will commit in resources. These resources include time, money, logistical support, training, and freeing up key people from other responsibilities. The last factor is often one that derails change. Upper management often automatically assumes that new responsibilities will just be added on to existing responsibilities. The results are usually lack of concerted effort, missed timeliness, extra stress, and possible burnout. People trying, or being assigned, to achieve planned change are almost always already busy. Adding extra burdens without freeing them from some of their regular responsibilities naturally increases stress, decreases productivity, and in many cases leads to logically unworkable situations. Yet this step is all too often missed, and people wonder why change management is often ineffective and stressful. Preferably, the responsibilities being relieved, the new responsibilities for change planning being added, and what is expected of the persons involved in change planning should be spelled out clearly.

Breaking down change into smaller steps. Once sponsor support has been ensured, the problem and proposed change should be reexamined to break these down into smaller, more specific formulations. For each of these, new and more specific formulations and goals need to be drawn up. Distinctions should be made between long-term goals and short-term goals. Should the change be handled as a global transformation, or should it be handled incrementally? Determination should also be made of whether to introduce the change systemwide or to experiment first as a pilot test in a selected specific entity. For instance, the change could be introduced in only one team, department, or level and the impact assessed. This experimental approach affords the luxury of an opportunity to work out bugs in the plan before wider application.

Involving change agents and persons effected by change. At the data gathering stage, the areas likely to feel the impact of change, be they people or procedures (usually they are both), should have been identified. If these individuals have not already been involved, steps should be taken to involve them. Ideally, people who are likely to be affected by the change should be included from the inception of the change process. In addition, it will be necessary to identify and include the appropriate change agents, both natural change agents and formal change agents such as managers and supervisors, either as members of the team or through ongoing dialog and communication. Once the problems, what is to be changed, and the goals have been specified clearly, some reassessment of required resources should be made, and sponsors should be apprised again of these more specific formulations and needs to ensure their continued support.

Developing the change plan. The next step may be developing the change plan. Some investigators (Janis & Mann, 1977) recommend developing a full range of scenarios and for each of these developing objectives, risks, costs, benefits, and the like. In reality, however, practical constraints usually allow the consideration of only those scenarios that from experience or logic appear most viable (Phillips, 1989; Simon, 1976). Nevertheless, it is helpful to play out at least two or three scenarios to understand the full implications of the changes being proposed and to arrive at the best kinds of change. Kilmann (1984) and Mason and Mitroff (1981) warn that with each scenario or strategy being proposed particular attention must be paid to underlying assumptions. For instance, change managers may assume staff loyalty or that staff will want a change without any data to back up these assumptions. Change strategies based on misguided assumptions have a great likelihood of blowing up in the faces of the change planners. In fact, they frequently do. This is where team members who dare to challenge each other regarding unvalidated assumptions become such an important insurance against failure.

After a change strategy has been decided, the team can move to the specifics of making assignments of who will do what and establishing a time table for the whole change plan. Although timely performance of assigned tasks should always be strongly emphasized, the plan should also have flexibility built in to accommodate new findings or changes that occur en route. One way to achieve this is to have preset, regular meetings of the change team to review progress, obstacles, and new developments and the impact of these on the original change plan. In addition, the plan should develop mechanisms to get ongoing feedback from the staff. Another way of increasing flexibility is assigning "go-to" persons who can either make on-the-spot decisions and report later to the change team or collect data on the problem for later deliberation by the team.

Addressing training needs. Yet another task of the change team is to identify what new knowledge and skills training will be necessitated by the change. The team will have to decide what training will have to be accessed outside the organization, how to access such training, and what training can be provided in-house. Weighing the costs and benefits of both sources becomes part of the planning process. Advantages of outside consultants include access to expertise not available in house and possibly better reception by staff because there is an assumption of greater objectivity. The advantages of in-house sources are that these sources are usually more accessible and less costly, these individuals know the company better, and again staff may be more accepting if the trainers are known and trusted.

Preparation for change implementation. There are several tasks that are necessary to prepare for change: preparing strategies to communicate change to staff, finding ways to involve staff meaningfully, finding ways to identify and defuse resistance, and planning to reward participation and support. These tasks are discussed in greater detail later in this chapter.

Building an evaluation component. A final component should always include an evaluation mechanism. Essentially, this component addresses the questions of how well the change plan is being implemented, whether the plan is successful, and what the impact of the changes put in place will be. The evaluation component should be able to yield both formative and summative data (Posavac & Carey, 1985; Rossi & Freeman, 1982). Formative data are data that come in on an ongoing basis that enable one to make midstream changes. The example of reducing staff at client and family conferences mentioned earlier illustrates this. That same evaluation system also was able to measure the impact of the introduction of dictaphones on report writing timeliness. Such evaluation capabilities are especially important when one is introducing change with the experimental method. One team could be the first to implement the change, with resultant data being analyzed to fine tune the plan for the rest of the organization. Summative evaluation provides data on final outcomes. Although formative evaluation focuses on the process of change, summative evaluation answers the outcome questions of whether the goals and objectives were met and how well they were met. To establish an effective evaluation system, goals and objectives should, in the first place, follow the oft repeated advice that they be written in a clear, specific, and measurable format. Unless they are clear, specific, and measurable, they cannot be measured, and evaluation becomes almost impossible.

Making the final decision. Once the change plan has been developed, it becomes time to make the decision of whether to implement the plan. This stage merely reflects on the previous steps to determine that all possible bases have been covered. It is also the time to check whether the conditions that had previously called for change still remain. If conditions have changed, appropriate modifications of the plan may be called for. In addition, it may be time to go back to sponsors with specifics to get their feedback and renewed commitment. This is often the time when resource needs are finally negotiated and expectations of what the team will require of upper management get spelled out.

Although the above steps have been presented somewhat sequentially, it is not necessary that this particular sequence be followed. Different problems or different change proposals may involve juggling the sequence as well as the pace of implementation. What is most important is that all the steps mentioned are covered.

Communicating the Change

Maintaining open communication regarding the change is crucial for successful change management and particularly to defuse potential resistance (Beilinson, 1991; Koontz & O'Donnell, 1976; Laplace, 1983; Lippitt, Langseth, & Mossop, 1988). Change managers are sometimes prone to withdrawing into a secret closet and taking extraordinary measures to enforce secrecy. This is probably the worst possible way to approach change. It engenders mistrust, fuels rumor mills, contributes to all kinds of false surmises and misperceptions, induces fear, and builds resistance even before the change can be announced.

Communicating change involves four dimensions: content, target, style, and timing. Who receives what information, the form in which they receive it, and when they receive it are important considerations (Beilinson, 1991; Kirkpatrick, 1986; Koontz & O'Donnell, 1976). Content should include the reasons for the change, the costs and benefits of changing, the process by which decisions were made, the probable and desired impact of the change, what is expected of the people who will be affected by the change, and publicizing sponsor support. For example, to prepare for changing or reducing health benefits one might present company information on the rising cost of health care within the organization, facilitate discussions on this topic, and share relevant articles. The more open and direct the information, the better. Preparing for the necessity of CARF accreditation could involve sharing information about how such standards are becoming the norm of the industry; how accreditation could boost the prestige, visibility, and financial success of the organization; how it could improve the quality of client care; and so on.

Target in this context refers to all people and areas affected by change. Although in general it is recommended that everyone receive any information that is not confidential or too cost prohibitive to disseminate, it is particularly important that the people most affected by the change be integrally involved in the communication loop. Because of the interconnectedness of brain injury rehabilitation, it is more than likely almost everybody will be affected. Some groups that may sometimes be overlooked, however, are the board of directors, members of the local community, outside agencies with whom the facility has association, outside consultants, and funding sources.

In general, the style that is most strongly advocated is free, open, and sincere communication moving in all directions throughout the organization. As Lippitt et al. (1988) put it, the communication needs to be "a 'warts and all' candidness that deals as fairly with large and small failure as with large and small success" (p. 111). Lippitt et al. (1988) consider communication the single most important factor in change implementation. Communication is not just telling or informing. It must create a common understanding among all parties (Kirkpatrick, 1986; Koehler, Anatol, & Applbaum, 1976; Laplace, 1983). Dalziel and Schoonover (1988) recommend that people at different levels be polled to determine whether there is common understanding of the communication. This will help ensure effective communication and will provide opportunities to correct misperceptions. In addition, the style and content of communication should be modified according to the specific target audience. People most affected by the change may need the most relevant information and should be invited to provide the most input. People most skeptical may need special attention to reinforce the importance of the change.

For change implementation to be successful, communication must run throughout all staff levels to connect all parties participating in the change process (Graham, 1985; Koontz & O'Donnell, 1976; Szilagyi, 1981). For example, managers must assist staff to stay focused on the reasons, goals, methods of implementation, benefits and costs, time lines, persons responsible, and expectations and impact of the changes. Staff communication to managers and is crucial to evaluate success and to identify trouble spots.

The final dimension is timing. Again, in general people should receive information sooner than later. Beilinson (1991) also recommends that the staff be prepared beforehand when hearing of changes. Regular channels that are most used by staff will prepare staff for when to expect more news or a schedule of updates on change planning and implementation could be posted. Timing should take into account particular situations. For example, a time of high census, when people are most busy, may not be the most appropriate time to announce new changes of procedure. Conversely, slower times at a facility may provide excellent opportunities to embark on important projects to keep staff involved instead of laying them off.

Identifying and Overcoming Resistance

Resistance to change can come from many different sources: perceived personal loss of security, money, pride, stakes, control, satisfaction, autonomy, contacts with friends, freedom, responsibility, authority, good working conditions, and respect; fear of criticism, extra effort being needed, more harm being done than good, and making mistakes; emotional blocks such as learned habits, inertia, needing stability and security, sense of personal inadequacy to handle change, resentment over lack of personal input, and resentment of authority; misconceptions regarding source, purpose, expectations, effects, and motives for change; institutional barriers such as entrenched bureaucracies, organizational structure, organizational culture, external stakeholders, lack of political support from the top, decision making and policy setting styles; inadequate resources such as space, time, money, personnel, and skills; incompatibility with mission, goals, policies, and procedures; ineffective reward or incentive systems; the very way the process of change is handled leading to lack of consensus, indifference, noncommittance or fence sitting, passive resistance, sabotage, blaming, and finger pointing; and finally, preoccupation with the present crisis or responsibilities (Calish & Gamache, 1981; Gibb, 1974;

Jones & Bearley, 1986; Kilmann, 1984; Kirkpatrick, 1986; Margolis & Fiorelli, 1984; Riggar et al., 1989). Riggar et al. (1989), in their review of organizational change literature, identify three major keys to reducing or eliminating resistance: participatory management, communication, and staff development and training.

Participatory management and open communication. Over and over again, the management literature stresses involving staff in program management empowering staff to make decisions and to take ownership in solving problems, genuinely seeking and using their input and assessments, and keeping them informed about how their input was used (Kanter, 1983; Kilmann, 1984; Lawrence, 1954, 1990; Peters, 1987). Of particular importance in the very beginning of planning change is including natural change agents and those persons who may be effected by change (Backer, 1986; Beckhard & Harris, 1987; Crimando et al., 1988; Dalziel & Schoonover, 1988; Kanter, 1983). As Lewis and Lewis (1983) put it, "involving people who have a stake in the outcome" (p. 29). Natural change agents are people in the organization who have influence and the respect of others not because of their position or title but simply by virtue of their natural leadership talents (Alinsky, 1971; Beckhard & Harris, 1987). These people must not be confused with formal change agents, such as directors, managers, and supervisors, who, by virtue of the authority invested in their position are decision makers and wield influence. Natural change agents have the power to make or break change implementation.

Participatory management (a common buzzword in management parlance), however, must not be used as a gimmick. Lawrence, whose 1954 article on overcoming resistance was reprinted as a classic in the *Harvard Business Review* in 1990, emphasized that participation is of value only if staff participation is genuinely sought and based on respect. As Galvin (1989) stresses, "Participation cannot be artificially created and should not be used as a device to manipulate participants or 'sell' them on a decision already reached by top management" (p. 141). Lawrence (1954, 1990) saw resistance not just as something to be overcome but as something of value. Not all resistance is bad. Sometimes it acts as a red flag for poor implementation or unseen problems and should be explored rather than ignored (Jones & Bearley, 1986). In fact, as Galvin (1989) notes, there are some changes in health care and rehabilitation that may deserve active resistance just as other changes may merit active support.

Training and staff development. For overcoming resistance and for the overall success of change implementation, training is the third crucial factor (Howell, 1989; Kanter, 1983; Rosow & Zager, 1988; Salyers, 1989). Training and education should be specific to what is needed as a result of the change, such as new skills or new procedures; should address the circumstances surrounding the change, such as the rationale for the change; and should include ongoing staff development. As Salyers (1989) writes, "Participation requires training. . . . Establishing and sustaining a comprehensive staff development and training system requires management to recognize that training does not interrupt work, but enables it. You always pay the price of process, or pay for its absence" (p. 142).

Obstacles to change. On the other hand, factors that tend to stifle change are overcentralization, conservation, emphasis on risk, scapegoating of leaders, staff turnover, low morale, loss of trust and confidence, restricted flow of communication, lack of training, absence of a clear plan for change, inaccurate communication, and lack of political support from the top (Bourgeois, McAllister, & Mitchell, 1978; Bozeman & Slusher, 1979; Cameron, Kim, & Whetten, 1987; Drucker, 1986; Kimberly, 1985; Kimberly & Quinn, 1984; Peters, 1987; Riggar et al., 1989; Starbuck, Greve, & Hedberg, 1978; Staw, Sandelands, & Dutton, 1981). Companies that do not emphasize people first will have a hard time implementing change (Dalziel & Schoonover, 1988; Peters, 1987). In rehabilitation there are sometimes management actions that overlook the fact that professionals are people first. The tendency is to deal with them primarily as employees. It appears that many managers forget that staff are people first and not robots that can be always counted on to be obedient, reliable, and loyal. All these attributes need to be earned by managers, not taken for granted as an expected part of the package when someone is hired.

Implementing Change

Earlier sections of this chapter deal with the formulation of change strategies. Although many people readily focus on formulation, implementation is just as important. The best conceived plans are useless or, worse, a waste of valuable resources and create more trouble than they were designed to alleviate unless exceptional care is taken in implementation (Schilit, 1987). Peters and Waterman (1992) stress that the most successful organizations are biased toward action while less successful companies are caught up in endless planning. In fact, they assert that companies that are ready to experiment and move even before plans are fully developed are companies that succeed. Managers who dabble endlessly in the formulation stage are less likely to effect change successfully because the conditions that earlier called for change themselves can change or deteriorate, assuming crisis proportions. Staff expectations of promised change begin to wane. Notions that the managers do not really care or they would move sooner begin to surface. Even suspicions that management does not know what to do or was hiding behind a pretense of planning change could become grist for the ever present rumor mills. Thus, although careful planning is important, implementation is the area most fraught with danger.

In brain injury rehabilitation, planning can become even more lengthy because crisis after crisis aborts scheduled meetings. As mentioned earlier, in effecting change, timing is crucial (Beilinson, 1991), and striking while the iron is hot is more than just a proverb. It is vital. Many other contextual and process variables also should be kept in mind. It is precisely because contextual and process variables are so important that they have been stressed repeatedly throughout this chapter and are discussed in some depth in the last section.

Preliminaries of implementation. Formulation is primarily informational, analytical, and technique driven, but implementation is behavioral, cultural, and structural (Bender et al., 1990). As stressed earlier, organizational changes should be initiated and driven from all persons within the organization, as well as consumers. In the best case scenario, implementation should begin even when change is first being conceived because the first step of implementation is letting the staff know that it is coming. All the steps of informing staff of potential change, gathering data from staff, involving them in planning and problem solving, and keeping them posted about the progress of planning are initial steps of implementation.

Johnson and Fredian (1986) break down implementation into three phases: the preannouncement phase, the transition phase, and the consolidation phase. The preannouncement phase was discussed earlier. The most important step in the transition phase is getting the support of key people. This requires, first and foremost, that sponsors remain fully committed to the plan and be ready to commit resources and their personal support. The other groups to be enrolled are the change agents and the people who will be affected by the change. Enlisting the support of these people was mentioned earlier. Ensuring that they remain committed is essential for the transition to succeed.

Establishing the transition team. The next step is putting the transition team together. This could be the planning team used earlier or a different team. It is important to include identified change agents and representatives of the various program sectors likely to feel the impact of change. The same guidelines for establishing a team and making sure that team members are not merely "yes men" apply to the transition team. Sponsors may or may not be part of the team so long as they make their full support of the team clear and public. However, a significant key to successful implementation is that management not only says it is in support but demonstrates that in its behavior. Managers should be the first to adopt and use new procedures.

Putting the plan into action. The next step is putting the plan into action. This consists of people doing their assigned tasks and reporting progress or problems back to the transition team. There should be a clear and uncompromising emphasis on performance and outcome (Drucker, 1986). Throughout implementation, it is important to keep selling the need for change, to maintain open communication, and to involve staff as much as possible (Johnson & Fredian, 1986).

Staff should be kept informed of procedures and schedules of the transition. They should have a person to go to as questions arise. Staff should be kept motivated by public announcements of progress being made. Finally, the plan to reward participation and support should be put in place (Nadler, 1981). Thank you notes, public recognition, and other reinforcements should be used to show appreciation. There is often a misconception that bonuses and other tangible rewards are the most effective staff reinforcers. Public recognition is often valued over monetary rewards, but the most effective reward is job satisfaction, the opportunity to do a good job and to succeed. Particularly for rehabilitation staff, any change that makes their job easier and makes it more possible to have a significant impact on the lives of persons with brain injury is their biggest reward. Injudicious use of bonuses and recognition can cause more trouble than benefit, but nobody would argue with a change that makes a job easier or success possible in their chosen profession. This is why it bears reiterating that staff should always be asked what would make their jobs easier or would help them succeed and that change should be inspired by this exploration or at least take it into account.

The consolidation phase. Successful implementation does not end with the transition phase. If the change is to take hold and stay, much attention should also be paid to consolidation. In behavioral plans used with clients, this is called maintenance and generalization. Consolidation should perhaps begin with evaluation of the transition. Did it work? How well did it work? What bugs surfaced that need to be corrected? How will they be corrected? What adjustments have become necessary, and how will they be effected? What new ideas have emerged that can improve on the original changes? How did the staff receive the new changes? If resistance has

emerged, how will it be addressed? Have there been improvements in quality and productivity? Were the goals of the transition met, and how well were they met? Were the needs of those impacted by the change met?

In addition, some celebration to retire the old and inaugurate the new may be in order. For instance, one facility held a dinner and distributed "We survived CARF" T shirts to celebrate their first accreditation by CARF. Be liberal with rewards and recognition of successful efforts.

Evaluation

Finally, once the transition has been completed and the changes are fully in place, a comprehensive summative evaluation of the change should be completed. This is not to say that evaluation should be held off until this stage. As has been stressed earlier, formative evaluation should be an ongoing feature of the whole process. At this final stage, however, the evaluation consists of an examination of how successful the change has been and how well the goals and objectives set earlier were accomplished.

Upon completion of the evaluation, the transition team should be disbanded. A full report or debriefing of their activities, accomplishments, and recommendations may be kept on record for use as a model for future change projects. The importance of consulting history to determine how change was handled before has already been emphasized. Documentation regarding the present change adds to this history. The better the documentation, the more useful it will be for future change planners. The evaluation may also reveal that other structures to continue or monitor the change are needed and should be installed.

Managing Change

Managing change is defined here as an organization's ability to effectively deal with unanticipated change. The challenge is how to posture the organization so that it is always able to deal with change. Strategies to manage unexpected change include being proactive, having a bias for action, valuing training, empowering staff, and establishing an ethic of change. These five strategies are explained below. All these factors are essential prerequisites of successful implementation of intentional change as well.

Being Proactive

A primary ingredient of managing change is establishing a proactive climate within the organization (Crimando et al., 1988; Smits et al., 1981). Every owner, administrator, or manager of a brain injury facility reading this would readily agree. Some pull their hair out trying to find ways to be proactive instead of crisis oriented. Others may actually believe that they already are proactive. Examine, however, the example of a staff and client schedule provided in Figure 16-1, which is an excerpt from an actual schedule of a treatment team (modified to protect confidentiality) in a residential facility. Therapists are indicated in the left column, and client initials or activities are given in the time and day slots. Empty boxes are for report writing and other such activities. Because it is driven in part by the need to achieve billable hours and to ensure client coverage, this schedule is fairly typical of schedules used in most facilities.

When one looks at this schedule and considers the constant need for team collaboration and problem solving, spontaneous visitations to the facility, the importance of responding quickly to client and family needs, and the many critical issues that require immediate attention throughout the day, it is not surprising that many facilities are crisis-oriented. Such a schedule shapes organizational behavior, in this case keeping it crisis oriented. How can such a schedule allow for a responsive and proactive climate when the organization is frequently, if not constantly, engaged in putting out fires? The free slots in staff members' schedules seldom coincide with each other, effectively negating any chance for spontaneous conferencing that may lead to proactive and creative ideas. In such a tight schedule, staff can waste much time in trying to get in touch with a fellow team member about an issue that cannot wait for the next team meeting. Sometimes, the chase can prove so unsuccessful that discussions get postponed, again reducing proactivity, increasing crisis potential, and decreasing the time available for program development. Of course,

this proclivity toward crisis orientation is compounded many times over for facilities with more than one team, especially with regard to interteam collaboration.

Somewhere in the schedule, there needs to be time when staff can congregate and troubleshoot. Such time slots need not coincide across the entire organization but should at least coincide for groups where cooperation and collaboration is essential, such as treatment teams, activity therapists, residential staff, and other similar groups.

This proposition may seem at first blush to be an arrangement that lessens productivity. Management may tend to frown on the loss of billable hours in the short run or even be suspicious that such time will be spent sharing complaints or venting or wasted in social intercourse unrelated to work (and what does such a fear say about management's view of its staff?). Such penny wise–pound foolish perspectives will kill proactiveness. Undoubtedly, some "off-task" time may occur, but it is highly likely that much of the time will also be spent catching up on information, troubleshooting, and other productive activities. In the long run such informal conferencing times increase productivity, especially when one considers all the time and effort spent on dealing with problems that might otherwise be avoided. Unstructured time can often lead to the identification of productive solutions. Such productive unstructured time was one of the keys to the Macintosh success story (Kawasaki, 1990). In fact, time spent among supportive colleagues may provide the needed respite that can forestall burnout and increase productivity.

Studying trends. In addition to these informal conferencing time slots, some person within the organization needs to be designated to watch for future trends. More important than having a designated person is having a reporting mechanism where trends that have been identified can be routed for study of their potential implications. For example, more than 15 years ago warnings were being raised about potential bank failures because of their overexposure to loans to Third World countries. About 10 years ago similar warnings were raised about the savings and loan industry. More pertinent to brain injury rehabili-

Week of:	Mon 8:30	Mon 9:30	Mon 10:30	Mon 1:00	Mon 2:00	Mon 3:00	Mon 4:00	Tue 8:30	Tue 9:30	Tue 10:30	Tue 1:00	Tue 2:00	Tue 3:00	Tue 4:00	Wed 8:30	Wed 9:30	Wed 10:30	Wed 1:00	Wed 2:00	Wed 3:00	Wed 4:00	Thu 8:30	Thu 9:30	Thu 10:30	Thu 1:00	Thu 2:00	Thu 3:00	Thu 4:00	Fri 8:30	Fri 9:30	Fri 10:30	Fri 1:00	Fri 2:00	Fri 3:00	Fri 4:00
Clinical Director		Mtg Psy		PE Mtg	Mtg VP	Mtg PD		Team Mtg	Ψ TE	Team mtg	Mtg pt/ot	Mtg COD		Mtg PD			Mtg PD	Safety committee		Mtg PD	Mtg VP	Conf Call	Admit Com	Evaluation Conference					MIS mtg	Ψ TE	Mtg COD	Planning Pres		Task Force Mtg	
Program Director	Team mtg	MIS mtg		Staff PA	Mtg WV	Mtg CM		Team mtg	Mtg RT		Conf Call		Resid mtg	Mtg CD	Team mtg		Mtg CD	Conf Call		Mtg CD	Conf Call	Team mtg	Ct Mtg	Admit Com	Evaluation Conference				Team mtg	Evaluation Conference				Task Force Mtg	
Case Manager	Team mtg		REPORTS	REPORTS	CM JW	Mtg PD	Fam Call	Team mtg	Fam Call	Fam Call	Conf Call	Fam Call	Resid mtg	Fam Call	Team mtg	Rep	CM DB	Ct FU	CM KH	Fam Call	Conf Call	Team mtg	Bills	Admit Com	Evaluation Conference		Fam Call	Fam Call							
Physical Therapist	Team mtg	PT TH	Sch	PT MM	PT SW		NR team	Home Evaluation			Mtg CD	PT NM	PT SW	PT RB	PT NM	PT TH	PT MM	PT OT	PT SW	PT AP	PT Conf Call	PT JW	PT ME	Admit Com	Evaluation Conference										
Occupational Therapist	Team mtg	OT CR	Sch	OT NM	OT PK	OT SW	NR team	Home Evaluation			Mtg CD	OT SW	OT KF	OT KF	OT DA	OT KF	OT KF	PT OT	OT PK	OT SW	OT KB	Mtg MG		OT ME	Evaluation Conference	OT SW	OT SW	OT CM	OT Evaluation DH Conference			OT CL	OT HW	OT SW	OT NM
Cognitive Therapist	Team mtg	Cog ME	Cog Th	Cog JW	Cog DB	Cog NM		Team mtg		Cog NM	Com Staff	Cog TH	Cog DB		Team mtg	Cog JW	Cog ME	Cog WV				Team mtg	Cog JW	Cog TH	Cog WV	Cog NM	Cog TW		Team mtg Evaluation Conference				Cog NM	Cog WV	
Recreation Therapist	Team mtg		TC mtg					Team Mtg PD			RT schedule		Resid mtg	Client input	Team mtg	RT schedule		Safety committee				Team mtg			Evaluation Conference		House mtg		Team mtg Evaluation Conference						
Behavior Therapist	Team mtg	BI WV		Staff PA	BI GW		Social Group	Social Team mtg	BI NM	BI WV	BI JW		BI staff		Team mtg	BI DB	BI TH	BI NM	BI TW	Mtg KJ	Social Group	Team mtg	BI KH	BI JW	Evaluation Conference				Team mtg Evaluation Conference			BI KH	BI TH	BI NM	BI ME
Psychological	Team Mtg CD	Psy NM		Psy RL	Mtg WV	Psy JW	NR team	Team mtg	PI team		Psy TW	Psy TW	Psy	Psy Mtg	Team mtg	Psy staff	Mtg TH	Psy JW	Psy NM	Support Group		Team mtg	Psy BT	Psy GW											

Figure 16-1 Weekly schedule.

tation is the fact that at least 8 years ago insurance companies were being scrutinized for financial viability given their overexposure to real estate loans. Some study of this trend in the context of the decade old trend of rapidly rising health care costs could have anticipated the effects of present cost-cutting efforts by insurance companies on health care.

An even more obvious trend is the aging of America. It is inevitable that facilities serving people with brain injury will begin to see more and more older clients seeking treatment in the next 10 to 15 years (Arokiasamy, 1992). What are the implications for brain injury rehabilitation? How will this age group affect vocational, recreational, activities of daily living, productive activity, community reintegration treatment, and outcome goals? How will therapist and client relationships change when clients happen to be as old as the grandparents of the therapists? The implications are enormous, but is the industry actively (or even remotely) considering them? Although it may be irksome to spend time examining such long-term trends, that is precisely what makes for proactive organizations. Even in the short term, how many brain injury organizations, many of which are privately owned, are studying the implications of the Americans with Disabilities Act (ADA)? It would be ironic if the first ADA-based suit filed were against a brain injury rehabilitation organization. As a final example, how many brain injury organizations are aware of and preparing for the traumatic brain injury act that is even now being considered in Congress? Becoming proactive requires some expenditure of resources in the present, but it mitigates the whipsaw effects of future change and makes an organization more ready to handle change. In fact, Drucker (1986) insists that organizations that are not ready to invest in the future will have a hard time surviving through the present.

Bias for Action

A second value that enables organizations to manage unexpected change is a bias for action. Peters and Waterman (1990), in their classic work *In Search of Excellence,* identified bias for action as one of the 10 common ingredients of the most successful companies in the United States. There are a number of obstacles that can impede action, including a cumbersome bureaucratic organizational structure and overcentralization of power (Bourgeois et al., 1978; Drucker, 1986; Kimberly, 1985). Within such organizations, action gets stifled by the number of levels that need to be negotiated before action can be authorized. Delegating authority for appropriate action to all organizational levels and removing hierarchical barriers enhance quick action (Drucker, 1986).

Other ways in which quick action is aborted include the creation of numerous committees, task forces, planning commissions, and other such groups that spend time in endless study of the situation and in planning (Peters & Waterman, 1990). Such groups help dissipate responsibility for action so that no particular person can be held accountable. Furthermore, they usually provide the illusion of action without anything tangible being accomplished. Minutes from these group meetings often highlight this point. A helpful exercise is to examine the minutes of such groups, preferably over a period of several meetings. Typically, such minutes will reveal recommendations to study (not resolve) a particular problem, postponement of particular action for some reason or another, decisions to wait for action from another committee, and often repetition and rehashing of the same issues. Such activity is not action. Often, different committees are established that deal with different facets of the same problem, with none being empowered to enact decisive action. The move to interdisciplinary teams is certainly a positive move in the direction of decisive action in addressing the needs of persons with brain injury. In other areas, however, particularly administration, such overlapping and overabundant groups may still exist. A first step toward establishing a bias for action is the examination of the need for all standing committees, task forces, and the like.

Sherman (1993) stresses the wide scale and continuous use of Do It Groups (DIGs) to encourage staff to vigorously attack organizational problems. The DIGs tackle small and manageable problems and have rotating membership.

They typically meet for one hour per week and convene for no longer than one month. They are quick action-oriented teams that must identify practical strategies for the improvement of a specific area. Participants are not to get stuck on perfectionist tendencies, must seek no-cost or low-cost solutions, and work under the expectation that 90 percent of all proposals will be approved by management. The DIGs meeting should be enjoyable and should achieve outcomes that build positive organizational momentum.

Organizations with a bureaucratic structure tend to become inexorably larger and larger. Not only do bureaucracies grow larger, they tend to routinize basic operations and to abhor change (Weber, 1947). If one stops to examine the thousands of layoffs being announced by company after company, one should wonder how these companies are going to manage with such drastic reductions of the work force? If they still manage to function, why in the first place did they need so many workers? A case in point is the recent announcement by General Motors that it would reduce its central office from 13,500 to 3,500. To be flexible enough to deal with unanticipated change, organizations need to stay lean, not wait for adversity to force chaos and cause layoffs. Many brain injury facilities can look back to an earlier time in their history when they were smaller and more agile. Decisions were made more quickly and were shared with more people in less time. As they grew, however, many grew vertically. For greater versatility and flexibility, it is recommended that growth be horizontal. Instead of hierarchical layers, a consortium of small, self-managed teams empowered to make decisions enhances the organization's ability to confront change (Drucker, 1986).

A second step in establishing a bias for action is setting clear accountabilities and evaluating performance by outcome rather than process. Some managers tend to get overinvolved in how things are going to be accomplished rather than assigning tasks and leaving it to the persons responsible to devise their own ways of accomplishing them. Not only should managers hold staff accountable for outcomes, they should set examples by taking decisive action themselves. Managers have a tendency to ignore complaints rather than considering their possible legitimacy (Dalziel & Schoonover, 1988). *People are never satisfied* is a phrase that is heard too often when managers get together. Even complaints that are distorted or exagerrated can become sources of information about real problems. Decisive action on the part of managers enhances the ethic of bias for action throughout the organization. If managers do not set the example of responding to the needs of others, how can they expect staff to be fully committed to the satisfaction of clients, families, or funding sources? In fact, in one facility where both client and staff satisfaction surveys were conducted, the similarity of items of dissatisfaction between the two groups was astounding. The complaints that clinicians had against the administration were the very same complaints that clients made against their clinicians. Clients, just like their therapists, complained that they did not have sufficient opportunities for providing input, did not receive enough information, and felt misunderstood.

The Value of Training

Another common characteristic among organizations that can best weather unanticipated changes is the resilience of their staff. According to London (1988), resilience is a combination of self-confidence, a desire to achieve, and a willingness to take risks. All these factors, especially the first two, can be improved by training. Despite much evidence that organizations that invest in training are more resilient and prosper (Brokaw, 1991a, 1991b), however, training is often one of the first things to be cut during hard times. From 1986 to 1990, productivity in the manufacturing sector grew by 3.3% annually while productivity in the service sector dropped by 0.4% annually (Mangelsdorf, 1991). This is partly because the average manufacturing company outspent business, health, and educational service companies by 20% to 40% in training (Mangelsdorf, 1991). Because the benefits of training are not immediately recognizable, training often receives inadequate attention. The better trained the staff and the more they know about their own work and the work of their counterparts, however, the more versatile and resilient they become. Such staff become more self-confident and more ready to take risks. In addition, expenditure on training makes staff feel more valued. This translates into staff loyalty and support for the organization during traumatic times. As discussed above, there can be no participation and therefore no empowerment without training (Drucker, 1986; Salyers, 1989). Training can be specific to new skills necessitated by particular changes, but it should not stop there. Ongoing training opportunities that enhance the personal and professional development of staff raise the versatility and caliber of staff in general, placing the whole organization in a better position to weather change.

How staff are treated when they make mistakes directly affects their willingness to take risks. This is fairly obvious, but managers in brain injury programs often create an environment where there is not much permission to make mistakes. In the training of both clients and clinicians, many stress that it is all right to make mistakes. The environment often disenchants anyone of this notion, however. Clients are frequently discouraged from taking risks, and those who make mistakes quickly receive behavioral consequences. On the other hand, staff who take risks run the danger of being criticized, both personally and professionally. The threat of liability that always hangs over brain injury rehabilitation programs strongly reinforces safety and a mistake-free environment. If mistakes get treated as learning opportunities, however, they foster a greater willingness among staff to take risks and also serve to strengthen a bias for action.

An Ethic of Change

The success of Japanese management and the comparative lack of success of American management over the last two decades has seen American management turn to Japan for some answers to its management problems. Among the most lauded solutions is just in time inventory (JIT), which has been widely discussed in business literature. Another concept, *kaizen,* which the Japanese consider more responsible for their success than JIT, has somehow eluded attention, however (Peters & Waterman, 1987).

Strangely enough, the *kaizen* concept was an American concept that was taken to Japan in the 1950s by Deming and Juran and revolutionized their industry while leaving U.S. industry comparatively untouched (Imai, 1986). Furthermore, JIT is only applicable to the manufacturing sector. *Kaizen* can be used readily by service sector industries such as brain injury rehabilitation. In recent times, the adoption of the *kaizen* philosophy has augured the turnaround of a number of large U.S. corporations, such as Xerox, Chrysler, and Motorola.

What is *kaizen?* Simply put, it is small improvements. More than that, it means ongoing improvement involving everybody (Imai, 1986). *Kaizen* is pretty much a household word in Japanese industry. When American managers think of change, they tend to think of large changes or innovations. In fact, it is highly probable that managers reading this chapter are thinking in terms of large-scale change and do not notice the little changes that are constantly occurring in their facilities. Examples of innovations and large-scale changes are the introduction of the computer, robotization, and organizational restructuring. *Kaizen,* on the other hand, refers to little improvements. For example, if the night staff places arrows marking the direction of the restroom, many clients will stop ringing the night bell to get staff to show them where the restroom is. Transforming a narrative log into easily used checklists is another example. Innovations are usually abrupt and volatile, involve a few champions of the project, are intermittent and nonincremental, require much investment in training and cost, and often involve scrapping the old and rebuilding. By contract, *kaizen* is gradual and constant; involves everybody; is continuous and incremental; requires little cost, effort, or training; and usually involves maintenance and improvement rather than scrapping and rebuilding.

Small improvements are constantly happening in brain injury facilities. The difference between this and the *kaizen* philosophy is that these improvements are scarcely noticed, whereas with *kaizen* they are celebrated and built into an ethic of change. Establishing such an ethic of change within brain injury facilities increases the facilities' ability to manage change and to build for the future.

Kaizen, or the ethic of change, has to become a central part of the value system of the organization. How do we establish such an ethic? *Kaizen* begins with the recognition of a problem. As Imai (1986) puts it, "Where there are no problems there is no potential for improvement" (p. 163). A problem is defined as anything that inconveniences anyone. Usually, the people who create the problem are not directly inconvenienced by it. Hence people are bothered by the inconveniences caused them but are not so bothered by the inconvenience they cause others. Problems, therefore, are better passed on to the next person. Under the ethic of change, the buck stops where the problem exists. In rehabilitation, then, a residential staff person suspecting a client of illegal drug use immediately takes action, even if the action is just a note to the case manager or the behavior specialist on the team. Each problem is seen as an opportunity for improvement. Such a commitment greatly enhances organizational functioning in at least two ways. One, problems get identified and resolved quickly instead of impacting on people all over the organization. Two, they get resolved before they assume crisis proportions.

The way to create such an ethic is first to reward staff for all such actions, preferably immediately, instead of dismissing this initiative as unimportant. Second, all resolutions of every problem, no matter how small, should be celebrated and rewarded. Third, adopt each improvement as a new standard of excellence. Fourth, involve everyone in such problem identification and resolution. All this both requires and facilitates participatory management and staff empowerment to take action. *Kaizen* is responsible for Toyota Motor Corporation generating 1.5 million suggestions a year and staff putting 95% of them to practical use (Imai, 1986). No problem or solution is too small or insignificant to be recognized. The maintenance engineer who places two rolls of toilet tissue in the restroom instead of one just to reduce the inconvenience to other staff should be properly commended and recognized. Such recognition leads to people taking greater initiative to fix the

little leaks before they become major roof jobs. Treatment team members nip problems in the bud instead of waiting for the next team meeting or until it becomes a serious issue. An organization with such an ethic builds quality into process instead of waiting for final outcomes.

Such an ethic has applicability even in the treatment of clients, where every small gain is celebrated instead of only the final outcome goals. Although this approach is almost second nature to rehabilitation professionals when they are working with clients, it does not seem to get generalized to nonclinical areas of life. Applying such an ethic to all areas and all persons within the organization makes the organization a better working place, increases productivity, and enhances the ability to avoid or withstand unanticipated change.

Coping with Change

The fact that change is an inescapable aspect of life has been made clear earlier in this chapter. That it is often a stressful fact of life also has been made clear. Therefore, being able to cope with change and to adapt to it is important. Change becomes a problem when one cannot find a way successfully to negotiate one's way through it. The ability to negotiate through a change or any stressor is not a skill one is born with; it is learned over time and with experience. Given the multitude of stressors from change that are an inherent part of brain injury rehabilitation, it behooves even the most experienced professional to take a proactive stance in an effort to control the effects of change. This proactive stance can also be referred to as prevention through preparation.

Taking Stock

Many staff members, especially those who are just out of school and new to the clinical setting, are dramatically affected by the stress associated with change because they have not taken the opportunity to make a personal inventory as to how they are affected by or react to various changes in their own lives. Both professional and personal sources of stress must be accounted for in this inventory process. As much as staff members are encouraged not to take work issues home and not to bring home issues into work, the two—home and work lives—are not able to be completely separated at all times (Quick & Quick, 1984).

Change affects people in different ways depending on their personality, problem-solving style, and capacity to handle transition and uncertainty. Developing a proactive approach to handling change starts with an examination of self and proceeds to development of strategies to cope that can be called into action in times of stress. Becoming self-aware includes understanding personal values, strengths, limitations, and needs and what causes one to become stressed.

To perform a personal inventory, one might start with the following:

- What are one's personal and professional goals?
- What is wanted from or valued in performing a given job?
- Is what is wanted from or valued in performing a job consistent with one's goals?
- Are changes to routine accepted and integrated or avoided?
- If change is avoided, what are the reasons for the avoidance?
- How are new assignments or challenges handled?
- What kind of support system, both inside and outside work, is available?
- Does one work best alone or as part of a team?
- Does one feel confident making a decision, or does one need a supervisor to do this?
- What are the sources of stress both in and out of the work setting (for example, finances or debt, personal relationships, family, children, company policies or expectations, problems with support staff, overwork, physical and psychological demands associated with providing rehabilitation, etc.)?
- How are times of increased stress handled?

By starting with the above points, many aspects of a person's life and position within the change situation are examined, and potential sources of increased stress are identified. This process is the foundation of developing coping strategies to handle stressful change. All too often clients are instructed that they must learn where their strengths and limitations are and how to ask for help when they need it. Professionals have a hard time taking their own medicine. Professionals also need to examine their strengths and limitations when it comes to stress management and coping with change. Clients are taught that they are ultimately responsible for taking care of and advocating for themselves. Yet it is not uncommon to see staff members not taking care of themselves, not paying attention to personal limitations, and burning out as a result.

Another aspect of developing personal awareness is paying attention to warning signs of ineffective coping. These may come in the form of depression, anxiety, lethargy, cutting corners in care, venting problems onto clients, quick tempers and impatience greater than usual, bickering, waking up in the morning and not looking forward to work, and increased absenteeism.

Increasing overall personal awareness is a good exercise to undertake for life satisfaction in general. It is especially helpful in coping with change, however, when that awareness is applied to a given situation that has to be faced and managed. Understanding one's boundaries of control in a given situation is a critical part of increasing awareness. Many times it feels as though there is no aspect of a given situation that is within our control. Plans are formulated without our input, decisions affecting us are handed down without explanation, and no other options appear available to us. Ultimately, the outcome may not be something we can control. Many of the aspects of getting through such experiences however, are well within our reach.

Developing Coping Strategies

After the personal inventory is done, the next part of personal change management is the examination and development of coping strategies.

Numerous investigators have outlined strategies to reduce stress at work and at home (Charlesworth & Nathan, 1984; Executive Health Examiners, 1985; Quick, Nelson, & Quick, 1990; Quick & Quick, 1984). These strategies can be broken down into three categories: strategies to prepare the person to deal with stress, strategies that can be applied to stressors in general, and strategies that can be applied to address specific situations. Underlying all these strategies is the notion of getting some measure of control over self, over general stressors, and over particular situations.

Preparing the person. The first category involves lifestyle changes such as getting enough exercise; eating regularly and establishing a proper diet; securing quiet time for relaxation or meditation; making time for self; developing a positive attitude; examining, refuting, and discarding negative attitudes; using constructive self-talk; developing special interests or hobbies; and ensuring that there is provision for leisure or recreation time. It is interesting to note that the word *recreation,* in essence, means re-creating or becoming new again. All these strategies recharge personal batteries and help a person face each day with new energy and vigor. It should be no surprise that these are also the prescriptions for good health. They flesh out the old Latin proverb *Mens sana in corpore sano:* "Healthy minds in healthy bodies."

There are also some things that usually do not help in coping with change effectively. In fact, they can make things worse. These are activities that drain energy, such as increased alcohol and drug use, addiction to overwork, preoccupation with griping or complaining, and panic reactions to decisions. If we find that we cannot get back into a constructive way of working, seeking help becomes important. Some facilities have staff assistance programs that can help. Otherwise, outside professional help or at least a valued and competent friend should be sought out for assistance.

Preparing for stressors in general. The second category consists primarily of good habits that mitigate the effects of stressors in general. These include structuring the work environment, keeping one's desk free of clutter, separating work and home issues, simplifying and avoiding complications with people and things, avoid procrastinating, exercising time management, learning how to delegate effectively, setting limits and sticking to them, preparing a realistic to-do list each day and rewarding oneself as things on the list get accomplished, prioritizing tasks, taking time outs as needed to regroup, minimizing disruptions of one's daily schedule, and developing and using support systems. It is a good idea sometimes to take a walk outside the facility or to go out to some quiet spot away from the work environment for lunch. The more these strategies become ingrained habits, the more effective and efficient one becomes, and the greater the control one exerts over external stressors. In addition, some things that are inadvisable are constantly working over lunch, setting unrealistic to-do lists, and forcing oneself to work without taking any breaks.

Strategies for specific situations. The third category involves strategies to use in dealing with particular stressful situations. When one is faced with such situations, it is important to gather relevant factual data as to the scource of stress as soon as possible, to recognize one's limits of control over the particular situation, to break down resolution strategies into smaller and more manageable parts, to seek help as needed, and finally to look for the humor in each situation. Finding appropriate humor in each situation releases physiological antistressors and reduces the tension of other people. Individuals also must learn their limits in situations beyond their control, learn to become detached, and learn to let go.

Nevertheless, there will be times when stress has become so chronic and severe that one is not even in a position to use these strategies. In such cases, one must be ready to seek outside help in the form of psychological or career counseling or medical attention (Quick & Quick, 1984). One may also have to make a decision to leave the job or situation temporarily on a leave of absence or permanently to find a less stressful job or position.

Cognitive therapists such as Beck (1967, 1971, 1976), D'Zurilla and Goldfried (1971), Ellis (1970, 1979a, 1979b), Mahoney (1974, 1977), Maultsby (1975, 1984), and Meichenbaum (1973, 1977) are in agreement that it is not particular events or changes that really cause stress but the way a person views or interprets the event. It is the same old story of looking at a cup as half full or half empty. A change can be viewed as a stumbling block or a stepping stone. Each perspective engenders its own set of responses and feelings, with negative perspectives leading to negative emotions and greater stress and positive perspectives resulting in eager anticipation and exhilaration over a new challenge. Depending on one's frame of reference, change can be viewed as something to be dealt with as a stressor, with negative implications forcing us to do things in a different way, or it can be viewed as a positive opportunity to expand our repertoire and learn something new. The perspectives are different, the former being potentially maladaptive, and the latter being constructive. Coping well with change depends largely on one's particular attitude toward the tasks at hand.

Not only is stress dependent on how one views an event, but it is also a function of how one views oneself (Beck, 1971; Ellis, 1970; Meichenbaum, 1977). If a person views himself or herself as weak, a failure, and unable to deal with change, then change is apt to be extremely stressful. On the other hand, for tough-minded optimists, change is yet another welcome challenge. Usually, views of self are reinforced by self-talk (Meichenbaum, 1977). Negative self-talk can be replaced by positive self-talk, which will help a person change his or her response to impending stressors. Ellis (1970) also strongly recommends challenging and refuting negative beliefs about oneself and replacing them with more positive and rational views of oneself. Hence the prescriptions for positive attitudes, constructive self-talk, and refuting negative beliefs recommended earlier are all strategies for dealing with change. This is an extremely condensed summary of cognitive strategies to deal with stress. For a more complete understanding of these strategies, the reader is referred to the works of the therapists referenced above.

CONTEXTUAL FACTORS

Change does not happen in a vacuum. It happens within a context. Whether the change proves to be damaging or beneficial depends partly on the context. A list of books and articles that provide formulas or recipes for dealing with organizational change can easily fill 20 or 30 pages. For successful change to happen, however, two contextual factors are of paramount importance: organizational culture and organizational structure (Benerder et al., 1990; Drucker, 1986; Peters, 1987).

Organizational Culture

Organizational culture is what Drucker (1986) calls the spirit of the organization. The importance of organizational culture or spirit cannot be overstated. As Drucker (1986) says:

> Management by objectives tells a manager what he ought to do. The proper organization of his job enables him to do it. But it is the spirit of the organization that determines whether he will do it. It is the spirit that motivates, that calls upon a man's reserves of dedication and effort, that decides whether he will give his best or do just enough to get by. (p. 144)

Change is not so problematic in organizations with high morale, resilience, open and trustful communication, a proactive climate, a tradition of cooperation, and a sense of ownership by every staff member. Conversely, even normally desired changes such as increasing revenue or adding new equipment can have adverse effects in an organization with poor spirit as staff anxiously wait for more surprises or suspiciously second guess management's motives. Even promotions or salary increases can stir controversy.

Therefore, before any magical formula for dealing with change can be implemented, managers need to take stock of their managerial style and understand the organizational culture they have created. There have been no systematic studies of management in brain injury facilities. Anecdotal data, however, suggest that management styles in brain injury rehabilitation, despite much protestation to the contrary, too often resembles Theory X rather than more progressive participatory management styles.

Theory X is based on the assumption that employees are uncommitted, lack motivation, and need to be driven (McGregor, 1960; Vogen-thaler & Riggar, 1985). No administrator of a brain injury rehabilitation organization would openly espouse such an orientation. They see themselves as promoters of open communication and participatory management. Yet how many brain injury organizations regularly conduct staff satisfaction surveys? Such a survey was conducted in 1990 at a brain injury facility that professed open communication, staff empowerment, and participatory management, among other things. Results of the survey showed staff morale to be extremely low. One item, staff satisfaction with how much input they had in administrative decisions, was rated 1.8 on a scale of 1 to 5 with 1 signifying extremely low and 5 extremely high. This score was inclusive of ratings from higher administrative staff, which edged the mean upward. Management's response was to decree the survey invalid, to excoriate the developer of the survey (who had designed all their previous surveys for other purposes), and to promise staff a more reliable and valid survey. To date, that promise has not been kept. Management continues to view itself as open and participatory, however. At another facility, staff scheduling was a continually harrowing problem, as it tends to be in most brain injury facilities. This facility employed a centralized scheduling system for its various programs. When a suggestion was made to the director of operations to involve staff in scheduling themselves, the immediate and almost instinctual response was "Oh, no! None of the staff would schedule themselves client contact hours." In other words, staff needed to be driven. Yet this facility too sees itself as a champion of participatory management.

Such anecdotal examples of entrenched denial in management abound. In a survey of 62 supervisors employed in social service, Erera (1992) discovered that supervisors found their own subordinates to be their primary source of emotional support and approval. Superiors were criticized for providing inconsistent and insufficient information and for withholding emotional and tangible support and approval. A number of studies cited by Erera (1992) had similar findings (Burke & Belcourt, 1974; Burke & Weir, 1980;

Etzion, 1984; French & Caplan, 1972). There is no reason to assume that this is not true for brain injury rehabilitation.

Open communication, participatory management, effective leadership, and trust are absolute essentials for managing change. There is perhaps no truer statement about American business management than that the vast majority of the time management works for the benefit of its staff, but the staff are the last to know. A close second to this statement in terms of its veracity is that management almost always thinks it keeps the staff informed, but the staff almost always say they never heard anything. Managers are often left perplexed by staff not having got the message because they are certain they have shared information. What is important is not whether management has informed staff but rather whether staff have heard (Dalziel & Schoonover, 1988).

Achieving Open Communication

One key to open communication is ongoing, continual sharing of information in good times and in bad (Beilinson, 1991; Case, 1991; Kanter, 1983; Welles, 1992). As Beilinson (1991) says, even "the effects of bad news are softened when management communicates with employees in good times too" (p. 15). A poignant example of this is the experience of Jim Ebright, Chief Executive Officer of Software Results, Inc. When his company saw sales drop 90% and he had to lay off workers, he was astounded when instead of being angry his laid-off workers consoled and tried to cheer him up. Ebright attributed this incredible support to the fact that he had always communicated openly about the company in good times and in bad, building credibility for himself and loyalty among his staff (Welles, 1992).

Open communication can be achieved through newsletters, management reports, regular open forums, bulletin boards, and other informational channels. Some factors to be considered in successfully sharing information include timing the moment correctly, ensuring that all who need the information receive it, and tailoring the information to meet the needs of those involved. An example of when these factors are violated is when the people who are to be reassigned or laid off are the last people to know. Open, ongoing discussions of difficulties as they arise provide a rationale for tough changes and give staff advance time to adjust. The worst case scenario is when staff find out bad news from sources other than their own management. In one recent case, staff of a brain injury facility found out about organizational changes from media reports. Remarkably, there continue to be many staff in health care, particularly in large institutions, that rely on media reports to get current information on anticipated changes. Such organizations rarely use staff input to generate alternative strategies and options for addressing pressing problems. Many managers have later regretted this approach when more desirable options were pointed out after the fact and when the long-term implications of change have materialized (e.g., substantial drops in morale, unanticipated turnover, and recruitment difficulty).

The greatest destroyer of open communication is frequent contrast between what is said and what is done. How can staff members whose management is acting as if everything is fine place any stock in management's commitment to open communication when they suddenly find out that major changes are imminent? Open communication dies as soon as mistakes and even disastrous decisions are treated euphemistically or glossed over as new directions, planned transitions, or necessary evolution. Managers' motive is certainly not to cause their staff pain when they keep their secrets. Instead, they are usually acting out of protective instincts, but the effects are the same: death of both open communication and shared investment in achieving organizational goals.

In the spirit of taking stock of the level of open communication, stop for a moment and think of the numerous secrets that you keep. If you are a manager or an administrator, think of how much you share plans for reorganization, financial status, client census, plans for expansion or downsizing, and problems with cash flow or bill collection. If you are a staff-level clinician, what kinds of secrets do you keep from management? If these lists are long, can you still say there is open communication within your facility?

Open communication must move in all directions and should not be restricted completely to the pathways defined by organizational charts. Getting staff to provide candid and timely feedback to managers can be problematic, however. How often has management genuinely requested feedback but, apart from many positive remarks and a gripe or two, never received much? How many times have commuication channels been kept open without being used? Yet according to Toyota Motor Chairman Eiji Toyoda, Toyota employees produce 1.5 million suggestions a year (Imai, 1986).

It is not enough for managers to request feedback. They must create systematic mechanisms for feedback to occur. Furthermore, how feedback is treated will determine the quality and quantity of future feedback. The staff satisfaction survey mentioned earlier is a clear example of a death knell for future feedback. Another documented example illustrates this further. Amid a rumbling of staff discontent, managers met with staff members in two open forums to hear all their issues. After much advocating by change agents within the organization, the staff members openly and graphically related their issues, one of which dealt with the impediments they faced in getting client reports out on time. Management clearly got the point that morale was in very bad shape. Two actions ensued. A few weeks after the open forums, staff received a memo that spelled out a list of punishments for continued late reports. A few months later, management, in great secrecy, designed a complete restructuring of the organization. With much aplomb they unveiled their new plan. Staff were aghast at how badly management had missed the mark. It must be pointed out that in both actions management acted out of the best of motives. Instead of involving staff in the problem solving, however, their plan only validated earlier staff misgivings about ever providing feedback.

There are many mechanisms to encourage feedback. The first, of course, is to make it clear that feedback is genuinely sought. A number of small measures can accomplish this. All feedback should be acknowledged by a reply to the person providing the feedback. Feedback could be published in the company newsletter. A regular reward system could be established that provides recognition or awards for the best suggestion of the month. Finally, feedback should result in some action or at least an explanation for why no action can be taken. A major reason for Toyota workers making 1.5 million suggestions for quality improvement a year is that 95% of these suggestions are put to practical use (Imai, 1986).

Achieving Participatory Management

It is amazing how often participatory management is heavily stressed in management literature. Peters (1987, p. 343), cites two quotations in support of his philosophy of participatory management. The first is from Rosabeth Kanter of the Harvard Business School: "Powerlessness corrupts: Absolute powerlessness corrupts absolutely." Within the context of rehabilitation, this quote means that removing staff's ability to self-direct, control, and shape key aspects of their work will, in effect, destroy their ability to effectively respond to consumer needs and to set standards of care of which they may be proud. Powerlessness will corrupt the spirit needed to meet the demands of rehabilitation. The second is from Frank Borman, former chairman of Eastern Airlines: "I'm not going to have the monkeys running the zoo." Perhaps it is telling that Harvard Business School is still a premier business school and that Eastern Airlines is a bankrupt and defunct airline. Peters (1987) believes that the chief reason for America's failure in world class competition is failure to tap the work force's potential while the Japanese and Germans have consistently sought to enhance labor's value and have sought competitive advantage through a philosophy of worker inspired, constant, small improvements (*kaizen*).

Managers in brain injury rehabilitation often believe that they have participatory management. Often this can be a delusion. For instance, any upper level manager would readily say that his or her organizational values promote hard work and merit. These may be the professed values. Monitoring staff discourse during informal gatherings, however, may soon show that the real value that ensures promotion (at least according to staff perceptions) is learning to say the right things to

management. Some staff in these situations have worked it down to a fine art to provide just the acceptable amount of opposition to lull managers into thinking that there really is participatory management and open communication. In these situations it is really conformity that is rewarded, and staff creativity and involvement are decreased.

Participatory management is a seductive but subtle concept. Staff creativity cannot be coerced; creativity has to be provided a nurturing environment in which to emerge and grow. Staff productivity and initiative cannot be milked; they must be enticed. Participatory management can happen only when real opposition is openly welcomed and when staff have real power to shape the various aspects of their work.

Most brain injury facilities have performance appraisal systems. How many of these systems provide for upward evaluation? Usually, supervisors evaluate their immediate supervisees, managers evaluate these supervisors, and so forth. Consequently, the most important person to whom a staff member needs to impress for advancement or job security is the person above him or her in the hierarchy. Hence the behavior that is reinforced is looking good to the person above you. A corollary system of evaluation by lower level staff of upper level management, with evaluations being included in the personnel files of these supervisors and managers, would help make people in the management roles more accountable to the people they supervise or manage. Now instead of achieving performance standards set by the people above them, they also need to be accountable to the people below them. Such a system has much potential to force managers to be more attentive to the needs of staff whom they supervise. Among items that can be profitably included in such upward evaluation are those that assess supervisor and manager skills and abilities in listening, motivating, praising, providing emotional and logistical support, articulating goals, and delegating authority; consistency; fairness; sensitivity to staff needs; decision making; openness to staff ideas; and bias toward action. Because of the power differential between managers and other staff, it is recommended that the evaluations be done anonymously. To enhance staff participation and open communication, management should publish the evaluations (as group data, not individual data, because individuals in upper management too have a right to privacy) and have a plan of how to use the data obtained. Seeing that their evaluations are taken seriously and result in real action is powerful motivation for staff to be more honest, open, and accurate in their evaluation.

Participatory management should not stop with staff members. Clients and families must also be involved. Again, instead of using these individuals as sources of information, many brain injury facilities tend to establish client advisory councils or other such bodies more to meet accreditation standards than as invaluable sources of input. For instance, having a client or two participate for 10 to 20 minutes during the interviewing process of new staff and using their input would help to give clients some say about who will be working with them. Additionally, it provides a first-hand glimpse of how the canditate relates to clients. The use of peer counselors is another example of meaningfully involving consumers in the treatment services of the facility. Financial supporters can also play a helpful role in assisting programs to be more knowledgable of and responsive to external pressures.

The following case study, adapted from Foster (1991), illustrates how difficult it is to maintain a climate of open communication and participatory management. A brain injury rehabilitation facility hired a new human resource administrator, Sheila. The company had recently made a commitment to open communication, participatory management, and staff empowerment. Sheila was asked to be part of that effort. One of the suggestions Sheila made was to turn over the publication of the internal company newsletter to the staff. A committee was formed and told that it was responsible for what went into the newsletter. After a couple of issues, one or two slightly risqué articles began to appear, but they were taken in good humor. That year the company finances made it impossible for the company to give cash Christmas bonuses. Instead, staff were given plastic cups and coasters with the company emblem on them as gifts. The newsletter committee thought it would be fun to

do an informal survey of what staff did with their gifts and to publish it. The article that appeared poked fun at management and their idea of the Christmas spirit. Many staff members enjoyed the article. Some administrative staff took offense, saying it was disrespectful and bad for discipline and morale. Soon much discussion and some argument ensued. Some staff wanted the newsletter shut down. Others said it epitomized open communication. Sheila was in a dilemma. What should she do?

This is a difficult dilemma and intentionally so. On the one hand, ceasing the newsletter would put an end to open communication. On the other hand, letting the newsletter go on in the same trend could lead to divisiveness and lower morale. Perhaps what such a dilemma offers is an opportunity for mutual discussion between staff and managers to clarify what open communication means for the organization as a whole, what the boundaries of open communication should be, and what obligations and responsibilities are incurred by persons choosing such modes of communication. It also can be an occasion to discuss the mission of the newsletter and mutually to establish editorial policies. Additionally, it can be an occasion for sharing mutual feelings toward the piece in the newsletter. People in management can express how they sincerely wanted to support open communication, how they wanted to show their appreciation of staff within their restrictive financial constraints, and how they felt slighted or taken advantage of in spite of their good intentions. Staff could explain their reasons and motives for their reaction. Finally, the dilemma can provide management with an opportunity to explore possible undercurrents of discontent and to take action. Such a discussion is itself an excellent example and model of open communication and a constructive way of encouraging staff to keep the good of the whole organization in mind.

Organizational Structure

In addition to organizational culture, the probability of successful change depends on organizational structure. A top-heavy or hierarchical structure involving layers of management is a poor environment for proactive approaches to change. The more vertical levels within the organization, the greater the bureaucracy and the greater paralysis of action. Not only is action too slow, it is often inappropriate and ineffective and creates more dissatisfaction than solutions.

This happens for a number of reasons. First, the more levels of management, the more people will be involved in getting approval for decisions. Authorization has to go up a long line and then come down that same long line again before action can be initiated. The Grace Commission, investigating government bureaucracy, was purported to have found that a single memo had to pass through 32 people for signatures before a decision could be approved. Closer to home, there is a documented case of it taking 2 weeks for staff to get approval to purchase a tube of toothpaste at a brain injury facility. At this facility, staff frequently bypassed this convoluted system and bought necessary items for clients with their own money rather than wait for the approval to spend what turned out to be the clients' own money.

A second problem is that the longer the decision-making line, the greater the distortion of the message (both the request going up and the permission coming down). A third, and perhaps more important, problem of vertical bureaucracies is that they ensure that the people with the greatest authority to make decisions are the furthest removed from the level where the problems occur. Vice versa, the front line staff with the most information about what is happening are the furthest removed from the level where enough authority to make decisions resides.

It is no surprise, therefore, that in this day and age many staff layoffs involve gutting middle management. Simply getting rid of middle management, however, does not ensure more streamlined and successful decision making. A hospital-based residential rehabilitation unit recently removed its program director level. This resulted in greater dissatisfaction and clinical staff feeling even more disconnected from senior management. One reason was that management, in planning the restructuring, had not fully appreciated the roles of liaison and buffer that the program director had provided. In removing

that level, they had severed their line of communication to the front line staff, did not have someone with credibility to present the needs of clinical and support staff to them, did not have someone to present their needs and plans to these individuals, and lost someone who had previously dissipated some of the friction between the two groups.

Another reason for staff dissatisfaction was that management had not involved the staff in making that decision. Instead they had employed outside consultants, who had also not consulted with the staff involved. A third reason for the failure of such changes involved the redistribution of power and responsibility that was previously held by the program director. Most often, such reorganization fails because most of the responsibility gets shifted down while the power or authority is further consolidated at the top. As a result, many staff may feel an increase in the burden of responsibility and a decrease in power to make decisions and end up feeling even more helpless. Managers do this over and over again, giving away responsibility but holding on to power. For action and successful change to occur, both responsibility and authority must move in the same direction and to the same persons or positions. Otherwise, it is an illusion to think that removal of a middle management level will lead to greater communication or streamlined decision making. Instead, the greater the authority on top, the greater the psychological distance from those below. Staff who had felt relatively comfortable venting to a middle manager might be too afraid to approach someone in top management.

CONCLUSION

Many organizations, in an effort to effect radical change, send staff out for training or hire consultants for training and internal development. Graduates of the new training return filled with enthusiasm. As Schaller (1972) says, however, instead of new brooms sweeping clean, new brooms get worn out. Often the new training and new trainees reenter systems and management practices that are resistant to change only to dismantle staff enthusiasm and initiative.

Many organizations, despite much protestation to the contrary, do not really want to change. They are invested in maintaining the status quo. Their primary mission is institutional survival, not new growth. Take for example mid-level supervisors who are sent for training to learn to coach rather than manage to establish open communication or to empower staff. The organization still keeps secret its profit and loss statements and its planned staff changes, or instead of openly and nondefensively admitting mistakes it euphemistically describes them as healthy changes. If organizations want to maintain old autocratic structures, then they should perhaps not consider the strategies suggested here. It should continue to handle change by edit rather than by participatory management. After all, one would certainly not recommend participatory management to the military. These organizations should perhaps concentrate on discipline and unquestioning loyalty.

For the multiple reasons mentioned throughout this chapter, however, the authors strongly recommend that organizations involved in brain injury rehabilitation follow the track of participatory management, open communication, and staff empowerment and the concept of the whole organization playing as a cohesive team with a common mission and purpose. Managers must be genuine in implememting this approach.

They must be resolved not to be threatened by potential reduction of their power and increased accountability to staff and consumers alike, but should be encouraged by the potential of complementary reductions in their burden, responsibility, and stress. They must be ready to provide the leadership necessary to fight the personal and institutional tendency to hold on to the old and to maintain the status quo. They must be ready to match the principles of shared and open management with sincere action and consistent new behavior. This requires the courage to welcome differing views, to encourage responsible risk taking, and to make room for mistakes. Brain injury rehabilitation organizations that genuinely follow the management philosophy espoused in this chapter will be better prepared to meet the challenges and changes of the next century. Also, managers that practice participa-

tory, open, empowering, and shared management will see the same principles trickle down to treatment resulting in improved therapeutic relationships among all staff members, persons with brain injury, and their families.

ACKNOWLEDGMENT

The authors thank Nancy Curole and Tamatha Foster for their invaluable assistance during the development of this chapter.

REFERENCES

Abramson, J. (1990). Tough teamwork. *Headlines: The Brain Injury Magazine from New Medico Head Injury System, 1,* 10–17.

Aitken, C., & Cay, E. (1975). Clinical psychosomatic research. *International Journal of Psychiatry in Medicine, 6,* 29–41.

Alinsky, S.D. (1971). *Rules for radicals.* New York: Random House.

Arnow, H.U., Desimone, B.S., & Wood, R.L. (1987a). Continuity of care in the traumatic brain injured patient: Part II: A system for gathering information. *Continuing Care, 6,* 20–22.

Arnow, H.U., Desimone, B.S., & Wood, R.L. (1987b). Traumatic brain injury: Discharge and beyond: Part III: Discharge and the recovery process. *Continuing Care, 6,* 26–29.

Arokiasamy, C.V. (1992, July 30). *TBI rehabilitation in the year 2000.* Paper presented at the South West Regional National Rehabilitation Association Conference, New Orleans, LA.

Arokiasamy, C.V., Benshoff, J.J., McLean, L.S., & Moss, G.L. (1992). Computer applications in program evaluation: Basic guidelines. *Journal of Rehabilitation Administration, 16,* 5–12.

Arokiasamy, C.V., Leja, J.A., Austin, G., & Rubin, S.E. (1988). The study of the future: A contemporary challenge for the rehabilitation counseling profession. In S.E. Rubin & N.M. Rubin (Eds.), *Contemporary challenges to the rehabilitation counseling profession* (pp. 317–330). Baltimore: Brookes.

Attkissen, C.C., Hargreave, M.J., Horowitz, & Sorenson, J.E. (Eds.). (1978). *Evaluation of human service programs.* New York: Academic Press.

Backer, T.E. (1986). Research utilization and managing innovation in rehabilitation organizations. In *Proceedings of national education forum: Achieving excellence in developing human resources* (pp. 11–16). Stillwater, OK: National Clearing House of Rehabilitation Training Materials.

Banja, J. (1990). Rehabilitation and empowerment. *Archives of Physical Medicine and Rehabilitation, 71*, 614–615.

Barczak, G., Smith, C., & Wilemon, D. (1987). Managing large-scale organizational change. *Organizational Dynamics, 16*, 23–35.

Beck, A.T. (1967). *Depression: Causes and treatment.* Philadelphia: University of Pennsylvania Press.

Beck, A.T. (1971). Cognition, affect, and psychopathology. *Archives of General Psychiatry, 24*, 495–500.

Beck, A.T. (1976). *Cognitive therapy and the emotional disorders.* New York: International Universities Press.

Beckhard, R., & Harris, R.T. (1987). *Organizational transitions: Managing complex change* (2nd ed.). Reading, MA: Addison-Wesley.

Beilinson, J. (1991). Communicating bad news. *Personnel, 68*, 15.

Benerder, D.A., Murphy, A.W., & Redden, J.P. (1990). Managing strategic change. *Health Care Supervision, 9*, 27–31.

Bourgeois, L.J., McAllister, D.W., & Mitchell, T.R. (1978). The effects of different organizational environments upon decisions about organizational structure. *Academy of Management Journal, 21*, 508–514.

Bozeman, B., & Slusher, E.A. (1979). Scarcity and environmental stress in public organizations. *Administration and Society, 11*, 335–356.

Brokaw, L. (1991a). Books that transform companies. *Inc., 13*, 30–40.

Brokaw, L. (1991b). The enlightened employee handbook. *Inc., 13*, 49–51.

Brooks, N. (Ed.). (1984). *Closed head injury: Psychological, social and family consequences.* Oxford, England: Oxford University Press.

Buckley, K.W., & Perkins, D. (1984). *Managing the complexity of organizational transformation.* Alexandria, VA: Miles Riber.

Bunker, D.R., & Wijnberg, M.H. (1988). *Supervision and performance: Managing professional work in human service organizations.* San Francisco: Jossey-Bass.

Burke, D.C. (1987). Planning and system of care for head injuries. *Brain Injury, 1*, 189–198.

Burke, R.J., & Belcourt, M.L. (1974). Managerial role stress and coping responses. *Journal of Business Administration, 5*, 55–68.

Burke, R.J., & Weir, T. (1980). Coping with the stress of managerial occupations. In C.L. Cooper & R. Payne (Eds.), *Current concerns in occupational stress.* New York: Wiley.

Burke, W., Wesolowski, M., & Zencius, A. (1988). Long term programs in head injury rehabilitation. *Cognitive Rehabilitation, 6*, 38–41.

Butt, L., & Gerber, D. (1987). Thematic staff pressures secondary to brain injury exposure: The question of stress and burnout. In M.E. Miner & K.A. Wagner (Eds.), *Neurotrauma: Treatment, rehabilitation and related issues* (pp. 161–171). Stoneham, MA: Butterworth.

Calish, I.G., & Gamache, R.D. (1981). How to overcome organizational resistance to change. *Management Review, 70*, 21–28, 50.

Cameron, K.S., Kim, M.U., & Whetten, D.A. (1987). Organizational effects of decline and turbulence. *Administrative Science Quarterly, 32*, 222–250.

Carpino, L., & Newman, J.F. (1991). Role assessment of the allied health rehabilitation team. *Journal of Rehabilitation Administration, 15*, 187–190.

Carrai, E.B., & Handford, H.A. (1983). Problems of hemophilia and the role of the rehabilitative counselor. *Rehabilitation Counseling Bulletin, 26*, 155–163.

Case, J. (1991). The knowledge factory. *Inc., 13*, 54–59.

Cervelli, L. (1990). Re-entry into the community and systems of posthospital care. In E.R. Griffith & M. Rosenthal (Eds.), *Rehabilitation of the adult and child with traumatic brain injury* (2nd ed., pp. 463–475). Philadelphia: Davis.

Chan, F., Matkin, R.E., Parker, H.J., & McCollum, P. (1988). Computer applications and issues related to their use in rehabilitation counseling. In S.E. Rubin & N.M. Rubin (Eds.), *Contemporary challenges to the rehabilitation counseling profession.* Baltimore: Brookes.

Charlesworth, E.A., & Nathan, R.G. (1984). *Stress management: A comprehensive to wellness.* New York: Atheneum.

Condeluci, A. (1988). *Community residential supports for persons with head injuries.* Washington, DC: United Cerebral Palsy Association.

Conder, R., Evans, D., Faulkner, P., Henley, K., Kreutzer, J., Lent, B., Maxwell, J., & McNeny, R. (1988). An interdisciplinary programme for cognitive rehabilitation. *Brain Injury, 2*, 365–385.

Conner, D.R. (1988). The myth of bottom-up change. *Personnel, 65*, 50–54.

Crimando, W., Riggar, T.F., & Bordieri, J. (1988). Proactive change management in rehabilitation: An idea whose time has been. *Journal of Rehabilitation Administration, 12*, 20–22.

Crimando, W., Riggar, T.F., Bordieri, J., Hanley-Maxwell, C., Benshoff, J.J., & Calzaretta, W.A. (1989). Managing organizational change: A review of the literature. *Journal of Rehabilitation Administration, 13*, 143–150.

Crimando, W., & Sawyer, H. (1983). Microcomputers in private sector rehabilitation. *Rehabilitation Counseling Bulletin, 26*, 26–31.

Cronbach, L.J. (1982). *Designing evaluations of educational and social programs.* San Francisco: Jossey-Bass.

Dalziel, M.M., & Schoonover, S.C. (1988). *Changing ways.* New York: American Management Association.

DeJong, C. (1979). Independent living: From social movement to analytic paradigm. *Archives of Physical Medicine and Rehabilitation, 60*, 435–446.

DePompei, R., Zarski, J.J., Hall, D.E. (1987). Systems approach to understanding CHI family functioning. *Cognitive Rehabilitation, 5*, 6–10.

Deutsch, P.M. (1988). Discharge planning: Structuring the home environment. In P.M. Deutsch & K.B. Fralish (Eds.), *Innovations in head injury rehabilitation* (pp. 16.00–16.203). New York: Bender.

Deutsch, P.M., & Fralish, K.B. (1988). Long-term supported living. In P.M. Deutsch & K.B. Fralish (Eds.), *Innovations in head injury rehabilitation* (pp. 15.00–15.100). New York: Bender.

Dixon, T.P., Goll, S., & Stanton, K.M. (1988). Case management issues and practices in head injury rehabilitation. *Rehabilitation Counseling Bulletin, 31*, 325–343.

Dolan, J. (1982). Ethics and politics of program evaluation. *Journal of Rehabilitation Administration*, 49–53.

Drucker, P.F. (1986). *The practice of management.* New York: Harper & Row.

D'Zurilla, T.J., & Goldfried, M.R. (1971). Problem-solving and behavior modification. *Journal of Abnormal Psychology, 78*, 107–126.

Egan, G. (1988). *Change-agent skills B: Managing innovation and change.* San Diego: University Associates.

Eisenberg, L. (1986). Health care: For patients or for profits. *American Journal of Psychiatry, 143*, 1015–1019.

Ellis, A. (1970). *The essence of rational psychotherapy: A comprehensive approach to treatment.* New York: Institute for Rational Living.

Ellis, A. (1979a). The basic clinical theory of rational emotive therapy. In A. Ellis & M.M. Whiteley (Eds.), *Theoretical and empirical foundations of rational-emotive therapy.* Monterey, CA: Brooks/Cole.

Ellis, A. (1979b). The practice of rational emotive therapy. In A. Ellis & J.M. Whiteley (Eds.), *Theoretical and empirical foundations of rational-emotive therapy.* Monterey, CA: Brooks/Cole.

Emener, W.G. (1989). Invited comments. *Journal of Rehabilitation Administration,*

Emener, W.G., Lauth, T.P., Renick, J.C., & Smits, S.J. (1985). Impact of government retrenchment on professionalism: The cases of rehabilitation counseling and social work. *Journal of Rehabilitation Administration, 9*, 45–53.

Erera, I.P. (1992). Social support under conditions of organizational ambiguity. *Human Relations, 45*, 247–264.

Etzion, D. (1984). The moderating effect of social support on the relationship of stress and burnout. *Journal of Applied Psychology, 69*, 615–622.

Executive Health Examiners. (1985). *Stress management for the executive.* New York: Berkley.

Executive Wealth Advisory. (1990). *Greater emphasis placed on business etiquette to build sales.* Des Moines, IA: National Institute of Business Management.

Field, T.F., & Norton, L.P. (1992). *Americans with Disabilities Act: Resource manual for rehabilitation consultants.* Athens, GA: Elliot & Fitzpatrick.

Fisch, R.O., Conley, J.A., Eysenbach, S., & Chang, P.N. (1977). Contact with phenylketonurics and their families beyond pediatric age: Conclusions from a survey and conference. *Mental Retardation, 15*, 10–12.

Florian, V., Katz, S., & Lahav, V. (1989). Impact of traumatic brain damage on family dynamics and functioning. *Brain Injury, 3*, 219–233.

Foster, D. (1991). The case of the team-spirit tailspin. *Harvard Business Review*, 14–25.

Fralish, K. (1988). Transitional living programs. In P.M. Deutsch & K.B. Fralish (Eds.), *Innovations in head injury rehabilitation* (pp. 14.00–14.100). New York: Bender.

French, J.R.P., & Caplan, R.D. (1972). Organizational stress and individual strain. In A. Marrow (Ed.), *The failure of success.* New York: Amacom.

Galvin, D.E. (1989). Invited comments. *Journal of Rehabilitation Administration*, 141–142.

Gans, J.S. (1983). Hate in the rehabilitation setting. *Archives of Physical Medicine and Rehabilitation, 64*, 176–179.

Gibb, J.R. (1974). Defensive communication. In R.S. Cathcart & L.A. Samovar (Eds.), *Small group communication: A reader* (2nd ed., pp. 327–333). Dubuque, IA: Brown.

Goodstein, L.D., & Burke, S. (1991). Creating successful organization change. *Organizational Dynamics, 19*, 5–17.

Graffi, S., & Minnes, P. (1989). Stress and coping in care givers of persons with traumatic head injuries. *Journal of Applied Social Sciences, 13*, 293–316.

Graham, R.J. (1985). *Project management: Combining technical and behavioral approaches for effective implementation.* New York: Van Nostrand Reinhold.

Growick, B. (1983). Computers in vocational rehabilitation: Current applications and future trends. *Rehabilitation Research Review,*

Hahn, H. (1983). Paternalism and public policy. *Society, 20*, 36–46.

Hahn, H. (1985). Disability policy and the problem of discrimination. *American Behavioral Scientist, 28*, 293–318.

Hartman, S. (1987). Patterns of change in families following severe head injuries in children. *Australian and New Zealand Journal of Family Therapy, 8*, 125–130.

Howell, P.B. (1989). Guest editorial: Will you thrive or just survive? *Journal of Rehabilitation Administration, 13*, 3.

Hyatt, J. (1991a). Ideas at work. *Inc., 13*, 59–60, 64–66.

Hyatt, J. (1991b). Mapping the entrepreneurial mind. *Inc., 13*, 26–31.

Imai, M. (1986). *Kaizen: The key to Japan's competitive success.* New York: Random House.

Jacisin, R.D., & VanKirk, D.S. (1989). Head injury: Innovations in day treatment. *Cognitive Rehabilitation, 7*, 12–15.

Jackson, C.N. (1985). Training's role in the process of planned change. *Training and Development Journal, 39*, 70–74.

Jacobs, H.E. (1989). Adult community integration. In P. Bach-y-Rita (Ed.), *Traumatic brain injury* (pp. 287–318). New York: Demos.

Jacobs, H.E. (1990). A rationale for family involvement in long term traumatic head injury rehabilitation. In D.E. Tupper, & K.D. Cicerone (Eds.), *The neuropsychology of everyday life: Issues in development and rehabilitation*. Hingham, MA: Kluwer Academic.

Johnson, H.H., & Fredian, A.J. (1986). Simple rules for complex change. *Training and Development Journal, 40*, 47–49.

Johnson, J.R., & Higgins, L. (1987). Integration of family dynamics into the rehabilitation of the brain-injured patient. *Rehabilitation Nursing, 12*, 320–322.

Johnston, M.V., & Cervelli, L. (1989). Systematic care for persons with head injury. In P. Bach-y-Rita (Ed.), *Traumatic brain injury* (pp. 203–222). New York: Demos.

Jones, J.E., & Bearley, W.L. (1986). *Organizational change—The Organizational Change-Orientation Scale (OCOS)*. Bryn Mawr, PA: Organization Design and Development.

Kagan, D., & Pietron, L.R. (1987). Cognitive level and achievement in computer literacy. *Journal of Psychology, 121*, 317–327.

Kanter, R.M. (1983). *The change masters: Innovations for productivity in the American corporation*. New York: Simon & Schuster.

Karol, R.L. (1989). The duration of seeking help following traumatic brain injury: The persistence of nonneurological symptoms. *Clinical Neuropsychologist, 3*, 244–249.

Kawasaki, G. (1990). *The Macintosh way*. New York: Harper Collins.

Kilmann, R.H. (1984). *Beyond the quick fix: Managing five tracks to organizational success*. San Francisco: Jossey-Bass.

Kilmann, R.H. (1989). A completely integrated program for creating and maintaining organizational success. *Organizational Dynamics, 18*, 5–19.

Kimberly, J.R. (1975). Environmental constraints and organizational structure: A comparative analysis of rehabilitation organizations. *Administrative Science Quarterly, 20*, 1–9.

Kimberly, J.R., & Quinn, R.E. (Eds.). (1984). *Managing organizational transitions*. Homewood, IL: Irwin.

Kirkpatrick, D.L. (1986). *How to manage change effectively*. San Francisco: Jossey-Bass.

Kissler, Y.D. (1991). *The change riders: Managing the power of change*. Reading, MA: Addison-Wesley.

Koehler, J.W., Anatol, K.W.E., & Applbaum, R.L. (1976). *Organizational communication*. New York: Holt, Rinehart & Winston.

Koontz, H., & O'Donnell, C. (1976). *Management: A systems and contingency analysis of managerial functions*. New York: McGraw-Hill.

Kraft, G.H. (1992). Variations on a theme: In defense of health care. *Archives of Physical Medicine and Rehabilitation, 73*, 211–219.

Laplace, M.A. (1983). Communication: They key to higher productivity and morale. *Journal of Rehabilitation Administration, 7*, 112–115.

Lawrence, P.R. (1954). How to deal with resistance to change. *Harvard Business Review*, 36–44.

Lawrence, P.R. (1990). How to deal with resistance to change. *Harvard Business Review*,

Leland, M., Lewis, F.D., Hinman, S., & Carrillo, R. (1988). Functional retraining of traumatically brain injured adults in a transdisciplinary environment. *Rehabilitation Counseling Bulletin, 31*, 289–297.

Levin, H.S., Benton, A.L., & Gossman, R.G. (1982). *Neurobehavioral consequences of closed head injury*. London: Oxford University Press.

Levy, A. (1986). Second-order planned change: Definition and conceptualization. *Organizational Dynamics, 15*, 4–20.

Lewis, J.A., & Lewis, M.D. (1983). *Management of human service programs*. Monterey, CA: Brooks/Cole.

Lippitt, G.L., Langseth, P., & Mossop, J. (1985). *Implementing organizational change*. San Francisco: Jossey-Bass.

London, M. (1988). *Change agents: New roles and innovation strategies for human resource professionals*. San Francisco: Jossey-Bass.

Luthans, F., Maciag, W.S., & Rosenkrantz, S.A. (1983). O.B. Mod: Meeting the productivity challenge with human resources management. *Personnel, 60*, 28–36.

Mahoney, M.J. (1974). *Cognition and behavior modification*. Cambridge, MA: Ballinger.

Mahoney, M.J. (1977). Personal science: A cognitive learning therapy. In A. Ellis & R. Grieger (Eds.), *Handbook of rational psychotherapy*. New York: Springer.

Mangelsdorf, M.E. (1991). Making it. *Inc.*, 20–24.

Margolis, H., & Fiorelli, J.S. (1984). An applied approach to facilitating interdisciplinary teamwork. *Journal of Rehabilitation, 50*, 13–17.

Maultsby, M.C. (1975, June). *The evolution of rational behavior therapy*. Paper presented at the First National Conference of Rational Emotive and Behavior Therapists, Chicago, IL.

Maultsby, M.C. (1984). *Rational behavior therapy*. Englewood Cliffs, NJ: Prentice-Hall.

Mayo, E. (1933). *The human problems of an industrial civilization*. New York: Macmillan.

Mayo, E. (1945). *The social problems of an industrial civilization*. Cambridge, MA: Harvard University Press.

McGregor, D. (1960). *The human side of enterprise*. New York: McGraw-Hill.

McKinlay, W.W., & Pentland, B. (1987). Developing rehabilitation services for the head injured: A UK perspective. *Brain Injury, 1*, 3–4.

McMahon, B.T., & Growick, G. (1988). *Preface. Rehabilitation Counseling Bulletin, 31*, 274-275.

Meichenbaum, D.H. (1973). Cognitive factors in behavior modification: Modifying what clients say to themselves.

In C.M. Franks & G.T. Wilson (Eds.), *Annual review of behavior therapy, theory, and practice.* New York: Brunner/Mazel.

Meichenbaum, D.H. (1977). *Cognitive behavior modification.* New York: Plenum.

Mullins, L.L. (1989). Hate revisited: Power, envy, and greed in the rehabilitation setting. *Archives of Physical Medicine and Rehabilitation, 70,* 740–744.

Nadelson, C.C. (1986). Health care directions: Who cares for patients? *American Journal of Psychiatry, 143,* 949–955.

Nadler, D.A. (1981). Managing organizational change: An integrative perspective. *Journal of Applied Behavioral Science, 17,* 191–211.

Naisbit, J. (1982). *Megatrends: Ten new directions transforming our lives.* New York: Warner.

Neufeldt, A.H. (1986). Managing change in rehabilitation services. In R.I. Brown (Ed.), *Management and administration of rehabilitation programs* (pp. 55–75). San Diego: College-Hill.

Peters, T. (1987). *Thriving on chaos.* New York: Harper & Row.

Peters, T., & Waterman, R. (1982). *In search of excellence.* New York: Harper & Row.

Phillips, J.S. (1989). Invited comments. *Journal of Rehabilitation Administration, 13,* 153.

Posavac, E.J., & Carey, R.G. (1985). *Program evaluation: Methods and case studies.* Englewood Cliffs, NJ: Prentice-Hall.

Prigatano, G.P. (1987). Effective traumatic brain injury rehabilitation: Team/patient interaction. In E.D. Bigler (Ed.), *Traumatic brain injury* (pp. 297–312). Austin, TX: Pro-Ed.

Quick, J.C., Nelson, D.L., & Quick, J.D. (1990). *Stress and challenge at the top: The paradox of the successful executive.* New York: Wiley.

Quick, J.C., & Quick, J.D. (1984). *Organizational stress and preventive management.* New York: McGraw-Hill.

Ridley, B. (1989). Family response in head injury: Denial . . . or hope for the future? *Social Science and Medicine, 29,* 55–561.

Riggar, T.F., Crimando, W., Bordieri, J., Hanley-Maxwell, C., Benshoff, J.J., & Calzaretta, W.A. (1989). Managing organizational change: A review of the literature. *Journal of Rehabilitation Administration, 13,* 134–140.

Riggar, T.F., Garner, W.E., & Hafer, M. (1984). Rehabilitation personnel burnout: Organizational cures. *Journal of Rehabilitation Administration, 8,* 94–104.

Riggar, T.F., Godley, S.H., & Hafer, M. (1984). Burnout and job satisfaction in rehabilitation personnel. *Rehabilitation Counseling Bulletin, 27,* 151–160.

Riggar, T.F., Hansen, G., & Crimando, W. (1987). Rehabilitation employee organizational withdrawal behavior. *Rehabilitation Psychology, 32,* 121–125.

Rimel, R.W., Jane, J.A., & Bond, M.R. (1990). Characteristics of the head-injured patient. In E.R. Griffith & M.

Rosenthal (Eds.), *Rehabilitation of the adult and child with traumatic brain injury* (2nd ed., pp. 8–16). Philadelphia: Davis.

Rogers, E.M. (1962). *Diffusion of innovations.* New York: Free Press.

Rosow, J.M., & Zager, R. (1988). *Training . . . the competitive edge.* San Francisco: Jossey-Bass.

Rossi, P.H., & Freeman, H.E. (1982). *Evaluation: A systematic approach* (2nd ed.). Beverly Hills: Sage.

Salyers, W.M. (1989). Invited comments. *Journal of Rehabilitation Administration, 13,* 142.

Schaller, L.E. (1972). *The change agent.* New York: Abingdon.

Schein, E.H. (1985). *Organizational culture and leadership.* San Francisco: Jossey-Bass.

Schilit, W.K. (1987). An examination of the influence of middle-level managers in formulating and implementing strategic decisions. *Journal of Management Studies, 24,* 271–293.

Schmitt, P., & Growick, B. (1985). Computer technology in rehabilitation counseling. *Rehabilitation Counseling Bulletin, 28,* 233–241.

Seligman, L., & Ceo, M.N. (1986). Multidisciplinary mental health treatment teams. In J. Palmo & Weikel (Eds.), *Foundations of mental health counseling* (pp. 145–165). Springfield, IL: Thomas.

Shaw, L.R., & McMahon, B.T. (1990). Family-staff conflict in the rehabilitation setting: Causes, consequences, and implications. *Brain Injury, 4,* 87–93.

Sherman, V.C. (1993). *Creating the new American hospital: A time for greatness.* San Francisco: Jossey-Bass.

Smits, S.J., Emener, W.G., & Luck, R.S. (1981). Prologue to the present. In W.G. Emener, R.S. Luck, & S.J. Smits (Eds.), *Rehabilitation administration and supervision* (pp. 1–19). Baltimore: University Park Press.

Stack, J. (1992). The great game of business. *Inc., 14,* 53–62.

Starbuck, W.G., Greve, A., & Hedberg, B.L.T. (1978). Responding to crisis. *Journal of Business Administration, 9,* 111–137.

Staw, B.M., Sandelands, L.E., & Dutton, J.E. (1981). Threat-rigidity effects in organizational behavior. *Administrative Science Quarterly, 26,* 501–524.

Stout, H. (1992, September 15). Physician group supports regulation of medical fees. *Wall Street Journal,* pp. B1, B7.

Szilagyi, A.D. Jr. (1981). *Management and performance.* Santa Monica, CA: Goodyear.

Thomas, J.P. (1988). The evolution of model systems of care in traumatic brain injury. *Journal of Head Trauma Rehabilitation, 3,* 1–5.

Toffler, A. (1970). *Future shock.* New York: Random House.

Toffler, A. (1980). *The third wave.* New York: Morrow.

Trieschmann, R.B. (1990). Sickness treatment or health care: Implications for head injury. *Journal of Head Trauma Rehabilitation, 5,* 57–64.

Uomoto, J.M., & McLean, A. (1989). Care continuum in traumatic brain injury rehabilitation. *Rehabilitation Psychology, 34,* 71–79.

U.S. Equal Employment Opportunity Commission (1991). *Americans with Disabilities Act.* Washington, DC: Author.

U.S. News and World Report (1991, September 23). How to fight killer health costs. pp. 50–58. Author.

Vogenthaler, D.R., & Riggar, T.F. (1985). Theory Z for rehabilitation administration. *Journal of Rehabilitation, 51,* 42–45, 79.

Walker, R.A. (1972). The ninth panacea: Program evaluation. *Evaluation, 1,* 45–53.

Weber, M. (1947). *The theory of social and economic organization* (A.M. Henderson & T. Parsons, Trans.). New York: Oxford University Press.

West, J. (Ed.). (1991). *The Americans with Disabilities Act: From policy to practice.* New York: Milbank Memorial Fund.

Yalom, I.D. (1985). *The theory and practice of group psychotherapy.* New York: Basic Books.

Young, J.A., & Smith, B. (1988). Organizational change and the HR professional. *Personnel, 65,* 44–48.

Index